FASCINATING
BIBLE
FACTS
FOR CHILDREN

PUBLICATIONS INTERNATIONAL, LTD.

Picture credits:

Animals Animals: John Chellman: 180 (bottom); E.R. Degginger: 183 (top left); Noah Satat: 186 (bottom); Dr. Nigel Smith: 174 (bottom); **FPG International:** Josef Beck: 52 (top); Louis Goldman: 35 (top right); Spencer Jones: 87 (left center); **International Stock:** Frank Grant: 33 (bottom); Michele & Tom Grimm: 155 (top); Michael Philip Manheim: 29 (bottom); Steve Myers: 184 (top); **Richard T. Nowitz:** 19 (top), 53 (center & top right), 60, 61 (bottom), 63 (top), 75 (left center), 78 (bottom), 79 (top right & bottom), 85 (left), 105 (top), 115 (right), 126 (bottom), 154 (right), 173 (top), 185 (bottom); **Zev Radovan:** 13 (bottom), 28 (bottom), 36 (top), 40 (bottom), 41 (bottom), 50 (left), 51 (left), 53 (top left), 54, 58 (bottom), 59 (top), 61 (top right), 69 (top), 70 (bottom), 75 (top & right center), 76 (bottom), 89 (right), 95 (top), 96 (top), 99 (top), 105 (bottom), 107 (top), 110 (bottom), 113 (bottom), 114 (bottom), 115 (left), 121 (bottom), 122 (bottom), 123 (bottom), 124 (top), 131 (right), 137 (bottom), 143 (bottom), 152 (right), 165 (top right & center), 166 (bottom), 181 (right), 182 (bottom), 188 (bottom); **SuperStock:** 191 (bottom).

Contributing Writers:
The Livingstone Corporation: Dr. James Galvin, Michael Kendrick, Amy Ronne, Robert Hosack, Terry Day, Andrea Kendrick, and Gary Knussman. The project members of Livingstone specialize in writing about biblical subjects, including contributions to the children's books *Bible for Little Hearts* and *Kid's Application Bible*.

Consultant:
Gary Burge, Ph. D., Department of Biblical, Theological, Archaeological & Religious Studies, Wheaton College

Front Cover Illustration:
Karen Pritchett

Illustrator:
Karen Pritchett

Contributing Illustrators:
Thomas Gianni
Randy Hamblin
Michael Jaroszko
Stephen Marchesi
Lyn Martin
Cheryl Roberts
Sally Schaedler
Gary Torrisi
Wild Onion Studios

Map Illustrator:
Myron Netterlund

Contents

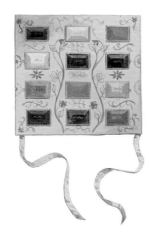

Introduction

EADING THE BIBLE is an ideal way to encourage positive thinking in a child's life. Unfortunately, many young readers approach this best-selling book with little enthusiasm. After all, what could possibly be interesting in a really old book with so many pages and such tiny type? *Fascinating Bible Facts for Children* provides the perfect answer to that question! With hundreds of facts taken directly from the Bible, and well-researched illustrations accompanying them, the Bible will come alive for any child.

Whether reading about the activities of biblical-era children, the various animals on the ark, or the frogs that hopped all over Egypt, *Fascinating Bible Facts for Children* provides intriguing facts and helpful background information to engage the minds and imaginations of young readers. Such spirited learning about biblical characters, customs, rituals, and daily living will jump-start their interest in reading and sharing more of the Bible.

A great topic for "show and tell," a source for evening Bible trivia games, or the subject of quiet reading on a road trip, this book will also provide hours of family entertainment. As a reference book it can help with homework, church classes, Bible studies, and dinner-table discussions. With this book as an introduction, the Bible itself will become more approachable and easier to understand.

Fascinating Bible Facts is organized into chapter topics that appeal to children. Each chapter contains countless facts and pictures that will inspire interest and continued

reading. The simplified excerpts are easy to comprehend and a building block to researching the rest of the story.

Fascinating Bible Facts for Children begins with Heroes of the Bible. Here children can get acquainted with the deeds of favorite biblical characters, including Abraham, Ruth, Moses and Aaron, David and Goliath, Samson, Mary, and Paul.

Accounts of lesser-known heroes are also included, all of which can be very exciting reading. These heroes rode fiery chariots, caused city walls to crumble, fought great battles, and made for some unlikely leaders.

Chapter 2, Religious Customs, presents the tradition of using smoke and incense in worship; prayer rituals; and reverence in the Tabernacle and synagogues. The reader will also encounter priests and Nazirites, dreamers and scribes, who were all important personalities in biblical times. They will learn about God's word and how it came to be written, celebrated, and passed on.

Chapter 3 is appropriately named Miracle Stories. It contains the well-known accounts of Creation, of Lazarus being raised from the dead, of Moses opening the sea, and of Jesus walking on water. The chapter also has spellbinding stories of food sent from heaven, powerful healings, and water

flowing from a rock. The miraculous birth and resurrection of Jesus are included as well.

Children will find differences and similarities between their lives and those of biblical characters in chapter 4, Everyday Life. For example, they will learn that families gathered at supper, the last meal of the day, to eat, talk, and tell stories, just as many families do today. Ordinary men and women wore clothing that was comfortable and practical. Others wore clothes that told of their privileged place in society. Soldiers, kings, and priests could be identified by the robes, tunics, or equipment they wore. Homes were often one-story stone houses with small windows, few rooms, and very little furniture. Rooftops were flat so that a variety of activities could take place there.

Chapter 5 gives various descriptions of Family Life. Though few children in biblical times had toys, they did play outdoor games with sticks, stones, marbles, and balls. They were expected to do chores and help their families earn a living, usually through farming. A boy was expected to become his father's apprentice, while girls were expected to help their mothers gather wood, bake, cook, and sew. Families also passed on values and spiritual training. At home, a child learned Scripture and heard stories about ancestors who served God. Elders encouraged children to follow their example. During these times, families often lived close to each other. In a typical community, a child might live near aunts and uncles, grandfathers and grandmothers, cousins, and extended family. Some relatives might even live in the same house.

A parable is a simple story often used by Jesus to explain a complicated spiritual matter. Chapter 6 is entitled Parables. Jesus would include everyday objects and common people in his stories to show what the Kingdom of God was like. Interesting facts from the parables of the weeds in the wheat, the mustard seed, the lost sheep, the rich fool, the prodigal son, the good Samaritan, the sower, and the rich man and Lazarus are brought out. Also featured in this chapter is an Old Testament parable that the prophet Nathan told to King David.

The final chapter, Animals in the Bible, explains the significance of camels, deer, doves, lambs, mules and donkeys, oxen, pigs, and even whales to the lives of common people. These animals were used for food, clothing, and farm work. But people also marveled at the strength, beauty, or intelligence of many of God's creatures. In biblical stories, animals often symbolized characteristics that humans admired or feared. David wrote about them in his Psalms, and Jesus included them in his parables.

Children will enjoy learning these and many other facts, taken primarily from the *Holy Bible, New Revised Standard Version.* Though entitled *Fascinating Bible Facts for Children,* readers of all ages will find wonder and amazement on every page. Share this book's surprises and its timeless lessons with a child today.

Heroes of the Bible

WHAT DO YOU THINK it takes to be a hero? Courage? Strength? Wisdom? The Bible shows us that heroes come in all shapes and sizes. A rich man was a hero, but a poor beggar was, too. A tough warrior was a hero, but so was a beautiful woman. Heroes were kind to others, and they listened to God. These heroes weren't always perfect, yet God was able to use them to show what wonderful things are possible when men, women, and even children love and obey him.

The Visitation

MARY WAS CHOSEN to be a very special mother—the mother of Jesus. One day, the angel Gabriel visited her. He called Mary "the favored one" and gave her an important message. Gabriel announced that the Holy Spirit would soon cause her to be with child. Mary was frightened and confused at first, because she was young, poor, and unmarried. How could she have a baby? Despite her worries, Mary believed the angel and was honored that the baby Jesus would be the Son of God. Mary told Gabriel that she would do what God asked of her. From that day, she rejoiced and looked forward to this wonderful blessing from God.

JOSEPH'S DREAM

Joseph was engaged to Mary. When he found out she was going to have a baby, he did not know what to do. Should he call off the wedding? Then, in a dream, an angel told Joseph that the baby was from God and to take Mary as his wife.

JESUS' BROTHER, JAMES

James was also Mary's child and the brother of Jesus. He may have doubted Jesus at first, but later he became a disciple and a brave leader in the early Church. He also wrote a letter, or epistle, to Jewish Christians giving them helpful instructions on how to live virtuously. This letter is found in the New Testament.

JESUS' EARTHLY FATHER

Joseph was Mary's husband and Jesus' father on earth. Joseph worked as a carpenter, and as Jesus grew older his father taught him how to build things out of wood. Joseph may have died early in life, because the Bible does not mention him after Jesus' childhood.

MAGNIFICAT

"Magnificat," which means "my soul magnifies the Lord," is the song Mary sang thanking God for the important task he was entrusting to her. It expresses the joy she felt after receiving the angel's tidings.

CHILDREN ARE SPECIAL

Jesus was tired. He had been traveling through crowded cities, healing the sick and teaching. When he sat down to rest, some children came up to him. The disciples shooed them away, thinking Jesus wouldn't want to be bothered. "Let the children come to me," Jesus said. He held the children and talked to them and blessed them. That day, the disciples learned how important children were to Jesus and how much he loved them.

Out on a Limb for Jesus

ZACCHEUS WAS A RICH and powerful man who wanted to hear Jesus speak. Because Zaccheus was short and could not see above the crowd, he scurried up a sycamore tree to catch a glimpse. To his amazement, Jesus knew his name and called to him to come down from the tree. He told Zaccheus that he was coming to his house for the midday meal. Zaccheus was happy, but the people in the crowd were not. Zaccheus had a bad reputation for cheating people. At dinner, Zaccheus admitted to Jesus that he had overcharged people on their taxes, and Jesus forgave him. Zaccheus gave back four times the money he had wrongly taken and promised to give half of all he owned to the poor.

A TRUE FOLLOWER

Nicodemus was an important leader in Jerusalem. He had heard rumors about Jesus and his miracles but wanted to find out more for himself. Afraid to be seen with Jesus, Nicodemus visited him at night. Jesus answered Nicodemus's questions clearly. After that, Nicodemus secretly began to believe in Jesus. After the Crucifixion, Nicodemus helped prepare Jesus' body for burial. People knew by this that he was truly one of Jesus' followers.

THE SADDUCEES

The Sadducees were a Hebrew religious group. They believed that only part of the Old Testament was true, and they did not believe in life after death.

JUST HYPOCRITES

Nicodemus belonged to the Pharisees, a group that followed religious laws very strictly. Jesus criticized some of them as hypocrites—people who say one thing but do another.

PROMISE OF SALVATION

Jesus reached out to the criminal next to him while he was dying on the cross. He saw the man's sincere faith and promised him salvation.

A typical village well in Judea

BARZILLAI'S DEVOTION

Barzillai was a wealthy man who showed kindness to King David. When David's son Absalom rebelled and drove his father out of Jerusalem, Barzillai gave food and shelter to the king, even though it was risky. After Absalom was defeated, David showed his thanks to Barzillai by bringing his son Chimham home to live in the palace.

HE DIDN'T PLAY FAVORITES

Important people weren't the only ones Jesus took time to talk to. One day, he met a woman drawing water from a well. This woman had a bad reputation, and because she was a Samaritan, she was hated by the Hebrews. Jesus was kind to her and told her about eternal life.

In the Wilderness

IT WAS TIME for the Hebrews' exodus from Egypt. They had been the Egyptians' slaves for more than 400 years. God chose Moses to lead them to a land of their own. It was a long and difficult journey, and Moses and his people spent 40 years in the wilderness. One day, there was loud thunder and bright lightning. A huge cloud came down on Mount Sinai. Fire spewed forth, and smoke billowed out as the mountain began to shake. All these things were happening because God was at the top of the mountain. He called for Moses to come up to him. There, God gave Moses the Ten Commandments. They were written on large stone tablets. These laws taught people how to worship God and to love and respect their fellow humans.

MOSES' BASKET

The little basket holding Moses was made of papyrus reeds and waterproofed with tar. These reeds could be found all along the Nile and sometimes grew as tall as 16 feet. Moses' basket kept him dry and was difficult to spot in the thick reeds.

AARON'S TALENT

Early in his life, Moses was helped by his older brother, Aaron. Moses had trouble talking. He spoke slowly and stuttered. But Aaron was good with words and knew how to talk to the multitudes. God let him speak for Moses, and so the brothers together spread the word of God.

A CLEVER GIRL

As a girl, Miriam secretly watched over her infant brother, Moses. Moses had been sent in a basket down the Nile to escape danger because the pharaoh had ordered that all Hebrew baby boys be put to death. One day, the pharaoh's daughter found little Moses and claimed him for her own. Miriam offered to find a woman to nurse the baby for the princess. Do you know whom she chose? Moses' own mother! And so they were reunited.

BROTHERLY TEAM

In the New Testament, another pair of brothers—Peter and Andrew—worked together. The two, who began their lives as fishermen, later became great leaders of the early Church.

THE EGYPTIANS AND THE ISRAELITES

Moses went to visit some Israelites who were being held captive by the Egyptians. He saw how badly the Israelites were being treated. Once, an Egyptian soldier brutally knocked a man down. Moses waited until no authorities were around, killed the soldier, and buried the body in the sand.

MOSES AND THE BURNING BUSH

Before Moses' journey into the wilderness, God spoke to him through a burning bush. The bush was engulfed in flames, but it did not burn up. When Moses went to investigate, God talked to him and told him there was important work for him to do.

Abraham's Son

ABRAHAM AND SARAH could not believe their ears. An angel from God told them they were going to have a son. Sarah laughed at the very idea. She and Abraham had wanted a baby all their lives, but now they were both very old. God kept his promise, however, and the following year, Isaac was born. Several years later, God tested Abraham's love for him by telling him to sacrifice the boy. Abraham obeyed God. He gathered wood and started to build a fire on the altar where offerings were made. When God saw that Abraham was doing as he had been told, he knew that Abraham's faith was sincere and stopped him just in time. Abraham noticed a ram caught in a bush. He took the ram and sacrificed it instead of his son whom he loved very much.

WHAT'S IN A NAME?

Sometimes God changed a hero's name to show that he or she had a new relationship with God. Abraham and Sarah were originally called Abram and Sarai. Others who were renamed included Jacob, whose name became Israel.

A GREAT HONOR

Sarah was the first woman to be listed in the Hall of Faith in Hebrews 11. This list celebrates people who lived by faith.

ISAAC'S SONS

Isaac, whose name means "laughter," married Rebekah and had twin sons, Jacob and Esau. Esau was born just before Jacob, so he was considered the firstborn. Esau was Isaac's favorite, while Rebekah favored Jacob.

MESOPOTAMIAN BRIDE

Abraham sent his servant to Nahor in Mesopotamia to find a bride for his son, Isaac. Mesopotamia had been the land of Abraham's birth. There the servant found Rebekah.

A VERY GOOD STEW

Esau returned from the hunt one day so hungry that he made a serious mistake in judgement. Jacob was cooking stew, and Esau traded his rights as the firstborn son to Jacob in exchange for a plate of stew.

WHO WAS MELCHIZEDEK?

After defeating several kings and rescuing his nephew Lot, Abraham met a king named Melchizedek. Melchizedek was king of the city of Salem and a "priest of the Most High God." Melchizedek gave Abraham bread and wine and blessed him. Abraham in return gave Melchizedek a portion of everything he had captured. Melchizedek is talked about in the New Testament book called Hebrews.

ISHMAEL

Ishmael was another son of Abraham. He became the father of a great warrior tribe, known as the Ishmaelites, who lived as nomads in the deserts.

The Flood

THE WORLD HAD BECOME an evil place. Noah and his family were the only ones still faithful to God. God warned Noah that He was sending a powerful flood and told him to build a large ark, or ship, filling it with pairs of every kind of animal. When people saw Noah building the ark, they laughed and made fun of him. They didn't believe that a flood was coming. Then, the waters came! It rained for 40 days and 40 nights, and everything on earth was destroyed. Noah and his family were kept safe and dry in the ship. When the flood was over, Noah sent a raven out the ark window to find dry land. A week later, he sent a dove. When the dove brought back an olive branch, Noah knew that it was safe to get out of the boat. Noah was thankful he had listened to God.

A VERY LARGE BOAT, INDEED

God designed the ark to be 450 feet long, 75 feet wide, and 45 feet high. More than 45,000 animals fit inside.

METHUSELAH

Methuselah, Noah's grandfather, was the oldest man in the Bible. He died at the age of 969.

The Jaffe Gate in the walls of Jerusalem.

NEHEMIAH'S FEAT

Another man in the Bible had a very tough job to do. Nehemiah wanted to rebuild the crumbled walls of Jerusalem. The walls were needed to protect the city from foreign armies. But Nehemiah's foes, who did not want Jerusalem to be strong again, tried to stop him. They mocked Nehemiah and threatened him. Still, Nehemiah kept on working and praying. God helped him, and the walls were rebuilt strong and sound—in just 52 days!

ABEL'S OFFERING

Abel was the first child to please God by obeying him. He gave God a lamb as an offering, exactly as God had asked him to do.

JOSIAH'S DISCOVERY

Josiah was an obedient king. One day, he discovered God's Word, which had been locked up in the temple for a long time. He read it and realized he needed to change. He cleaned up the temple and told the people to get rid of their idols and worship God instead.

THE FIRST MARTYR

Stephen was a wise Christian who loved to talk about God. But many people—especially religious leaders—hated his message. While he was speaking one day, an angry crowd stoned him to death. Stephen was the Church's first martyr, that is, a person who is killed for his beliefs.

Joseph's Story

JACOB HAD MANY CHILDREN, but Joseph was his favorite. To show how much he loved Joseph, Jacob gave his son a brightly colored coat. Joseph's brothers became angry and jealous. Joseph also had a special ability. He was able to tell people what their dreams meant. This talent made his brothers even more jealous. They devised an evil plan to sell Joseph into slavery. After Joseph was gone, they told their father that he had been killed. Years later during a famine, the brothers went to Egypt to beg sacks of grain from the governor. Imagine their surprise when they discovered that this important official was their own brother, Joseph! The brothers were so happy that they began weeping with joy and went back to tell their father the good news.

LABAN'S DECEPTION

Jacob wanted to marry a beautiful woman named Rachel, but first he had to work for her father, Laban, for seven years. Then the wedding finally took place. However, the next day, Jacob realized Laban had tricked him. He had married Rachel's sister, Leah, instead. Jacob worked seven more years to marry Rachel.

ISAAC'S BLESSING

Isaac was very old. Before he died, he needed to give a special blessing, called the birthright, to his firstborn son, Esau. This would allow Esau to receive an inheritance and lead the family. But Isaac, who was nearly blind, was tricked into blessing the wrong son—Esau's twin brother, Jacob. God had important plans for Jacob: His family would grow big enough to form a whole nation.

SAMUEL'S CHILDHOOD

Hannah had wanted a baby for a long time, because children were a sign of God's favor. Hannah promised God that if she had a son, she would give the child back to become God's helper. Samuel was finally born to Hannah, and when the child was three years old, his parents were true to their word and took him to live at the temple. They would miss him very much, but they were glad to keep their promise.

ELI'S CHOICE

Eli was the priest at the temple. Because his sons were evil, they could not take his place. Eli trained Samuel to become a priest instead.

RUTH AND NAOMI

Ruth made a promise—to always take care of her mother-in-law, Naomi. Ruth left her own home-land and friends to do this.

THE SUFFERINGS OF JOB

Job was a wealthy yet good man, but God permitted Satan to test Job's faith. Job became very sick. He lost all of his money. Then, his ten children were killed. Still, Job vowed that he would not turn away from God. God blessed him, and Job's health and fortune were restored.

Jonah's Mission

NINEVEH WAS A WICKED CITY. God told Jonah to go there to tell the people they would be destroyed. Jonah disobeyed and boarded a ship heading away from the doomed city. A

terrible storm blew up, causing the boat to almost capsize. The sailors were afraid they would drown. Jonah knew that the storm was his fault because he was running from God. Jonah told the sailors to throw him into the ocean. When they did, the storm stopped! In the water, Jonah was swallowed by a great fish. Jonah prayed while he was inside the fish, thanking God that he had not drowned. After three days and three nights, the fish spit him out, and Jonah hurried to Nineveh. The people heard his message and turned to God.

THE MAN FROM ETHIOPIA

God sometimes sent his messengers to specific people. An angel told Philip to go to a certain road exactly at noon. A chariot came along carrying an important man from Ethiopia who happened to be reading the scriptures. God prompted Philip to ask the man if he understood what he was reading. The man did not. So Philip sat down and explained the scriptures to him. The man continued his journey, but now he believed in Jesus.

BOOKS OF THE PROPHETS

The Bible contains many books written by prophets. The Major Prophets wrote books that were lengthy. These prophets were Isaiah, Jeremiah (who also wrote the book of Lamentations), Ezekiel, and Daniel. The books written by the Minor Prophets were shorter. These prophets were Hosea, Joel, Amos, Obadiah, Jonah, Micah, Nahum, Habakkuk, Zephaniah, Haggai, Zechariah, and Malachi.

PROPHET AS MESSENGER

Jonah was a prophet. This is like a messenger, or someone chosen by God to speak his words for him. God's prophets told people his message.

SPECIAL MESSENGER

John the Baptist was God's special messenger. He wore strange clothes and ate strange food, but it was he who spread the word that the Messiah was coming.

SWEET WORDS

The prophet Ezekiel had a vision in which God told him to eat a scroll. It tasted like honey! God then told Ezekiel to take his message to the Hebrews.

JEREMIAH'S TRIBULATIONS

Jeremiah was another prophet sent to tell people to obey God. But no one listened. Once, some angry people threw him into a deep well and then looked down and laughed at him. But after Jeremiah was rescued, he continued to preach obedience to God.

A SIGN TO GIDEON

Gideon was afraid that he would fail in doing God's work. One night he set out a piece of wool. In the morning, if the wool was wet though the ground was dry, it would be a sign that God would help him. Gideon received the sign he needed.

The Secret of His Strength

SAMSON WAS FAMOUS for his great strength. He used it to fight the Philistines. A woman named Delilah tricked Samson into telling her the secret of his power. Samson told Delilah that if his long hair were ever cut, he would become weak. Delilah told the Philistines, who then cut Samson's hair and captured him. Months later, Samson was brought to a temple feast so that the Philistines could mock him. By then his hair had grown long again. Samson asked God to strengthen him one more time, and he pushed hard against the pillars of the temple. They came crashing down, killing Samson and his enemies.

AQUILA AND PRISCILLA

In ancient times, it was often dangerous simply to be friends with someone who spread the teachings of Jesus. Aquila and his wife, Priscilla, helped the apostle Paul. Paul said they often risked their lives for him. He thanked God for such good friends as these.

ESTHER'S CHARM

King Ahasuerus was looking for a new queen and issued a decree asking that all beautiful women in Persia come to his palace. Among them was Esther, a Hebrew slave. Esther's beauty and sweetness won the king's heart, and he made her his wife.

PERSIAN KINGS

There are three major Persian kings mentioned in the Bible: Cyrus, who conquered Babylon; Darius, who led battles and also built buildings, canals, and highways; and Darius's son, Xerxes (sometimes called Ahasuerus), who helped protect the Jews from Haman, an evil official.

THE WICKED HAMAN

Mordecai was Esther's older cousin, a government official who refused to bow down to Haman, the prime minister. Haman became so mad that he plotted to kill all Jews. Mordecai asked his cousin for help. Nobody knew Esther was a Hebrew. She risked her life by alerting Ahasuerus of Haman's evil plan. The king ordered Haman put to death, and the Jews were saved.

THE COURAGEOUS HANANI

Hanani was a courageous prophet. In obedience to God, he delivered an unwelcome message to King Asa of Judah. The king became angry and put Hanani in chains.

THE KINGDOMS OF ISRAEL

The Jewish people were forced to leave their homeland several times in history. In Egypt, they were held for nearly 400 years (1805–1446 B.C.). In 722 B.C., Assyria captured the Northern Kingdom of Israel. Most of the people living there were forced to leave, and most never returned. Then in 586 B.C., Babylon occupied the Southern Kingdom of Judah. The people were again forced to move and serve another king in a foreign land.

25

Deborah's Triumph

DEBORAH WAS ISRAEL'S only woman judge. The people respected her wisdom and followed her advice. The Canaanites, under the lead of General Sisera, had been provoking the Israelites for 20 years. Deborah asked Barak, the head of Israel's army, to lead an attack against Sisera's men. Barak agreed but only if Deborah would help him. They faced great odds. Sisera had 900 iron chariots! Deborah and Barak were confident that God would be with them. They led 10,000 men down the slopes of Mount Tabor and into battle. God caused the Canaanites to become very afraid. The soldiers began jumping out of their chariots and running away. That day, with God's help, the Israelites were victorious.

VICTORY SONG

In celebration of their great victory, Deborah and Barak sang a song. In it they praised God and gave him the credit for their success. Some of the words to the song were:

Praise the Lord!
Israel's leaders bravely led;
The people gladly followed!
Yes, bless the Lord!
Listen, O you kings and princes,
For I shall sing about the Lord,
The God of Israel.

DORCAS'S RETURN

There were many other good women in the Bible who served God. A woman named Dorcas was renowned for doing kind things for people, especially the poor. She made robes and coats for people who had no money. When she died, the people were very sad. They showed Peter all the wonderful clothes she had made them. God helped Peter bring Dorcas back to life. After that, many people believed in the Lord.

A KIND ACT

Mary and Martha were two sisters who were very devoted to Jesus. Once Mary wanted to show Jesus how important He was to her. She took costly scented oil and poured it on Jesus' feet and wiped the feet with her hair. This kind act pleased Jesus and surprised everyone.

THE IMPORTANCE OF FAITH

When Martha's brother, Lazarus, died, Martha was disappointed that Jesus had not arrived in Bethany in time to save him. Jesus asked her if she believed that he was the Lord of Life and that anyone who believes in him will rise again. Despite her disappointment, Martha fervently declared her faith in Jesus. Jesus then made Lazarus rise from the dead.

LYDIA'S GENEROSITY

Lydia was a wealthy woman from Thyatira who sold expensive cloth for a living. On Paul's missionary trip to the eastern Mediterranean, she was the first person to become a Christian. After that, she let her home be used for meetings of the faithful and gave Paul and his friends a place to stay.

HEAVY METAL

Soldiers wore body armor when going into battle. A heavy metal coat covered the body, including a special protective covering for the neck. A leather and metal helmut protected the head. Heavy shields were also used to deflect the enemy's arrows.

27

The Battle of Jericho

JOSHUA HAD BEEN MOSES' second-in-command for many years. One day, Moses told Joshua to take his place. Now, it was Joshua's responsibility to lead the Hebrews to conquer the lands God had promised them. It would be difficult, but Joshua believed in God. At Jericho, God gave Joshua and his army specific instructions. For six days they were to march around the city once. Priests carrying trumpets were to lead the procession. On the seventh day, the men were to march around seven times, with the priests sounding the trumpets. Then, the priests were to sound one long note, and all the men were supposed to shout. The soldiers did exactly as God said, and Jericho's walls tumbled down.

JERICHO'S WALLS

In Joshua's day, sturdy stone walls protected cities from their enemies. In Jericho, the walls were up to 25 feet high and 20 feet thick.

Part of the walls of Jericho, c. 8500–4500 B.C.

RAHAB'S BRAVERY

Rahab lived in a house in Jericho and risked her life by hiding two spies who were from Joshua's army. When Jericho's king came looking for them, she helped the spies escape through a window. Because of her bravery, Joshua spared Rahab and her family when the city was destroyed.

MUSIC AS A WEAPON

Like Joshua, Jehosaphat used an unusual battle tactic. A choir marched in front of his army singing a hymn to God. When the enemy soldiers heard the music, they started fighting each other and destroyed themselves. Jehosaphat had depended on God and believed him when God promised victory.

CALEB'S REPORT

Caleb was one of Joshua's closest friends. Long before the battle of Jericho, Caleb was sent with a group of spies into Canaan, the Promised Land, to see if it was safe for the Hebrews to enter. The other spies came back with bad reports—they thought it looked too danger-ous. They claimed there were giants in the land. But Caleb took a stand. He said that they should do as God commanded and go forth to battle.

THE WORLD'S OLDEST CITY

Jericho was first occupied in 9000 B.C. It was an oasis in the Jordan Valley, and it was called the City of Palms in the Bible. The Israelites captured it under Joshua. It lay as a sparsely inhabited ruin for more than 1,000 years, and then it was rebuilt by King Herod.

Bees emerge from a honey-laden comb.

THE LAND OF MILK AND HONEY

The report by Caleb and the spies about the Promised Land did not just talk about giants. The report also described Canaan as a country flowing "with milk and honey." That phrase has since come to mean a place rich in promise as well as in resources.

Saul and the Witch of Endor

AT WAR WITH THE PHILISTINES, a frightened Saul asked God for help in defeating his enemies. But he received no answer from God. Saul's advisers told him to consult the Witch of Endor. Saul knew that going to the witch was wrong. After all, he was the one who had made the rule that banned all witches and fortune-tellers from the land. So, he waited until after dark to go see her, and he wore a disguise. Instead of his royal robes, he wore ordinary clothing. The witch called up the spirit of Samuel who told Saul that he would lose the battle and die the next day. At this news, Saul fell to the ground, paralyzed with fear. The witch's predictions did come true. Saul and his sons died on the battlefield.

SAUL'S TRANSFORMATION

Saul was the first king directly appointed by God. He was handsome and courageous and a good king—at first. But he soon stopped listening to God. Saul appointed David to his court but became jealous of him and tried to kill him. God protected David, and he became the next king.

DAVID'S BEST FRIEND

Jonathan, Saul's son, was not like his father. He was a close and loyal friend to David. He once saved David's life by hiding him from the king.

DAVID, THE GIANT-KILLER

Everyone was afraid of the giant Goliath. This Philistine was over nine feet tall and was dressed head to toe in heavy armor. But David knew that God would help him fight Goliath. He took one smooth stone, put it in his sling, and flung it at his enemy. The stone hit Goliath on his forehead, and the giant fell over. The soldiers of Israel then won a great victory over the Philistine army.

ABSALOM'S FATE

Prince Absalom was David's son. He was anxious to take his father's place, but God wanted David to remain as king. One day, while riding his donkey, Absalom became entangled in a tree by his hair. He could not escape. Some of Absalom's enemies found him and killed him. Absalom would never be king.

DAVID'S SONGS

When he was afraid, David often wrote songs, known as Psalms. In Psalm 54:4–7, he wrote, "But God is my helper. He is a friend of mine! He will repay my enemies for their evil. Do as you promised and put an end to these wicked men, O God. Gladly I bring my sacrifices to you; I will praise your name, O Lord, for it is good. God has rescued me from all my trouble and triumphed over my enemies."

THE WISEST MAN EVER?

Solomon was another famous king. He was known as the wisest man who ever lived. Once, two women brought a baby to him, each claiming it was her own. Solomon said to cut the baby in two and give half to each woman. But one woman cried out, "No! Give her the child—don't kill him!" In this way, Solomon had discovered who the real mother was and gave the baby to her. The real mother would not have allowed her baby to be harmed.

Daniel and the Lions

A NEW LAW WAS WRITTEN in the land of Babylon. No one could pray to any god or human, except to Darius. Daniel knew about this, but he went home and prayed in his room three times a day. This was just as he always did. Some men overheard Daniel's prayers and rushed back to tell the

King. Having no choice but to follow the new law, King Darius ordered Daniel to be cast into a den of hungry lions as punishment. He hoped that Daniel's God would protect him. And, behold, a wonderful thing did happen. The lions could not seem to open their mouths! They did not harm Daniel one bit. The next morning, King Darius was overjoyed to find that Daniel was still alive. Daniel was removed from the pit of lions without a scratch on him. He immediately gave thanks to God.

DARIUS'S DECREE

King Darius was relieved that Daniel was not killed. He ordered the men who had reported on Daniel to be put in the lions' den, where they were killed. Darius issued a decree telling everyone of Daniel's miracle and how wonderful and powerful Daniel's God was.

JOASH'S RESCUE

When Prince Joash was a baby, his wicked grandmother wanted to kill him. But God asked Joash's aunt and uncle to protect him. They rescued the child and hid him in the temple until he was seven years old. Joash loved God and later became a king.

ELISHA AND NAAMAN

Naaman, an army commander, was very sick. A little servant girl who lived in Naaman's house told him that Elisha, God's prophet, could make him well. Elisha told Naaman to wash in the Jordan River seven times. At first Naaman refused. When Naaman finally did as Elisha asked, God healed him.

LOT AND HIS WIFE

God also rescued Lot from danger. Lot lived in Sodom, a city full of wicked people. God resolved to destroy the city but first promised to spare faithful Lot. God rained fire and burning tar from the sky. He told Lot and his wife to run from the city as fast as they could—and not to look back. But Lot's wife looked over her shoulder. For this, she was turned into a pillar of salt.

GEHAZI'S MISTAKE

Because Elisha had advised Naaman to wash in the Jordan to be healed, Naaman wanted to give Elisha a gift. Elisha refused. Secretly, Gehazi, Elisha's servant, went to Naaman. He lied and said that Elisha changed his mind and wanted the gift after all. Naaman gave Gehazi a great deal of money, which he hid in his home. When Elisha learned of the lie, Gehazi and his family were stricken with leprosy.

The cobra—deadly and poisonous

THE FLIGHT INTO EGYPT

When Jesus was a baby, God protected him, too. King Herod wanted to kill all baby boys born in Bethlehem at that time. Jesus' parents took him to Egypt to keep him safe.

ONCE BITTEN

Jesus' follower Paul was once bitten by a deadly snake. But God protected him from its poison, and Paul did not die.

Paul Mends His Ways

AT ONE TIME, Paul had been one of the great enemies of the Church. He actually hurt and killed Christians. Paul was walking down the road to Damascus when Jesus, now glorified, appeared to him in a bright light. The light was so bright that it blinded Paul. Jesus told Paul not only to stop persecuting believers but also to begin believing in God. A few days later in Damascus, a man named Ananias had a vision from God. God told him what had happened to Paul. He told Ananias to find Paul and help him. At first, Ananias did not want to help, because he knew that Paul had once been mean to Christians. Ananias did what God asked and found Paul. He prayed for Paul, and Paul's sight was restored. From that day on, Paul believed in God and started telling others about the Good News of Jesus Christ.

EHUD'S CLEVER BREAK

There are other stories of escapes in the Bible. Ehud had killed a cruel Moabite king. He managed to lock the door and escape. Because the door was locked, the guards didn't discover for several hours that their king was dead. This gave Ehud time to gather his armies. He then led his men to conquer the unsuspecting Moabites. Because of Ehud's actions, Israel was a peaceful land for 80 years.

UNCONVENTIONAL ESCAPE

Paul had not been a Christian for very long before he was telling people about Jesus. This made the Jewish leaders in Damascus so angry that they vowed to kill him. One night, Paul's friends helped him escape by lowering him in a basket through a window in the city's wall.

The Appian Way near Rome

NOT AN EASY JOB

After Paul's escape over the Damascus wall, he traveled around the world preaching about Jesus. In the New Testament, you will find letters that Paul wrote to Christians in many different cities. Wherever Paul visited, crowds gathered to hear him, and many of his listeners became believers in Jesus Christ. Paul discovered that doing God's work wasn't always easy. Because of his faith, he was beaten and jailed many times.

EPHESIANS

One of the letters Paul wrote was to the church at Ephesus, the capital city in the Roman state of Asia. In the Bible, the letter makes up the book of Ephesians. In this letter, Paul tells about God's purpose and plan for the world. Two chapters explain how husbands, wives, and children should act.

WHEN IN ROME...

One day in Jerusalem, the crowd became angry at Paul. Officials arrested him and were about to beat him when they discovered that Paul was a Roman citizen. By law, Roman citizens could not be beaten unless they had been proven guilty of a crime. Paul was released and used the opportunity to tell the Jewish Council about God.

Oil to Spare

A POOR WIDOW once owed money. She was told that if she did not pay, her sons would be taken from her. The widow had nothing. There was famine in the land, and she did not have food—only a small jar of olive oil. The prophet Elisha told her to gather all the jars and pots she could find. She even borrowed some from her neighbors. He told her to pour the oil into them. The tiny jar filled each container to the brim! The oil ran out after all of the pots had been filled.

The thankful mother sold the oil to pay her debt so she could keep her children. There was enough money left over to live comfortably for a long time. God had used Elisha in a miraculous way.

Figs on the tree

ISAIAH'S CURE

King Hezekiah had been told that he would die, but he prayed that God would heal him. The prophet Isaiah made a medicine out of figs, and Hezekiah recovered.

SPECIAL DELIVERY

Prophets can also benefit from miracles. When Elijah hid in the desert from his enemies, God sent ravens to bring him food to eat.

SPIRITUAL HEALER

Once, a paralyzed man asked Jesus to heal him. But when Jesus saw how much faith the man had, he not only made him well but also forgave his sins. This amazed the religious leaders. It showed them that Jesus could heal the spirit and was indeed the promised Messiah.

A LAME MAN WALKS

As one of Jesus' disciples, Peter spread the word that Jesus had died for people's sins and had returned from the dead. One day, Peter met a crippled beggar outside the temple. The man asked for money, but Peter gave him something better. Through God's power, he commanded the man to walk. Peter took the beggar's hand and pulled him to his feet. At that moment, the man's legs became strong, and he walked without help.

DELIVERANCE

The faithful Enoch was also touched by a miracle. God was so pleased with how Enoch had lived his life that he swept him up to heaven—before Enoch could die.

ONLY ONE WAS GRATEFUL

Once, Jesus healed ten men who had leprosy (a very serious and crippling disease), but only one returned to thank Jesus for making him well again. We don't know that man's name, but he was a hero for remembering to give proper thanks and praise to God.

Religious Customs

SOMETIMES WE FEEL CONFUSED or even bored when we don't understand what is going on during a church service. If Hebrew children had not been taught the religious law and Scriptures at home, they might have felt the same way about the religious rites and customs of their day. By making an effort to understand the

customs and practices of the Hebrew nation, we can learn the way in which the people of Israel lived and worshiped.

Washed Clean

JOHN THE BAPTIST was Jesus' cousin. He baptized many people who had become Christians. These new believers were usually baptized in the Jordan River. John used this ceremony to show that a person was sorry for their sins and to symbolize that God had washed that person clean. One day, Jesus came to John and asked to be baptized. At first John refused—he didn't feel right baptizing Jesus. He thought Jesus should baptize him instead! Jesus told him it was very important, and John baptized Jesus. Jesus was baptized not because he was sinful but to be a good example. He wanted to show that he too should obey God. After Jesus' baptism, a dove appeared. Jesus heard God's voice from heaven telling him that he loved him and was pleased with him.

WATER IS SYMBOLIC

Baptize comes from a Greek word that means to "dip" or "immerse." A person being baptized is often entirely submerged under the water, and then brought back up. Many Christians, however, only sprinkle water on the person. Baptism is a symbolic death, burial, and resurrection. It is to remind us of Christ's death on the cross, burial in the tomb, and resurrection three days later.

A child is immersed during its baptism.

PETER'S PREACHING

Once, the apostle Peter gave a long and powerful sermon. He had just received the Holy Spirit, who gave him wisdom and just the right words to say to glorify God. Peter told the audience to turn to God for forgiveness and salvation. That day 3,000 people who became believers were baptized!

JESUS THE ANOINTED

Did you know that the word *Christ* means "anointed"? Jesus' followers called him by this Greek name so that others would understand who he was. The title of Christ told people that Jesus had been chosen for a special mission, and it showed that he had a sacred relationship with God the Father.

SPECIALLY CHOSEN

Anointing with olive oil was a special custom. It showed that a person had been appointed to do God's work. Only certain people could be anointed. Usually, they were kings, prophets, or priests who were about to begin the task God had given to them.

OIL'S MANY USES

Olive oil was used for anointing but had many common uses as well. The oil was used in cooking, for grooming a person's hair and skin, and as fuel for lamps.

ANOINT A PILLAR?

Jacob, a famous leader in the Old Testament, once anointed a stone pillar. When Jacob came to Bethel, God appeared to him and said his name would be changed to Israel, which means "one who struggles with God." To commemorate this event, Jacob built a stone pillar on the spot where the vision had appeared. He then poured wine over the pillar as an offering and anointed it with olive oil.

DAVID IS SUMMONED

King David's anointing was surprising. The prophet Samuel was told by God to go to Bethlehem and anoint one of Jesse's eight sons to be the new king. David was called in to meet Samuel only after his seven older brothers had been rejected by the prophet. When Samuel met David, God told him that David was the right one, and the prophet immediately anointed the boy.

Olive tree

In the Presence of Greatness

THE MAGI TRAVELED A LONG TIME to find Jesus, who had been born in Bethlehem. The book of Matthew says that when they finally reached him, they knelt down and worshipped him. That must have looked strange—three grown men bowing down to a little baby. But the wise men realized that this was no ordinary baby. They knew that they were in the presence of a great king. Kneeling, or even falling face-down on the ground, was a way of showing respect to a king. Some countries today still have kings, and people bow when coming into their presence. People also prayed on their knees to show their respect for God. The Bible sometimes calls this bowing the knees.

Many Christians throughout history, as well as believers today, have made it a practice to pray on their knees, humbly coming before God.

NO GENUFLECTING

Angels are majestic beings, but one shouldn't kneel down before them. The apostle John learned this after he had a vision of heaven. He was so impressed that he wanted to worship the angel who was guiding him. The angel told John not to worship him but to honor God instead.

EZRA'S CONFESSION

Ezra was a priest and teacher who called Israel to become a nation again. He was a great leader, known for his faith in God. Ezra was upset when he learned that the Jews had disobeyed God and married foreigners. He confessed the sins of his people before God, and Ezra's prayer caused many other people to gather and ask God's forgiveness.

PRAY FROM THE HEART

The best way to pray is the simplest. As Jesus said, talk to God when you're in a quiet place—so you can truly speak from the heart.

TEARFUL FAREWELL

When you know somebody well, it's hard to say good-bye. That's what happened when the apostle Paul said farewell to the leaders of the Church in Ephesus. He had been with them for three years, helping to start a following. The leaders knelt to pray and even wept with Paul as he took his leave.

IN GETHSEMANE

On the night before he was to die on the cross, Jesus' heart was greatly troubled. He knew he would be facing a trial the next day and had to be prepared for the outcome. He went to the Garden of Gethsemane, where he knelt and prayed to God for guidance and strength. Soon, however, the faithless Judas Iscariot— who had betrayed Jesus to the Romans— arrived with a group of soldiers to arrest him.

THE SOLDIERS' IGNORANCE

Unlike the magi, the Roman soldiers at Jesus' trial showed no respect for their prisoner. They knelt, but only to mock him. They also struck him and spat upon him.

43

A Little Help from His Friends

CAN YOU HOLD YOUR ARMS in the air for even five minutes? Moses once held his hands up for an entire day. The Israelites were fighting the Amalekites, a nation known for being hostile and evil. Moses stood high on a hill watching the battle. As long as he held up his hands in prayer, Israel was winning. But when he rested his hands at his sides, the Amalekites began winning. Keeping his arms raised was hard work, but Moses did not give up. When he became exhausted, Aaron and Hur brought a stone for him to sit on. Then they stood on each side of him and held his hands up so that he could continue praying. By sunset, Israel had won the battle. God promised Moses that this victory was just the beginning. Although the Amalekites would remain Israel's enemy for hundreds of years, they would finally be destroyed.

GOD'S BLESSING

Lifting the hands was often a way of bestowing God's blessing in biblical times. According to Luke, Jesus's last act on earth was to lift his hands and bless his disciples.

GOOD REASON FOR THANKS

Paul no doubt lifted his hands in thanks when he recovered his sight. He had been struck blind for three days after he saw Jesus in a bright light near Damascus. When Paul's eyesight was healed, he arose and was baptized, and from that moment, he became a devoted follower of Jesus.

THE RAINBOW'S PROMISE

Prayers are not always to ask God for something but sometimes to thank and praise him. After the great flood, in which all on earth but those aboard the ark perished, Noah said a prayer of thanks to God for allowing him and his family to be saved. God then pledged that he would never again send such a devastating flood. As a sign of his promise, God created a rainbow in the sky.

A GOOD ATTITUDE

The apostle Paul taught his young disciple Timothy that attitude was important in prayer. He said that people should pray, "lifting up holy hands without anger or argument."

JACOB'S GOOD FORTUNE

Jacob once used staffs of poplar, plane, and almond trees to make himself wealthy. He had an agreement with his father-in-law, Laban, that he would receive any speckled or spotted sheep or goats. (It was believed that an animal that saw something spotted would produce spotted offspring.) Jacob then peeled white streaks in the staffs and put them in the animals' drinking troughs. God blessed Jacob's efforts. He soon owned a huge herd of spotted and speckled animals!

NO MAGIC TRICK

Moses and Aaron possessed staffs with extraordinary powers. When God chose Moses to lead the Jews out of Egypt, Moses was afraid. God displayed his might by changing Moses' staff to a snake and back again. Later, Aaron changed his rod to a snake to demonstrate God's power before Egypt's pharaoh.

SYMBOL OF GOD'S POWER

Did you know that in the Bible the staff or rod had mostly religious significance? It stood for God's presence and protection, his healing power, and sustenance.

The Church's Birthday

GOD SOMETIMES USED DREAMS to speak to his prophets. Joel thought there would be a time when many people would speak like prophets and have dreams or visions. Hundreds of years later, the apostle Peter was at Pentecost (a special feast) when he remembered Joel's words. On that day, the disciples were praying when they heard a noise that sounded like wind. Then, little flames appeared above their heads. They all began speaking in different languages—ones they had never spoken before. These signs told them that the Holy Spirit of God had come upon them. The Holy Spirit filled the disciples with the power to glorify God. The flames went away, but the Holy Spirit stayed in their hearts to help them and comfort them. This event was called the baptism of the Holy Spirit. After Pentecost, thousands of people became followers of Jesus. We remember that special Pentecost today as the birthday of the Church.

TIMELY DREAM

Joseph dreamed that he should take Mary and young Jesus to Egypt to escape King Herod's wrath. After Herod died, the family returned and settled in Nazareth.

SOLOMON'S DEAREST WISH

King Solomon may have been the wisest man in the Old Testament, but how did this come about? God asked Solomon in a dream what thing he most wanted. Solomon, as a new king, asked for wisdom to rule his people fairly and with honor. God was pleased and granted his request.

PROPHETIC DREAM

God used dreams to keep people from harm. He warned Abimelech, the Philistine king, not to marry Abraham's wife. Abimelech listened, and his life was spared.

JOSEPH'S DREAM COMES TRUE

Joseph, Jacob's favorite son, got in trouble for a dream he had in which he was ruling over his older brothers. In the dream brothers grew jealous and sold him as a slave to passing travelers. Joseph ended up in Egypt. Years later, he did indeed rule over his brothers, just as his dream had foretold.

DANIEL'S VISIONS

Daniel may be the Bible's most famous dreamer. Not only did he solve the mysterious dreams of two kings, but he had visions of the future.

Special Messenger

GOD SOMETIMES USES ANGELS to rescue people from danger. One day, the apostle Peter was arrested and imprisoned by King Herod. This evil king hated Christians. He had already killed the apostle James, and Peter was next! The night before Peter was to be executed, God dispatched an angel (a word that means "messenger") to help him. Peter was asleep, double-chained between two soldiers. More soldiers were guarding the prison gate. The angel awakened Peter and told him to get up. Peter's chains slipped to the ground, and he followed the angel. He could not believe what was happening—he thought he must be dreaming! Then, the prison gate opened on its own, and Peter walked out. Peter realized that God had sent the angel to save him. Peter returned to his friends, who were surprised and overjoyed. They could not believe that Peter was alive!

FEARSOME GUARDIAN

Angels often enforced God's will. After Adam and Eve were banished from Eden, an angel with a fiery sword stood guard at the gate to keep them from returning.

GLORIA IN EXCELSIS DEO

Imagine seeing a choir in the sky! That's what the shepherds saw and heard the night Jesus was born. The angels' "Gloria" is recalled in the Christmas carol "Hark, the Herald Angels Sing."

DREAM OF VICTORY

A dream about bread inspired a general to victory. Gideon, an Israelite leader, overheard two enemy soldiers talking about a dream one of them had experienced. In his sleep, the soldier had seen a large barley cake roll into a camp and destroy it. The second soldier interpreted the dream as a sign that Israel would win the forthcoming battle. Thus inspired, Gideon led his army to a great victory over the much larger Midianite army.

ALL CREATURES GREAT AND SMALL

Not all visions made immediate sense. Peter was once told in a vision to eat some "unclean" animals that had been lowered from heaven on a sheet. Because Hebrew law did not allow him to eat such animals, Peter did not understand the vision. Later, he realized that he should regard everything God made as good—even supposedly unclean beasts. This insight helped the disciple see that God loved all people, whether Jew or gentile.

FIERY SERAPHIM

Angelic visions could sometimes be fearsome. The prophet Isaiah once envisioned fiery angels in the temple surrounding God's throne. These six-winged angels were known as seraphim, a word that means "to burn." The sound of their voices shook the temple and frightened Isaiah.

MYSTERIOUS VISITOR

Angels did not always say who they were. Abraham discovered this when three men visited him in his tent. Since travelers often had to journey across hot, dry stretches, Abraham tried to be a good host and offered them food and drink. Later, one of the men told Abraham that he would have a son. This promise was fulfilled a year later when Isaac was born.

Duty Bound

THE HEBREWS TOOK GREAT CARE to learn God's law. Their traditional way for reminding themselves of important Bible passages was to wear phylacteries, also called frontlets. These were long strips of leather to which a small 1½-inch leather box was attached. In the box were square pieces of parchment that had parts of the Jewish law written on them. The boxes were then strapped to the person's wrist and forehead. One box rested on the head between the eyes, symbolizing control over the mind by God's word. The other box was worn on the left arm opposite the heart, showing that the person loved the Lord with all his heart. Some men wore the phylacteries all day and night, but most wore them only during prayer. By wearing these unique boxes, the Hebrews literally fulfilled Moses' command in Deuteronomy to bind the law to their hands and foreheads.

Phylacteries are strapped to the foreheads of these worshippers.

AARON'S ROLE

Aaron, Moses' older brother, was the first high priest of the nation of Israel. He had assisted Moses during the exodus from Egypt and later was chosen by God to perform the religious duties of the Israelites. He and his sons received distinctive clothing. In addition, Aaron wore a turban on which was written "Holy to the Lord." Aaron's most important task was to make sacrifices for all of Israel on the yearly Day of Atonement, or Yom Kippur.

RICH ROBES

The high priest wore special clothes when offering sacrifices to God. The outer garment was called an ephod, and it was made of richly embroidered linen. High priests also wore a breastplate encrusted with 12 jewels. Each stone bore the name of one of Israel's tribes.

THE BIGGER THEY COME

Abiathar was a priest who won great favor, only to lose it all. He was high priest during David's reign, and he stayed loyal during Absalom's rebellion. Later, however, he conspired to crown David's son Adonijah king even before David was dead. Instead, Solomon became king and punished Abiathar by removing him from his post.

FAR FROM IMPARTIAL

Caiaphas was the high priest who presided over Jesus' trial. Like the other scribes and council members who sought false testimony against the Nazarene, he believed Jesus should be put to death.

Rabbi

RABBIS AND PRIESTS

Jewish priests worked in the Temple, holding worship services and offering sacrifices. But a priest's most important duty was to teach the law of God to the people. In the same way today, rabbis teach people the Jewish law and how to apply it to their lives. Rabbi means "teacher."

WOMEN PRIESTS

There are no women priests mentioned in the Bible. This does not mean that women were inferior to men, but in those days there were very clearly defined roles for men and women. In the New Testament, women began gaining more equality with men in ministering in the church. Believing Jesus was the Messiah had already set them apart. Appointing women to high positions would have caused further division.

Moses' Language Lessons

DID YOU KNOW THAT the oldest writings were made up of little pictures? People who lived in Middle East lands long before Moses were the inventors of the first written languages. When Moses was educated in Egypt, he would have used a picture alphabet, known as hieroglyphics, to write sentences on a scroll. The characters, or letters, consisted of both living creatures and everyday objects. Some of the pictures resembled an owl, a man in a chair, a hand, a boat, a hawk, a chicken, a leg, a feather, and a moon. The characters could be written horizontally or vertically, to be read from left to right or right to left, depending on which way the animal and bird symbols were facing (the proper way was to read toward their faces). This system of writing was difficult to learn. Usually only wealthy people could afford the time—usually several years—to master the art of writing.

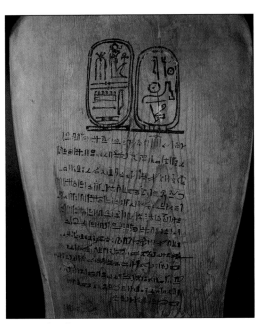

Hieroglyphics

SWEET AND SOUR

Books aren't meant to be eaten, but the Bible records a couple of instances when a scroll was eaten by a prophet. The last book of the Bible, Revelation, describes the time when the apostle John ate a little scroll, which tasted sweet in his mouth because it recorded the word of God. However, the scroll turned sour in his stomach because it told of the destruction God would rain down at the end of the world.

THE EARLIEST BOOKS

Scrolls were the equivalent of books in ancient days. People wrote on long strips of parchment or leather rolled onto a stick for ease in carrying.

Ink pot

WRITING IMPLEMENTS

People in biblical times usually had to write with a sharpened reed, or stylus, on clay. Their other choice was to make brush pens from reeds and use ink derived from soot.

NOT ALL LAWS ARE GOOD LAWS

A Persian king who was married to the Hebrew Esther mistakenly approved several bad laws. These laws allowed people to kill Jews and take their property. The king soon commanded that new and fairer laws be written to protect the Jews and then had these laws sealed on scrolls for posterity.

A Scribe works on a scroll.

JOSIAH'S SECRETARY

Scribes, or secretaries, were common in ancient times. They worked for kings, prophets, and apostles. In fact, Shaphan, a secretary to King Josiah, played a role in the religious revival of Judah. It was Shaphan who read a dusty scroll containing God's law to the king. When Josiah heard what had been read, he put an end to idol worship.

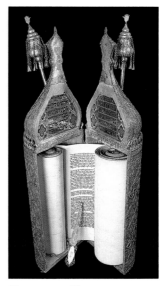

Fancy scroll

THE EARLIEST PAPER

Most of the material for scrolls came from wetlands. In Egypt there was a watery delta that was lush and green all year round. That's where papyrus plants grew. Their stems were cut into strips and glued together to make paper.

DISCOURAGING WORDS

One Old Testament king, Jehoiakim, was so angry at the news he received that he burned the scrolls that held the message. This news was a warning from the prophet Jeremiah that God was displeased with the sins of the people of Judah. When the scrolls were burned, Jeremiah had his scribe, Baruch, write the words on a new scroll. This time, Baruch added warnings from Jeremiah that the king would be punished for his actions.

53

Skilled Craftsmen

CRAFTSMEN WERE VITAL to building the Tabernacle according to God's requirements. The directions Moses received were detailed, and skilled people were needed to carry them out. Bezalel was chosen for the job. The Bible says that he was filled "with divine spirit, with ability, intelligence, and knowledge in every kind of craft." Bezalel could design objects out of gold, silver, and bronze. He was also a woodcarver and jewelry maker. Besides these talents, Bezalel was an expert at engraving, weaving, and embroidering fine linen cloth. Bezalel used his God-given abilities not only to construct and furnish the Tabernacle but to tailor the priest's clothing as well. Bezalel hired other talented men and women to help him. Many people donated materials—such as gold, wood, and purple cloth—to help build the temple. The workers finally told the people to stop bringing gifts. They had more than enough to finish the temple!

WHAT'S A TABERNACLE?

The word tabernacle has two meanings in the Bible. It refers to a meeting tent for worship as well as the much larger Tabernacle that housed the Ark of the Covenant.

A HAPPY FESTIVAL

The Jews had a number of religious festivals. One of them was the Festival of Tabernacles. During this event, each person or family made a small shelter or booth. The holiday celebrated the autumn harvest of grapes and olives. The little booths of branches and leaves reminded the people of God's protection during their years of wandering in the desert to reach the Promised Land. It was the Israelites' happiest festival.

A shelter from the Festival of Tabernacles

GROUP EFFORT

The Israelites took a collection so that the Tabernacle could be built. They contributed gold, silver, bronze, animal skins, leather, oil, spices, and precious gems.

ARK OF THE COVENANT

The Ark of the Covenant was a holy object that could not be touched. Even priests had to carry it with long poles. One day while the Ark was being moved, the oxen carrying it stumbled. A man named Uzzah tried to catch the Ark and died instantly.

SHOWBREAD

Bread kept in the Tabernacle was so special that it was carried on gold trays and eaten only by priests. Called showbread, it was replaced every Sabbath with fresh loaves.

THE GREATEST TREASURE

The most important item in the Tabernacle was the Ark of the Covenant. It was a wood chest covered inside and out with gold and holding the two tablets of the Ten Commandments, among other items of significance. It later rested in Solomon's temple. The Ark disappeared after the temple was seized by the Babylonians.

Solomon Honored

DAVID WANTED TO REPLACE the Tabernacle with a more permanent temple, but God would not allow it. That honor fell instead to David's son Solomon. Solomon spared no expense in building the temple. He used the most expensive materials and the most talented builders. He even traveled to other nations for advice and special supplies. After seven years of careful construction, the Temple was finished. It was a beautiful sight, for it had gold walls and floors, intricately carved stone, and elaborate embroidery. At the entrance to the temple were

two giant pillars, called Jachin and Boaz. As wonderful as the temple was, not all of the people ruled by Solomon were happy with him. To pay for the temple (and his own expensive palaces), Solomon charged higher taxes. Still, Solomon became famous for his temple. For hundreds of years, people remembered him for it.

JESUS IN THE TEMPLE

When Jesus was 12, he went with his parents to Jerusalem for Passover. Joseph and Mary started back home, but, after a day's travel, they became worried when they discovered Jesus was not with them! They went back to Jerusalem and finally found Jesus. He was in the temple asking the teachers questions and telling them about God.

A THRILLING SPECTACLE

The dedication of Solomon's temple was a thrilling event, for the building was the first permanent place of worship for the Jews. The temple replaced the Tabernacle, which had housed the Ark of the Covenant for centuries. After the festivities and King Solomon's prayer, fire issued from heaven and consumed the sacrificial meat on the altar. God then filled the temple with bright light and smoke, showing that he was present.

BABYLON'S INVASION

Solomon's spectacular temple was destroyed when the Babylonians invaded Jerusalem in 586 B.C. They robbed the temple of much of its gold and silver and burned both city and temple to the ground. The temple was rebuilt in a much simpler style about 80 years later.

THE IMPORTANCE OF COMPASSION

Jesus often visited or taught in the synagogue, which in Greek means "a place for gathering together." It was the place where the Jews worshiped God every week. Jesus drew great crowds whenever he visited a synagogue, and he also healed many people. One synagogue leader became angry with Jesus for healing a man on the Sabbath, the day of rest. Jesus responded by saying that showing compassion was more important than abiding by a set of rules.

SACRED GROUND

As a boy, Jesus spent several days talking with the teachers in the temple. As a man, he threw merchants out of the temple for selling animals and birds for sacrifice at a profit. Jesus proclaimed that the temple was a place of worship, not a den of thieves.

TEMPLES vs. SYNAGOGUES

The Jewish people first met in the temple for worship. But while in exile, they began worshipping at synagogues. The synagogue had no priests, and no sacrifices were offered. The synagogue also served as a place to study Jewish teachings, as a school to teach Hebrew, and as a community gathering place.

Sacrificial Bread

IN THE OLD TESTAMENT, grain (or meal) offerings were sacrificed on the altar to remind the people that their food came from God. The grain (usually wheat) was either uncooked or ground into flour to make bread. The bread, baked with oil and flour but without yeast, would be shaped into loaves or wafers. Bread made this way was called unleavened bread. Sometimes, the grain offering was simply parched green ears of grain. Oil, frankincense, and salt were often mixed with the grain. To present this type of offering to the Lord, the grain was brought to the priest at the door of the tabernacle. He would take a handful of grain and mix it with the oil. The priest would put the offering on the altar where it would be burnt with one of the animal sacrifices. Then, the priest would eat the rest of the meal offering in the tabernacle.

HOLY OBJECTS

Censers were used to carry the coals upon which incense would be burned. Priests used these tools in the temple, and they were considered holy objects. The first censers were made of brass, but the ones in Solomon's temple were made of gold.

Censers

A VALUABLE SPICE

Frankincense was valued as a spice in biblical times. It was frequently used for incense and was one of the spices the magi gave to the baby Jesus. Frankincense was created from a strong-smelling gum from the balsam tree. Bringing frankincense to Jesus showed that the wise men were paying him great honor.

Tropical tree of the Myrtaceae family

FOUR HORNS OF THE ALTAR

One type of altar used for making sacrifices was a square pillar with four horns at each of its upper corners. A part of the blood from the sacrifice was to be placed on these horns. A person who was a fugitive could take hold of the horns and find protection and refuge.

SECRET RECIPE

People often use secret recipes for cooking ordinary foods, but the Hebrews could not copy the recipe for worship incense. It was reserved for holy uses. The incense was a mixture of the spices stacte, onycha, galbanum, and frankincense. These were blended with salt and beaten into a powder. God warned that this mixture could not be used for any purpose except worship. Anyone who violated this command would be cut off from the people.

YOM KIPPUR

The most important day of the year for the Jews was Yom Kippur, or the Day of Atonement. The people would not work or eat all day but instead pray for cleansing from their sins. Only on this day could the high priest enter the holy of holies in the tabernacle.

INCENSE AS PRAYER

In the Bible, prayer is compared to incense. The apostle John describes a scene in heaven where the elders hold incense bowls that are "the prayers of the saints."

Origin of Passover

EGYPT HAD ALREADY EXPERIENCED nine plagues—the river turned to blood; thousands of frogs appeared; dust turned into crawling lice; swarms of flies attacked; animals caught diseases; people were covered with boils; damaging hail fell; locusts covered the land; and Egypt was completely dark for three days. Then the Lord said he was sending one more plague, worse than any of the others: The eldest child in every family throughout the country would die. But God promised that the Jewish children would be saved. When the plague came, an angel killed all Egyptian first-born, but the children in homes that had lamb's blood smeared over the door were spared. The event became known as Passover, for the angel had "passed over" the Hebrew camp. The festival of Passover reminded the Jewish people of God's goodness to them in Egypt. It is still celebrated today.

A WEEKLONG EVENT

Passover today is celebrated over seven or eight days. The first and last days are the most important, and no work is done on them.

Passover meal

THE HEBREWS' "THANKSGIVING"

The Passover meal was the most important one for the Hebrews, much as Thanksgiving would be for us. Everything had to be just right. The roast lamb would serve 10 to 20 people. Four cups of red wine were used. Bitter herbs and bread made without yeast reminded the people of how hard it had been to live in Egypt. Scriptural passages from the book of Exodus and Psalms were read to recall the first Passover.

PASSOVER AND EASTER

The Christian Easter is always held on the first Sunday after the Jewish Passover. Passover's date varies, but it always comes at full moon in March or April.

RENEWING A CUSTOM

How exciting to find something you've lost! King Josiah of Judah learned about Passover from old scrolls his high priest found. He held the festival for the first time in many years.

Torah scrolls

BARABBAS GOES FREE

The Romans who governed the Jews in Judea had a custom of releasing a prisoner during Passover. Pontius Pilate, the Roman governor, had offered to release Jesus because he had found Jesus innocent of wrongdoing. The crowd instead wanted Barabbas, a murderer, set free. Jesus was later crucified at Golgotha.

JESUS' OBSERVANCE

As a boy, Jesus went to Passover in Jerusalem every year with his parents. Later, Jesus shared Passover with his disciples. In fact, the Last Supper was celebrated during Passover. In one of his letters, Paul compared Jesus' death on the cross to the lamb traditionally sacrificed at Passover.

The cenacle in Jerusalem, the site of the Last Supper

The Nazirite Vow

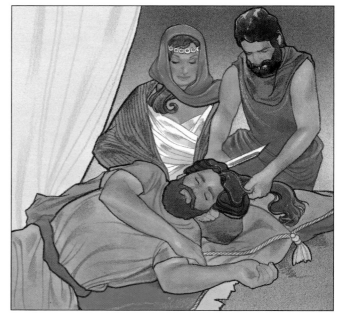

A NAZIRITE WAS A MAN OR WOMAN who made a special promise to God. The Nazirite vow could be taken permanently, or for as little as 30 days. They were to show their devotion and service to God by following three certain rules. First, Nazirites pledged not to cut their hair, and if they were men, to shave their beards. When the time of the vow was over, the hair would be cut and burned on the altar. (Samson was a famous Nazirite who was weakened after Delilah cut his hair.) Second, Nazirites were not to eat or drink anything associated with grapes—including raisins and wine. Third, a Nazirite was never to touch a dead body. Most people volunteered to take the vow, but sometimes a parent would take it for their children, making them Nazirites for life.

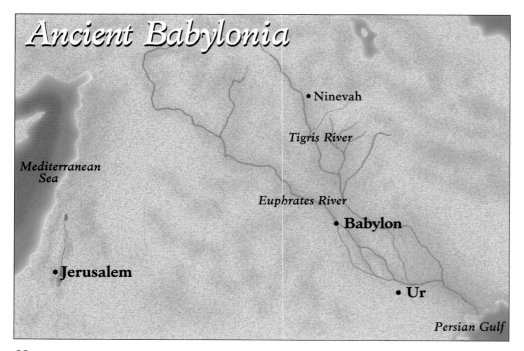

PRIDE HAS ITS PRICE

King Nebuchadnezzar of Babylon once grew his hair as long as eagle feathers. The king, who thought too highly of himself, had been admiring the empire he had built when a heavenly voice announced his judgment. The king was driven from the palace and went mad. He lived outdoors like a wild animal, and his hair and nails grew incredibly long. Finally, he humbled himself, and his kingdom was restored.

HANUN'S INSULT

Beards were a mark of maturity and respectability in ancient Israel, but one king, Hanun of Ammon, was determined to offend Hebrew custom, including the wearing of beards. When King David sent ambassadors to deliver friendly greetings, the Ammonite, who thought the men were spies, cut off their beards and slashed their robes. This angered David, who went to war against Ammon. Hanun suffered a great defeat and never troubled Israel again.

BEARDS AND HAIR

The Hebrews cared a great deal about the appearance of their beards and hair. To distinguish themselves from non-Christians, Hebrew men did not cut their hair at the temples or trim the corners of their beards.

Hebrew males did not cut their hair at the temples.

HAIR ETIQUETTE

Does it matter if your hair is long or short? What about wearing a hat? These don't matter so much to us, but they did to women long ago. It was considered shameful for women to show their hair in public.

GIFT OF DEVOTION

Have you ever given a very expensive gift to someone you love and respect? A sinful woman once did that by pouring expensive perfume on Jesus' feet at a wealthy man's home—then using her beautiful long hair to wipe his feet. Her act was a sign of devotion.

TOUCHY SUBJECT

When some rowdy youths teased the prophet Elisha for being bald, he brought a terrible curse upon them. Forty-two of them were mauled by bears.

Miracle Stories

THE BIBLE IS FILLED WITH STORIES of miracles—from the beginning of the Old Testament to the final events of the New Testament. Moses, prophets such as Elijah and Elisha, Jesus, Peter, Paul, and the early Christians performed amazing acts that showed God's power. Astonishing miracles were performed: Paths opened through rivers and seas; a small amount of food fed thousands of people, and Jesus calmed the sea with a single word. This chapter is filled with wonderful stories that are still talked about today!

John's Vision

JOHN ONCE HAD A VISION. In it the old earth and sky had disappeared and a new Jerusalem, or a new earth, came down from heaven to replace it. This city was made of gold as clear as glass. There was a wall made of layers of gems, and there were gates made of thousands of pearls. The city was as beautiful as a bride at her wedding! It also had a refreshing river where the water of life flowed through the streets and a tree grew fruit all year long. The city did not need a sun or moon to light it, because God himself was the light. Best of all, in this new city there was no more death, sorrow, crying, or pain! God will actually bring this wonderful city to earth someday, but only those who believe in him will get to live there.

GOD CREATES HEAVEN AND EARTH

The creation story includes God's words, "Let there be light." Until these words were spoken, there was only empty darkness. Water was everywhere, so on day two, God separated heaven from the waters. On the third day, he let the waters gather so that dry land appeared.

GENESIS AND JOHN

Like the first book of the Bible, Genesis, the gospel of John starts with, "In the beginning." But John's focus is on Jesus, the Word that "became flesh and dwelt among us."

NO LOVE LOST

No wonder most people don't like snakes. Satan took the form of a serpent when he tempted Eve. After the fall from grace, God put a curse on the snake and made it crawl on its belly. God also said that there would be trouble between the serpent and Eve's children.

HEAVEN'S MEANINGS

The word *heaven* can mean three things: the "atmosphere"; "the sky with stars, moon, and sun"; and "the place where God dwells."

A PERFECT WORLD?

When Adam and Eve listened to Satan rather than God, the Bible says sin entered the world, affecting God's perfect creation. There was sickness, suffering, and death. But the apostle Paul said creation would someday be set free, for God would make it perfect again.

THE POWER OF WORDS

Just as God spoke the word and the world was created, Jesus could cure by simply declaring a person well—even from a distance. A Roman centurion wanted his servant healed from a paralyzing, painful illness. Jesus offered to go to the centurion's home to see the sick man, but the Roman didn't feel worthy to have Jesus come into his home. Jesus just said the word and the servant was healed.

Favored by God

THE ISRAELITES WHO FLED EGYPT were very frightened. They were pursued by more than 600 chariots and horsemen. Pharaoh had called out his entire cavalry for the chase! However, God was on the Israelites' side because the Egyptians did not honor him and refused to listen to his warnings. Moses told the people not to be afraid. He promised them that they would be speechless with amazement at how God would help them. Then, God gave Moses the power to open a path through the Red Sea. A wind blew all night, drying the path. In the morning, the Israelites passed through, but the Egyptians were close behind! Suddenly, God caused the Egyptians' chariot wheels to fall off and scrape in the dirt! Once the Israelites had made it safely across, God told Moses to stretch his hand over the parted waters. The waters quickly closed over the Egyptian warriors, drowning them all.

PARTING THE WATERS

God provided a miraculous escape for the Israelites from the pharaoh's army. He opened a path through the Red Sea and allowed them to cross over to the Sinai Desert.

ENTERING THE PROMISED LAND

Another miraculous parting of the waters occurred at the Jordan River when the Israelites entered the Promised Land. The priests carried the Ark of the Covenant. When they stepped into the water, the river parted, and the Hebrews crossed safely to the other side.

A PATH THROUGH THE JORDAN

The prophets Elijah and Elisha once crossed the Jordan River after Elijah struck the water with his mantle, causing the river to part to both sides.

RESCUED FROM THIRST

God once saved an army of Judah and Israel from dying of thirst. He filled a valley with water, even though no rain had fallen.

The Jordan River

MIRACLE OF PURIFICATION

Elisha miraculously purified a contaminated spring. A group of men from the city of Jericho told the prophet that the spring water was bad and that the land was suffering because of it. Elisha had them bring him a bowl filled with salt, which he then threw into the spring. As he did so, he declared that God had cleansed the water and that the land would recover. On that very day, the water became pure again.

PAUL'S SHIPWRECK

The apostle Paul once had a frightening experience while at sea. On his way to Rome to stand trial for his beliefs, Paul's ship ran into a storm and broke apart. God told Paul that he and his fellow travelers would make it to shore safely—and, indeed, all were saved.

"What Is It?"

CAN YOU IMAGINE EATING the same food every day for a week? Probably not, but the Israelites ate the same food for 40 years in the desert! It was a food from heaven called manna. When the Israelites first saw the strange white flakes, they asked, "What is it?" And that is what *manna* actually means—"What is it!" It was used for baking cakes, or it was cooked like cereal. Each morning the Hebrews gathered the honey-tasting wafers that covered the ground, but they did

not gather manna on the Sabbath. The people soon began to complain about the miraculous manna— they wanted meat instead. Next, God caused millions of quail to fall into the camp. There were so many quail that each person gathered 100 bushels! But some of the people became greedy and overate. God caused a plague to come upon those who were selfish, and they died.

ONE OMER

When God provided the manna, he told everyone to gather what they needed— one omer for each person in their family. An omer was a measurement equal to about two quarts. The people who disobeyed and gathered more than an omer had none left over, but the people who gathered less always had plenty!

ZERO PERCENT HUMIDITY

The Sinai Desert is very dry, and some parts receive less than two inches of rain a year. Several months can pass without a drop of water falling.

The wilderness of Sinai

WATER FROM THE ROCK

After the Hebrews were freed from slavery in Egypt, they were forced to wander without water in the desert. Angry, they complained to Moses, who called upon God for help. At God's command, Moses hit a rock with his staff. The rock split open and out gushed enough water for all the people and their livestock.

JESUS' MANY NAMES

In the New Testament, Jesus is called the spiritual rock that the people drank from, the fountain of living water, the bread of life, and Immanuel, which means "God is with us." He is also called the Way to the heavenly Father, the Truth, and the Life. Another of his names is Promised One, because Jesus is the one who God promised would die and rise again to take away people's sins.

TELLING NAMES

Moses called the desert place where he struck the rock with his staff Massah and Meribah, meaning "testing" and "quarreling," because the people complained so much. They had found fault with their leader and cried, "Is the Lord among us or not?"

Ancient Egypt

Mediterranean Sea

• **Damascus**

•Hazor
Sea of Galilee

Dothan•
Shechem•

Jordan River

Jerusalem•

Dead Sea

Beersheba •

• **On**

• **Memphis**

Nile River

WANDERING ISRAELITES

Did you ever wonder why the Hebrews wandered in the desert for so long when there were faster and more direct ways to get to Canaan from Egypt? The Israelites' tricky route often helped them avoid their enemies. Also, God used that 40 years to teach them many important lessons.

No Contest

AFIERY DISPLAY OF GOD'S POWER involved the priests of Baal, an idol worshipped by the people of Canaan. They thought that Baal ruled over their land and animals and that it was Baal who caused the rain that watered their crops. Sometimes the Hebrews were tempted to worship Baal too, but many of God's prophets warned them about worshipping false gods. One day, on Mount Carmel, a contest was held to see whether Baal or Israel's God could light an altar fire. First, Baal's priests tried. They shouted to their god from morning until night and cut themselves with knives, but nothing happened. Next, it was Elijah's turn. He dug a trench around the altar and soaked it with four barrels of water. When Elijah prayed, God sent fire from heaven that burned up not only the sacrifice, but also the wood, stones, dust, and water!

ALAS, BABYLON

Nebuchadnezzar was one of a number of powerful kings who ruled the Babylonian empire. The main city, also known as Babylon, was located between the Tigris and Euphrates rivers in what is now Iraq. Its first great king was Hammurabi, famous for creating a system of laws. Later monarchs expanded the empire from the Persian Gulf to the Mediterranean Sea. Not long after Nebuchadnezzar's rule, Babylon was captured by the Medes and Persians.

JUDAH'S SUBJUGATION

Long before Jesus' birth, the nation of Judah was conquered by Babylon, and many were sent to live in Babylonian settlements. A privileged few became advisers to the king.

NEW NAMES

When Hananiah, Mishael, and Azariah entered the service of the Babylonian king, they received new names: Shadrach, Meshach, and Abednego. They were chosen for their handsomeness and intelligence.

SHADRACH, MESHACH, AND ABEDNEGO

King Nebuchadnezzar of Babylon once commanded everyone to worship a huge golden idol. His servants Shadrach, Meshach, and Abednego refused. The king was furious and ordered them to be thrown into a red-hot furnace. The three said God would be able to save them. How astonished Nebuchadnezzar was when he saw them walking around in the furnace unharmed! When he told the three Hebrews to come out, they didn't even have the smell of smoke on them.

REFINING METAL

The Bible often compares testing and trials to being refined in a furnace. The intense heat of the furnace separates pure metal from dross, or waste material.

HANDWRITING ON THE WALL

Belshazzar was a Babylonian king described in the book of Daniel. He was not humble and had little regard for God. During a feast, a mysterious hand wrote on the wall that God was putting an end to Belshazzar's kingdom. Belshazzar was killed that very night, and his kingdom was taken over by Darius the Mede.

Humble Beginnings

HUNDREDS OF YEARS before Jesus was born, God told his prophets that he would send a deliverer to save Israel. But who would have guessed the Savior's humble origins? Joseph and Mary traveled to Bethlehem to pay taxes. During the journey, Mary realized that her baby would be born soon. When they reached the town, they found it crowded with people arriving for the census. Joseph asked for lodging at the village inn, but it was full. The only place available to spend the night was a stable. There, in dark surroundings among the cows and donkeys, the King of kings was born. After Jesus was born, Mary laid him in a manger—a feeding box filled with hay for the animals to eat. Everyone expected that the Messiah would be born in royal surroundings, or at least a soft, clean bed, but God had other plans.

WINE FROM WATER

Jesus' first miracle happened at a wedding in Cana of Galilee. When the wine ran out, Jesus told the servants to fill up the water jars. When it was served, it was found that the water had turned to wine—very good wine. In fact, it was the best that had been served all day!

MADE IN HEAVEN

By performing his first miracle at a wedding, Jesus showed respect for marriage. Marriage was God's idea. The Bible says God made marriage so that people would not be alone and so they could work together to make a safe place for children. Jesus said it was God's plan that if a man and woman got married, they should stay together and love and care for each other for the rest of their lives.

Contemporary wedding ceremony in Israel

EPHESIANS 5:18

"Don't drink too much wine; for many evils lie along that path; be filled instead with the Holy Spirit, and controlled by him." Ephesians 5:18

Animal-skin containers

NEW WINE IN NEW SKINS

Dried animal skins made good wine containers—but only if new wine was put into new wineskins. Old skins could not be used because they would burst during fermentation.

Israeli school children press grapes.

WINEMAKING

Wine was made in a winepress—a large square pit or a stone basin carved from bedrock. Grapes were gathered and dumped into the press. Then the people would stamp on the grapes in their bare feet while singing and clapping joyfully. The juice pressed out of the grapes flowed into a collecting basin.

TOO MUCH OF A GOOD THING

The Scriptures call wine a good gift. Jesus used it with his disciples at the Last Supper, and Paul suggested that Timothy use it to cure stomach problems, perhaps because the drinking water was impure. At the same time, the Bible also warns against drinking too much wine and getting drunk. Joy, it says, should come from the Lord.

Try, Try Again

PETER, A FISHERMAN BY TRADE, knew all the secrets to catching fish— and yet, one night, he and his friends fished for hours and didn't catch a thing. The next morning, Jesus told Peter to try again. This time, Peter's net became so full of fish that it started to tear! Peter's friends brought their boats, and they became so filled with fish that they nearly sank! Peter fell to his knees and thanked Jesus. Another time, Peter and the disciples were fishing when a man on the shore told them to throw their net on the right side of the boat. When they did, it became heavy with fish. When they got to shore, the man was cooking a breakfast of fish and bread for them over a fire. They were surprised to realize that the man was actually Jesus. He had returned to them after rising from the dead.

AN ENDLESS SUPPLY?

God kept a widow's flour and cooking oil from running out during a drought. He told Elijah to ask her for a piece of bread. She had only enough flour and oil to make one small loaf for her son and herself, but Elijah promised that God would provide for her. So she made Elijah a cake of bread and found miraculously that there was enough for her and her son, too. For many days they continued to eat, and the flour and cooking oil did not run out.

BREAD AND WINE

Christians use bread to celebrate communion, or the Eucharist, in order to remember Jesus' death. The small amount of bread and wine or grape juice are not meant to feed a person's physical hunger but rather to represent spiritual food.

A wine jug

FEEDING THE MULTITUDES

Twice Jesus fed large crowds of people with very little food. He blessed a boy's lunch and broke it into pieces. He kept giving pieces to his disciples to give to the people. Everyone ate and was satisfied, yet there were 12 basketfuls of leftovers! Another time, Jesus fed 4,000 with just seven loaves of bread. Seven baskets of leftovers were gathered afterward.

THE LOAVES AND THE FISHES

The food Jesus provided for a crowd of some 5,000 men, women, and children came from a boy's lunch of only five barley loaves and two fish, which probably were dried and salted.

WORRY NOT

Matthew 6:25 states, "Don't worry about things—food, drink, and clothes. For you already have life and a body—and they are far more important than what to eat and wear." The Bible also says if God cares enough to provide food for the birds, he will surely provide for us, too.

PICKING GRAIN ON SABBATH

The Sabbath was supposed to be a day of rest—not work. But one time on the Sabbath, Jesus and his disciples were walking through a grain field. Because they were hungry, they picked some grain to eat. People immediately accused them of breaking the law. Jesus reminded them that obeying God was more important than following rules. He had created the Sabbath, and he had the authority to do what he wanted on the Sabbath.

Have No Fear

HAVE YOU EVER SEEN ANYONE walk on top of water? One night, Jesus sent his disciples across the lake in their boat. He was going into the hills to pray and would follow them later. The disciples started out, but soon strong winds began to blow, and the waves grew rough. While attempting to row hard against the wind, the disciples were terrified to see someone walking on the water. They thought it was a ghost! How relieved they were to see it was Jesus. Although they had watched him perform the miracle of feeding the 5,000 only the day before, they were still surprised that Jesus could do such a miraculous thing. Jesus called out to them, "Take heart, it is I; have no fear." When he climbed into their boat, the wind stopped. "You really are the Son of God!" they exclaimed.

SKILLED FISHERMEN

At least six of Jesus' disciples were fishermen and knew about boats, lakes, and fishing. The boats they used were small sailboats that they rowed when there was too much or too little wind. The disciples were accustomed to being on the lake after dark since they fished at night.

SEA OF GALILEE

The Sea of Galilee was also called Lake of Gennesaret, Sea of Tiberias, and the sea of Chinneroth. It is about 13 miles long, 7 miles across, and 695 feet below sea level. The Jordan River flows into the Sea of Galilee on the north. From Galilee's southern shore, the Jordan flows into the Dead Sea.

A fisherman casts his nets in the Sea of Galilee.

"WHY DID YOU DOUBT?"

When Peter saw Jesus walking on the water and heard his comforting voice, he also wanted to walk on the water. With Jesus' encouragement, Peter boldly climbed out of the boat and began walking toward him. But when the disciple saw the waves being whipped by the wind, he lost courage and began to sink. Jesus quickly grabbed him, but he was disappointed in Peter's lack of faith: "O man of little faith, why did you doubt?" Later, Peter's strength and growing faith were to make him a leader of the early Church.

The Dead Sea and its formations of salt caps

DEAD SEA

The Dead Sea is a large lake in southern Israel. It is called dead because it is so salty that nothing can live in it. The lake is about 50 miles long and 10 miles across, and in some places, more than 1,000 feet deep! The sea is so dense that people easily float in it. The zig-zagging Jordan River, which stretches 200 miles long, connects the Dead Sea to Sea of Galilee.

THE ROCK

Simon, one of Jesus' first and closest disciples, was renamed. Jesus called him Peter, or Cephas, which both mean "rock."

LOT'S WIFE

A 60-foot salt pillar on the shore of the Dead Sea is called Lot's Wife—after the woman who disobeyed God and was turned into a pillar of salt.

A salt mount near the Dead Sea called Lot's Wife

A Terrible Storm

THE BOOK OF REVELATION says that sometime in the future God will punish those who have disobeyed him and refused to acknowledge his lordship. Seven "bowls" of God's wrath will be poured on the earth. The first will cause everyone to break out in terrible sores. With the second, the oceans will become like blood and everything in them will die. With the third, the rivers and springs will become blood. The fourth bowl will cause the sun to scorch and burn, and with the fifth, the earth will be completely dark. The sixth bowl will unleash evil spirits and demons. God's seventh bowl of wrath will cause a terrible storm,

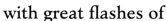

with great flashes of lightning, peals of thunder, and 100-pound hailstones. This storm will also produce the worst earthquake that the world has ever seen. The Bible says that the world will fall in heaps of rubble—and even the mountains will be flattened.

WHAT'S REALLY IMPORTANT

Jesus said people look at the sky and predict the weather. But he said it's more important to know God's word so they can know what's coming in life.

PLAGUE OF HAIL

One of the ten plagues suffered by Egyptians in Moses' time was a great hailstorm that ruined crops and killed livestock. The Scriptures state that it was the worst storm ever to hit Egypt.

WELCOME RAIN

A storm that people were happy to see came after three years of drought. Because King Ahab and Queen Jezebel were leading the people in worship of Baal, Elijah the prophet said there wouldn't be any rain until he said so. After the people admitted their sin and got rid of the followers of Baal, God finally sent a soaking rain.

"WHERE IS YOUR FAITH?"

Storms didn't bother Jesus. On a trip across the lake with his disciples, Jesus once fell fast asleep. Suddenly a gale blew up, and the boat was in danger of being sunk. The disciples were frantic as they saw Jesus peacefully sleeping. They yelled to wake him up, saying they were going to drown. Jesus told the wind and the raging waters to stop, and everything became calm. Then he asked his disciples, "Where is your faith?"

EZEKIEL'S STORM

The prophet Ezekiel witnessed a whirlwind that brought forth a great fiery cloud. Eventually, strange creatures with strange features emerged. Some of the most bizarre imagery in the Bible occurs in Ezekiel's description.

WRATHFUL STORM

God used a storm to show his displeasure. The Lord wanted his people to look to him for guidance and protection. But they told the prophet Samuel they wanted a king. Samuel predicted disaster. He said the Lord would send a storm to show his anger. Even though it was the dry season, it poured that day.

Jairus's Daughter

WHEN JAIRUS, A SYNAGOGUE LEADER, asked Jesus to heal his 12-year-old daughter, Jesus gladly agreed. But before Jesus arrived, messengers came and reported that the child had already died. Jesus insisted on going anyway, telling Jairus not to be afraid and to trust him. When Jesus reached the house, he found many people weeping and wailing in mourning. "Stop crying," Jesus told the people. "She is not dead, she is only asleep." The people laughed and scoffed because they all knew she was dead. Then Jesus told the crowd to leave and went into the girl's room with her parents and three of his disciples. Then Jesus took the girl by the hand and told her to get up! She jumped up and walked around, completely healed. Jesus even told her parents to give her something to eat!

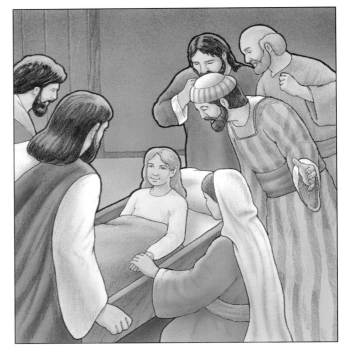

NOT OUT FOR GLORY

Jesus performed miracles to help people, not to impress them. Often he took only Peter, James, and John with him and told the person he healed not to tell anyone.

RITUAL MOURNING

In biblical times, mourning for the dead usually began at the moment of death and continued uninterrupted until after the burial. Often, professional mourners were hired to join with the family. These mourners were usually women who, to show their misery, wept, cried out loud, beat their chests, pulled out their hair, threw dust on their heads, tore their clothing, and put on a rough, uncomfortable fabric called sackcloth.

AN EXORCISM

Jesus was especially kind to women and children. A Greek woman whose daughter was possessed by an evil spirit begged him to drive the demon out. Jesus tested her faith by saying he should help the Jews first. But she was persistent: She asked for just a crumb of his goodness and power for her child. Jesus told her to go home because the demon had left her daughter. When the woman arrived, she found that her daughter had recovered.

AT ARM'S LENGTH

In order to keep themselves ceremonially clean, the Jewish leaders kept themselves separate from the gentiles, or non-Jews.

THE WOMAN FROM SHUNEM

A woman from Shunem had only one son, who died. She asked the prophet Elisha for help. Elisha prayed and then covered the boy with his body, laying mouth to mouth, eyes to eyes, hands to hands. He could feel the boy's body getting warm. Elisha got up and walked around, then repeated his actions. Finally the boy sneezed seven times and opened his eyes.

WOMAN'S PLACE

God's instruction to his people was clear in his provision for the protection and well-being of women. However, the male-dominated Middle Eastern culture in general did not give women much political or legal power. For a woman to make a request of an authority figure took much courage.

FALLEN ANGELS?

Demons, or evil spirits, may have been the angels who sided with Satan when he rebelled against God. In the New Testament, there are many incidents of Jesus casting out demons from people. Once, he cast a demon out of a boy after his disciples had failed to do so. The boy's father begged Jesus to help his son, and Jesus cured him that very hour.

Blind Bartimaeus Healed

BARTIMAEUS WAS A BEGGAR along the road in Jericho. Like most blind people in the ancient world, he depended on charity to survive. When he heard a crowd passing by one day, he asked what was happening. Someone told him that Jesus was coming! Bartimaeus called to Jesus for mercy, but the people yelled at him to keep quiet. Bartimaeus didn't listen and only yelled louder, "Son of David, have mercy on me!" "Son of David" was a popular way of addressing Jesus as the Messiah. It shows that this blind beggar truly knew who Jesus was. When Jesus reached the spot where the beggar was sitting, he stopped and asked him what he wanted. Bartimaeus answered that he wanted to see. "Your faith has healed you!" Jesus said, and immediately Bartimaeus could see. He followed Jesus down the road, praising him. And all the people who saw what had happened praised God, too.

BLIND LEADING THE BLIND

Jesus pointed out of the foolishness of a blind person following another blind person. He was speaking not of physical sight but of spiritual matters.

AN EYE-CATCHING PHRASE

A figure of speech can get a person's attention. Jesus said that if your right eye makes you sin by looking at evil, you are to "pluck it out and throw it away." He was teaching that sin is so harmful to us that we should do everything we can to avoid it.

A woman draws water from the ancient Pool of Siloam.

A BEGGAR IS MADE TO SEE

Jesus once healed a blind beggar by making a lump of mud from saliva and dirt. He put it on the man's eyes, then told him to go wash in the Pool of Siloam. The beggar's neighbors were stunned to see him walking around, able to see.

NO HOMETOWN HEALING

Once when Jesus was teaching in Nazareth he said, "Surely you will quote this proverb to me: 'Physician, heal yourself! Do here in your hometown what we have heard you did in Capernaum'" (Luke 4:23). Jesus said that he wasn't doing miracles in Nazareth because no prophet would be accepted in his own hometown.

HEALING BATHS

Bethesda was a special pool in Jerusalem where people came to be healed. Water for the pool came from an underground spring, which occasionally bubbled. People would try to be the first one in the water when the bubbling started. They believed that the water would make the first person well.

"PICK UP YOUR MAT AND WALK!"

Thirty-eight years is a long time to be lame. That's how long one man in Jerusalem had been an invalid. He would lie near the Pool of Bethesda—the name means "house of kindness"—hoping for someone to lower him into the healing waters. When Jesus saw him, he asked the man if he wanted to get well, then simply told him, "Get up! Pick up your mat and walk!" Incredibly, the man was healed.

Lazarus Raised

J ESUS' FRIEND LAZARUS had been very sick. Although Jesus loved him very much, he did not go to him immediately but stayed in another town for two days. In the meantime, Lazarus died and was buried. When Jesus finally arrived in Bethany, Lazarus had been dead for four days. Lazarus's sisters, Mary and Martha, were sad and disappointed that Jesus had not come sooner, but they also believed that it was not too late for a miracle! When Jesus saw how sad they were, he cried, too. The sisters took Jesus to their brother's tomb where they rolled away the stone at its entrance. Jesus prayed and shouted, "Lazarus, come out!" Then, wrapped in grave clothes, Lazarus walked out of his own tomb. Jesus had chosen not to heal his dear friend when he was sick but to raise him from the dead to show his disciples and others his power over death.

HEALING INFLUENCE

Sometimes people were healed without Jesus even touching them or saying a word. At Gennesaret, people brought their sick family members to Jesus just to touch the edge of his cloak so that they would be made well again.

LEPER COLONIES

Leprosy was a terrible, disfiguring skin disease common in biblical times. People who had it were called lepers. They had to live outside of cities with other lepers until they got better or died. If people without the disease came near them, the leper would cry out, "Unclean! Unclean!" to warn them.

PETER'S SICK RELATIVE

Jesus cared about women. One day, he went home with Peter from the synagogue. There they found Peter's mother-in-law sick in bed with a high fever. Jesus spoke to her and, taking her by the hand, helped her up. Immediately the fever left her, and she felt well enough to help serve a meal.

Medicinal herbs

HEALING HERBS

In biblical times, there were physicians, as there are today, to help the sick. Medicines were derived from herbs and plants. These natural substances could ease pain, clean cuts, and soothe aches and pains. Some plants used as medicines were coriander, myrrh, myrtle, galbanum, gall, aloe, and olive oil.

PAUL'S HEALING POWERS

God used the apostle Paul to heal people by using clothing and handkerchiefs that the apostle had touched. When sick people touched these items, they became well, and the demons that possessed them left.

THE POWER OF FAITH

The woman must have felt desperate. She had been bleeding for a dozen years, but no doctor had been able to help her. She saw Jesus in a crowd and thought if she could just touch his garment, she would be healed. As soon as she touched his robe, she could tell that she was well. Jesus also knew that something had happened. He understood that an act of goodness had passed from him. He told the woman her belief had healed her and to go in peace.

Hopeful Tidings

JESUS HAD TOLD HIS DISCIPLES many times that he would die and rise from the grave, but they did not understand. After Jesus had died and been buried, some women followers went to the tomb Sunday morning to apply more spices to the

body. They were shocked to discover that Jesus was not there and that the large stone to the door of the tomb was moved away! Two angels told the women that Jesus was not there because he had come back to life! The women ran to tell the disciples, but the disciples did not believe them. That evening, the disciples were meeting together in a locked room when suddenly Jesus was standing in the midst of them! He showed them the wounds in his hands and side from the crucifixion. The disciples finally realized that Jesus had risen from the dead, and they were overcome with joy.

A SIGN OF DEATH

When Jesus was crucified, the Roman soldiers didn't have to break his legs, as they did with the others, for Jesus was already dead. Instead, they pierced his side with a spear, and blood and water came out—a sure sign of death.

BURIAL RITUAL

In New Testament times, a body was prepared for burial by washing it and wrapping it in new linen strips. Aromatic spices, such as myrrh and aloe, were layered between the wrappings. About 100 pounds of spices were used for Jesus' burial shroud.

HEALING BONES

On their way to bury a man, some Israelites saw a gang of bandits. Frightened, they threw the corpse into Elisha's tomb. When the dead body touched Elisha's bones, the man came back to life.

ETERNAL LIFE

The Scriptures are filled with accounts of people being raised from the dead by prophets, by Jesus, and by his followers. But all eventually died again. The apostle Paul said that flesh and blood cannot inherit the kingdom. Instead, like a seed, the body dies to give birth to a new form that cannot die or decay. For those who believed in Christ, the apostle Paul said that death would be "swallowed up in victory."

JOSEPH OF ARIMATHEA

Joseph of Arimathea was rich enough to have a tomb cut from rock—and generous enough to have Jesus buried there. The body, wrapped in grave clothes, was laid on a stone slab inside the tomb. Then a large, flat rock was rolled in front of the opening. The stone was heavy and extremely difficult to remove.

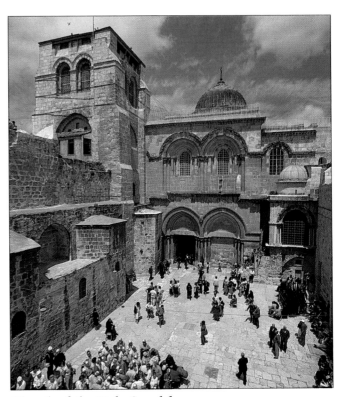

Church of the Holy Sepulchre

HOLY SEPULCHRE

Today in Jerusalem there is a Church of the Holy Sepulchre. It is possible that the tomb used by Jesus lies under this church.

EUTYCHUS'S FALL

Once when Paul was preaching, a young man named Eutychus went to sleep on a window ledge. The unfortunate fellow fell to the ground and died. Paul put his arms around Eutychus and brought him back to life.

89

Everyday Life

WE OFTEN THINK THAT DAILY LIFE in biblical times was very different from our life today. There were no refrigerators, televisions, radios, or automobiles. Their lamps were oil, not electric. Their transportation was by ship and camel instead of by car. Their rulers were kings instead of presidents. On the other hand, families ate meals together, dressed up for special occasions, and liked to visit with each other. There were games and books to read. Actually, life in biblical times may not have been so different after all.

The Last Supper

THE BIBLE TELLS of a special meal called the Last Supper. It is the final meal Jesus ate with his disciples the night before he died. The supper took place on Thursday evening of Passover Week in the upper room of a house in Jerusalem. Jesus and his disciples ate, sang Psalms, and prayed. On this occasion, Jesus said two surprising things. He said that Judas would betray him and that Peter, his close friend, would deny that he ever knew him. Both of these things came true just as Jesus predicted. At the Last Supper, Jesus took the bread and wine and gave them meanings. From that point on, they would remind people of Jesus' death on the cross. The bread would be a reminder of his body, and the wine would be a reminder of his blood. Christians throughout history have continued to take part in the Lord's Supper, sometimes called Communion, to remind them of the sacrifice Jesus made for them.

HOLY GRAIL

The Holy Grail was the cup supposedly used by Jesus at the Last Supper. It became the subject of many legends during the Middle Ages. In King Arthur's court, an empty seat was reserved at the Round Table for the knight who found the Grail. The cup has never been found.

GATHERING AT MEALS

People in biblical times worked very hard all day and looked forward to supper. The lamps would be lit, and the family would gather to eat, talk, tell stories, and maybe even sing. Then they would go to bed. Jesus often ate meals with friends and strangers, and then he joined them in conversation.

A THOUGHTFUL GIFT

In addition to eating food, people in the biblical era gave food as gifts to friends and family. Because food was sometimes hard to get, it was considered valuable and, therefore, a thoughtful gift.

WHAT'S FOR DINNER?

Meals were cooked over a wood fire. People ate bread and a variety of fruits and vegetables. Fish was common, while meat was usually saved for special occasions. When the word *meat* is used in the Bible, it usually means "food." Nuts, herbs, and cheese made from goat or sheep milk were also tasty favorites in biblical times.

TABLE MANNERS

Tables in Jesus' day were long and narrow. People would sit on benches or chairs or, if the table was low, on rugs or mats. Sometimes dinner guests would even recline, lying on low couches with their head near the table and their body propped up on one elbow.

THE STAFF OF LIFE

Bread was a necessity at every meal. It is referred to hundreds of times in the Bible. The round, flat loaves of the day were made of wheat or barley.

The Last Straw

IN ANCIENT EGYPT, Israelite slaves worked all day to make bricks for the Pharaoh's building projects. The bricks were made of clay, which was mixed with straw to give the bricks more strength and durability. The bricks were formed by hand, or in a wooden mold, and then baked in the sun until they were hard. If the slaves did not make a certain amount of bricks each day, they would be punished. At first, Pharaoh supplied straw for the workers. But one day, he told them they would have to gather their own straw and make even more bricks! The people tried to do as Pharaoh asked, but it was impossible! There was not enough time to gather straw and make bricks, too. But Pharaoh showed no mercy and beat them for falling short. Finally, the slaves rebelled against the Pharaoh and began their escape out of Egypt.

LIFE AT THE TOP

Rooftops on houses were flat in biblical times. People used them for drying flax and fruit. They washed clothes there and wove fabric. Roofs were also places to sleep when it was hot and places to pray when one needed privacy. Rooftops in cities were so close together that a person running from danger could jump from one roof to another, then escape down the stairs of the last house in the row.

SIMPLE HOUSES

Most houses in biblical times were one story high. Their thick walls were made from cut stone. Windows were small and did not have glass.

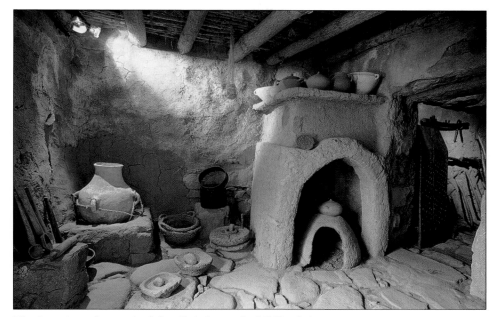

The interior of a typical family's home in biblical times

HOME SWEET HOME

The houses of well-to-do families usually had four rooms. People would enter through an open courtyard where fragrant flowers and plants grew. At the end of the house was a large living and sleeping room. A table, a chair, and a reed mat for sleeping were basic furnishings. The rich might also have a couch or a bed.

FOLLOW INSTRUCTIONS!

Jesus once told a story about a wise man who followed directions and built his house on solid rock. But a foolish man built his house on the sand. When a storm came with rain and wind, the foolish man's house came crashing down, while the wise man's dwelling was left standing. Jesus said it was important to follow his directions.

TOP SECRET

The first Christians worshipped together in their own homes. These gatherings were usually held in secret because of enemies who wanted to destroy the new religious movement.

DID JESUS HAVE A HOME?

Did you know that Jesus had no place to live? The Bible says that even foxes had holes and birds had nests, but Jesus had no home of his own.

Sense of Style

WOMEN WORE TUNICS during biblical times, although they were longer and more tailored than the man's tunic. Women liked to add decorative designs to their clothing by embroidering with colorful thread around the neckline. A woman would never leave home without wearing an upper mantle over her tunic. This was a large piece of material that wrapped around the head and upper body. It could be made of warm wool for winter or light linen for summer. The mantle could be used as a veil, as a shawl, or even as a bag. Sometimes the mantles had a padded ring on top enabling the woman to carry a pitcher of water on her head. Both men and women wore jewelry including earrings, nose rings, and rings on toes, ankles, and wrists. In ancient Egypt, women wore cosmetics made of paints and dyes. Wooden combs, clay perfume bottles, and bronze mirrors were also used by Egyptian women.

Gold jewelry, mid-second millenium B.C.

THE BASIC TUNIC

The tunic was the main item of clothing in biblical times. It was a simple, long undergarment, something like a shirt. It draped over one shoulder and went down to the knees or ankles. Made of either wool or linen, tunics could be adapted for warm and cool weather. Beneath the tunic, a linen loincloth or waist cloth was worn. Men may have worn a scarf wrapped around the head as protection from the sun.

CAREWORN

Sackcloth was a rough material made of goat's hair. People would wear it when they were very sad or grief-stricken or to show that they were sorry for their sins.

ONE IS ENOUGH

In the book of Luke, John the Baptist says that if a man has two tunics, he should give one away to a person who has none.

WARM AND SNUG

The Bible says that baby Jesus was wrapped in swaddling clothes when he was born. These were not really clothes but cloth wrapped tightly around a baby to keep it warm and secure. It was also believed that swaddling protected a baby's body. Newborn babies today are still comforted by being swaddled in a blanket.

LOOKS AREN'T EVERYTHING

God told the prophet Samuel that what people look like on the outside is not important. God does not judge people by their appearance or the clothes they wear. Instead, he looks at what is inside—their thoughts and attitudes.

AN UNFRIENDLY WAGER

After Jesus died on the cross, the soldiers wanted his tunic. They threw lots to decide who would keep it.

Outside with the Shoes!

SANDALS COULD NEVER be worn indoors in biblical times. When people came inside, they removed their sandals, but their feet were very dirty from walking on dusty roads. To welcome visitors, the host would bring a basin of cool water and wash and dry the feet of their guests. Jesus once washed the disciples' feet as a symbol of humility and love. He wanted to show them that, no matter how great a person is, they still need to serve others by being kind and helpful. Another way the host would honor his guest was to serve him the best morsel of food he had.

SOMETHING TO LEAN ON

People in biblical times spent a lot of time walking. They often used a staff or walking stick to guide them. A staff was usually four to six feet long and made from a peeled vine branch. Travelers used a staff for climbing, for clearing twigs or rocks in a rough path, to kill snakes, or to lean on when they grew tired.

BAGGING IT

Travelers also carried a bag. This was usually made of animal skin and carried over the shoulder like a purse. It held food for the journey.

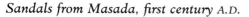

Sandals from Masada, first century A.D.

ON HALLOWED GROUND

Did you know that God once told a man to take off his sandals? In the desert, God appeared to Moses in a burning bush. He told him to take off his shoes because he was standing on holy ground. Moses obeyed to show his deep respect for God.

FOOTWISE

Sandals were common footwear in biblical times. They were made of a piece of leather or wood cut in the shape of a foot and tied with leather straps. In big households, it would be a servant's job to untie the straps of the sandals. John the Baptist admired Jesus so much that he said he did not feel worthy enough even to untie Jesus' sandals.

JUDGMENT DAY

God also told Isaiah to take off his shoes—and his clothes, too! Isaiah walked barefoot (and naked!) as a symbolic act to show people that God's judgment was near.

NOW YOU SEE IT...

When Moses obeyed God and threw his staff on the ground, it turned into a snake! When he picked up the snake, it became a staff again.

MIRACULOUS STAFF

God helped Aaron use his staff to perform miracles. When Aaron put his staff in the Nile, it and all the other bodies of water in Egypt turned to blood. Another time he struck the dust with his staff, and the dust throughout Egypt became lice!

Festive Garb

GARMENTS WORN FOR FESTIVALS and feasts were similar to everyday clothing, but they were more colorful and decorated with fancy embroidery. They were usually made of fine linen rather than wool. At weddings, guests were given a special robe to wear at the banquet. If a guest refused to wear it, the host of the wedding would be offended and think that the guest did not want to take part in the festivities. The Israelites sometimes added special tassels to the corners of their outer garments, with a blue thread attached to each tassel to remind them of God's commandments. Jewish men today wear special four-cornered prayer shawls with these tassels.

Priests in biblical times wore clothing that was very colorful and expensive—linen tunics with beautiful belts made of blue, purple, and scarlet. The high priest wore an expensive breastplate made of gold and costly linen and decorated with expensive stones.

BUNDLED UP

Men who traveled needed warm garments to protect them against the cold. Elijah wore a coat made of animal skins. John the Baptist wore one of camel's hair.

VALUABLE APPAREL

Cloaks were a valued possession in biblical times. Since they were expensive, most people owned only one. They used it as a sack to carry things in, as a place to sit, and as a promise to pay a debt. The prophet Elijah once put his cloak on Elisha's shoulders to show that Elisha would be the next ruler. Later, when Elijah went to heaven, he left his cloak behind for Elisha.

WEDDING CHIC

Brides in biblical times wore rich and beautiful dresses. The book of Proverbs describes one wedding dress as "woven with gold." The bride also wore jewels and a veil. The groom would be dressed in a festive robe and might have worn a garland of flowers around his neck.

DRESSED TO THE NINES

The Pharisees liked to stand out in a crowd. They wore expensive linen garments with bright embroidery. The hems of their robes were wide and decorated with long tassels.

A BELT'S MANY USES

Men and women often wore belts around their tunics. Some belts were made of leather and were used as purses for money. Jonathan gave his friend David a belt that could hold a knife or sword. The prophet Agabus took Paul's belt and bound his own feet and hands with it to demonstrate how the apostle would be treated if he returned to Jerusalem. What he said came true, because Paul was taken into custody by the Romans occupying Jerusalem.

WHITE WAS SPECIAL

A robe, or stole, was worn for special occasions. People in heaven were said to wear pure white robes to show that Jesus had washed away their sins.

OF CLOAKS AND COATS

Cloaks were worn over tunics for extra warmth. Many people did not own blankets and used their cloaks for cover at night.

On Guard

ROMAN SOLDIERS WERE SENT TO GUARD Jesus' tomb after his death. The tomb was already secured by a large stone at its only entrance. There was a wax seal placed on the joint of the stone. If anyone tampered with the tomb, their crime would be obvious since the seal would be broken. But these precautions weren't enough for Pilate. He wanted guards posted at the tomb's entrance as well. Pilate knew that Jesus had predicted he would rise again. He was afraid that the disciples would steal Jesus' body and then tell everyone that he had risen from the dead. The guards took their job very seriously. If anything did happen to Jesus, they would be held responsible and severely punished, even killed. The sealed and guarded tomb did not stop Jesus. After three days, he rose from the dead, just as he had promised.

ON THE OFFENSE

The catapult was often used in Roman battle. This heavy machine had a wooden arm that hurled burning javelins and rocks into enemy territory.

AGAINST THE ODDS

The Hebrews often found themselves outnumbered and ill-equipped during battle. But with God's help they were often victorious— even when the odds were against them.

ROMAN GEAR

A Roman soldier would wear a jacket of metal plates over his chest and back, while a bronze helmet protected his neck and forehead. Cheek guards protected his jaw, and colored plumes helped tell friend from foe in battle. Favorite weapons were the gladius, a two-edged sword, and the javelin, a six-foot-long pointed spear.

BATTLE READY

Soldiers in the Old Testament were well prepared for battle. Each soldier wore a leather and metal helmet, a coat of heavy armor, and a protective covering around the neck. They also carried heavy shields. Horse-drawn chariots were used in battle because of their speed. A soldier's main weapons were spears, swords, and slingshots, but warriors were also skilled with a bow and arrow. They were good enough to shoot accurately while riding in a bumpy chariot!

TORTOISE FORMATION

Sometimes, when marching into battle, Roman soldiers would lock their shields together to form a solid wall or roof. The soldiers' rectangular shields formed a pattern that resembled a turtle's shell, and so this became known as the tortoise formation.

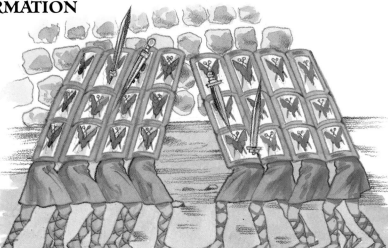

WORDS AS WEAPONS

"Telling lies about someone is as harmful as hitting him with an axe, or wounding him with a sword, or shooting him with a sharp arrow." Proverbs 25:18

A Troublemaker

IN THE BIBLE, kings were chosen by God to rule over cities and nations. Before kings, judges made important decisions for the people. For a long time, the Israelites lacked any king other than God himself, and they began to complain. God

told Samuel to warn them that a king would only cause trouble. God wanted to be their only ruler. An earthly king would disappoint them and not always rule them well. When the people still did not listen, God told Samuel to appoint Saul as the first Hebrew king. After Saul, David became king, and after David, Solomon. These were the three best-known kings of Israel. Later, the kings of Israel and Judah became increasingly evil and wicked and wanted the people to worship idols. A king usually had a wife (or wives!) and lived in a palace surrounded by personal attendants, officials, and bodyguards.

OLD TESTAMENT KINGS

The Old Testament books of First and Second Kings tell about the Kings of Judah and the Kings of Israel from the end of King David's reign until Jerusalem was destroyed.

EGYPT'S GREAT HOUSE

"Pharaoh" is the general title used in the Bible for the kings of Egypt. It means "great house," referring to the palace where the king lived. Many pharaohs are mentioned in the Bible, even a woman named Hatshepsut. Hatshepsut inherited her position and led Egypt for 17 years.

The enormous pyramids at Giza remind us of that ancient Egyptian civilization.

HE ASKED FOR IT

The pharaoh most often mentioned in the Bible is Ramses II, who enslaved the Israelites. God warned Ramses many times to free the Hebrews. When the king would not listen, God sent plagues upon Egypt, including hordes of frogs, swarms of mosquitoes and flies, destructive hail, voracious locusts, and a blinding dust storm.

A WONDER OF THE WORLD

When pharaohs died, they were often buried in stone pyramids. It is amazing that these elaborate and monumental tombs were built by hand using simple axes, chisels, and saws.

An Egyptian coffin is unearthed.

THE TASTE TEST

Two of the most important men in a pharaoh's court were his baker and his cup bearer. The baker was in charge of preparing the pharaoh's meals. The cup bearer would taste all of the pharaoh's food and drink before it was served to make sure it had not been poisoned. It's no surprise that a pharaoh was likely to have more than one cup bearer throughout his reign!

ANCIENT COFFINS

The Egyptians and Philistines often buried their dead in large clay coffin-like boxes. The top third or half of the box was cut away so the body could be inserted, and the top was then replaced. On the front of the coffin, a likeness of the deceased person's face was molded in clay.

105

It's in the Stars

ASTROLOGERS WERE ALSO CALLED MAGI, or wise men. Magi was the name of an ancient religious group who predicted the future and had the special ability to study and understand the meaning of star formations and the movement of planets. Later, people who seemed to have an unusual ability or intelligence were called magi. The most

famous magi, or wise men, in the Bible were the three who came to worship Jesus. When these astrologers saw a special star in the east, they knew the Messiah had been born. They followed the star for thousands of miles, until they reached Bethlehem. Although most Nativity scenes show the wise men and the shepherds kneeling at the manger together, this probably did not occur. It is more likely that Jesus was already one or two years old by the time the wise men reached him. The Bible says that when they found him "their joy knew no bounds!"

A SOLITARY LIFE

In the Bible, sheep were used for their wool, milk, and meat. A shepherd cared for and protected these valuable animals. He would lead the flocks, sometimes over long distances, to find food and water. He would find them shelter during storms or on cold nights. The sheep recognized their shepherd's voice and came when he called. Lonely young men, shepherds would often pass the time by playing a flute, sitting at a campfire, or singing songs.

O LITTLE STAR OF BETHLEHEM

What was this mysterious star of Bethlehem? Some think it was a comet; others say it may have been the planets of Jupiter, Saturn, and Venus shining together. Still others believe it to have been a supernova. Ancients charted it as a conjunction of Jupiter and Saturn in the constellation of Pisces, which is probably the best explanation.

A USEFUL TOOL

Shepherds used a slingshot for a number of purposes. If a sheep had gone astray, the shepherd would fling a rock that would land in front of the animal, startling it into going in the right direction. A slingshot was also used, along with a club, to ward off lions and bears that attacked the flock.

Ancient wall carving of a man firing a slingshot, c. ninth century B.C.

FIT FOR A KING

The three wise men presented Jesus with precious gold; frankincense, an expensive perfume from the bark of a terebinth tree; and myrrh, a sweet-smelling gel found on shrubs in the desert.

THOSE WAYWARD SHEEP

Sheepfolds were stone-walled enclosures built to keep the sheep from wandering away at night. The shepherd would sleep at the sheepfold entrance.

THE GOOD SHEPHERD

In the Bible, Jesus is called the Good Shepherd and the people who followed him his sheep. Jesus loved and cared for the faithful, and just as a shepherd might die while trying to protect his sheep from harm, Jesus was willing to die for his "sheep" so that they could be saved. In Psalm 23, David, a shepherd himself, describes God as a wonderful shepherd to him, guiding and protecting him throughout his life.

Stone Throwing

PEOPLE WHO DISOBEYED certain parts of God's law were sometimes punished by stoning. Rocks were hurled at the accused person until they died. Once Paul was in Lystra when the crowd became angry and began stoning him. Taken for dead, Paul was dragged from the city. Paul's friends were amazed when he stood up and went back into the city! At a stoning, three witnesses needed to testify that the person had committed a crime. Two of these witnesses had to throw the first stone. Once, a crowd brought an adulterous woman to Jesus, demanding that she be stoned. Jesus answered, "If any one of you is without sin, let him be the first to throw a stone at her." One by one every person left. They knew they could not judge her because they were sinners themselves. Jesus told the grateful woman to go on her way and sin no more.

HELPING THE NEEDY

Beggars were a common sight in biblical times. They would ask for money outside the temple or along the roads near cities. Most beggars were unable to work. They may have been lame or blind or sick. But Jesus saw beyond the beggars' dirty and tattered clothes. Jesus said that if people were in need, they deserved whatever help people could give them.

ALMS TO THE POOR

Alms were voluntary gifts of money or food to the poor. Jesus taught to give alms but to do it quietly, without letting others know.

CRUEL AND UNUSUAL

Most prisoners were criminals, but many Christians were jailed, too, simply because of their religious beliefs.

TERRIFYING PLACES

Prisons in biblical times were dark, underground dungeons, usually with no windows. One famous prison mentioned in the Bible was carved out of rock. Prisoners were shackled with chains and often forced like slaves to do hard work. In ancient days, prisoners were guilty until proven innocent and rarely received a fair trial. Several books in the New Testament were written by people who were in prison.

CORPORAL PUNISHMENT

Roman prisoners were sometimes beaten with a scourge, a wooden-handled instrument with three leather straps studded with small pieces of iron. After being beaten, prisoners were often placed in stocks, which were wooden frames with holes just big enough for the ankles or wrists.

EGYPTIAN JAILS

In ancient times, muddy pits sometimes served as prisons. A room in the inner court of the temple or a guarded room outside in the palace courtyard could be a prison, too. Joseph endured an Egyptian prison for two years. Egyptian prisoners wore heavy iron collars and painful shackles.

A World Traveler

KING SOLOMON BUILT A FLEET of ships to transport valuable materials from other lands. He harbored his ships at Ezion-geber on the tip of the Red Sea. This location became a trading post. Soon Solomon was sending his ships to buy and sell around the world. Often his ships carried copper and iron to Ophir and returned with rare and expensive items.

The round trip—about 1,250 miles each way—took three years! To build the temple, King Solomon imported cedar, cypress, and gold from the city of Tyre. His ships also brought him ivory, silver, chariots, precious stones, peacocks, horses, and even monkeys! He paid for these treasures with wheat, oil, or silver shekels. About a century after Solomon died, King Jehoshaphat started building ships again. Unfortunately all his ships were wrecked in a terrible storm, and for a time shipbuilding came to an end.

A WICKED CITY

Corinth was a famous seaport noted for its wickedness. Paul wrote two famous letters to the Christians in this city, encouraging them to live more piously.

The Temple of Apollo at Corinth

UNWISE JOINT VENTURE

King Jehoshaphat of Judah was a wise ruler who loved God, but he made a mistake when he joined with the wicked King Ahaziah of Israel to build trading ships. A prophet named Eliezer told Jehoshaphat that his plans would be ruined. Sure enough, the ships were later wrecked and the partnership ended.

STRANGE DISAPPEARANCE

The city of Tarshish is mentioned often in the Scriptures. It was a famous port city reported to have vast wealth, especially gold. Surprisingly, no one today knows for sure where Tarshish was located.

GRACEFUL DESIGN

The sterns and bows of Philistine ships were carved in the shape of a bird's long neck. These ships, which were oarless, were sometimes used in battles at sea.

HAZARDS OF TRAVEL

Most people did not travel by ship. The Hebrews were afraid of the water, thinking that it held mysterious powers. They had good reason. The sea was unpredictable, and travel by boat was extremely dangerous. The apostle Paul was shipwrecked at least three times and once spent a whole day and night in the sea! But travel on foot could be hazardous, too. Travelers had to contend with robbers and wild animals, as well as hunger and cold weather.

SHIP TO SHORE

One day, an enormous crowd gathered to hear Jesus. He could not even find a place to stand. So he got into a boat and spoke from there while the people listened from the shore. Jesus and his disciples often used fishing boats to travel from town to town.

Music as Medicine

THE HARP IS THE FIRST MUSICAL INSTRUMENT mentioned in the Bible. It had a triangular wooden frame with strings stretched between the wood. The number of strings varied—as few as 12, or as many as 40. The strings could be played by hand or with a special pluck called a plectrum. Simple strings could be made of twisted grasses, but better strings were made from dried animal intestines. The lyre was similar to the harp, but it was smaller in size and had only a few strings. The lyre made soft, beautiful music. David liked to play the harp while watching his sheep in the fields. He eventually used his musical abilities to write many of the Psalms in the Bible. When David worked for King Saul, he would often play the harp for the King if he was troubled or sad. The beautiful music calmed and soothed Saul. Today, harp music is still known for its tranquil effects.

"JUBAL"-ATION?

The Bible tells us that Jubal was the first musician. This descendant of Cain invented the harp and the flute.

FOR ALL OCCASIONS

Music was used for many purposes throughout the Bible. People sang happy songs to celebrate military victories and sad songs to mourn the death of a loved one. Music could be heard at festive occasions like wedding banquets and a king's coronation. Jesus enjoyed music, too. He and his disciples often sang hymns. Psalm 150 says that people should praise the Lord with every instrument they have.

A LOUD AND JOYFUL NOISE

Music was an important part of worship in the temple. Orchestras of instruments such as flutes, tambourines, trumpets, cymbals, and drums would play. They accompanied singers, dancers, and actors. Some of the Psalms were actually songs sung at worship or special ceremonies.

SING A SONG

Singing during temple worship was often done in parts—with different groups alternating lines of the songs. Lamech sang the first song in the Bible.

SHINING LIGHTS

When it is dark, can you hide a brightly lit city that stands on a hill? No! Jesus says Christians are to shine just as brightly: "Don't hide your light! Let it shine for all; Let your good deeds glow for all to see so that they will praise your heavenly Father." Matthew 5:16

A LAMP UNTO MY FEET

Early lamps were small clay bowls filled with olive oil. A flax or wool wick floated in the oil. Some fancier lamps tapered into a spout, with the wick emerging at the end. The lamps held little oil and needed much refilling. Oil lamps did not shed much light and were put on a lamp stand to brighten a bigger area. Jesus said that the Bible is like a lamp—it lights our path by revealing God's wishes and keeps us from stumbling in the "darkness" of evil and sin.

Oil lamp from the Hellenistic Period.

A Simple Life

THE NOMAD'S TENTS were made of cloth woven from black goat hair, which kept out the rain and the heat. Nine poles supported the tent, dividing it into two rooms—one for women and children, and one for men and guests. The "houses" were small and cramped since many people slept in the same room. Beds were straw or wool mats. The nomadic diet consisted of goat's milk cheese and sometimes meat stews. Life as a nomad wasn't easy. Each family worked hard every day gathering food or tending animals. At harvest time or sheep-shearing time, whole families pitched in and helped. There were the daily tasks of cleaning, baking, spinning, weaving, and fabric dying to take care of as well. Nomads were happy when they found an oasis because it provided them with water, fruit, and shade.

A NOMADIC EXISTENCE

Abraham lived a nomad's life at several points in his life, but he liked to stay in one place for as long as he could. For ten years, he camped in an oak grove near Hebron.

NO FIXED ADDRESS

Nomads traveled and lived in the desert in Old Testament times. The nomadic life probably came about as shepherds were forced to leave depleted pastures in search of grazing land for their flocks. They would move from place to place and live in tents for shelter. Occasionally, nomads would raid cities or offer their services when a king needed an army.

A nomadic campsite

A PERFECT WORLD

In the Bible, the prophet Isaiah said that God's kingdom would someday be like a wonderful oasis. After the world has passed away, only beautiful and good things would exist—no sickness, no misery, and no death. Only people who have put their faith in God would inhabit this perfect world.

A date-palm oasis in the Negev Desert

WELCOME RELIEF

The Middle East has several deserts—large, open areas covered with sand, rocks, and scrub. Deserts are generally hot and dry, but sometimes rain or springs of water create an oasis, where beautiful flowers, green grass, and lush plants grow, creating a paradise in the wilderness.

Date-palm trees

HIGHLY PRIZED

Date-palm trees thrived around an oasis. The trees produced dates, a fruit valued for its juicy and delicious meat.

JERICHO'S SPRINGS

Jericho was an oasis town built around springs of water. The same springs are still bubbling today, supplying the town with fresh water.

Family Life

IN MANY WAYS, the Bible is a book about families. Families were close-knit and shared in the work, worship, and celebrations of the community. Brothers and sisters, mothers and fathers, and aunts and uncles often lived under the same roof or in nearby houses. From their families, a boy or girl would learn God's word, valuable skills, and customs that they would pass to the next generation. Families were also a source of help and security during hard times. In this chapter, you will learn how families in biblical times lived—and how they resemble our families today.

Buying Back the Firstborn

OLD TESTAMENT LAW made it clear that first-born males belonged to God as a reminder of what happened in Egypt. This was because during the exodus from Egypt, all the Egyptians' firstborn sons died, but God saved the firstborn sons of Israel. From then on, it was thought that the firstborn should be set apart for God. Forty days after being born, the baby had to be presented to a priest. The parents would have to "redeem," or buy back, the child by making an offering. This amount was usually five pieces of silver. Jesus' parents, Mary and Joseph, followed this custom, too. They brought the infant Jesus to the temple and presented him to the Lord. The Holy Spirit had told an old man named Simeon to come to the temple that day because Jesus would be there. Simeon held Jesus in his arms and praised God. He had waited all of his life to see the son of God.

A SIGN FROM ABOVE

A Hebrew couple's greatest desire was to have children. To be childless in biblical times was said to be a sign of God's disfavor.

THE MARVEL OF LIFE

Psalm 139 has a beautiful passage about how human life is created. David, who wrote the psalm, praises God because he had been "fearfully and wonderfully made."

MIDWIVES

Physicians only helped women in childbirth when it was an emergency. Instead, experienced women called midwives cared for women undergoing labor. They gave advice, provided remedies, and took care of the new baby. Usually, they were friends or relatives of the family. A midwife was with Rachel as she died giving birth to Jacob's son, Benjamin.

AN OLD BELIEF

An old superstition claimed that mandrake roots had magical qualities, including the power of fertility. Leah received mandrakes from her son, Reuben, and she and her husband, Jacob, soon had another child.

BIRTH RITUAL

A newborn was cared for according to several established customs. After birth, the umbilical cord was cut and tied. The midwife then washed the baby and rubbed salt, water, and oil on the baby's skin. She then wrapped the baby in a cloth blanket and presented it to the father. The mother would begin nursing the baby a little while later. After a week, the baby was washed and rubbed again and placed in new swaddling clothes.

JUMPING FOR JOY

Even before he was born, John the Baptist recognized Jesus. Jesus' mother, Mary, who had learned that she would have a child, went to visit her relative, Elizabeth. (Elizabeth was also expecting a baby who would grow up to be John the Baptist.) When Elizabeth heard Mary's greeting, her baby leaped for joy in her womb!

Trick Question

THE SADDUCEES WERE A GROUP of Jewish priests. They were rich and important men who differed from other Jewish groups in several ways: First, they believed that only the first five books of the Old Testament were true; second, they did not believe in life after death; and third, they did not believe in angels or spirits. The Sadducees became angry that so many people were following the teachings of Jesus. They began plotting to destroy him. One day, they tried to make Jesus look foolish by asking him a question about marriage in heaven. They told the story of a woman who, after her husband died, married each of the man's brothers in turn. The Sadducees then asked Jesus which man would be the woman's husband in heaven. Jesus surprised them all by saying that in heaven there was no marriage, for men and women would be like angels.

THE GO'EL

A go'el was the head of an extended family. If a woman's husband died without leaving any children, the go'el was supposed to marry the woman so that she could produce heirs.

HELPMATE

A hard-working wife was considered a great help to her husband. It was commonly believed that a man could rise to leadership only if his wife were sensible and talented.

A FATHER'S DUTY

Besides providing food and shelter, a husband was the family's religious leader, responsible for instructing his children in Moses' teachings.

BAD ADVICE

Like Job, his wife was very sad about losing her children and her home. But unlike Job, she did not trust in God's goodness. She told Job to curse God and die. Job refused. He did not believe he should accept only the good things in life and not the bad.

MORE—OF EVERYTHING

Some men in Old Testament times took more than one wife. Sometimes they did this to have more children, but the practice caused problems. For example, there was jealousy among the wives, added expenses, and disputes among the children. In fact, unless a man was wealthy, he usually had only one wife. Lamech is the first man with two wives mentioned in the scriptures. King Solomon had more than 700 wives. Many came from other countries and were blamed for leading Solomon into idolatry.

City of Corinth

AN EVANGELIST TEAM

Aquila and his wife, Priscilla, met the apostle Paul in the city of Corinth. They were Jewish Christians who had been forced to leave the city of Rome. They were also evangelists—that is, they worked to spread the news about Jesus' resurrection and tried to persuade others to become Christians.

A Christian Heritage

TIMOTHY MAY BE THE ONLY PERSON in the Bible whose family had three generations of Christians. His mother, Eunice, and grandmother, Lois, were Jewish Christians who most likely led Timothy to the faith and taught him the Scriptures. The name Timothy means "one who honors God." As a young man, Timothy left Lystra to join Paul on a missionary journey. Paul became so fond of his young disciple that he considered him a son. Paul wrote two letters to Timothy that are part of the New Testament. In the first letter to Timothy, he gives Timothy, now a preacher, advice on choosing church leaders and running the church. In the second letter, Paul knows that he is nearing the end of his life. He asks Timothy to come and see him before he dies. In this loving, final letter, Paul gives his last instructions and encouragement to his dear friend Timothy.

CHILD'S PLAY

Matthew 11:16–17 mentions children that played "wedding" and "funeral." These imitation games are the only children's games mentioned in the New Testament.

KIDS WILL BE KIDS

Many children in biblical times, especially those who had no toys, played outdoor games using sticks, stones, marbles, and balls.

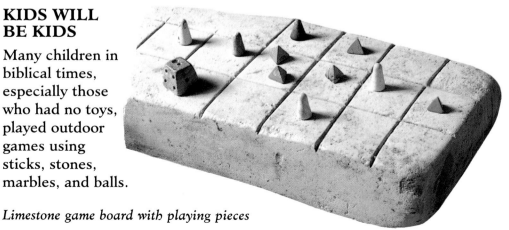

Limestone game board with playing pieces

BOARD GAMES

Board games were played in many ancient cultures from the biblical era. One of the oldest was the Royal Game of Ur, and it may have been played as early as 1800 B.C. Games similar to chess and checkers have also been found. Many games used two-sided or four-sided dice.

Lots made of stone and bone

YES, NO—OR WAIT

Jews did not allow gambling, but casting lots was often allowed as a way of finding out God's will. In fact, the high priest wore on his breastplate a pouch containing two stones known as the Urim and Thummin. They may have been flat stones that were black on one side and white on the other. The way the stones landed indicated an answer to a question: Two whites meant "yes," two blacks "no," and a black and a white meant "wait."

SORE LOSER

Samson once told a riddle to the men of his wedding party and said that if they couldn't answer it, they would have to give him a large gift. The men threatened Samson's wife until she told them the answer. When Samson lost the bet, he was so angry that he killed 30 men.

ADULT RECREATION

Adults in biblical times took time out for games, too. Many games were related to running, wrestling, and shooting slingshots or bows and arrows.

Reciting Scripture

B Y JESUS' TIME, schools followed a regular system for teaching and memorizing the Scriptures. The most important text taught and recited was a prayer called the Shema. This was actually a quotation of three passages from the books of Numbers and Deuteronomy. It was repeated morning and evening by men. By age 12, all Jewish boys were required to have this prayer memorized. But because the Shema was prayed so frequently, it soon began to lose its meaning. Jesus warned, "Don't recite the same prayer over and over as the heathen do, who think prayers are answered only by repeating them again and again" (Matthew 6:7). Another important text was the hall'el Psalms (Psalms 113–118). Students also read and learned the Creation account from Genesis and teachings from the book of Leviticus. Students met in the same room and often recited their passages aloud at the same time.

A boy reads a passage from the Torah.

RELIGIOUS LEARNING

The first purpose of education in Hebrew culture was to instill a love for God and respect for his law. Most education occurred at home.

STUDYING THE WORD OF GOD

Psalm 119, the longest of all the Bible's psalms, is a poem about the delights of studying God's word. Its form is also unusual. It is an acrostic verse in which each section starts with a different letter of the Hebrew alphabet.

THE HAZZAN

The responsibility for keeping the scrolls in the synagogue was considered so important that it was assigned to a kind of librarian called a hazzan. He took out the scrolls to be read in worship and returned them afterward. Jesus handed scrolls to a hazzan after reading from the book of Isaiah.

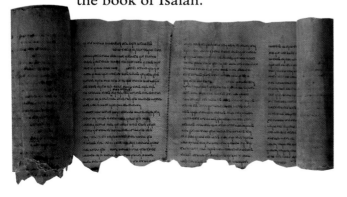

TORAH'S MEANING

A word related to the Torah is *yarah*, meaning "to shoot an arrow." Like an arrow, the Torah aims toward the mark of a right relationship with God.

SYNAGOGUE SCHOOLS

Synagogue schools began sometime after the Jews were exiled to Babylon in the sixth century B.C. These schools met apart from the regular times of synagogue worship. Only boys six years or older were allowed to attend, and they learned sitting at the feet of their teacher. Classes typically began early in the day, recessed during the hottest part of the day, and resumed for a few hours in the afternoon.

SCRIBES AND SCROLLS

Scribes carefully hand-copied the Scriptures onto pages of parchment. The pages were glued together to form long scrolls—some 35 feet long!

The temple scroll

125

Surprise Catch

Fish have been caught with a line and hook for thousands of years, but Peter once reeled in a surprise. One day when Peter arrived in Capernaum, the temple tax collectors came to him asking if Jesus paid taxes. All Jewish males were required to pay a temple tax to help take care of the temple. Tax collectors set up booths to collect these taxes. Peter mistakenly answered that Jesus did pay taxes. But just as kings paid no taxes, Jesus the King owed no taxes. When Jesus learned of Peter's answer, he told him to cast a hook into the sea and to open the mouth of the first fish he found. In it was a coin! Peter used the coin to pay the temple tax for both himself and Jesus. Jesus did not want to offend those that did not understand that he was truly a king.

MAGDALA

The business of selling and trading fish developed rather late in Israel's history. Galilee became a center for this activity. Several cities on the shores of this great lake became known for their fish trade. The name of one of them, Magdala, actually means "fish salting."

FISHING NETS

Large drag nets several hundred yards long were hauled into shore by each end after fishing. Fishermen spent much time washing, drying, and mending their nets.

A fisherman retrieves his net.

126

HUNTING HISTORY

Hunting has been around since the beginning of man. In Genesis, Nimrod is called a "mighty hunter" and a man blessed of God.

LIKE FATHER, LIKE SON

Hunting was a common way to get food, but it was dangerous work. Often large pits were dug to trap bigger animals. Smaller game might be killed with a spear or bow and arrow. Hunting was a skill passed from father to son. Genesis mentions Esau as a hunter, and his father, Isaac, admired Esau's skill. Once, Isaac told Esau to take his bow and quiver, hunt game, and prepare a favorite meal after which Isaac would give his son a blessing.

FISH GATE

One of the entrances to Jerusalem was called the Fish Gate. It is thought that fish from the Sea of Galilee were brought into the city to be sold at market.

FISHING IN PAIRS

Many fishing boats during New Testament times could hold no more than four men. Often a team of two worked together, one steering and the other tending the net. It is not unusual to find Jesus calling some of the disciples in pairs, since many of them were fishing teams: Peter and Andrew worked together, as did John and James. Matthew lists the disciples in pairs. This also may have been the way they sat in the boat as they sailed with Jesus.

Unspoken Agreement

ONE DAY ELISHA WAS PLOWING his field. He was just finishing a field when something unusual happened. Suddenly, Elijah, God's prophet, walked over and placed his cloak on Elisha's shoulders and walked away. No words were said, but Elisha understood that he was being called by God to be a prophet. Elisha ran after Elijah and said he would leave as soon as he said goodbye to his mother and father. Then, Elisha returned to his oxen, killed them, and used the wood from the plow to build a fire and cook their meat. By getting rid of his oxen, Elisha was showing God that he was serious about serving him—without the oxen he could no longer farm. Elisha and the other plowmen sat down and had a big feast. After the feast, Elisha left home to begin God's work.

EVEN RAVENS GET FED

To remind his listeners of God's love for them, Jesus talked about ravens. They did not plant or harvest, yet God fed them. Thus did God feed those who loved him.

HOW FAITH GROWS

The apostle Paul once compared the job of gaining new believers to sowing seeds. One Christian would plant a seed, another would water it, and God would bring about growth.

THE FIRST TILLER

Cain is the first farmer mentioned in the Bible. He is called a "tiller of the soil," meaning he used a tool to break up the ground before planting.

THE CUSTOM OF GLEANING

Moses taught that the harvest should be for everyone, including the poor and outsiders. When the harvest was gathered, much food was left behind in the fields. After the harvesters left, the poor were allowed to collect, or glean, what had been dropped or left on the stem. The Old Testament heroine Ruth and her mother-in-law, Naomi, were gleaning when they met Ruth's future husband, Boaz.

FALLOW LAND

Old Testament law provided for good planting practices. Long before anyone understood agricultural science, Hebrew farmers were commanded to let the land lie fallow, or empty, every seven years. Farmers could sow seeds or harvest grapes every six years, but the seventh year was a year of rest for the land. Any food that happened to grow could be taken, however. The practice resembled the Hebrew custom of resting every seventh day.

THE FIRST FRUITS

The harvest was a time of celebration in ancient Israel. But God did not want his people to forget that he was responsible for the abundant crops. Therefore, the people had to bring the first fruits of the season to their priest as an offering. The Israelites were not allowed to eat any of the harvest until this ceremony was performed.

Moses' Kindness

DID YOU KNOW THAT MOSES met his wife by being kind and helpful? Reuel, who was sometimes called Jethro, was a shepherd and priest who lived with his seven daughters in Midian. In Bible times, girls had chores to do, especially if their father had no sons. One day, Reuel's daughters came to the well to fill the water troughs for their family's flock, but other shepherds chased the girls away. Moses, who had been resting near the well, came to their rescue. He defended the girls and even watered their flocks for them. When the girls returned home, Reuel asked them how they had finished their chores so quickly. When they told their father of how Moses had helped, Reuel insisted that they invite him for dinner. Eventually, Moses came to live with Reuel's family, and Reuel gave him his daughter, Zipporah, to be his wife.

CHILDREN'S CHORES

Boys and girls in biblical times were taught to do chores by their parents. Girls learned such things as baking, spinning, and weaving, while boys learned specific job skills such as farming or carpentry. Usually a boy would grow up to have the same occupation as his father.

KEEPING BUSY

Boys were taught the importance of hard work at an early age. One well-known proverb declares, "A slack hand causes poverty, but the hand of the diligent makes rich."

TIME TO LEAVE

Jonathan asked a boy to perform an unusual chore to save his friend David. He told the youngster to fetch arrows he had shot into the air. The place where the arrows landed indicated whether or not it was safe for David to return to the palace where Saul lived. By the way the boy gathered the arrows, David knew he had to leave.

THRESHING

After a crop was harvested, it had to be threshed, which meant beating the grain with sticks or grinding it under big stones or heavy threshing sledges. The purpose was to separate the kernels of grain from the straw.

Winnowing

CHILD LABOR

Children began working long days in the fields at an early age. The poorer the family, the more the extra help was needed. Sometimes boys and girls became servants to rich land-owning families. The Jewish leader Nehemiah was once asked to help some poor families. Not only were they losing fields and vineyards to richer neighbors, but their children were forced to work for others just to get enough food to live. Nehemiah convinced the rich farmers to stop this practice.

SEPARATING THE WHEAT FROM THE CHAFF

Winnowing separated the good parts of the grain (wheat) from the waste parts (the chaff). To separate the chaff from the wheat, a person would work in a large open area and toss the grain into the air. The wind would blow away the lighter chaff, while the heavier grain would fall to the ground to be collected. Winnowing followed threshing.

Joseph's Special Talent

AFTER HE WAS SOLD by his brothers, Joseph ended up in Egypt. There, an official named Potiphar bought him. Joseph was a skilled apprentice and soon was in charge of Potiphar's household. However, Joseph was accused of a crime he didn't commit and ended up in prison. He had been imprisoned for a few years when the pharaoh asked him to interpret the meaning of a dream. Pharaoh dreamed about seven fat cows that were grazing in the grass. Then, seven very skinny cows came and ate the fat ones! Pharaoh had another dream about seven plump stalks of grain and seven shriveled stalks of grain. In this dream, the withered stalks swallowed up the fat ones. Joseph told Pharaoh what his dreams meant: Egypt would experience seven years of prosperity, followed by seven years of famine.

Joseph's answer impressed the pharaoh so much that he made Joseph his second-in-command.

SALAD DAYS

Daniel, Shadrach, Meshach, and Abednego were apprenticed to be servants to the king of Babylon. During their training, they were supposed to eat the rich food of the king's table. They asked if they could eat a diet of vegetables and water instead. At the end of ten days, they were healthier than the other apprentices.

DISHONEST JUDGES

Samuel's attempt to bring up his sons as good apprentices ended in failure. Both of them became judges who took bribes and did other dishonest things.

GRAVE CONSEQUENCES

Nadab and Abihu were sons of the high priest Aaron. They were apprentices for the important job of leading the nation in worship and offering sacrifices to God. But neither followed strict instructions for burning incense at the altar. Displeased, the Lord caused a fire to come from his presence that destroyed them both.

NOT INVITED TO ATTEND

When the prophet Samuel visited Jesse's sons, the youngest, David, was left to tend sheep in the fields. His father thought he was too young to meet such an important guest.

THE SON OF A CARPENTER

A son was expected to follow in his father's footsteps. Jesus learned the skills of woodworking from his father, Joseph. His neighbors remembered him as a carpenter's son.

PAUL'S CHANGE OF HEART

Mark is best known as the writer of the Gospel of Mark. As a young man, he was apprenticed to help Paul and Barnabas in their travels to spread God's message. But Mark may have become homesick, for he left Paul and the others and returned home. Later, Paul refused to take Mark with him on a journey because he thought Mark was unreliable. Paul eventually changed his mind and came to appreciate Mark's abilities again.

Zelophehad's Daughters

DAUGHTERS WERE ALLOWED to inherit land only if their father had no living sons. Zelophehad did not have any sons—but he had five daughters named Mahlah, Noah, Hoglah, Milcah, and Tirzah. When Zelophehad died in the wilderness, the daughters asked to be given their father's property. Moses took the case before the Lord, who agreed that Zelophehad's daughters should keep their father's land. And so the women (along with their five great-uncles) were given an inheritance of ten sections of land. But others in Zelophehad's tribe complained that the land would be lost, or greatly reduced, if the daughters married outsiders from another tribe. So Moses ruled that the daughters could marry any man they liked—as long as he was from within their own tribe. Zelophehad's daughters agreed and were married to men in their tribe of Manasseh. Their inheritance remained in their tribe.

FRESH BREAD, BAKED DAILY

Baking bread was a daily chore for women in ancient days. Bread was made of wheat, rye, barley, or millet and usually baked on flat stones that had been heated. In later times, some families used ovens. One kind was an earthenware dish that was placed upside down over a fire. The bread cakes were baked on the curved surface. Another kind was shaped like a cone. Bread cakes were placed on the inside of the cone as the coals burned.

SLEEPLESS DADS

Did fathers worry about their daughters' future? As most marriages were arranged during the biblical era, most fathers did not have to worry about that. However, they probably worried that their daughters might marry but not have children.

WOMAN'S WORK

In Proverbs 31, a king named Lemuel gave a description of the accomplished woman, which he had learned from his mother. The ideal woman prepares food, spins cloth, buys land, plants crops, gives to the needy, makes fine clothing, and sells cloth to merchants.

NO SUCH THING AS DIVORCE?

Jesus taught that marriage was intended to be permanent. But divorce, in certain circumstances, was allowed in biblical times. In Deuteronomy, Moses lists reasons for divorce.

NO TIME FOR DOLLS

Girls were supposed to help their mothers with chores around the house. A girl might gather wood for a fire, press dough into cakes, or sew clothing.

CHILDLESSNESS

In biblical times, being childless was a woman's greatest misfortune. Childless women mentioned in the Bible are Sarah, Rebekah, Rachel, Hannah, and Elizabeth. The Lord eventually blessed each of these women with a child. Psalm 113:9 states, "He gives the barren woman a home, making her the joyous mother of children."

It Was Meant to Be

IN ANCIENT TIMES, it was very unusual for a man not to marry. Boys could legally marry when they were over age 13, and girls when they were over 12 years of age. These marriages were often arranged by the parents of the bride and groom. Abraham, who lived in Canaan, did not want his son Isaac to marry a local woman, since Canaanites were known for idol worship. He sent a servant to the land of his relatives to find a bride for Isaac. The servant prayed for God's guidance and traveled to Nahor, where he found Rebekah. Without ever having seen the groom, Rebekah agreed to travel back to Canaan and marry Isaac. Arranged marriages, however, did not always mean that the men and women had no say as to whom they would marry. Shechem and Samson both asked their parents to arrange marriages with a particular girl.

MISTAKEN IDENTITY

Most brides were carried on a litter in the parade that preceded the wedding. They wore beautiful clothing, decorated with jewels. It was traditional for the bride to wear a heavy veil throughout the ceremony. Jacob was tricked into marrying Leah because he thought his beloved Rachel was under the veil!

BROKEN PROMISE

King Saul ordered David to kill a hundred Philistines as the price for marrying his daughter Michal. Saul figured David would be killed instead, but the young man did what Saul asked. The king broke his word by giving Michal's hand to another, but years later, after Saul was dead, David got his bride back.

A HEAVENLY MARRIAGE

Weddings are often used to describe the Kingdom of God in the New Testament. Jesus told several parables about weddings to show the joy and celebration of life in heaven. Paul carried this idea further in his letters. He compared the church to the bride of Christ, with Christ himself being the bridegroom. And John, in his vision known as the book of Revelation, watched a great celebration in heaven so loud it sounded like thunder. He called it the marriage of the Lamb.

Silver shekels, 66–70 A.D.

WEDDING TABOO

It was generally forbidden for Hebrews to marry foreigners. It was feared that a spouse might introduce strange customs and idol worship into the marriage.

BRIDE PRICE

In Old Testament times, it was customary for the groom to pay the bride's father a bride price. In most cases, money was paid, but the bride price could also be a gift or pledge of service.

LENGTHY FESTIVITIES

Weddings were festive events that often lasted a week. The book of Tobit, written about 200 B.C., describes a wedding feast that lasted 14 days.

Respected Elders

IN BIBLICAL TIMES, elders had a reputation for wisdom and learning and were highly respected. They were expected to provide leadership to their families and communities. In Jesus' time, the Sanhedrin was a Jewish court made up of elders, priests, and scribes. They had the final say in religious matters, in collecting taxes, and in certain criminal cases. In the New Testament, Paul writes about the qualities that elders in the church needed to have. They included being hardworking, thoughtful, orderly, hospitable, gentle, kind, and full of good deeds. An elder was supposed to have well-behaved children. An elder was not to be a heavy drinker, quarrelsome, or greedy for money.

LENGTHY LIVES

People in the Old Testament often lived extremely long lives. Methuselah lived longer than any other person in the Bible. He died when he was 969 years old! Other men who had long lives were Adam (930), Seth (912), Mahalalel (895), Jared (962), and Lamech (777).

ELDERS AT THE GATE

Elders were called on to settle disputes and enforce laws. Some elders in cities were chosen as judges and sat at the city gates. They ruled on cases there because that's where people commonly gathered to do business. In the early Church, elders were a group of men chosen to lead local Christians. Today, many churches are still ruled by elders.

A TIME FOR GRIEVING

Like weddings, funerals in biblical times lasted for many days. They began with a period of wailing and weeping, often in loud voices. Clothes might be torn to show grief. The burial took place quickly because the body rapidly decayed in the hot weather. Bodies were placed in caves or in carved-out tombs. Sometimes the tombs even had round, rolling stones in front of them to keep strangers out. Jacob's funeral, recorded in Genesis, involved 40 days spent preserving the body and 70 days weeping.

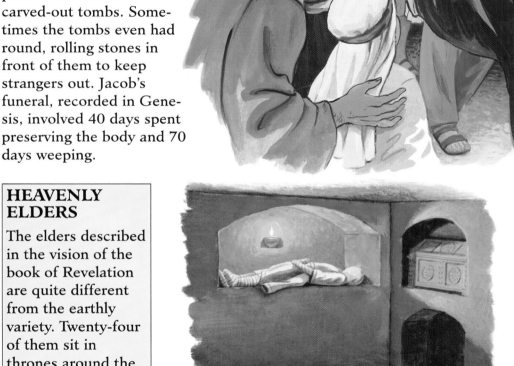

HEAVENLY ELDERS

The elders described in the vision of the book of Revelation are quite different from the earthly variety. Twenty-four of them sit in thrones around the great throne of heaven, and each elder wears a white robe and a crown of gold. They sing songs of praise to the Lamb, another name for Jesus.

ANCIENT BURIALS

Dead bodies were well cared for in ancient times. Corpses were washed, anointed with spices and oils, and wrapped in linen cloths or bandages with a separate face cloth. Not being buried was the ultimate humiliation. The evil queen Jezebel was killed and left in the street, and her flesh was eaten by dogs.

OUT OF BONDAGE

Elders are first mentioned in the book of Exodus. Moses talked with them about God's command to lead the Israelites out of Egypt.

Family Plots

MOST FAMILIES HELD ONTO A PLOT of land for generations. A man named Naboth had a vineyard on the outskirts of a city near King Ahab's palace. One day King Ahab decided that he wanted Naboth's land for a garden. The king offered money, or a trade for a better piece of land, but Naboth refused to sell the vineyard that had been in his family for many years. King Ahab became angry. He refused to eat and sat in his bed pouting. When the king's wife, Jezebel, saw how upset he was, she arranged for Naboth to be killed so that Ahab could take the vineyard. The prophet Elijah discovered the crime and predicted that God would cause great harm to come to King Ahab. Upon hearing this news, Ahab became distraught. The Lord kept his word, and eventually Ahab and all of his descendants were destroyed.

DIVVYING UP THE LAND

When the 12 tribes of Israel entered the Promised Land, some people inherited land based on promises made hundreds of years earlier. Others cast lots to divide up the remaining territory.

THE ROOT OF ALL EVIL

A man who wanted his brother to divide a family inheritance with him asked for Jesus' help. Instead, Jesus warned the man how greed and possession can ruin a soul.

WHO INHERITS?

A man who had more than one wife could face problems in passing land to his sons. Normally, the eldest son from any marriage would receive the biggest inheritance. But custom allowed the son of a first wife to receive the inheritance, even if he had been born after the son from a later marriage.

GOOD STEWARDS

Stewardship involves the management of divinely given resources in a godly and responsible manner. It doesn't mean humans can do whatever they want. Instead, they are to take care of things in a way that God would approve. Stewardship might include treating animals kindly, giving to others in need, or tempering justice with mercy. In the New Testament, Paul says that stewards are to be trustworthy.

THE YEAR OF JUBILEE

According to Old Testament law, the Israelites were to celebrate the year of jubilee every 50 years. During that year, no crops were to be sown or harvested. More important, any land that had been sold was to be returned to the original owners. Also, slaves were to be freed, and all debts canceled. The jubilee was intended to narrow the gulf between the rich and the poor. Sadly, there is no evidence that Israel ever celebrated it.

THE LEVITES

The tribe of Levites received no land when they entered the Promised Land. They lived as priests in cities and depended on the gifts that other tribes were supposed to provide.

Sisera's Death

A TENT PEG BECAME A WEAPON in the hands of a woman named Jael. The army of the Canaanite general Sisera had been destroyed, but Sisera had escaped. Jael offered to let Sisera hide in her tent to remain safe. Sisera trusted Jael—after all, her husband, Heber, was loyal to his army. But, Jael was actually plotting Sisera's doom! First Jael covered Sisera with a blanket to make him comfortable. Next she gave him a drink of milk. Then, when Sisera was sound asleep, Jael crept close and drove a tent peg through his head and into the ground, killing him. The prediction of Deborah, a godly leader and judge, had come true: She had said that the honor of conquering Sisera would go to a woman. Jael, the woman who killed Sisera with a tent peg, became a heroine of the Israelites.

KEEPING WARM AND DRY

Tents in biblical times resembled the ones we see today. They were made of animal skins or cloth sewn together and stretched over poles. A popular fabric for tents was goat's hair. When moisture fell on goat's hair, the fabric swelled, creating a tighter seal and keeping the people inside dry. The cloth was anchored to the ground with pegs made of wood or stone. Tents typically held only a few items—cushions, cooking utensils, and lamps.

FATHER OF TENT DWELLERS

Tent dwellers have been in biblical lands from the earliest days. Genesis names Jabal, a descendant of Cain, as the father of all who live in tents.

A TOUGH LIFE

People who lived in tents did not have an easy life. Most longed for something more permanent and secure. In the same way, Paul told Christians that their bodies were tents. One day they would be replaced with glorious heavenly bodies that would not get sick or grow old.

STILL IN DEMAND

By the time of the early Church, most people lived in houses. But enough people needed tents that a person could make a good living making and selling them. The apostle Paul made tents to raise money for his missionary journeys and to support himself as he worked to start new groups of followers.

RECHABITE WAY OF LIFE

The Rechabites were a clan of tent dwellers who lived in the desert. They followed the rules of their ancestor Jonadab, who said his people were never to live in houses, drink wine, or plant vineyards. The Rechabites lived in tents for more than 200 years and settled in Jerusalem only because of the threat of an invading army. When the prophet Jeremiah offered them wine, they refused. God held the Rechabites up as an example to the people of Judah. He wanted the same kind of obedience from them.

The wilderness of Sinai

THE ISHMAELITES

Ishmael was the son of Abraham and Sarah's servant Hagar. He became the father of the Ishmaelites, a tribe of fierce nomads who lived in tents in the Sinai wilderness.

Parables

WE ALL HAVE DIFFERENT WAYS OF LEARNING. Some people like to memorize lists of facts. Others like to make up word games to learn ideas. Jesus understood another way that helped people remember his teachings—he told stories. He would use everyday objects and situations and compare them to the Kingdom of heaven. These stories Jesus told are called parables. They taught people how they should treat others and love God. Jesus also used para-bles to show people how they could enter the Kingdom of God.

Nathan's Parable

To CONFRONT KING DAVID for his sin with Bathsheba, the prophet Nathan told the king a parable. In a certain city, there were two men. One was very rich and owned many flocks of sheep and herds of goats. The other was a poor man who owned nothing but a little lamb. This little lamb meant the world to him. He even fed it from his plate and held it in his arms like a baby. One day, the rich man had a guest and needed something to cook for dinner. Instead of killing a lamb from his own flocks, he took the poor man's only lamb, slaughtered it, and served it to his guest. When David heard the story, he was appalled! Nathan told David that he had done something just as bad, because he had taken Bathsheba from her husband even though David already had many wives.

LENGTHY REIGN

David became king of Judah in 1010 B.C. and reigned for 40 years. In 1003 B.C., he became king over all of Israel and ruled for 33 years.

DAVID'S TROUBLES

Nathan predicted that David's family life would always be troubled. His words came true. First, the child he had with Bathsheba died. Then his son Amnon was killed by his half-brother, Absalom, after Amnon had attacked Absalom's sister Tamar. For years, Absalom and David did not speak to each other. Then Absalom led a bloody rebellion against his father that ended in Absalom's death. At the end of his life, David watched his sons Solomon and Adonijah fight over the throne.

SPEAKING FOR GOD

A prophet is someone who speaks on God's behalf and warns people of the results of not obeying God. Nathan, speaking in the name of the Lord, had been sent to confront David.

PERSUASIVE WOMAN

Later in life, Nathan asked Bathsheba to use her influence to make sure her son Solomon became king. She persuaded David to stop another son, Adonijah, who had assumed the throne without David's knowledge.

WHAT'S A PARABLE?

The word *parable* comes from a Greek word meaning "to place beside." A parable is literally a comparison of two objects. We find parables throughout the Bible, but most are found in the teachings of Jesus. In fact, the gospels relate more than 30 parables.

WORDS TO LIVE BY

The Ten Commandments were God's laws to the Israelites. They are found in two Old Testament books, Exodus and Deuteronomy. Four of the laws describe how people are to treat God. The other six tell how other people should be treated. David broke many commandments by coveting Bathsheba, who was Uriah's wife.

The Sower

JESUS ONCE USED THE PARABLE of the sower to show how people respond to the word of God. A farmer was sowing seed in his field to grow a crop. But as he was scattering the seed, some fell beside a path, and birds came and ate it. Some more seed fell in a rocky area, and the plants quickly died. Other seeds fell in a thistle patch, which choked the plants as they grew. But some of the seeds fell on good soil and produced a crop that was 100 times as large as what the farmer had originally planted! Jesus explained that the seed that did not grow represents people who hear God's word but do not respond. The seed that grew in good soil represents people who believe and obey God's word, and then go and tell others about him.

THE MASTER TEACHER

Jesus is sometimes known as the Master Teacher. Unlike the rabbis, he didn't teach in the temple but instead usually taught outside, speaking to large crowds and using parables and stories to make his point.

JESUS' UNUSUAL PULPIT

Jesus told the parable of the sower from a boat on the Sea of Galilee. So many people had gathered to hear him that day that he climbed into a fishing boat near the shore so everyone could see him.

WEEDS AMONG THE WHEAT

In the parable of the weeds among the wheat, a farmer planted a field of wheat, but later an enemy sowed weeds in the same soil. As the crop matured, the workers noticed the weeds and asked their master, "Shall we pull them up?" The master told the field hand to let the weeds grow because when the harvest came, the weeds would be separated and burned. This parable shows how God will separate those who love and obey him from those who do not.

LANGUAGE LESSONS

Telling stories was one of Jesus' favorite ways of teaching. More than a third of Jesus' sayings recorded in the Bible are parables.

SOWING SEEDS

A sower in biblical times carried his seed in a large shoulder bag. The seed was not planted in the field in straight rows as it is today. Instead, the farmer would take handfuls of seed from his bag, and toss it on the ground as he walked along.

GETTING THE POINT ACROSS

Most people in Jesus' day were farmers. Thus, the parable about planting seed would have had special meaning to his listeners. By speaking to them about a task most of them knew well, he was able to get across his message.

149

The Fig Tree

ONCE WHEN JESUS WAS PREACHING to the people about repenting for their sins, he used the parable of the fig tree to help them understand. In this story, a man planted a fig tree in his garden. Each day he would check the tree to see if there was any fruit. Three years passed, but still there were no figs. Disappointed, the man told his gardener to chop the tree down. But the gardener asked the man to give the tree one more chance and to be patient for one more year. The gardener promised to give the tree extra care and protection. If the tree still did not have fruit in one year, then it would be destroyed. Jesus is like this caring gardener—patiently waiting for people to "bear fruit" by living godly lives. Like the gardener in the story, he will not wait forever.

THE MUSTARD SEED

In Jesus' time, the mustard seed was the smallest seed used by Palestinian gardeners and farmers. Under the right conditions, it could sprout into a ten-foot-tall plant. Thus, when Jesus told the parable of the mustard seed—in which a man plants a small seed that becomes a huge plant—he was trying to show the growth that is possible in the Kingdom of God.

EDIBLE GREENS

Mustard, beets, and radishes were popular in the Mediterranean world. Mustard was unique in that the leaves, flowers, and seeds were all eaten for food. The mustard plant grows quickly and easily in a variety of climates. A thick-stemmed plant, it was an important cash crop in the Holy Land.

THE VALUE OF FAITH

Jesus compared faith to a mustard seed. He said that faith as tiny as this seed could do tremendous things—even move a mountain!

Mint

SPICE OF LIFE

Cumin, mint, and dill were other plants used for spices in Jesus' day. So strict were the Pharisees in observing their rules that they set aside a tithe, or a tenth, of their spices for God. But Jesus criticized them for doing these minor things without being just or charitable.

A VINE AND ITS BRANCHES

Jesus once compared himself to a vine and his disciples to the branches. No branch can bear fruit by itself. In the same way, the disciples could do nothing unless they remained attached to God. The grapevine is a fruitful plant, because many grapes are produced from a single vine. Sometimes, however, branches that do not bear fruit are pruned back. God, then, is like a gardener who must sometimes prune, or discipline, his people.

VINEYARDS

Vineyards were usually located on a hillside and were protected by a wall. There were also high watch towers with booths at the top. At harvest time, families sometimes lived in these booths. Grapevines grew on trellises or walls so that the heavy fruit would not drag on the ground.

151

Can't Take It with You

DID YOU KNOW THAT JESUS taught about money? Jesus says that trying to get rich is a waste of time. He said that riches will fly away as though they had wings like a bird! In the book of Matthew, Jesus warned that treasures accumulated here on earth do not last. Money and valuables can be lost, stolen by thieves, ruined by the rain or hot sun, or even eaten by insects. In his Sermon on the Mount, Jesus told the crowd to build up treasures in heaven—that is, good works that please God and help others. Jesus said, "For where your treasure is, there your heart will be also." Jesus also told the people that it is impossible for man to love money and love God, too. They would hate one and love the other.

Built near where Jesus gave the Sermon on the Mount

JESUS' HILLSIDE SERMON

Matthew 5–7 is called the Sermon on the Mount because it was given by Jesus on a hillside near Capernaum.

ONLY A MENTION

There are four Gospel accounts of the life of Jesus in the New Testament, but the phrase "Kingdom of Heaven" is used only in the book of Matthew. The phrase "Kingdom of God," however, is found throughout the Gospels.

THE TREASURE IN A FIELD

In the parable of the treasure in a field, a man was digging in a field when he stumbled upon a great treasure. He reburied the treasure, sold all he had, and purchased the field—making him the owner of the treasure, too. And so it is with the Kingdom of heaven. According to Jesus, people may not see the treasure God has given them right away, but eventually they realize its worth and will give up anything for it.

THE PEARL OF GREAT PRICE

In the parable of the pearl of great price, a merchant was looking for fine pearls one day when he found a rare pearl of great value. He sold everything he had so that he could buy it. The meaning of the parable is that the Kingdom of heaven is of utmost value, and people should be willing to follow the Lord, giving up everything to attain salvation.

STASHING IT AWAY

Why was treasure buried in the middle of a field? The answer is simple. There were bankers in ancient times, but no banks as we know them today. Thus, it was quite common for the wealthy to hide valuables in their fields.

PEARLS BEFORE PIGS

Jesus said that trying to teach holy things to people who did not want to hear them was like giving expensive pearls to pigs.

The Great Catch of Fish

MANY MEN IN JESUS' DAY fished for a living. Jesus used fishing as an illustration in the parable of the fishing net. In this story, fishermen cast a net in the lake and gathered all sorts of fish—valuable and worthless. Then, they pulled the net on shore and sorted the fish—saving the good, edible fish and throwing the bad ones away. The story illustrates God's final separation of the godly people from the wicked in a last great "harvesting" of souls. At the end of the world, angels will separate the evil people from the good people. Parables like "The Great Catch of Fish" must have made Jesus' listeners uncomfortable. In this final dividing of the faithful from the unfaithful, there will be much sorrow and despair. It will be a full and final judgment.

FISHING WITH NETS

Fishing is frequently mentioned in connection with the Sea of Galilee. One popular method involved the use of a circular casting net, which was thrown either from a boat or while standing in shallow water. At the end of each workday, the nets had to be washed, mended, and hung to dry.

Fish from the Sea of Galilee

MULLET AND BARBEL

Both the Old and New Testaments often refer to fish. Two common types that were eaten for food were the striped mullet and the barbel.

Mussels—"bad" fish in biblical times

TRAPPED LIKE AN ANIMAL

Nets were used in biblical times for trapping animals as well as catching fish. The prophet Isaiah once compared the conquered people of Israel to an antelope caught in a net.

HANDS OFF!

In Jesus' day, good fish were those allowed to be eaten according to Jewish law. "Bad" sea creatures—those without fins and scales—could not be touched.

A PLAGUE ON THE NILE

The first judgment that God visited upon Egypt was the plague of blood. In this terrible curse, the water of the Nile River was turned to blood, and all the fish died.

EZEKIEL'S VISION

In an amazing vision, the prophet Ezekiel saw a river of healing, swarming with fish and sea creatures. Similar to rivers mentioned in the books of Genesis (in the Garden of Eden) and Revelation, this special river symbolizes the blessings that flow when a person's life becomes one with God.

155

The Lost Sheep

CHEATERS, NOTORIOUS SINNERS, lying tax collectors—these people often came to hear Jesus. Sometimes he would even eat dinner with them. This made the religious leaders angry. They felt that Jesus should not associate with such people. So Jesus told them this story: There was a man who had 100 sheep. One day, one of the sheep wandered away and was lost. The man immediately left behind the 99 sheep to search for the one that was lost. When he found it, he joyfully carried it home on his shoulders and invited his friends to his house to celebrate. The man was much happier about finding the one lost sheep than about all the others that were safe at home. So it is in heaven, where there is greater rejoicing over one lost sinner who returns to God than over the many faithful people who have never strayed away.

THE LORD IS MY SHEPHERD

The deep concern of the shepherd for his lost sheep is reminiscent of the care provided by the shepherd in Psalm 23. The psalm, written by King David, compares God to a protecting shepherd who leads and comforts his flock.

ANGELIC REJOICING

Angels are heavenly beings created by God to serve him. The work of good angels—those who obey God—includes standing in his presence and worshipping him. Also, as ministering spirits they actively assist and protect creation. In the parable of the lost sheep, Jesus indicates that the angels rejoice each time a sinner turns to follow God.

THE LOST COIN

In the parable of the lost coin, Jesus told the story of a woman who owned ten silver coins but lost one of them. She lit a lamp, swept the house, and searched high and low until she found it. When she finally recovered the coin, she called all her friends and neighbors together and said, "Rejoice with me, for I have found the coin I had lost." Like the parable of the lost sheep, this story was told to show the rejoicing in heaven over one sinner who turns back to God.

BRIDAL COINS

Brides in the Middle East typically received wedding gifts from their fathers. A common wedding gift might be silver coins with holes drilled in them so they could be worn on a necklace or headdress.

DRACHMA

The ten silver coins mentioned in the parable of the lost coin were drachmas, Greek coins worth about a day's wages each. Thus, a lost coin really was worth searching for!

A LITTLE LIGHT ON THE SUBJECT

The typical Judean peasant hut had no windows, a low entrance door, and an earthen floor. Thus, it makes sense that the woman in the parable had to light a lamp to search for the missing coin.

157

The Rich Man and Lazarus

JESUS ONCE TOLD THE STORY of the rich man and Lazarus to teach the consequences of selfishness. The rich man lived in complete luxury, while Lazarus was a diseased beggar. One day, Lazarus lay outside the rich man's door, hoping to get some scraps from the rich man's table. But the rich man paid no attention to him. Eventually, Lazarus died and went to heaven where he was comforted. The rich man died, too, but he was sent to hell. While there, he saw Lazarus, a long distance away. In anguish, the rich man pleaded for Lazarus to bring a drop of water to cool his tongue. But the spirit of Abraham reminded the man that he had everything he wanted all his life, while Lazarus had nothing. He sadly told the man that he and Lazarus were now separated by a valley that could not be crossed.

THE RICH YOUNG MAN

"What must I do to get to heaven?" a rich young man asked Jesus. He had already obeyed all of Jesus' commandments. "Sell everything you have, give the money to the poor and follow me," Jesus answered.

The man went away very sad, because he could not do as Jesus asked.

WHICH LAZARUS?

Two men named Lazarus are found in the New Testament. The better-known Lazarus, according to the book of John, was a real person that Jesus raised from the dead. The Lazarus of the parable is probably a fictitious character. Interestingly, he is the only person in Jesus' parables to have a name.

HADES

In New Testament times, Hades, or hell, was the place where the dead went to await final judgment. It was believed that both the righteous and the wicked rested there, though they were separated by a huge gulf. It was believed that people in one area could see and talk with those in the other.

THE PHARISEE AND THE TAX COLLECTOR

Jesus told the parable of the conceited Pharisee and the crooked tax collector who went to the temple to pray. The Pharisee began to pray loudly, shouting so that everyone could hear him. He bragged about how good he was and boasted that he was not a sinner. But the tax collector wept and prayed sincerely, admitting he was a sinner and begging for God's mercy. Jesus said that the sinner, not the Pharisee, was forgiven that day.

THE RICH FOOL

In this parable, Jesus taught about greed. A rich farmer planted a crop and had a bountiful harvest. The yield was so large that the farmer had no place to store the crops. So, he decided to build bigger barns. The man was confident that he had enough grain stored away to last him the rest of his life. But God told the selfish man that he would die that night, and that his plans would amount to nothing. And so it is for those whose hearts are not rich with the love of God. Putting money before God endangers a person's soul.

AGAINST THE GRAIN

Jesus constantly surprised—and upset—the Pharisees with his teachings, which usually went against their traditions. The story of the Pharisee and the tax collector contradicts their belief that wealth was a proof of righteousness.

The Wedding Banquet

THE PARABLE OF THE WEDDING banquet tells the story of a king who sent out invitations to a wedding banquet held for his son. When everything was ready, the king sent his servant around to collect the guests. But everyone started making excuses. One man had just bought a piece of land that he needed to inspect. Another said he had purchased five oxen and needed to try them out. Another said he couldn't attend because he had just been married. Angry, the king sent his servant into the streets of the city to invite everyone he saw—even the beggars! Finally, the banquet hall was filled with guests. The lesson of the parable is that we should not make excuses when God calls us to join him at his banquet. He invites us and is eager for us to be with him, but it is up to us to come.

TWO INVITATIONS

It was the custom in Jesus' day to send two invitations when parties were given. The first invited the guests, while the second indicated that all was in readiness.

THE WATCHFUL PORTER

Jesus told the story of the man who went on a trip to another country. The man gave his employees tasks to do and told his gatekeeper to keep a sharp lookout for his return—it could happen morning, noon, or night! Jesus' message to the people was to always watch for his return.

THE SHEEP AND THE GOATS

The story of the sheep and the goats is a parable about judgment. Jesus, referring to himself as the Son of Man, promised to divide the nations into sheep and goats. Jesus separates his true followers—the sheep—from those who only pretend to believe in him—the goats. The sheep show kindness to strangers, visit those in prison, and give to the needy. The goats do none of these things. The sheep are rewarded with eternal life, while the goats are punished.

ALL IN GOOD TIME

The Pharisees practiced fasting, or going without food to show devotion to God. They asked Jesus why his followers didn't do the same. Jesus compared himself to a bridegroom and his disciples to guests at a wedding banquet. No one would fast during such a happy party. The time for fasting would come when the bridegroom had gone.

FORGIVE AND FORGIVE

A king demanded his servant to repay a large debt. When he failed, the king ordered the man and his family be sold. The servant begged for mercy, and the king freed him, canceling his debt. Soon the servant saw someone who owed him a little money and dragged him to jail. Someone saw them and told the king. The king jailed his servant until his debt was paid. Jesus said this is how God would treat us if we didn't forgive each other.

The Ten Maidens

THE KINGDOM OF HEAVEN was illustrated in the parable of the ten bridesmaids who took their lamps to meet the bridegroom. Only five of the women remembered to bring extra oil for their lamps, but the other five did not. The bridegroom was late, so the women lay down to sleep. "The bridegroom is coming!" someone shouted at midnight. When the bridesmaids ran to meet him, the lamps of the foolish women sputtered and went out. The wise women did not have enough oil to spare, so the foolish women left to buy more for themselves. When the groom arrived, the banquet began without the foolish bridesmaids. When they came back, the door was locked and the groom told them to go away. The meaning of the parable is that Jesus—the groom—wants everyone to be prepared for his return.

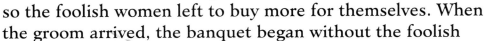

MOVABLE FEAST

It was common for the groom to go the bride's house for the wedding. Later, the bride and groom, accompanied by a parade, would go to the groom's house for a feast.

THEY TURNED TAIL

Torches were important in Gideon's victory over the Midianites. Gideon's 300 men surrounded the enemy camp, each carrying a trumpet and a torch. When the time for battle came, each blew the trumpet and lit a torch. The Midianites saw the torches, panicked, and deserted.

LAMPS

The most common form of lamp fuel was olive oil. Most lamps could hold enough oil to burn through the night. However, someone usually had to get up several times in the night to tend the wick, which was made of flax or a piece of linen.

WEDDING GOBLET

It is believed that during a wedding ceremony the bride and groom drank from the same goblet before smashing it to the floor. This was a sign of their wedding vows.

LONG ENGAGEMENT

In biblical times, marriage involved two events: the betrothal, or engagement, and the wedding. Jewish custom dictated a lengthy betrothal period, but the engagement promise was considered as serious as the actual marriage vows. While the wedding itself did not include a religious ceremony, it's likely that betrothal required a public promise of commitment and faithfulness by bride and groom.

NIGHT LIGHT

The saucer lamp was the most popular style of lamp during the period. However, because it spilled easily, it was not suitable for night travel, so a torch was probably used for that purpose.

The Prodigal Son

THE PARABLE OF THE PRODIGAL SON told the story of a man and his two sons. One day, the younger son demanded his share of the inheritance. After getting his money, the son left

home and spent it all on parties and sinful living. With no money left for food, the young man began to starve. So he went and persuaded a farmer to hire him to feed his pigs. When even the pig's food began to look good to him, the young man realized he had made a terrible mistake. He decided to return to his father and admit he had been wrong. His father saw him coming from a distance and ran to hug and kiss him and to welcome him home. And so it is with God, who fully forgives those who are truly sorry for their sins and welcomes them back to him.

ESPECIALLY FAVORED

In ancient Israel, the firstborn son received special preference. According to the book of Deuteronomy, a father dividing his estate was to give the eldest son twice the amount of property as other sons.

ABOUT AS LOW AS YOU CAN GET

According to Jewish law as dictated in the book of Leviticus, the pig was an unclean animal, neither to be eaten nor to be sacrificed. Thus, when the prodigal son was forced to feed pigs, he had sunk to the lowest level. Not only was the work unpleasant, but he was doing something a faithful Jew would never do.

ONLY IN LUKE

Several of Jesus' parables are found in more than one place in the gospels. However, the well-known parable of the prodigal son is found only in Luke.

THE GOOD SAMARITAN

In the parable of the good Samaritan, a man was on a journey when he was robbed, beaten, and left for dead at the side of the road. Ignored by two religious leaders that passed by, the man was finally noticed by a Samaritan. The Samaritan bandaged the man, took him to an inn, and even paid the innkeeper to care for him. This story—intended to inspire love of one's neighbor—may have shocked some of Jesus' Jewish listeners who thought we only had to love the people familiar to us. But Jesus says that our neighbors are also people who are different from us.

SAMARITANS

Samaritans were people who lived in Samaria, a region north of Jerusalem or Judea. They accepted only the Pentateuch (first five books of the Bible) as Scripture. The Samaritans were descendants of Jews who had married people from other nations. The Jews living in Palestine looked down on Samaritans as unrighteous people. When Jesus showed love for the Samaritans, it made many people angry.

Samaritan priest with Pentateuch

Old road between Jerusalem and Jericho

JERUSALEM TO JERICHO

Roads, such as the one from Jerusalem to Jericho, were usually just dirt paths that became rough and muddy when it rained. The pathways of the dirt roads changed as travelers looked for smoother ground to cross. Traveling these roads was dangerous, because thieves often lurked in the shadows waiting to rob unsuspecting travelers.

SOUR GRAPES

Some Pharisees were complaining that Jesus welcomed sinners and even ate with them. Jesus may have been telling the parable of the prodigal son for their sake. The strict Pharisees would not have rejoiced over a sinner who had returned to God.

165

The Workers in the Vineyard

A VINEYARD OWNER went out early one morning to hire workers. He agreed to pay them a nice sum. A few hours later, the owner was walking through town when he noticed several men looking for work. He hired the men and sent them to his fields. He hired more men at noon, some more at three o'clock, and even more at four o'clock! When evening came, it was time for the men to be paid. The owner then did something surprising. He paid all the workers the same amount, even those who had worked only a few hours. The men who had worked all day complained of being cheated. The owner reminded them that they had agreed to work for the amount they were paid. The point of the parable of the vineyard workers is that God's grace is always available. Those who choose it later, rather than earlier, are no less favored.

THE FIRST VINTNER?

Like his father, Noah was a farmer. The Bible says that he was the first person to plant a vineyard. Thus, he may have been the first to make wine from grapes.

Denarii

A DENARIUS SAVED . . .

A denarius was a Roman coin, and the drachma was a Greek coin. Both were equal to a typical day's pay in New Testament times.

PLENTY OF TLC

Vineyards thrived in the mountain regions of Samaria and Judea and were usually surrounded by a wall of stones to keep out pests. Vines needed much care to be fruitful. They were pruned every spring, and the ground around them was weeded and plowed regularly.

166

A WARNING TO JUDAH

The book of Isaiah compares the nation of Judah to a vineyard in which God digs the soil, clears the rocks, plants vines, builds a watchtower, and makes a winepress. Despite his care, Judah produces wild grapes—sour fruit that is useless. Isaiah's message was a warning: If the people of Judah did not turn away from sin, their land would be ruined by enemies.

WHAT IS A TALENT?

A talent was not a coin. It was a unit of measure that refers to a weight of about 30 kilograms. In the parable of the talents, it would mean a large amount of money and represent several years' wages.

APPEASEMENT

When Babylon captured Judah, the commanding officer gave many vineyards to the poor. This was done to make the poor grateful to the Babylonian rulers and thus prevent future rebellion.

PARABLE OF THE TALENTS

Jesus taught that we are to use our time and resources wisely. In the parable of the talents, a man going on a trip loaned his servants money to invest while he was gone. Two of the servants invested wisely, doubling their money. But one servant hid his money in the ground and gained nothing.

WATERED-DOWN WINE

In Old Testament times, wine was drunk at full strength, but the Greek practice of diluting wine became popular in Palestine around the time Jesus was born. Wine would be mixed with water and often spiced with cinnamon, honey, or herbs.

The Widow and the Judge

JESUS ONCE TOLD HIS DISCIPLES a story to illustrate the importance of constant prayer and to encourage them to keep praying until their prayers were answered. The story was the parable of the persistent widow. A widow was owed money, but she had no way of collecting it. Seeking help, she went to a city judge who only ignored her. The woman did not give up. She continued to go to the judge time after time. Finally, the judge became so weary of the woman's requests that he agreed to help her! Jesus told his listeners, "If even an evil judge can be worn down like that, don't you think God will surely give justice to his people who plead with him day and night? Yes! He will answer them quickly!"

LIMITED DISCRETION

The judges who lived in Jerusalem in Jesus' day had the power to settle their cases without interference from Rome. However, they could not have a person executed. That was left to a Roman official called a procurator. The punishment a procurator might hand down included crucifixion, public whipping, or a lifetime at hard labor in the mines. The council that tried Jesus turned him over to Pontius Pilate so that he could be crucified.

WHAT JUDGES DID

In the Bible, the word *judge* can have two meanings. It can refer to a person who tries cases and punishes wrongdoers, such as the man in the parable of the widow and the judge. Or it can mean a national hero—such as Gideon, Samson, or Deborah, who saved Israel from an enemy. The book of Judges is a collection of stories about such heroes.

THE WIDOW'S OFFERING

Another widow described in the gospels is the poor woman who gave two copper coins to the temple. Jesus told his disciples that she had given more than the rest because she gave all she had.

THE WIDOW ANNA

Anna was a prophet who lived in the temple and had been a widow most of her life. Before she died, God allowed her to see the Messiah, the baby Jesus.

GOD WILL BE THERE FOR YOU

In the parable of the friend at midnight, Jesus asked his listeners to imagine going to the house of a friend late at night to borrow bread. Even though your friend and his family are asleep, he gets up to give you what you need because you asked for it. This is why Jesus said, "Knock and it will be opened to you." God is always ready to hear what you need in prayer.

ESPECIALLY DESERVING

Both the Old and New Testaments emphasize that widows and orphans deserve special care. As in the parable of the Widow and the Judge, they had no one to plead their cases in court.

Animals in the Bible

THE BIBLE MENTIONS OVER 100 varieties of animals. Some had strange names. Others had curious habits. One animal could drink 25 gallons of water in a few minutes. Another creature swallowed a man whole and kept him inside its stomach for three days! But animals were not only remarkable for the amazing things they could do. Animals were valuable to the people of biblical times because they provided clothing, food, and transportation. Read on to learn more fascinating facts about the creatures of the Bible.

The Making of a King

DONKEYS ONCE PLAYED an important role in a king's life. Saul was the son of a rich man who owned many donkeys. Nearly every family in biblical times, even the poorest, owned a donkey, but to have many donkeys was a sign of wealth. One day, the rich man's donkeys wandered off. Saul and a servant were sent to find them. They searched everywhere without success. Finally, the servant suggested that they ask the prophet Samuel, who lived in a nearby town. When they entered the city, they met Samuel coming toward them. He told Saul that the donkeys had been found and then puzzled him by saying, "You own all the wealth of Israel now!" What Saul didn't know was that God had told Samuel to make him the new king. Samuel took Saul to a banquet, anointed him, and told him the surprising news.

PALM SUNDAY

The final week of Jesus' life began when he rode a donkey into Jerusalem. Along the way, people placed palm branches and their cloaks in the road—a sign of respect—and shouted, "Hosanna!" Today, many churches remember this event on Palm Sunday.

BALAAM'S STRANGE ENCOUNTER

Balaam was a prophet who worked for the king of Moab. He had been ordered to curse the Israelites. On a journey, Balaam began beating his donkey because it had stopped in the road. The donkey turned and spoke to him! Only then did Balaam realize that an angel had been blocking the path. Balaam quickly agreed to do what the angel said.

HARD WORKERS

Mules and donkeys were useful animals that could pull a plow, push a grindstone, or carry people to faraway places. They could live on little water and not much food.

Donkeys can haul heavy loads.

THE FOUR HORSES

The book of Revelation talks about the four horsemen of the Apocalypse. The horses are different colors and symbolize God's judgment at the end of the world. Some say that the white horse represents the conquering Christ. The red horse represents war; the black horse, famine and death; and the pale horse, disease, famine, and wild animals.

DIRECTIONAL GUIDES

In Psalm 32:9 the writer warns, "Do not be like the horse or the mule which have no understanding, but must be controlled by bit and bridle or they will not come to you." God wants believers to willingly let him guide them.

INSTRUMENT OF WAR

In biblical times, the horse was used mainly for warfare—Hebrew farmers almost never used them for plowing. A horse-drawn chariot was the most feared weapon of the ancient world, for it combined speed with the deadly accuracy of archers who rode in them. The Israelites were not supposed to own horses because God feared they might develop a love for war. King Solomon did not follow this advice—he owned 12,000 horses, imported from Egypt.

A HORSE IS A HORSE . . .

The Bible mentions horses in terms of war, though they were also used for transportation, most often to pull chariots. Riding horses does not seem to have been common.

Only Human

PAUL AND BARNABUS got an unexpected reception when they arrived in Lystra. After Paul had miraculously healed a man, the people of the city thought they were Zeus and Hermes, two popular gods in the Roman world. Legend has it that when these gods once came to Lystra, no one welcomed them except for an old couple. In retaliation, the gods killed everyone in the city but rewarded the old couple. Now, when the people of Lystra saw the miracles of Paul and Barnabas, they thought that they were being revisited by Zeus and Hermes. Remembering what had happened before, they immediately welcomed Paul and Barnabus. They brought oxen and wanted to sacrifice them to the two missionaries. Paul and Barnabas tore their clothing and begged the people to understand that they were mere humans. Even so, the crowd did not listen and nearly went ahead with the sacrifice!

BEAST OF BURDEN

A Hebrew farmer would prize an ox more than a modern farmer might prize a tractor. An ox could plow fields, thresh and grind grain, pull heavy wagons, and drive a water wheel.

A farmer uses his ox to plow a field.

OUT OF STEP

In biblical times, a farmer was not supposed to place an ox and a mule together for plowing. The different strides of each animal were likely to cause injury to the mule.

HIGHLY PRIZED

Oxen in the Middle East varied greatly in size and shape. Some had long horns, others short horns, and a few breeds had none. They could be all white, white with black patches, or entirely red. All the breeds supplied milk, which was made into butter and cheese for their owners. Because oxen were so valuable, laws protected them. For instance, a person could not watch a neighbor's ox wander off and do nothing: They had to report what they had seen so the animal could be brought back. In the Ten Commandments, God said that we shouldn't covet our neighbor's oxen.

CRIME AND PUNISHMENT

The Old Testament had many laws that set punishment and fines for owners of animals that injured people. An ox that had killed a person was supposed to be stoned to death. If the animal had a history of hurting people and if the owner ignored the problem, then the owner could be fined—or even executed.

EXCEPTION TO THE RULE

Wells that were dug into the earth often became a hazard for animals. Because God wanted all animals to be treated with kindness, an ox that fell into a well was to be rescued at once, even if it was the Sabbath, a day of rest. As Jesus pointed out, even the strict Pharisees rescued their animals on the Sabbath.

One Hump or Two

CAMELS WERE JUST AS IMPORTANT as sheep, cows, and donkeys in the Old Testament. Camels have been described as unintelligent and quarrelsome, but they were a necessity for people living in desert areas. They were used to transport both goods and people, and each could carry 600 pounds or more. Although camels were slow-moving, they could still travel 60 to 75 miles in a day. The camels mentioned in the Bible were from Arabia and were accustomed to the hot, dry climate of the Middle East. They were easy to tell from other breeds because they had only one hump. The more familiar two-humped camels are the Bactrian variety. This species is bigger, heavier, and has more hair than the one-humped camel. These camels are native to Asia and are usually found in colder climates. The hair shed by camels was usually saved and woven into cloth.

NARROW IS THE WAY

Jesus said that it was harder for a camel to pass through the eye of a needle than for a rich man to enter the Kingdom of heaven.

ADAPTED TO THE DESERT

The camel is amazingly well suited to work in the desert. Its long eyelashes and efficient eyelids keep the blowing sand from blinding it. It can go for days without water and can digest the toughest desert plants. When food is not available, the camel can live off the fat stored in its hump.

A DIFFERENT SORT OF TRAIN

A caravan is a long train of camels that travels through the desert from city to city. Merchants usually traveled this way, because it was safer and better for business to travel in groups. Many caravan routes went through Israel, for it was on the main route between Egypt, Arabia, and Mesopotamia. Joseph was sold by his brothers to a caravan of Ishmaelites. Also, the queen of Sheba once assembled a huge caravan to take costly gifts to King Solomon.

A TEDIOUS CHORE

Giving water to camels was no easy job. A thirsty camel can drink more than 25 gallons of water in ten minutes. When Abraham's servant asked God to show him the ideal wife for Isaac, he wanted a sign. That sign would be the woman who offered to water his camels as he sat near a well. Rebekah displayed that kindness. When she offered to water the camels, she showed herself to be kind and thoughtful—and hard-working.

WALKING ON NAILS

Camels' feet appear to be encased in divided hooves, but they have nails instead. The camel was forbidden food for Israelites because it does not have divided hooves.

TWICE AS RICH

Before Job's trials began, he owned some 3,000 camels—which meant that he was a very rich man, indeed. By the end of the story, Job had gained twice that number.

THEY MISSED THE POINT

The Pharisees followed religious rules, but some of them missed the important things that God required. Jesus said it was like straining a gnat from a drink but then swallowing a camel.

177

Vicious Attack

IN BIBLICAL TIMES, the Syrian brown bear was commonly found in the hills and forests of Israel. When hungry, the bear was a threat to sheep and goats, and shepherds had to protect their flocks against it. A group of disrespectful young men once had a fatal run-in with two female bears. The young men were teasing the prophet Elisha, mocking him and making fun of his bald head. They did not want to listen to his message from God. Suddenly two she-bears tore out of the woods and attacked the young men, killing 42 of them! The bears that came after the youths may have been defending their young cubs. It is also possible that they had been startled by all the shouting. But, most likely, the bears were sent by God as judgment against the evil young men.

STAR GAZING

The constellations Ursa Major (Big Bear) and Ursa Minor (Little Bear) have been watched for thousands of years. Job describes the God who made the constellations known as the Bear and Orion.

UNBEARABLE FOOL

The book of Proverbs says that it is better to meet a she-bear robbed of her cubs than to catch a fool in the middle of something he shouldn't be doing.

NOT A PICKY EATER

The Syrian bear is probably the one described in the Bible, standing six feet tall and weighing more than 500 pounds. Its diet included plants and animal flesh, although most of the time it lived on fruits and berries. When food ran low—usually in the winter—the bear was more likely than at other times to threaten a farmer's livestock. The Syrian bear has disappeared from Israel, but it still lives in other parts of the Middle East.

BOY VS. BEAR

Shepherds often had to defend their flock from wild animals, including the bear. To persuade Saul that he could fight Goliath, David told him that he struck down bears that had caught his sheep. If one came after him, he would grab it by the jaw and kill it!

PEACEABLE KINGDOM

What will the Kingdom of God look like? The prophet Isaiah painted a picture of the peace that will reign on earth. In the book that bears his name, he says that the bear and the cow will graze together. The fierce lion will eat straw like the ox, and the wolf will live with the lamb. Even a child will be able to play near a nest of poisonous snakes without being harmed.

FEARSOME BEAST

The false prophet who appears in the book of Revelation is a fearsome creature. He looks like a leopard, with the feet of a bear and the mouth of a lion.

Samson's Strength

LIONS IN BIBLICAL TIMES were a threat to both humans and animals. Proverbs 30:30 describes the lion as the king of the animals who won't turn aside for anyone! But a man once proved himself to be stronger than a lion. Samson and his parents were on their way to the city of Timnah when Samson was attacked by a young lion. Samson did not have a weapon, but the Lord gave him power, and in an amazing show of strength, Samson ripped the lion's jaws apart with his bare hands. On his way back home, Samson saw the carcass of the lion still lying by the side of the road. In it he discovered a swarm of bees and lots of honey. Samson took some honey to eat on the way home. Later he gave some to his parents but did not tell them where he had gotten it.

PERSIAN LIONS

Persian lions were about five feet long. They had heavy manes and tails about 30 inches long. They could not climb and were active at night.

The lion—a favorite of kings

HUNTING BIG GAME

King Darius of Media and Persia, who lived about 550 B.C., kept a large collection of captured lions in his park. This is probably the lions' den that the prophet Daniel was thrown into. Other kings stalked lions for sport. Assyrian rulers hunted from chariots while footmen prodded the cats into the kings' range.

APPEASING THE HEBREWS' GOD

When Israel was conquered by Assyria, most of the Israelites were moved to other lands. In an effort to colonize Israel, Assyria sent settlers to take the land and establish homes. But soon after the settlers arrived, many were killed by lions. A messenger told the king of Assyria that they had upset Israel's God, so they sent a Hebrew priest back to Israel to instruct the settlers on how to properly worship God.

Seal casting with imprint of lion

KINGS AND LIONS

Lions were a favorite of kings. Lions were used in hunting, and Ramses II was said to have kept a tame lion that went with him into battle.

THE BAND OF THIRTY

Benaiah was one of the Thirty, a band of David's warriors known for their bravery. Once, Benaiah went into a snowy pit to kill a lion.

REGAL SPLENDOR

King Solomon's throne must have been an impressive sight. It was made of ivory and overlaid with gold. On the side of the seat were armrests and two lions of gold. Twelve more lions stood on the sides of the six steps that led to the throne. It was said that nothing like it had ever been constructed in any kingdom.

The Gadarene Swine

WHEN JESUS CAME TO THE COUNTRY of the Gadarenes, he met a man who had been possessed by demons for a long time. The man wore no clothes and lived chained up in a cemetery among the tombstones. The demons were so strong that the man often broke his chains and ran through the hills screaming and cutting himself. Jesus commanded the demons to leave the man. The demons begged to be sent into a herd of pigs on a nearby hill. Jesus agreed, and the demons rushed into the animals, which then plunged over a cliff and drowned in the sea below. Every person in the city came to see what had happened. They found the man who had been possessed fully clothed and sitting calmly at Jesus' feet. Sadly, this frightened the Gadarenes, and even though they had witnessed a miracle, they told Jesus to go away and leave them alone.

DEFINITELY NOT KOSHER

The pig was a forbidden animal, according to the dietary laws of Israel. One who kept a herd of pigs was not allowed to enter the temple. A person who had to get rid of a dead pig had to wash every piece of clothing afterward.

Excavated figure of a pig's head

A WASTE OF TIME

Jesus told his followers not to cast their pearls—of wisdom—before swine. Pigs could not appreciate the beauty of pearls and would only trample them. So it is with people who have no interest in God's message. It is useless to try to persuade them, because their minds are closed.

Wild boars

A BIT OF A BOAR

The wild boar ruined crops by eating or trampling them. The boar, which is like a large hairy pig, could be brown, gray, or black. It had only four teeth that continued to grow throughout the animal's life.

DEER ANTLERS

The antlers of the fallow deer were large and flattened out. They resembled an open hand, palm up, with its fingers spread out.

FLEET OF FOOT

The red, the fallow, and the roe were types of deer in biblical times. The red deer was most common and was served on King Solomon's table daily.

GOD QUENCHES THIRST

King David once said, "As the deer pants for water, so I long for you, O' God." As a deer depends on water to live, we depend on God.

183

The Wings of an Eagle

SEVERAL TYPES OF LARGE BIRDS of prey are mentioned in the Bible, including vultures and eagles. Since the two birds were usually observed from a distance, it was hard to tell the difference. The Hebrew word for eagle means "to tear with the beak." The eagle is the largest flying bird in Israel today, and its wingspread can exceed eight feet. The Bible often speaks of the eagle's power and beauty. Isaiah 40:31 says, "They that wait upon the Lord shall renew their strength. They shall mount up with wings like eagles. . . ." In Proverbs, Solomon marvels that one of the things too wonderful for him to understand is how an eagle glides through the sky. The eagle was also known for the care of its young. In the book of Deuteronomy, God's protection of the Israelites is compared to a soaring eagle that has spread its wings, carrying its young eaglets on its back.

Golden eagle

IMPERIAL AND GOLDEN

Varieties of eagles include the imperial eagle and the rarer golden eagle. The golden eagle can fly three or four miles in only ten minutes.

OF SHEEP AND LAMBS

In the Bible, people are often compared to sheep, because people tend to wander from God and put themselves in danger. The prophet Isaiah says, "We, like sheep, have gone astray." Jesus is often compared to the Passover lamb that has been sacrificed for his people. The book of Revelation refers to Jesus as the Lamb no less than 37 times. Revelation also talks about the lamb with the seven horns who lifts the scroll with the seven seals from the hand of God.

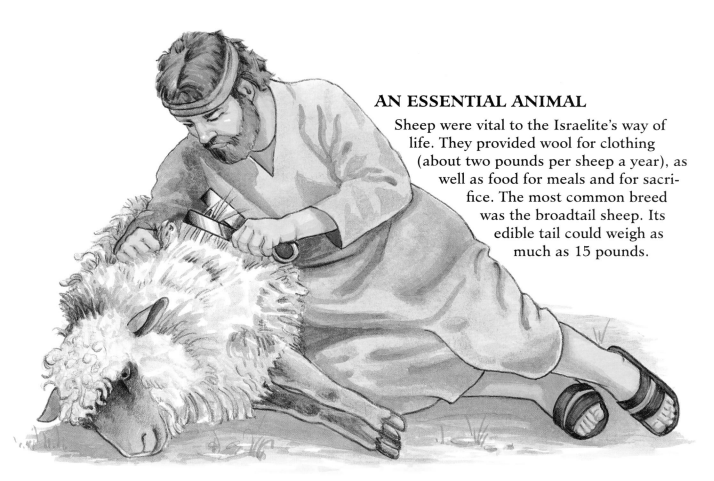

AN ESSENTIAL ANIMAL

Sheep were vital to the Israelite's way of life. They provided wool for clothing (about two pounds per sheep a year), as well as food for meals and for sacrifice. The most common breed was the broadtail sheep. Its edible tail could weigh as much as 15 pounds.

Ram

RAM'S HORNS

The ram's horns are two to three inches in diameter and were used as sharp weapons. Once removed they were used as trumpets or as oil containers.

A FESTIVE OCCASION

Sheep shearing was usually held after the summer grazing. It was a festive time during which friends and neighbors were invited to celebrate. Nabal held a feast in his house after the shearing, and Absalom used the celebration to lure his brother, Amnon, to his death.

DANGEROUS ERRAND

Jesus told his disciples that he was sending them out as lambs in the midst of wolves. It was another way of saying that there were many who would hate them and their message.

Let Them Eat Quail

QUAIL, WHICH ARE SMALL GAME BIRDS (related to turkeys and pheasants), are only mentioned a few times in the Bible. In one account, Moses and Aaron were leading the Hebrew nation through the western portion of the Sinai Desert, when the people became very hungry. They complained that Moses and Aaron brought them out to the desert to starve to death. They even said they wanted to go back to Egypt where they had been enslaved because at least there they would have meat and bread to eat. The Lord heard their complaints, and he appeared to Moses in a bright cloud. He told Moses that as a sign that he was their God, each evening they would have enough meat and each morning they would have enough bread. That same evening God sent so many quail that they were all over the camp—and in the morning there was enough bread for all.

BLESSING OR CURSE?

Huge flocks of quail migrate over the Sinai region after spending the winter in Africa. Exhausted from the flight, the quail can be easily caught.

THE HOOPOE BIRD

The hoopoe bird appears only twice in the Bible, where it is listed among the birds forbidden as food. The hoopoe was beautiful, but it smelled rancid and had filthy eating and nesting habits. Hoopoes are still common in Israel today and like to nest in holes found in houses and buildings.

Hoopoe bird

186

MANY MEANINGS

Doves are mentioned more than any other bird in the Bible. Actually, the Hebrew word for dove is used to describe several species of pigeons. The prophet Jeremiah noted that the bird's arrival was a sign of spring and that the dove would often build its nest in a high place. Because of its faithfulness to its mate, the turtledove was also a symbol of love. In the Song of Solomon, "dove" is used as an affectionate name for the beloved.

THE OLIVE BRANCH

After the torrential rains stopped, Noah released a dove from the ark to see if it could find dry land. When the bird brought back an olive branch, Noah knew land was close by.

THE HOLY SPIRIT

Throughout the history of the Church, the dove has been a symbol of the Holy Spirit. This association comes from the story about Jesus' baptism. As Jesus was coming out of the water, the heavens opened and the Holy Spirit, in the form of a dove, descended and alighted on him.

CEREMONIAL OFFERING

When a newborn boy was brought to the temple for dedication, the mother was to bring a yearling lamb and a pigeon or dove for the purification ceremony. If she was poor, however, two doves or pigeons were acceptable. When Mary brought Jesus, she offered two doves, a sign that she was probably poor.

Leviathan

THE WORD LEVIATHAN refers to a variety of large sea creatures in the Bible. In the book of Job, the leviathan is very likely a crocodile. The creature described has a large body, thick skin, and powerful jaws and teeth—and is impossible to catch or even harm. Job realizes that he is powerless against this fearsome animal that God created. Crocodiles were plentiful in the Nile River in biblical times. Long ago, a Roman writer named Pliny referred to a place in the Holy Land called Crocodeilopolis, meaning "crocodile city." In the book of Ezekiel, the crocodile is referred to as a "mighty dragon lying in the middle of the rivers." In other books of the Bible, however, the leviathan is not a crocodile but a porpoise or whale. The book of Genesis says that whales, or "great sea animals," were among the first living things created by God.

SYMBOL OF THE FISH

The earliest Christians used the symbol of a fish as a secret sign to identify other believers. It was not yet safe to follow The Way (the teachings of Jesus), so believers could simply trace a fish in the sand and watch for acknowledgement. The Greek word for fish is *ichthus*. It is an acrostic for "Jesus Christ, God's son, savior," words that sum up Christian beliefs. The fish symbol (⌖) has been found in early Christian catacombs (underground passages and tombs) of ancient cities of the Roman Empire.

Mosaic floor from the Church of the Loaves and Fishes

RESURRECTION

The whale was a symbol of Jesus' resurrection. He predicted that, just as Jonah was in the fish for three days, he would be in the earth three days before rising again.

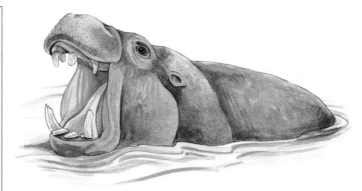

A WHALE OF A FISH STORY

What sort of fish swallowed Jonah? It may have been a toothed whale, which has a stomach large enough to hold a person. Others believe that God created a large fish specifically to swallow Jonah. Still others believe that the story is symbolic of something else (such as the capture of the kingdom of Judah). The important thing to remember is that the experience changed Jonah. After his experience, he went to Ninevah, the capital of Assyria, and fulfilled the command God gave him.

BEHEMOTH

Another baffling creature mentioned in the Bible is the behemoth. It too appears in the book of Job. However, experts are fairly certain that it is a hippopotamus. Job says this creature eats grass like the ox, has bones that are like tubes of bronze, and wades in rivers—even ones as wide and deep as the Jordan.

THE UNICORN

The King James version of the Bible mentions unicorns several times. The actual animal was probably an oryx, sometimes called a wild ox. This animal was a small white antelopelike creature with two long, straight, sharp-edged horns. The oryx nearly became extinct, but it is being restored in Israel by wildlife conservationists.

DRAGONS

Dragons are mentioned in the Old and New Testaments. These were not the types of dragons pictured in fairy-tale books but were more likely serpents or mythological monsters. Dragons often symbolized evil. In the book of Revelation, a dragon with seven heads and ten horns symbolizes Satan.

Symbol of Healing

WHEN MOSES FOUND HIMSELF again listening to complaints from the Israelites, the Lord sent poisonous serpents among the people to punish them. The serpents were described as "fiery" since their fatal poison killed so quickly. Many of the Israelites were bitten and died. The rest of the people cried out that they were sorry they had sinned, and they begged Moses to do something. God told Moses to make a bronze serpent and place it on a pole. If a person was bitten, he or she simply needed to look at the bronze snake in order to live. It was not the snake itself that healed the people, it was their belief that God could heal them. Later in the Bible, this bronze serpent was destroyed because the people had started to worship it. Jesus compared himself to the bronze serpent. His sacrifice on the cross would provide the way for others to live if they would only look to him.

THAT ANCIENT SERPENT

The first and last books of the Bible both compare Satan to a serpent. In the book of Revelation, we read that Satan, "that ancient serpent," will be thrown into a lake of fire.

VARIETY OF SNAKES

The ancient Hebrews were familiar with a number of venomous snakes, among them the horned sand snake (adder), the horned viper, the puff adder, and the Egyptian cobra. Most Middle Eastern snakes live on a diet of frogs and small animals. Some vipers differ from snakes in that they bear their young live rather than hatch them from eggs.

RELIGIOUS SNAKES

Both Jesus and John the Baptist referred to some hypocritical Pharisees as snakes. John called these particular Pharisees snakes because they were not humble before God. Jesus called them a "brood of vipers" because of their lying and hypocrisy. Like snakes, they spread poison and death wherever they went.

FEARSOME STING

Scorpions are fearsome creatures varying from two inches to around nine inches in length. Their tail bears a stinger that can poison and paralyze. Several Bible passages—particularly in the book of Revelation—refer to the painful sting of the scorpion. When Reheboam became king of Israel, he wanted the people to know that he would be even more severe than his father, Solomon, and promised to give out discipline "with scorpions."

LOOKS CAN DECEIVE

When curled up tight, a scorpion can look like an egg. Thus, the passage in the book of Luke, which speaks of God's openness to those who seek him: "What father among you, if his son . . . asks for an egg, will give him a scorpion?"

SWARMING HORNETS

In the Old Testament, armies sent by God into battle were sometimes described as hornets. The vast armies would "swarm" in and drive out their enemies.

Hornets' nest

191

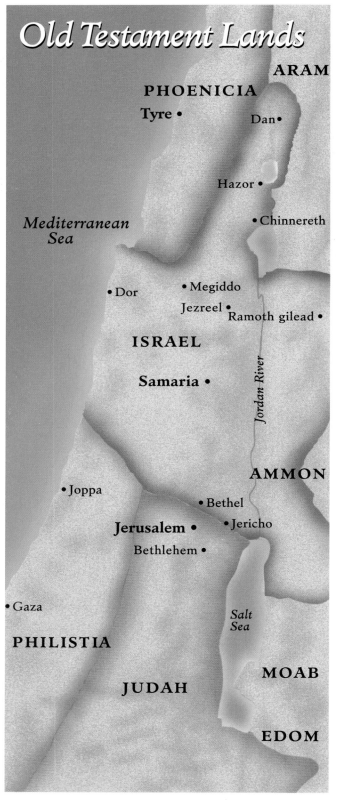

Old Testament Lands

ARAM

PHOENICIA

Tyre •

Dan•

Hazor •

• Chinnereth

Mediterranean Sea

• Dor

• Megiddo

Jezreel •

• Ramoth gilead •

ISRAEL

Samaria •

Jordan River

AMMON

• Joppa

• Bethel

Jerusalem •

• Jericho

Bethlehem •

• Gaza

Salt Sea

PHILISTIA

MOAB

JUDAH

EDOM

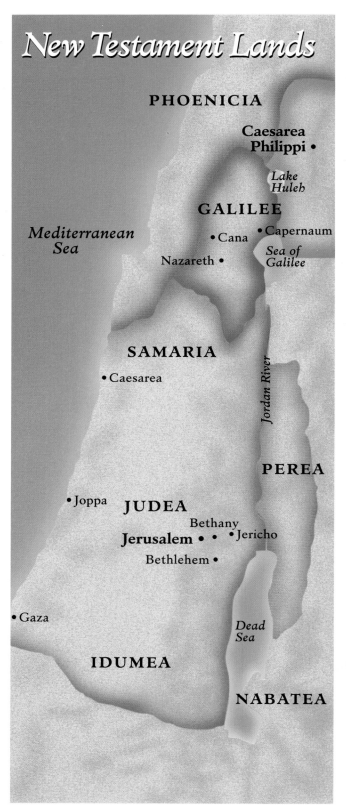

New Testament Lands

PHOENICIA

Caesarea Philippi •

Lake Huleh

GALILEE

• Cana

• Capernaum

Nazareth •

Sea of Galilee

Mediterranean Sea

SAMARIA

• Caesarea

Jordan River

PEREA

• Joppa

JUDEA

Bethany

Jerusalem • •

• Jericho

Bethlehem •

• Gaza

Dead Sea

IDUMEA

NABATEA

MARKETING

3rd edition

Rosalind Masterson & David Pickton

MARKETING
an introduction

MORE THAN JUST A BOOK...

3rd edition

Rosalind Masterson & David Pickton

MARKETING
an introduction

MobileStudy · companion website · S

- Videos
- Podcasts
- Web links
- Practice quizzes

- Revision PowerPoints
- Chapter summaries
- Interactive eBook
- Bonus chapter on careers in marketing

LEARN HOW YOU LIKE.

Check out the extensive FREE online resources to support your study at **www.uk.sagepub.com\masterson3e**

or just scan this QR code

Want to learn more? See More than just a book on page xx

Praise for the Second Edition

'This is a really exciting introductory text that brings to life the key principles of marketing. It is packed with good examples of marketing in practice and students will find it highly accessible.'
Pauline Maclaran, School of Management, Royal Holloway University of London

'A very good course support that also offers students interesting and updated case studies to study in groups during tutorials. This book provides a good balance of theoretical concepts and managerial insights to offer the students a comprehensive introduction to the vast subject of marketing.'
Veronique Pauwels-Delassus, IESEG School of Management

'Great book. It provides an excellent overall understanding of the marketing discipline. It shows how to apply the key marketing concepts to different situations by using several interesting up-to-date examples and illustrations which makes this book very easy to read. It is a great book for any undergraduate student who wishes to have an overview of the key elements of marketing.'
Magdalena Gonzalez Triay, School of Business and Management, Gloucestershire University

'Love this book! It's quirky, funny and entertaining – ideal for students new to marketing and I think the students will engage well with it. I like the fact that it isn't too "Americanised", so will appeal to the UK students. It is set out well and easy to follow and ties in nicely with the syllabus.'
Hilary Bishop, School of Business and Law, Liverpool John Moores University

'As a course team we felt that this book met our students' needs, the chapters were of a manageable size and that it fitted well within a 12-week introductory course. The case studies were interesting and the online material accessible for both the students and the lecturers.'
Charlotte Lystor, Winchester Business School, Winchester University

3rd edition

Rosalind Masterson & David Pickton

MARKETING
an introduction

§SAGE

Los Angeles | London | New Delhi
Singapore | Washington DC

Los Angeles | London | New Delhi
Singapore | Washington DC

SAGE Publications Ltd
1 Oliver's Yard
55 City Road
London EC1Y 1SP

SAGE Publications Inc.
2455 Teller Road
Thousand Oaks, California 91320

SAGE Publications India Pvt Ltd
B 1/I 1 Mohan Cooperative Industrial Area
Mathura Road
New Delhi 110 044

SAGE Publications Asia-Pacific Pte Ltd
3 Church Street
#10-04 Samsung Hub
Singapore 049483

Editor: Matthew Waters
Development editor: Amy Jarrold/Robin Lupton
Assistant editor: Nina Smith
Production editor: Sarah Cooke
Copyeditor: Martin Noble
Proofreader: Sharon Cawood
Indexer: Silvia Benvenuto
Marketing manager: Alison Borg
Design: Francis Kenney
Digital content assistant: Isabel Drury
Typeset by: C&M Digitals (P) Ltd, Chennai, India
Printed and bound in Great Britain by Ashford
Colour Press Ltd

Third edition first published 2014
Second edition first published 2010. Reprinted 2011
First edition first published by McGraw-Hill 2004

Library of Congress Control Number: 2013941666

British Library Cataloguing in Publication data

A catalogue record for this book is available from
the British Library

ISBN 978-1-84920-570-2
ISBN 978-1-84920-571-9 (pbk)

Brief contents

Contents

PART ONE

This Is Marketing   3

1 Marketing today   5

2 The marketing environment 49

PART TWO

Making Sense of Markets   95

3 Buyer behaviour   97

A message from the authors

Dear reader,

We're really excited about this new edition of *Marketing: an introduction* and hope to pass on that enthusiasm to you too – not just with our third edition, but with marketing as a subject and as a career. This edition has been thoroughly updated, and some of the chapters have undergone major revision because we've found a better way to cover the subject (take a look at the environmental analysis illustrations running through chapter 2). The text comes with an interactive eBook which links to current examples and other online resources, mobilestudy (accessing a mobile optimised website) and a comprehensive companion website which includes slides, test questions, interviews with marketers and a comprehensive tutors' guide – all designed to make the learning easier.

Marketing is clearly the fun side of business (at least we think so), although it does of course have a serious purpose. Without good marketing, most organisations would not survive. Even not-for-profit organisations like charities and government departments use marketing techniques. Many people equate marketing with advertising, but that is just one small part of the subject. Marketers develop and manage new products; nurture valuable brands; build and maintain relationships with customers, consumers, distributors; develop pricing strategies; do market research; devise ways to grow companies; negotiate sponsorship deals; run events; expand product ranges – all this as well as communicating with people via mass media advertising, public relations, personal selling, websites and social networking media, e-mail and many other communications channels.

Our book covers all of this and more. We wrote it for first year undergraduates (though this isn't an actual requirement – anyone can read it). We wanted to introduce the subject whilst inspiring you to want to know more. We hope we've achieved that; why not read the book, use the Sage companion website, and let us know?

Rosalind and David

About the authors

ROSALIND MASTERSON was a Principal Lecturer at De Montfort University until 2013. She has taught extensively, and has been subject and programme leader, at both undergraduate and postgraduate levels. This book came about as part of an extensive redesign of the university's core first-year undergraduate module: *Principles of Marketing*. She has taught, and been external examiner, at a number of universities during an academic career spanning twenty years.

Rosalind's commercial experience includes sales and marketing positions within IBM and marketing management for an IT consultancy. She ran her own marketing consultancy and freelance copywriting business for ten years.

Rosalind is a Chartered Institute of Marketing Chartered Marketer, a Member of the Academy of Marketing and a Fellow of the Higher Education Academy.

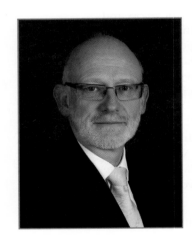

DAVID PICKTON is Honorary Academic Fellow at De Montfort University having been founding member of its academic Marketing Department and its Head. He is Visiting Academic at the Universities of Birmingham, UK, and Vienna, Austria. He has been visiting lecturer and external examiner at over 20 universities in the UK and internationally.

He is an Editorial Board member of the *Journal of Marketing Communications, Innovative Marketing Journal* and *Marketing Intelligence and Planning*, and, previously, on the *Journal of Brand Management* and *Corporate Communications: An International Journal*. He has written numerous articles and contributed to various academic texts.

His commercial experience includes marketing management positions on both the client and agency sides of industry, directorship of his own business consultancy and providing executive marketing and management training.

His professional affiliations include Fellowships of the Chartered Institute of Marketing, the Royal Society of Arts and the Higher Education Academy.

Acknowledgements

The authors would like to extend their warmest thanks to the contributors to chapters in the first edition of this book:

Tony Garry

Len Tiu Wright

Kit Jackson

Phil Garton

Lynn Stainsby

Tracy Harwood

Also to Chris Vaughan-Jones for his much appreciated input to Chapter 5, 'Marketing research', in this edition.

Publisher's acknowledgements

The publishers would like to extend their warmest thanks to the following individuals for their invaluable feedback on the Second Edition and comments on draft material for the Third Edition.

Cecelia Cassinger, University of Essex

Chavi Chen, IESEG School of Management

Charlotte Lystor, University of Winchester

Christine Mullin, Glasgow Caledonian University

Dan Frost, Umeå University

David Harvey, University of Huddersfield

Delane Osborne, Curtin University

Hilary Bishop, Liverpool John Moores University

Ioannis Kostopoulous, University of Bedfordshire

Lindsay Williams, Oxford Brookes University

Prithwiraj Nath, University of East Anglia

Rania Badr El Din Mostafa, Damanhour University

Steve Mawson, Salford University

Susan Scoffield, Manchester Metropolitan University

William Mott, University of Wolverhampton

Yue Meng-Lewis, Bournemouth University

Introduction to the focus themes

Throughout this book there are focus boxes that relate the chapter's subject matter to certain key marketing themes. The boxes are:

- e-focus
- global focus
- b2b (business-to-business) focus

- ethical focus
- customer focus
- expand your knowledge.

The themes have been chosen to reflect marketing's current major preoccupations. Marketing is a broad subject that overlaps with many other business functions: corporate strategy, human resource management, operations management, research and development, design and corporate communications. It also draws on many other academic disciplines, for example: psychology, economics, management strategy, intercultural relationships, media studies and sociology.

e-focus

e-focus explores digital innovations and online campaigns

The Internet presents businesses with numerous challenges and opportunities. It has far-reaching effects throughout the business world, affecting the ways that businesses communicate with their customers, their suppliers, their own staff. The Internet has shortened supply chains by cutting out trade intermediaries such as wholesalers and retailers, and allowing manufacturers to deal directly with their end customers. It has broadened the geographic reach of companies by providing a fast, cheap way to communicate with customers in other countries. It has increased the levels of competition in many industries, and the ways in which firms compete, by making it easier for companies to get into new markets and for smaller companies to compete with larger ones for business. For example, Amazon did not exist pre-Internet but it is now a serious global competitor in bookselling. It has taken enormous amounts of trade away from the more established bookshops, and is rapidly branching out into other areas too.

Web pages provide a shop front to the world. Many companies now do very well without a high-street presence. Online, everyone looks the same size so there is no immediately obvious disadvantage for a smaller firm like there is for a smaller shop. It still has to deliver the goods, of course, as only a few businesses manage to do that online (e.g. software and music downloads, and services such as banking).

E-marketing does not stop at the Internet. Further new communications technologies are being developed all the time. Mobile phones are now seen as marketing media with smartphones opening up further possibilities. The digitisation of television has radically changed the way we watch TV – and how organisations use it to reach customers.

Throughout this book we will take the opportunity to reflect on the impact of new technologies and how they can be used to market goods and services.

e-focus boxes:

global focus

There is a widely held view that all marketing today is international. If this is not quite universally true now, it is certainly the way the trend is going. Almost all large firms have to deal with foreign competitors either in their home markets or abroad or both. Foreign rivals may not be much in evidence in the local shop, but foreign products are, and it may be foreign-owned supermarkets that are taking away its customers.

However, there are a large number of small to medium-sized businesses that have little or no dealings outside their own country. Many services businesses (e.g. cleaning, consultancy, law, accountancy, hairdressing and plumbing) have no significant international dimension. Will they all be crushed by the march of the multinationals? It seems unlikely that everyone will desert their regular hairdresser (especially those that make home visits and therefore have very low costs and, consequently, low prices), or that individuals and small business people will prefer to hand over their tax returns to an anonymous corporation or Internet service rather than the accountant round the corner.

All businesses, however small, need to be aware of the forces of globalisation though. They need to look out for new competition, new products and services and new opportunities. (See Chapter 2 for more about monitoring changes in the organisation's environment.)

The patterns of trade are changing. The twentieth century was the era of free trade, with richer countries pushing for the lowering, or abolition, of barriers to trade between nations, such as import duties, quotas (specified maximum amounts of imported goods), embargoes (bans on certain imported products) and subsidies (grants to producers that make home-produced goods cheaper). The twenty-first century may well prove, at least in its early part, to be a time of reconsolidation, but along new lines. Countries are clamouring to join trading blocs such as the European Union (EU), the North American Free Trade Association (NAFTA), the Association of South East Asian Nations (ASEAN) and Mercosur (an alliance of South American nations). Between them, the EU and NAFTA account for the bulk of world trade. Within their borders, member countries conduct trade on preferential

global looks at marketing examples from around the world

terms. For example, within the EU, there are no import taxes and EU citizens can move to any country to work without obtaining work permits.

b2b (business-to-business) focus

b2b highlights examples of business-to-business (b2b) marketing

Marketing grew from a start in consumer goods – in particular, FMCG (fast-moving consumer goods). The term FMCG describes products that move off the shelves fast, i.e. they are bought frequently and so shops need to restock them regularly. These are everyday products such as soap, washing-up liquid, toothpaste, shampoo, breakfast cereal and bread – low-cost, kept in the cupboard all the time, items. Because of this heritage, modern marketing techniques favour the selling of these kinds of items to individuals for their own use. It is also the type of shopping that most people are more familiar with, so they usually relate to it better than b2b.

ACTIVITY

Look around your room. What items can you see that both a business and an individual might buy? How might their uses of the items differ? Where would they go to buy them?

When you want to buy something, the decision is usually yours although you may consult other people, particularly if you are not paying the whole cost yourself. Within organisations, it is rarely just one person who makes the decision on any significant purchase. There is a group of people involved who are referred to as a decision-making unit.

Take the example of a new car. There may be the fleet manager (who will specify which cars may be bought), the buyer (who will choose a supplier and negotiate terms), the finance department (which will set the budget and pay the invoice) and, of course, the person who is actually going to drive the car: the user. A potential supplier may have to deal with all these people and more. (See Chapter 3 for more on decision-making units.)

With all these people involved, purchasing decisions can become long and complicated. There are often forms that must be filled in, committee meetings called, procedures that must be followed. The organisation is likely to have rules about how many suppliers must be invited to bid for a contract. All of them must get a fair chance, and so there are more rules and procedures to ensure that this happens. It is a lot more complex than when you decide to buy a new printer for your PC.

However, just consider how much more money businesses have to spend than individuals. Large companies spend millions every year. When they do buy the everyday items that we do (pens, paper, sticky tape, etc.), they buy them by the crate. This is a good market to be in.

b2b focus boxes:

 ## ethical focus

Different businesses operate according to different ethical codes. There was a time when it was considered perfectly acceptable for an employer to own his workers and their children, yet now such a practice would cause outrage. Ethics change with the times. There are a number of different ethical models under which an organisation can operate.

ethical illustrates sustainability and ethical practices

There are different views on who should be the main beneficiaries of business activities. Many companies are ostensibly run for the sole benefit of their owners or shareholders, whose primary requirement is likely to be profit. In practice, though, a business cannot run without workers, and so they must benefit too, usually through wages or salaries. Then again, if the firm's products and/or services do not benefit anyone, why would customers buy them? So perhaps a firm is run primarily for the benefit of customers?

The stakeholder view of business ethics takes all of these interests, and more, into account. The argument is that the benefits to all of an organisation's stakeholders should be considered by the management team.

When an ethical position is generally accepted within a country, it is likely to be formalised by the passing of a law. Regulations and codes of practice are watered-down laws. They still reflect what is generally accepted as right or wrong. There are many laws governing marketing, e.g. product liability, consumer protection, trades descriptions, pricing, anti-competitive practices. There are regulations and codes of conduct covering advertising, sponsorship, sales promotion, Internet trading, telesales, data protection and many other marketing activities. For example, the UK Sale of Goods Act requires goods that are delivered to be the same as the ones that were shown to the customer. This is particularly important for mail order where the pictures and descriptions must be accurate.

Products can be unethical. There are a number of products that are banned in most countries (e.g. recreational drugs). Many would argue that cigarettes should not be on sale either. Sales of some products are severely restricted (e.g. guns, alcohol – which is banned in some countries – and strong medicines).

Unethical pricing practices include fixing prices so that consumers are forced to pay too much. This usually involves collusion between competitors (e.g. as a cartel) or the existence of a monopoly or a severe shortage of goods. In wartime, there are people who exploit other people's misery by charging dearly for essential goods, and so they become rich.

Too low a price may be considered unethical too. The outlawing of dumping is called for at meetings of the WTO (World Trade Organisation) and there are now severe restrictions on its legality. Dumping is an anti-competitive practice whereby a company exports its products at a very low price and so undercuts competitors in the target country. The local companies are then unable to compete and eventually go out of business, and so jobs and wealth are lost in that country. The low price is, of course, unsustainable. The company that has dumped the products will either raise its prices or will stop exporting, so the residents of the dumped-on country end up with either no products of that type or more expensive ones.

Professional marketers, and marketing associations, such as the Chartered Institute of Marketing, strive to behave ethically towards all their organisation's stakeholders. There are still those who doubt their motives, however, and consider their caring stance to be enlightened self-interest or just good PR.

ethical focus boxes:

 ## customer focus

 customer analyses the customer and how to meet their needs

Customers are at the heart of what marketers do. That old saying 'the customer is king' is still often quoted and it is true that good customer service is often a key to sales. There is a distinction between customers and consumers, both of whom are vital to business success. A customer is someone who buys the firm's products. However, they may not actually use the products themselves. The eventual user of the product is called a consumer.

Consumers are important influencers on purchase decisions even if they do not make the actual decision on what to buy (see Chapter 3 for more on this). For example, children's toys, particularly those designed for young children, are usually bought by other members of their family or by friends. They are the customers but the child is the actual consumer. Food is often bought by one or two members of a household, the ones doing the shopping that week, but will be consumed by everyone in the house. A person may be a customer but not a consumer, or a consumer but not a customer, or both consumer *and* customer.

This distinction is even more important in business markets where there may be a professional buying department. They buy everything the organisation needs, but mostly the products are used by other people. One person may sign an order for 50 000 staples – but they are not going to use them all themself. In b2b marketing, the term 'user' is used instead of 'consumer'.

customer focus boxes:

EXPAND YOUR KNOWLEDGE

These boxes contain references to further reading to help you understand better the points raised in the book. Some of the references are well accepted articles that have shaped and often changed marketing thinking over the years; they are marketing classics that have been influential in developing marketing thought. The considerations contained within them are still relevant today and still shape our thoughts and understanding and are especially useful for students first learning about marketing. Marketing has travelled a long way from its early beginnings, but a far richer appreciation of marketing is gleaned by understanding its roots and how it has branched into the discipline it is today.

Other articles in the expand your knowledge boxes are of more recent publication. Their inclusion allows readers to delve more deeply into specific areas and into some of the latest thinking that has influenced or is influencing marketing thinking now.

More than just a book

MARKETING: AN INTRODUCTION OFFERS A RANGE OF LEARNING RESOURCES IN THE TEXT AND ONLINE

Chapter contents lists allows you to see what will be covered in each chapter at a glance, helping you to dip in and out of the book as you need.

Chapter introduction challenges encourage you to start thinking like a marketer from the start by posing you with real-life marketing problems to solve. Hints on how to successfully meet these challenges are at the end of each chapter.

Activities exercise your analytical and critical thinking skills by inviting you to complete a small task relating to the chapter either on your own or with classmates, friends and family.

Glossary terms for key marketing concepts appear in the margins for easy reference. These terms and more are also available in the glossary in the back of the book.

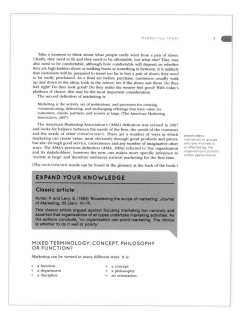

Expand your knowledge refers you to further reading to support assignments, exams and literature reviews.

Case studies throughout the chapters bring marketing theory to life.

Chapter summaries sum up the key concepts covered in the chapter to help ensure you are meeting your learning objectives.

Reading around provides illustrations of concepts covered in the chapter and prompts to think more deeply about the subject.

GO ONLINE AND GET INTERACTIVE

Marketing is everywhere. You encounter it all day, every day, but you won't always have your textbook to hand.

Not to worry. You now have the flexibility to learn how, when and where you want if you purchased *Marketing: an introduction* with 12 months **FREE** access to the **interactive eBook**.

How it works. A unique code on the inside front cover of this book gives access to an online version of the text on VitalSource Bookshelf® and allows you to access the book from your computer, tablet, or smartphone. You can make notes and highlights which will automatically sync across all your devices.

What makes the book interactive?

Your textbook is dotted with coffee cups alerting you to different types of additional online resources.

To get the most out of the great interactive features in the textbook, think GREEN.

When using your interactive eBook simply click on the web links printed in the text, or click on the coffee cups to:

remember

green means GO! ▶

 Watch videos to get a better understanding of key concepts and provoke in-class discussion.

 Peruse a dedicated Pinterest page to find a wealth of topical real-world examples of marketing that you can relate to your study.

 Visit websites and access templates to help guide students' study.

 Listen to the Daily Grind – a podcast series where recent graduates and marketing professionals talk about the day-to-day of marketing and specific marketing concepts.

HOW TO USE THE COMPANION WEBSITE AND MOBILESTUDY

You can also access all the additional resources in the book on the companion website via your computer at **www.sagepub.co.uk/masterson3e.** If you would prefer to revise on the go, all student resources are also available on MobileStudy, a mobile-friendly version of the companion website – designed for smartphones and tablets – allowing you to study when and where you want.

STUDENT RESOURCES AVAILABLE ON THE COMPANION WEBSITE AND MOBILESTUDY

- **Videos** to help you gain a better understanding of key concepts and provoke in-class discussion.

- Interactive **practice questions** to test your understanding.

- Hundreds of links to useful **websites** and **templates** to help guide your study.

- Access **SAGE Marketing Pins**, SAGE's Pinterest page, giving you access to regularly updated resources on everything from Branding to Consumer Behaviour.

- **Daily Grind podcast series** to learn more about the day-to-day working life of a marketing professional.

- A **bonus chapter on careers in marketing** to not only support your study, but your job search and future career.

- **PowerPoints** summarising each chapter to help you revise for exams.

LECTURER RESOURCES ON THE COMPANION WEBSITE:

- **PowerPoints** highlighting key concepts – including figures and tables from the book – are ideal for lecturers.

- **Tutor's Guide** detailing the key objectives of each chapter and outlining suggested activities to promote class discussion.

- **VLE Testbank cartridges** allowing you to easily upload resources to your university's Virtual Learning Environment (VLE).

3rd edition

Rosalind Masterson & David Pickton

MARKETING

an introduction

This is Marketing

This Part Contains:

WHAT THIS PART IS ABOUT

The term 'marketing' comes literally from market: a place where traders go to sell and customers come to buy. Sellers have always tried to show their products to advantage, and buyers have always looked for good value. This has not changed. However, marketing has come a long way since the days when traders travelled around the market towns with their goods packed in a wagon.

The first part of this book looks back at marketing history to show where the marketing discipline has come from in order to shed light on its strengths and limitations. It explains why marketing is more important today than it was in earlier times. It looks at how marketing has evolved into such a sophisticated business discipline and also briefly considers the key aspects of modern marketing.

All business organisations, and most non-commercial organisations too, are built around four main business functions: marketing, finance, operations (or manufacturing) and human resources (HR). Marketers must work with their colleagues from other disciplines in order to make the best use of the resources available. However, no organisation exists in isolation. It has to interact with other organisations and with individuals. Successful marketing depends upon a thorough understanding of the context in which the organisation is operating. Good marketers will be prepared for changes in their world and so they are constantly scanning their marketing environment and making changes to their plans.

Marketing today 1

MARKETING CHALLENGES

At the start of each chapter in this book, you will find several challenges. They are there to help you see the significance of the chapter you are about to read. You aren't expected to know how to deal with the challenges now; just bear them in mind as you read the chapter and see what you can find that helps.

- You tell friends who are studying sciences that you are doing a marketing course. One says, 'You're studying advertising, what fun.' Is he right? Is marketing just another name for advertising?
- You are the marketing manager for a large university. Funds are always short. A local bar owner has offered the university Registry a substantial amount of money for its list of student names and addresses so that he can text them with a very tempting offer to visit the bar. The Registry wants your advice.
- You are a sales assistant in an electronics store. The shop is in a quite poor area and business is slow. You have a lot of DVD recorders that are getting harder to sell now that there are newer technologies available. The manager tells you to sell them hard and offers the sales staff bonuses for every recorder sold. Other salespeople are selling more than you are but they are telling customers that this is the latest technology.
- Winston Smith installs CCTV systems for a living. He is self-employed and all his jobs are one-offs. Today he's very annoyed because he's just seen someone else adding to one of his systems. The customer was pleased with the work Winston did but couldn't remember his name, so he got someone else in when the system needed enlarging. How could Winston have got that job himself?

INTRODUCTION

A market is a place where things are bought and sold. It is often defined as a place where buyers and sellers meet.

Marketers are the sellers. They set out their stalls, displaying goods to their best advantage, and then try to attract buyers. Of course, modern marketing is rather more complex than a street market, but it is still about attracting customers, serving them well, competing with others and making a profit (usually). Marketing is a customer-focused discipline centred on an exchange between two (or more) parties. That exchange is at the centre of marketing activity and is usually of products for money. Good marketing brings about fair exchanges where both sides feel that they have got good value.

In this chapter, marketing is introduced through a brief look at how it evolved to become what it is today. We will consider current marketing issues and where marketing might be tomorrow.

Some organisations see themselves as marketing companies, while others see themselves as primarily manufacturers, or as financially excellent, or perhaps as innovators. They may have different strategic orientations but all businesses need customers, ideally loyal ones. Customer retention and brand loyalty will be introduced here.

Towards the end of this chapter, there are overviews of some of the key developments in modern marketing.

Definition
of
Marketing

WHAT IS MARKETING?

The two most commonly quoted definitions of marketing come from the Chartered Institute of Marketing (CIM) and the American Marketing Association (AMA).

The first definition of marketing is:

> The management process which identifies, anticipates and satisfies customer requirements efficiently and profitably. (Chartered Institute of Marketing, n.d.)

This definition stresses the need for management action to understand what customers really want from products. A product must meet customer needs physically (e.g. it should work), psychologically (e.g. they should feel good about owning it), financially (e.g. they should be able to afford it) and timewise (e.g. it should not take too long to actually get it). For the company, this may involve considerable market research and analysis.

© Dave Pickton

Traditional markets are the origin of the term 'marketing'.

Take a moment to think about what people really want from a pair of shoes. Clearly, they need to fit and they need to be affordable, but what else? They may also need to be comfortable, although how comfortable will depend on whether they are high-fashion shoes or walking boots or something in between. It is unlikely that customers will be prepared to travel too far to buy a pair of shoes; they need to be easily purchased. As a final act before purchase, customers usually walk up and down in the shop, look in the mirror, see if the shoes suit them. Do they feel right? Do they look good? Do they make the wearer feel good? With today's plethora of choice, this may be the most important consideration.

The second definition of marketing is:

> Marketing is the activity, set of institutions, and processes for creating, communicating, delivering, and exchanging offerings that have value for customers, clients, partners, and society at large. (The American Marketing Association, 2007)

The American Marketing Association's (AMA) definition was revised in 2007 and looks for balance between the needs of the firm, the needs of the customer and the needs of other **stakeholders**. There are a number of ways in which marketing can create value, most obviously through good products and prices, but also through good service, convenience and any number of imaginative other ways. The AMA's previous definition (AMA, 2004) referred to 'the organisation and its stakeholders', however the new one makes more specific reference to 'society at large' and therefore embraces societal marketing for the first time.

stakeholders individuals or groups who are involved in, or affected by, the organisation's actions and/or performance

(The **emboldened** words can be found in the glossary at the back of the book.)

EXPAND YOUR KNOWLEDGE

Classic article

Kotler, P. and Levy, S. (1969) 'Broadening the scope of marketing', *Journal of Marketing*, 33 (Jan): 10–15.

This classic article argued against focusing marketing too narrowly and asserted that organisations of all types undertake marketing activities. As the authors conclude, 'no organisation can avoid marketing. The choice is whether to do it well or poorly.'

MIXED TERMINOLOGY: CONCEPT, PHILOSOPHY OR FUNCTION?

Marketing can be viewed in many different ways. It is:

- a function
- a department
- a discipline
- a concept
- a philosophy
- an orientation.

First, let's distinguish between the marketing 'function' and the marketing 'department'. Function is a wider concept. It embraces all marketing activity within the organisation – whether or not it is carried out by members of the marketing department. The department is a defined part of the organisation in which specialist marketers work. They report to marketing managers and directors who lead the department. The distinction is important because, in a truly market-orientated organisation (see below for an explanation of market orientation), everyone will think marketing and, at least some of the time, carry out marketing-related activities.

For example, reception staff could be said to play a key role in the maintenance of a company's image and the building of relationships with customers; they do not report to the marketing manager, are not part of marketing staff, but they do perform a marketing function as part of their job. See Exhibit 1.1 for the most common marketing activities.

The 'discipline' of marketing is of primary interest to students and their tutors. Discipline means 'field of study' (Allen, 2000). Organisations are more likely to consider marketing as a function or a department.

Exhibit 1.1   Marketing activities

Marketing research and analysis – *where and who we are now*

Market research – who are our customers and what do they want?
Competitive research – who are our competitors and what do they do?
What is our position in the market? (market share, customer views)
Organisational research – what are we good at? (organisational strengths)
What are we bad at? (organisational weaknesses)
What have we done that worked well in the past? (e.g. promotions)
Are we risk takers?

Objective setting – *where and who we want to be*

Targets – e.g. market share, profits, sales, brand image, brand awareness, numbers of sales outlets, locations where products are available (at home and abroad), new product launches, product updates, customer satisfaction levels...

Marketing tasks – *how we are going to make it happen*

Planning – selecting and scheduling marketing tasks
Staff – suitably selecting and training
Budgets – allocating to activities
Promotional activities – advertising, PR, sales promotions, sales force support, direct marketing, packaging, website, etc.
Sales – finding new customers, getting repeat business
Pricing – setting prices, discounts, credit terms, etc.
Distribution – stock holding, packaging, shipping, order handling, etc.
Product management – development, dropping old products, standardisation, adaptation to suit different customers, etc.
Branding – branding strategy, maintaining brand image, logos, colours, etc.

Market entry – selling in new markets (directly or through a third party)

Customer service – loyalty schemes, complaints handling, after-sales service, warranties and guarantees

Customer management – customer database, events/actions designed to build relationships

Collecting feedback and controlling activities – *how we will keep track of things*

Objectives – have they been achieved? Are they likely to be achieved?

Customer feedback – complaints, compliments, recommendations, repeat buys, satisfaction surveys

Checklists and deadlines – have things happened on time?

Market position – are we doing better/worse than our competitors?

Academic researchers are more concerned with the marketing 'concept', marketing 'philosophy' and market 'orientation'. The distinction between these terms is sometimes unclear. They are used differently within different texts and journal articles. Sometimes they are even used interchangeably with no real distinction drawn between the terms, for example Dibb et al. (2006: 17) define the marketing concept as:

> the philosophy that an organisation should try to provide products that satisfy customers' needs through a co-ordinated set of activities that also allows the organisation to achieve its goals.

However, Hooley et al. (1990) suggest that the marketing concept is a process, rather than a philosophy (or way of thinking) and Jobber also sees the marketing concept as a process, i.e. something that organisations do, defining it as:

> the achievement of corporate goals through meeting and exceeding customer needs better than the competition. (Jobber, 2006: 5)

These differences in definition are less important than the principles behind marketing – and are not something to be too concerned about at this stage. An awareness that such terms are often substituted for each other, without there being any great significance to the way they are used, is all that is required.

Market orientation is another term that gets thrown into this mix. An organisation's strategic orientation provides 'the guiding principles that influence a firm's marketing and strategy making activities' (Noble et al., 2002: 25) and so determines how it will interact with its marketplace. Orientation literally means the way a person, or organisation, faces. Market-orientated firms, then, look to markets and markets are made up of buyers and sellers, so a truly market-orientated organisation ought to be both customer and competition facing. (Strategic orientations are covered in more detail below.)

For the purposes of this textbook, the terms 'marketing concept' and 'marketing philosophy' will be used in a similar way. Market orientation will be used to describe those firms that have embraced the marketing philosophy (or concept) and use it to inform all their activities and strategies. So a true market orientation requires marketing actions, not just thoughts or intentions.

EXPAND YOUR KNOWLEDGE

McDonald, M. (2009) 'The future of marketing: brightest star in the firmament, or a fading meteor? Some hypotheses and a research agenda', *Journal of Marketing Management*, 25 (5/6): 431–50.

Good marketing has always come from a deep understanding of consumer needs and expectations, however in the early twenty-first century 'marketing' is often seen as 'mismarketing' in practice. The blame rests largely with the use of disreputable tactics such as spamming, misleading advertising and hard selling. A few bad marketers are in danger of giving the whole discipline a bad name. In his article, Malcolm McDonald makes some suggestions for possible new initiatives/directions for marketing, including some ideas about the name 'marketing' itself.

WHAT MARKETING IS NOT

advertising
a persuasive communication paid for by an identifiable source and addressed to the whole of a target audience without personal identification

marketing communications
another name for promotion; communication designed and implemented to persuade others to do, think or feel something

The world, even the business world, has some erroneous ideas about what marketing is. It is worth being aware of these (it may save you some confusion) as it is important to be clear that marketing is not just selling, advertising, promotion or marketing communications. Let's take selling first. Although the idea of selling pre-dates that of marketing, for some years now selling has generally been viewed as a part of marketing, an important part. The underlying aim of most marketing activity is to make sales. However, this could be said to be the underlying aim of most business activities. After all, where is the profit without sales? The clear importance of commercial organisations making sales has led to a counter-movement where sales is held to be a discrete function worthy of a sales director on the Board – though this may be a consequence of a more limited view of the nature of marketing.

Selling is about persuading customers to buy and this may involve either a hard sell or a soft sell. Hard selling is pushy, an aggressive stance that is usually resented by customers and is therefore not a good tactic if you want them to come back again. It is often used in selling items that people are reluctant to buy, such as replacement windows. A soft sell, just as it sounds, is a gentler approach – more persuasive.

Peter Drucker, a world-renowned marketer, once famously said: 'The aim of marketing is to make selling superfluous.' If the product is something that the customer actively wants to buy, then a hard sell is unnecessary.

ACTIVITY What does BOGOF stand for?

If you don't know, look it up in the glossary at the back of the book. (All terms in bold text can be found in the glossary and terms are defined in the margins when first used in each chapter.)

So selling is a part of marketing, but not all of it. In fact, it would be more accurate to say that selling is a part of marketing communications or promotion (these are alternative terms for the same thing), and that marketing communications is part of marketing. Marketing communications (promotion) will be covered in more depth in Chapter 8. It is a collective term for all the activities that an organisation undertakes to promote its products to its customers. Such activities may include holding press conferences, designing appealing packaging, making promotional offers such as prize draws and BOGOFs, supporting websites, sponsoring sports teams and advertising, which means that advertising is only part of marketing communications, which in turn is part of marketing. Clearly, there must be more to marketing than just advertising. So what is included in marketing besides promotional activities?

global focus: The hard sell

It may seem obvious that the soft sell is the better sales technique, but it depends. In many countries, and some situations, a hard sell is needed. It may even be part of the local culture. If you have ever been a tourist anywhere, but particularly in a less-developed country, then you will almost certainly have been subjected to a hard sell. Trinkets, local crafts, postcards, boat tickets, even accommodation, are thrust at tourists as soon as they arrive anywhere. Many sales are made (and many are later regretted by the new owner of a stuffed donkey or undrinkable local liqueur).

Holiday souvenirs are typical one-off transactions.

One of the biggest areas of marketing is market research (see Chapter 5). Research is vital in understanding customer needs, buyer behaviour (see Chapter 3) and how to design goods and services to meet those needs. Without new product development (see Chapter 6) a company will die. Marketing is also concerned with getting the right products to the right place at the right time, and so distribution (place) is key (see Chapter 9). Those products also need to be at the right price (Chapter 10) or they will not sell.

brand
'the intangible sum of a product's attributes: its name, packaging, and price, its history, its reputation, and the way it's advertised' (David Ogilvy)

competitive advantage
something about an organisation or its products that is perceived as being better than rival offerings

Although marketing definitions tend to be centred on customers, marketing is also about understanding your competitors (competitive intelligence) and devising strategies to beat them. Strong branding is a competitive strategy that is often used today. Think of the sportswear market; it has some of the strongest, most valuable **brands** – Nike, Adidas, Reebok, Sergio Tachini, Umbro, Head. There are many of them but some are stronger than others and therefore have a **competitive advantage** over their rivals. Yet how much is there to choose in terms of quality, value for money, even style, between Nike shorts and those made by Adidas?

Marketing, then, encompasses a large number of business activities. An examination of Exhibit 1.1 will give you more detail on its scope.

customer focus: The right relationship

Think back to the earlier example of hard selling to tourists. Tourists are, by their very nature, not in a place for very long. They are often actively seeking mementoes and gifts on which to spend their money. Is it better for vendors to build a relationship with the tourists or to make a quick sale?

Many of those souvenirs are made in factories and workshops in other parts of the country (or even in other countries altogether). Think about the craftsperson hundreds of miles away. Should he or she be selling hard to the street vendor or would it be better to develop a relationship so that he or she can rely on selling more products next month?

BEFORE MARKETING

In a subsistence economy, such as the poorest in the world today, there is very little trade. Only when people have a surplus of goods do they swap them with other people for different things. So if farmers have an abundance of apples, say, they may go to market and try to trade them for something else. If they have only enough to feed their own families, there will be no apples left over for others to buy. So markets, and marketing, are only found where the economy has developed beyond these very early stages.

In Europe, before industrialisation, the emphasis was on making enough goods to supply people's needs, not on persuading them to buy them. There is no need to be persuasive when there are not enough shoes, soap or sugar to go round any-way. There was a time when goods were produced in small quantities, sold locally and farmers or craftspeople sold everything they made. There were enough local buyers and no need for the expense, and risk, of travelling to find more custom. So marketing is a relatively new discipline.

Those markets were **supply-led**, not **demand-driven**. That is, the challenge lay in producing enough to meet customers' needs rather than in persuading customers to choose your products. However, as factories opened and towns developed, there were more goods available and the city workers became more reliant on buying things from others to meet their needs. They did not have land on which to grow their own vegetables or keep animals. They needed to buy food with the wages they earned. Farms became larger and so produced surpluses that could be sold at market. Smaller farmers sold their surplus food to intermediaries, who would take it to market for them, where it would be sold alongside other products from other parts of the country, or even overseas.

This represented a major change in the way that goods were sold. Sellers no longer had direct contact with their buyers; there were agents and shopkeepers in between. This had two effects: first, it meant that they were not as aware of customers' requirements, relying as they did upon these intermediaries, and, second, it meant that customers no longer knew their suppliers – they only knew the shopkeepers or stallholders.

So the smarter producers made conscious efforts to find out what customers wanted – i.e. they began to conduct rudimentary **market research** (largely through those same intermediaries). Some also badged their products so that customers could recognise them. These makers' marks were an early form of branding.

The new factories brought with them an even more significant change. Their new mass-production techniques meant that there was a greater supply of products and that they were cheaper. Initially, the focus was still on finding more efficient ways to produce larger quantities as people queued up to buy all these new cheap products. There was more than enough demand to keep the early factories going. However, technology continued to improve and the volume of products available grew until there was no longer a shortage but a surfeit of almost everything. Today's suppliers cannot rely on people to buy everything they produce. They have to compete for customers. In such a situation, they need good marketing skills.

There are still a few supply-led markets though. Some modern products are in short supply just by their nature (e.g. precious stones or antiques), others by design (e.g. limited-edition prints or collectibles). Have you ever struggled to buy a concert or football match ticket? Perhaps you have even paid more than the face value? These are modern-day, supply-led markets.

MARKETING BEGINNINGS

Before mass production, value for money, pleasant service, a shop sign, a maker's mark and a reputation built by word of mouth were enough to keep a business afloat. Modern marketing is clearly more complex than that, although those early

supply-led
shortages of goods mean that suppliers can dictate terms of business

demand-driven
a surplus, or potential surplus, of goods to be sold gives buyers more power

market research
the systematic gathering, recording, and analysing of customer and other market-related data

History of Marketing

Marketing had to evolve to cope with the increased supply of goods from mass production techniques.

good-business principles are still valid today. More sophisticated marketing techniques were originally developed for the everyday, high-volume products of the new mass-production techniques: washing powder, toothpaste, shoe polish, soap, foodstuffs, etc. They were easier to make and so there were more companies making them. At the same time, transport improved. There were roads, railways and canals available to ship goods to other parts of the country. Consumers had lots of choice and competition became an issue.

These mass-produced products acquired brand names, had posters and press advertisements, were sold on special offer, and were adjusted to suit customer tastes and to be better than rival products. Manufacturers clearly could not sell such large volumes to so many customers directly and so the intermediaries, the shopkeepers and **wholesalers** became more significant. They were persuaded to stock products (and perhaps not to stock rivals' products), to display them more prominently, to recommend them to customers. So a number of factors led to the birth of modern marketing, the main ones being:

wholesaler
a reseller, buying products in bulk to sell on to other businesses in smaller quantities

- breakthroughs in production technology
- advances in the technology for transporting goods (particularly railways)
- social changes such as the move away from the countryside and into towns
- increased competition.

These forces still drive marketing today. Modern technological breakthroughs (such as the Internet) still have the power to change the way we sell goods and services. Air freight has made it possible to have fresh foods from around the world. It means we can have tropical fruits in northern Europe all year round. The changing age profile of our population means more products are developed for, and aimed at, older age groups. In many parts of the world, people are leaving rural areas and heading for the towns to find work. They have to buy food that they might previously have grown for themselves. They need housing and transport, etc. Competition now is global; it is no longer limited to rivals based in the same town, or even the same country. European Union (EU) companies compete fiercely with each other across the region – and across the world. The wealth of Europe attracts American, Canadian, Japanese, Chinese, African and Asian competitors. Almost all countries across the world are home to at least some internationally competitive companies.

You will learn more about how these forces shape marketing – and indeed our world – in later chapters, particularly Chapter 2 which looks at the marketing environment. 'Global focus' boxes throughout the text will provide further insights into the nature of global competition.

DEMAND AND SUPPLY

The concepts of **demand** and **supply** are fundamental in business – and in marketing. The word 'demand' causes some confusion. It is being used here in its economic sense, i.e. it means what people will buy, not just what they would like if only they could afford it, find it, etc.

Today, most markets are demand-driven. This means that the amount of goods made available for sale is dependent upon the customers and how much they will buy. In a supply-led market, the amount of goods available would depend on how much could be produced.

In a supply-led market, the most successful companies will be those that are the most efficient producers. Everything they can make will be bought. However, in a demand-driven market, companies have to compete for custom, hence the modern-day importance of marketing. It is the job of marketers to stimulate demand, to provide the goods and services that people want, and to persuade them to buy.

Ideally, demand should equal supply exactly. At this point firms maximise sales without having anything left over. The point where the supply curve and the demand curve cross (see Exhibit 1.2) is called the equilibrium point. At this price, customers will want to buy just exactly the amount that suppliers want to sell. Take the example of a book publisher. The easiest way to make sure that all its books are sold would be to produce fewer books than demanded. However, this would mean that some customers will be unable to get copies and the publishing firm will miss out on potential sales and so make less profit. It would be in its interest to print more books.

demand
quantity of goods that customers actually buy at a certain price, i.e. sales

supply
quantity of goods that sellers are prepared to put on the market at a certain price

Era of Demand Marketing

Exhibit 1.2 Demand and supply

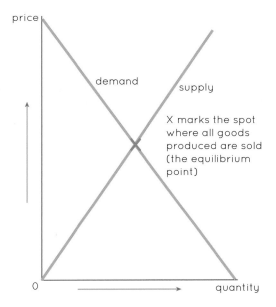

Exhibit 1.3   Equilibrium

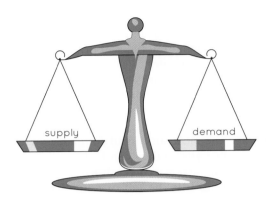

EXCHANGES

exchange
when two parties
swap items
perceived to be of
approximately equal
value

It is often said that marketing is about managing the **exchange** process. If you exchange something, you part with something of value (e.g. a product or an idea) in return for something else of value. The 'something else of value' is, of course, usually money, though it could be another product.

Clearly, there must be two parties to an exchange: the seller and the buyer. Each wants to exchange something for something else that they value more. So the car that the customer is buying must be a car that he or she wants more than the money he or she will part with in order to obtain it, and the car dealer would rather have the money than the car standing on the forecourt. This may sound obvious, but it is a concept worth remembering as you move on to more complex marketing ideas. This valued exchange is at the heart of marketing. If we cannot offer customers goods and services that are worth more to them than whatever they have to give up to obtain them, then we will not sell much.

Good marketing will create and maintain mutually beneficial exchange relationships. They may be very short-term relationships, if the sale is a one-off, or ongoing ones if a company is looking for repeat business. To be sure of repeat business, a company needs to make its customers loyal and loyalty should, of course, be a two-way street. The company needs to be consistent in its good treatment of its customers if it wants the same in return. (See below and Chapter 11 for more on customer loyalty.) This idea of ongoing relationships with customers will be revisited many times throughout this book, particularly in the CRM (customer relationship management) focus boxes and below, under the subheading 'Relationship marketing'.

Customers give up more than just money. They give up time: the time taken to check out the other options, to test drive other cars, for example. They put in effort that could have been expended doing something else. They have to weigh up the pros and cons of each possible car in order to make their decision. Sometimes customers will pay more for something just because it is less hassle, or quicker, or safer, or for any number of other good reasons. For example, train tickets are cheaper if booked in advance, but it is often just not convenient to book ahead. Many products can be bought more cheaply on the Internet, but many people do not yet trust Internet sales. Vegetables are usually much cheaper when bought

Exhibit 1.4   An exchange of value

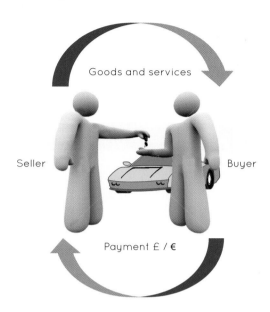

from a market stall than from supermarkets, but still you see lots of people with supermarket carrier bags full of them.

Customers take a risk when they hand over their money for a product. The product may not do the job it is being bought for, or may not work at all. It may go out of fashion. It may not suit them or other people may not like it. A good salesperson recognises this and tries to reassure customers that the risk is minimal and worth taking.

MARKETS

A **market** is a place where buyers and sellers meet. The term is often made more complex, but it is worth hanging on to that simple definition.

There are lots of different markets (e.g. consumer markets, industrial markets, b2b markets, overseas markets). These are broad groups of buyers and sellers, and they can be narrowed down into smaller groupings such as product type (e.g. **white goods** market) or customer type (e.g. youth market) or a combination (e.g. children's clothing market). Often, when people refer to 'markets' they are using the term interchangeably with 'customers'. However, a market needs sellers too and so any thorough study of a market should also include the seller – and its competitors. Exhibit 1.5 provides a framework for categorising markets.

STRATEGIC ORIENTATIONS

Different organisations take different approaches when it comes to achieving their objectives. Almost all (the successful ones anyway) will have a strategy to guide

market
a composite of individuals or organisations that have a willingness and ability to purchase products; a market can consist of a single or multiple segments

white goods
large electrical household appliances such as fridges and washing machines (traditionally coloured white)

their future actions but there are many ways to achieve success. The strategies themselves, and the thinking behind them, vary. If an organisation has embraced a marketing philosophy, then the needs and wants of its customers, coupled with a recognition of what competitors offer them, will be the driving force behind its thinking. That organisation will be market-orientated.

Exhibit 1.5 Market classifications

Market	Typical purchase descriptions	Purchase
B2C (business to consumer) markets	Personal purchases	E.g. household weekly shop
Industrial markets	Things that will be used in the making of other things	E.g. glass to go into headlights for cars, cooling fluids for machinery
B2B (business to business) markets	Things for use in the course of another business	E.g. delivery vans
Not-for-profit markets	Purchases and marketing activities by charities, government organisations, trades unions, clubs and associations, etc.	E.g. as other organisations
Government markets	Purchases by central government, local government, health services, schools, public libraries, armed forces, police, etc.	E.g. office supplies
Reseller markets	Goods to be sold on, e.g. by retailers, wholesalers, distributors, dealers, etc.	E.g. anything found for sale in a shop
Overseas markets	All above categories – but in other countries or outside the home country's trading bloc (e.g. EU)	Could be anything at all
Internal markets	Other divisions, subsidiaries or employees of the organisation itself	E.g. own product sales (usually at discounted prices), services provided by one division for another in the same organisation

However, 'market' is not the only strategic orientation an organisation could adopt. Exhibit 1.6 shows some of the other options.

Many textbooks ascribe these orientation strategies to specific eras, usually making production the earliest and 'market' the most recent. However, there are still organisations that are product- or production-orientated, even though market orientation is widely accepted as better in terms of business performance.

Cooperative and financial orientations are beyond the scope of this book. The next section goes into detail on the other, more marketing-related orientations. Production is included as it often appears in marketing texts, though it is out of favour with modern-day management thinkers. Societal orientation is included because of its links with **corporate social responsibility (CSR)** and positive corporate image.

corporate social responsibility (CSR) 'the responsibility of enterprises for their impacts on society' (European Commission, 2011)

Exhibit 1.6 Strategic orientations

Orientation	Focuses on	Typical objectives
Production	Production efficiency	Higher profits through reduced costs
Product	Product quality and features	Increased sales through product improvements
Sales	Sales techniques and advertising	Sales volume – often short-term
Customer	Customers' needs	Increased long-term sales through customer loyalty, positive image
Marketing	Customers' needs and competitors' strategies	Long-term profits through good customer relations and a sustainable competitive advantage
Cooperative	Workers' needs	Long-term job security, good working conditions
Financial	Financial ratios and other measures	Return on investment (ROI), higher share prices and dividend payments
Societal	Society's well-being	Environmental regeneration, community welfare

PRODUCTION ORIENTATION: PUTTING THE FACTORY FIRST

Firms that have a production orientation focus on production efficiency. They try to make their products and services as quickly as possible and at the lowest possible cost. A production-orientated firm will take great pride in its production facilities, which may well be state of the art.

Ford: Mass Production Evolution

Such firms place great emphasis on **economies of scale** and so are likely to be large-scale producers. It is usually most cost-effective to produce a large amount of a product because it makes it worthwhile to have the largest, fastest machinery or specialist tools, gains bulk discounts on component parts, and enables workers to concentrate on certain tasks and so become expert in them. This efficiency often comes at the cost of product range. If a firm is making a huge quantity of one product, then it cannot also make others. In fact, it is in the interest of such a firm to offer its customers limited product choice. The most famous example of a production orientation is the original Ford car, the Model T, of which Henry Ford is alleged to have

economies of scale unit costs fall as larger quantities are produced; a cost advantage associated with large organisations

said, 'They can have any colour they like, so long as it's black.' This lack of consideration for customer requirements means that a production orientation is not in keeping with the marketing philosophy. However, today, technological developments are making it possible to achieve production efficiency and lower production costs without the need to go into large mass-production quantities.

PRODUCT ORIENTATION: PUTTING THE PRODUCT FIRST

Firms with a product orientation are concerned with making the best possible product. They put great effort into product development and improvements, adding new features, expanding ranges, improving quality, etc. Their view is nicely summed up by the nineteenth-century American philosopher and poet Ralph Waldo Emerson, who asserted that if someone can build a better mousetrap than anyone else can, the world will beat a path to their door. This is often used as an indictment of marketing communications – showing it to be unnecessary. However, there are a number of flaws in this product-orientated view, not least that the world can only beat that path to your door if it knows about the mousetrap and where to get one. So communication in some form is required. If you build a better mousetrap, chances are that someone will steal your idea – or build an even better one, or make a cheaper one. Technology moves on and it is hard to keep ahead of the competition even with groundbreaking new ideas. Also, sometimes the mice just get smarter.

EXPAND YOUR KNOWLEDGE

Classic article

Levitt, T. (1960) 'Marketing myopia', *Harvard Business Review*, 38 (Jul/Aug): 45–56.

Levitt, T. (1975) 'Marketing myopia: a retrospective commentary', *Harvard Business Review*, Sept/Aug: 1–14.

The first of these two articles is one of the most widely read and quoted articles in marketing. In it, Levitt argued that companies needed to define the nature of their business in a wide sense if they were to best highlight the competitive forces that surrounded them and avoid demise. He warned about the dangers of marketing short-sightedness. In the second article, written some 15 years later, he revisits the issues and considers the use and misuse that has been made of marketing myopia, describing its many interpretations and hypothesising about its success.

In his famous article 'Marketing myopia', Levitt (1960) stated that product-orientated industries inevitably died. The example he used was that of the North American railways, which believed themselves to be in the railroad business and were therefore surprised when they lost all their customers to airlines. They had not appreciated that they were all in the transport market.

Product-orientated firms believe that, if they provide a good quality product at a reasonable price, then people will buy it without much further effort on the firm's part. This concentration on product improvement has its advantages. For example, it may well produce groundbreaking new products. Many technology companies are product-orientated; they produce new computers, machinery, gadgets and gizmos, believing that other people will be as caught up in the invention and its cleverness as its designers are.

Sometimes this works. Vacuum cleaner manufacturer Dyson is a modern example of a successful product-orientated firm. After all, people find it hard to imagine products or services that do not currently exist. Someone – often someone with technical expertise – has to come up with the ideas before they can run them past potential customers to check their likely popularity. Imagine a world without DVDs. Would you have come up with such an idea? How about recorded music generally? That is only a twentieth-century invention. Before that, if you wanted to hear music, you had to learn to play an instrument, or befriend others who could. If you had only ever known communication over distance by letter, would you have asked for a mobile phone? (See Chapter 6 for more on product innovation.)

Of course there are some basic needs that we know we want fulfilled, even without imagining new technology. For example, we want cures for a number of diseases, from cancer and HIV through to the common cold. We want to be able to get to places faster and more reliably. Many of us want to be slimmer. Often, it is more useful to ask people what they want to be able to do, what desires they have, rather than what new products they would like.

Technological breakthrough products, then, usually require a leap of imagination, and faith, on the part of their providers. Most of these products fail in the market-place. The ones that do succeed tap into a real customer need, either a pre-existing one that was being met less well (or not at all) previously, or a need not previously recognised (e.g. to be able to talk on the phone, hands-free of course, while driving a car).

Other situations where product orientation may be effective are when there is little effective competition or a shortage of that type of product – for example, where a company has a patent, as Dyson had on its vacuum cleaner technology, or a monopoly, as many train operators have in their designated areas or under the terms of their franchises. Product-orientated companies that do not have these advantages may need to do some very hard selling.

SALES ORIENTATION: SAYING THAT THE CUSTOMER COMES FIRST

Firms that are sales orientated spend a lot on sales training, sales aids and support materials (brochures, presentations, etc.). They do a lot of **sales promotion** (short-term special offers such as 'buy one get one free', coupons, competitions) and often use hard-sell advertising ('amazing special offer', 'this week only', 'never

Marketing Myopia

sales promotion short-term special offers and other added-value activities, e.g. two for the price of one

before available to the public', etc.). They are likely to have a large salesforce that may be quite pushy. Such firms seem to believe that customers will not want to buy their products unless they are pushed into doing so. They are trying to over-come customers' reluctance to buy. Double-glazing firms and timeshare sellers are often sales orientated.

The emphasis here is on the seller's need to shift stock or to make the targets, rather than on customers' needs. However, as part of the heavy sales drive, the salespeople may pay lip-service to marketing – perhaps by calling sales managers 'marketing managers' (as IBM used to do) and by taking an interest in the customer's requirements (so they can sell them other products). This may really just be part of their sales technique, a way of generating rap-port with a prospect. Sales-orientated firms are far more interested in their own needs than those of their customers and their salespeople often have high quotas of products to sell with the prospect of large commissions if they succeed. So the success of a sales-orientated firm depends largely upon the skill of its salesforce.

Sales-orientated companies are stuck in the old transaction exchange way of thinking (see above). Pushing a customer to buy something that they may not really want or need, and may later regret, is no way to build a relationship.

CUSTOMER ORIENTATION: ACTUALLY PUTTING THE CUSTOMER FIRST

Many writers do not distinguish between customer orientation and market orien-tation – but there is a key difference. A market is made up of buyers and sellers so, within this text anyway, a market orientation will be taken to include serious consideration of the competition.

A customer orientation is held by most to be essential to long-term success. How strange, then, that so few organisations are customer-orientated. Many pay lip-service to the idea but fail to gear their systems to satisfying customers, focus-ing too much on the needs of the organisation itself instead.

An organisation has a number of types of customer. A company that focuses on end customers, without considering trade customers, may find that its products are not actually available for sale (trade customers include **retailers**, **wholesalers**, distributors, and import and export agents).

The move to a true customer orientation is not easy and takes a long time. Organisations typically experience considerable resistance from individual departments and employees. Any organisational change has to be managed carefully to ensure that it is accepted and works, but turning an organisa-tion around, so that all its processes are geared towards the customer, can be particularly gruelling and may cause major conflict. An organisation's orientation is a feature of its culture. Organisational culture can loosely be described as 'the way we do things around here'. The procedures an organisation follows are evidence of its culture. The culture may be formal (as in many banks) or informal (as in many software companies). It may be traditional (like Harrods) or contemporary (like, say, Virgin Radio). The tone of it is often set by the chief executive or founder and their lead influences the behaviour of all members of the organisation – all success-ful members that is.

retailer
a sales outlet that deals with end customers, e.g. a shop

wholesaler
a reseller, buying products in bulk to sell on to other businesses in smaller quantities

An organisation's culture is possibly the hardest thing about it to change. It can be a source of great strength but, if it is too rigid, it can hold an organisation back and prevent it from moving with the times (as happened with IBM in the late 1980s). Changing an organisation's culture is rather like asking you to become another nationality – and to behave appropriately, forgetting all of your original beliefs and behavioural patterns. You would have to learn to like different food, support a different football team (possibly a whole new sport), maybe wear different clothes, talk another language, etc. Very few firms have yet managed to adopt a true customer orientation that permeates their whole organisation. Do not underestimate the obstacles in their way.

MARKET ORIENTATION: PUTTING THE CUSTOMER FIRST, WHILE WATCHING THE COMPETITION

Market and Product Orientation

A true market orientation requires a focus on both customers and competitors. Marketing is about providing products and services that meet customers' needs, but it is also important to do that better than your competitors. Many marketers believe that there is a third, vital, component of a true market orientation, and this is coordination between the different functions of the business. Kohli, Jaworski and Kumar (1993: 467) defined market orientation as:

> the organisation-wide generation of market intelligence pertaining to current and future needs of customers, dissemination of intelligence horizontally and vertically within the organisation, and organisation-wide action or responsiveness to market intelligence.

Much recent evidence suggests that organisations that are market orientated enjoy better overall performance than those with other orientations and marketing practitioners see clear-cut benefits from the adoption of this orientation. This is in no small part due to these organisations' emphasis on marketing research. They use their superior market information to find new marketing opportunities in advance of the competition.

Market-orientated organisations take marketing research seriously. Research is essential to an understanding of customers and their needs. It may not be formal marketing research; many smaller companies are able to maintain personal contact with their customers, which is by far the best way to get to know them. Larger companies have to find more cost-effective ways to understand their much larger customer base. These may include customer satisfaction surveys, websites, loyalty schemes, owners' clubs, helplines and customer service desks.

Market-orientated firms take a long-term view of their markets and the products and brands they develop to serve them. Not for them the quick fix that will make this year's sales targets at the expense of next year's – that's a tactic more likely to be employed by a sales-orientated company. For example, if you were an industrial machinery salesperson with a quota of sales to make before the year end, achievement of which would gain you a large bonus, then you would want a customer to order sooner rather than later. However, suppose the customer said they could only afford the smaller machine this year, but if you wait until their next financial year they would buy the larger, newer model. Might you offer them discounts and other incentives to order early so that you get your bonus and your company makes its targets (and makes you a hero)? Then, next year, when the new, improved model comes out, how welcome is that customer going to make you? Will they buy any more from you? Probably not.

The advantages of a market orientation are:

- better understanding of customer needs and wants
- better customer relations
- a better reputation in the marketplace
- more new customers
- more repeat purchases
- improved customer loyalty
- more motivated staff
- a competitive edge.

However, the other orientations should not all be dismissed out of hand – they may work for specific organisations in particular circumstances (Noble et al., 2002). Technology companies, such as Apple Inc, can become market leaders through their product focus while others, such as The Body Shop, are successful thanks to their societal marketing orientation (see below).

Societal
Marketing
Concept

consumer
the individual end-
user of a product or
service

SOCIETAL MARKETING ORIENTATION: PUTTING CONSUMERS AND THEIR SOCIETY FIRST

Societal marketing involves meeting customers' needs and wants in a way that enhances the long-term well-being of **consumers** and the society in which they live. Some of the products and services on sale today (e.g. cigarettes) are known to be bad for consumers. Some are damaging to our environment, either in use or in production (e.g. cars). Organisations that adopt a societal marketing orientation recognise the wider implications and responsibilities of marketing and take them into account when formulating strategies. For example, they may design packaging that is minimal, made from recycled materials and biodegradable. Their product design may take into account how the product can be disposed of at the end of its life. Their advertising will encourage responsible product use, for example, they would not encourage children to over-indulge in high-sugar treats. The Co-operative Bank's mission statement commits it to being 'a responsible member of society by promoting an environment where the needs of local communities can be met now and in the future' (Co-operative Bank, n.d.).

Cynics would say that societal marketing is just another marketing ploy: responding to a current trend. Societally orientated companies may be motivated by enlightened self-interest or they may have a genuine desire to do good. Consumers are beginning to choose organic foods and other green products, and these are proving lucrative niche markets as customers seem prepared to pay a little more for them (not too much more, though).

EXPAND YOUR KNOWLEDGE

Classic article

Kohli, A.K. and Jaworski, B. (1990) 'Market orientation: the construct, research propositions and managerial implications', *Journal of Marketing*, 54 (April): 1–18.

Narver, J. and Slater, S. (1990) 'The effect of a market orientation on business profitability', *Journal of Marketing*, 54 (Oct): 20–35.

Both of these pairs of authors are the early researchers of market orientation. Each has taken a slightly different perspective to the elements which best characterise market orientation and that may be used in its evaluation. Much of the work that has followed, both by these authors and others, has taken its directions from these early works.

FOCUSING ON CUSTOMERS

IBM: The Customer is King

'The customer is king!'

This is a rather sexist and hackneyed phrase, but it has a serious point: companies cannot exist without customers. It would therefore seem to make sense to design the company around the customer, gearing everything to serve the customer better. This focus on the customer is at the heart of good marketing and is one of the hallmarks of a market or customer orientation (see above).

It is important that employees recognise that they are there to meet customers' needs and wants rather than their own. It is no good a delivery person standing on the doorstep and saying 'But this is the best time for me to deliver' if it is not a good time for the customer. It is equally important that investors recognise that without the customer there is no company. A few years ago, Gerald Ratner was widely reported as saying that his firm's products were of poor quality and not what he would buy. The firm's share price, and Mr Ratner's standing, plummeted.

Not all customers are of equal value. In fact, it is possible for some customers to actually cost the company money. This is the reason behind the closure of uneconomic shops, bus services and post offices in some rural areas. There are customers but they do not use these services frequently enough, or pay enough for them, to cover the company's costs.

Ted Talks: The Voices of Twitter

Sometimes there are good reasons for continuing to support loss-making customers, either temporarily or as part of a customer group that includes more profitable customers that can support the losses made.

Perhaps:

- this is a new customer and the company wants to nurture them, hoping that they will become a good customer in the future
- the company is trying to break into a new market, perhaps in a different country, and can afford to sustain losses for a while
- there are considerable social benefits (often in the case of rural services) that outweigh the financial considerations.

ethical focus: Know when to stop

Diageo (the company that makes Guinness and Smirnoff vodka) ran an unusual ad campaign. Titled 'Know when to stop', the TV campaign encouraged people to drink less. Diageo claimed it was part of its corporate social responsibility programme.

The drinks industry has been heavily criticised in recent years for not doing enough to tackle problems caused by drink, particularly drink-driving and under-age, excessive drinking. Anti-drinking charities welcomed the campaign as a step in the right direction but pointed out that it didn't amount to much when set against the £200 million (€280 million) or so that is spent each year on alcohol advertising in the UK.

Whose responsibility do you think it is to promote sensible drinking – if anyone's?

CUSTOMERS OR CONSUMERS?

There is a distinction between customers and consumers, both of whom are vital to business success. A customer is someone who buys the firm's products. However, they may not actually use the products themselves. The eventual user of the product is called the consumer.

ACTIVITY

Think about paper. Who buys it? What for? How many different types of customers and consumers can you list? What do they want from paper?

Consumers are important influencers on purchase decisions, even if they do not make the actual decision on what to buy (see Chapter 3 for more on this). For example, children's toys, particularly those designed for young children, are usually bought by other members of their family or by friends. They are the customers but the child is the actual consumer. Most perfume is bought as a gift, usually from a man to a woman. So while perfume consumers are clearly predominantly female, perfumiers' customers are mainly men. A person may be a customer but not a consumer, or a consumer but not a customer, or both consumer *and* customer.

MARKETING'S CHANGING EMPHASIS

In its short history, marketing has moved its focus from the immediate sale to the preservation of future sales. Good marketing practice today involves thinking beyond the one-off sale. It means longer-term planning and that makes it a more complex process to manage.

TRANSACTIONAL MARKETING

There is still a place for the one-off sale that is sometimes referred to as **transactional marketing**. Here there is no intention to continue a relationship. Both parties are satisfied by that one sale and they go their separate ways. A **transactional exchange** is likely to be appropriate where the product is a basic commodity, such as salt, or an occasional purchase, such as a house. Alternatively,

transactional marketing focuses on the immediate sale

transactional exchange a one-off sale or a sale that is conducted as if it were a one-off

---

b2b focus: Dave the decorator

Dave the decorator has a thriving business. He is booked up at least six months in advance. He doesn't need to advertise as word of mouth brings in all the business he needs. Many of his customers are regulars, so impressed by his work that they wouldn't dream of employing anyone else, and most certainly wouldn't do the decorating themselves.

Dave has a lot of experience in interior decorating and so has become an expert on which paints and papers look best in which situations and which last longest. People ask Dave for his opinion on their proposed colour schemes and for his recommendation on types of paint.

Currently, Dave favours an eggshell finish rather than gloss for woodwork. He thinks it looks smarter and says it doesn't fade as quickly. He dislikes ceiling paper and thinks some of the supposedly better wallpapers are overpriced.

People say you can tell Dave's work, not just by the quality of the finish, but by the trademark eggshell woodwork, the plain ceilings and the brand of paper.

So, from Dulux, Crown or any wallpaper manufacturer's point of view, who is the key customer here – consumer or trade?

the circumstances of the exchange may dictate that it be transactional. For example, the buyer may just be passing through, a visitor to the area. The seller may only have one thing to sell, perhaps a private car or furniture that is no longer wanted, or they may be winding a business down.

RELATIONSHIP MARKETING

> Relationship marketing is a long-term, continuous series of transactions between parties. (Doyle, 2002)

relationship marketing
a long-term approach that nurtures customers, employees and business partners

When it was first proposed, relationship marketing was a revolutionary idea that turned sales and marketing on their heads. No longer were end-of-year sales figures the prime measure of success, companies wanted to look ahead to next year and the year after that. Could they count on repeat business from this year's customers?

The other new and exciting thing about relationship marketing was that these long-term relationships were to be built not just with customers, but with all members of the supply chain, both upwards and downwards. The key to maximising long-term profitability was seen to lie not just with loyal customers, but also in ongoing relationships with suppliers. Keeping the same suppliers not only makes for more pleasant, comfortable working relationships, but also saves the time and risk involved in finding new ones. It can have more direct benefits as well. A supplier who is secure and has a good working relationship with the buyers is more likely to be flexible and to try harder.

Although the term 'relationship marketing' can be traced back to Berry (1983), the importance of building long-term customer relationships really became apparent from some groundbreaking studies in the 1990s. Researchers found that retaining customers for just a little longer increased a company's profitability significantly and also that it was much cheaper to hold on to existing customers than to find new ones. Loyal customers may prove a company's best form of promotion: they tell their friends about their good experiences with the company and so word of mouth spreads. Who would you be more likely to believe when they recommend a product – a friend or the company's salesperson?

EXPAND YOUR KNOWLEDGE

Payne, A. and Frow, P. (2005) 'A strategic framework for customer relationship management', *Journal of Marketing*, 69 (4): 167–76.

In this article, the authors develop a conceptual framework for customer relationship management (CRM) that helps broaden the understanding of CRM and its role in enhancing customer value and, as a result, shareholder value. The authors explore definitional aspects of CRM, and they identify three alternative perspectives of CRM.

RETAINING VALUABLE CUSTOMERS

Long-standing, regular customers can be valuable assets. They buy more products, tell their friends good things about the company (word of mouth advertising), are less time-consuming (because they already know how to handle orders with the company and they trust its products) and less likely to be put off by a price increase. It costs approximately five times more to attract a new customer than it does to keep an existing one happy. **Customer relationship management (CRM)** has evolved in response to this need to retain customers and increase their value to the company.

There is a school of thought that takes CRM as a set of technological tools that capture customer information and enable an organisation to use it to market its products more effectively: 'the application of technology to learning more about each customer and being able to respond to them one-to-one' (Kotler, 2003: 34). This is really just a sophisticated form of **database marketing**. It enables a company to **cross-sell** (i.e. sell existing customers additional, different products) and **up-sell** (i.e. sell customers a more expensive version of the product) but customer relationship management is more than just technologically enhanced customer service. It is the use of procedures and management techniques that enhance the customer's experience of the organisation, build loyalty and contribute to long-term profitability. It is about attracting and keeping the right customers. Technology is an enabler and not a main driver – if you have a poor value proposition you are not going to gain or keep too many customers (Woodcock et al., 2000).

It is as important to be skilled in ending relationships as it is to be able to maintain them. A customer will end a relationship that no longer has value. The organisation must be prepared to be similarly ruthless. Some customers, particularly long-standing ones, can in fact cost the firm money.

It is often said that 20% of a firm's customers generate 80% of its profits (the Pareto principle). The other 80% of customers only account for 20% of profits and so may not justify the time and money spent on servicing their needs. This is not a hard-and-fast rule, of course; for example, new customers take up a lot more time than older ones who know the ropes, but a firm must still have new customers if it wants to grow and thrive. They may well turn into profitable customers in time.

If the relationship is good enough, then some of those regulars may become loyal or even brand ambassadors, i.e. people who feel strongly enough about the brand to recommend it highly, and frequently, and without even being asked. Exhibit 1.7 illustrates these different stages.

customer relationship management attracting and keeping the right customers

database marketing the use of computerised information used for targeted marketing activities

cross-selling persuading a customer to buy

up-selling persuading a customer to trade up to a more expensive product

Exhibit 1.7   Customer loyalty

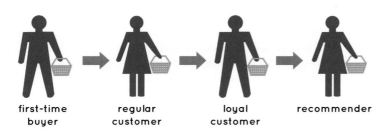

first-time buyer → regular customer → loyal customer → recommender

customer focus: An expanded definition of customer relationship management

Crm is about:

- finding the right customers – i.e. those with an acceptable current and future net value
- getting to know them – as individuals or groups
- growing their value as customers (if appropriate)

- retaining their business – in the most efficient and effective way.

It is achieved by companies enabling their people, processes, policies, suppliers and customer-facing technologies to manage all customer interactions proactively during each stage of the customer life cycle in a way that enhances each customer's experience of dealing with the company.

SOURCES: Woodcock et al. (2000)

---

marketing mix
(see 4Ps, 7Ps) the basics of marketing plan implementations, usually product, promotion, place, price, sometimes with the addition of packaging; the services marketing mix also includes people, physical evidence and process

4Ps
a mnemonic (memory aid) for the marketing mix: product, promotion, place, price

Van Hook:
Fundamentals
of Marketing
presentations

Loyalty is an emotional attachment. Not all regular customers are loyal, and a strong brand is not enough to create loyalty on its own (although it helps). For example, customers may buy products regularly just because they are cheap or convenient, and when something else becomes available, either more cheaply or more conveniently, then they may switch. Someone who usually buys milk from their local petrol station is unlikely to be a loyal customer, just a rather disorganised person who runs out of milk a lot. They could be lured away quite easily by milk delivery or another, more convenient, retail outlet.

See Chapter 11 for more detail on branding and brand loyalty.

INTRODUCING THE MARKETING MIX

One of the most enduring, and popular, concepts in marketing is the marketing mix. The Mix is the basic marketing toolkit that marketers use to implement their marketing plans. It is most commonly known as the 4Ps: product, promotion, price and place.

This 4Ps mnemonic was first proposed by Jerome E. McCarthy in 1960 and, despite some criticism over the years, it is still taught in universities and used in practice today. However, with the increasing dominance of service products, and the importance of the service elements of physical products, the preferred framework today is the 7Ps, first popularised by Bernard Booms and Mary Jo Bitner in 1981. The 7Ps add physical evidence, people and process to the original 4Ps.

The 4Ps (or 7Ps) sound deceptively simple but each P covers a range of marketing ideas and theories. A product is so much more than the item you buy. The product that is offered to customers includes its packaging, its brand and its supporting services, and the decision to buy it may have more to do with those things than with the make-up of the item itself. Promotion (or marketing communications) is so much more than just advertising which is, in any case, considerably more subtle than simply saying 'buy this'. Place is about getting the right products to the right people at the right time and about making it easier for customers to buy the products. Without a price, a product is a gift. Set the wrong price (either too high or too low) and products may not sell at all.

Decisions about the 4Ps should not be made in isolation. The Ps need to fit with each other. An exclusive product, such as a designer suit or a Bang and Olufsen stereo, commands a high price, is sold in upmarket shops, or delivered to your door in a smart van, and should be high quality. An everyday product, such as shampoo or cat litter, should do its job reliably, be inexpensive and be widely available. If just one of the Ps is out of sync, then the whole of the product offering will be devalued.

Each of the 4Ps has its own chapter in this book while the additional 3Ps that make it up to 7 are covered in Chapter 7 (Service products). Chapter 11 then brings them all back together to demonstrate how they can be used to build brands.

MARKETING TODAY AND TOMORROW

Looking ahead, what is happening in the world of marketing? This section considers some of the things that are changing the way marketing is carried out. Most of these things are interrelated; each supporting and encouraging other changes. Some are external influences on marketing, such as the major developments in technology. Some are to do with the ways in which people's behaviour and lifestyles are changing as they respond to these developments. Marketers have at least to react to these changes; at best they are proactive in seeking out and taking advantage of new marketing opportunities.

DIGITAL TECHNOLOGIES

The Internet has had a significant impact on our lifestyles and on the way that many companies market their products. Firms look to it for competitive edge and cost savings. Some organisations, e.g. Amazon, eBay and Google, **only** deal through the Internet, while most follow a more flexible business model that incorporates both online and offline customer contacts – so-called bricks and clicks operations.

Shoppers in the UK make a greater proportion of their purchases online than any other developed nation. According to the Boston Consulting Group (BBC, 2012), in 2010 approximately 13.5% of all purchases in the UK were made over the Internet. This is projected to rise to 23% by 2016. The worldwide growth in online retailing is largely due to improved financial security for payments, which reassures customers as well as cutting the costs of fraud, faster connections and more sophisticated databases which enable retailers to serve their customers better.

The Internet has made international marketing a realistic aim for all sizes of business in all sorts of markets. It is hard for a small, offline retailer to compete with larger companies but the World Wide Web is a great equaliser: web pages are much cheaper to design and maintain than huge chains of stores. This changes the fundamental nature of competition in many markets.

promotion
another name for marketing communications, one of the 4Ps, communication designed and implemented to persuade others to do, think or feel something

price
how much each product is sold for

place
one of the elements of the marketing mix, concerned with distribution, delivery, supply chain management

7Ps
a mnemonic (memory aid) for the services marketing mix: product, promotion, place, price, process, people, physical evidence

physical evidence
the tangible aspects of a service, e.g. a bus ticket, shampoo (at the hairdressers); one of the 7Ps of services marketing

people
one of the elements of the marketing mix, concerned with distribution, delivery, supply chain management

process
one of the 7Ps of the services marketing mix; the way in which a service is provided

However, Internet marketing is not just about e-tailing. Digital technology has opened up a world of marketing communications opportunities through: websites, online advertising (e.g. Google ads), emailing, blogging, texting, tweeting, mash-ups, online video content and social media sites. Some of the more innovative uses of e-marketing in consumer markets include brand placement in computer games. If you have played 'Pro Evolution Soccer' on the PlayStation, you will have seen adverts around the animated pitch for Reebok and Canon. Marketers can text barcodes to smartphones which retailers will accept instead of paper discount vouchers. Vouchers can also be distributed through websites such as Groupon, Dealcloud, Vouchercloud and Wowcher, which have sprung up to facilitate and take advantage of this new marketing activity.

It is not only consumer companies that are taking advantage of the opportunities created by digital technologies. Gleanster, a company that researches and 'benchmarks best practices in technology-enabled business initiatives' (**www.gleanster. com**) has identified the most popular social media channels used by top performers in b2b marketing. These are shown in Exhibit 1.8. Ninety-three per cent of b2b marketers ranked measuring return on social media campaigns as their number one challenge with respect to social media marketing.

Exhibit 1.8

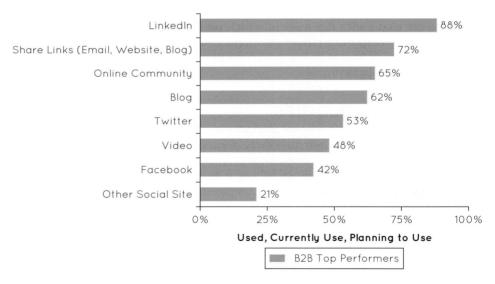

SOURCE: Gleanster Research

m-marketing

The 4G system is now already in use in over 30 countries and will provide speeds that are up to 10 times faster than 3G, effectively eliminating download wait times and allowing new applications such as mobile high-definition TV, high-quality video conferencing and sophisticated video gaming. A 4G mobile

e-focus: No more empty fridge

In 2012, Tesco trialled a new way to interact with their customers. Four, large, touchscreen, virtual grocery stores at Gatwick airport allowed holidaymakers to order food which Tesco would deliver to their homes on the day they returned.

Customers could view a range of everyday products by scrolling through moving screens on large virtual fridges. By scanning the barcodes with their smartphones they could then add their chosen products to their online baskets, book a home delivery slot and checkout.

Welcome home from Tesco!

Ordering groceries for homecoming.

connection (with the right hardware of course) will make surfing the net on a phone or tablet as quick as surfing at home on a PC. Global consultancy Deloitte predict that worldwide smartphone sales will be 1 billion in 2013, bringing the number of active phones with either a touchscreen or an alphabet keyboard to 2 bn by the end of the year – though about 20% of these phones will rarely, if ever, be used to go online (Garside, 2013). With increased usage of all this mobile technology, the reach of mobile marketing is expanding. Mobile marketing is on its way to becoming mainstream.

e-consumers

One of the most interesting consequences of the rise of the Internet is the change it has made to the way we buy and sell, and even to **who** buys and **who** sells. The lines between buyer and seller have blurred as consumers find it easier to become sellers. eBay is one of the biggest business successes of the twenty-first century. It has grown from relative obscurity to being a household name. Anyone can now buy or sell online through eBay, Amazon Marketplace and other sites. So, if consumers can sell to other consumers (c2c), where will businesses make up their lost profits? A number of business models are emerging to take advantage of this trend. For example, Amazon and eBay have always charged commission on third-party sales. Amazon now also offers a trade-in service for books and video games. A third party takes the unwanted items and the seller receives an Amazon gift card to spend on more Amazon products. These are all variants of offline models of agency and secondhand sales. Digital technology has also enabled some rather more sophisticated consumer-driven business models such as crowd-sourcing and open market models. Peer-to-peer (p2p) sites like bigbarn.co.uk – whose stated mission is to 'reconnect consumers with their local producers, direct, or through local retailers, and encourage local trade, giving farmers a better deal and consumers fresher, cheaper, accountable food' (BigBarn, 2012) – cut out business intermediaries and allow both farmers and individuals to trade directly with consumers.

This important area of e-marketing is considered throughout the book in the inset e-focus boxes.

EXPAND YOUR KNOWLEDGE

Jeon, S., Sung, T.K. and Dong, H.L. (2011) 'Web 2.0 business models and value creation', *International Journal of Information and Decision Sciences*, 3 (1): 70–84.

Includes discussion of: crowdsourcing, social networking, mashup, product customisation, and open market models.

Marketing automation

Digital technologies enable some very sophisticated ways of capturing data and developing databases that can be used to manage customer and prospect interactions and support. As the number of channels through which customers and companies can communicate and transact has exploded, there has been the increasing need for marketers to find ways to track all of this traffic. Market research and analysis is becoming increasingly automated. In May 2012, Forrester Research published a report that investigated the use of marketing automation which they defined as:

> Tooling and process that help generate new business opportunities, improve potential buyers' propensity to purchase, manage customer loyalty, and increase alignment between marketing activity and revenue.

In their research, they identified that marketers see automation as a critical technology in its own right and that they planned to make greater use of automated activities. They also identified that to manage and take advantage of the increasing use of technology, marketing departments are developing new organisational structures which require marketers with specialist skills in IT, web development, marketing operations, applications, and database management.

The international nature of the Internet has made it possible to locate call-centres anywhere in the world. Operating out of countries such as India, where wages are lower than they are in Western nations, has huge cost-saving potential but is unpopular with many customers. Automated call handling is an even cheaper alternative, but that is even less popular. As companies have tried to drive down costs in search of higher profits, both ideas have become widely used, but at what price for customer relationships? Some companies are now returning to a more old-fashioned idea of service. The HSBC subsidiary bank First Direct boasts that customers always get through to a real person – no automated call-handling systems there. For First Direct, this is a key competitive difference from other banking services, although it should be noted that they have no branches so their customers do not actually receive personal, face-to-face service.

SOCIAL CHANGE

Social change is one of marketing's key emerging themes, according to the Chartered Institute of Marketing. In part, this is due to the changing demographic profiles of the population. People are living longer and choosing to use their discretionary income in different ways. Targeting the greys, i.e. the over 50s, is relatively new to marketers who have courted the youth market for many years but, for a number of product areas, these 'baby-boomers' are growing markets with substantial buying power. They represent over a third, and are the fastest growing part of the population in a number of developed countries. The greys are likely to remain a key market demographic for some time.

The markets within developed and developing economies are also experiencing new behaviours in the younger populations of Generation X (those who succeeded the baby-boomers, born around the 1960s to 1980s) and Generation Y (those succeeding Generation X, born around the late 1980s to early 2000). These generations (and the one that follows) have grown up with the opportunities offered in the new digital age. Technologies that were unthought-of when their parents were young are taken for granted as part of their daily lives: computer gaming, social networking, MP3 players, smartphones, tablets and e-books. 'Apps' have become part of the language and increasingly the means by which people interface with the world. Technology has changed the way people chat, the way they meet new people, the way they socialise generally and what is considered socially acceptable – or not.

SOCIAL NETWORKING MEDIA

The many electronic technologies and software packages now available have, of course, changed the way people communicate. They have also changed the way the marketers communicate. One of the rules of good marketing is that it should put the customer at its heart. So marketers study the way that consumers behave and try to ensure that their brands become a valuable part of their lives.

It used to be that media owners (e.g. television companies, newspapers, cinemas) controlled all the significant means of communication, but that is no longer true. The digital marketplace has encouraged peer-to-peer (p2p) communications which have radically altered marketing and communications. Marketing relationships are no longer just between the company and the customer or the company and the media; now customers are communicating with other customers about brands. It is important that marketers understand these evolving decision-making networks (see Chapter 3 for decision-making). Customers are adopting 'ISIS' behaviours – Information Searching, Information Sharing. They are searching the Web, reading the news, and asking questions on social networks. They take more notice of the advice of their peers than they do of official brand communications or mainstream media. Social media strategist Paul Gillin says;

Baby Boomer v Generation Y.

'In the past, we believed buyers were ignorant and it was up to us to educate them. Today, they're smart and self-educated. They no longer need us' (Silverpop, 2012). He believes the biggest change in recent years is the rapid growth of peer engagement and that marketers need to have a robust, customer-centric online presence and learn to leverage the peer network. The balance of power has shifted from sellers to buyers.

COMMUNICATIONS OVERLOAD

Advanced technology has brought some additional problems with it. As the costs of reaching people have fallen, thanks largely to electronic (especially digital) communication technologies, so everyone seems to want to talk to as many people as possible. This desire to communicate is not limited to marketers. Organisations and individuals are sending and receiving more messages than ever before. Take personal web

 e-focus: The baby bloggers

Even young children are sharing their views with the world. Holly Pope of Oxford has become a book critic. Her blog, Childtastic Books, offers her thoughts on books she is reading at school and at home. Martha Payne shares her views of primary school dinners in her blog, NeverSeconds. Although it only started in May with posts of photographs, descriptions and ratings of sometimes unhappy school lunches, six weeks into her blogging the local council banned her from taking photographs in the school canteen but by then her blog had gone viral and made international headlines. Within 24 hours the council had reversed its decision. After only 12 weeks the blog has had almost 7.5 million hits and invites guest bloggers to post each week. It receives contributions from around the world. The blog, which links to a JustGiving site, has so far made £110,000 for the charity Mary's Meals, which helps feed 650,000 children every day in 16 countries.

Now hundreds of children in Britain are creating their own blogs scrutinising everything from fashion to school sports days. Data from Ofcom and EU Kids Online show that 15% of 12–15-year-olds are now blogging.

Based on Francesca Angelini, *Sunday Times* article 'The baby bloggers', 29 July 2012.

pages and blogs, for example; never before have so many people broadcast their lives and views so frequently and so publicly.

One consequence of this is that we are all sent many more messages than we can possibly deal with. The average Briton or American gets approximately 3000 marketing messages a day and the majority feel overwhelmed and are becoming increasingly negative towards advertising messages in particular (Benedictus, 2007). Consumers have to block out the majority of this bombardment in their own self-defence and that presents an additional challenge to marketers who have to find ways to cut through the clutter and be heard.

Marketers have responded to this difficulty in getting heard in a number of ways. Some try to get closer to their customers, either through strategic use of Customer Relationship Management (CRM) or through integrating their brands into consumers' lifestyles (see lifestyle branding below). Others look for more original media through which to convey their marketing messages. Anything that is capable of carrying a message to an audience can be construed as a marketing communications medium and so marketers have lots to choose from and vie with each other to dream up unique media (Pickton and Broderick, 2004). Advertising messages have been written on bus tickets, on the edge of steps, on web pages, in the sky, on the sides of buildings (by laser), and on people's heads, cars and houses.

In a communications world so heavily influenced by peer engagement, marketing communications cannot be a monologue. Marketers need to hold conversations with their customers and consumers and to integrate their brands into people's lives. Modern marketers want to understand and plan the customer journey in relation to all customer touchpoints with the company and its brands. There is a focus on the customer experience and how the relationship between customer and company or brand developed over time. It is about understanding each and every point of contact, actual and potential, and weaving these understandings together. Again, technology has a major role to play in gathering, storing and using the data that can be used for these purposes.

MARKETING METRICS

In the past marketing has been accused of not proving its worth. As a management discipline it has suffered from an unwillingness or inability to analyse and evaluate its effectiveness and efficiency. Marketing metrics is about measuring marketing performance and using the information to improve its management. In today's increasingly cost-conscious and efficiency-driven businesses, it is important for marketers to know how to use marketing analytics to justify marketing expenditure. 'Soft metrics' such as brand awareness, consumer opinions, page impressions, search rankings and reach need to be joined with 'hard metrics' such as distribution penetration, sales, returns and profits. Quantitative measures need to be used alongside qualitative measures. Database, digital and analytical technologies have made all kinds of data easier to collect, e.g. customer transaction data and customers' specific use of web content. However, analysing and using such data to improve marketing decisions requires new marketer skills. Other business disciplines expect marketing to deliver measurable results.

customer journey
a customer's experience of the brand, incorporating all the customer's brand-related interactions and emotions; this journey can be mapped as an aid to planning

touchpoints
all a customer, user or consumer's contacts or interactions with a brand including communications and actual use

ethical focus: Stealth marketing

Have you heard the buzz? Did you recognise it or did you think that stranger who so kindly recommended a drink, a club or a place to eat was on the level? Perhaps they were, but then again they may have been part of a buzz marketing campaign.

Buzz marketing is a variant of word-of-mouth marketing but sometimes, instead of friends and relatives recommending products to you, people are paid to do it. They seem like one of the crowd but they have infiltrated it deliberately in order to sell products.

For example, when a Premiership football club launched a text message service, it was struggling to persuade fans to sign up. They advertised the service in programmes and on the website, and employed a troop of attractive young women to hand out leaflets on match days, but still fans were resistant to parting with 25p a message to find out the latest club news. So the club decided it was time to hire professionals in the form of a local marketing agency.

'We got a group of 14 or 16 actors, who were all football fans,' explained Graham Goodkind, founder and chairman of the Sneeze Marketing Agency. 'And they went round bars and clubs around the ground, in groups of two, saying that one of their mates had been sacked from work because he kept on getting these text messages and talking to everyone about it, and his boss had had enough and given him the boot. So they were going round with this petition trying to get his job back – kind of a vaguely plausible story.

'And then the actors would pull out of their pocket some crumpled-up leaflet, which was for the text subscription service. They'd have a mobile phone in their pocket, and they'd show them how it worked. "What's the harm in that?" they'd say. And they could have these conversations with lots of people – that was the beauty of it. Two people could spend maybe 20 minutes or half an hour in each pub, working the whole pub. We did it at two home games and reckon we got about 4000 people on the petition in total.'

Subscriptions to the club's texting service soared – though the petitions went straight in the bin.

In the USA, marketers have been paying people to spread marketing messages by word of mouth for some years. A little known sausage brand became much better known after a holiday weekend when hundreds of people arrived at barbecues with packets of sausages and enthusiasm for their low fat recipe. They were invited guests at the parties, but paid agents for the sausages.

Stealth marketing is often criticised as unethical, although its professional proponents usually stop short of breaking any laws. The buzz marketers themselves defend it as a necessary tactic to reach increasingly cynical and media-literate consumers in these over-communicated times. They also say that there are few, if any, complaints. But then if the marketing is stealthy enough, people just don't realise that it's marketing at all.

SOURCES: Benedictus, 2007; Walker, 2004

LIFESTYLE BRANDING

In the twentieth century, many organisations moved from a product focus to a customer focus (see strategic orientations above); even public sector organisations started to regard the people who received their services as customers, although there is a considerable backlash against this now. For example, it really may not be helpful for probation officers to regard their charges as customers or teachers to treat schoolchildren as such. Towards the end of the century, the term 'brand' became more commonly used than 'product'. Now almost everything is branded. Even public services have logos and mottoes and are endowed with brand values.

Traditional brands, with their values based on the organisation's and the product categories, are being overtaken by lifestyle brands. This can be seen as the next step in the goal of true customer orientation. Brands are developed with the values of a particular consumer group in mind and the resultant products slot into, and enhance, those consumers' lifestyles. Lifestyle brands usually have loyal customers who use the brand to declare their identity, or membership of a group. Abercrombie and Fitch, Mini, Harley Davidson, Nike and Virgin are all lifestyle brands and their consumers are generally proud to be associated with them. If consumers identify closely with a brand, it becomes easier to launch new products, even those in a different category. For example, designers such as Calvin Klein have made successful inroads into perfumery. Youth culture has particularly strong, though changeable, values that are shared the world over, making global youth lifestyle brands, such as Adidas, possible. Not all global products aimed at the youth market are by any means lifestyle products though, much as the brand owners might like to think that they are. McDonald's has tried hard to achieve this status but it just does not have the appeal that makes people want to be identified with it (Kiley, 2005). Would you wear their clothes or carry their logo with pride?

It is not yet clear what, if anything, will replace branding as the competitive weapon of choice for twenty-first-century companies. There is a trend towards more socially responsible marketing (though for many organisations this is currently no more than a token gesture, a chance to be seen as doing the right thing), and cynics would say that this is merely another positive image projection for competitive effect. It may be that firms seek to build even stronger relationships with their customers (see 'Relationship marketing' above), though, again, there is evidence that customers do not always want to have relationships with their suppliers. In fact, increasing numbers choose the anonymity of the Internet marketplace in order to avoid personal contact with sellers (O'Connor and Galvin, 2001).

ACTIVITY

Visit The Body Shop's website at **www.thebodyshop.com.** In what ways is the company trying to improve our well-being? Why do you think it does that?

CONSUMERISM

In the Western world, we have more material wealth, more stuff, than any society has ever had before. The amassing of goods is seen as a sign of success. Expensive, desirable possessions confer status. Consumerists believe that it is economically desirable to consume (i.e. eat, drink, use) more and more. Modern production techniques mean that we have more than enough of everything. Every day, Western businesses and households throw away millions of excess goods. In the meantime, there are parts of the world that are so poor that they are short of basic necessities: food, water, clothing, shelter. This disparity provokes envy and conflict, yet still, even where governments have the will to do so, it is difficult to even things out.

With this surplus of goods, the power has shifted to consumers. Today, most producers of goods and services are more reliant on their customers than the other way around. A customer can usually go to another supplier but, for the supplier, a replacement customer is harder to find. This would suggest that customers have the upper hand but this is not always true. Large customers, which are usually big companies, can indeed dictate terms to their suppliers. UK supermarkets have such dominance in the food market that they can demand low prices, specially packed products and frequent (often several times a day) deliveries. However, it is harder for an individual consumer to make demands on a large corporation. Even with the current levels of competition for customers, just one customer among thousands is not so significant a loss.

As a consequence, just as workers formed trade unions in the early twentieth century, consumers in the latter half of that century got together and formed pressure groups. The power of numbers can make large corporations listen. Organisations such as the Consumers' Association have significant influence. The media can make an impression too – even the largest of multinationals wants to protect its reputation. Most newspapers have consumer advice columns and are prepared to take on any size of organisation, as are television programmes such as the BBC's *Watchdog*.

ECO-CONSUMERS

M&S
Schwopping
ad

Working in
environmental
marketing

Many of today's consumers share concerns over sustainability and the future of the planet. Citizens and their governments are worried about environmental issues such as energy consumption, waste and pollution. The rise of eco-concern directly challenges the assumption that greater consumption (i.e. we should eat more, drink more, use more) is economically and ethically desirable. For many, marketing is one of the villains here but, actually, responsible marketing has a great part to play in helping the environmental cause.

Companies are more keenly aware of their corporate social responsibilities (CSR). While responsible business benefits society, CSR activities also create opportunities to gain added marketing and competitive advantage. There are brands whose values are built on sound environmental principles. For example, Ecover uses natural, sustainable resources for both ingredients and packaging and does less harm to the environment. One brand of toilet paper advertises the fact that for every tree used in its manufacture, three more trees are planted.

Increasing numbers of brands display their Fairtrade credentials proudly on their packaging – and increasing numbers of consumers look for that distinctive logo when choosing products. The Fairtrade mark declares that the producer is an ethical company which actively supports sustainability and fairness to suppliers from less developed countries.

EXPAND YOUR KNOWLEDGE

Kaur, G. and Sharma, R.D. (2009) 'Voyage of marketing thought from a barter system to a customer centric one', *Marketing Intelligence and Planning*, 27 (5): 567–614.

This article charts the developments that have taken place in marketing thinking and provides an extensive review of much of the relevant literature.

SUMMARY

This chapter has been an introduction to the marketing concept and its development as well as to this textbook. We have looked at what marketing is, and what it is not. Marketing has been defined and the modern marketing concept explained. The origins of marketing should be helpful in understanding how the discipline has developed and why.

An organisation's strategic orientation has a huge influence on how, and what, decisions it makes. Some organisations put their products at their heart; others focus on customers. Those with a market orientation put their customers first, while keeping a close eye on the competition, but this does not mean that firms must be market-orientated in order to do any marketing at all. Almost all organisations, even those that are clearly production-orientated, must do some marketing in order to survive.

Some basic economics, notably the theory of demand and supply, has been considered. Economic theory is highly relevant to marketing and informs much of what marketing managers do. Marketing is based on the idea of an exchange of equal value – usually an exchange of products for money, but rarely for money alone. Customers give up their time and the opportunity to buy other things when they buy something. They also take risks. The product may not work, it may not be good value, others may think them foolish for buying it, it may not suit them after all. Marketing can help reassure customers and reduce their perceptions of the risks inherent in a product purchase.

Customer relationship management is a key concept in modern marketing and this chapter introduced it through the concept of relationship marketing. Relationship marketing takes a long-term view of both customers and suppliers. This contrasts with transactional marketing, which sees sales as one-off events.

This book has been carefully designed to help those new to marketing as a subject. As well as the questions and case studies that you would expect to find in a textbook of this type, we have included challenges, activities and focus boxes. The focus themes are key marketing issues and they, along with the focus boxes you will see throughout the text, should help build a bridge from your academic studies to the marketing practitioner's world – and your future marketing career.

CHALLENGES REVIEWED

Now that you have finished reading the chapter, look back at the challenges you were set at the beginning. Do you have a clearer idea of what's involved?

HINTS

- See 'definitions' and 'what marketing is not'.
- Good marketers always act ethically; also, check the Data Protection Act 1998.
- This is an ethical challenge: is it right to sell outdated technology? Would it be taking advantage of a vulnerable group? What would be a better strategy?
- Customer retention and CRM, database marketing; if he had kept in touch, then his customers would have known how to find him; also, a simple sticker on the cameras might have helped!

READING AROUND

JOURNAL ARTICLES

Jeon, S., Sung, T.K. and Dong, H.L. (2011) 'Web 2.0 business models and value creation', *International Journal of Information and Decision Sciences*, 3 (1): 70–84.

Kaur, G. and Sharma, R.D. (2009) 'Voyage of marketing thought from a barter system to a customer centric one', *Marketing Intelligence and Planning*, 27 (5): 567–614.

Kohli, A. and Jaworski, B. (1990) 'Market orientation: the construct, research propositions and managerial implications', *Journal of Marketing*, 54 (April): 1–18.

Kotler, P. and Levy, S. (1969) 'Broadening the scope of marketing', *Journal of Marketing*, 33 (Jan): 10–15.

Levitt, T. (1960) 'Marketing myopia', *Harvard Business Review*, 38 (Jul/Aug): 45–56.

Levitt, T. (1975) 'Marketing myopia: a retrospective commentary', *Harvard Business Review*, Sept/Aug: 1–14.

McDonald, M. (2009) 'The future of marketing: brightest star in the firmament, or a fading meteor? Some hypotheses and a research agenda', *Journal of Marketing Management*, 25 (5/6): 431–50.

Narver, J. and Slater, S. (1990) 'The effect of a market orientation on business profitability', *Journal of Marketing*, 54 (Oct): 20–35.

Payne, A. and Frow, P. (2005) 'A strategic framework for customer relationship management', *Journal of Marketing*, 69 (4): 167–76.

BOOKS AND BOOK CHAPTERS

Baker, M. (ed.) (2008) 'One more time – what is marketing?', in *The Marketing Book* (6th edn). Oxford: Butterworth Heinemann/Chartered Institute of Marketing, Chapter 1.

Davis, E., Bannatyne, D., Meaden, D., Jones, P., Farleigh, R., Paphitis, T. and Caan, J. (2007) *Dragons' Den: Success, from Pitch to Profit*. London: Collins.

Silk, A. (2006) *What is Marketing?* Boston: Harvard Business School Press.

JOURNALS

Journal of Marketing
European Journal of Marketing
Journal of Marketing Management

MAGAZINES

Marketing Week
Marketing
The Marketer (Chartered Institute of Marketing magazine)
(Most libraries will have these magazines – possibly online – ask your librarian.)

WEBSITES

www.brandrepublic.co.uk
www.cim.co.uk – website for the Chartered Institute of Marketing, including lots of information and articles and an excellent glossary.
www.mad.co.uk

SELF-REVIEW QUESTIONS

1. Define a market. (See p. 6)
2. Is marketing an alternative term for advertising? (See p. 10)
3. What is another term for marketing communications? (See p. 10)
4. Why is marketing less important when there is a shortage of goods? (See pp. 12–13)
5. Give five examples of FMCG items. (See the Introduction)
6. Why is it desirable for a product's demand and supply to be in equilibrium? (See p. 15)
7. Why is value such an important part of an exchange? (See p. 16)
8. List five advantages of a market orientation. (See p. 24)
9. What is relationship marketing? (See p. 28)
10. What are the five focus themes that run through this book? (See the Introduction)

Mini case study: Liverpool relaunched

Read the questions, then the case material, and then answer the questions.

Questions

1 What problems did Liverpool face in attracting tourists? (Use the information in the case study, but you may also want to look up Liverpool, and rival cities, on the Internet.)

2 How could good marketing help to overcome these problems?

3 Write a short piece (approx. 200 words) on Liverpool for inclusion in a tourist guide. You should identify different aspects of the city that will appeal to different types of visitor.

4 How could relationship marketing help Liverpool to attract more visitors?

In its heyday, as England's busiest port, Liverpool saw the launching of many fine ships but, with those glory days long gone, the city was in need of a relaunch itself.

For years Liverpool had suffered from jokes and abuse and for being more famous for its sense of humour than its work ethic. TV programmes such as *Bread*, *Brookside* and *The Fast Show* built a picture of Liverpool as a city of lazy benefit fraudsters and chancers. As a result, most tourists, shoppers and business travellers avoided it, fearing for their wallets and their safety. Yet locals always claimed that the Northern city's poor image was invented by London-based media and that the truth was very different.

A golden opportunity to put things right came in 2008 when Liverpool became the European Capital of Culture. Over £2 billion was invested in the city to fund such ambitious plans as reinventing rundown Paradise Street as a suitable venue for a variety of entertainments, including street theatre and music. The rejuvenation of Liverpool was one of Europe's biggest regeneration projects. The impressive waterfront and the city's fabulous architecture were cleaned up and shown off. New facilities were provided. New hotels were built. This was Liverpool's chance to show the world what a great place it really was.

Liverpool has always had a lot to boast about. As well as writers such as Beryl Bainbridge, Willy Russell, Alan Bleasdale, Catherine Cookson and Roger McGough, Liverpool has produced many pop-cultural icons. More artists with number-one hits were born in Liverpool than in any other British city. Its most famous sons are, of course, The Beatles. These symbols of the 1960s first played at the Cavern club – now redeveloped as a Beatles museum. The National Trust now owns John Lennon's childhood home (a gift from his widow, Yoko Ono-Lennon) and opened it to public view. Liverpool Football Club has been one of the country's premier clubs for decades. Comedians as diverse as Ken Dodd, Jimmy Tarbuck and Lily Savage all hail from the city. Cilla Black started her days (as Priscilla White) singing in Liverpool, and more recent music exports include Echo and the Bunnymen, Atomic Kitten, Space, the Lightning Seeds, the Coral and Cast.

Unusually for a city, Liverpool has been abroad itself. Its wealth of architectural styles and the grandeur of its buildings have made it an ideal film double for a number of European cities, including Moscow, Dublin, Paris and, most surprisingly, Venice. The most dramatic aspect of Liverpool has always been best viewed from the Mersey. It is, of course, the UNESCO listed waterfront with its 'three graces': the Royal Liver Building, the Cunard Building and the Port of Liverpool Building, which together form one of the world's most well-recognised skylines. Liverpool's docks were once among the busiest anywhere and the Albert Dock remains so, though now it is

Liverpool's waterfront.

home to thriving bars, restaurants and shops, upmarket apartments and the Tate art gallery rather than ocean-going ships.

Even with all these advantages, if the city was to make it on to every tourist's must-see list, it had a lot of image rebuilding to do. A spokesperson for the City Council said, 'People just haven't been listening. Unemployment is reducing and it is one of the safest cities in the country. Liverpool has art galleries, shopping centres and trendy bars. We are also close to becoming the film capital of Britain with the number of films shot here. I don't see why it should be a problem marketing ourselves to the UK and abroad.'

Liverpool was a smash hit as Capital of Culture in 2008 and has managed to build on that success. It has been named in the top three UK city break destinations for the second successive year by readers of travel bible, *Condé Nast Traveller Magazine*, and was recently voted the best loved of Britain's non-capital cities.

SOURCES: BBCi, n.d.; Liverpool City Council, n.d.; Liverpool 08, n.d.; Singh, 2003; Visit Liverpool, n.d.

REFERENCES

Allen, R. (ed.) (2000) *New Penguin English Dictionary*. Harmondsworth: Penguin.

American Marketing Association (AMA) (2007) *Community* 'AMA definition of marketing', American Marketing Association. Available at: **www.marketingpower.com/ Community/ARC/Pages/Additional/Definition** (accessed 06/11/09).

American Marketing Association (AMA) (2008) 'The American Marketing Association releases new definition for marketing'. American Marketing Association. Available at: **www. marketingpower.com/AboutAMA/Documents/American%20Marketing%20 Association%20Releases%20New%20Definition%20for%20Marketing.pdf** (accessed 03/08/13).

Bagozzi, R.P. (1975) 'Marketing as exchange', *Journal of Marketing*, 39 (Oct): 32–9.

BBC (2012) 'UK is the "most internet-based major economy"', available at: **www.bbc.co.uk/ news/business-17405016** (accessed 11/08/12).

BBCi (n.d.) Capital of Culture (web page). Available at: **www.bbc.co.uk/capitalofculture** (accessed 10/08/03).

Benedictus, L. (2007) 'Psst! Have you heard?', *The Guardian*, 30 January, available at: **www. theguardian.com/media/2007/jan/30/advertising.marketingandpr**.

Berry, L.L. (1983) 'Relationship marketing', in L.L. Berry, G. Shostack and G. Upah (eds), *Emerging Perspectives on Services Marketing*. Salt Lake City, UT: American Marketing Association.

BigBarn (2012) 'Discover real local food', available at: **www.bigbarn.co.uk** (accessed 20/05/13).

Booms, B.H. and Bitner, M.J. (1981) 'Marketing strategies and organisation structures for service firms', in J. Donnelly and W.R. George (eds), *Marketing of Services*, American Marketing Association, pp. 51–67.

Chartered Institute of Marketing (CIM) (n.d.) *Marketing Glossary*. London: Chartered Institute of Marketing. Available at: **www.cim.co.uk/cim/ser/html/infQuiGlo.cfm?letter=M** (accessed 11/06/07).

Co-operative Bank (n.d.) *Social Responsibility*. Available at: **http://www.co-operative. coop/corporate/ethics-and-sustainability/sustainability-report/social- responsibility/** (accessed 17/02/14).

Dibb, S., Simkin, L., Pride, W.M. and Ferrell, O. (2006) *Marketing Concepts and Strategies* (5th European edn). Boston, MA: Houghton Mifflin Company.

Doyle, P. (2002) *Marketing Management and Strategy*. Harlow: FT/Prentice Hall.

European Commission (2011) 'Enterprise and industry, corporate social responsibility'. Available at: **http://ec.europa.eu/enterprise/policies/sustainable-business/ corporate-social-responsibility/index_en.htm** (accessed 03/08/13).

Garside, J. (2013) 'Smartphone sales to hit 1 billion a year for first time in 2013', *The Guardian, Technology*, Sunday, 6 January 2013; available at: **http://www.theguardian. com/business/2013/jan/06/smartphone-sales-1bn-2013** (accessed 17/02/14).

Hooley, G.J., Lynch, J.E. and Shepherd, J. (1990) 'The marketing concept: putting theory into practice', *European Journal of Marketing*, 24 (9): 7–24.

Jeon, S., Sung, T.K. and Dong, H.L. (2011) 'Web 2.0 business models and value creation', *International Journal of Information and Decision Sciences*, 3 (1): 70–84.

Jobber, D. (2006) *Principles and Practice of Marketing* (4th edn). New York: McGraw-Hill.

Kaur, G. and Sharma, R.D. (2009) 'Voyage of marketing thought from a barter system to a customer centric one', *Marketing Intelligence and Planning*, 27 (5): 567–614.

Kiley, D. (2005) 'Not every brand is a lifestyle brand', *Business Week*, 5 July.

Kohli, A.K. and Jaworski, B. (1990) 'Market orientation: the construct, research propositions and managerial implications', *Journal of Marketing*, 54 (April): 1–18.

Kohli, A.K., Jaworski, B.J. and Kumar, A. (1993) 'MARKOR: a measure of market orientation', *Journal of Marketing Research*, November: 467–77.

Kotler, P. (2003) *Marketing Insights from A to Z*. New York: John Wiley & Sons.

Kotler, P. and Levy, S. (1969) 'Broadening the scope of marketing', *Journal of Marketing*, 33 (Jan): 10–15.

Levitt, T. (1960) 'Marketing myopia', *Harvard Business Review*, 38 (Jul/Aug): 45–56.

Levitt, T. (1975) 'Marketing myopia: a retrospective commentary', *Harvard Business Review*, Sept/Aug: 1–14.

Liverpool City Council (n.d.) *Liverpool, European Capital of Culture*. Available at: **www.liverpool.gov.uk** (accessed 10/08/03).

Liverpool 08 (n.d.) *2008 Highlights*. The Liverpool Culture Company. Available at: **http://www.liverpool08.com/** (accessed 17/02/14).

McCarthy, J.F. (1960) *Basic Marketing. A Managerial Approach*. Homewood, IL: Richard D. Irwin.

McDonald, M. (2009) 'The future of marketing: brightest star in the firmament, or a fading meteor? Some hypotheses and a research agenda', *Journal of Marketing Management*, 25 (5/6): 431–50.

Narver, J. and Slater, S. (1990) 'The effect of a market orientation on business profitability', *Journal of Marketing*, 54 (Oct): 20–35.

Noble, C.H., Sinha, R.K. and Kumar, A. (2002) 'Market orientation and alternative strategic orientations: a longitudinal assessment of performance implications', *Journal of Marketing*, 66 (4): 25–39.

O'Connor, J. and Galvin, E. (2001) *Marketing in the Digital Age*. Harlow: FT/Prentice Hall.

Payne, A. and Frow, P. (2005) 'A strategic framework for customer relationship management', *Journal of Marketing*, 69 (4): 167–76.

Pickton, D. and Broderick, A. (2004) *Integrated Marketing Communications* (2nd edn). Harlow: FT/Prentice Hall.

Silverpop (2012) 'CMOs Speak: how to navigate the crazy new world of marketing'; available at: **www.silverpop.com** (accessed July 2012).

Singh, S. (2003) 'Can Liverpool set the record straight?', *Marketing Week*, 12 June.

Visit Liverpool (n.d.) 'Liverpool Tourist Information'. Available at: **www.visitliverpool.com** (accessed 05/12/09).

Walker, R. (2004) 'The hidden (in plain sight) persuaders', *The New York Times*, 5 December, available at: **www.nytimes.com/2004/12/05/magazine/05BUZZ.html?_r=2&**.

Wilson, K. (1996) 'Managing the industrial sales force of the 1990s', in B. Hartley and M. Starkey (eds), *The Management of Sales and Customer Relations*. London: International Thomson Business Press.

Woodcock, N., Starkey, M. and Stone, M. (2000) *The Customer Management Scorecard: A Strategic Framework for Benchmarking Performance Against Best Practice*. London: Business Intelligence.

Visit the companion website on your computer at **www.sagepub.co.uk/masterson3e** or MobileStudy on your Smart phone or tablet by scanning this QR code and gain access to:

- **Videos** to get a better understanding of key concepts and provoke in-class discussion.
- Links to useful **websites and templates** to help guide your study.
- Access **SAGE Marketing Pins (www.pinterest.com/sagepins/)**. SAGE's regularly updated **Pinterest** page, giving you access to regularly updated resources on everything from Branding to Consumer Behaviour.
- **Daily Grind podcast series** to learn more about the day-to-day life of a marketing **professional**.
- Interactive **Practice questions** to test your understanding.
- A **bonus chapter on Marketing Careers** to not only support your study, but your job search and future career.
- **PowerPoints** prompting key points for revision.

3rd edition

Rosalind Masterson & David Pickton

MARKETING
an introduction

The marketing environment

2

CHAPTER CONTENTS

ENVIRONMENTAL CHALLENGES

The following are illustrations of the types of decision that marketers have to take or issues they face. *You aren't expected to know how to deal with the challenges now*; just bear them in mind as you read the chapter and see what you can find that helps.

- You work in the marketing department of a multinational which has a large investment in East Africa. Your company often considers pulling out. Can you devise a system for monitoring the often volatile situation there?
- You are the manager of a small chain of cafés. Business has been a bit slower this year than it was last, but you are better off than many of your competitors, some of whom have gone out of business. Do you know why that happened to them? Are you in danger too?
- You work for an oil company and Greenpeace protesters are currently camped outside the refinery. They are protesting over a proposed new pipeline and no one at the oil company seems surprised that they are there. In fact, the counter-arguments were prepared in advance and the press release has gone to all the newspapers. Greenpeace kept its intentions a secret, so how was this possible?
- You work in banking and a colleague has just come up with a new service idea that has got the whole bank talking and will probably get him a promotion. It takes advantage of a new IT product that IBM has just announced. Why didn't you come up with that idea?

INTRODUCTION

The word 'environment' has come to be associated with conservation; with the green movement. However, that is not the sense in which the word is used in this chapter. The *New Penguin English Dictionary* (Allen, 2000) defines environment as 'the circumstances, objects, or conditions by which somebody or something is surrounded', and this is closer to the way the term is used in marketing.

Organisations do not operate in isolation. They have to take account of other organisations and individuals in their plans and in their day-to-day dealings. They operate within a specific marketing environment which is changing all the time. Managers always need to be aware of what is going on in the world around them. They have to identify trends within their organisation's environment and make plans. To do this, they will need good information gained from sound marketing research (see Chapter 5). They will need to have a clear idea of exactly who their market is both currently and potentially (see Chapter 4) and what potential their product has. They need to have a solid understanding of their customers, the ways in which they use products, how they relate to brands, and how they choose what to buy (see Chapter 3). If a company is to be successful, then it is vital that it understands its competitive environment well. Without up-to-date knowledge of what competitors are doing, and of how well that is working, how can a company make its own marketing plans? All this information feeds into product development, the setting of prices, the design of distribution networks and choice of retailers, the creation of promotional campaigns and the development of a distinctive, desirable brand.

This chapter will consider the nature of the marketing environment and explain how to monitor changes within it. There are a number of frameworks available to help with the organisation of this environmental information and this chapter will introduce the PRESTCOM analysis tool (see below for an explanation). The analysis of an organisation's current situation forms the basis for strategic planning and we will touch on that – though it is covered in more depth in Chapter 12. Another analysis tool used here is one of the best known in management: the SWOT analysis (see below).

MARKET DYNAMICS

MARKET LEADER OR MARKET LED?

Some companies are said to be market led, others to be market leaders. Strictly, the market leader is the company that sells the most. It is important to be clear which market you are referring to when talking of a market leader. Cadbury's may well be the market leader in chocolate in the UK but not in the USA, where it is more likely to be Hershey's, or in any other European country, each of which has its own favourites.

The term 'market leader' is often used more loosely, however, to refer to a firm that leads the way in a market. This may be in terms of setting prices, releasing innovative products, devising new forms of promotion, moving into different market segments, or any number of other ways of starting an industry trend. Such leaders are not necessarily large organisations. Often the recognised market leader is a smaller firm that is more innovative (e.g. Dyson and its vacuum cleaners), or that has more expertise (e.g. some specialised consultancy and accountancy firms), or has exceptional talent (e.g. fashion designers such as Stella McCartney).

If a company takes its lead from other firms within its market, it is called a market follower. Market followers watch competitors closely and learn from their successful ideas and strategies. This does not mean that they produce only me-too designs or campaigns, only that they wait for more radical ideas to be tested by others first and cash in on their research experience. This strategy is not limited to new inventions, for example some fashion chains send people out to other stores to see what they have on display and what seems to be selling before placing their own orders for stock.

A company that has ambitious growth plans and aspires to be market leader, is called a market challenger and is likely to attract a more severe reaction from the current market leader.

Followers are, by definition, second (or third, fourth, etc.) into a new market and therefore do not usually get the benefit of **first mover advantage**. Often, the first significant company to move into a market becomes the leader. It can be hard to dislodge as it is the brand people know, the one they tried first and presumably liked – or there would be no market.

Coca-Cola was the first company to make a cola drink and it still outsells all others in most countries. The Body Shop was the first to build a retailing chain around the idea of more ethically produced toiletries. Amazon was the first company to sell books online with a view to making a large business of it, and it had the resources and skills to make that dream a reality. All these firms have first mover advantage.

However, being first into the market does not guarantee success as many IT and Internet companies have found. Sometimes the first in is a very small company which is unable to exploit the market to the full, or which may make mistakes, thus letting another, larger or more able company steal the high ground. Peter Doyle (2006) lists the four most common mistakes made by market pioneers, i.e. the first in:

- marketing mistakes, e.g. misjudging who will want to buy the product and so targeting it at the wrong market segment
- product mistakes, e.g. technical or design flaws and limitations that challengers can exploit
- first-generation technology, e.g. market challengers can incorporate the very latest technology into their products, perhaps leaving the pioneer behind
- resource limitations, e.g. the pioneer may be a smaller company whose resources are therefore limited and who can be outgunned by a larger challenger.

The first company bears the brunt of the risks and so may fail where later companies succeed. If it is successful, it is likely to attract the attention of larger competitors. A highly praised Internet browser called Netscape pre-dates Microsoft Internet Explorer. Which one do you use? Market leaders are constantly challenged by the other firms who wish to supplant them. These market challengers employ a number of strategies, and adopt a number of positions, in order to achieve their goal of market leadership. Some challengers are small, but they can be very large. PepsiCo is a market challenger, constantly harrying Coca-Cola and trying to steal some of Coke's **market share**. Most market leaders are large, although it is

first mover advantage
the first significant company to move into the market often becomes the market leader and can be hard to dislodge from that position

market share
a firm's sales expressed as a percentage of the total sales of that type of product in the defined market

market segment
a group of buyers
and users/consumers
who share similar
characteristics and
who are distinct from
the rest of the market
for a product

possible to be a small market leader. It depends on how large your market is. Niche brands sell into small, well-defined market segments so it is common to find a small brand leading the way. For example, Bentley by no means lead the car market, but they are one of the leaders of the prestige car market.

It is easier to challenge a market leader in the early stages of a market's development before the leader has built significant economies of scale which bring their costs down and make it very hard for others to compete on price. Internet Explorer does have viable competition, e.g. Firefox, but despite the efforts of enthusiastic Firefox users, and of people who are anti-Microsoft on principle, Internet Explorer still dominates the market.

EXPAND YOUR KNOWLEDGE

Classic article

Oxenfeldt, A.R. and Moore, W.L. (1978) 'Customer or competitor: which guideline for marketing', *Management Review*, Aug: 43–8.

Many commentators have emphasised the importance of recognising the significance of competitors as well as customers to effective marketing. Many naïve views have been developed about marketing by placing too much emphasis on the importance of customers alone. Even though customers are clearly important, there are other factors that have to be balanced for marketing to be carried out well. This is an early article which highlights the need for companies to tune into the competition and balance this with a customer-orientated approach.

ASSET-LED MARKETING

asset-led marketing
basing marketing
strategy on the
organisation's
strengths rather than
on customer needs
and wants

Not all organisations are marketing focused, so they cannot be said to be either led by the market or driven by it. For example, some companies are said to be **asset led**. These companies concentrate on doing what they already have the resources and skills to do, rather than looking for market opportunities and adapting to fit them. The asset in question might be equipment, people, contacts, a distribution network, shops – almost anything. In the UK, many shoe repairers also cut keys, and frequently now take in dry cleaning. They have suitable shop premises to do this. Their shops are major assets to be exploited. Many universities rent out rooms in their halls of residence to tourists in the summer months, using an asset that would otherwise stand empty. Theatres, museums and art galleries rent out their foyers for upmarket parties. Did any of these organisations conduct research to discover people's needs and then design their offerings to fit? No, they realised they had spare space and came up with something profitable to do with it.

It is not just spare space that can be exploited profitably. IBM realised it had hundreds of highly trained management and computing personnel whose skills could be offered to clients as consultants. Many years ago, when textile production was dying in the UK, the factory owners realised that the same machines could be used to knit tea bags.

So, is it best to build your strategy around what your customers want, or around the assets you already have? This is an occasion where companies look for the best of both worlds. The ideal is to meet your customers' needs while making the best possible use of all your assets.

Sometimes circumstances allow you to be more proactive about this, e.g. when moving or building new premises. When Leicester City Football Club had its new stadium built, for instance, it incorporated private rooms of various sizes into the design so that it could develop its business of hiring out space for meetings, lunches and other functions.

Picture courtesy of Leicester City Football Club

Leicester City Football Club making full use of its assets.

SUPPLIERS AND DISTRIBUTION PARTNERS

An important feature of market dynamics is the way in which products actually get to customers. Most businesses use intermediaries to help with product distribution. These intermediaries are the links between producers and their customers and consumers. Transport companies such as FedEx, UPS, Parcelforce, DPD, DHL, TNT, Eddie Stobart, Norbert Dentressangle physically deliver goods to customers on behalf of producers. Agents, wholesalers and retailers may also be part of the **distribution channel**. Some markets have developed their own particular **supply chains**. The distribution of pharmaceuticals, especially prescription drugs, is heavily controlled: usually customers have to visit licensed pharmacists to obtain them. New cars are typically sold through **franchised** dealerships dedicated to specific car manufacturers. By contrast, fast moving consumer goods are sold through extensive distribution channels so that customers can buy them almost anytime, anywhere. Chapter 9 (Place) describes distribution in detail.

distribution channel
a chain of organisations through which products pass on their way to a target market

supply chain
the network of business and organisations involved in distributing goods and services to their final destination

franchise
a form of licence; the franchisee pays for the rights to run a business that has already been successful elsewhere, in a new territory and benefits from the expertise of the original owners (franchisors)

STAKEHOLDERS

There are a large number of individuals and groups that exist within a company's environments and that have an interest in the company and its activities. These are its stakeholders. Freeman (1984) defined stakeholders as 'any group or individual who can affect or is affected by the achievement of an organisation's activities'. All organisations have a large number of stakeholder groups and they will be different for each one.

b2b focus: Going shopping

Have you ever bought Coke from Coca-Cola, toothpaste from MacLean's, shampoo from L'Oreal, fish fingers from Birds Eye, a camera from Canon, a printer from HP, or a mobile phone from Nokia? The answer is most likely 'no', even if you have bought these products before. These are all manufacturing companies and they use different channels of distribution. As end customers, we buy these products from retailers such as Tesco, Boots, ASDA Walmart, Amazon, who buy directly from manufacturers. Or we may go to smaller retailers who buy from wholesalers who in turn buy from the manufacturers, sometimes through **agents**. So even though Coca-Cola, Pepsi Cola, Proctor and Gamble and Unilever are among the world's biggest consumer goods companies, we have never bought anything from them – at least not directly!

Typically, stakeholder groups include:

agent
represents other businesses and sells products on their behalf; does not usually hold stock or take ownership of the goods, just takes orders and is paid a commission

- customers (who buy goods and services)
- consumers (who use the goods and services – for further discussion of the distinction between customers and consumers, see Chapter 1)
- employees, including directors
- pensioners, i.e. ex-employees who receive their pension income from the firm
- suppliers of goods and services, e.g. advertising agencies, raw materials providers
- distributors, e.g. wholesalers, retailers, agents
- government (local and central)
- local community, from whom customers, employees and pressure group members (e.g. local residents' organisations) may be drawn
- shareholders, who own the company
- pressure groups, e.g. trade unions, consumer groups
- bankers, who may have lent the company money
- other investors, e.g. venture capitalists
- professional bodies, e.g. the Chartered Institute of Marketing.

public relations (PR)
planned activities designed to build good relationships and enhance an organisation's or an individual's reputation

These groupings are very like the potential audiences that **PR** people sometimes refer to as publics.

Stakeholder groups will want different things from the firm, and often their objectives for the firm conflict. For example, customers usually want the best quality but at the lowest possible price. Shareholders, on the other hand, will want the company to make high profits so that their dividends are higher and their shares are worth more. Pressure groups such as Greenpeace will want the company to spend money on protecting the environment and will consider any resulting increase in prices, or decrease in profits, as perfectly acceptable. Trade unions may want higher wages and better working conditions. This will, again, push up the company's costs and so it may have to raise its prices (which the customers will not like) or cut its profits (which the shareholders will not like). Setting objectives, developing strategies and managing situations in a way that resolves the conflicts between these differing stakeholder groups are key management tasks that can use up much time and effort.

EXPAND YOUR KNOWLEDGE

Finlay-Robinson, D. (2008) 'What's in it for me? The fundamental importance of stakeholder evaluation', *Journal of Management Development*, 28 (4): 380–8.

The paper presents an overview of the relevance and value of stakeholder analysis and provides a list of key factors for consideration when carrying this out.

The idea of a firm having a responsibility towards its stakeholders is relatively new in management thinking. Previously, a company's prime duty was thought to be to its shareholders, or owners, alone. This led to many organisations' main objective being short-term profit maximisation, which was often not in its best interests in the longer term. Current managerial thinking takes account of other stakeholder groups when setting the organisation's direction. Just how far to take this has become a moral question that has prompted significant debate.

ENVIRONMENTAL INFORMATION

Strategic Planning Business Case Study

Organisations build up information on what is happening in the world around them so that they are better able to deal with any threats to their business or to take advantage of any new opportunities before their competitors do.

A firm's environment is commonly split into two parts: its external environment and its internal environment. Things that happen in the external environment are largely outside the firm's control and so are referred to as **uncontrollables** (or 'uncontrollable variables'), e.g. wars, crop failures, a change of government, new technology. The internal environment ought to be more easily controlled and so occurrences within it are often referred to as **controllables** (or 'controllable variables'), e.g. skill levels of employees, available finance, product range.

Environmental information is used in two main ways:

1 As input to the planning process
2 As part of ongoing analysis of marketing opportunities and threats (environmental scanning).

uncontrollables
events, issues, trends, etc. within the external environment that are outside the firm's control

controllables
events, issues, trends, etc. within the internal environment

global focus: Not so sweet

Tate & Lyle is one of the oldest brands in the UK. It dates back to 1921 when Mr Tate merged his sugar cube business with Mr Lyle's business, best known for the golden syrup that is still a favourite flavour for pancakes today. By 1939, Tate & Lyle's Thames factory was the largest sugar cane refinery in the world and the brand has gone from strength to strength ever since. By 2007, the company operated 65 production plants in 29 countries, but profits were sliding and the company seemed about to lose its blue-chip status.

Tate & Lyle were no longer just sugar refiners. Over the years, the company had diversified into food additives, such as citric acid, starches, and animal and fish feed. Their research and development division had been highly productive and had made a number of major breakthroughs, including, in 1976, the invention of a superior, zero calorie, sugar substitute called Sucralose. This revolutionary product has since been renamed Splenda but, though sold around the globe, it is still solely manufactured and sold by Tate & Lyle.

Despite such diversification, sugar remains at the heart of Tate & Lyle's business and therein lies its problem. Governments and researchers throughout the world say that too much sugar is not good for hearts, nor for health generally. Obesity is at crisis levels in many Western countries – notably the USA and the UK, which are key Tate & Lyle markets. Consumers generally are watching their weight – and therefore their sugar intake. These trends in the political and social environments are proving costly for Tate & Lyle. Splenda should have saved the company but apparently it just tastes too good – too much like the real thing. Consumers expect their diet and lite drinks to taste more artificial. Then there's the consumer backlash against additives and artificial flavourings – poor Splenda just cannot win.

Much of Tate & Lyle's business is conducted in the USA and the weakness of the dollar has meant that US profits translated into fewer pounds than in previous years. A further problem with the company's US connections has arisen in the regulatory environment. The European Union has banned imports of US corn gluten (a by-product of maize that is used as animal feed) after some was found to have come from a genetically modified source. The problem gluten was not actually supplied by Tate & Lyle, but they are suffering from the fallout anyway as they are unable to import their gluten into the EU and, because of the resultant glut of the product in the USA, prices there have fallen dramatically. Meanwhile, in Europe, the price of maize (a key raw ingredient for Tate & Lyle) has shot up and so, with higher costs to deal with, profits are being further squeezed.

So Tate & Lyle's current marketing environment is not a sweet one.

Based on Finch (2007)

INPUT TO THE PLANNING PROCESS

Particularly during the planning process, it is useful for a firm to have a framework in which to place its environmental data. It can then assess the data's impact and what to do about it. For example, a firm would want to identify its key competitors and investigate their strategies; it is then in a position to develop counter-strategies if necessary. It would want to know about the lives of its customers, so that it could develop products and services to meet their needs.

Planners do not stop at just identifying relevant trends or competitors. They take the environmental data, feed it into a situation analysis and so arrive at a fuller understanding of the organisation's current situation on which they can build their plans.

ENVIRONMENTAL SCANNING

Wise organisations continuously scan their environments so that they can keep up with changes and are ready to deal with market developments, be they good or bad. This is an ongoing research exercise. The collected data helps build a better picture of their world. Perhaps they will find that a new law or regulation is being proposed and that it will affect their interests adversely. Take, for example, the proposals by various government organisations to increase taxes on 4 × 4 vehicles, the so-called 'gas guzzlers'. These are highly profitable products for many car companies and so they have been lobbying to get the proposals scrapped or watered down, while at the same time taking account of a likely fall in sales (or a total ban) when making their plans. Some firms have research departments, or employ outside research consultants, to scan their environment. However, most do this on a more ad hoc basis.

Some managers rely on personal contacts for their environmental knowledge, possibly because it can be difficult to get hard facts on external environmental trends (economics, for example, has never been an exact science). These personal sources are supplemented by, or cross-checked in, newspapers, magazines, trade journals and other secondary sources (for sources of secondary data, see Chapter 5). The approach that academic commentators recommend, however, is to analyse the external environment as a team, i.e. to consult a range of employees from senior managers to the most junior staff. This way the firm benefits from a wide range of viewpoints and is more likely to identify key things that will affect it in the future (Mercer, 1995).

How do managers decide what is, and what is not, relevant?

Taken to its extreme, the whole world and everything in it can be considered as having an impact upon the organisation – particularly if it is a very large organisation such as IBM or Unilever. Clearly it is not practical to study absolutely everything and so the management team must initially decide what sorts of things to include – a number of models have been developed to help them do this: e.g. PEST, SLEPT, PRESTCOM. Brownlie (2000) proposed the process for environmental scanning seen in Exhibit 2.1.

Unfortunately in the hectic world of business, sometimes pressing matters take precedence over long-term thinking. Many organisations have come unstuck

situation analysis
an investigation into an organisation or brand's current circumstances to identify significant factors and trends; the most common framework used is SWOT (Strengths, Weaknesses, Opportunities, Threats)

Environmental Scanning

lobbying
a means of influencing those with power, particularly politicians and legislators

secondary data
data previously collected for other purposes that can be used in the current research task

Exhibit 2.1   Environmental scanning process

monitor	✓ trends, issues and events ✓ develop a list of relevant sources to check regularly
identify	✓ factors (trends, issues, events, etc.) that are significant to the organisation ✓ set, and regularly review, criteria to determine what is likely to be significant and what is not
evaluate	✓ the impact of the identified factors upon the organisation's operation in its current markets
forecast	✓ what is likely to happen next? ✓ examine future threats and opportunities presented by the identified and evaluated factors
assess	✓ the impact of those threats and opportunities on the firm's medium- and long-term strategies

by not looking beyond the requirements of current decision-making. The firm's most immediate operating environment (customers, suppliers, distributors, etc.) is likely to change rapidly and to receive more management attention than its wider environment (Brownlie, 2000). For example, sales of red meat have been falling for some time. There have, of course, been a number of health scares associated with the eating of meat (high cholesterol, BSE, foot and mouth disease, excess growth hormones, etc.). It would be easy for farmers to blame their troubles on these scare stories. At the same time, however, many people are eating more chicken or fish, rather than red meat, for more general health reasons and, in many countries, significant numbers of people are becoming vegetarian. These people are unlikely to return to their meat-eating habits when the latest scare dies down.

SOURCES OF ENVIRONMENTAL INFORMATION

- companies' own records (these may not be accessible to outsiders)
- market research reports: these may be specially commissioned, or more general reports can be bought from organisations such as Euromonitor, Mintel and Keynote
- newspapers (archives available online) and magazines; news stories should be triangulated, i.e. checked with at least two other independent sources
- trade magazines and newsletters, e.g. *The Grocer, Computer Weekly*
- documentaries: again these should be checked
- government reports and statistics; usually available online, e.g. **www.europa.eu** for the European Union
- trade organisations, e.g. the European Association of Aerospace Industries or the Chartered Institute of Marketing
- international bodies and committees, e.g. OECD (Organisation for Economic Cooperation and Development) who publish comparative statistics on many topics for most countries or the WTO (World Trade Organisation)

- trade unions, e.g. UCU or Unison or the TUC
- company websites; information from here should be checked – remember that these are really company publicity
- news organisation websites, e.g. Reuters or the BBC
- consultancy firms: some of these publish reports that can be accessed freely, e.g. KPMG, PWC, McKinsey and Co.

MARKETING ENVIRONMENT MODELS

The data that an organisation collects through its environmental research must be analysed. This process involves sorting the data, categorising it and then looking for trends, changes in trends, patterns, dangers and opportunities. There are a number of models of the marketing environment that an organisation can use to help it to analyse environmental data. Relevant factors are put into one or another of the categories within each model. These models are known by their acronyms (the words that are created by the letters that make up the model).

Probably the best-known environmental model is PEST:

Political
Economic
Social
Technological.

Using PEST analysis to support Decision Making

Common variants are STEP, SLEPT and PESTEL. The L in the last two acronyms stands for legal. The extra E in PESTEL can be environmental or ecological. All of these models are ways of looking at a firm's external environment. The **macroenvironment** is the term favoured by economists and refers to the broadest external environment in which a firm operates.

Many textbooks ignore these environmental acronyms, which might suggest that PEST and its variants have had their day. However, they are a useful *aide-mémoire*. Perhaps their current lack of favour can be attributed to the fact that most omit so much that is important (e.g. the microenvironment), along with a tendency to follow them too slavishly rather than use them as prompts. There is no need to invent things in order to fill every box. If there is nothing of significance happening in one of the categories, then it should be passed over. The important thing is to have thought everything through.

It is important not to get muddled over this term 'environment'. It is commonly used to refer to nature or green issues but that is not what it means here. Green issues are highly relevant in a firm's planning of course, but they present a bit of a problem as to where they should be placed within the model. Should the natural environment even have its own heading in an environmental analysis? Does it fit well under some, or all, of the other headings? Certainly there are political aspects to environmentalism, especially when lobbyists such as Greenpeace, Friends of the Earth or (perhaps at the other end of the political spectrum) the Countryside Alliance are involved (the Countryside Alliance is an organisation that campaigns to preserve certain traditional aspects of British country life, such as hunting).

macroenvironment the broad, external influences that affect all organisations in a market, e.g. the political situation in a country

The natural environment underpins all the other marketing environment categories.

Regulation is relevant in terms of laws and codes governing issues such as pollution or recycling. The using, or spoiling, of irreplaceable natural resources has economic implications. Social attitudes towards green issues are changing. Technology has the power to harm or heal the natural world. Being seen to be greener than rival firms can give a company a valuable competitive edge – there is a significant minority of customers who choose environmentally friendly products.

The natural environment affects an organisation in numerous ways. Whether this means it should be treated separately or within the context of other forces is a choice the analyst must make. It will probably depend upon the nature of the organisation, its products and the rest of its operating environment. In this book green issues will be considered where they are relevant within other categories. In this way, their important influence can be considered more seriously and widely. PEST, and its variants, only cover *part* of the organisation's external environment. Marketers must consider all of the external environment and the internal environment as well. The more immediate environment is what economists refer to as the microenvironment. It comprises competitors, distributors, suppliers and the organisation's own internal resources.

The macroenvironment refers to broad influences that affect all organisations in a market, whereas the microenvironment contains influences specific to the nature of the business, its suppliers, marketing intermediaries, customers and competitors.

So PEST does not give the whole picture: it only covers the macroenvironment. In order to complete the picture, Wright and Pickton (cited in Pickton and Broderick, 2001) proposed a more comprehensive, environmental model: PRESTCOM. PRESTCOM provides a framework for the analysis of both the macro and micro environments (see Exhibit 2.2).

PRESTCOM

PRESTCOM is an acronym that stands for:

Political
Regulatory
Economic
Social
Technological
Competitive
Organisational
Market.

Over the following pages, each of these categories will be considered in turn. As examples of what to include under each PRESTCOM heading, at the end of

Exhibit 2.2   PRESTCOM

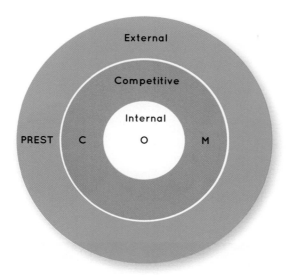

each section there will be a couple of factors or trends taken from an analysis of Cadbury in 2012. This is not a **complete** PRESTCOM for Cadbury, just an illustration of how to do the analysis.

THE MACRO ENVIRONMENT

The macroenvironment, which is external to the organisation, is represented graphically in Exhibit 2.3.

THE POLITICAL ENVIRONMENT
Players in the political environment include:

- government – i.e. domestic government bodies (central, regional and local, and government-appointed committees), supranational government bodies (e.g. the EU) and foreign governments
- government departments, e.g. Department of Trade and Industry (UK), Directorate General for Competition (EU)
- industry bodies and watchdog committees, e.g. OFCOM (UK), European Food Safety Authority, European Data Protection Supervisor (EU)
- special interest and pressure groups – i.e. political organisations that exist to further a cause (e.g. Friends of the Earth) or the interests of a particular group of people (e.g. trade unions)
- political parties.

These groups affect an organisation and its operations in a number of ways. The philosophy of the government in power sets the business climate. Government policy has a direct effect on the way in which businesses are allowed

Exhibit 2.3   The macroenvironment

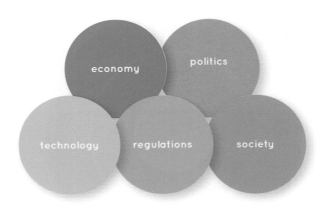

Demonstrations are a common form of political protest.

to operate. For example, some governments are characterised as interventionist and others as non-interventionist. The interventionists are far more likely to interfere in the running of businesses, for good or for bad.

Things to look for in the political environment include:

- the political orientation of the government, e.g. left wing or right wing? Democratic or authoritarian?
- the stability of the political situation – how likely is it to change and how radically? Examples of radical change include coups or war; a less radical change might be an election or a passing on of power such as happened in North Korea when Kim Jong-il appointed his son Kim Jong-un to replace him as Supreme Leader
- existing and proposed government policies, e.g. commitment to austerity measures to reduce debt, reducing people's reliance on state benefits, encouraging home ownership, support (or non-support) for same-sex marriage, attitudes to environmental conservation
- specific business-related attitudes and policies (the attitude may help you to predict new policy), e.g. grants for small business start-ups, links with trade unions, attitudes towards foreign investment, e.g. China has strict controls on foreign firms

- import and export restrictions
- membership of a trading bloc, e.g. the European Union
- views on the operation of the market (e.g. are they pro a free market, where the laws of supply and demand dictate product availability and prices, or likely to intervene to influence supply or prices)
- the government's own commercial dealings; governments have huge spending power but many have at some point followed a policy of giving their own country's suppliers preference when placing their orders
- the relationship between governments, e.g. some Middle Eastern governments are unwilling to allow trade with the West.

In the UK elections of 2010, no one political party gained a majority of seats and so, for the first time since the Second World War, a coalition government was formed. After 13 years of a Labour government, this was quite a change and caused a great deal of uncertainty. A right-wing government could be expected to cut taxes and the public sector – but how would Conservative policies be affected by having to accommodate the more liberal views of their new Lib Dem partners?

In Greece in 2012 there was a lot of political unrest as the Greeks took to the streets to oppose the austerity measures imposed by the EU as the price of an economic bail-out. In France also, the people revolted against the constraints of debt reduction policies and elected a new president.

ethical focus: A government takeover: nationalisation

Perhaps the most extreme form of government intervention is when a government takes over a business or part of a business – often without consultation or adequate compensation. This is called nationalisation. In 2012, the Bolivian government decided to nationalise TDE (Transportadora de Electricidad), a subsidiary of the Spanish company Red Electrica de Espana (BBC News, 2012). Of course, Spanish officials objected strongly, just as others had done before them. Nationalisation is an ongoing government policy in Bolivia. In 2008 they took back control of telephone company Entel from its foreign owners. Previously, they had seized control of a BP oil pipeline and other foreign-owned gas and oil fields. The Bolivian government believes that all basic services should be publicly owned (BBC News, 2008).

In contrast, a non-interventionist government may scale down all of these things, and even privatise previously nationalised industries. Right-wing governments tend to be less interventionist than more left-wing, or socialist, governments. Generally speaking, communist governments exert the most control of all.

The European Union

global focus: The European Union

The largest trading bloc in the world is the European Union (EU), which generates approximately 20% of global exports and imports while being home to only 7% of the world's population (European Commission, 2012a). Additionally, the members of the EU have a common tariff, i.e. they all charge the same amount of duty on goods imported from outside the EU. This prevents other countries from shipping goods into a country with lower taxes and then taking advantage of the lack of barriers within the EU to move the goods on.

In 2012, there were 27 member states in the EU. The dates in brackets show when the country joined:

- Austria (1995)
- Belgium (founding member, 1957)
- Bulgaria (2007)
- Cyprus (2004)
- Czech Republic (2004)
- Denmark (1973)
- Estonia (2004)
- Finland (1995)
- France (founding member, 1957)
- Germany (founding member, 1957)
- Greece (1981)
- Hungary (2004)
- Ireland (1973)
- Italy (founding member, 1957)
- Latvia (2004)
- Lithuania (2004)
- Luxembourg (founding member, 1957)
- Malta (2004)
- Netherlands (founding member, 1957)
- Poland (2004)
- Portugal (1986)
- Romania (2007)
- Slovakia (2004)
- Slovenia (2004)
- Spain (1986)
- Sweden (1995)
- UK (1973)

The following are candidate countries who have started, or will soon start, accession negotiations:

- Croatia
- Iceland
- Macedonia
- Montenegro
- Serbia
- Turkey

(European Commission, 2012b)

European Union Parliament Building.

SOURCES: European Commission, 2012b

© newphotoservice/Shutterstock

This is clearly an important time to be keeping up with political events and assessing the possible impact of future policy changes.

Cadbury: example of political factors

- Governments and health organisations, especially in the UK, are taking action over rising obesity levels. Medical professionals have launched a campaign to combat the problem on five fronts: action that may be taken by individuals, the environment, clinical interventions, fiscal measure and education (Academy of Medical Royal Colleges, 2012).
- The UK government's call to action on obesity encourages food producers to sign up to the calorie reduction pledge (Department of Health, 2012), which has implications for Cadbury's current products and new product development.

Working on the Cadbury account

THE REGULATORY ENVIRONMENT

The actions that an organisation can take are constrained by the rules imposed upon it and by the duties it owes to other organisations or individuals. These rules and duties may be formalised as laws (e.g. the Human Rights Act 1998) or as codes of practice (e.g. those governing what is, and what is not, acceptable in advertising) or they may be merely accepted behaviour (e.g. an advertising agency not handling competing clients). For marketers, the regulations and codes of practice set by professional and industry bodies can be just as significant as laws. It is important to know, for example, what is permitted when making price offers, setting competition rules, offering sales promotions, making advertising claims, designing packaging, commenting on competing brands, etc. All of these things, and more, will need to follow professional codes of practice.

Laws and regulations vary from country to country. There are very few laws that span borders and, contrary to popular belief, there is no international body of law or international court that covers all trading agreements between companies. Increasingly, there are supranational laws and bodies within trading blocs, e.g. the European Union, but in the main, individual countries' laws still apply and so it is vital that companies from different countries agree which country's rules should apply to a contract at the outset. This variety of laws in countries is one of the things that makes international marketing additionally complicated. Take sales promotion laws as an example: in some countries, such as Britain, it is perfectly acceptable to entice customers to buy your product by giving them a money-off voucher. In other countries, such as Germany, this is not allowed.

Although the parties to the contract can choose which country's law applies to an international contract, they cannot opt out of another country's laws and regulations concerning the product itself and its sale within that country. It is important to understand the laws and business regulations of any country with which you hope to trade. Ignorance is rarely a defence in law and unwary companies who assume that judicial systems and laws in all countries are the same are likely to earn themselves hefty fines – or even find their employees imprisoned.

Things to look for in the regulatory environment include:

- new laws and regulations
- changes in laws or regulations: either in content or punishments
- new legal institutions or other bodies, e.g. courts, advisory committees – OFTEL
- changes in the way regulations are administered, e.g. a move away for the Financial Services Authority.

Laws are developed by governments, or the judiciary, and usually take a long time to come into force. This gives organisations (or at least those that have identified the proposed laws through their environmental scanning) an opportunity to try to influence the content of laws during their development. This activity is called lobbying.

Lobbying is a means of influencing the politicians. It is often employed by pressure or interest groups (e.g. trade associations) rather than by individual firms. The tobacco industry and farmers both have strong lobbies in many EU countries. Trained lobbyists identify the key members of committees that are debating the proposed changes in law and put their arguments to them. They hope to persuade the committees to make favourable changes or to drop any harmful proposals altogether. In Britain, the tobacco lobby has been particularly effective: even when it had been agreed that cigarette companies should no longer be allowed to sponsor sports, it managed to get motor racing and snooker exempted. More recently, alcohol producers lobbied to try and prevent stricter rules on the advertising of alcoholic drinks being imposed, and the UK TV industry successfully lobbied advertising regulators and the UK government to get **product placement** rules relaxed. In 2012, banks came under increasing pressure from proposed legislation such as the potential financial transaction tax. In response, Barclays decided to appoint an EU-level Public Affairs agency to complement its recent appointment of Cicero in the UK and lobby on its behalf.

product placement arranging for products to be seen, or referred to, in entertainment media, e.g. during TV or radio programmes, films, plays, video games

Cadbury: example of regulatory factors

- EU regulations specify the permitted ingredients in chocolate and cocoa products intended for human consumption, including the maximum permitted vegetable fat of 5% (Europa, 2012); this has had more impact on UK brands, which traditionally have lower cocoa levels, than it has on their European rivals.
- UK regulations prohibit schools from providing chocolate or other sugary snacks in school (Department for Education, 2012).

THE ECONOMIC ENVIRONMENT

The E in PRESTCOM refers to the macroeconomic environment – *not* to the internal costs of firms. All firms are affected by changes in their macroeconomic environment. The macroeconomic environment is what is commonly referred to in newspapers as 'the economy'. It is made up of all the buying and selling that goes on in a country (the national economy) or in the world (the global economy). Economic trends today are increasingly global rather than affecting a country in isolation, and this makes it harder for countries to manage their own economies. Most Western governments publish data on economic trends, as do professional organisations such as the Chartered Institute of Marketing (CIM) and international bodies such as the Organisation for Economic Cooperation and Development (OECD).

Things to look for in the economic environment include:

Addicted
to Risk

- stage in the **trade cycle**, e.g. boom or recession?
  - o Booms are the good times, characterised by high consumer spending and business profits, and low unemployment. Unfortunately, this increase in demand for goods and services may lead to shortages and so to raised prices (inflation) and the need to import more while exporting less (balance of payments deficit).
  - o A recession is likely to follow. Consumers cannot afford the high prices and so demand falls. Businesses find they have surplus capacity and cut back, so unemployment rises, and consumers have even less money to spend. It is a vicious circle (see Exhibit 2.4). Traditionally, food retailers do comparatively well in hard times, but those who sell luxuries suffer.
- rates of inflation; these have a big impact on prices
- unemployment figures; again this helps work out the potential market, and also indicates what kind of products (luxury or basic) might do well
- household disposable income figures and trends; these indicate whether or not people are likely to be able to afford a product
- availability of credit; both consumer and business; European austerity measures including the UK credit crunch have restricted consumer and business borrowing, making it harder for them to spend; clearly this has a massive knock-on effect on sales – especially of non-essential items
- the country's approach to **social costs**; how much might your company have to contribute?
- business taxes, e.g. VAT (purchase tax) which affects prices and corporation tax (on a company's profits)
- import tariffs; firms that trade internationally have to take account of import duties (taxes) and other import barriers when devising their marketing plans
- membership of trading blocs, e.g. EU, NAFTA, ASEAN. There are no import tariffs for EU countries trading with each other.

trade cycle
patterns of economic activity consisting of boom, downturn (recession), slump (depression), upturn (recovery); also know as the 'business cycle'

social costs
the costs incurred by society generally as a result of business processes or decisions, e.g. the clearing up of pollution, the provision of transport infrastructure

Most firms will hold off new product launches during a recession and it is almost certainly not the time to launch the latest luxury model. It may, however, prove a good time to launch cut-down, budget versions of products, e.g. the no-frills version of a mass-market car or super-economy class on an airline. Prices are likely to need careful monitoring and may need to be changed more often than in better economic times. It is important to remember the negative implications of

Exhibit 2.4   The trade cycle

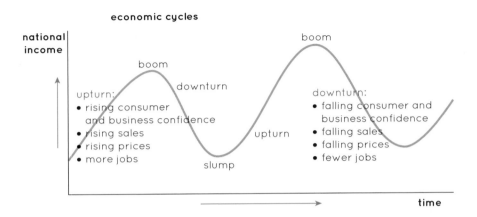

reducing prices though. For example, a low price may be associated with lower quality (see Chapter 10).

Just as some companies are said to be recession-proof, so are some individuals (i.e. the very rich). Businesses that target wealthy consumers, e.g. top designers such as Christian Dior and luxury goods makers such as Rolex, are less likely to suffer significant drops in sales because of downward shifts in the world economy. Income distribution is as important as average income. In some countries (e.g. Saudi Arabia) a small proportion of the population controls the bulk of the country's considerable wealth.

A firm that understands the economic environment in which it operates is far better placed to take advantage of changes in income and spending. Even a recession can be turned to competitive advantage by well-informed and talented marketers.

EXPAND YOUR KNOWLEDGE

Woodall, T. (2012) 'Driven to excess? Linking calling, character and the (mis)behaviour of marketers', *Journal of Marketing Theory*, 12 (2): 173–91.

The author has identified the need for a new approach to marketing that takes account of the changes in the marketing environment, notably: recession, increased emphasis on business ethics and shifting social agendas.

Available at: http://mtq.sagepub.com/content/12/2/173.full.pdf+html

Cadbury: example of economic factors

- Inflation rates are rising in many European countries leading to higher prices for chocolate bars: 49% of UK chocolate eaters would cut back if the price of a bar rose substantially (Mintel, 2012).
- Ongoing recession/low growth rates have resulted in generally lower disposable incomes: less money to spend on luxuries such as chocolate. However, chocolate is possibly recession-proof, i.e. in hard times, consumers spend more on low-price luxuries such as chocolate and overall European sales, although sluggish, are not falling (KPMG, 2012).

THE SOCIAL ENVIRONMENT

The social environment encompasses trends and changes in society, i.e. things that are happening to people. Next to the technological environment, this is the area that has perhaps seen the most changes over the last 50 years. Populations have exploded in some parts of the world (notably China and India), while declining in others (notably the Western nations). This has put a massive strain on the resources of some countries, while the richer nations try to close their doors to a potential flood of immigrants.

IBM:
Future of
Marketing

Things to look for in the social environment include:

- population figures
- age profiles, e.g. many Western nations have ageing populations while in some African countries, where life expectancy is relatively low, the bulk of the population is under 35
- gender balance; ratio of men to women
- lifestyle changes, e.g. a move to urban living, an increase in leisure time, ways in which people spend their time, how people interact (e.g. through online social networking)
- cultural differences, e.g. changes in how children are brought up, changes in men's and women's roles
- religions.

The way we live our lives is changing all the time and products, and marketers, must keep up. It is not so long ago that most women were housewives. Now nearly 70% of UK women are in employment (Goodridge, 2006). In the past, marketers could just target all women's products and household items at housewives. It is not so easy now. They have to address a variety of different types of women, with different lifestyles and different requirements. The result of this has been a boom in **convenience goods**, such as cleaning wipes and ready meals. It has also led a retail revolution as shoppers seek convenience through home delivery services, mail order, Internet shopping and personal shoppers.

convenience goods
products that customers buy frequently and think little about

Cadbury: example of social factors

- Over half (53%) of the UK population are either over-weight or obese, despite increased understanding of the health risks associated with this (Mintel, 2012).
- UK sales of Fairtrade chocolate confectionery grew from £18 million in 2005 to £343 million in 2010 (Fairtrade Foundation, 2011), reflecting the population's increased concern over the ethics of what they buy.

e-focus: Made for sharing

Did you know that there are **hundreds** of social media and network sites worldwide? The top ones are Facebook, Twitter and MySpace but others include Qzone (second most popular site in China), LinkedIn (sixth most popular site in the Netherlands) and Ameblo (eighth most popular site in Japan). Given the popularity of these sites, it seems easy to believe that everyone must be linked in some way over the Internet. While this is not literally true, it is undoubtedly the case that the new technologies that have driven the development of social media in terms of both hardware and software, have had a major impact on social behaviour. They have affected how we communicate with each other and the things we buy. In turn, this has had a huge effect on how marketing is conducted. Consumers exert an ever more powerful influence over the marketplace. Online communities can be powerful consumer interest groups: YouTube shows videos of some of the best and the worst consumer experiences. Customer reviews are posted on Amazon. Friends share their thoughts (and they are not always complimentary) about their latest product purchases, Twitter captures what is going on moment by moment, perhaps from a restaurant or an event while blog sites encourage dialogue over product use. Marketers who ignore the social and market impact of these technologies and social behaviours run the risk of becoming famous for all the wrong reasons.

THE TECHNOLOGICAL ENVIRONMENT

In the last two centuries, technology has changed at an unprecedented rate. In the developed nations, people have moved from a way of life based on agriculture, to industry with its mass production, and on to jobs in a microprocessor-based service economy. The Most Developed Countries (MDCs) are now becoming post-industrial information- and communication-based societies.

Rates of technological advancement vary across the world. It would be expected that the MDCs would have all the latest technology while Lesser Developed Countries (LDCs) lagged behind – and this is generally speaking true. However, international marketers must be careful about making assumptions about countries' readiness to accept types of goods based on their level of economic development alone. It is not uncommon to see colour televisions and satellite dishes in basic homes in poorer countries. Such luxuries can be status symbols that people are prepared to go without basics in order to obtain. There is also the phenomenon of technology skipping, where a developing country misses a whole generation of technology and jumps in at the next level. For example, in parts of Africa mobile phones are common while there are no landlines – the distances are too great to make it viable to install telephone wires. Never make assumptions about other countries – always check.

What to look for in the technological environment:

- new types of technology, especially information technology (IT) or computers but also production technology
- changes in transport, e.g. high-speed train lines
- changes in communications technologies, e.g. the increased presence of large digital screens in shopping centres
- convergence of technologies, e.g. that of computers and telecommunications to produce smartphones
- increased availability of existing technologies, e.g. of high-speed communications networks (e.g. broadband) or of digital television
- new software, especially where there are changes in lifestyle, e.g. social media networking, personal web pages and blogs
- green technologies, e.g. electric cars, solar panels, better recycling facilities.

Burberry: Smartphone Marketing Strategy

Technology has made parts of the world much richer but, from the nineteenth-century factory wreckers to the twentieth-century print workers (who went on strike against the introduction of computerised printing equipment in the 1980s), technological change has always been resisted.

EXPAND YOUR KNOWLEDGE

Järvinen, J., Tollinen, A., Karjaluoto, H. and Jayawardhena, C. (2012) 'Digital and social media marketing usage in b2b industrial section', *Marketing Management Journal,* 22 (2): 102–17.

This paper presents an overview of the usage, measurement practices and barriers surrounding digital marketing in the era of social media. It also provides a useful summary of other studies in the b2b sector.

It is not just businesses that are affected by changes in technology: consumers' lives would be radically different if technology had not progressed at the pace it has. Houses would be colder and a lot less convenient. The kitchen would be a very different place in which to cook. Hygiene standards would be lower as hot water would be a more complicated treat. There would be fewer home offices if the recent advances in communications and personal computing had not happened.

ACTIVITY

Look around your room. Are there any items in it that wouldn't have existed 20 years ago? What about ten years ago? And of the things that did exist, would you have been likely to own them?

Technological change has far-reaching effects. Its impact can be felt right across the external environment. Technology, and the ability to innovate, are key determinants of competitiveness.

Many external factors could reasonably be placed in several of the PRESTCOM categories. For example, there are overlaps between the technological environment and the social environment. Think, for example, of the different views on the use of mobile phones in public, or noisy personal stereos. There are still recycling resisters and climate change deniers but many have changed the way they live to try and conserve the earth.

There is increasing concern about the way we have exploited the planet on which we live. Any responsible analysis must take into account the impact that a firm's marketing will have on the world around us – the Earth is rich in resources but these are not limitless. There is a growing trend towards only harvesting things that can be replaced or regrown. Wooden and paper goods proudly declare it if they are made from sustainable sources. Organic food has become big business in the UK, where consumers are worried about pesticides and genetically modified (GM) products.

3D Printed
Jumbo Jet

The technological environment has to be watched very carefully. Most environmental changes happen quite slowly, over a considerable period of time, but a technological breakthrough can change an organisation's prospects overnight. Long-established businesses often lose their market leadership to younger rivals with better technology.

Swiss watches used to be reckoned to be the best in the world, until the Japanese put microprocessors in theirs. IBM, once the undisputed leader in almost all forms of computing, lost out to Microsoft's more user-friendly Windows operating system. Cars and planes harmed the railway industry and vinyl has become a niche market thanks to the invention of CDs, which have in turn lost out to downloads, iPods and other multimedia devices. How long will DVDs be on our shelves?

Cadbury: example of technological factors

- Scientists are searching for healthier versions of chocolate and there have been a number of successes in this area, along with product innovations such as bubbly chocolate which is pumped with air and crispy chocolate bars made with puffed rice.

- Advances in packaging improve the shelf life of the bars and the ability of the chocolate to withstand heat. Kraft are working on packaging that is easier to re-seal which it is hoped will have the effect of encouraging people to eat less at one sitting (Brooks, 2012).

THE COMPETITIVE ENVIRONMENT

Michael Porter on the Five Forces

The competitive environment (see Exhibit 2.5) is part of the external environment.

Some industries are more competitive than others. For example, the rivalry between UK supermarkets is high, with frequent price undercutting and heavy promotional activity. Some firms are arch-rivals. Often these companies are vying for each other's **market share** – perhaps to take over as the market leader. PepsiCo and Coca-Cola, for instance, compete fiercely, as do Nike and Adidas. Other companies may opt for **coopetition** i.e. they cooperate, most commonly in research and new product development, up to a point. The finishing touches on the Citroen C1, the Toyota Aygo and the Peugeot 107 may be different but they are basically the same car (*Top Gear*, 2008).

Another example, this time from the market research world, is that of AC Nielsen and Symphony IRI, both internationally renowned market research companies, especially in the field of consumer packaged goods (CPG) marketing. Despite a history of bitter rivalry and long-running court battles over anti-competitive practices, the companies formed a coopetition alliance in order to develop, recruit and retain a shared **consumer panel**. They shared the panel members but not

market share
a firm's sales expressed as a percentage of the total sales of that type of product in the defined market

coopetition
when competitors cooperate with each other for mutual benefit, e.g. by sharing research costs

consumer panel
a primary research technique that seeks the views, attitudes, behaviour or buying habits of a group of consumers

Exhibit 2.5   The competitive environment

competitors
- direct
- close
- substitute
- indirect

the data. Each company uses the panel to collect their own data on household purchases and use.

EXPAND YOUR KNOWLEDGE

Dagnino, G. and Padula, G. (2002) 'Coopetition strategy: a new kind of interfirm dynamics for value creation', The European Academy of Management Conference, Stockholm, vol. 9, May, pp 9–11. Available at: http://ecsocman.hse.ru/data/977/644/1219/coopetition.pdf

This paper proposes a definition of coopetition, advances a typology of coopetition and clarifies the role of coopetition strategy within strategic management, organisation theory and managerial practice.

The first thing to work out is: who are the competition? Competitive products can be categorised as: direct, close, substitute or indirect.

Direct competition

A direct competitor offers a product or service that is similar to the company's own. For example, Heineken is a direct competitor to Carlsberg, just as Coca-Cola is to Pepsi.

Close competition

A close competitor offers a similar product – one that satisfies the same need. Other soft drinks, such as Tango, can be said to be close competitors of Coca-Cola and Pepsi. Close competition might be said to extend to any drink, in fact.

Substitute competition

These are products that are different from the company's own, but might be bought instead. Again, they satisfy the same or similar needs. An ice cream is a substitute product for a chocolate bar – either can be eaten as a sweet snack.

Indirect competition

This is competition in its widest sense. People have limited amounts of money to spend and so all products compete for that spending ability. A woman may go out to buy a jacket but then see an irresistible pair of shoes. If she does not have the money for both, the jacket and shoes are in competition.

Firms analyse the competitive environment to see how they compare with rivals, and to try to understand their competitors' strategies – what they are doing now and what they intend to do in the future. This is essential if the firm is to develop counter-strategies and maintain, or improve, its market position.

Substitutes for a cross-channel trip: plane, ferry and Eurostar.

EXPAND YOUR KNOWLEDGE

Classic article

Slater, S. and Narver, J. (1994) 'Does competitive environment moderate the market orientation-performance relationship?', *Journal of Marketing*, 58 (Jan): 46–55.

These authors have been instrumental in maintaining a research interest on issues related to market orientation. In this paper, they address issues pertaining to the effect of competitive environment on the adoption of orientation.

Things to look for in the competitive environment include:

- the main competitors
- the relative strengths of competitors, e.g. in terms of resources or control of the distribution channel
- who is the market leader?
- how the companies or brands compete, e.g. on price or through product differentiation
- the ferocity of the competition; frequent price wars or very high marketing spends suggest high levels of competition
- the nature of competitive products – are they direct, indirect, close or substitute (see above)? – and the relative strengths of those products
- the structure of the industry, e.g. is it dominated by one or two large companies or brands or are there lots of small ones (a fragmented industry)?
- competitors' action and intentions.

Despite the growing internationalisation of business, a company entering a new market is likely to find itself facing at least some new competitors. For example, Coca-Cola and Pepsi Cola lead the market in most countries across the globe, except in India. In India, the favoured cola drink was Thums Up. Coca-Cola was finding it unusually hard to compete against Thums Up and Pepsi at the same time. The strategy they eventually settled on was to buy the Thums Up company.

Cadbury: example of competitive factors

- The UK confectionery market is dominated by Kraft (owners of Cadbury's), Mars and Nestle who have 76% market share between them. Thornton's and Ferrero are 4th and 5th respectively (Mintel, 2012). There are a number of successful niche players, notably in high end products, e.g. Hotel Chocolat; in ethical products, e.g. Montezuma's; and in healthier products, e.g. Tasty Little Numbers.
- Innovation is an important competitive weapon in this market with twice the number of new product launches in 2011 than in 2010. Own label products, such as supermarket brands, are a significant contributor to the increased consumer choice, accounting for 44% of new product launches (Mintel, 2012).

THE ORGANISATIONAL ENVIRONMENT (THE INTERNAL ENVIRONMENT)

The organisational heading in the PRESTCOM analysis is the only one that concerns internal factors, i.e. things that are particular to the company in question. This includes the organisation's structure as well as its assets (people and their skills, money, brands, buildings and machinery, etc.).

Exhibit 2.6   The internal environment

There are five basic functions within a business (see Exhibit 2.6), of which marketing is one. It is important that these functions work well together and support each other. This requires good communication between staff and a culture that encourages interaction and mutual support. If all functions display a **customer orientation** (see Chapter 1), then this harmony will be easier to achieve. One of the key things that the company wishes to achieve from this cooperation is a consistent image.

In analysing an organisation's internal resources, the analyst is looking for sources of advantage and disadvantage. For the purposes of marketing planning, these should be of relevance to the marketing function (although that does not mean that they will always be contained within the marketing department).

Things to look for in the organisational environment include:

- key products and brands
- the quality of personnel, e.g. do they have the best engineers?
- staff turnover; do they keep their key staff?
- the state of the company's finances and the size of budgets
- production facilities, e.g. are they the most advanced in the industry? Are they out of date?
- comparative costs; which will affect prices and profits
- strength of the company's balance sheet; are they secure? Can they afford to invest?
- reputation
- suitability of premises, e.g. is the shop attractive?
- strength of the Research and Development (R&D) department
- facilities, e.g. do they own factories or contract out to others? Do they have their own shops?
- location of outlets
- access to transport.

customer orientation the whole organisation is focused on the satisfaction of its customers' needs

Cadbury: example of organisational factors

- Cadbury sponsored the Olympic Games in London 2012, describing themselves as 'Official Treat Provider' (Cadbury, 2012).
- Cadbury has a strong corporate brand name in the UK and across the world, as well as a wide range of well-known, popular branded products. Some, e.g. Dairy Milk, are Fairtrade products.

THE MARKET ENVIRONMENT

The market environment is part of the external environment. In modern marketing terms, the word 'market' is most often used to refer to customers or consumers. Increasingly, the recipients of goods or services are referred to as customers even when they are not paying, as in the case of charities and other not-for-profit organisations. This is an attempt to improve the effectiveness of organisations by focusing their attention on the people they exist to serve (see the section on customer orientation in Chapter 1).

Markets can be classified according to the customers within them. The major customer groups are described below:

- Individuals, i.e. consumer markets: where private individuals buy goods for their own use, or perhaps to give to someone else. For some purchases, a distinction can be made between customers (who pay for products) and consumers (who use the products). For example, children's clothes are bought by adults (customers) but worn by children (consumers) – both groups are important.
- Businesses, which may be either industrial or b2b (business to business):

  o Industrial buyers use the products they buy as an ingredient, or component, in the making of something else (e.g. Peugeot buying tyres to fit on to new cars) or to contribute directly to the manufacturing process (e.g. oil for machinery). Those tyres could, of course, have been bought by an individual to replace the worn-out tyres on their own car, and that would be a consumer purchase and come from a different source (and be almost certainly more expensive).
  o Organisations also need general supplies, office stationery, etc., which they use rather than make something with it. The sale of such goods is a b2b market.

- Government/public sector – governments are extremely large customers, spending millions on goods and services annually.
- Resellers, i.e. those who sell on the products they buy to someone else, such as wholesalers, distributors, dealers, franchisees (see Chapter 9).
- Overseas markets, i.e. all the above, but in other countries.

Exhibit 2.7   Markets

Things to look for in the market environment include:

- who the customers, consumers, users are; develop customer profiles
- how purchase decisions are made
- what the key influences are on purchase choices
- how brand loyal customers are
- motivations to buy
- how much typical customers spend, and how often
- size of the market for the products in question; in terms of sales volume and sales value
- customers' media habits, e.g. do they read newspapers? which ones? how much time do they spend surfing? do they have smartphones, iPads, etc.?
- customer attitudes to the products, the company, other relevant factors, e.g. green issues.

sales volume
the quantity of goods sold, expressed in units, e.g. 2 million apples

sales value
the revenue derived from items sold

EXPAND YOUR KNOWLEDGE

Classic article

Kotler, P., Gregor, W. and Rogers, W. (1977) 'The marketing audit comes of age', *Sloan Management Review*, 18 (2): 25–43.

Key areas of marketing are identified and put together in a comprehensive 'audit'. The audit forms an essential part of the analysis process that will eventually form the basis of marketing plans.

customer focus: A computer with a personal touch

Probably the most significant influence on marketing in the last decade of the twentieth century came from the technological environment. The Internet has had a huge effect on the way we market goods and services. A debate has raged over whether the Internet is a whole new marketplace or just another channel to market or new medium. That debate seems to have settled down now in favour of new channel/new medium, but still the impact of this technology has been greater than that of previous innovations, such as telemarketing.

The power of the computing technology behind the Internet has allowed companies to collect enormous amounts of information on visitors to their sites. What's more, they can use this information to address customers on an individual basis. This personalised, one-to-one marketing is far more subtle and effective than the old direct mail techniques ever were. Where *Reader's Digest's* mailers would address you by name throughout the text, Amazon's website knows who your favourite authors are and what kind of music you like. You get personal recommendations, your own page showing which items you've looked at – even an invitation to sell your past purchases online, with an estimate of their worth.

Cross-selling is so much easier with all that computer power behind you. Before a visitor checks out of Amazon's site, a list pops up: 'Other customers who bought items in your basket, also bought...'

Cadbury: example of market factors

- 77% of British people eat snacks between meals. Chocolate remains a favourite snack and is viewed as an inexpensive indulgence by many (Mintel, 2012).
- The European and North American chocolate market is seasonal with peaks at Easter and Christmas. Chocolate, especially luxury chocolate, is increasingly given as a gift (Mintel, 2012).

THE INTERNATIONAL MARKETING ENVIRONMENT

The PRESTCOM model can be adapted for use in international situations, along with the addition of three Cs:

Political   +
Regulatory   **M**arket
Economic   **C**urrency
Social   **C**ulture
Technological
Competitive
Organisational
Country

PRESTCOM

The international marketing environment is very much more complex than the domestic one – not least because no two countries are alike and researchers therefore need to conduct PRESTCOM analyses for each and every country in which the company trades (see Exhibit 2.8).

Exhibit 2.8 International environments

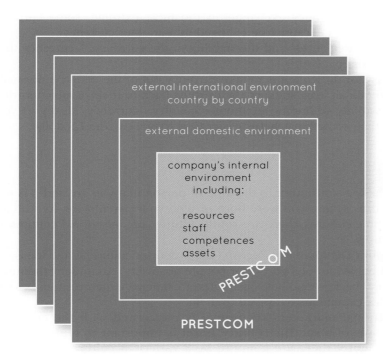

THE THREE CS

Country

A country's history and geography should be taken into account when designing and implementing plans.

Things to look for include:

- the relationship between countries; Britain has very good relations with a number of its ex-colonies (many of which belong to the Commonwealth), but not with all, e.g. Zimbabwe
- geography and climate can affect a country's suitability for certain products and the ease, or otherwise, with which they can be distributed; some countries are remote and inaccessible, e.g. Tibet, which is politically inaccessible as well as being surrounded by the Himalayan mountains
- infrastructure, e.g. transport links, business agencies, distributors; e.g. many landlocked African countries have roads that are too rough to carry trucks of goods safely to their destinations.

Currency

Most countries have their own currency and products will normally have to be sold in that currency.

Things to look for include:

- the ease of currency exchange; at the most extreme, some currencies are unconvertible, i.e. cannot be changed into another currency
- exchange rates; levels and the stability of the currency; a currency that varies wildly is risky
- how easy, or difficult, it is to take currency out of the country; normally, firms want to take at least some of their profits back to their home countries
- the possibility of trading in another country's currency, ideally to your own; failing that, something that is easier to manage, e.g. the US dollar.

Culture
(Geert
Hofstede)

Culture

Culture is a key contributor to the kind of person that you are and it is not solely determined by where you were born or who your parents are. As well as ethnic or geographic cultures, there are youth cultures, organisational cultures and religious cultures.

The *Oxford Dictionary of English* (2005) defines culture as 'the ideas, customs, and social behaviour of a particular people or society'. An understanding of a person's cultural background helps marketers to anticipate their responses to products and to tailor campaigns to appeal to them.

International marketers are primarily concerned with the culture shared by the people of a specific country, but it is important to remember that even within a country there are going to be a variety of cultures. Just take a walk down London's Oxford Street and see if you think all the people there share the same cultural background – well, perhaps they are all part of a consumer culture at least.

ACTIVITY

Visit a place that is popular with tourists or, if that's not possible, watch one on television or just imagine one. How do the people there differ from each other? How do you know that they are from different countries? Can you tell (without actually asking them) where they are from?

Things to look for include:

- language
- beliefs
- attitudes
- customs

- superstitions
- uses for products
- the way the people of a country live.

When language lets us down, we often try sign language, or gestures instead, but there is no more a universal understanding of gestures than there is of words. In many countries it is extremely rude to point, whereas in others it is just a normal way to indicate something. On the Indian subcontinent, people shake their head for yes and nod for no; in Europe, it is the other way around. The holding up of the index and middle fingers (or even just the middle finger) is very rude in the UK, but a sign that is not readily understood elsewhere. It can make it quite dangerous for foreigners to count on their fingers in Britain. Even in the UK, it makes a huge difference if you hold the hand the other way, palm out, as the two fingers then symbolise peace. And, if we go back to the end of the Second World War, when British Prime Minister Winston Churchill first used the gesture, he was not being rude – his two fingers symbolised victory.

© Reg Speller/Hulton Archive/Getty Images

Winston Churchill's V for Victory.

ACTIVITY

Choose three countries (one can be your own) and investigate their most popular sporting event(s). You can do this either through an Internet search or by discussing sport with people who have been involved, either as players or spectators, in other countries. What happens around the match/race/contest? What do spectators do? Does anything happen on the pitch/court/track etc. that is extraneous to the sporting action (e.g. cheerleading)? What does this tell you about the similarities and differences between the peoples of those countries?

These cultural differences make the world a more interesting place but are a minefield for unwary international marketers.

SITUATION ANALYSIS

It is very hard (and usually spectacularly unsuccessful) to plan a route ahead without an understanding of the starting point. Take the example of a journey to London. The travel agent is going to need to know the journey's starting point before they can possibly recommend a method of travel. It makes a big difference whether the traveller is currently in Paris, New York or Leicester.

Similarly, a company needs to know where it stands at the moment before it can make plans to improve its position. Acquisition of another chain might well be a suitable way for a large chain of stores with a dominant market position to grow, but a smaller chain, with fewer resources, is unlikely to be able to do this.

Planning using SOSTAC

An analysis of the current situation is the starting point for most plans. It tells a firm where it is now.

The basic planning process looks like this:

Where are we now?
(situation analysis)

↓

Where do we want to be?
(objectives)

↓

How will we get there?
(the plan)

↓

Are we on the right route?
and
How will we know when we've arrived?
(evaluation and control)

There are a number of techniques and models that the organisation can use to analyse its situation, the most widely used of which is a SWOT analysis. This analysis is based on organising environmental data gleaned from a PRESTCOM environmental analysis.

ACTIVITY

Pick a company that is in the news. What has been going on in its environment that has helped put it there?

SWOT

A SWOT analysis is a general management tool rather than being peculiar to marketing. However, it is widely used as a basis for marketing planning. Selected environmental variables from the PRESTCOM analysis (see page 60) are placed under one of the four SWOT headings:

Strengths   internal, i.e. under the organisation's control, e.g. well-developed brand

Weaknesses   internal, i.e. under the organisation's control, e.g. small budget

Opportunities   external, i.e. not under the organisation's control, e.g. favourable fashion trend

Threats   external, i.e. not under the organisation's control, e.g. unfavourable fashion trend

Strengths and weaknesses are internal factors, while opportunities and threats are external. So, only organisational factors go into strengths or weaknesses; the rest of the PRESTCOM analysis is external and so feeds into opportunities or threats.

A strength is something that the firm has, or something that it does, that is better than its competitors. For example, a stronger brand name would be a strength.

A weakness is the opposite of a strength: something that the firm has (or does not have) or does that is worse than the competition. For example, an outdated product range would be a weakness.

Threats and opportunities are part of the external environment and therefore an organisation will have far less (if any) control over them.

A threat is something that is going on in the firm's external environment that is likely to cause it problems. The drinks industry is threatened by proposed regulations that will make it much more difficult to promote alcohol.

An opportunity is the opposite of a threat: it is something that is going on in the external environment that is likely to be good for the organisation. For example, an upturn in the economy is an opportunity for many firms.

Opportunities have deliberately been left until last as they seem to be the cause of much student confusion. It is important to realise that the word 'opportunity'

Social
Media
SWOT
Analysis

SWOT analysis
a situational
analysis tool
that assesses the
organisation's
strengths and
weaknesses
(internal) and
opportunities and
threats (external)

is being used in a very particular way here: *an opportunity is not an action*. It is not something that the firm could *do*. It is just something good that is happening outside that the firm might be able to take advantage of – somehow.

Further examples of possible opportunities are:

- the election of a government that is pro-foreign trade in one of the firm's export markets
- the relaxation of rules governing what can and what cannot be sponsored
- low interest rates
- a baby boom
- digital iTV
- a competitor going out of business
- a new store opening locally.

Not all of these opportunities will apply to all organisations. For example, the last one (the new local store) may only be of relevance to local suppliers – but, to them, it is clearly a great opportunity. They may be able to sell more. How they go about persuading the store to stock their products (if indeed they decide that they want to do that) comes further along in the planning process. The SWOT analysis just identifies that an opportunity exists.

A comprehensive SWOT analysis would take account of all elements of PRESTCOM, however a SWOT analysis should be concise, covering key factors only. Strengths and weaknesses should focus on competitive advantages or disadvantages. Opportunities and threats should be significant to the organisation.

sponsorship giving financial aid, or other resources, to an individual, organisation or event in return for a positive association with them, e.g. the Coca-Cola Cup

 Using SWOT analysis at work

ACTIVITY

Pick one of the following companies (or choose your own) and make a list of relevant PRESTCOM trends, issues, events (i.e. environmental variables). Then categorise them under the SWOT headings. Choose from:

- Microsoft
- Virgin
- Gap
- Vodafone.

When you've completed the exercise, check the following points:

- Do all your strengths/weaknesses come from the 'organisation' heading? Are they all particular to the firm and (mainly) its responsibility?
- Do all your opportunities/threats come from the external environment (the other PRESTCOM headings)? Do they all affect other companies too?
- Are any of your opportunities actions or things the company can do? If so, then they are strategies or tactics, *not* opportunities!

- Does the same factor appear under more than one SWOT heading? If so, think about this in more detail. For example, if interest rates appear as opportunities and threats, it may be that low interest rates could be an opportunity and high interest rates a threat.

RANKING
SWOT analysis does not stop at listing the relevant variables under their correct headings – that is just the start. The next task is to rank the variables in order of their importance to the company.

MATCHING
The really interesting bit of the SWOT analysis comes during a process called matching. The firm looks for opportunities that play to its strengths (that match them). If there is an opportunity that matches a strength, then these will be key to the company, and objectives and strategies will be built upon them. For example, AOL merged with Time Warner and so gained access to its cable pipes. This coincided with increased interest from customers in broadband services (such cable pipes are needed to deliver broadband). The pipes were an AOL strength, while broadband presented the company with an opportunity. The two matched. The exploitation of this opportunity became a key part of its marketing strategy.

It is also important to watch out for threats that prey upon weaknesses. These are significant threats, and action needs to be taken to reduce their effect. Let's take the example of AOL again. AOL grew into one of the biggest Internet service providers (ISPs) by offering a standard, suits everyone, style of service. As the Internet market matured, people wanted different types of product, e.g. home users wanted something simpler and with more support. AOL did not have this. The standardised service was a weakness that was unfavourably matched by the market's new demand for different types of service.

SUMMARY

No organisation exists in isolation. What is happening in and around it largely determines its ability to succeed in achieving its goals. Monitoring changes in the environment helps a company to spot key opportunities and threats, and forms the basis for sound marketing planning. Some firms do have formal processes for the collection of environmental data but many gather their information in a more ad hoc manner, relying on the judgement and contacts of managers.

There are a number of acronyms that can be used as frameworks for the analysis of the external environment. The one proposed here is PRESTCOM, which encompasses not just the macroenvironment, but the competitive and internal environments as well.

The key environments to be monitored are: political, regulatory (or legal), economic, social, natural, technological, competitive, the organisation itself (internal), distribution and customers (market). When an organisation is trading internationally, it will have to assess these environments in its home country and in all the others in which it trades.

For many firms, the technological environment is a key determinant of competitive edge. Technological change may speed economic growth; provide a means for innovation; alter the way people work, spend their leisure time and even how they think. It can also make an organisation more efficient. Often, technologies, such as production and transport, have an impact upon the natural environment that may need to be watched out for.

Environmental data can be input into a situation analysis using a framework such as SWOT. This categorises and prioritises the information, and so identifies the key opportunities and threats that the organisation should address. That situation analysis then becomes the base upon which the organisation's marketing plans are built.

CHALLENGES REVIEWED

Now that you have finished reading the chapter, look back at the challenges you were set at the beginning. Do you have a clearer idea of what's involved?

HINTS

- Think about PRESTCOM and environmental scanning.
- Again, think about environmental scanning and SWOT and whether the failure of some cafés presents your business with an opportunity.
- This company should have been monitoring groups like Greenpeace, and could therefore have predicted such action and put contingency plans in place.
- There are any number of reasons why you might not have been as creative as your colleague, but one of them may be that you were not keeping up with relevant changes in the technological environment.

READING AROUND

JOURNAL ARTICLES

Dagnino, G. and Padula, G. (2002) 'Coopetition strategy: a new kind of interfirm dynamics for value creation', *The European Academy of Management Conference*, Stockholm, vol. 9, May, pp. 9–11.

Finlay-Robinson, D. (2008) 'What's in it for me? The fundamental importance of stakeholder evaluation', *Journal of Management Development*, 28 (4): 380–8.

Järvinen, J., Tollinen, A., Karjaluoto, H. and Jayawardhena, C. (2012) 'Digital and social media marketing usage in b2b industrial section', *Marketing Management Journal*, 22 (2): 102–17.

Kotler, P., Gregor, W. and Rogers, W. (1977) 'The marketing audit comes of age', *Sloan Management Review*, 18 (2): 25–43.

Oxenfeldt, A. and Moore, W. (1978) 'Customer or competitor: which guideline for marketing?', *Management Review*, Aug: 43–8.

Pickton, D. and Wright, S. (1998) 'What's SWOT in strategic analysis?', *Strategic Change*, 7 (2): 101–9. (A critical commentary of SWOT analysis.)

Slater, S. and Narver, J. (1994) 'Does competitive environment moderate the market orientation-performance relationship?', *Journal of Marketing*, 58 (Jan): 46–55.

Woodall, T. (2012) 'Driven to excess? Linking calling, character and the (mis)behaviour of marketers', *Journal of Marketing Theory*, 12 (2): 173–91.

MAGAZINE ARTICLES

Cadwalldr, C. (2012) 'Satellites in the shed? TEDGlobal announces the new DIY revolution', *The Observer*, Sunday, 1 July 2012; available at: **http://www.theguardian.com/technology/2012/jul/01/build-satellite-shed-new-diy-revolution** (accessed 17/02/14) – possible social and technological futures.

Loo, T., Wu, M. and Huang, F. (2013) '10 Chinese consumer trends', *Admap*, February; available at: **www.warc.com** (accessed 23/07/13).

BOOKS AND BOOK CHAPTERS

Harvard Business School (2006) 'Competitor analysis', in *Marketer's Toolkit: The 10 Strategies You Need to Succeed*, Harvard Business Essentials series. Boston: Harvard Business School Publishing Corporation, Chapter 3.

Worthington, I. and Britton, C. (2009) *The Business Environment* (6th edn). Harlow: Prentice Hall.

MAGAZINES

The Economist

WEBSITES

www.cia.gov/library/publications/the-world-factbook/ – the Central Intelligence Agency's (CIA) view of the world.

www.europa.eu – statistics and other information on the European Union.

www.oxygen.mintel.com – consumer and market insights; you will need a subscription to view full Mintel reports or your university may well have one.

www.statistics.gov.uk – check out the latest UK social trends.

www.wto.org – the World Trade Organisation's website.

SELF-REVIEW QUESTIONS

1. Define marketing environment. (See p. 50)
2. What are uncontrollables? (See p. 55)
3. What are the two ways in which environmental information is used? (See p. 55)
4. How is environmental data gathered? (See p. 57)
5. What does PRESTCOM stand for? (See p. 60)
6. Name three ways in which the political environment can impact upon a firm's marketing operations. (See p. 62)
7. List four characteristics of a downturn that would adversely affect a firm's ability to sell its goods. Why is that? (See p. 68)
8. What are social costs? Why do some people think that companies should account for them? (See p. 67)
9. Under which PRESTCOM heading would you place changes in a country's transport infrastructure, e.g. new high speed rail links? (See p. 71)
10. List and describe four types of competition. (See pp. 73–4)
11. What are the five main internal functions of a business? (See p. 77)
12. What is an opportunity within a SWOT analysis? What is the key difference between opportunities and threats, and strengths and weaknesses in a SWOT analysis? (See pp. 85–6)

Mini case study: Haircare: hygiene or high fashion?

Read the questions, then the case material, and then answer the questions.

Questions

1 Using the information in the case, and information from other sources e.g. Mintel or Keynote, do a PRESTCOM analysis for L'Oreal.

2 Now do a SWOT analysis.

3 If you were a marketing consultant, what advice would you give to a haircare company? Your suggestions should be based on your analysis of the case and they should all be *explained* and *justified*.

For some, choosing haircare products is simple. After all, the point is to end up with clean hair, isn't it? So the cheapest shampoo will do. Other people spend significant amounts of time and money on their haircare. They don't just buy shampoo, but look for the very best in conditioners, styling products and dyes. After all, you wear your hair every day, don't you? So why wouldn't you take at least as much time with it as you do in choosing your clothes.

Fashions in hairstyles change as often as those in clothing styles. Celebrity hairstyles can make the news and attract as much comment as their clothes, bags and shoes do. The film and pop stars who make the trends often have their own personal hairdressers on hand, but most people cannot afford such luxury and so they need help from gels, mousses and other miracle products to make their curly hair poker straight or to coax their straight hair into curls. Then, thanks to all that frequent washing and blow-drying, their heat-damaged hair needs yet more products to make it shine.

The fashionistas have added value to the haircare sector but this market has been adversely affected by changes in the economy. The first decade of the twenty-first century has seen one of the deepest recessions in living memory. Many jobs have been lost, pay packets have shrunk and people have had to give up some of their luxuries, e.g. trips to the hairdresser. Shampoo is an essential purchase for most people but shoppers have been buying own labels and cheaper brands or value packs, or looking out for price promotions. Clever shoppers wait for the promotions and then stock up with their preferred brands. Western Europe's ageing population is another problem for the haircare brands because older consumers tend to wash their hair less frequently and use fewer products. Conditioner sales have been even worse hit than shampoos; some consumers have cut conditioning from their haircare routine altogether. Women are still far more likely to buy conditioner than men; just over one-third of men use this type of product, compared with three-quarters of women.

Manufacturers have also had to deal with increasing consumer concern about the negative environmental impact of haircare products which find their way into oceans and water supplies. Recycling of packaging is also an issue.

Global demand for L'Oreal's premium brands, which include Lancôme and Kiehl's, has fallen sharply. Retailers have cut their orders and some manufacturers have responded with lower prices to try to stimulate sales. In an attempt to revitalise the market, L'Oreal's scientists are developing new products for mass-market brands, such as Maybelline New York and L'Oreal Paris.

In 2007, retail sales of shampoo and conditioner reached £706 million, dropping to £700 million in 2008 and Mintel predicts they will fall further. Shampoo has the biggest share of the market with sales of £391 million in 2009.

Hairdressers have also been hit hard as women visit them less often. Some of the premium haircare brands have responded to this trend by launching products with salon-finish quality or longer colour maintenance benefits.

This is a highly segmented market presenting marketing opportunities for a variety of differentiated products. Shampoos are available for different hair types, hair colours and hair lengths. Frizzy hair can be tamed or thin hair volumised. Older hair can be rejuvenated or children's sensitive eyes protected from accidental contact with shampoo. Combined shampoo and conditioner products such as Elvive 2 in 1 were in decline before the recession hit and manufacturers seem to be phasing them out. L'Oreal still markets these products to children and men, but has dropped them from most of its adult women's ranges. They tend to be more popular among men who want convenience rather than the more exotic benefits promised by so many female brands. Nivea have responded to this need with Men Active 3: a combined shower gel, shampoo and shaving foam.

Procter & Gamble is very strong in this sector with a 36% market share. Brands such as Head & Shoulders and Herbal Essences are long-time favourites with customers and P&G has continued to innovate through the recession and has kept up its advertising. It launched a new range of men's haircare products under its Gillette brand name and these are building market share. Although women still spend far more on haircare, there is a growing trend among men, especially younger men, to purchase more grooming products.

Johnson & Johnson is another key competitor. Its strong brand positioning in babycare makes it ideally placed to take advantage of opportunities presented by the rising number of under 4-year-olds in the UK.

Unilever has been pushing its Timotei brand, launching variants including Golden Highlights, Soft & Smooth and Strengthen &

Shine. It also extended its Dove brand with the addition of the Therapy range, offering colour protection and intensive conditioning.

Meanwhile L'Oreal cut its ad budget for the Garnier Fructis brand and focused its attention instead on its Elvive brand, possibly because of its purchase of The Body Shop in 2006. Sales have dropped by almost 54% since 2007, according to Mintel.

SOURCES: Keynote, 2008; Mintel, 2009; WARC, 2009; Wood, 2009.

REFERENCES

Academy of Medical Royal Colleges (2012) 'Medical profession united in fight to defuse obesity time-bomb'. Available at: http://www.aomrc.org.uk/about-us/news/item/medical-profession-united-in-fight-to-defuse-obesity-time-bomb.html (accessed 17/02/14).

Allen, R. (ed.) (2000) *New Penguin English Dictionary*. Harmondsworth: Penguin.

BBC News (2008) 'Bolivia nationalises energy firms'. Available at: news.bbc.co.uk/1/hi/business/7378803.stm (accessed 28/02/10).

BBC News (2012) 'Bolivia takeover: Spain dismayed by TDE nationalisation'. Available at: www.bbc.co.uk/news/world-latin-america-17922069 (accessed 05/05/12).

Brooks, J. (2012) '£6m Kraft pack will make Dairy Milk re-sealable', *Packaging News*, 3 January.

Brownlie, D. (2000) 'Environmental scanning', in M.J. Baker (ed.), *The Marketing Book* (4th edn). London: Butterworth Heinemann, pp. 81–107.

Department for Education (2012) 'Departmental advice for school food in England: Food-based standards for school food other than lunch'. Available at: www.education.gov.uk/aboutdfe/advice/f00197541/departmental-advice-for-school-food-in-england/food-based-standards-for-school-food-other-than-lunch (accessed 19/06/12).

Department of Health (2012) 'Calorie reduction pledge delivery plans published'. Available at: https://responsibilitydeal.dh.gov.uk/f4-delivery-plans-published/ (accessed 17/02/14).

Doyle, P. (2006) *Marketing Management and Strategy* (4th edn). Harlow: FT Prentice Hall.

Dagnino, G. and Padula, G. (2002) 'Coopetition strategy: a new kind of interfirm dynamics for value creation', The European Academy of Management Conference, Stockholm; available at: http://ecsocman.hse.ru/data/977/644/1219/coopetition.pdf (accessed 29/06/12).

Europa (2012) 'Summaries of EU legislation: cocoa and chocolate'. Available at: http://europa.eu/legislation_summaries/consumers/product_labelling_and_packaging/l21122b_en.htm (accessed 19/06/12).

European Commission (2012a) 'The economy'. Available at: http://europa.eu/about-eu/facts-figures/economy/index_en.htm (accessed 05/05/12).

European Commission (2012b) 'Member states of the EU'. Available at: http://europa.eu/about-eu/countries/index_en.htm (accessed 05/05/12).

Fairtrade Foundation (2011) 'Fairtrade and cocoa: commodity briefing'. Available at: http://www.fairtrade.org.uk/includes/documents/cm_docs/2011/C/Cocoa%20Briefing%20FINAL%208Sept11.pdf (accessed 17/02/14).

Finch, J. (2007) 'How Tate and Lyle went sour', *The Guardian*, 29 September, p. 41.

Finlay-Robinson, D. (2008) 'What's in it for me? The fundamental importance of stakeholder evaluation', *Journal of Management Development*, 28 (4): 380–8.

Freeman, R. (1984) *Strategic Management: A Stakeholder Approach*. London: Pitman.

Goodridge, P. (2006) 'Labour market analysis and summary'. London: HMSO. Also available at: **www.statistics.gov.uk/downloads/theme_labour/LMT_Dec06.pdf** (accessed 20/07/07).

Järvinen, J., Tollinen, A., Karjaluoto, H. and Jayawardhena, C. (2012) 'Digital and social media marketing usage in b2b industrial section', *Marketing Management Journal,* 22 (2): 102–17.

Keynote (2008) *Marketing Assessment Clothing and Personal Goods: Men's and Women's Buying Habits*. London: Keynote.

Kotler, P., Gregor, W. and Rogers, W. (1977) 'The marketing audit comes of age', *Sloan Management Review*, 18 (2): 25–43.

Kotler, P., Armstrong, G., Saunders, J. and Wong, V. (2001) *Principles of Marketing* (3rd European edn). Harlow: Pearson Education Ltd.

KPMG (2012) 'Consumer markets: the chocolate of tomorrow'. Available at: **https://www.kpmg.com/UK/en/IssuesAndInsights/ArticlesPublications/Documents/PDF/Market%20Sector/Retail_and_Consumer_Goods/chocolate-of-tomorrow.pdf** (accessed 17/02/14).

Mercer, D. (1995) 'Simpler scenarios', *Management Decision*, 33 (4): 32–40.

Mintel (2009) *Shampoos and Conditioners – 2009 – UK*. London: Mintel.

Mintel (2012) *Chocolate Confectionery – 2012 – UK*. London: Mintel.

Oxenfeldt, A.R. and Moore, W.L. (1978) 'Customer or competitor: which guideline for marketing?', *Management Review*, Aug: 43–8.

Oxford Dictionary of English (2005) Oxford: Oxford University Press.

Pickton, D. and Broderick, A. (2001) *Integrated Marketing Communications*. Harlow: FT Prentice Hall.

Shearman, S. (2012) 'Cadbury's Olympic sponsorship leads to 2.5m social media fans, Marketing. Available at: **http://www.marketingmagazine.co.uk/article/1147152/cadburys-olympic-sponsorship-leads-25m-social-media-fans** (Accessed 17/02/2014).

Slater, S. and Narver, J. (1994) 'Does competitive environment moderate the market orientation-performance relationship?', *Journal of Marketing*, 58 (Jan): 46–55.

Top Gear (2008) 'Credit Crunch City Cars', available at: **www.topgear.com/uk/car-news/crunch-city** (accessed 20/06/12).

Usiner, J.C. and Lee, J.A. (2005) *Marketing Across Cultures* (4th edn). Harlow: FT Prentice Hall.

WARC (2009) 'FMCG giants target male consumers', *WARC News*, 9 September. Available at: **www.warc.com/News/TopNews.asp?ID=25645** (accessed 10/09/09).

Wood, Z. (2009) 'L'Oreal shares jump 10% after firm beats profit forecast', *The Guardian*, 28 August.

Woodall, T. (2012) 'Driven to excess? Linking calling, character and the (mis)behaviour of marketers', *Journal of Marketing Theory,* 12 (2): 173–91.

Visit the companion website on your computer at **www.sagepub.co.uk/masterson3e** or MobileStudy on your Smart phone or tablet by scanning this QR code and gain access to:

- **Videos** to get a better understanding of key concepts and provoke in-class discussion.
- Links to useful **websites and templates** to help guide your study.
- Access **SAGE Marketing Pins (www.pinterest.com/sagepins/)**. SAGE's regularly updated **Pinterest** page, giving you access to regularly updated resources on everything from Branding to Consumer Behaviour.
- **Daily Grind podcast series** to learn more about the day-to-day life of a marketing **professional**.
- Interactive **Practice questions** to test your understanding.
- A **bonus chapter on Marketing Careers** to not only support your study, but your job search and future career.
- **PowerPoints** prompting key points for revision.

3rd edition

Rosalind Masterson & David Pickton

MARKETING

an introduction

Making Sense of Markets

This Part Contains:

3 Buyer behaviour

4 Market segmentation, targeting and positioning

5 Marketing research

Successful marketing depends upon a thorough understanding of customers and consumers, their worlds and their needs. Consequently, marketers spend much time, effort and money on research and analysis. They draw on other social science disciplines to shed further light on their customers' behaviour: economics, psychology and sociology in particular. Such in-depth market understanding confers a valuable competitive advantage.

WHAT THIS PART IS ABOUT

Part II goes behind the scenes and looks at the forces that shape an organisation's marketing activities.

Buyer behaviour 3

BUYER BEHAVIOUR CHALLENGES

The following are illustrations of the types of decision that marketers have to take or issues they face. *You aren't expected to know how to deal with the challenges now*; just bear them in mind as you read the chapter and see what you can find that helps.

- You have developed a brand new product that is a technological breakthrough: a communications implant. A computer chip inside the person's ear is voice-controlled and transmits music, phone calls and other sounds: rather like an internal iPhone. A screen on a wrist strap is optional. It's your job to persuade people to try it. Which types of people are most likely to be the first to use such a product and how would you persuade them to do so?
- You are the product development manager for a small, local brewery. You are hoping to develop a new type of beer that will appeal to people who currently rarely, if ever, drink beer. The marketing director has asked you to identify what influences people when they are deciding whether or not to try a new drink. What sorts of things will you consider?
- You are attempting to sell a computer system to a large government department. You have to give a presentation to the end-users of the computer system, the head of department, the IT manager and an accountant. What criteria do you think they will use to assess the suitability of your computer? Who else should you target within the organisation and who do you think has the most influence?
- *The Apprentice* is a BBC television programme in which young business people compete for a job with Lord Sugar. In one episode, the teams were asked to sell expensive lollipops at a zoo. One contestant's approach was to hand a lollipop to a small child, ask if the child liked it/wanted it – and then charge the parents. What do you think of that idea?

INTRODUCTION

There are a number of well-known sayings about customers, e.g. 'The customer is king' and 'The customer is always right', and it should hardly come as a surprise that marketers invest a great deal of money and effort into finding out about their customers. A company that understands its customers well is far more likely to bring successful products to the market than one that operates on false assumptions.

In Part I the difference between consumers (users) and customers (buyers) was explained. It is important to appreciate the difference. Sometimes customers and consumers are different people, perhaps because a customer buys something for other people to use. Sometimes they are the same. However, it is popular convention when considering buyer behaviour to use these terms interchangeably, which does help distinguish between organisational markets and consumer markets. Following this convention, for the purposes of this chapter, 'customer' and 'consumer' will be used interchangeably unless otherwise specified.

The first part of this chapter focuses on consumers as individuals within a market. It explores how consumers purchase products: how they decide what to buy, and the various stages they may go through in reaching that purchase decision. The chapter goes on to examine what influences them, considering both internal factors (such as their personality or their motivation for buying the product) and external factors (such as friends and family).

Many purchases are made by organisations rather than individuals. The way organisations make decisions is considerably more complex, not least because there are likely to be a number of people involved. The second part of the chapter will look at organisational buying behaviour.

Buyer Behaviour (CIM)

consumer models representations of consumer buying behaviour, usually as diagrams

THE CONSUMER BUYER DECISION PROCESS

Marketers spend large amounts of time and money on attempting to find out how consumers respond to different elements of the marketing mix. There have been many attempts to portray these responses through the creation of **consumer models** of buyer behaviour. These aim to provide frameworks for explaining the stages that consumers pass through in their decisions on whether or not to purchase a product or service.

Engel, Blackwell and Miniard's (2006) model (see Exhibit 3.1) is a well-known example.

Exhibit 3.1 shows the key stages that a consumer passes through in deciding whether or not to buy a product. Although it is more relevant to new or difficult purchases, the model is useful as an aid to understanding all purchases because it shows all the factors facing a consumer when deciding what to buy. The next part of this chapter will look at these stages in more detail.

NEED/PROBLEM RECOGNITION

The decision to buy something begins with a potential customer recognising that they have a problem or an unfulfilled need. This person realises that there is a difference between their current (or actual) state and their desired state (see Exhibit 3.2). In other words, they want something. The trigger for this need may be an internal factor, such as being hungry or thirsty and therefore needing food or drink, or it may come from an external source, such as a suggestion from a friend (e.g. 'let's have a drink'), an advert or the display in a shop window.

Exhibit 3.1   The buyer decision process

SOURCE: adapted from Engel et al (2006)

In this model, and in most other need or problem recognition models, the problem does not have to be serious or life-threatening. For example, imagine you are watching TV and an advert for crisps appears. This may stimulate a desire for a snack even though you are not hungry. There is no serious problem here, you are not even really hungry, but there is a discrepancy between your actual state (snack-less) and your desired state (eating crisps). You have recognised a problem that could be solved by a packet of crisps.

Exhibit 3.2   The process of problem recognition

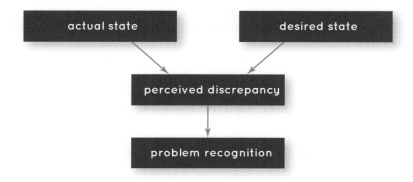

SOURCE: Wilkie, 1990

© Dave Pickton

Sweets at a supermarket checkout are designed to be external triggers to stimulate impulse purchases.

Sometimes the stimulus of a need or problem and its answer are more subtle. The stimulus may well come from inside, perhaps being based on a feeling. For example, some people eat ice cream when they are miserable. The trigger is feeling miserable, the need is to feel better and the ice cream is the means – but clearly something else is happening in their heads between the recognition that they were feeling low, and the decision to make themselves feel better by buying something. Then yet another thought pattern kicked in, which made the decision on what to consume to solve the problem. These decisions are much harder to understand, and to predict, than the simple 'I am thirsty so I will drink' type.

If marketers understand consumers' needs, it is more likely that they will be able to offer goods or services that will satisfy those needs. Clearly it would also help if the marketer understood what was likely to generate and influence those needs. Then they could develop an appropriate marketing mix for the customer.

INFORMATION SEARCH

Once consumers have recognised that they have a need, or a problem, they look for information on how to fix it. This is the information search stage of the decision-making process. The required information may be found internally or externally.

An internal search involves accessing memory and using previous experience. So, for example, if the consumer had felt the need to clean the kitchen sink before, and a particular brand of cleaner had worked well then and so solved the problem, they might buy it again. However, if no satisfactory solution is found within the consumer's memory, then they may have to look for new information elsewhere. External sources of information include, but are not limited to:

- personal sources, such as family and friends
- social networks and online forums
- commercial sources, such as shop assistants, websites and adverts (interestingly, someone who is considering buying, for example, a new laptop PC, tends to notice laptops and adverts for laptops when they might never have registered them before)
- third-party reports, such as magazine comments, newspaper editorials, Watchdog reports, blogs, reviews or webpages.

awareness set
a number of products or brands that may satisfy a customer/ consumer need or solve a problem

The result of this searching, both internal and external, will be that the consumer is aware of a number of different possible solutions to the problem. This list of products may be quite long and is called their **awareness set**, i.e. all the products/ brands that they know of that are possibilities. The rest of the decision-making process is all about cutting that list down until just one product remains – and is bought. Gathering information about the strengths and weaknesses of different products will help turn an awareness set into a more manageable list of serious possibilities (evoked set).

evoked set
the products or brands from which a person will make their purchase choice

ACTIVITY

Choose a product from those below and write out a list of all the brands you have heard of, i.e. build up your own awareness set for that product:

- football boots
- holiday companies
- mascara
- PCs
- tennis racquets
- razors.

Now cut the list down to the brands you would consider buying (your evoked set). What were your choice criteria?

A common objective of advertising is to make consumers aware of products (i.e. to get them in the consumer's awareness set) and to provide consumers with the information they need to make a decision or at least to progress the product to their evoked set. Marketers need to know where the consumers within their target market look for information: newspapers, websites, magazines, Facebook, retailer sites, Google search, etc., and the relative importance of these sources to the consumers. They can then help consumers to make their purchase decision by making sure that the necessary information is easily available.

EVALUATION OF ALTERNATIVES

Ethical Consumers: FairTrade

Once a consumer has discounted the non-starters in their awareness set, e.g. those products that are too expensive, or not available or just really not their style, they start assessing the remaining evoked set of products to see which will work best, i.e. they evaluate the alternatives. An evoked set is a small subset of the consumer's awareness set, which in turn is likely to be only a small part of the total number of alternatives on offer (Howard and Sheth, 1969). Evoked sets differ from consumer to consumer and over time for the same consumer but marketers need to get their products within these sets if they want to make a sale.

The consumer examines the benefits that can be derived from each product's features and considers how well they are likely to satisfy the need (or solve the problem). For example, a drink with a high sugar content (a product feature) has the benefit of providing quick energy and tasting good. The downside is, of course, potentially rotten teeth and excess weight. Different consumers will attach different degrees of importance to different attributes of the product, e.g. a person's view of the high sugar content may depend upon their propensity to put on weight.

e-focus: e-disinformation: Kentucky Fried Monster

The Internet has changed the way many of us decide what to buy and when and where to buy it. Users can browse the Web looking for information, and can also share the information they have with others. Potential customers are able to access not only the official company websites, but also impartial consumer watchdog websites (such as www.which.co.uk), Internet chat rooms, blogs, discussion boards and personal web-pages where information and opinions are available from people who have bought, or at least have opinions about, products and the organisations which supply them. Potential buyers are no longer reliant upon company-controlled sources.

However, the Internet has no official, central controlling body. Anyone can set up a website and post almost anything on to it. While reputable host organisations have rules governing the content within their own sites, no one checks up on all the myriad blogs, boards and emails that have blossomed across the Net. People can say pretty much anything about anyone with little risk of being taken to task about it. This has caused problems for some organisations who have been the subject of hoaxes. These untrue stories may be malicious, but they are usually just mischievous.

One such hoax is the famous chicken-less KFC story which was widely circulated by email. It appeared in a number of variants, one of which is reproduced below. Please do note that the University of New Hampshire denies that any such study ever took place.

'Many people, day in and day out, eat at KFC religiously. Do they really know what they are eating? During a recent study of KFC done at the University of New Hampshire, they found some very upsetting facts.

'First of all, has anybody noticed that just recently, the company has changed their name? Kentucky Fried Chicken has become KFC. Does anybody know why? We thought the real reason was because of the "FRIED" food issue. It's not. The reason why they call it KFC is because they cannot use the word chicken anymore. Why? KFC does not use real chickens. They actually use genetically manipulated organisms. These so called "chickens" are kept alive by tubes inserted into their bodies to pump blood and nutrients throughout their structure. They have no beaks, no feathers, and no feet. Their bone structure is dramatically shrunk to get more meat out of them. This is great for KFC because they do not have to pay so much for their production costs. There is no more plucking of the feathers or the removal of the beaks and feet.

'The government has told them to change all of their menus so they do not say chicken anywhere. If you look closely you will notice this. Listen to their commercials, I guarantee you will not see or hear the word chicken. I find this matter to be very disturbing. I hope people will start to realise this and let other people know.

'Please forward this message to as many people as you can. Together we [can] make KFC start using real chicken again.' (University of New Hampshire, n.d.)

Such hoaxes can cause severe damage to a business and it is hard to get the refutation published as widely as the original story.

For more information on how to spot a hoax, and to see further examples, visit w w w . hoaxbusters.org/.

'Salient attributes' are those that the consumer associates with the product and considers to be important.

It is important to realise that the products in a consumer's evoked set may not be the same kinds of products or even seen as direct competitors by their suppliers. For example, a consumer who wants to relax with a drink may have wine and tea in that same set of possibilities.

Sometimes, consumers may reduce their evoked set to a tighter shortlist which they will test further; they might test drive a few cars for example, or ask for references from a couple of lawyers. This final shortlist is referred to as a consideration, or **purchase consideration set** (see Exhibit 3.3).

The way consumers evaluate products varies from person to person and according to the specific buying situation. They narrow down the possibilities by assessing the products' distinguishing features against their choice criteria (i.e. the things the product must have if it is to solve their problem). They are likely to use a variety

purchase consideration set the mental shortlist of products or brands from which a person will make their final purchase choice

Exhibit 3.3 Moving towards the purchase consideration set

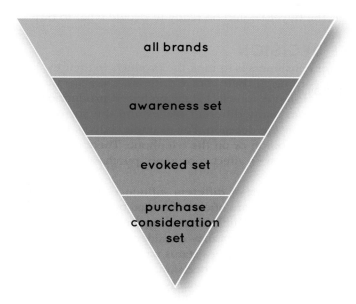

SOURCE: Adapted from Wilkie, 1990

Exhibit 3.4   Criteria for evaluating alternatives

Criteria	Includes
Performance related	Reliability Quality Longevity Specification Style Comfort Taste
Financial	Actual price Price of extras Value for money Credit terms Running costs Depreciation
Social	Status Reputation Perceived image Social acceptability
Personal	Self-image Level of risk Ethics Emotional appeal

of both formal and informal criteria in making their final choice. Typical choice criteria include: price, reliability, service, quality, environmental friendliness, speed of delivery, fashion, status and image (see Exhibit 3.4). Once they have evaluated the alternatives, the buyer should be ready to decide what to buy – if anything.

PURCHASE DECISION

The next stage for consumers is to rank the products in their evoked sets in order of preference (according to their choice criteria). They are then ready to make a **purchase decision**, i.e. to select their preferred product or brand. Purchase decisions are made in many different places and the surroundings can be an important influence on the decision. For example, buyers may be in a shop, on the Internet, at an exhibition or on the telephone. There are, however, a number of influences that are likely to affect consumers' purchase decisions wherever they are (see Exhibit 3.5).

There are a large number of different influences on purchase decision. For example, purchase intentions are often influenced by the attitudes of other people: friends, family, partners, etc. Think of a young teenager going shopping for new clothes with parents. The parents may consider price and reliability to be more important criteria than the teenager's status or self-image. Unexpected situational factors may interfere with purchase decision, e.g. a particular product size or colour may be sold out and so the consumer is forced to make a re-evaluation. These influences are considered in more depth later in the chapter.

purchase decision
the selection of the preferred product to buy

Exhibit 3.5   From evaluation of alternatives to purchase decision

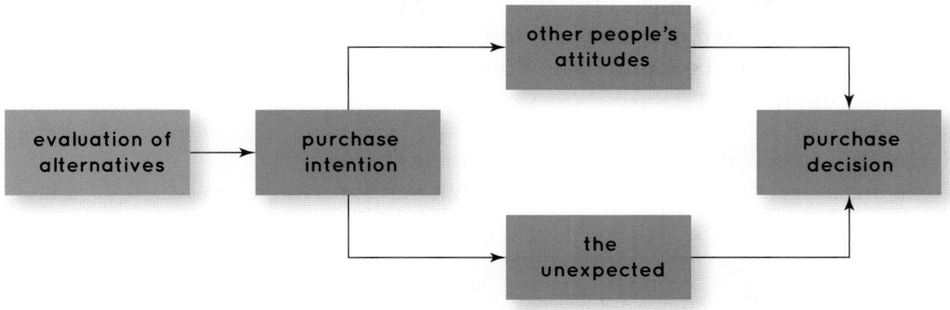

PURCHASE

Making the decision to buy a particular product is one thing; actually buying it is another. How many times have you gone out with the express intention of buying one thing, only to change your mind in the shop and buy something else? People rarely come out of supermarkets with just the things that were on the list. Marketers continue to try and influence potential customers right up to the point where the purchase is made – and sometimes beyond. **Point of sale** materials and sales promotions (e.g. special offers) are favourite ways to try and change a person's mind.

point of sale (POS) the place where a product or service is bought

POST-PURCHASE EVALUATION

The post-purchase stage of the decision process is particularly important to marketers as it determines whether or not the consumer will purchase the product again and how they will influence other people in terms of purchasing the product. According to Smith and Taylor (2004), consumers tell up to 11 people of a bad experience but only 3 or 4 of a good one. This **word of mouth** is extremely important to organisations, which try and harness its positive power as effective advertising. Unfortunately, it is even more difficult to counteract bad word of mouth than it is to encourage the good. (See Chapter 8 for more on word of mouth.)

word of mouth individuals passing on information, experiences or promotional messages to each other; see also viral marketing

Consumers evaluate the product they have purchased in terms of what was promised (e.g. in the adverts or by sales assistants in shops) before they purchased it, and how it actually performs. There are three common outcomes of this:

- disappointment – the consumer is unlikely to repurchase the product
- satisfaction
- delight – the consumer is likely to repurchase the product, will talk favourably to others about the product, and will pay less attention to competing brands when watching adverts (and will not feel the need to try them).

Sometimes, when a consumer has invested a lot of time, effort and money into the purchase decision, or when there are many similar alternatives available, they may experience feelings of doubt about whether they have made the right

post-purchase dissonance
when a consumer is psychologically uncomfortable about their purchase

decision. For example, friends may question their decision: 'How much did you pay for that? I could have got you it for half the price.' Based on the work originally conducted by Leon Festinger (1957) on cognitive dissonance, in marketing this is called **post-purchase dissonance** and means that a customer is psychologically uncomfortable with their purchase. Consumers attempt to reduce this feeling of doubt by either:

- ignoring information that undermines their choice
- paying more attention to information that supports their choice.

ACTIVITY

Have you ever bought something and, afterwards, wondered if you have done the right thing? Think back to a time when this has happened. How did it make you feel? What did you do about it? Did you still look around the shops for the same item or go online to search? Did you discuss your purchase with your friends? Did they agree with you? What if they did not? If you found something that might have been better, what did you tell yourself?

According to research on post-purchase dissonance, we are quite good at finding ways to convince ourselves that we made the right original choice. Did you convince yourself? Did anything the company did help?

So marketers' jobs do not end when a customer makes a purchase. They need to reinforce that purchase decision in order to reduce any cognitive (or post-purchase) dissonance and to stimulate positive word of mouth and encourage repeat purchases. Marketers can minimise post-purchase dissonance by setting expectations correctly before the purchase and providing reassurance afterwards. Some of the ways they do this are by:

- ensuring salespeople and other means of promotion (e.g. advertising) do not exaggerate the product features (over-promise)
- allowing consumers to sample or test the goods prior to purchase so that they know what to expect from the product
- helping customers in the early stages of product use, e.g. with installation, training, etc.
- providing reassurance through advertising, good **public relations** and community building (e.g. owners' clubs)
- offering excellent after-sales support, advice lines, etc.

public relations (PR)
planned activities designed to build good relationships and enhance an organisation's or an individual's reputation

Clearly, the appropriateness of these techniques depends upon the category of product. Firms are unlikely to offer much in the way of after-sales service for small items like chocolate bars – nor do consumers need it. This sort of service is traditionally offered for larger items, with higher levels of involvement (see below), such as computers, DVD recorders and cars.

TYPES OF CONSUMER BUYING DECISION

The buyer decision model should not be taken as an absolute, infallible process showing all the stages that consumers pass through every time they buy something. Clearly this is not the case. Sometimes stages of the process are missed out or they may be worked through in a different order. A major factor affecting the flow and the formality of the decision-making process is the situation in which the purchase is being made. There are three main types of buying situation:

- routine problem solving
- limited problem solving
- extended problem solving.

Routine problem solving is where a consumer buys a product on a regular basis and there is no lengthy decision-making process. Packets of crisps and bars of chocolate are routine purchases. There is very little financial (or any other) risk associated with the purchase of these products and so the consumer does not usually think too much about them.

With *limited problem solving*, the product is purchased less frequently and is likely to be more expensive and expected to last longer. Typical examples of limited problem-solving products are electrical products such as TVs. These types of product usually involve more deliberate decision-making.

Infrequently purchased expensive items, such as houses and cars, call for *extended problem solving*. It is important to the consumer to make the right choice and so they spend time searching for relevant information and evaluating alternatives. Consumers normally have a high level of involvement in these purchases.

LEVELS OF INVOLVEMENT

Consumer
Involvement

Some purchases are more important than others. This may be because they are expensive items, or risky or perhaps life-changing. Certain products help to define their owners and there is therefore a strong emotional involvement in the product. The consumer's level of involvement in a purchase decision has a direct bearing on how much time and effort they put into making the decision as to what to buy, where and how. If a purchase is important to the buyer, (e.g. a new car) then they will think harder about and take more time over it, i.e. they are more likely to follow a lengthier, more complex decision-making process. However, when the purchase is of little importance or is a routine purchase (e.g. a sandwich), consumers will often use short-cuts, or choice tactics, to reduce the time and effort they expend in their decision-making process (see Exhibit 3.6).

Both factual and emotional considerations add to the level of involvement a consumer has with a purchase decision. Facts such as cost and the role the product will play in the consumer's life are clearly important and may vary from consumer to consumer, even for the same product group. For example, someone buying a bag

Exhibit 3.6   Purchase decision stages and levels of involvement

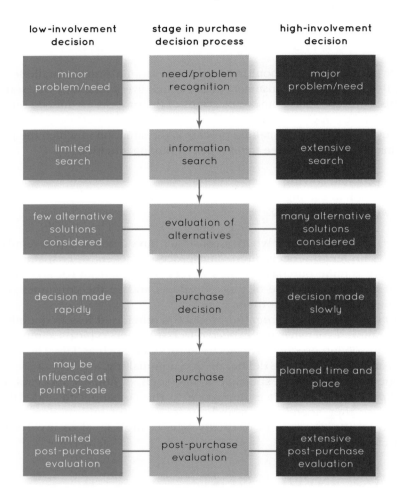

for occasional use in carrying papers will invest less money and time than someone who is buying a briefcase that they intend to use every day for work. Emotional involvement with a decision is just as important while being less easy to predict or control. Research suggests there are four factors that affect a consumer's level of involvement with a product purchase (see Exhibit 3.7):

1   *Self-image*: where the consumer thinks that a product will affect the way they see themselves (e.g. cars and clothes), then involvement levels are likely to be higher.

2   *Perceived risk*: where the consumer thinks there are risks in making a wrong choice. This may be financial risk because the product is expensive, physical risk if the product is potentially dangerous, functional risk if there is a worry

that the product may not work properly, social risk if there are concerns about how others might react to the purchase, or psychological risk if there is the possibility of a wrong decision or one that might make the consumer feel stupid in some way. If risk levels are high, then levels of involvement are likely to be high as well.

3 *Social factors*: where the consumer thinks that a purchase may affect their social acceptability to others or cause them embarrassment (e.g. being seen in the right [or wrong] nightclub), then involvement levels are likely to be higher.

4 *Hedonism*: where the consumer thinks that the purchase may be capable of delivering a high degree of pleasure (e.g. a holiday), then involvement levels are likely to be higher.

Exhibit 3.7   Factors affecting level of involvement

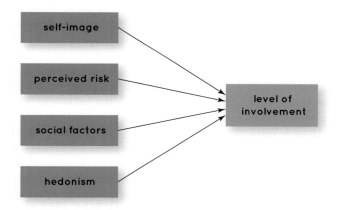

SOURCE: Laurent and Kapferer, 1985

The buying situation and the consumer's level of involvement (see above) both affect their purchase behaviour. Another key influence on how people go about deciding what to buy is how different the competing products are perceived to be. Four major types of buyer behaviour can be seen in Exhibit 3.8.

Exhibit 3.8   Four types of buyer behaviour

	high involvement	low involvement
siginificant difference between brands	complex buying behaviour	variety-seeking buying behaviour
little difference between brands	dissonance-reducing buying behaviour	habitual buying behaviour

SOURCE: Based on Assael (1987)

1 *Complex buying behaviour*: consumers who are making complex decisions usually want to learn (covered later in the chapter) a great deal about the product they are buying as they move through the decision-making process. From this learning develop **beliefs**, and then **attitudes**, about the product type before making a decision to purchase. These consumers have a high level of involvement with the product decision and perceive significant differences between brands. The purchase of an e-book reader would usually prompt complex buying behaviour.

2 *Dissonance-reducing buying behaviour*: if the consumer thinks there is little difference between brands, they put less effort into collecting brand information and may just shop around. Having seen what is readily available, and checked prices, availability, delivery, etc., they are able to make a decision to purchase relatively quickly. These consumers do have a high level of involvement with the product, but think all brands are similar. It is called dissonance-reducing behaviour because the brand comparisons are intended to reduce the chance of post-purchase dissonance resulting from regretting a purchase when a better deal or product is spotted later. The purchase of airline tickets might well fall into this category.

3 *Variety-seeking buying behaviour*: sometimes it is good to have a change, to try something different. There are certain product categories where people are known to buy a different thing next time deliberately, e.g. sandwiches. Marketers attempt to encourage variety seekers to switch to their product through lower prices and sales promotion (e.g. a meal deal). These consumers have relatively low levels of involvement with the product but do perceive brands to be quite different from each other. Many low-value personal products, like shampoo or shower gel, prompt variety-seeking behaviour.

4 *Habitual buying behaviour*: some purchases are routine or always on the shopping list. Consumers spend very little time thinking about these – they just drop them into the supermarket trolley. Marketers try to make this easy for them by dominating shelf space in supermarkets. This way they can encourage repeat purchases and avoid substitution (i.e. consumers buying alternatives) because their product is not to hand. These consumers have a low level of involvement and perceive little difference between brands. Low-value food products like bread and eggs usually fall into this category.

ACTIVITY

Think of three items from each of the following categories that you have purchased, or used, recently:

- a food or snack item that you purchase regularly
- an expensive item such as a TV or CD player
- an emergency or distress purchase.

For each of these, make notes on the following:

- How did the need arise?
- How long did it take to make a decision?
- How many alternatives did you consider?
- How did you choose between them?
- Was it the sort of purchase or consumption your friends would make?
- Would you say the purchase was a high- or low-involvement product? Why?

customer focus: Shall we dine-in or eat-out?

Many predicted that luxuries such as eating in restaurants would be one of the first things consumers would cut out when the recession began to bite. However, UK restaurants have done surprisingly well through the recession years.

Partly this is because of recent changes in consumer attitudes to leisure activities and to food. Eating out is a major social activity that people are reluctant to give up. And they like good food too. Cookery shows are one of the most popular TV formats – and it seems the more upmarket they are, the better. Apparently consumers aspire to be great chefs.

The recession has had some impact on eating habits though. It is the cheaper end of the restaurant market that has seen a sales increase while the more expensive sector has remained steady. People are trading down and looking for bargains. This bargain hunting extends to food shopping too. Supermarkets offer masses of sales promotions designed to keep consumers spending. Some promotions are designed to encourage shoppers to put more in their baskets, e.g. three for the price of two; others are trying to cash in on the popularity of restaurant food. Most supermarkets have followed M&S's lead and produced versions of the M&S 'Dine in for £10' meal deal. These present the best of both worlds: restaurant quality menus at home-cooking prices.

An understanding of the consumer's level of involvement with their products helps marketers to serve their customers better. Consumers will be actively searching for lots of information about high involvement products and marketers need to provide it in a format that these consumers can find easily and study at their own pace (e.g. webpages, newspapers, magazine adverts).

When selecting low-involvement products, consumers are often passive in their information search. They do not actively search for information so marketers attempt to create, and increase, awareness of their product and to reinforce its positive attributes. Television is often used to advertise low-involvement products because of the opportunity this provides for repetition and reinforcement, and because of the large amount of people who, potentially, will see the advert (think about how many people watch, say, *Coronation Street*).

INFLUENCES ON CONSUMER BUYER BEHAVIOUR

Having looked at the consumer buyer decision process, and the different types of consumer buying decision, the next section of this chapter will look at the internal and external factors that may influence these.

INTERNAL INFLUENCES ON CONSUMER BEHAVIOUR

Although markets can be broken down into distinct groups (or segments – see Chapter 4) of customers who are alike in many ways, these groups are clearly made up of individuals with their own, unique characteristics. The next section of this chapter looks at what these characteristics are and how they affect individuals' buying behaviour.

Personality theories, types and tests

Personality

The term **personality** describes a person's distinguishing psychological characteristics, which lead them to respond to situations in particular ways. **Personality** consists of all the features, behaviours and experience that make individuals unique and distinctive. It is often described in terms of personality traits, such as dominant, sociable, introvert or extrovert. Personality is often related to self-image or the concept of self and one of the fundamentals of self-image is that a person's possessions (e.g. clothes, books, CDs) reflect their identity. For example, new acquaintances commonly check out each other's CD collections or books in order to form an opinion of that individual.

Perception

Two people seeing the same advertisement may react to it differently because they perceive the situation differently. Even the same individual may perceive the same advertisement differently at different times. Imagine how you would react to an advert for a snack when you are hungry and compare that to when you have just eaten.

Perception is the process by which people select, organise and interpret sensory stimulation (sounds, visions, smell, touch) into a meaningful picture of the world. There are three main processes that lead to the formation of individual perceptions.

Selective attention is the process by which stimuli are assessed and non-meaningful stimuli, or those that are inconsistent with our beliefs or experiences, are screened out. This has major implications from a marketing perspective. For example, it is estimated that the average person is exposed to 1500 advertisements per day. Only 5–25% of these advertisements catch the attention of the individual; the rest are screened out. Marketers use various techniques (such as colours, contrasting backgrounds and foregrounds, centre of vision) to ensure their advertisements are given attention.

Selective distortion occurs when consumers distort or change the information they receive to suit their beliefs and attitude. One of the many challenges that marketers face when communicating with audiences is to understand how this selective distortion is likely to work and then either avoid it or make use of it so that their message gets through as intended. This careful presentation of the message is called **information framing**. For example, in most of Europe

personality
a person's distinguishing psychological characteristics that lead them to respond in particular ways

perception
the process by which people select, organise and interpret sensory stimulation (sounds, visions, smell, touch) into a meaningful picture of the world

selective attention
the process by which stimuli are assessed and non-meaningful stimuli, or those that are inconsistent with our beliefs or experiences, are screened out

selective distortion
occurs when consumers distort or change the information they receive to suit their beliefs and attitude

information framing
the ways in which information is presented to people to ensure selective distortion does, or does not, happen

we associate blue with cool and red with hot. Many bottled waters use blue to indicate their cooling ability whilst chilli-flavoured snacks usually favour red packaging or writing.

Consumers remember only a small number of the many messages they see and hear. This is called **selective retention**. People tend to remember messages that support their existing beliefs and attitudes better than those that do not. For example, the message 'dieting makes you fat' is more likely to be remembered, and acted on, by those who hate dieting than by those who are in favour of it.

Perception and memory are closely associated with learning.

Learning

Learning describes changes in an individual's behaviour that arise from their experiences. Marketers are keen for consumers to learn from promotion so that they know which product to buy and why. Learning can take place in a number of ways (see Exhibit 3.9).

Classical conditioning

Classical conditioning uses an established relationship between a **stimulus** and a **response** to that stimulus to evoke or teach people to have the same response to a different stimulus. The most famous example is that of Pavlov's dogs. Pavlov, who was a renowned nineteenth-century psychologist, rang a bell at the dogs' mealtimes. The dogs learnt to associate the bell (the stimulus) with food and their response was to salivate. After a while, they always salivated on hearing the bell – even if no food was forthcoming. Clearly the application of classical conditioning in marketing is more sophisticated than it was for Pavlov's dogs. Marketers may put a stimulus alongside their brand in order to create an association and so build brand awareness. For example, music is often used in advertising. If the association is strong enough, as many jingles are, then just hearing that tune will bring the brand to mind.

selective retention
the way consumers retain only a small number of messages in their memory

learning
changes in an individual's behaviour arising from their experiences

classical conditioning
the process of using an established relationship between a stimulus and a response, which can then be used to evoke the same response

stimulus
something that provokes a reaction, activity, interest or enthusiasm

response
a reaction to a stimulus

Introduction to Classical Conditioning

Exhibit 3.9   Types of learning

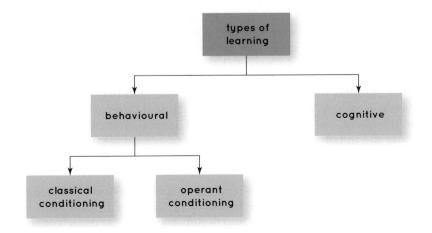

Exhibit 3.10   The classical conditioning approach to influencing product attitudes

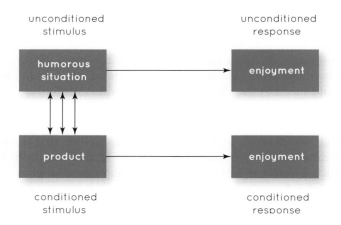

Operant or instrumental conditioning

operant conditioning (instrumental conditioning) the learner's response produces a reinforcing stimulus

Operant conditioning (also known as **instrumental conditioning**) also requires a link between a stimulus and a response. However, with operant conditioning, the correct response receives a reward (positive reinforcement) while an incorrect response may receive punishment (negative reinforcement). Think about house-training a puppy – this is usually done through operant conditioning. The learning may not be so simple as to be an absolute; the stimulus that results in the highest reward is the stimulus that is learnt. Marketers will try to increase the likelihood of the right response, e.g. buy a product regularly, through positive reinforcement such as special offers for regular customers.

While classical conditioning is useful in explaining how consumers may learn simple kinds of behaviour, operant conditioning is much more useful in determining more complex, goal-desired behaviour. The learned behaviour results from expectations of the rewards (or penalties) that may be received or have been received through previous experiences. Through operant conditioning, an association is made between a behaviour and a consequence of that behaviour, even when the initial stimulus is no longer present.

For example, the *Financial Times* (*FT*) sells its paper to students for 20p instead of 85p. The reduced-rate *FT*s are distributed on campus and, because it is at a reduced rate, students purchase it (desired response) and because it has desirable properties (i.e. may help with their studies) it is thought useful (positive reinforcement) and the likelihood of it being purchased again increases (see Exhibit 3.11), even without the initial stimulus of the discount.

Cognitive learning

cognitive learning active learning using complex mental processing of information

Both classical and operant conditioning are forms of behavioural learning involving stimuli and responses; **cognitive learning** however involves the complex mental processing of information. The cognitive learning approach sees people as problem solvers who actively look for information that will help them. The

Exhibit 3.11 Operant conditioning over time

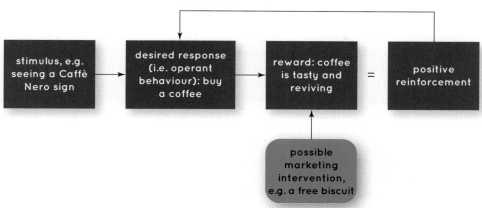

previous section on the consumer buyer decision process presumes that at least some cognitive learning takes place. Creativity and insight are important if this way of learning is to be successful (Solomon et al., 2010). There are a number of types of cognitive learning including rote learning, where two concepts are associated with each other through repetition without conditioning (e.g. slogans with products), and vicarious learning, which involves learning from others, i.e. without direct experience or reward, e.g. finding out about products through word of mouth.

Exhibit 3.12 Maslow's hierarchy of needs

SOURCE: Based on Maslow (1943)

Motivation and values

Motivation involves a complex relationship between needs, drives and goals. A motive is a need that is sufficiently pressing that the person is driven to seek satisfaction of that need. According to Maslow, these needs can be placed in a hierarchy in terms of their relative importance (see Exhibit 3.12).

An individual will try to satisfy the most important needs of survival first (the bottom row). When these needs are met, they will stop being motivators and the individual will then try to satisfy the next most important need, i.e. the one at the next level up in the hierarchy. For example, an individual who is starving will have no interest in anything else until their hunger is satisfied. Someone in danger of dying of thirst will drink from a dirty pool – and only later worry about whether that was a safe thing to do. Once a person has satisfied their basic physical and safety needs, then, and only then, will they look for the company of others. Human beings are social animals and so socialising with others is important – but not as important as staying alive. Not satisfied with having friends, a decent social life, romance, people next look for esteem, for the approval and even admiration of others. Typically we do this through our work, or our wealth, but certain products also fulfil this need. Sports cars are not bought just because their drivers want to break speed limits; they are objects of desire and provoke envy in others. They enhance the status of the driver. The final level, self-actualisation, is the hardest to reach. It involves the fulfilment of dreams and ambitions. This is a general model of motivation. It was not created with marketing in mind and Maslow did not envisage its use as a marketing tool. However, many modern ads have dream fulfilment at their heart, positioning their product as the answer to prayers – and not always with tongue in cheek. Many car (and holiday) ads appear to fall into this category, such as the 'Volvo C70 feel' campaign where the car takes them above the clouds (this advert, and many others, can be viewed at **www.tellyads.com**).

There are a number of criticisms of this model. Firstly, it is important to remember that it was not developed for marketing. It is useful for marketers in that it helps categorise products by the kind of need they are trying to fulfil and stimulates further thought on how these products should therefore be positioned and advertised, however any attempt to apply it too rigorously to a marketing situation is likely to raise more questions than it answers. Secondly, it is difficult to work out the extent to which one need needs to be fulfilled before someone is ready to move on to the next level, and also to measure that level of fulfilment in an individual (Schiffman et al., 2008). Thirdly, the model can also be criticised as being reflective of certain Western cultures only. Other cultures may not be as materialistic or individualistic and may therefore have different priorities (Solomon et al., 2010), for example raising the relative importance of social needs.

It is clearly important that marketers should understand the motives that drive consumers to purchase products. Those motives determine how consumers choose products and such knowledge enables marketers to design product offerings that have the best chance of being chosen. Consumer motives can also be used to group potential customers together and so to segment markets (see Chapter 4). As an example, consider the purchase of a mobile phone: while some people's primary motive may be to be contactable in an emergency, others may consider it an important tool for socialising or a status symbol. The phone's advertising would need to take this into account.

EXPAND YOUR KNOWLEDGE

Hyllegard, K.H., Yan, R-N., Paff Ogle, J. and Attmann, J. (2010) 'The influence of gender, social cause, charitable support, and message appeal on Gen Y's responses to cause-related marketing', *Journal of Marketing Management*, 27 (1–2): 100–23.

This study examined the influence of gender, type of social cause, amount of charitable support, and message appeal on Gen Y consumers' attitudes and purchase intentions towards an apparel brand in the context of cause-related marketing.

Attitudes and beliefs

Attitudes and beliefs are acquired through the experience of doing things and the resultant learning process. A belief is a thought that a person holds about something, usually based on knowledge, opinion or faith. Beliefs are important to marketers because beliefs about certain products or brands may affect a consumer's choice criteria. Attitudes are important because they have strong links to behaviour – although consumers sometimes do the opposite of what their attitude suggests they might, e.g. someone who believes strongly in healthy, organically grown food might still buy a cheaper version of a product.

An attitude describes a person's consistently favourable or unfavourable evaluation, feelings and tendencies towards an object or idea. From a marketing perspective, this attitude may be directed at a product or brand (i.e. the object) and thus will be reflected in their behaviour (i.e. whether they purchase the product or not). Attitudes can be discovered by asking the person how they feel about the brand.

Williams (1981) suggests that attitude comprises three components: cognitive, affective and conative. The cognitive attitude relates to **beliefs** about a product; the affective attitude relates to positive and negative **feelings** associated with the product; the conative attitude is the link with **behaviour** (i.e. attitude X is likely to lead to behaviour Y). It is this link between attitude and behaviour that is of prime interest to the marketer, e.g. how a positive attitude towards a product can be translated into a purchase decision, or how someone with a negative attitude can be prevented from taking undesired actions such as posting a poor review. One of the most common advertising objectives is to create favourable attitudes just as a common aim of customer service representatives is to prevent the consequences of negative attitudes, e.g. by offering something extra or free to compensate for something that went wrong.

EXPAND YOUR KNOWLEDGE

Laran, J. and Tsiros, M. (2013) 'An investigation of the effectiveness of uncertainty in marketing promotions involving free gifts', *Journal of Marketing,* 77 (2): 112–23.

This paper examines the effects of not being sure what the free gift will be on the cognitive, conative and affective aspects of consumer decision-making.

Consumer
psychology
in a recession

culture
the set of basic values, perceptions, wants and behaviour learnt by a member of society from family and other institutions

high-context culture
one where communication must be interpreted according to the situation; much of the message is in the context rather than being explicitly expressed in the words

low-context culture
the information to be communication is put into words explicitly; there is little need to take account of the surrounding circumstances

EXTERNAL INFLUENCES ON CONSUMER BEHAVIOUR

The previous section looked at how the consumer buyer decision process might be influenced by internal factors; this section will consider some of the many external influences on this process.

Culture

Culture manifests itself through such things as customs, art, language, literature, music, beliefs and religion. As children grow up, their society provides them with a framework within which they are able to develop acceptable beliefs, value systems and cultural norms (see Exhibit 3.13).

Within any culture, there will be subcultures. A subculture is a group of people with shared value systems based on common life experiences and situations. These shared value systems may come from ethnic origin, geographic areas, life stage, lifestyle or religion. Subcultures often form very important market segments (see

Exhibit 3.13   Elements of culture

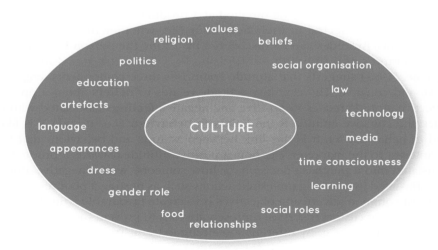

global focus: High- and low-context cultures

The noted anthropologist Edward Hall (cited in Usunier and Lee, 2009) is responsible for the introduction of the concepts of **high-context** and **low-context** cultures into the study of international exchanges. In a high-context culture, such as Japan, it is important to take account of the situation in which something is said. The words alone may not convey the true meaning of the speaker. It is difficult for most Northern Europeans to decode this, but it is important to be aware that 'first we must do x' or 'I'll let you know next week' might well actually mean 'no', depending on the circumstances in which it is said, who is saying it and where they come from. On the other hand, a North American (low context) will have no compunction in saying 'no' if they do not want to make the deal, and will see that as commendable honesty and straight-dealing rather than as shocking discourtesy. The use of language in extreme low- and high-context cultures can be as different as its use in technical manuals and in poetry: the first tries to make the meaning as clear as possible through words alone; the second works on a number of different levels and requires interpretation by someone familiar with the poetic form.

The following are usually considered low-context cultures:

- USA
- Canada
- Germany
- Switzerland
- Austria
- Scandinavian countries
- Australia
- New Zealand.

The following are considered to be high-context:

- Latin American countries
- Middle Eastern countries
- Japan.

The British are the source of some confusion, especially to Americans, who assume a greater similarity between these two peoples than there really is. (There is an old saying: two peoples divided by a common language.) Britain fits into the middle of the high/low-context spectrum thanks to the British tendency towards understatement and euphemism, as well as the demands of courtesy which make some statements too bold.

Another country that causes problems in categorisation is France. The French language has long been considered the ideal diplomatic language because it can be precise or vague according to the speaker's wish (Usunier and Lee, 2009).

Chapter 4). For example, MTV has a global format that appeals to youth culture across the world.

Reference groups

Reference groups are groups of people to which an individual belongs or wants to belong. These groups may be formal or informal, e.g. sports clubs, professional bodies such as the Chartered Institute of Marketing (CIM) or the gang that goes for a drink after work on Fridays.

These reference groups can have a significant influence on consumer purchase behaviour. They can be classified into three main types:

1   Membership groups are groups that an individual already belongs to and therefore have a direct influence on their behaviour.
2   Aspirant (aspirational) groups are those groups to which an individual would like to belong; they identify with them but there is no face-to-face contact, e.g. an amateur footballer may aspire to be part of a professional club.
3   Disassociative groups are groups to which the individual does not want to belong or be seen to belong. For example, an upmarket shopper may not wish to be part of a discount club no matter how good the deals are.

These people almost certainly share certain personality traits and belong to a particular reference group.

Little Mix in the 2012 X Factor final: talent show contestants are an aspirant group for many people.

Ed Keller;
'Mouthing
off'

reference groups
the groups to which an individual belongs or aspires to belong

EXPAND YOUR KNOWLEDGE

Wei, Y. and Yu, C. (2012) 'How do reference groups influence self-brand connections among Chinese consumers? Implications for advertising', *Journal of Advertising*, 31 (2): 39–53.

The reference groups considered in this paper include both in-groups (membership groups) and out-groups (aspirational, dissociative and neutral groups).

Reference groups may influence consumers in at least three ways:

1 They expose the consumer to new behaviours and lifestyles.
2 They may influence the consumer's self-concept (e.g. they want to be accepted and fit in with a particular group).
3 They may create pressures to conform to the group norms that affect product or brand choice.

customer focus: Harley riders

Harley-Davidson is perhaps the most distinctive motorcycle in the world – and it inspires extreme devotion. If you own a Harley, you are a member of an elite club and this is a feeling the company recognises and fosters.

Visit its website (www.harley-davidson.com or www.harley-davidson.co.uk) or one of its other international sites, and see how it builds that community feeling.

There is welcoming information and tips for new riders. You can post photos and so build up an online photo album of you, your friends and, of course, your bikes. You can join HOG (the Harley Owners Group) and so get access to special information and invitations to join in at special events. This brand community of Harley owners, and would-be owners, is a privileged, membership group.

How important a reference group is to a consumer will vary depending on the nature of the product. It tends to be most important for conspicuous purchases. A product is conspicuous if:

- it is exclusive and therefore noticeable; many designer brands will fall into this product category (e.g. Rolex, Lacoste)
- it is consumed in the public domain and other consumers may see it, e.g. drinking a particular brand of bottled beer in a nightclub.

Exhibit 3.14 shows how group influence may affect brand choice for four types of product.

Online social networks

Not all consumers use social networking sites but most do and usage is growing. Of the population of Western Europe 54.4% used social networks in 2012 and this is projected to rise to over 60% by 2014 (European Travel Commission, 2012).

Exhibit 3.14   Group influence on brand choices

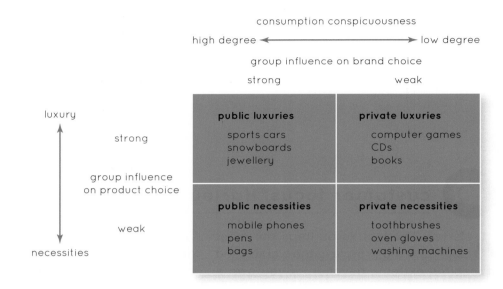

SOURCE: Bearden and Etzel, 1982

According to Mintel (2012) younger people are more likely to use social networks than older people. Nevertheless, over half of the over-65s who use the Internet visit social networking sites.

Social network interaction can have a powerful influence on consumer behaviour. It works in a number of ways:

- Each network or group that a person belongs to is a membership reference group (see above) and as such the opinions of the group are respected and members will try to conform.
- Comments and reviews on the site can be an instantaneous form of word of mouth.
- Brands may have their own pages; members of these pages (who may only have to 'like' the page to join) are in effect a **brand community**, i.e. a group united around a brand with which they have a strong relationship. They may feel ownership of the brand and will be motivated to protect it and to convert others to it.

brand communities a group of people, usually consumers, formed on the basis of their shared admiration for a particular branded product or range of products, e.g. the BMW owners' group

Consumers play different roles within social networking sites. Some are far more active and involved than others and it is these people who are likely to have the stronger influence over consumer behaviour. Research done by Forrester Research categorised Internet users according to their social networking behaviour. The seven categories of social media user range from 'creator' to 'spectator' and finally 'inactive'. 'Creators' actually create online content for spectators to read. In between, there are 'conversationalists' who do things like update their status in Facebook regularly or tweet, 'critics' who write reviews and post comments on other people's blogs etc., 'collectors' who may add tags or vote and 'joiners' who

What is your Social Media Personality?

maintain their profile on one or more sites but do little else (Li and Bernoff, 2011). These classes of networkers are placed on a ladder with the most active being the highest up. These opinion leaders and opinion formers are valuable allies and great potential brand ambassadors.

opinion leaders
individuals who are often asked by people they know for advice for information

opinion formers
individuals with specialist skills or expertise who have influence over others, often through the media

ACTIVITY

Think about the people you know and the things you do regularly. What reference groups do you belong to? How do they influence you as a consumer – or how do you influence the other members of the group?

Family

Family members are a strong influence on a buyer's behaviour over their whole lifetime, i.e. not just during the time they live in the family home. Family influence can be divided into one of two categories: family orientation influence and family procreation influence.

brand ambassador
someone who is passionate and knowledgeable about a brand and recommends it to others; this may be an employee, a celebrity endorser, or a customer acting independently

ethical focus: Pester power

The pre-school market is estimated to be worth around £5 billion a year and, if you add those areas where children influence their parents' purchases the most (areas such as clothing, food, leisure activities, holidays, etc.), that estimate rises to up to £30 billion a year. The Advertising Code of Practice has been tightened in an attempt to prevent advertisers from directly encouraging children to ask for things. However, think about the number of collectable toys, usually based on cartoon films, that are offered by fast-food restaurants, or tins of spaghetti in the shape of children's favourite characters, such as the Tweenies or Postman Pat. The Market Research Panel suggests that the five biggest causes of pester power are:

1 TV advertising

2 Free promotional gifts

3 Attractive packaging

4 Licensed characters (e.g. Postman Pat)

5 In-store samples.

Family orientation influence is the influence parents exert over their children, even when there is no longer any interaction. This may be at a general level in terms of values and attitudes towards product types (e.g. whether you view a car as a status symbol or as a functional product to get you from A to B), or at a more specific level (e.g. continuing to purchase the same brand of coffee as your parents did).

Family procreation influence consists of the more direct influences on daily buying behaviour that family members exert upon one another. This is continually evolving with changing social conditions and working patterns. For example, the increase in the number of working mothers has meant the rise of latchkey kids – i.e. children who arrive home from school before their parents arrive home from work and who prepare a snack or tea for themselves. Such consumers have particular requirements for food products, e.g. ease of preparation.

EXPAND YOUR KNOWLEDGE

Lawlor, M.-A. and Prothero, A. (2011) 'Pester power – a battle of wills between children and their parents', *Journal of Marketing Management*, 27 (5–6): 561–81.

The authors investigate children's views on pester power in contrast to other research that has concentrated on parental perspectives.

Consumer buying roles

Within groups such as families, or flatmates or clubs, many purchase decisions are made by the group, not just one individual. Consumers fulfil different roles in making purchase decisions and these roles can change depending upon what is being purchased. For example, parents may pay for their children's clothes but leave it to them to decide what to buy, whereas the children may pay for their own sweets but within rules set by their parents.

The roles that individuals play in a decision include: influencer, customer and consumer. An *influencer* may make suggestions, offer advice or an opinion. Children are frequently influencers within a family although it may be someone from outside the group who exerts influence: a friend, or a salesperson perhaps. A *customer* is the person who actually buys the products or the person who has the final say. In a family group, this is often one or both parents. The *consumer* actually uses or eats the product. For example, the whole family would consume a Disneyland, Paris experience.

e-focus: Purchase decision making: the social media effect

Has the way we buy things changed as a result of our social media networking? Apparently it has. Of course we buy many things online, but technology has made quite an impact on the other stages of the purchase decision module too.

The Internet provides us with so much information that it can be a challenge to sift and assess it all to decide which brands should be placed in our consideration sets. So are there short cuts? Yes there are. We can ask our friends; see what they've bought and what they like. Some of those friends are close friends, some are just Facebook friends – and some are brands. Digital and social media have prompted consumers to expect more from brands. Not only must brands be available when and how consumers want them but they must also engage in conversations about themselves, and their competitors, and help consumers to find their way through that overload of information.

Many consumers have a mental picture of any market they are interested in, of the similarities and difference between competing brands. They may be quite expert in the relative merits of tablets, airlines or fashion designers. They use the additional information and advice they get online to confirm or revise that mental picture. That information may be received passively, e.g. through brand-initiated marketing communications, or may be actively sought, e.g. through search engines or online review sites. Opinions and emotional support can come from friends, family members, experts, journalists or the brands themselves. This can happen at any stage in the decision-making process so brand communicators have to be flexible in both what they communicate and how they do it. A consumer who is on the point of deciding which smartphone to buy might need the reassurance that they know other people who have that phone rather than pages of information on what you can do with the device. Someone who is unsure whether they would read an online newspaper is more likely to be swayed by a demonstration of how it works, or how it fits into their lifestyle, than by a comparison of the different papers available.

With all that online information to process, and all those friends to consult, consumers are constantly updating their mental market pictures. That means that when they want to buy a product, they are quite likely to know already which one is their kind of brand.

SOURCES: Powers et al. (2012)

ACTIVITY

Using the example of a Friday night out, who carries out the roles of influencer, customer and consumer?

EXPAND YOUR KNOWLEDGE

Classic article

Kotler, P. (1965) 'Behavioural models for analyzing buyers', *Journal of Marketing,* 29 (4): 37–45.

Kotler offers five approaches/models to analysing and understanding buyer behaviour from Marshellian economics to Veblen social constructs (Veblen originated the term 'conspicuous consumption' so beloved of marketers) and organisational buying behaviour.

Staying ahead
by meeting
changing
consumer needs

THE CONSUMER BUYER DECISION PROCESS FOR NEW PRODUCTS

The sale of new products presents special challenges to the marketer. Consumers may view new products as riskier than tried and tested alternatives. They may not properly understand what they are for or how to use them. They may not see a need for them. This section will explore how consumers approach the purchase of new products:

A new product may be defined as a good, service or idea that is *perceived* by potential customers as being new (see Chapter 6 for more on new products). Consumers have to go through a number of mental processes (see Exhibit 3.15) when deciding whether to buy a new product:

- *Awareness*: the consumer becomes aware of the product but does not have any information about it.
- *Interest*: the consumer actively seeks information about the new product if they think it may be of use to them.
- *Evaluation*: the consumer decides whether or not they should try the new product.
- *Trial*: the consumer tries the new product on a small scale to judge its value.
- *Adoption*: the consumer decides to make full and regular use of the new product.

Marketers need to plan how they can aid potential consumers to move through the various steps by, for example, providing information or having a trial or testing plan.

Exhibit 3.15   The stages of buyer readiness

INDIVIDUAL DIFFERENCES AND NEW PRODUCTS

Individuals differ in their attitudes to new products generally: some are excited by the idea of something new, others are a little scared. Consumers' willingness to try new products also varies according to the nature of the specific new product. For example, while some people may love to try new food or have the latest fashions, they may not be so willing to buy the latest Smartphone or book a space shuttle flight. This has led marketers to classify consumers into a number of product adoption categories (see Exhibit 3.16), as follows:

- *Innovators* (2.5%) are consumption pioneers who are prepared to try new ideas.
- *Early adopters* (13.5%) are often opinion leaders within their reference groups. Opinion leaders are those individuals who have special skills, knowledge, personality or other characteristics, and exert influence on others (e.g. DJs).
- The *early majority* (34%) are quite adventurous in their decision making and, as a result, adopt new ideas before the average person.
- The *late majority* (34%) are more sceptical. They adopt new products only after most have tried them.
- *Laggards* (16%) are conservative and suspicious of change. They adopt a new product only when it has become something of a tradition in itself.

Marketers research and identify the characteristics of the various groups and tailor their marketing mix and, in particular, their advertising messages accordingly.

The models looked at so far relate to consumer purchases. The next section will look at the way organisations purchase products.

Exhibit 3.16   Product adoption categories

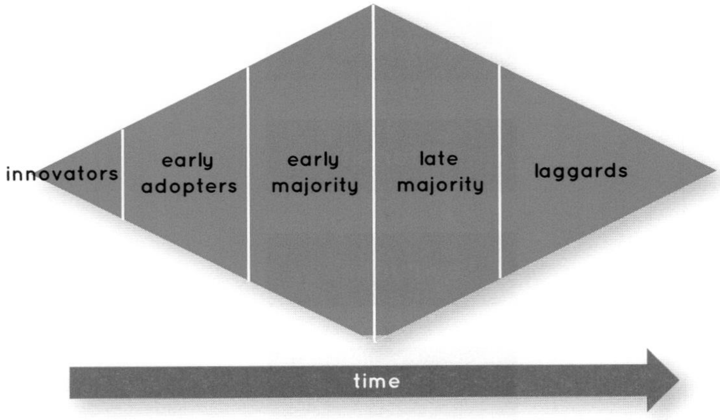

| innovators | early adopters | early majority | late majority | laggards |

time

SOURCE: Based on Rogers, 2003

TYPES OF ORGANISATION AND THE PRODUCTS THEY PURCHASE

Purchases made in the business to business (b2b) market are usually larger than the business to consumer (b2c) market. When a consumer buys a car, that b2c transaction is only the final stage of a number of b2b purchases that make up the supply chain involved in producing and distributing cars (see Chapter 9 for more on the supply chain). What is more, consumers usually buy cars one at a time. A business may buy hundreds for its company car fleet. Business customers tend to place much bigger orders.

This section of the chapter looks at organisational customers and how their buying decisions are made, who is involved and what criteria they use.

EXPAND YOUR KNOWLEDGE

Classic article

Rogers, E.M. (1976) 'New product adoption and diffusion', *Journal of Consumer Behaviour*, 2: 290–301.

Rogers is the recognised proponent of this important marketing concept and model that is sometimes referred to as *innovation diffusion* and which has widespread application in marketing practice.

As well as many of the things that consumers purchase, organisations purchase a diverse and complex range of goods and services. These include:

- utility services (such as water, electricity and broadband)
- raw materials (such as steel, cotton and chemicals)
- component parts (such as chips, switches and valves)
- capital items (such as buildings and machines)
- MRO goods (i.e. maintenance, repair and operations goods such as cleaning materials and tools)
- professional services (such as legal and financial advice).

CHARACTERISTICS OF ORGANISATIONAL MARKETS

There are many similarities between business markets and consumer markets but there are also a number of key differences between these two types of market. They typically differ in terms of:

- market structure
- nature of demand
- complexity of the buying process.

MARKET STRUCTURE

It is important to establish how many customers there are in a consumer market. That is the first step towards estimating potential sales. This is also key in b2b or industrial markets but it is crucial to understand how big and how influential those customers are.

INDUSTRIAL CONCENTRATION

In b2b markets, there are normally fewer buyers but they are far larger in terms of purchasing power. Compare the selling of computers to the consumer market with selling dedicated computer systems to car manufacturers. There are fewer customers but they are more easily identifiable and they buy more.

GEOGRAPHICAL CONCENTRATION

Some industries have a strong geographical concentration. This may have arisen due to the availability of resources (e.g. steel manufacturing in Sheffield), because of political incentives (e.g. EU grants) or for historical reasons (e.g. financial services in London).

NATURE OF DEMAND

Remembering that demand in this sense means **actual sales**, b2b demand for products can be more complex than consumer demand. The demand for b2b products is: derived, often joint, usually relatively inelastic and may fluctuate considerably. Each of these ideas is briefly explained below.

Derived demand

All business demand is derived demand, i.e. demand that ultimately comes from (or is derived from) the demand for the final product. The demand for steel panels is derived from the demand for cars, which ultimately depends on how many the end consumer wants to buy.

Joint demand

Joint demand is demand that is linked with the sales of other organisational products. So, the demand for tyres has a strong link to the demand for cars.

Inelastic demand

Some b2b sales are not very price sensitive. Businesses do of course want to save money and will shop around for the best deal, but if the purchase is a relatively trivial one, a price rise will not affect overall sales very much. Inelastic demand is where the sales of a product are largely unaffected by price changes, especially in the short run. For example, the tyres on a jumbo jet's wheels are one small component of the overall cost of the finished product. A rise in the price of tyres will not affect the overall demand for jumbo jets. (See Chapter 10 for a fuller explanation of inelasticity of demand.)

Fluctuating demand

Demand for goods and services tends to fluctuate more rapidly in b2b markets. This is at least partly because it is derived demand and even joint demand (see above) and so subject to a range of market forces. When a firm has a large order, it wants products to help satisfy it. When business is slow, there is no need to buy in as much.

THE COMPLEXITY OF THE ORGANISATIONAL BUYING PROCESS

The purchasing habits of organisations are rather different from those of individuals. Typically, businesses:

- buy in larger quantities
- negotiate harder on delivery terms
- expect reduced prices for bulk buying
- may require tailored products
- are harder to please
- have more people involved in making the decision to buy
- have longer, more complex decision-making processes.

Businesses buy in larger quantities just because they are buying goods and services for more people. An individual may buy one or two ballpoint pens; a company would need several boxes just so that each employee can have one. If the goods they are buying are actually for use in their production process (e.g. Birds Eye buying rice as an ingredient for its ready meals) or for selling on (as shops do), then they will have to buy enough for all their customers.

If a consumer orders something, such as a new CD or a new computer add-on, then usually they want it to arrive quickly, just because they cannot wait to play it or plug it in. Businesses have a more pressing need to know that their orders will arrive on time. A company's whole production process may well depend on having sufficient rice to make its paella, or there may be just one time slot, say a national holiday, when it can install its new computer hardware without too much disruption. So businesses tend to insist on particular delivery times and, if their orders are large enough, suppliers will comply.

Organisations are well aware that they are more valuable customers than individual purchasers. Often they expect something in return. They may settle for superior customer service, or they may insist on a discount as an incentive to place a large order.

Some business customers will ask for their own version of a supplier's products. For example, Zanussi makes special washing machine models for selected UK high-street stores such as Dixons. There are a number of reasons why businesses may want this. In the case of Dixons, it would almost certainly be to confer a competitive advantage by offering a model that other stores do not have. Businesses may want cars in the company colours or pens with their name on. They may want the rice they buy to be of uniform size so that they can be sure it will all cook through when they cook it in a large batch. It would not usually be worth the supplier's while to customise its products for an individual customer, but for a large organisation? That is a different matter.

The business buying process tends to be more formal and often involves professional purchasers who adopt sophisticated purchasing systems. Very often, organisations will have policies and guidelines (e.g. a purchasing policy) as to whether purchasing should be centralised or decentralised, and from a single supplier (single sourcing) or a number of suppliers (multiple sourcing). All these policies have advantages and disadvantages.

ORGANISATIONAL BUYING SITUATIONS

There are three main types of organisational buying situation. These may be viewed on a continuum ranging from a straight re-buy, through modified re-buy, to new task at the other end of the scale (see Exhibit 3.17).

Exhibit 3.17   Types of organisational buying situations

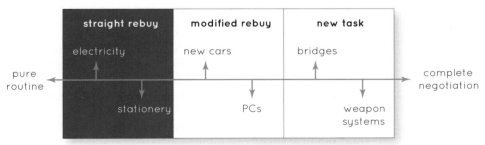

SOURCE: Adapted from Enis, 1980

- A straight re-buy is where the buyer routinely reorders a product without any change to the order whatsoever. There may even be an automatic reordering system. Straight re-buys are usually low risk, frequently purchased and inexpensive items (e.g. stationery or paint).
- A modified re-buy is where the buyer wants something to be slightly different from the previous purchase. This may be the product specification (such as colour, size or technical specification) or the price or the terms (such as delivery time).
- A new task is a first-time purchase. This is the most complex category of purchase with the most involved, and sometimes lengthy, decision-making process. This is often something that is infrequently purchased or is high risk, e.g. expensive products such as computer systems, or it may be that the organisation is trying a new supplier or has introduced something new to its business, e.g. a lighting manufacturer who has introduced a new range of energy-saving lights.

THE BUYING CENTRE

buying centre comprises all the individuals that participate in the business buying decision process

In any sizeable organisation, there are likely to be a number of people involved in any purchase. The **buying centre** is not an actual department or formal group, it is a way of looking at all the people who participate in a business buying decision process and assessing their roles and information needs. Buying centres vary depending on the nature of the purchase and of the organisation.

Individuals within a buying centre fulfil one or more of the following roles. These roles may be formal, i.e. part of their jobs, or informal: they have volunteered or been asked to look into a purchase on a one-off basis. Typical roles within the organisational buying centre (or decision-making unit) are outlined below:

Initiators:	people who first identify the need for the product and communicate it to the others, e.g. a dissatisfied canteen customer who complains that there are no healthy choices on the menu.
Users:	members of the organisation who will actually use the purchase, e.g. administrators using computers.
Influencers:	individuals whose opinions may contribute to the final choice of purchase. Their influence may be related to their expertise (e.g. an IT specialist) or it could be of a more informal and/or personal nature.
Buyers:	the individuals who actually make the purchase, or select and approve suppliers, and negotiate the terms of the purchase. In larger organisations there will be a professional buying department.
Deciders:	individuals (e.g. the boss) who have formal or informal powers to select or approve suppliers.
Financiers:	the individual or department who holds the budget which will fund the purchase.

Gatekeepers: individuals who have some control over the flow of information into the organisation. These may include buyers, technical personnel (e.g. IT experts) or receptionists.

THE ORGANISATIONAL BUYING PROCESS

Individuals within the organisational buying process have their own personal agendas, motives and dynamics. It is important to remember that they are individuals and that each must be understood and treated as such. Organisations do not make decisions – people do. The organisational buying process is longer and more complex than the consumer one (see Exhibit 3.18).

Exhibit 3.18   The organisational buying process

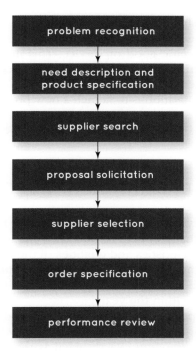

Kotler et al. (2012) identify seven stages in the organisational buying process. This lengthy and complex process is more representative of the way organisations go about making large or significant purchases. A routine order for paperclips, or the booking of train travel for an employee, will be much quicker and more straightforward. However, the initial decision of which stationery supplier to use for paperclips may well have gone through all these stages.

Courtesy of ExCel London

Many business customers visit trade exhibitions to find new products or suppliers.

PROBLEM RECOGNITION

An individual, or group, within an organisation identifies a problem that may be solved by acquiring a specific good or service. This may be an entirely routine operation, such as reordering stationery, or a much more complex operation, such as purchasing a capital item (e.g. a fork-lift truck).

For example, if an organisation is to launch a new product, then to do so it may need new manufacturing systems or new component parts for it. External factors that influence the choice of product and supplier may be trade press, exhibitions or sales representatives.

GENERAL NEED DESCRIPTION AND PRODUCT SPECIFICATION

Having identified that they have a need, the organisation needs to think it through and describe it in a way that will help to find the right solutions. This description includes the general characteristics and qualities of the required product in terms of what it has to do, e.g. the manufacturing equipment must be capable of making six varieties of cake, all the same size but with different ingredients, and must be ready to start production within the year.

An organisation will specify the attributes that a product should have. This is very different from the situation in consumer markets, where much of the enjoyment of shopping is not knowing exactly what is required, but seeing what is available. The product specification will often incorporate aspects such as colour, material quality, performance levels and its compatibility with other components. This may require external assistance from, for example, consultants if the product is of a technical nature.

SUPPLIER SEARCH

The buyer organisation then searches for the best vendor (selling organisation) to supply the product to the specification requested. This may be done using trade directories, brochures kept on file, exhibitions, Internet searches or through recommendations (or word of mouth).

PROPOSAL SOLICITATION

The next stage is for the organisation's specialist buyer to invite suitable prospective suppliers to submit proposals. These proposals may range from catalogues to formal presentations and substantial written proposals, dependent upon the value and importance of the potential order.

SUPPLIER(S) SELECTION AND COMMITMENT

The buying organisation then reviews the proposals from the prospective vendors and, based on pre-specified criteria, selects one. The selection criteria usually revolve around attributes such as delivery times, product quality, prices, and possibly even honest corporate behaviour. Companies have, historically, used a number of suppliers as this enables them to obtain price concessions. However, increasingly, companies are working more closely with a smaller number of suppliers and, as a result, expect preferential treatment.

ORDER SPECIFICATION

The buyers finalise the order in terms of product specification, quantities, delivery times, price, etc., and forward it to the supplying organisation(s).

b2b focus: Developing a relationship

In recent years, much emphasis has been placed on the importance of buyer–seller relationships and how these may be a source of competitive advantage. The emphasis is on long-term, collaborative relationships between a small number of suppliers and customers. Building trust between organisations is essential to maintaining such relationships.

Ford (1980) proposed the following model of relationship development:

Pre-relationship stage: this stage involves the buyer evaluating potential new suppliers.

Early stage: potential suppliers are in contact with buyers to negotiate trial deliveries.

Development stage: deliveries of the product increase as trust and understanding develop between the buyer and the seller.

Long-term stage: the buyer and seller are mutually dependent.

Final stage: the relationship has become institutionalised.

Decisions need to be made as to the level of relational development required, since it is clearly a waste of valuable resources to invest in unwanted or unprofitable relationships. Technical support, increased access to expertise, better service levels and risk reduction are some of the benefits to the two organisations that need to be considered.

PERFORMANCE REVIEW

The final stage is performance review. The buying organisation assesses the performance of the supplying organisation and its products, and decides whether to use them as a supplier in the future.

ORGANISATIONAL PURCHASE CRITERIA

Organisational purchase criteria are usually much more rational, functional and objective than consumer criteria. Criteria such as price, conformity to product specification, quality, reliability and customer service levels, and continuity of supply are likely to be used. However, organisations are composed of individuals who have their own personal goals and motives. Therefore, more intangible, or implicit, criteria may also be important. Such criteria may include preferential treatment, which in turn may lead to useful professional relationships between individuals within, and between, organisations.

EXPAND YOUR KNOWLEDGE

Classic article

Webster, F.E. and Wind, Y. (1972) 'A general model for understanding organizational buying behaviour', *Journal of Marketing*, 36 (Apr): 12–19.

Sheth, J.N. (1973) 'A model of industrial buyer behaviour', *Journal of Marketing*, 37 (Oct): 50–6.

Both of these articles focus on organisational buying behaviour in contrast to consumer market behaviour. The significant factors that influence the eventual buying decision are explored.

SUMMARY

Markets are made up of individual people and organisations. In consumer markets (b2c), these people vary enormously in terms of gender, age, income, education, personality, perceptions, attitudes and many other factors. Marketers need to understand the processes that consumers go through when making purchase decisions: the stages they go through and the criteria they may use. These decisions are influenced by internal factors, such as motivation, attitude and perception, as well as external factors such as family, friends and culture.

Organisational (b2b) buying is more complex than b2c buying. Organisations vary in terms of size, culture, purchasing policy and many other factors. Organisational buying tends to be much more objective and rational than consumer decision-making, to the extent that it may be over-bureaucratic. It is important for marketers to understand the processes that businesses go through and who is involved in purchase decisions.

Before developing a marketing strategy, all these factors must be understood and taken into account. Without this understanding, the marketing organisation is unlikely to exert as much influence as it might have during its customers' decision-making processes.

CHALLENGES REVIEWED

Now that you have finished reading the chapter, look back at the challenges you were set at the beginning. Do you have a clearer idea of what's involved?

HINTS
- Product adoption categories – characteristics of innovators
- Influences on consumer buying behaviour
- Organisational decision-making unit (buying centre) and organisational buying process
- Thinking about the roles the child and its parents play in the purchase process, what reaction would you expect from the parents whose roles have been usurped? What is the likely impact on future business? Is the sales technique used ethical?

READING AROUND

JOURNAL ARTICLES

Belk, R. (1988) 'Possessions and the extended self', *Journal of Consumer Research*, 15 (2): 139–68.

Foxall, G. (1984) 'Consumers' intentions and behaviour', *Journal of Market Research Society*, 26 (3): 231–41.

Hyllegard, K., Yan, R-N., Ogle, J.P. and Attmann, J. (2010) 'The influence of gender, social cause, charitable support, and message appeal on Gen Y's responses to cause-related marketing', *Journal of Marketing Management*, 27 (1–2): 100–23.

Kotler, P. (1965) 'Behavioural models for analyzing buyers', *Journal of Marketing,* 29 (4): 37–45.

Laran, J. and Tsiros, M. (2013) 'An investigation of the effectiveness of uncertainty in marketing promotions involving free gifts', *Journal of Marketing,* 77 (2): 112–23.

Lawlor, M-A. and Prothero, A. (2011) 'Pester power – a battle of wills between children and their parents', *Journal of Marketing Management,* 27 (5–6): 561–81.

Maslow, A. (1943) 'A theory of human motivation', *Psychological Review,* 50 (4): 370–96.

Rogers, E. (1976) 'New product adoption and diffusion', *Journal of Consumer Behaviour,* 2: 290–301.

Sheth, J. (1973) 'A model of industrial buyer behaviour', *Journal of Marketing,* 37 (Oct): 50–6.

Webster, F. and Wind, J. (1972) 'A general model for understanding organizational buying behaviour', *Journal of Marketing,* 36 (Apr): 12–19.

Wei, Y. and Yu, C. (2012) 'How do reference groups influence self-brand connections among Chinese consumers? Implications for advertising', *Journal of Advertising,* 31 (2): 39–53.

MAGAZINE ARTICLES

Whelan, M. (2013) 'The schizophrenic shopper', *Admap*, February, London: WARC.

Wilson, J. (2013) '10 rules for social media research', *Admap*, April, London: WARC.

BOOKS

Hanna, N., Wozniak, R. and Hanna, M. (2009) *Consumer Behaviour: An Applied Approach*. Dubuque, IA: Kendall Hunt Publishing Co.

For more on b2b, see:

Ford, D., Gadde, L-E., Håkansson, H. and Snehota, I. (2006) *The Business Marketing Course: Managing in Complex Networks*, 2nd edn. New York: John Wiley & Sons.

Li, C. and Bernoff, J. (2011) *Groundswell: Winning in a World Transformed by Social Technologies*. Boston, MA: Harvard Business Review Press.

Quart, A. (2003) *Branded: The Buying and Selling of Teenagers*. London: Arrow.

JOURNALS

Advances in Consumer Research
Journal of Consumer Research

MAGAZINES

Ethical Consumer (Ethical Consumer Research Association)
Which? (The Consumer Association)

WEBSITES

www.acrwebsite.org – the Association of Consumer Research, which has an interesting section for marketers.

www.mintel.co.uk – Mintel provides a range of market research reports, to which many libraries subscribe.

VIDEO

The Money Programme (December 2005) 'Primark: King of No Frills Fashion'. London: BBC.

The Secret Lives of Students from TV Thinkbox; available at: www.thinkbox.tv/server/show/nav.852 (accessed 22/07/12).

SELF-REVIEW QUESTIONS

1. What are the main stages of the consumer decision-making process? (See p. 99)
2. List the three main types of buying situation and the types of product that might be included in each of them. (See p. 107)
3. What are the four main types of consumer buyer behaviour? (See pp. 109–10)
4. What are the major internal influences on consumer buying behaviour? (See pp. 112–13)
5. What are the main types of learning process? (See pp. 113–14)
6. Name the stages of Maslow's hierarchy of needs. (See p. 115)
7. What is the difference between an attitude and a belief? (See p. 117)
8. List the key roles in the organisational buying centre. (See p. 132)
9. What are the main categories in the consumer product adoption model? (See pp. 127–8)
10. What are the main organisational buying situations? (See p. 131)
11. What are the main characteristics of organisational markets? (See pp. 129–30)
12. What are the main stages of the organisational buying process? (See p. 133)

Mini case study: Getting there

Read the questions, then the case material, and then answer the questions.

1 Identify all the people involved in the two purchase decisions outlined in the case study: Duncan's Paris journeys and the couple's holiday plans. Comment on these people's roles and information needs. Explain and justify your answer.

2 What factors, internal and external, are likely to influence Duncan's decision about Paris? How?

3 Apply the decision-making framework to Annie and Duncan's holiday decision, picking relevant information out of the case and adding to it from your own knowledge (e.g. of information sources) if you can. What is likely to influence the outcome of each stage? How can marketing techniques assist the couple in their decision-making?

Technological breakthroughs in transport have had an even more dramatic impact on the way we live our lives than those in communication. Mass air travel is perhaps the biggest contributor to the changes, opening up possibilities that were impractical, or at least extremely time-consuming, in the past. Before the advent of commercial airlines, a trip from Europe to South Africa or Australia took months.

For some time, the emphasis in our hectic and stressed-out world, has been on getting from A to B as quickly as possible. Travellers have tended to favour the plane and the car as the speediest modes of transport. Cars were also preferred to public transport as they were considered more comfortable, more convenient and of higher status. The late Baroness Thatcher, formerly Margaret Thatcher, the UK Prime Minister, famously remarked in a 1986 government debate: 'A man who, beyond the age of 26, finds himself on a bus can count himself as a failure', yet today governments are encouraging the use of public transport rather than cars while environmental pressure groups advocate trains and boats rather than planes. Whether or not such green policies will prevail, will depend upon consumer attitudes and behaviour.

Many people are switching from plane to train in order to reduce their carbon dioxide emissions. Eurostar's Business Premier class, which has a 10-minute check-in facility and a work-friendly environment on board, has become increasingly popular with busy executives. In 2009, Eurostar's daily ticket sales were approximately £1.85m and rising, the growth coming mainly from business travel.

Boarding the Eurostar.

© Eurostar ID Brand Library

Richard Brown, Chief Executive of Eurostar, commented: 'The growth in traveller numbers clearly indicates that concerns about the environmental impact of short-haul air travel, combined with the worsening experience of flying, are prompting more people to look for a greener and easier way of travelling to the Continent.'

Eurostar is leading the way in an image change for train travel generally. Its excellent punctuality record, with 95% of trains arriving on time in 2009 (before the Christmas crisis), has been a key factor in changing attitudes towards train travel.

The service has got even better since the new terminus at St Pancras opened. Journeys from St Pancras International are at least 20 minutes quicker than before. Passengers are whisked from London to Paris in just 2 hours 15 minutes and London to Brussels in only 1 hour 51 minutes. When compared to the time it takes just to get to the departure gate at a UK airport (upwards of two hours), the train looks even more attractive.

Duncan Scott travels from London to Paris on business at least once a week. He has always taken a taxi to Heathrow airport (a journey of about 10 miles) and then flown from there. At Charles de Gaulle airport, he gets another taxi to his destination in Paris. However, his friends are starting to harass him about his carbon footprint – some seriously, some light-heartedly. His girlfriend, Annie, has done the research and found that he could walk to his local tube station, catch a tube to Kings Cross Railway Station, stroll through the smart shops and cafes of St Pancras International and from there take the Eurostar to Paris Nord in the heart of the French capital. Then he could take the Metro, though it would mean two changes and would take about three-quarters of an hour, or he could take a taxi which would be quicker. Annie thinks he should take the Metro but Duncan dislikes being underground and is worried about getting lost.

He is also concerned that the train may actually cost more and that his firm will be reluctant to pay for it. The travel department, who book everything, are notoriously inflexible and cost-conscious. However, he is playing golf with his boss and the Finance Director soon and has promised Annie that he will raise the issue. He hasn't dared tell her about the Finance Director's attitude to trains. According to him, train travel is for other people. He flies, drives his Bentley or is driven by someone else – usually someone wearing a peaked cap.

As well as trying to reorganise Duncan's travel arrangements, Annie is worried about Duncan who seems stressed and in need of a good holiday (they haven't had one for nearly a year). She can only take one week off work so they need to spend as little time travelling as possible so that they have enough time at their destination. Duncan thinks they should fly but is leaving the decision to Annie. She is worried about what her friends will say if she flies, given the fuss she has been making about Duncan flying to Paris. One of her friends, Irene, is a travel agent and she is trying to find suitable ferries and trains for them to get to their first-choice destination, Austria, where they had planned to hike. So far it is not looking hopeful. Irene has suggested they go to France or Holland instead. There is the possibility of hiring a barge in Holland,

(Continued)

(Continued)

which really appeals to Duncan. Annie would prefer horse riding in the Camargue, although her mother is absolutely against it, claiming that it is far too dangerous. She suspects that they will end up cycling somewhere as a compromise and she is content with that – as long as they don't have to fly.

Travel decisions have been dominating Annie and Duncan's lives. Their flat is liberally scattered with brochures, the PC seems to be permanently linked to travel sites and they get at least two messages a day from travel agents. When Duncan gets home from a long day, made longer by a security alert at Heathrow, he finds Annie excitedly waving two tickets to Amsterdam (ferry and train). Her mother has decided to treat them to a Dutch canal trip.

With thanks to Eurostar, 2007

REFERENCES

Assael, H. (1987) *Consumer Behaviour and Marketing Action*, 6th edition. Boston, MA: Kent Publishing Co.

Bearden, O. and Etzel, M. (1982) 'Reference group influence on product and purchase decisions', *Journal of Consumer Research*, 9 (2): 183–94.

Engel, J., Blackwell, R. and Miniard, P. (2006) *Consumer Behaviour*, 9th edn. Fort Worth, TX: The Dryden Press.

Enis, B.M. (1980) *Marketing Principles*, 3rd edn. Santa Monica, CA: Goodyear.

Eurostar (2007) 'Press release: Eurostar revenues rise as travellers go for high speed rail'. Available at: **http://www.eurostar.com/uk-en/about-eurostar/press-office/press-releases/2007?page=2** (accessed 17/02/14).

Festinger, L. (1957) 'A theory of cognitive dissonance', in J. Sheth, B. Mittal and B. Newman (1999) *Customer Behavior: Consumer Behavior and Beyond*. Fortworth, TX: The Dryden Press.

Ford, D. (1980) 'The development of buyer–seller relationships in industrial markets', *European Journal of Marketing*, 14 (516): 339–54.

Howard, J.A. and Sheth, J.N. (1967) 'A theory of buyer behavior', in R. Moyer (ed.) *Changing Marketing Systems ... Consumer, Corporate and Government Interfaces: Proceedings of the 1967 Winter Conference of the American Marketing Association*. Washington, DC: AMA.

Howard, J.A. and Sheth, J.N. (1969) *Theory of Buyer Behavior*. New York: John Wiley & Sons.

Hyllegard, K.H., Yan, R-N., Paff Ogle, J. and Attmann, J. (2010) 'The influence of gender, social cause, charitable support, and message appeal on Gen Y's responses to cause-related marketing', *Journal of Marketing Management*, 27 (1–2): 100–23.

Kotler, P. (1965) 'Behavioural models for analyzing buyers', *Journal of Marketing*, 29 (4): 37–45.

Kotler, P., Keller, K.L., Brady, M., Goodman, M. and Hansen, T. (2012) *Marketing Management*, 2nd edn. Harlow: Pearson.

Laran, J. and Tsiros, M. (2013) 'An investigation of the effectiveness of uncertainty in marketing promotions involving free gifts', *Journal of Marketing*, 77 (2): 112–23.

Laurent, G. and Kapferer, J. (1985) 'Measuring consumer involvement profiles', *Journal of Marketing Research*, 22 (Feb.): 41–53.

Lawlor, M-A. and Prothero, A. (2011) 'Pester power – a battle of wills between children and their parents', *Journal of Marketing Management*, 27 (5–6): 561–81.

Li, C. and Bernoff, J. (2011) *Groundswell: Winning in a World Transformed by Social Technologies*. Boston, MA: Harvard Business Review Press.

Maslow, A.H. (1943) 'A theory of human motivation', *Psychological Review*, 50 (4): 370–96.

Mintel (2012) *Social Media and Networking – UK – May 2012*. London: Mintel International.

Powers, T., Advincula, D., Austin, M.S. and Graiko, S. (2012) 'Digital and social media in the purchase-decision process: a special report from the Advertising Research Foundation', *Journal of Advertising Research*, 52 (4): 479–89.

Rogers, E.M. (1976) 'New product adoption and diffusion', *Journal of Consumer Behaviour*, 2: 290–301.

Rogers, E.M. (2003) *Diffusion of Innovations*, 5th edn. New York: The Free Press.

Schiffman, L.G., Kanuk, L.L. and Hansen, H (2008) *Consumer Behaviour: A European Outlook*. Harlow: FT/Prentice Hall.

Sheth, J.N. (1973) 'A model of industrial buyer behaviour', *Journal of Marketing*, 37 (Oct): 50–6.

Smith, P.R. and Taylor, J. (2004) *Marketing Communications: An Integrated Approach*, 4th edn. London: Kogan Page.

Solomon, M.R., Bamossy, G., Askegaard, S. and Hogg, M.K. (2010) *Consumer Behaviour: A European Perspective*, 4th edn. Harlow: Pearson Education.

University of New Hampshire (n.d.) 'Kentucky Fried Chicken Hoax'. Available at: **www.unh.edu/BoilerPlate/kfc.html** (accessed 22/07/07).

Usunier, J-C. and Lee, J.A. (2009) *Marketing Across Cultures*. Harlow: FT/Prentice Hall.

Webster, F.E. and Wind, Y. (1972) 'A general model for understanding organizational buying behaviour', *Journal of Marketing*, 36 (Apr): 12–19.

Wei, Y. and Yu, C. (2012) 'How do reference groups influence self-brand connections among Chinese consumers? Implications for advertising', *Journal of Advertising*, 31 (2): 39–53.

Wilkie, W. (1990) *Consumer Behavior*. New York: John Wiley & Sons.

Williams, K.C. (1981) *Behavioural Aspects of Marketing*. London: Heinemann Professional Publishing.

Zaichkowsky, J.L. (1985) 'Measuring the involvement construct', *Journal of Consumer Research*, 12 (3): 341–52.

Visit the companion website on your computer at **www.sagepub.co.uk/masterson3e** or MobileStudy on your Smart phone or tablet by scanning this QR code and gain access to:

- **Videos** to get a better understanding of key concepts and provoke in-class discussion.
- Links to useful **websites and templates** to help guide your study.
- Access **SAGE Marketing Pins (www.pinterest.com/sagepins/)**. SAGE's regularly updated **Pinterest** page, giving you access to regularly updated resources on everything from Branding to Consumer Behaviour.
- **Daily Grind podcast series** to learn more about the day-to-day life of a marketing **professional**.
- Interactive **Practice questions** to test your understanding.
- A **bonus chapter on Marketing Careers** to not only support your study, but your job search and future career.
- **PowerPoints** prompting key points for revision.

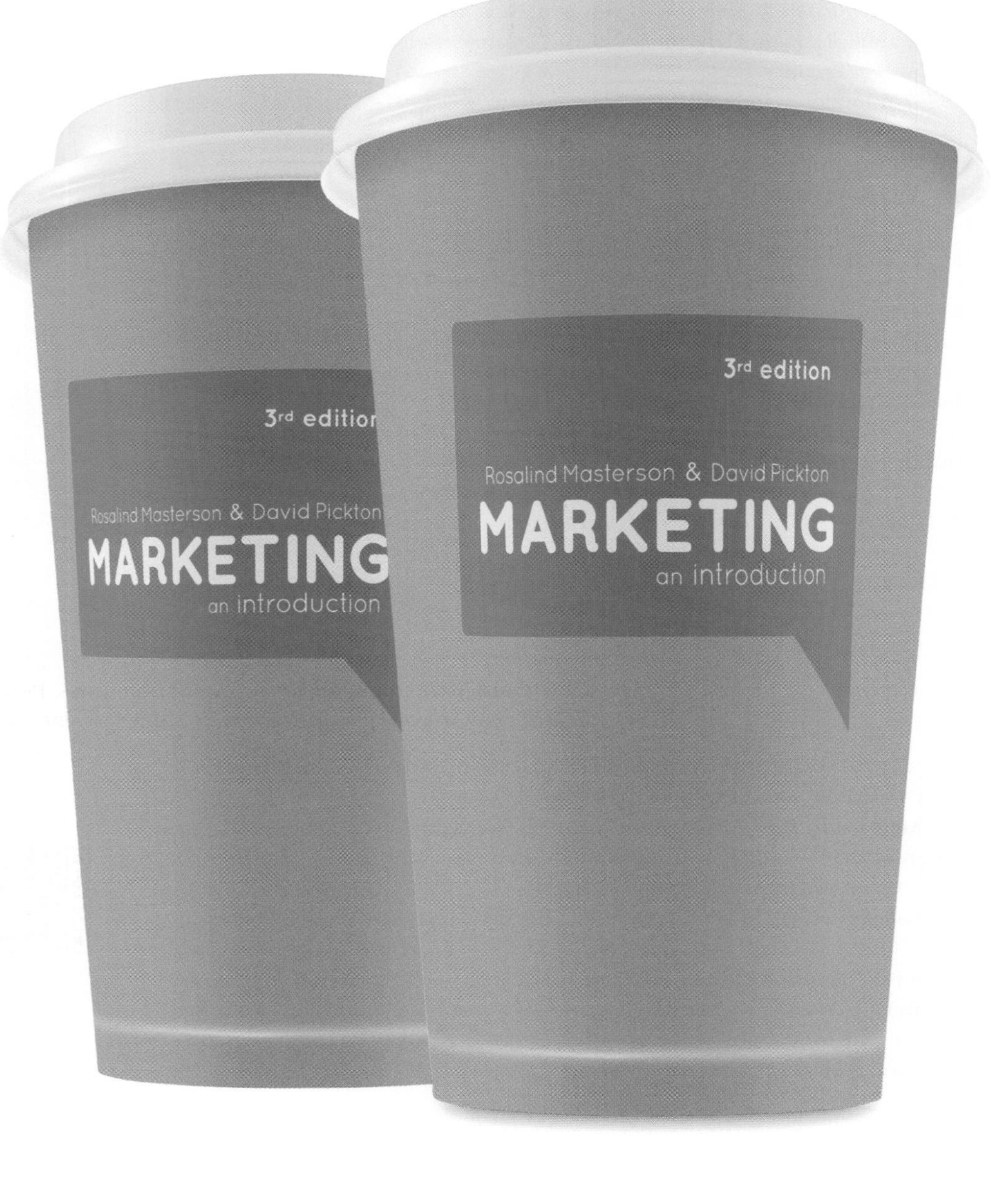

Market segmentation, targeting and positioning

4

MARKET SEGMENTATION CHALLENGES

The following are illustrations of the types of decisions that marketers have to take about market segmentation. *You aren't expected to know how to deal with the challenges now*; just bear them in mind as you read the chapter and see what you can find that helps.

- You have just joined the marketing department of a car company. Your managing director has asked your advice about the launch of a new product. The investment to date on product development has been large and high sales targets have been set. Should you try to appeal to as wide a market as possible, aiming to attract as broad a cross-section of customers as possible?
- You are the marketing director of a loss-making brewery. You need to develop new products to revitalise the business. How will you choose what type of beer to sell and to whom?
- You are a marketing manager for a firm of solicitors. Research has indicated that you are operating in a marketplace where people see little difference between rival solicitors' services. How could you develop a deeper understanding of what customers want and so find more profitable opportunities?
- You work in a travel agency. Recently published market research has revealed the existence of a variety of different types of holidaymaker. What criteria will you use to identify and describe these different types of holidaymaker?

market segmentation
the process of dividing a total market into subgroups (segments) such that each segment consists of buyers and users who share similar characteristics but are different from those in other segments

INTRODUCTION

Marketers are interested in satisfying the wants and needs of customers and consumers but not everybody wants the same things. This poses a problem for marketers. Marketing the same goods or services to everybody is unlikely to be successful but providing something unique for each individual will be too expensive. There has to be a compromise, and fortunately there is. Marketers can take advantage of the fact that some people share similar wants and needs. These people can be grouped according to their similarities. **Market segmentation** is about breaking up a market into sections (segments) so that marketing effort can be focused better towards particular segments. This is efficient and effective marketing.

The process of market segmentation requires accurate information on customers and potential customers and this is found through market research (see Chapter 5). It is important to understand which buyer characteristics (see Chapter 3) are significant in the purchase of the product in question. For example, it is quite common to split markets into male and female, but this is not likely to be the best way to do it if you are selling PC supplies.

In practice, there are different ways of segmenting a market and the approach taken will depend on the nature of the market and the way in which a company

These shoppers may all be part of a consumer market but their needs and wants are likely to vary significantly.

b2b (business to business)
business dealings with another business as opposed to a consumer

target marketing (targeting)
the selection of one or more market segments towards which marketing efforts can be directed; sometimes called market targeting

positioning
the place a product (brand) is perceived to occupy in the minds of customers/consumers of the relevant target market relative to other competing brands

wishes to deal with it. The way a company segments a **b2b** market will be different from the way a company segments a consumer market.

Market segmentation is not where the process ends, however – it is just the beginning. Having identified the different segments in a market, decisions have to be made about which ones to target and how many to target. This is referred to as **target marketing** (or simply targeting). These decisions lie at the very heart of marketing decision-making as they affect the full range of marketing activities undertaken. In choosing targets, marketers have to consider competing brands and position their own brands in such a way as to reduce unnecessary direct competition. This is called brand, or competitive, **positioning**.

This chapter emphasises the need to determine which markets are attractive, and explores different approaches to the important STP process of segmentation, targeting and positioning.

MARKET ATTRACTIVENESS

Choosing which markets to focus on, based on their **market attractiveness** to the organisation, is one of the most fundamental aspects of marketing. It involves a matching process based on an assessment of:

- market opportunity – to identify what is possible
- competitive advantage – to determine the degree of challenge
- the objectives of the organisation – to confirm what the organisation wants to achieve.

These assessments are essential inputs to an organisation's marketing strategy. How many market opportunities are selected will depend on the thinking of top management and the objectives of the firm. Some firms will want to be innovators and will be keen to search out new opportunities; some will be followers and quickly imitate the leaders (see Chapter 2). Others will consider themselves to be risk averse and will therefore be slow to adopt change. Ironically, this strategy may actually be riskier because they are failing to move with the times.

To stand the best chance of achieving marketing success, a thorough understanding of the market is absolutely necessary. It is unusual for an organisation to attempt to capture an entire market. It is more likely to target one or more segments of that market: usually those segments that seem to offer the best chance of high profits. Not-for-profit organisations also employ segmentation and targeting techniques in order to make more effective use of resources and increase their chances of achieving their objectives (e.g. fundraising or client/patient service).

WHAT ARE MARKETS?

Markets are people. Or, more accurately, a market consists of individuals or organisations that have a willingness and ability to purchase products. A market can consist of a single segment or multiple segments.

Even though markets may be described in terms of products, such as the 'drinks market', 'car market' or 'market for nuclear power stations', it is important that marketers never forget that markets are composed of people.

In basic marketing terms, markets are composed of customers (buyers) and consumers (users) but will also include other groupings as well, such as sellers and competitors (see Chapter 1). In terms of segmentation, targeting and positioning, we are particularly concerned with understanding customers (actual and potential) and consumers (actual and potential). Markets are, without doubt, very complex environments, as was shown in Chapter 2, and identifying markets only in terms of customers can overlook one other important dimension: that of the role of consumers. While customers are strictly the purchasers of products, consumers are the users. Marketers need to address the needs of both.

There are dangers associated with focusing **solely** on customers. Firstly, not all customers are the same or want the same things. A product that is ideal for one customer may be no good at all for another (think about films or clothes). Secondly, customers are not necessarily consumers. The users of goods and services may not be the actual customers (buyers). For example, toys are often bought by parents but used by their children. Who should we design the toy for? Who should we aim the advertising at? Similarly, some products, e.g. boxes of chocolate, jewellery, perfume, are often bought as gifts. The customer is buying the product with someone else in mind.

Industrial goods and services are almost never bought by the people who will actually use them. Organisations have buying departments to make the purchases the business needs.

market attractiveness
an assessment of how desirable a particular market or market segment is to an organisation

segments
distinct parts of a larger market; customers and consumers in each segment share similar characteristics

customer
a buyer of a product or service

consumer
the individual end-user of a product or service

Members of a supply chain, such as agents, wholesalers and retailers, buy things to sell on. They may be the first link in a chain of buyers but they are not the eventual consumers.

So yes, customers are important, but so are the final consumers or users of the products. Marketers need to address the needs of them all.

WHY SEGMENT AND TARGET MARKETS?

The tribes we lead

One of the most profound realisations to strike any marketer is that there is a great diversity among customers. (Louden and Della Bitta, 1993: 30)

mass-marketing delivering the same marketing programme to everybody without making any distinction between them

Mass-marketing, i.e. selling the same thing in the same way to everyone, is largely a twentieth-century idea. It relied on large numbers of customers/consumers sharing sufficiently similar needs and wants. This is not the approach in the vast majority of today's markets any more than it was in the distant past. As pointed out by Lindgren and Shimp (1996), mass-marketing is a very recent phenomenon. Up until the early 1900s, most goods were produced to meet the needs of specific customers, but as populations and demand grew, this became an inefficient process. Henry Ford, founder of the Ford Motor Company, is frequently attributed with developing and popularising the concept and the technology of mass-production. He standardised his production techniques and his products (even if there is now some doubt over whether he actually said 'you can have it any colour you want so long as it's black') to achieve economies of scale. The consequence of these lower production costs per unit was cheaper cars but it only worked so long as the cars were very similar in design. This mass-production strategy therefore led inevitably to the mass-marketing strategy of one product (the Model T), in one colour (black), at one price ($360) to the entire market.

In times of scarce supply of products, customers will make do with whatever is available. In many countries today, there is an over-supply of most products. Those markets are demand-driven, rather than supply-driven (see Chapter 1). As a consequence, markets are fragmenting and moving away from mass-marketing to more targeted approaches. Under such circumstances, trying to apply mass-marketing techniques, offering a single product and single marketing programme across the total market, while achieving economies of scale, runs the risk that few customers will be adequately satisfied (Dibb and Simkin, 1996). In contrast to mass-marketing, some now talk of **mass-customisation** to refer to the way in which, even in very large markets, organisations are being challenged to tailor their product offerings almost to meet individual needs. Once again, technology is being harnessed to provide solutions.

mass-customisation tailoring product offerings almost to meet individual needs

Marketers need to recognise that potential customers/consumers want different things, and that this creates opportunities to develop different markets and sub-markets *and* to develop different marketing programmes for each. So numerous and diverse are people's requirements that it would be impossible for any single organisation to satisfy everybody. This creates competitive opportunity and the potential for competitive advantage.

Although everybody is different, people do at least have some similarities and this allows companies to direct their efforts with greater effectiveness, efficiency and economy.

e-focus: Getting to know your target market

Simple marketing research and analysis, coupled with a basic understanding of market segmentation and targeting principles, can result in more effective marketing.

Many organisations regularly collect and store valuable customer information in databases. Many also fail to make the best use of that information which can reveal valuable insights into customers and potential customers – or students.

Further Education (FE) colleges are on tight budgets and so it is tempting for them to use a uniform marketing communications approach which treats all potential students the same. Clever use of the information they already have in their database could help them to target students more precisely.

The first step is to purge the database, removing duplicate entries, gone-aways and incomplete records. It is vitally important that data is clean and current.

The next step is to decide on a segmentation approach. For an FE college, which runs trade and vocational courses, GCSEs and A levels, it might be effective to segment by demographic and lifestyle characteristics. At one college, an analysis of the database showed that students on trade courses tended to be in their late teens or early twenties, of average affluence, unmarried with one or two children, usually working in craft or trade occupations and with practical activities such as DIY and home computing or computer gaming as hobbies. GCSE or A-level students were usually younger, living at home, single with no children, working part-time in unskilled jobs with music, dancing, reading and gaming as hobbies.

A good next step would be to see where these groups of people tend to live. This can be done by subscribing to a geo-demographic data-provider such as Mosaic or ACORN. They have systems to match those demographic profiles to local postcode areas. Targeted mailings, showing the right kind of courses, could then be sent to potential students. Website information could also be tailored to each profile, making it easier for potential students to find courses of interest and the other information they need.

Better targeting reduces junk mail and spam by only sending relevant information to the right people. That means a lot fewer people throw the mail in the bin – and get irritated by the sender. In this scenario, it could also reduce the number of prospectuses and other materials wasted on people with no interest, while at the same time improving enquiries and enrolments – and the college's image.

WHAT IS MARKET SEGMENTATION?

Market segmentation is the splitting of a market into smaller groups (segments) so that marketers can better direct or focus their efforts. Segmentation can be defined as: 'the process of dividing a total market into subgroups (segments) such that each segment consists of buyers and users who share similar characteristics but are different from those in other segments'.

Segmentation: A NIVEA case study

Ideally, from the marketing point of view, a segment would be those people who share the same buying behaviour and practices in **every** respect, but this is not possible. Instead, marketers make use of a variety of measures or techniques to find groups of people who are similar enough in the ways that count. It is possible, therefore, to segment a market (i.e. the customers for a product) according to age, where people live, their interests and lifestyles: anything that is relevant. In business-to-business (b2b) marketing, organisations can be segmented according to their location, industry grouping, etc. Much as marketers would love to measure and model every buyer and their purchase and product usage behaviour, this is not practical on a large scale. These segmentation approaches, or variables, are an indication of similarities between customers. A fuller description of the variables used as bases for segmentation follows after the next section which discusses the main factors that make for a good segment to target.

CRITERIA FOR DETERMINING GOOD MARKET SEGMENTS

Today there is a wealth of information available to marketers to help them segment markets. It is important to make sure that the segments you identify are the best ones. Good segmentation should meet particular criteria which are outlined below. The segments should be:

- *Measurable* – marketers need to know how many potential customers are in each segment. If it is not measurable, a segment cannot be assessed for its size and profit potential.
- *Homogeneous* (similar) within the segment – the customers/consumers in a market segment should be as similar as possible in their likely responses to marketing mix variables.
- *Heterogeneous* (different) between segments – the customers/consumers in **different** segments should be as different as possible in their likely responses to marketing mix variables. The less overlap there is between segments, the better.
- *Substantial* – the segment should be big enough to be profitable (or otherwise be capable of meeting the objectives of the organisation).
- *Accessible* – segments need to be reached and served effectively, not only in terms of delivery of product but also in terms of communication with the members of the segment. This can often be a problem. It may not be possible, for instance, to arrange new, or rearrange existing, distribution systems cost-efficiently to reach a chosen segment (Dibb and Simkin, 1996), for example if your factory is in Central England and the new target is in Tasmania. If your identified target is ex-gamblers with retired racehorses, how would you identify and communicate with them?
- *Operational* – the segmentation approach adopted should be useful in designing **specific** marketing mixes for each segment. If you end up taking the same approach for multiple segments, what was the point? The stability of the segment in the short, medium or long term is also important.

All these things should be used to evaluate whether or not a segment is suitable for targeting. Dibb and Wensley (2002) make the point that other important considerations also have to be borne in mind if a market segmentation analysis is to be turned into effective marketing action:

- the commitment and involvement of senior managers within the organisation
- the readiness of the company to respond to market change
- inter-functional/departmental coordination
- the need for well-designed planning.

In practice, companies operate with limited and imperfect information and resources. It is not always possible to meet all of the criteria above. Under such circumstances, the challenge is to consistently improve so that better segmentation (and subsequently targeting, which will be discussed later) can be achieved.

SEGMENTATION APPROACHES

There are many ways to approach the segmentation of a market. Although the approaches can be used singly, it is common to use them in combination. Exhibit 4.1 shows how this works to produce a much more focused segment for targeting. Variables used singly would still represent a fairly indiscriminate market, while, used collectively, a more clearly defined segment emerges.

A summary of the different approaches to segmentation in consumer markets is given in Exhibit 4.2 and each approach is then described in greater detail in the sections that follow. Segmentation approaches in business markets will be considered later in Exhibit 4.7.

Exhibit 4.1   Using multiple segmentation variables

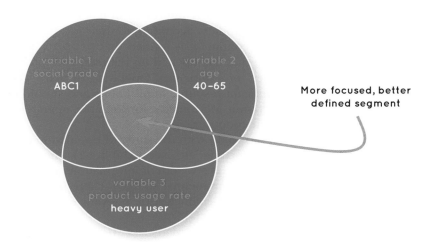

Exhibit 4.2   The main variables used as bases to segment markets

Consumer (b2c) markets	Examples of variables
• Geographic segmentation	Country, region, city, urban–rural
• Demographic segmentation	Age, gender, family size, life stage, e.g. family life cycle (FLC), religion, race, nationality, education, ethnic group, income, socio-economic grouping: A, B, C1, C2, D, E
• Geo-demographic segmentation	House type and house location (e.g. ACORN, MOSAIC)
• Psychographic segmentation	Lifestyles, values, motives, personalities, e.g. VALS
• Mediagraphic segmentation	Media habits (i.e. TV viewing, papers read, etc.)
• Behavioural segmentation	
purchase occasion	Day-to-day purchase, special occasion
benefits sought	Value for money, service, status, quality, brand image
usage rate	Heavy, medium, light user
user status	None, ex, potential, first time, regular user
readiness stage	Unaware, aware, informed, interested, desirous, intending to buy, bought, used
attitude to product	Enthusiastic, uninterested, positive, negative
involvement	Low involvement, high involvement (see Chapter 3 for more details)
adopter type	Innovator, early adopter, early majority, late majority, laggard
loyalty status	Total, strong, medium, light, none

demographic segmentation markets segmented by population characteristics such as age, gender, occupation and income

geographic segmentation markets are segmented by countries, regions and areas

Geodemographics and Class

SEGMENTATION IN CONSUMER MARKETS

Geographic and **demographic segmentation** are probably the most popular forms of segmentation. Marketers are clearly interested in where their customers are physically located. Grouping customers according to their location, e.g. their neighbourhood, town, country or continent, is termed **geographic segmentation**. In many markets, the Internet has opened up national and international opportunities to even the smallest of companies. Operating in many countries or areas, however, can have significant resource implications and should only be entered into after careful consideration. McDonald's, for example, operates around 22,000 restaurants in 109 different countries.

Demographic segmentation has to do with the study of population characteristics (such as gender, occupation, income, etc.; see Exhibit 4.2). These variables are relatively easy to measure and there is a wealth of information on them readily available from both government and commercial sources. There is a wide range of demographic variables: any personal characteristic relevant to the product in question may be used.

For example, if you are a manufacturer or retailer of shoes, size of feet would be relevant; or size of waist if you make clothing. Clothing retailers Long Tall Sally

global focus: The world is getting smaller

The world is getting smaller, or so it seems, with improvements in transportation and telecommunications technologies. Writer Marshall McLuhan invented the term 'global village' to describe this process and how it means that information can travel around the globe almost instantly. International trade is increasing as trade barriers are lifted. Through websites, email and mobile communications, and greatly improved physical distribution operators, even the smallest company can attract and satisfy international customers.

Moving into international markets is not without its problems, though. Even greater attention to segmentation is needed to ensure success. Around 230 nations each have their own unique cultures, subcultures, languages, customs, ethics, beliefs, religions and demographic patterns. All these differences complicate the segmentation process, especially as the quantity and quality of relevant information will vary significantly from country to country.

and High and Mighty use size to segment and target the women's and men's market respectively, and focus on larger sizes only. Life stage is another useful variable and an example of this is the **family life cycle** (FLC), which is described in the customer focus box on pp. 155–6. In this segmentation, the stages in the family life cycle create different needs. Young families have very different purchasing behaviour and leisure activities than solitary survivors. An alternative life-stage grouping is that developed by BMRB-TGI who identify 12 different life-stage segments and a 13th unclassified group:

family life cycle
a form of market segmentation based on the recognition that we pass through a series of quite distinct phases in our lives

- Fledglings – 15–34, not married and have no childrren; living with own parents
- Flown the nest – 15–34, not married, do not live with relations
- Nest builders – 15–34, married, do not live with son/daughter
- Mid-life independents – 35–54, not married, do not live with relations
- Unconstrained couples – 35–54, married, do not live with son/daughter
- Playschool parents – Live with son/daughter and youngest child 0–4
- Primary school parents – Live with son/daughter and youngest child 5–9
- Secondary school parents – Live with son/daughter and youngest child 10–15
- Hotel parents – Live with son/daughter and have no child 0–15
- Senior sole decision makers – 55+, not married and live alone
- Empty nesters – 55+, married and do not live with son/daughter
- Non-standard families – Not married, live with relations, do not live with son/daughter, and do not live with parents if 15–34
- Unclassified – Not in any group.

Source: Kantar Media

social grading
segmentation
by occupation of
head of household;
the typical
classifications used
are A, B, C1, C2, D
and E groups

Groups of occupations (usually of heads of households) can be used to segment markets according to **social grading**. In the UK, the best-known groupings are: A, B, C1, C2, D and E. Exhibit 4.3 shows these groupings and how the UK population has changed over time with a greater proportion representing the higher earning professional groups (ABs) and a lower proportion in the C2, D and E categories.

Exhibit 4.3   Social grading

Occupational Groups		Percentage of population 2010
A	Higher managerial, administrative and professional	4
B	Intermediate managerial, administrative and professional	22
C1	Supervisory, clerical and junior managerial, administrative and professional	29
C2	Skilled manual workers	21
D	Semi-skilled and unskilled manual workers	15
E	State pensioners, casual and lowest grade workers, unemployed with state benefits only	8

SOURCE: NRS data, 2010

These socio-economic groupings are sometimes inaccurately referred to as social classes, which is a related and overlapping concept but has wider connotations than just the occupational measure that is used in social grading.

Social grading has proved to be a particularly useful segmentation variable as it is used widely in market research and in the collection of government statistics. This means that there is a wealth of data available to the marketer that relates social grades to buying behaviour, disposable and discretionary income, media habits, hobbies and interests – all the sorts of things that marketers need to know. Unfortunately, social grading is not very good at determining discrete segments that are homogeneous within the group and heterogeneous between the groups (see 'Criteria for determining good market segments' on p. 150), which is an important aspect of market segmentation. The information may be fairly easy to collect and it may be widely available, but it is limited in its usefulness. Despite this, it remains popular but it is advisable to combine demographic variables to make a more focused market segment, as shown in Exhibit 4.1.

National
Readership
Survey:
Lifestyle data

To summarise, the thinking behind demographic segmentation is that age or life stage or occupation, etc. are factors that will tend to affect buying and usage behaviour. For example, a wealthy lawyer will shop for clothing very differently from a student. A 20-year-old male will exhibit different purchase and use behaviour from a 50-year-old female.

Geo-demographic segmentation has become an increasingly popular method for segmenting consumer markets. It combines aspects of both geographic and demographic data (hence its name). Developed first in the early 1980s by the

customer focus: Stages in the family life cycle

Newly living together.

Family life-cycle segmentation is based on the recognition that a person passes through a series of quite distinct phases in their life, each typified by a different set of circumstances, and within each they display some very different behaviour. Each stage gives rise to, or is associated with, different needs, social behaviour and purchasing patterns. The buying and consumption needs of a family with a young child or children (Full Nest I) are very different from those of an older couple with no children (Empty Nest II). Since its first inception, there has been far greater emphasis placed on the buying and influencing behaviour of children and, given the increasing longevity of life, the Empty Nest and Solitary Survivor stages.

Full nest I.

Stages in the family life cycle

Stage	Characteristics
Bachelor	Young, single, not living at parental home, few financial burdens, recreation orientated – holiday, entertainment
Newly living together	Young couple, no children, well off financially, two incomes – purchase home, home household consumer durables
Full Nest I	Youngest child under 6, home purchase is significant emphasis, increasing financial pressures, may have only one income, purchase of household necessities

Full nest II.

People at different stages in the family life cycle.

Solitary survivor II.

(Continued)

(Continued)

Full Nest II	Youngest child over 6, financial position improving, some working spouses		interest in travel and leisure pursuits
Full Nest III	Older married couple with dependent children, financial position better still, replace household furnishings and products	*Empty Nest II*	Older couple, no children at home, retired, drastic cut in income, medical services emphasised
		Solitary Survivor I	Still working, income good but likely to sell home
Empty Nest I	Older married couple, no children at home, home ownership is peak, renewed	*Solitary Survivor II*	Retired, low income, special needs for medical care, affection and security

ACTIVITY

For each of the stages in the family life cycle, identify a range of different goods and services you think are most likely to appeal.

Acorn

Mosaic UK

CACI organisation, ACORN (A Classification Of Residential Neighbourhoods) makes use of household census data (data collected by the government on the total population) and specifically focuses on where people live and what types of house they live in. Using sophisticated statistical techniques, it has been possible to 'cluster' the population into defined groups according to two variables: house location and house type. The implication is that the area and the sort of house we live in say something about the sort of people we are and, importantly for the marketer, the sort of things we do, buy and use. We can contrast this with social grading, which attempts to relate the sort of people we are and the things we do with our occupations (and income). Geo-demographic systems that have already analysed and grouped the population for every area in the country (in all large economies) are commercially available to the marketer to analyse a huge range of markets. Examples include: ACORN, MOSAIC, Euro-MOSAIC, GlobalMOSAIC, PIN and SuperProfile (details of MOSAIC's 15 main groups and examples of their 67 types are provided in Exhibit 4.4). Significantly, geo-demographic groupings have been extensively cross-referenced with other shopping and behaviour databases. In the case of MOSAIC, these include the Target Group Index (TGI) and BARB data (see also Chapter 5) so that the actual buying and media habits of these groups are widely known and analysed. The geo-demographic systems that are offered for commercial purposes, such as

ACORN and MOSAIC, are updated frequently so it should be noted that the categories and details are subject to change.

ACTIVITY

Walk around an area of housing you are familiar with. Using the brief MOSAIC descriptions given in Exhibit 4.4, try to guess what categories the types of house fit into. How much do the houses vary? How many different categories can you identify? Alternatively, if you are an Apple iPhone, iPod Touch or iPad user, you can download the free MOSAIC app and if you know the postcodes for the area you can insert these for immediate geo-demographic descriptions. Compare the descriptions with your impressions of the area.

Psychographic segmentation attempts to measure and understand people's lifestyles, values, personalities and/or their psychological characteristics. As an approach, it more directly addresses the issue of understanding buyer and usage behaviour through an understanding of the buyers and users themselves. It is a particularly useful approach for creating a more detailed understanding of particular segments within an overall market and can be used with other approaches, such as demographic segmentation.

psychographic segmentation using lifestyles, values, personalities and/or psychological characteristics to split up markets

For example, classifying shoppers into different types, as follows, is an interesting and useful lifestyle approach:

- the convenience shopper
- the recreational shopper
- the 'shop-till-I-drop' shopper
- the price-bargain shopper
- the store-loyal shopper
- the traditionalist shopper
- the outgoing/individualistic shopper
- the quality service shopper
- the socially conscious shopper
- the other directed shopper (concerned about asking others for opinions).

Working in shopper marketing

A popular consumer classification model is VALS™ which uses a combination of psychology and demographics to help marketers best target their customers. Originally developed by SRI International and now owned and operated by Strategic Business Insights (SBI), the most recent US version of VALS™ segments individuals age 18 and older into eight consumer groups on the basis of their demographic and psychological characteristics. The main dimensions of the framework are primary motivations on the horizontal axis and resources on the vertical axis. Exhibit 4.5 shows the eight types grouped into three primary motivations: ideals, achievement and self-expression. The extent to which these primary motivations may be realised is affected by an individual's physical, emotional and psychological resources.

VALS

Exhibit 4.4   MOSAIC geo-demographics

Group	Approx.% population	Approx.% households	Description	Examples of types within each group
A	4.3	3.5	Alpha territory	A01 Global power brokers A02 Voices of authority
B	9.5	8.2	Professional rewards	B06 Yesterday's captains B10 Parish guardians
C	4.8	4.4	Rural solitude	C11 Squires among locals C13 Modern agribusiness
D	9.2	8.75	Small town diversity	D17 Jacks of all trades D 18 Hardworking families
E	3.4	4.3	Active retirement	E20 Golden retirement E23 Balcony downsizers
F	13.2	11.2	Suburban mindsets	F26 Mid-market families F27 Shop floor affluence
G	5.3	5.8	Careers and kids	G30 Soccer dads and mums G32 Childcare years
H	4.0	5.9	New homemakers	H34 Buy-to-let territory H36 Foot on the ladder
I	10.6	8.7	Ex-council community	I 38 Settled ex-tenants I41 Stressed borrowers
J	4.5	5.1	Claimant cultures	J42 Worn-out workers J43 Streetwise kids
K	4.3	5.2	Upper floor living	K48 Multicultural towers K49 Rehoused migrants
L	4.0	6.0	Elderly needs	L50 Pensioners in blocks L53 Low-spending elders
M	7.4	7.4	Industrial heritage	M54 Clocking off M55 Backyard regeneration
N	6.5	7.0	Terraced melting pot	N60 Back-to-back basics N61 Asian identities
O	8.8	8.5	Liberal opinions	O63 Urban cool O67 Study buddies

SOURCE: Based on Mosaic UK (as at May 2012). MOSAIC is a registered trademark of Experian Ltd

Exhibit 4.5   VALS™ segmentation

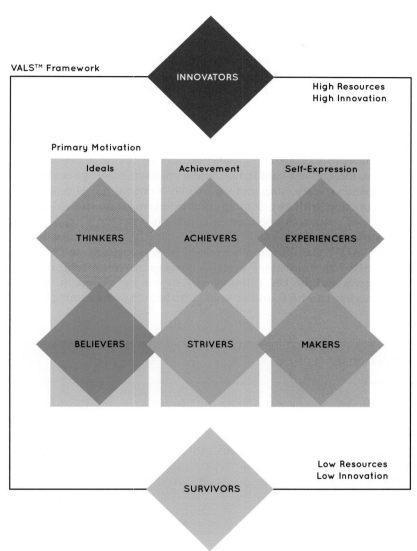

SBI describe their primary motivations and resources as follows:

US VALS™ consumer segment descriptions
Innovators are successful, sophisticated, take-charge people with high esteem
Thinkers are mature, satisfied, comfortable and reflective
Believers are strongly traditional and respect rules and authority
Achievers have goal-oriented lifestyles that centre on family and career
Strivers are trendy and fun-loving
Experiencers appreciate the unconventional
Makers value practicality and self-sufficiency
Survivors lead narrowly focused lives

Primary Motivation

The concept of primary motivation explains consumer attitudes and anticipates behaviour. VALS includes three primary motivations that matter for understanding consumer behaviour: ideals, achievement and self-expression. Consumers who are primarily motivated by ideals are guided by knowledge and principles. Consumers who are primarily motivated by achievement look for products and services that demonstrate success to their peers. Consumers who are primarily motivated by self-expression desire social or physical activity, variety and risk.

Resources

A person's tendency to consume goods and services extends beyond age, income and education. Energy, self-confidence, intellectualism, novelty seeking, innovativeness, impulsiveness, leadership and vanity play a critical role. These psychological traits in conjunction with key demographics determine an individual's resources. Various levels of resources enhance or constrain a person's expression of his or her primary motivation.

While the VALS™ classification described here is focused on US and Canadian consumers, SBI has equivalent systems for Japan, Venezuela, the Dominican Republic, Nigeria and the UK; China is currently in development. More details of the VALS™ models can be found at **www.strategicbusinessinsights.com/vals**.

ACTIVITY

Visit the SBI website (**www.strategicbusinessinsights.com**) and make notes on each of the eight types identified in the VALS™ model. As an additional fun exercise, try out the survey questions for yourself (although you should remember that the survey can only accurately type respondents who are English speaking and acculturated in the US or Canada).

VALS™

Arts
audiences:
Insights
(Arts Council
England)

behavioural segmentation dividing a market into subgroups (segments) of customers/users according to how they buy, use and feel about products

Behavioural segmentation groups customers and consumers according to how they buy, use and feel about products and can be very effective in identifying segments.

The growth of out-of-town and edge-of-town supermarkets and shopping malls has changed shopping behaviour. As most shoppers travel by car, it has been possible to increase the size of bulk packaging of such items as soap powders as they only have to be transported to the car park. In contrast, social changes and growth in what the Henley Centre for Forecasting has previously described as the 'secular household', in which individuals 'do their own thing', have resulted in increased sales of pre-packaged meals for one that can be prepared quickly in the microwave.

customer focus: Behind the camera

Some manufacturers in the camera industry make use of behavioural segmentation in designing their models.

Point-and-clickers look for ease of use, reliability and auto-settings so that the camera effectively takes all of the guess work out of taking photos.

Budget buyers look for value for money and more 'bang for their bucks'.

Gadget freaks just can't have enough of those twiddly bits, buttons and menus, and look for extra functionality.

Settings junkies really want manual controls and overrides of the auto settings or lots of auto settings to choose from to suit each photo occasion.

Professionals and serious enthusiasts are looking for high performance, which probably means auto and manual control, digital SLR, high-specification body and lenses, superior photo chip and data capture in compressed and non-compressed formats as standard.

Behavioural segmentation can involve many different variables, as indicated in Exhibit 4.2, and these can include product or brand loyalty, frequency of purchase or rate of consumption, attitudes towards the product, whether the product is perceived as a high-involvement product, in which great care will be taken over the purchase, or a low-involvement product that may be bought more out of habit (see Chapter 3), what the customer is buying the product for – general use or a special occasion such as a party – and so on. For example, the chocolate market could be segmented into individual consumption (e.g. small bars), sharing (e.g. larger bars, boxes) and gift purchases (e.g. fancier boxes).

> **high-involvement purchases**
> purchases that customers expend time and effort on, usually high cost or high risk, e.g. cars, holidays, wedding dresses

> **low-involvement purchases**
> products that customers spend little time or effort in choosing, often low cost, low risk or regular purchases, e.g. toothpaste, washing-up liquid, jam

EXPAND YOUR KNOWLEDGE

Classic article

Haley, R.I. (1968) 'Benefit segmentation: a decision-oriented research tool', *Journal of Marketing*, 32 (Jul): 30–5.

Haley introduces the concept of segmenting on the basis of the benefits offered by the brand as a legitimate new approach.

Loyalty status is increasingly used as a segmentation variable. As the value of maintaining loyal customers has become more widely recognised, degrees of loyalty have become more relevant to marketers. In today's market environment, it is difficult to believe in totally loyal customers. Even those that hold loyalty cards frequently hold such cards from a variety of competitors. One way of classifying customer loyalty (and therefore segmenting the market) is as follows:

Hard-core loyals: have absolute loyalty to a single brand or company, e.g. always buy Heinz ketchup.

Soft-core loyals: divide their loyalty between two, or sometimes more, brands or companies, e.g. sometimes buy Heinz ketchup, sometimes Waitrose, but never anything else.

Shifting loyals: brand-switch, spending some time on one brand, or favouring one company, and then moving to another, e.g. usually buy Heinz ketchup, then try supermarket own brands, usually returning to Heinz.

Switchers: show no brand loyalty, maybe purchasing products that are the lowest price or on special offer.

User status (which may vary from non-user to regular user) and usage rate (light usage to heavy usage) are similar to loyalty status but loyalty requires more than regular usage (see Chapter 1). Clearly a consumer who never uses a brand cannot be described as loyal, but these non-users may be exactly who the company wishes to target. Alternatively, they may target occasional users in an effort to make them buy the product more regularly. User/usage behaviour is therefore something to which marketers should pay particular attention. As the importance of longer-term customer relationships has become more widely recognised, the concept of customer lifetime value has gained more attention. The use of customer databases allows organisations to maintain vast amounts of data on their customers' purchasing habits and segment different customer groups accordingly.

The actual benefits sought by customers/consumers is another interesting way of distinguishing between them. The key benefit for some might simply be a low price, for others, ease of use. In the toothpaste market, there are numerous products aimed at different benefit groups. Sensodyne is for sensitive teeth. Pearl Drops is for tooth whitening. Eucryl is for smokers. Most toothpaste brands have developed sub-brands to appeal to users seeking different benefits: tartar and plaque control, fresh breath, reduced cavities, whiter teeth, etc. Each relevant benefit describes a substantial market segment and provides a great market opportunity.

customer lifetime value
a calculation of the long-term worth of a customer using estimates of expected purchases

ACTIVITY

Visit a supermarket and choose a category of heavily branded products such as soap, detergents or toiletries. Take a close look at the different brands and their packaging, and identify what benefits each is trying to emphasise. Think about the different ways the competing products are trying to be positioned in terms of the similarities and differences in the benefits they claim to offer. Can you identify the sort of different behavioural characteristics they appeal to?

Exhibit 4.6   Categories of adopter

Category	Characteristics	Percentage of the population
Innovators	Risk-takers, often affluent and well educated	2.5
Early adopters	Adopt early, are opinion leaders in their communities and a source of information about new things	13.5
Early majority	Follow the lead set by the early adopters, delay while making sure of new ideas and things	34
Late majority	Older than average and often less well educated, tend to be more sceptical, more traditional and more comfortable with older values	34
Laggards	Suspicious of innovation, often associated with low education and low income, often social outsiders	16

The **product adopters model** (see Chapter 3) is another way of conceptualising purchasing behaviour and identifying distinct market segments. Researchers have found that people are fairly consistently adventurous, or not so adventurous, in their purchase and consumption behaviours. These findings have been linked to particular **personality** and behavioural tendencies. Marketers have found this way of segmenting the market can be very insightful and helps to explain why product sales follow the typical product life-cycle curve that is described in Chapter 6. As new products to the market are launched, they appeal to innovators who are quick to respond to novel ideas. Over time these products are adopted by each of the adopter categories in turn until those new products become dated and really only appeal to the laggards, who are the slowest to accept new ideas and change. Therefore, it is possible to modify marketing activities to best appeal to each of the groups in turn as the product is first launched, becomes accepted in the marketplace and, eventually, declines in popularity. Exhibit 4.6 briefly summarises the different adopter groups.

product adopters model (product diffusion model) categorises product buyers/users according to their take-up rate of new products

personality a person's distinguishing psychological characteristics that lead them to respond in particular ways

EXPAND YOUR KNOWLEDGE

Bruning, E.R., Hu, M.Y. and Hao, W. (2009) 'Cross-national segmentation: an application to the NAFTA airline passenger market', *European Journal of Marketing*, 43 (11/12): 1498–1522.

The authors propose an approach to international segmentation that identifies meaningful cross-national consumer segments focused on airline passengers.

**FMCG (fast-moving
consumer goods)**
low-value items
that are bought
regularly (the shelves
empty quickly), e.g.
toothpaste

SEGMENTATION IN BUSINESS MARKETS

Segmentation principles apply in just the same way to business markets, both b2b (business to business) and industrial markets. Although marketing is most commonly associated with consumer markets (b2c) and even more particularly with fast-moving consumer goods (FMCG) markets, a great deal of marketing is b2b. B2b markets underpin consumer markets as manufacturers rarely sell direct to consumers; instead they sell to wholesalers or retailers or other supply chain intermediaries (see Chapter 9). Take Coca-Cola or Unilever, for example. They rarely, if ever, have dealings with consumers; their goods are instead sold in shops. They do, however, invest a lot of money in advertising to consumers of course, and so are still interested in consumer market segmentation and targeting.

Coca-Cola is really a b2c company even though it does not sell direct; true b2b organisations sell their products to other organisations, for use within those organisations and so it is these that need to be segmented. B2b market segmentation can be done using similar approaches to those for consumer markets, but there are some additional ones – for example, the type of business or industry they are in, and size of business (see Exhibit 4.7).

In b2b markets, the segmentation variables can be grouped into macrosegmentation variables and microsegmentation variables (as shown in Exhibit 4.7). As with segmentation in consumer markets, a well maintained and comprehensive database will make the job much easier and more cost-effective.

Exhibit 4.7 Segmentation approaches in business markets

Business-to-business (b2b) markets	Examples of variables
Macrosegmentation variables	
• Geographic location	country, region, city, urban–rural, industrial estate
• Type of organisation	manufacturer, service, government, local authority, private, local, international
• Industry grouping/business sector	standard industrial classification (SIC), e.g. textiles, computing, telecommunications, etc.
• Customer size	large, medium, small, key customer
Microsegmentation variables	
• User status	none, ex, potential, first time, regular user
• Trade category	agent, wholesaler, retailer, producer
• Benefits sought	economy, quality, service
• Loyalty status	total, strong, medium, light, none
• Readiness stage	unaware, aware, informed, interested, desirous, intending to buy, bought, used
• Adopter type	innovator, early adopter, early majority, late majority, laggard
• Purchasing practices	centralised, decentralised, tendering
• Buy class	straight rebuy, modified rebuy, new task

Shapiro and Bonoma (1984) proposed a detailed, nested approach in which they identified five general segmentation bases arranged in a nested hierarchy. The process of segmentation should work from the more general outer area (macrosegmentation) towards the more specific inner area (microsegmentation), probing deeper as it goes (see Exhibit 4.8).

1 *Demographic variables* are used to give a broad description of the business segments based on such variables as location (which Shapiro and Bonoma included as a demographic, rather than geographic, variable), size of business, type of business and business sector (e.g. SIC code; for details see below).
2 *Operating variables* enable a more precise identification of existing and potential customers within demographic categories. User status and technologies applied might be considered here.
3 *Purchasing approach* looks at customers' purchasing practices (e.g. centralised or decentralised purchasing). It also includes purchasing policies and buying criteria, and the nature of the buyer/seller relationship.
4 *Situational factors* consider the tactical role of the purchasing situation, requiring a more detailed knowledge of the individual buyer, others involved and the specific buying situation. This might include potential order size, urgency of order and any particular requirements.
5 *Personal characteristics* relate to the people who make the purchasing decisions. Different customers may display different attitudes to risk and different levels of loyalty to suppliers.

Exhibit 4.8   The nested approach to b2b segmentation

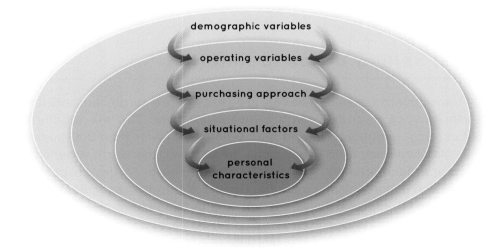

EXPAND YOUR KNOWLEDGE

Classic article

Shapiro, B.P. and Bonoma, T.V. (1984) 'How to segment industrial markets', *Harvard Business Review*, May–Jun: 104–10.

The difficulty of segmenting industrial markets has dissuaded companies from trying despite the benefits derived from so doing. This article explores the ways of segmenting industrial markets and proposes a nested hierarchy approach.

SIC (Standard Industrial Classification) system of classifying products by allocating numbers (codes) to every product category, industry or business sector

target market a group of buyers and consumers who share common needs/wants or characteristics and upon whom the organisation focuses

A great deal of information on b2b markets and their segmentation is available. For example, type of business/industry will be defined by industrial classifications, such as the SIC (Standard Industrial Classification), which governments use to categorise companies. Government publications summarise this data and company details can readily be found in a wide range of business directories. The SIC system simply allocates unique numbers to every industry or business sector. The first digit, or couple of digits, indicate the broad industry area. The succeeding digits provide greater detail and are more specific about individual products or product groupings. Exhibit 4.9 shows example details of UK SICs by providing just the first digit of the code, showing the major industry and service areas. The North American SICs (North American Industry Classification System – NAICS) code examples in this exhibit show how the code number is built up from the general to the specific. European SICs and other countries' SIC approaches adopt similar principles.

b2b focus: Selling buses to America

Approximately 5000 transit buses are sold per annum in North America to some 350 transport authorities. Segmentation in this b2b bus market has historically involved the macrosegmentation approach, namely focusing on customer size and geographical variables. Essentially, the most important consideration has been the size of the bus fleet. Transport authorities with over 750 buses are considered large, authorities with between 200 and 750 are medium, and authorities with fewer than 200 buses are small. In addition, the North American market is divided into 11 geographical regions. Research into microsegmentation characteristics in this market has revealed two new approaches to segmentation. The first highlights the importance of the purchase decision process and the second highlights the importance of the product evaluation process, which emphasises the significance placed by buyers on particular product features. Six distinctly different decision process segments and a further six product feature segments have been identified. These new ways of segmenting b2b markets are providing far greater insight into marketing issues, and overcoming the criticisms voiced and difficulties faced over not being able to adequately operationalise segmentation approaches into marketing strategy (Dibb and Wensley, 2002).

Crittenden, Crittenden and Muzyka (2002) described these two different groups of segments as follows:

Decision process segments

- The rider-conscious and low-cost bid segment

- The government regulation-prone advanced design bus (ADB) lovers' segment
- The low-cost bid and manufacturer reputation segment
- The staff-poor ADB big spenders' segment
- The large, new-look buyers' segment
- The 'opinions of others and not dollars count' segment

Product feature segments

- The drive train and not drivers segment
- The cool climate drive train and not drivers segment
- The rider-sensitive and forget the fuel segment
- The more rider-sensitive and less driver-sensitive segment
- The power-hungry segment
- The style conscious and cool segment

Exhibit 4.9 Standard Industrial Classifications (SICs)

UK SIC code	Description
0	Agriculture, forestry, fishing
1	Energy and water-supply industries
2	Extraction of minerals and ores (excluding fuels), manufacture of metals, mineral products and chemicals
3	Manufacture of metal goods, engineering, vehicles
4	Other manufacturing industries
5	Construction
6	Distribution, hotels/catering, repairs
7	Transport and communication
8	Banking, finance, insurance, business services, leasing
9	Other services

NAICS code	Description
	The first two digits of the NAICS code show the Major Group Category, for example:
20-39	digits in this range are for the Manufacturing Industry Division
34	these first two digits give the industry group code for 'Fabricated metals'
342	the addition of the third digit, 2, gives the industry group code for 'Cutlery and hand tools'
3423	the addition of the fourth digit, 3, gives the specific industry code for 'Hand and edge tools'
34231	the addition of the fifth digit, 1, gives the product class code for 'Mechanics hand service tools'
342311	the addition of the sixth digit, 1, gives the specific product code for 'Pliers' so allocating Code 342311 to a company (among any other codes it might also be allocated) would indicate that it was a manufacturer of pliers

TARGET MARKETING

target marketing (targeting) the selection of one or more market segments towards which marketing efforts can be directed; sometimes called market targeting

Target marketing involves making decisions about which part of the market an organisation wishes to focus on. It follows from market segmentation, in which the total potential market is subdivided according to its characteristics. Targeting is then the choice of which single segment or group of segments the organisation wishes to select. A **target market**, therefore, would actually be better described as a target submarket or target segment.

EVALUATING A SEGMENT FOR TARGETING

Targeting market segments: Australia Case Study

There are five principal characteristics that will make a market segment particularly attractive for targeting but, before selecting, the organisation must undertake a full PRESTCOM analysis (see Chapter 2), which will include consideration of its own company resources and capabilities, its strengths and weaknesses, the competition and the company's objectives. The characteristics of an attractive segment are that it includes one or, preferably, more of the following:

1 has sufficient current and potential sales and profits
2 has the potential for sufficient future growth
3 is not over-competitive
4 does not have excessive barriers or costs to entry or exit
5 has some relatively unsatisfied needs that the company can serve particularly well.

It should be noted that the distinction here is really about the way in which a company focuses its marketing efforts towards those customers (targets) that it really believes will give it greatest success. Customers from outside the target can, of course, be accepted, but these will not be the focus of attention. The result could be that companies may miss some potential customers that lie outside the target but, within their limited resources, they will have directed their efforts in ways that they have decided are likely to be most effective and cost-efficient. Wise marketers recognise that trying to appeal to *everyone* may well have the effect of not appealing successfully to *anyone*.

EXPAND YOUR KNOWLEDGE

Romaniuk, J. (2012) 'Five steps to smarter targeting', *Journal of Advertising Research*, 52 (3): 288–90.

The author offers five ways to make your targeting smarter, such as making your target market definitions evidence-based and including as many people as possible in your target market group.

REASONS FOR TARGETING AND POSITIONING

The rationale behind the process from market segmentation to targeting to positioning is a logical development of the marketing concept that was introduced in Chapter 1. As all marketing authors emphasise, segmentation, targeting and positioning are key decision areas in marketing and strategic planning, and are the foundation of successful marketing management.

Applying the principles outlined in this chapter allows organisations to handle market diversity by focusing resources on particular customer/consumer groups. Having a better understanding of the media habits, buying behaviour and product use of subgroups of the market creates the opportunity for organisations to fine-tune their offerings, allocate scarce resources more effectively, and provide the basis for strategic marketing decisions. Analysis of the market allows organisations to improve their competitiveness, exploit market gaps, avoid or reduce direct competition, and develop their competitive advantage. In short, they are fundamental parts of good marketing, facilitating marketing effectiveness, efficiency and economy. How well an organisation then puts these to use is an implementation issue that will be affected by managerial willingness and ability.

IPA:
Touchpoints

TARGETING STRATEGIES

Having analysed the chosen market and determined the attractiveness of the various segments in that market, a decision then has to be made concerning which segments to target. Exhibit 4.10 illustrates the different **targeting strategies** visually.

targeting strategies
used to select a single target market or a group of target markets

UNDIFFERENTIATED MARKETING

Undifferentiated marketing is where the market is believed to be composed of customers/consumers whose needs and wants from the product being offered are fundamentally the same, i.e. there is no basic difference between them, they are undifferentiated. This is mass marketing: a single marketing programme is used for all. Although this may result in lower costs, it is very difficult to satisfy all customers/consumers with one product or marketing mix. An organisation using undifferentiated marketing may also be providing an excellent opportunity for its competition to capture a portion of its sales by appealing to the desires of specific

undifferentiated marketing
where the market is believed to be composed of customers/consumers whose needs and wants from the product are fundamentally the same

b2b focus: The gnome experiment

Some segments are harder to target than others. This is particularly true in b2b marketing where segments are likely to be small, spread out and not well served by any one media channel. Many good products fail because they just aren't well known enough.

The gnome experiment for Kern.

The well-travelled gnome looks a bit chilly at the South Pole.

Kern and Sohn make scales, balances and weights for schools and laboratories. Their products are technically excellent, delivering highly accurate measurements. However, their market was commoditised. To customers, a scale was a scale – they expected all scales to be accurate and didn't see any advantage to any particular brand. Kern and Sohn's challenge was to raise awareness of their brand and of the technical superiority of their products – within a clearly defined, narrow market segment: schools and laboratories.

The solution proposed by the Ogilvy agency was the 'world's first mass-participation global gravity experiment'. How better to appeal to the world's scientists? The agency enlisted the scientific community's help to test the following hypothesis; 'if Earth was a perfect sphere of uniform density, then gravity would be consistent. But it's not, which means gravity varies wherever you go. So can we chart those discrepancies using just a basic-range Kern scale?'

Ogilvy produced a chip-proof garden gnome and, through a combination of social media, blogs, company websites and traditional media, invited scientists and existing customers across the world to weigh the gnome and send it on. The gnome travelled in his own suitcase, carefully protected and accompanied by a basic Kern scale calibrated to the gravity of his hometown in Germany. His temporary hosts recorded his local weight online before re-packing him.

The gnome travelled to 152 countries generating 1445 new sales leads, 65% of which were from the two key target markets: schools (45%) and laboratory-based scientists (25%). He returned home in May 2013 and is now retired – but you can watch the film of his travels on YouTube: http://www.youtube.com/watch?v=XVxEVMvwCvM

SOURCES: Kern (2013); Ogilvy Public Relations (2013).

market segments. For example, if a company only sold blue jeans, it would be giving away all the potential customers for other-coloured jeans. Few, if any, products are marketed totally in this way. Usually, some form of differentiation takes place, even if only on a small scale. Products such as the original Coca-Cola and Pepsi-Cola are reasonable examples of undifferentiated marketing, although it should be recognised that some modifications are made to the marketing, and even the product's

ethical focus: Leave our kids alone!

Should companies be allowed to target children with advertising for their products? Should marketing activity be allowed in schools? The answers to these questions depend on who you ask. Many big companies, e.g. soft drinks manufacturers, argue that children are their main consumers and so yes, of course, there should be adverts aimed at them and heavily branded vending machines in schools. The National Union of Teachers estimated that advertisers spend over £300 million per year advertising to children in UK classrooms. Companies want to catch consumers young and build the relationships that may keep them loyal to the brand throughout their lives.

Specialist agencies, such as TenNine, exist to reach this highly desirable market. TenNine are a media agency specialising in 'ethically responsible messaging' targeted at young people. Their clients include: Nike, Adidas, Orange, Tesco and Unilever. So they also say yes, targeting children is OK, but many parents would say no.

The parents' argument is that advertising uses sophisticated techniques to play on our emotions, our insecurities, our need to be respected, our need to be loved – techniques that are just too powerful, and potentially harmful, to be let loose on kids.

TenNine's counter-argument is that they display relevant and responsible messages and help large companies to support the school curriculum by providing equipment and product samples.

This curriculum support might include distributing Revlon perfume samples to pupils as support for PSHE (personal, social, health and economic) and, even more puzzlingly, PE (physical education) classes. Many school sports teams proudly display a sponsor's logo on their kit while drinks vending machines are splashed with logos and can even talk about the products they sell. Cadbury's withdrew their offer of free sports equipment when the Food Commission revealed that pupils would have to eat 5440 chocolate bars, containing 33 kg of fat and nearly 1.25 million calories, to qualify for a free set of volleyball posts.

In the UK, advertisements for food high in fat, sugar or salt cannot be broadcast during children's television programmes. But they can be fired at children from UK websites – and these foods may well be on the lunch menu at school.

What do you think? Should marketing be allowed into schools?

SOURCES: Clark (2004); Monbiot (2013).

Exhibit 4.10   Targeting strategies

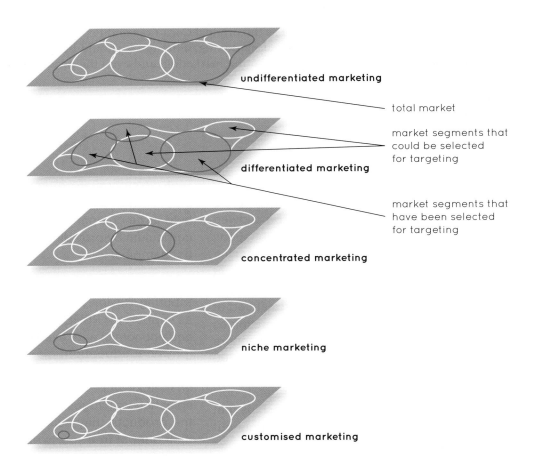

recipe, in different countries. Both companies have also recognised the potential of particular benefit segments within the market and so, by selling Diet Coke in the USA and the UK (Coca-Cola Light in most other countries), Coke Zero, Diet Pepsi, Pepsi Max, Caffeine-free etc., they become differentiated marketers instead.

There can be advantages to following an undifferentiated strategy. Lindgren and Shimp (1996) pointed out that an undifferentiated marketing strategy can enable an organisation to build and maintain a specific image with customers/consumers, minimise its production costs, achieve greater efficiencies and be able to offer its products at competitive prices (or otherwise achieve higher profit margins). They cite three instances, in general, when a mass, or undifferentiated, marketing strategy is most appropriate:

1 When the market is so small that it is unprofitable to market to just a portion of it.
2 When heavy users are the only relevant target because they make up a large proportion of the market.
3 When the brand dominates the market and appeals to all segments of the market, thus making segmentation unnecessary.

DIFFERENTIATED MARKETING

Differentiated marketing is when differences between market segments are recognised and two or more target markets are selected, each receiving a different marketing programme. The Ford Motor Company is a good example of an organisation that uses a differentiated target marketing strategy effectively. By developing a range of models, from the Ka to the Galaxy, it is able to meet the needs of a wide range of people. Most large organisations have adopted the principles of differentiated marketing, even if the specific approaches they have adopted vary (see Chapter 11, on branding strategies). Even the Coca-Cola Company, as an organisation, has adopted a differentiated approach to its total business. It has a number of other drinks brands as well as Coke including: Sprite, PowerAde, Minute Maid, Fanta and Lift.

Exhibit 4.11   Continuum of targeting strategies

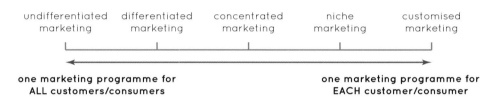

one marketing programme for
ALL customers/consumers

one marketing programme for
EACH customer/consumer

CONCENTRATED MARKETING

Concentrated marketing targets a single market segment. If that market is relatively small, well defined and very focused, it is called a **niche market**. In the car market, this might be Aston Martin or Morgan. **Customised marketing** goes a stage further and makes a product offering for one individual. In consumer markets, this may be for one-off products that are hand-built to a customer's specification. Tailors will custom-make suits or bridal gowns. Architects will design and build a new house to a client's exact specifications. This degree of targeting is more frequently found in b2b markets, especially for large-value orders such as a factory, an engineering project or the organising of a special event on behalf of a company.

Targeting strategies can therefore be seen as a continuum of strategies ranging from the very broad to the very narrow (see Exhibit 4.11).

differentiated marketing differences between market segments are recognised and two or more target markets are selected, each receiving a different marketing programme

concentrated marketing where only one market segment is chosen for targeting

niche market a market segment that can be treated as a target market; a small, well-defined market, often part of a larger market

customised marketing producing one-off products/ services to match a specific customer's requirements, e.g. a made-to-measure suit or the organisation of a product launch party

How I Built
A Fashion
Brand
With No
Experience

Customisation in the car market.

EXPAND YOUR KNOWLEDGE

Johnson, G.D. and Grier, S.A. (2011) 'Targeting without alienating: multicultural advertising and the subtleties of targeted advertising', *International Journal of Advertising*, 30 (2): 233–58.

Targeting by its nature focuses on some to the exclusion and possible alienation of others. This paper examines a way to target a specific minority group while maintaining resonance among the broader audience.

POSITIONING

Positioning follows naturally from the targeting decision, and forms a direct link between the target marketing strategy and marketing programmes. When the organisation has selected its target markets, but before it develops marketing plans and programmes, it needs to ensure that it fully understands customer/consumer perceptions of the competing brands. A detailed analysis of the target market(s) can show not only how the other offerings are perceived, but also where the organisation's own brand might fit. Customer perceptions are typically a consequence of their previous knowledge and experience of the brands themselves **and** of the companies that own them. Apple, for example, creates close links between itself as a company and its brands (e.g. iPhone, iPod, iPad). See Chapter 11 for more about branding.

Positioning refers to the place a brand is perceived to occupy in the minds of the target market relative to other competing brands. It has been referred to as a battle for the hearts and minds of customers/consumers. Companies usually have a range of brands, i.e. a **product (or brand) portfolio** (see Chapters 6 and 11). Companies may well have more than one version of a product within their portfolio, e.g. Thomas Cook offer a wide range of holidays for customers to choose between. When deciding whether or not to offer a new holiday for sale, they will want to make sure it adds something new to the portfolio. If it is just going to take sales away from an existing product, what would be the point? If the new holiday product is for a different, or underserved, part of the market, then it is far more likely to add to profits. Alternatively, it could be aimed at an existing market segment, but positioned differently so that it attracts new people.

For example, if Thomas Cook already had enough hotels rooms in Mallorca to satisfy all their customers, there would be no point in contracting for more unless they would attract **extra** customers. Say they have lots of hotels suitable for families, they do not need any more, but perhaps a hotel that did not cater for children would attract people without children. These people would be a new target market segment.

Alternatively, it might be worth taking on another family hotel if families would perceive it as significantly different to the existing holiday offerings, perhaps as a watersports centre rather than a beach hotel, or as more suited to children under 5 while the other hotels were better for older children, or as a place for parents who

product portfolio
all a company's or strategic business unit's products

want some peace but with the reassurance that their children are safe and happy and being well looked after by someone else. Then the hotel would be positioned differently. Families would see it differently and others might book.

ACTIVITY

Visit the websites of major car companies and look at their product portfolios. Who do you think these different cars are aimed at (their target market)? How do they compare to each other, and to other manufacturers' competing cars, in terms of image?

Exhibit 4.12 shows how the VW/Audi Group (VAG), which makes the Skoda, Seat, Volkswagen and Audi brands, have differentiated these brand families through careful positioning so that they do not compete directly with each other. VAG refer to these as product platform developments. Although the brands in Exhibit 4.12 are compared with each other on the basis of price and cost-leadership/differentiation,

Exhibit 4.12   VAG brand differentiation

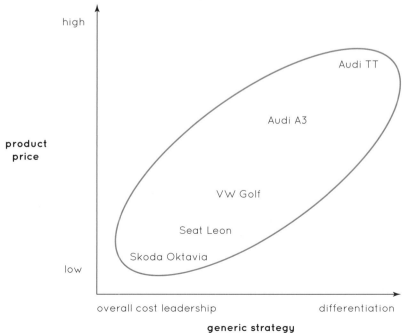

the actual process of creating brand differentiation and distinctiveness (and, thereby, positioning the brand in the marketplace) involves many more marketing dimensions and heavy reliance on marketing communications to create specific brand identities and images. Before VAG acquired ownership of Skoda, it had a very poor image. VAG changed that image through improved design and quality and an excellent advertising campaign. The result has been that Skoda is now accepted as a credible brand that competes well with many other mid-range vehicles. It has certainly captured market share from competitors and has won industry awards in the process.

ACTIVITY

An activity earlier in this chapter suggested a visit to a supermarket to investigate different brands. Think about that activity now or carry out the activity again but this time specifically look for brands made by the same company. You might look at carbonated drinks such as Coke, Lilt and Fanta, for example. But there are many other product groups you could choose. Consider what each brand is trying to achieve, how it is positioned and whether the brands are likely to appeal to the same target customers. Consider what the manufacturing company is trying to do in marketing such similar brands and the extent to which the company could be competing against itself.

perceptual map
results from the perceptual mapping process and shows brands' relative positions (also called a brand map, position map or space map)

Multi-attribute Attitude Mapping (MAM)
a form of perceptual mapping comparing a product's key features (according to their importance to target customers) with features offered by competitive brands

Multidimensional Scaling (MDS)
a form of perceptual mapping that establishes similarities and differences between competing brands

PERCEPTUAL MAPS

Rothschild (1987) highlights two particularly important techniques in ascertaining customer/consumer perceptions relative to competing bands. These are both represented visually as perceptual maps, which are also called brand maps, position maps or space maps. The first technique is Multi-attribute Attitude Mapping (MAM) and the second is Multidimensional Scaling (MDS), both of which sound more complex than they really are. Both forms of analysis can be presented pictorially, which makes the comparison between brand perceptions very straightforward.

MULTI-ATTRIBUTE ATTITUDE MAPPING (MAM)

MAM is achieved by first determining the key features or attributes of products in a group – for cars these might include fuel consumption, style, comfort, etc. People are asked to assess competing brands against these attributes by indicating how important each attribute is (from high to low) and how each brand is rated for each attribute (from high to low). The attributes may be given a score out of 10. It is important to ensure that only members of the target market(s) are asked for their perceptions. The views of the general population are not relevant to this analysis. The findings might then be presented as shown in Exhibit 4.13. The horizontal lines indicate how important each of the six identified attributes are perceived to

e-focus: Facebook friend or LinkedIn connection?

There are thousands of social networking sites on the Internet, many of them targeted at specific market segments. Facebook, YouTube and Twitter are amongst the best known sites. They have a broad appeal; anyone can join from anywhere in the world – young and old, affluent and poor, men and women, introverts and extroverts, conversationalists and spectators.

Some other sites are more specifically targeted at certain groups or types of people. These are following a niche targeting strategy. LinkedIn is a network for professionals and businesspeople. It is positioned as the site for business-networking, career progression and job seeking. Established in 2003, it now has more than 200 million registered

users in over 200 countries. Mumsnet's target membership is clear from its strap line: 'by parents for parents' (though it's possibly not the best name to appeal to fathers). Gapyear helps gap year students and backpackers to stay in touch, ask for help and advice, and meet other travellers. Goodreads is for book-lovers who share reviews and recommendations. MySpace used to be a serious rival to Facebook but, having lost that battle, it has repositioned, with considerable help from its association with Justin Timberlake, as a site for music-lovers and sharers.

How many social networking sites are you on? If you use more than one – why do you? Who are your sites targeting and how are they positioned?

be, and the relative position of brands A, B, C, D and E are shown against each of these attributes. Also shown is what is deemed to be the ideal position according to the respondents. This is identified as brand 'I'.

Using this map, the company can compare its brands to its competitor brands and also to the ideal position, i.e. the target market's perfect version of the product. Brand C, for example, is near the ideal position regarding price, while brand A is close to the ideal position regarding low running costs. None of the brands appears to be close to the ideal regarding style and comfort, although brand C greatly exceeds the expected ideal for performance.

Rothschild (1987) emphasised a further benefit of the MAM approach. If a number of people are involved in a purchase then they may hold different views about the importance of specific attributes because of their particular interests or perspectives. The views of the different **decision-making unit (DMU)** members can be isolated, rather than being aggregated into the total data, and a multi-attribute attitude map produced for each. He quotes an industrial market example to illustrate this:

> The most important attributes for the engineer are related to the technical specifications of the product, while the purchasing agent is most concerned with price issues. In such a case the firm can develop a technical ad for

decision-making unit (DMU)
all the individuals who participate in and influence the customer's purchase decision

Exhibit 4.13 Possible Multi-attribute Attitude Map for a compact car

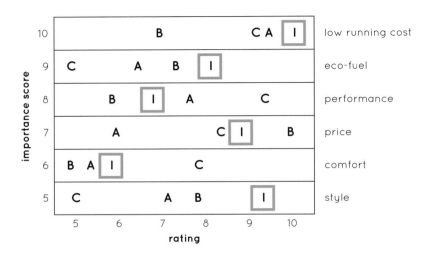

engineers and deliver it in *Engineering Digest*, while developing a price/value ad for purchasing agents that can be delivered in *Purchasing Agents Weekly*. (Rothschild, 1987: 89)

MAM is a useful tool in analysing and determining positioning. It is easy to implement; it identifies which attributes are important to customers/consumers; it identifies how competitors are perceived in relation to each other and to an ideal; and it provides further insight into positioning strategies for different customers/consumers within the target market. This understanding of the different perceptions of product attributes can help in identifying benefit segments (i.e. target markets identified using the segmentation variable *benefits sought* – see the earlier section on segmentation), which may then be specifically catered for by launching new products, changing marketing programmes and repositioning just for them.

MULTIDIMENSIONAL SCALING (MDS)

Multidimensional Scaling is a popular approach to visualising brand positions. For example, eight competing brands of soap are compared by asking members of the target market to consider the brands in groups of three. This is known as **triadic comparisons** and is a technique that is used because it is easier for respondents to compare such groups rather than try to consider all the brands together in one go. The respondents simply have to say which two of the three are most similar or, in other words, which they feel is the odd one out. The respondents do not have to work out why they feel this, it is enough that they can choose. All combinations of three brands are assessed in this way and a picture is developed of how similar or dissimilar the brands are to each other. These relative positions are analysed by a computer multidimensional scaling program, which takes into account all the responses and plots the brands' aggregate positions on a chart. The resulting map (see Exhibit 4.14) shows how close the brands are to, or how far away from, each other (hence the reason why these maps are sometimes referred to as space maps).

triadic comparisons technique used in perceptual mapping in which three products are compared to each other at a time

Exhibit 4.14   A possible perceptual map for soaps

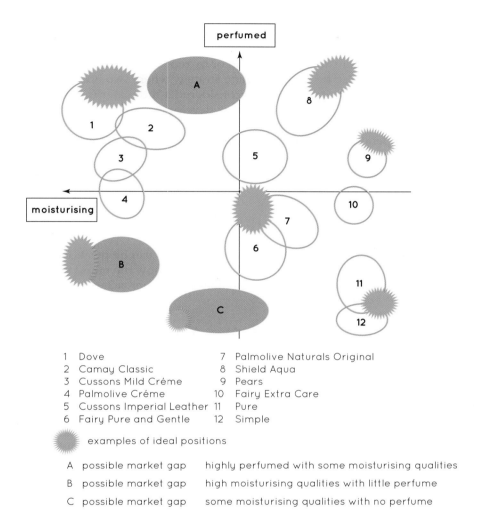

1   Dove
2   Camay Classic
3   Cussons Mild Créme
4   Palmolive Créme
5   Cussons Imperial Leather
6   Fairy Pure and Gentle
7   Palmolive Naturals Original
8   Shield Aqua
9   Pears
10   Fairy Extra Care
11   Pure
12   Simple

examples of ideal positions

A   possible market gap   highly perfumed with some moisturising qualities

B   possible market gap   high moisturising qualities with little perfume

C   possible market gap   some moisturising qualities with no perfume

The map at this stage would not have any axes. These are added by the researcher using their judgement to guess the major underlying reasons for the respondents' perceptions. In Exhibit 4.14, the differentiating attributes appear to be the perfuming and moisturising qualities of the soaps.

Respondents can be asked about their ideal product and their responses plotted on the map. As might be anticipated, there is rarely a single ideal product. The result will be a range of ideal positions according to the different preferences expressed. These preferences will tend to cluster however into a similar area, as shown by the circles in Exhibit 4.14. The larger the size of circle, the more people have expressed that ideal preference.

For the purposes of this text, the actual mechanisms of how perceptual maps are constructed are not too important. What is important is to recognise that such maps are used and what they represent. The positioning of competing brands helps to assess how close the competition is and also shows possible market opportunities by identifying ideal positions and market gaps. Market opportunities can be exploited by launching a new brand or by repositioning an existing brand. Repositioning may also be an appropriate strategy where two brands appear to be too close together. (Repositioning is considered a little later in this chapter.)

A much simpler, if less accurate, way of developing a perceptual map is to pre-select the axes and ask respondents to place brands on the map where they think each competing brand should lie. This is often used as an approach when first trying to illustrate the development and use of such maps to marketing students, but it should be clearly understood that this is not a methodologically sound approach.

repositioning involves moving existing perceptions to new perceptions relative to competing brands

POSITIONING STRATEGIES

There are a number of different ways in which a brand can be positioned against its competition. These strategies are largely to do with how the brand is promoted through advertising and other marketing communications approaches (see Chapter 8), and are outlined below.

Positioning on attributes/product features. A common way to position is to differentiate from other brands by emphasising a brand's distinctive product feature(s), e.g. Head & Shoulders shampoo eliminates dandruff while Ecover products help save the planet.

Positioning by price/quality. For some brands, high price or high quality is emphasised, while others are promoted for their relatively low prices or adequate quality. Stella Artois beer has previously been advertised as 'Reassuringly expensive'. Value for money is often used as a positioning strategy although this does not always clearly differentiate the brand well from other offerings, e.g. ASDA promotes 'ASDA price' while Tesco promotes 'Every little helps'.

Positioning for specific usage occasions, e.g. After Eight mints have consistently been promoted as an after-dinner chocolate.

Positioning on benefits or needs, e.g. Comfort fabric conditioner claims to reduce the need for ironing. BBC iPlayer promises to make the unmissable unmissable – even if you missed it when it was shown on TV.

Positioning by the product user, e.g. Hello Kitty is a brand for girly-girls while Louis Vitton is for fashionistas.

Positioning against another brand or with respect to a competitor or competitors, e.g. John Lewis is 'never knowingly undersold' and Budweiser is 'the king of beers'.

Positioning with respect to another product class. Rather than showing a direct comparison against another brand, the positioning can be against a product class, e.g. the 'I Can't Believe It's Not Butter' brand is a spread that clearly compares itself to butter.

ACTIVITY

Choose a number of different hotel chains (such as Holiday Inn, Travelodge, Best Western, Hilton, Sheraton, Holiday Inn Express, Hyatt) and consider how they each try to position themselves within the market. What are the marketing features that suggest their positions? Write a brief description of the market position of each and discuss your ideas with a colleague or friend.

EXPAND YOUR KNOWLEDGE

Toften, K. and Hammervoll, T. (2009) 'Niche firms and marketing strategy: an exploratory study of internationally oriented niche firms', *European Journal of Marketing*, 43 (11/12): 1378–91.

This paper explores how internationally orientated niche firms define and choose their markets and customers and how they position their products

REPOSITIONING

Repositioning is the marketing process of moving a brand from its current position to a new one in people's minds – relative to competing brands. Repositioning may be a good response to competitor activity or other changes in the marketplace. It may involve relatively minor shifts in perception or moving into totally new segments.

McDonald's has been trying to reposition itself as a healthier fast food brand.

Hellmann's mayonnaise found that sales were decreasing not just through competition with other mayonnaise brands but through competition with other dressings. The market for mayonnaise was being attacked and Hellmann's was losing out. Initially, changes to its promotional activities repositioned mayonnaise in relation to other dressings such as salad creams. Mayonnaise sales increased, but not only for Hellmann's – it had improved the market for its competitors, too. The company's next task was to position itself favourably compared with its mayonnaise brand rivals, and this it succeeded in doing.

Johnnie Walker, Keep on Walking

Johnson & Johnson's Baby Shampoo brand used to be specifically positioned for baby/infant use. To widen the market, the company successfully repositioned

customer focus: A truly great beer

There are risks associated with repositioning and, as a strategic approach, if the brand is already well established and strong, repositioning may be unwise and difficult to achieve. What is important is the effect on current and potentially new customers. However, where it is triggered by falling sales or the anticipation of faltering performance, repositioning may be a necessity. Löwenbräu was a successful beer before attempts to reposition it caused it to falter. Originally positioned as 'a truly great German beer', it was exported out of Europe. When the brand was bought by the American company, Miller, from Philip Morris, the new owners decided that they would not be able to continue importing it quickly enough and started brewing it in the USA. The position was changed to 'a truly great American beer' but this was at odds with the beer's established perception. Production issues led to the change of position and Miller had to spend millions of dollars creating a new position after losing a truly great position.

it as an adult, gentle, frequent-use shampoo. It achieved this without sacrificing its original position and now maintains two quite distinct positions within the market. This is difficult to do and rarely works. So successful was the strategy that the company extended it to its other baby products and enjoys similar success with its Baby Oil and Baby Powder brands.

Ecover, who make environmentally-friendly cleaning products, were losing sales in the recession and successfully repositioned from 'a brand for hippies' to a mainstream brand. They also increased their share of the green market by 7% suggesting that the repositioning had not alienated their core customers (Davidson, 2012).

THE FIVE-STAGE PROCESS FROM MARKET SEGMENTATION TO POSITIONING

There is an identifiable, step-by-step process by which companies can move from an initial understanding of their total market through to determination of their own brand positions. Exhibit 4.15 shows the full five-stage process.

There is a logical progression from one stage to another. The total potential market is analysed and market segments are identified. Through an understanding of the market segments, the market attractiveness of each can be determined and one or more segments can be targeted. Further analysis can reveal the perceptions of the potential customers and consumers in the target(s), and so the relative positions of competing products (brands) can be assessed. The complete analysis can then be used as a foundation for selecting appropriate marketing strategies and tactics, leading to the implementation of specific marketing activities and actions.

Exhibit 4.15   Stages in the market segmentation, targeting and positioning process

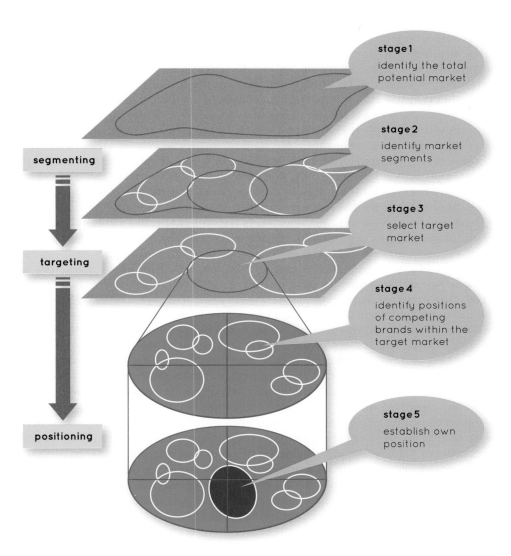

SUMMARY

Market selection is one of the most fundamental aspects of marketing. The choice will be affected by what market opportunities seem to be available matched against a company's objectives, its resources and its assessment of its general business environment (which can be undertaken through the use of PRESTCOM analysis).

Whether they are b2c or b2b, markets consist of customers and consumers, but no single company can fulfil the needs of all customers. While individuals are of course different, people do have some similarities in terms of some of their habits, lifestyles, preferences, where they are located or, in the case of b2b, what type of business they are in, etc. An understanding of these similarities can be used to divide a total market into subgroups that each consist of customers and consumers (buyers and users) who share similar characteristics and are different from people in the other subgroups. This process is called market segmentation.

There are many ways to segment markets and this chapter has briefly described the use of geographic, demographic, geo-demographic, psychographic and behavioural segmentation in the case of consumer markets and macro- and micro-segmentation approaches in the case of b2b markets. It is up to marketers to decide which of the segments are attractive enough to target. This is the process of targeting or target marketing.

A number of different targeting strategies have been described in this chapter: undifferentiated (mass) marketing, differentiated marketing, concentrated marketing, niche marketing and customised marketing. A useful way to think of them is as a continuum from undifferentiated, where there is no targeting and the product is considered suitable for all (e.g. copper), to totally customised, in which the product is provided on a totally individual basis (e.g. a handmade wedding dress).

Having identified one or more potential target markets, an understanding of customer/consumer perceptions of the competing brands in those target(s) is necessary so that the most appropriate marketing activities can be determined. This is the process of positioning and is achieved by firstly carrying out a detailed analysis of the target market(s) so that an appreciation of competing offerings and where one's own brand might fit into the market can be developed. Positioning is very much about understanding customer and consumer perceptions of the brands on offer. These are then plotted on a perceptual (brand) map. An in-depth understanding of the brands competing in the target market(s) is essential in determining the best positioning strategy.

Positioning is not a one-off activity. It may become necessary to reposition the brand later in order to minimise competition. Marketers should carry out regular checks on their brands' perceived positions and those of key competitors.

The chapter ends by bringing all these concepts together into the complete segmentation-to-positioning five-stage process, which starts by identifying the total potential market and goes on to the identification of market segments, the selection of target market(s) and the identification of the positions of competing brands within the target market(s), and finishes by establishing one's own position within the target market(s).

CHALLENGES REVIEWED

Now that you have finished reading the chapter, look back at the challenges you were set at the beginning. Do you have a clearer idea of what's involved?

HINTS
- Segmentation and targeting strategies
- Differentiated or undifferentiated?
- Perceptual mapping
- Segmentation bases.

READING AROUND

JOURNAL ARTICLES

Bruning, E., Hu, M. and Hao, W. (2009) 'Cross-national segmentation: an application to the NAFTA airline passenger market', *European Journal of Marketing*, 43 (11/12): 1498–1522.

Haley, R. (1968) 'Benefit segmentation: a decision-oriented research tool', *Journal of Marketing*, 32 (Jul): 30–5.

Johnson, G. and Grier, S. (2011) 'Targeting without alienating: multicultural advertising and the subtleties of targeted advertising', *International Journal of Advertising*, 30 (2): 233–58.

Romaniuk, J. (2012) 'Five steps to smarter targeting', *Journal of Advertising Research*, 52 (3): 288–90.

Shapiro, B. and Bonoma, T. (1984) 'How to segment industrial markets', *Harvard Business Review*, May-Jun: 104–110.

Toften, K. and Hammervoll, T. (2009) 'Niche firms and marketing strategy: an exploratory study of internationally oriented niche firms', *European Journal of Marketing*, 43 (11/12): 1378–91.

MAGAZINE ARTICLES AND BEST PRACTICE GUIDES

Davidson, N. (2012) 'Ecover's makeover', *Admap*, December, London: WARC.

Franklin, E.T. (2012) 'Consumer segmentation: subculture targeting', *Admap*, June, London: WARC.

Puddick, M. (2012) 'WARC best practice guide: how to write brand positioning statements'. Available from **http://www.warc.com/** (accessed 14/04/13).

BOOKS AND BOOK CHAPTERS

Brown, E. (2012) 'Networks', in *Working the Crowd: Social Media Marketing for Business,* 2nd edn. Swindon: BCS – The Chartered Institute for IT, Chapter 5.

Dibb, S. and Simkin, L. (2007) *Market Segmentation Success: Making It Happen!* New York: Haworth Press.

Pickton, D. and Broderick, A. (2004) 'Identifying target audiences and profiling target markets', in *Integrated Marketing Communications*, 2nd edn. Harlow: FT/Prentice Hall, Chapter 17.

WEBSITES

www.artscouncil.org.uk/what-we-do/research-and-data/arts-audiences/arts-based-segmentation-research/ – the UK Arts Council explains how segmentation works in the arts – with a quiz.

www.caci.co.uk – for information on ACORN.

www.experian.co.uk – for information on MOSAIC.

http://www.sportengland.org/about-us/ – Sport England segments sports players (and non-players).

www.strategicbusinessinsights.com/vals – for information on VALS psychometric segmentation.

SELF-REVIEW QUESTIONS

1. Broadly speaking, it is suggested that marketers should address three areas of concern when assessing market attractiveness. What are they? (See p. 147)
2. What is the difference between market segmentation and target marketing? (See pp. 149–50)
3. What are the main criteria for assessing how good a market segment might be? (See p. 150)
4. What are the main bases that can be used for segmenting consumer markets? (See p. 152)
5. What is social grading and how is it measured? Is it the same as social class? (See p. 154)
6. What is geo-demographic segmentation? (See pp. 154–5)
7. Why are lifestyles useful for segmentation purposes? Identify an example of lifestyle segmentation. (See p. 157)
8. Why is behavioural segmentation a useful approach for marketers? Identify some examples of behavioural segmentation variables. (See pp. 160–2)
9. What are the main bases that can be used for segmenting business markets? (See p. 164)
10. Why should macrovariables be used before analysing microvariables in business markets? (See p. 164–5)
11. What is the difference between targeting and positioning? (See p. 167 and 174)
12. What is the difference between mass marketing and niche marketing? (See p. 169 and 173)
13. Under what conditions is mass marketing an appropriate marketing strategy? (See p. 172)
14. What is the five-stage process from market segmentation to positioning? (See p. 183)

Mini case study: Auto-Tecnic GmbH

Read the questions, then the case material, and then answer the questions.

Questions

1 What is this product really? Hint: Marketing has to do with matching product offerings with customer/consumer demands. Review the benefits that Peter's product provides. Do not be happy with Peter's view that this is only a garage door-opening device. Reappraise his definition of the product and identify as many possible uses for the product as you can (some uses may be in industrial and commercial situations).

2 For each use you have identified, what segmentation variables would you use to segment the market?

3 Consider Auto-Tecnic's situation and resources. What target market or target markets would you advise the company to focus on?

Auto-Tecnic is a small German company founded and run by a clever electronics engineer, Peter Schneider. He has built his successful, though small, business over the past five years by undertaking subcontract work for large electronics companies. The work has mainly involved producing small control devices (automatic switches, timers, etc.) in response to his business customers' requests. Peter's expertise is valued by the organisations with which he has dealt.

Having returned from trips outside Germany, Peter noticed an increase in the number of homes making use of automatic garage doors. Drivers would either press a button on a device kept in the car, which activated a switch in a door-opening mechanism fitted to the garage door, or a device would be fixed in the car that automatically triggered a sensor as the car approached, which then operated the garage door-opening mechanism.

With his electronics expertise, Peter designed a better electronic system than the ones he had seen on his trips. His system contains extra security features that ensure constantly changing but synchronised coding between the transmitter (fixed in the car) and the receiver (fixed on the garage door). In other words, other people should not be able to activate the opening switch. In Peter's system, the garage door would automatically open as the car approached the receiving sensor. Peter has arranged for his system to be patented.

Peter recognises his limited understanding of marketing; his skills lie in technical electronic product development. He is convinced, however, that his new product idea will be profitable. As a first stage, he has asked you, as marketing consultant, to advise him how to define his market – just who would be interested in buying and using his product? He realises that, as with any product, his system is unlikely to have universal appeal.

REFERENCES

Anon (2007) 'Nectar case study', *Marketing*, 13 June: 35.

Bruning, E.R., Hu, M.Y. and Hao, W. (2009) 'Cross-national segmentation: an application to the NAFTA airline passenger market', *European Journal of Marketing*, 43 (11/12): 1498–1522.

Clark, S. (2004) 'Advertising in schools', *The Times Education Supplement*, 25 June, available from www.tes.co.uk/article.aspx?storycode=396901 (accessed 08/04/13).

Crittenden, V.L., Crittenden, W.F. and Muzyka, D.F. (2002) 'Segmenting the business-to-business marketplace by product attributes and the decision process', *Journal of Strategic Marketing*, 10 (1): 3–20.

Davidson, N. (2012) 'Ecover's makeover', *Admap*, December, London: WARC.

Dibb, S. and Simkin, L. (1996) *The Market Segmentation Workbook: Target Marketing for Managers*. London: Routledge.

Dibb, S. and Wensley, R. (2002) 'Segmentation analysis for industrial markets: problems of integrating customer requirements into operations strategy', *European Journal of Marketing*, 36 (1/2): 231–51.

Haley, R.I. (1968) 'Benefit segmentation: a decision-oriented research tool', *Journal of Marketing*, 32 (Jul): 30–5.

Johnson, G.D. and Grier, S.A. (2011) 'Targeting without alienating: multicultural advertising and the subtleties of targeted advertising', *International Journal of Advertising*, 30 (2): 233–58.

Johnson, R.M. (1971) 'Market segmentation: a strategic management tool', *Journal of Marketing Research*, Feb: 13–18.

Kantar Media, available at: www.kantarmedia.co.uk

Kern (2013) 'The Gnome Experiment', available from www.gnomeexperiment.com (accessed 08/05/13).

Lindgren Jr, J.H. and Shimp, T.A. (1996) *Marketing: An Interactive Learning System*. Fort Worth, TX: The Dryden Press.

Louden, D.L. and Della Bitta, A.J. (1993) *Consumer Behavior*, 4th edn. New York: McGraw-Hill.

Monbiot, G. (2013) 'Hey advertisers, leave our defenceless kids alone', *Guardian*, 15 April, available from www.guardian.co.uk (accessed 08/04/13).

Ogilvy Public Relations (2013) 'Case study: Kern the gnome experiment', available from www.ogilvyprlondon.com (accessed 08/05/13).

Pickton, D.W. and Broderick, A. (2004) *Integrated Marketing Communications*, 2nd edn. Harlow: FT/Prentice Hall.

Romaniuk, J. (2012) 'Five steps to smarter targeting', *Journal of Advertising Research*, 52 (3): 288–90.

Rothschild, M.L. (1987) *Marketing Communications*. New York: DC Heath.

Rogers, E.M. (2003) *Diffusion of Innovations* (5th edn). New York: The Free Press.

Toften, K. and Hammervoll, T. (2009) 'Niche firms and marketing strategy: an exploratory study of internationally oriented niche firms', *European Journal of Marketing*, 43 (11/12): 1378–91.

Shapiro, B.P. and Bonoma, T.V. (1984) 'How to segment industrial markets', *Harvard Business Review*, May–June: 104–10.

Smith, W.R. (1956) 'Product differentiation and market segmentation as alternative marketing strategies', *Journal of Marketing*, 21 (1): 3–8.

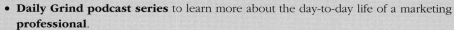

Visit the companion website on your computer at **www.sagepub.co.uk/masterson3e** or MobileStudy on your Smart phone or tablet by scanning this QR code and gain access to:

- **Videos** to get a better understanding of key concepts and provoke in-class discussion.
- Links to useful **websites and templates** to help guide your study.
- Access **SAGE Marketing Pins (www.pinterest.com/sagepins/)**. SAGE's regularly updated **Pinterest** page, giving you access to regularly updated resources on everything from Branding to Consumer Behaviour.
- **Daily Grind podcast series** to learn more about the day-to-day life of a marketing **professional**.
- Interactive **Practice questions** to test your understanding.
- A **bonus chapter on Marketing Careers** to not only support your study, but your job search and future career.
- **PowerPoints** prompting key points for revision.

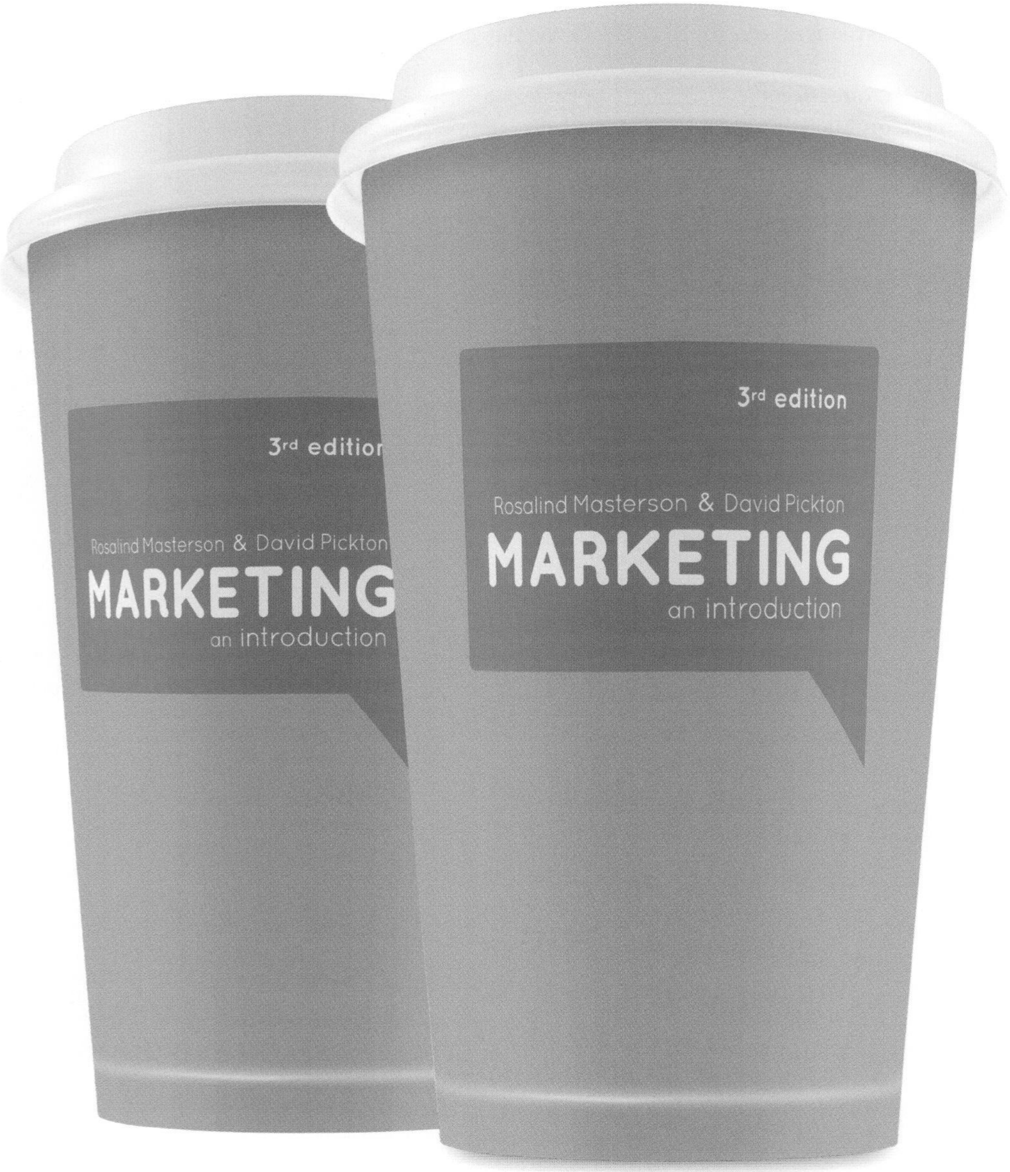

Marketing research  5

MARKETING RESEARCH CHALLENGES

The following are illustrations of the types of decision that marketers have to take or issues they face. *You aren't expected to know how to deal with the challenges now*; just bear them in mind as you read the chapter and see what you can find that helps.

- You run a travel agency. You have found a fabulous hotel in the Swiss Alps that you have never used before. However, the hotel wants to know how many rooms to reserve for you for next season. What information do you need to work this out, and how will you collect it?
- Your company's skateboard sales have been falling steadily over the last two years. How would you make a case to a sceptical managing director that the expense of research into the causes of the fall would be worthwhile?
- The editor of a lad's mag, a monthly magazine read by men and women (e.g. the men's wives and girlfriends), has invited you to research the attitudes of readers to its contents. How would you do this?
- Your company is hoping to launch a new beer and wants to find out what would be popular across Europe. This is difficult because different European countries traditionally drink different types of beer. However, recently you have seen an Italian drinking British beer, a British man drinking French beer and a Swede drinking German beer. You need to get views from a huge number of beer drinkers to be sure you get the complete picture. It is not practical to interview every beer drinker in Europe. What could you do?

INTRODUCTION

If any plan is to be successful, it must be based on good intelligence. If you want to change something, first you must understand exactly what it is currently. To understand a marketing situation, and its future possibilities, you must have good information about it, i.e. you have to conduct marketing research.

The environmental analysis discussed in Chapter 2 (the marketing environment) is only possible if there is sufficient data available. The segmentation processes described in Chapter 4 are totally dependent upon sound market intelligence. How can a company design products, develop advertising campaigns, set prices, choose outlets, encourage customer loyalty or build its brands without information about its customers, its competitors and the worlds they inhabit?

This chapter will outline the research process, list typical areas for marketing research and examine the techniques used by researchers to gather data. Much of this data is personal, some of it is sensitive and so market researchers have to be careful of their research subjects' wishes, rights and potential reactions. Market researchers should be honest, open and, above all, ethical in their dealings with research subjects.

Finally, the chapter briefly considers one of the main purposes of all this research and analysis: forecasting marketing trends.

ACTIVITY

Reflecting on previous chapters, write a list of all the things you might need to research in the following situations:

- starting up a small, top-quality ice cream business and hoping to sell to local businesses (shops, restaurants, etc.)

- a top brand of perfume is losing market share

- a firm of accountants is considering setting up a new office in a different town.

If you can, compare lists with someone else. Why do you want to know these things?

DEFINITIONS

Marketing research covers the investigation of a broad range of activities (see below). The terms 'marketing research' and 'market research' are today used interchangeably – although some might argue that market research is narrower in scope, focusing on customers and consumers, whereas marketing research covers the whole of the marketing process.

The Market Research Society (MRS) definition embraces all types of data gathering and investigations for market and social research:

Research is the collection and analysis of data from a **sample** of individuals or organisations relating to their characteristics, behaviour, attitudes, opinions or possessions such as consumer and industrial surveys, psychological investigations, observational and panel studies. (Market Research Society, n.d.)

This definition uses various research techniques as illustration. These will be explained below. It also refers to 'a sample'. Sampling is an important concept in marketing research. It is rarely possible to investigate everyone in the world, or even everyone in your target market, so researchers assess a subset, or sample, of the people (or products, or whatever the thing to be researched is) instead. It is important to ensure that this sample is big enough and broad enough to be fully representative of the whole – otherwise the resulting research will be flawed. Sampling methods are explained in more detail below.

Philip Kotler offers a much shorter definition. Marketing research is: 'the systematic design, collection, analysis and reporting of data and findings relevant to a specific marketing situation facing the company' (Kotler et al., 2012).

Note the phrase 'specific marketing situation' here. Marketing research is not a general activity, it is targeted, it has specific objectives. There is a good reason why it is being done.

sample
a smaller number of people, or cases, drawn from a population that should be representative of it in every significant characteristic

THE USE AND VALUE OF MARKETING RESEARCH

UK research market worth over £3bn

Marketing research is a planned activity. It is carried out methodically so that the results are supported by evidence that can be checked by others. Marketing research provides vital information for key marketing decisions, e.g. which products should be developed, how they should be packaged, what price should be charged, how they should be distributed, who they should be aimed at, what benefits and features customers would want and how the products should be promoted. In order to make these decisions, marketing managers need to know (among other things): what competitors currently offer, what their reactions might be to these new

Exhibit 5.1 Market research expenditure (in millions of US dollars, 2008)

Top six largest markets (2008)	Value (in millions US$)	Market share	Growth rate (adjusted for inflation)
Europe	16,066	49%	0.9%
North America	9629	30%	-2.1%
Asia Pacific	4538	14%	2.1%
Latin America	1700	5%	5.6%
Middle East and Africa	529	2%	1.1%
WORLD	32,000	100%	0.4%

SOURCE: ESOMAR, 2008.

IBM:
Smarter
Analytics

products, what would make customers buy these products in preference to those of their competitors and how retailers will respond (e.g. will they be prepared to stock the new products?) Without marketing research it would be very difficult to make such decisions. Marketing research is so important to good marketing that organisations spend billions on it each year (see Exhibit 5.1).

EXPAND YOUR KNOWLEDGE

Lukas, B.A., Whitwell, G.J. and Heide, J.B. (2013) 'Why do customers get more than they need? How organizational culture shapes product capability decisions', *Journal of Marketing,* 77 (1): 1–12.

It is a fundamental marketing principle that products should be designed to match customers' needs, yet many products are over-designed, i.e. they *more* than meet those needs. This paper examines why.

THE MARKETING RESEARCH PROCESS

Marketing research is a continuous process of information gathering and analysis into which ad hoc marketing research activities may also be fitted as and when management problems arise. Exhibit 5.2 shows the stages involved in the marketing research process.

Exhibit 5.2   The marketing research process

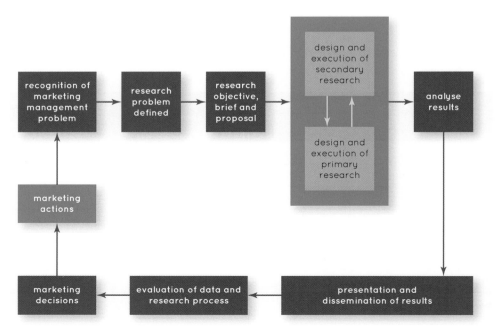

1   Recognise the marketing management problem.
    The starting point for the research process is the recognition of a marketing
    problem. Perhaps there has been a loss of sales or market share? It could be
    that there are problems with distribution or that customers are choosing to
    shop elsewhere.

2   Define the research problem.
    Once the marketing management problem has been recognised and understood,
    it needs to be restated as a research problem. This may require some background
    information. For example, a local authority may be concerned that few people
    shop locally, preferring large, out-of-town superstores and malls. Neighbourhoods
    are becoming rundown as shops close. The research problem, at its broadest, is
    to find out why customers shop outside their local community. More specifically,
    the research will investigate: who tends to shop outside, what local shopping
    is available, customer attitudes to the local facilities, what might make people
    change their shopping habits, and what are the costs and benefits involved from
    the points of view of the shoppers, the local shop owners, the supermarket own-
    ers and developers, etc. These are research questions to be answered.

3   Set research objectives, write research brief.
    The next step is to set research objectives. These provide a clearly defined
    direction for the research activity. From the objectives, basic decisions can be
    made as to the form the research will take, including the use of both secondary
    and primary research (see below). Management will need to think through the
    resources required and set a suitable budget. There is a trade-off to be made
    here between cost and certainty. The more information managers have, the
    better the decisions they can make, but costs rise as the research goes on and
    on, and so a reasonable budget must be set.
        Organisations do not always undertake their own research. Frequently, they
    employ research agencies to carry out some or all of the research tasks. These
    agencies will need to be thoroughly briefed on what is required. The agency
    then expands the brief into a complete research proposal, i.e. a document that
    details exactly what they propose to do. An agreed proposal makes it much
    less likely that misunderstandings will arise in the future and also encourages
    the agency to take more responsibility for the research.

4   Carry out research (design and execution).
    Secondary research (also known as desk research) should always be con-
    sidered *before* primary research (also known as field research) is under-
    taken. If the right information already exists, then it may be possible to answer
    a number of the research questions and address the research problem through
    secondary research alone. This would make primary research unnecessary,
    saving time and money.
        There are many sources of secondary information and the Internet has made
    them easier to find and to use. There are also many primary research methods,
    the most commonly used being surveys (see below for primary and secondary
    research – pp. 205–9).

5   Analyse data.
    As the data from the research is gathered, it is collated and analysed. The type
    of analysis will depend on the nature of the data and the information and

**secondary research
(desk research)**
the search for good-
quality data that has
been validated and is
now published for use
by others

**field research (primary
research)**
carried out specifically
for the research task in
question

answers required. Analysis, especially qualitative analysis, can be very subjective. However, it is important for analysts to be as objective as possible. Quantitative analysis claims greater objectivity thanks to the mathematical techniques it employs, but even this is dependent upon the skills of, and the decisions made by, researchers and analysts.

One way of looking at analysis is to think of it as a sense-making process. Analysis is the means by which raw data (e.g. the number of people who shop out of town on a Tuesday) is converted into valuable information (e.g. which are the most popular shopping days and why) that can be used for marketing decisions.

6   Present and disseminate results.
There is little value in researchers keeping their findings to themselves. After the sense-making process of analysis, the results need to be shared and made available to all staff who could benefit. Some of the results may be considered confidential and so restricted access is needed. However, the more usual problem is to ensure findings are distributed widely, are well understood and acted upon. Researchers are expected to comment on the quality of the findings (in terms of confirming their accuracy, validity and reliability (later in this chapter on page 226) and make appropriate recommendations related to the findings to management.

7   Evaluate data and research process.
Evaluation should not be limited to the results themselves but should extend to the whole research process. Has the research brief been fulfilled? Has this been done within budget? On time? Have the results shed light on the management problem? Could it have been done better?

8   Make marketing decisions and carry them out.
The purpose of research is to make well-informed decisions and to improve marketing actions, e.g. raise prices or develop a new product. These changes will elicit a response from the market which may then form the basis of a new marketing research cycle.

EXPAND YOUR KNOWLEDGE

Classic article

Brien, R.H. and Stafford, J.E. (1968) 'Marketing information systems: a new dimension for marketing research', *Journal of Marketing*, 32 (Jul): 19–23.

An article that emphasises the need to view marketing research as an integrated system rather than ad hoc research projects.

ETHICS IN MARKETING RESEARCH

Good marketing research always takes account of the ethics of the situation. Over recent years, professional body (e.g. the Market Research Society) codes of conduct have been strengthened by changes in laws and regulations covering data protection and freedom of information. Codes of behaviour for researchers are about honesty, openness and respect for respondents' privacy, and are mostly common sense. There have been some unscrupulous marketing research practitioners in the past and the activity continues to carry the stigma created by unethical salespeople claiming to be carrying out research as a selling tactic. When approaching potential respondents, a researcher should clearly identify who they are, that they are carrying out research, and the broad purpose for which the research is being conducted. Confidentiality should be assured or, if it is not, the respondent's permission must be acquired. Similar ethical considerations should be borne in mind when recording, analysing and reporting research findings. The storage of data will be affected by legal controls such as those covered by the UK Data Protection Act 1998.

MRS
Guidelines

A full version of the Market Research Society Code of Conduct can be found on their website (**www.mrs.org.uk**). Other professional bodies related to marketing research in other countries will also have their own versions of the codes.

AREAS OF MARKETING RESEARCH

Marketing research is used to investigate a number of different marketing areas including:

- the marketing environment (see Chapter 2)
- competitors
- consumer behaviour
- business buying behaviour
- sales
- distribution
- products and brands
- pricing
- advertising and promotions
- media habits.

MARKETING ENVIRONMENT RESEARCH

Organisations need to understand the wider environment in which they are operating. For example, an analysis of social trends may reveal opportunities for new products while an in-depth understanding of government's attitude to businesses may enable a company to foresee a business threat such as tighter (or looser) new regulations. Research in this area can be quite general and is most likely to be secondary. (See Chapter 2 for more on the marketing environment and PRESTCOM analysis.)

COMPETITOR RESEARCH

It is clearly important for an organisation to know as much as it reasonably can about who its competitors are and what they are doing. This includes not only their past and current activities, but also indications of their future plans.

The cola blind taste test is perhaps one of the most famous pieces of commercial research ever, although it was used mainly as advertising for Pepsi Cola. Pepsi claimed that in blind taste tests the majority of people preferred the taste of Pepsi. Yet they still buy more Coca-Cola. Why do you think that is?

Try this at home. Can you tell the difference? Are you surprised by which tastes best?

CONSUMER BEHAVIOUR RESEARCH

Customer and consumer research is largely concerned with their decision-making processes, attitudes, preferences, repurchasing patterns and with how consumers use products. Why do some people buy and others don't? Why do some shop around and others remain loyal to one supplier? What role do brands play in consumers' lives? Analysing consumer behaviour has led to a large and valuable body of knowledge that draws heavily on other disciplines such as psychology and sociology (see Chapter 3).

Nightclubs as research labs

Over recent years, there has been an explosion of customer data collection activities fuelled through the growth and availability of more advanced technologies. Modern computing power, in terms of storage and processing of data, has meant that companies can easily capture data on all customer transactions: what is bought, by whom, how frequently, by what means and where. Tesco, for example, makes good use of customer transaction data to segment their customer base and provide highly targeted offers based on buying and usage behaviour.

IBM: Business Analytics

BUSINESS BUYING BEHAVIOUR RESEARCH

In business markets, goods and services are bought either for use and consumption within the customer organisation or for resale. This is a vast area of research because it involves all organisations that buy and sell from each other, from one-person companies to huge **multinationals** and government corporations. Business-to-business (b2b) research includes research into government and **public sector** organisations and their buying behaviour as well as into commercial companies. Institutions such as local authorities and hospitals are large buyers and users of goods and services and may have complex buying procedures and decision-making criteria.

multinationals corporations with subsidiaries in multiple countries

public sector government-owned organisations

SALES RESEARCH AND FORECASTING

One of a marketing manager's most important and most complex tasks is sales forecasting. Developing a new product, entering a new market or making changes to any of the elements of the marketing mix is risky. Organisations need to predict how customers will react and also what competitors' retaliatory strategies might be. A costly failure can be disastrous for an organisation. Equally, standing still with no change brings its risks. Marketing management is about basing decisions for change on sound information obtained through professional marketing research.

It is hard to predict sales precisely but the better the information the forecast is based on, the better the chance that it will be accurate. Most sales forecasts are based on previous sales figures so that is the first piece of information required. Managers will want to know about the total market sales (i.e. the sales of competitive products as well as their own) so they can work out an overall market growth rate and their own market share. They will also need to factor in such things as changes in the marketing environment (see Chapter 2) and new product launches (their own and competitors').

Of course, the past is not always an accurate guide to the future and forecasts of future sales are a vital part of business planning. There are a number of ways businesses can try to see ahead. A customer **survey** of purchase intentions is an excellent way although it is more practical for b2b than for consumer goods. The salesforce are also a good source of information, although they tend to underestimate in order to get a lower sales target (and possibly to earn more commission by over-achieving it).

Methods of estimating future sales vary according to how frequently a product is likely to be purchased and should incorporate first time, replacement and repeat sales (Kotler et al., 2012). For example, washing machines and cars are infrequent purchases whereas coffee is a frequent purchase. Taking washing machines as an example, people setting up their first home may be buying for the first time. Later on, they may need to replace that machine. Knowing the likely life of the machine will help the company to estimate when that will happen. For FMCG (fast-moving consumer goods) such as shampoo, repeat sales may be the most important element of the forecast.

Forecasting can be defined as the estimation of the future value of a variable (most commonly sales). A key assumption is that a relationship **does** exist between the variable being forecast (the dependent variable) and the other one or more variables that are being measured against, i.e. the independent variable(s). For example, it is assumed that growth in sales is in some way related to advertising. Spreadsheets may be used to plot trends and compounded growth rates.

Marketing activities are designed ultimately to deliver sales and so sales forecasting is a key input to marketing planning.

> **survey**
> direct questioning of market research subjects

DISTRIBUTION RESEARCH

Distribution research is carried out by manufacturing companies and producers into their use of intermediaries (warehouse operators, wholesalers, insurance and financial brokers and agencies, retail store outlets) to find out how to get the best service for customers. There may be many intermediaries in a supply chain (e.g. in the food chain, from farm to fork). Distribution research can discover where companies could improve their selling functions or increase the selling effectiveness of their distribution outlets, perhaps by helping distributors with promotions or providing training in the use of products.

Manufacturing firms require information to assist them with decisions such as: the kinds of outlets to sell through; which territories to sell in and what field supervision and training are required. For retailers, research is crucial to help with management decisions about siting new stores, in-store layouts, car parking, stock quantities, deliveries, etc.

> **distribution**
> the processes involved in moving goods from the supplier to the customer or user

As with all these categories of research, it is common for companies to appoint research agencies to investigate their selling activities and the effectiveness of sales outlets and distribution networks. Some research companies undertake research like this under their own initiative and sell their findings to interested companies, e.g. AC Nielsen's retail audits.

New product development techniques

PRODUCT AND BRAND RESEARCH

Much of product research is about testing the design concept, performance, ease of use, reliability, special features, appearance and packaging of products. Researchers also ask customers and consumers about brand superiority, in terms of qualities, higher prices and appeal. This helps to create distinctive brands and unique selling propositions (USPs). Many of the products we use daily have been tested with customers by marketing researchers before their release onto the market. New product development is an important part of marketing and marketing research has a key role to play in each of the stages of development (see Chapter 6), whether this be research into new technologies, competitor products, screening, concept testing, market potential analysis, market segments, consumer preferences, etc. Marketing research has been fundamental to the expansion of many industries, including computer gaming, digital television and mobile phones, however FMCG industries such as food and drink consistently top the list as the most researched categories.

unique selling proposition (USP) a clear point of differentiation for a product/service

---

customer focus: Visit Scotland

Tourism agency VisitScotland used qualitative market research to optimise a pan-European marketing campaign. It needed to know what consumers would respond to and whether different approaches would be required for Germany, France and Spain. Research agency, Nunwood, set up two workshops in each country, for walkers, tourers and city breakers (based on previous research which identified these segments). Discussions centred on possible objections to Scotland as a holiday destination, such as lack of awareness of what it could offer. Responses to images of Scotland were used to elicit views. A key was that consumers' interests were similar in all three countries. This justified a single pan-European campaign.

A second round of research was carried out to evaluate different creative executions. Print ads and inserts were released across Europe. Return on investment increased compared to earlier campaigns. Brochure requests increased by 68% in Germany and 126% in France. There were an extra 180,000 hits on the French and German websites. Such was the success of the project that it won the award for Outstanding Research at the Marketing Research Society Annual Awards.

SOURCES: McLuhan, 2006.

Research is not confined to physical, manufactured goods but also extends into the service industries (see Chapter 7). These industries (e.g. financial services, travel, tourism and leisure, media, public services and utilities) have generated considerable work for marketing researchers. Marketing research has helped insurance companies and banks such as Aviva, Virgin Money and First Direct to provide new services and products both online and offline. In the travel sector, low-cost airlines such as easyJet and Ryanair were developed in response to well-researched customer needs. Customers are regularly asked for their opinions on a range of services from beauty care and therapy to secondhand book sales.

Larger companies usually have their own market researchers who regularly and systematically check the performance of the company's own products. Market analysts use audit data (see 'Secondary research' on page 205), sales data and other secondary sources in this to monitor markets, looking for customer and usage trends, and sometimes spotting gaps in the market that may be profitable opportunities for the company.

PRICING RESEARCH

Product sales are often highly sensitive to price movements and so pricing research is important to many firms. Research tests customers' reactions to price changes, competitors' price changes, price promotions, seasonal prices, and differences in expected price bands for different sizes, packaging and quantities. Even prestige, branded products, such as Gucci and Calvin Klein, are susceptible to price competition when there are reasonably priced quality substitutes available. Demand can be price elastic when there is choice, as there is with many household cleaning products (see Chapter 10 for an explanation of elasticity). The manipulation of prices is risky because of the competitive forces in play, so pricing research is done to establish just how much customers would be prepared to pay.

ADVERTISING AND PROMOTIONS RESEARCH

Advertising and promoting big brands such as Nike and Reebok is very expensive and so companies use marketing research to help ensure they meet their objectives and reduce the risks. Marketing research not only uncovers customers' desires and needs, it also provides data such as customers' personal details, which companies can use to target their mail-order offerings. Customer data feeds into crucial marketing decisions such as which market segments (see Chapter 4) to target and how best to appeal to them. Research in this area includes pre- and post-testing of communications, tracking studies, media planning research, readership/viewership/listenership surveys, exhibition and sponsorship evaluation, direct marketing communications research, including the use of e-communications and the design of customer offers.

MEDIA HABITS

Not only do marketers need to know who their customers might be, they need to know how best to communicate with them. This is where an understanding of their media habits comes in; what, where, when and how much they read, watch, and listen to. Media habits are in many ways an integral part of our behaviour, we 'consume' media constantly and there is a huge amount of data collected almost continuously (on the Internet this is done automatically). All the main media have audited data covering their use. In the UK, the Broadcasters' Audience Research

substitutes
other products that might be bought as alternatives; they satisfy the same or similar needs

price elastic
when the demand for a good changes significantly after a price change, e.g. price goes up by 10%, demand falls by 20%

elasticity
a significant response to changes in a marketing variable, most commonly price; quantity demanded changes by a greater percentage than the percentage change in price (i.e. if the price rises, the revenue falls)

pre-testing
evaluating the effectiveness of an aspect of a marketing campaign with its target audience before release

post-testing
evaluating the effectiveness of an aspect of a marketing campaign with its target audience after release

tracking
marketing effects are monitored over time

Social Media Habits

Board (BARB) provides information on television viewing habits, the Joint Industry Committee for National Readership Surveys (JICNARS) sponsors research covering the readership of print and online, the Radio Joint Audience Research (RAJAR) provides similar information for radio. There are similar organisations for cinema and video, and out of home (OOH). All the main media – from the local press to national TV, from poster sites to websites – will have detailed profiles of their audiences (which they use to encourage advertisers). But not only is media habit information vital in itself – it is collected with other research data to create much richer insights into customer behaviour. For example, Touchpoints is described as a consumer-centric, multimedia database which provides a detailed view of consumers and their media behaviour, giving a unique view of people's daily lives and how their media usage fits into these patterns. The Target Group Index (TGI) covers 18 broad product/service areas of 4000 brands in over 500 product fields involving over 720,000 interviews annually in over 60 countries. Information is collected on respondents' demographics (e.g. age, sex, income, education, etc.), their attitudes, beliefs, values and opinions, and on their consumption of press; satellite, cable and digital TV; radio; cinema; OOH and the Internet.

Non-
Response
Bias In
Survey
Sampling

SAMPLING

population
a complete group
of people, cases or
objects which share
similarities that
can be studied in a
survey

A sample is a smaller group of research subjects used to represent the whole of the research **population** to be studied. Qualitative research samples are small and are used to explore subjects or consider them in depth rather than to draw **general** conclusions about the research population as a whole, whereas quantitative research samples should be large enough, and representative enough, to allow researchers to draw general conclusions about the population being studied.

Sampling process:

1   define research population
2   determine appropriate sample size
3   choose sampling method
4   select sample

The first step in sampling is to define the research population from which the sample can be drawn.

The second step is to determine the appropriate sample size. How many people need to be surveyed? Then the researcher must choose a sampling method and finally select the actual research subjects (people, products, companies, etc.) to be approached.

It is important that the characteristics of the sample should be as close to those of the population as possible, as the sample is meant to be representative of the population from which it is drawn.

There are several sampling methods available to researchers (see below). Random (or probability) sampling approaches are well-suited to statistical analysis. Non-random (or non-probability) methods can deliver quantified results but care has to be taken in making presumptions about how representative they are of the wider population. Subjects chosen through a probability sample should have a

customer focus: Sampling

Imagine that you want to find out how children spend their money. Clearly, you cannot question all the children in the country, so you will try to find a representative sample. Then you can ask this subset of children questions and scale-up to get a close approximation of the picture across the whole country. You establish (perhaps through a smaller qualitative study) that the key factors that influence what children buy are:

- their gender (boy or girl)
- their age.

The country's child population breaks down as follows:

- 52% are girls
- 20% are 0–3 years
- 20% are 4–6 years
- 30% are 7–12 years
- 30% are 13–15 years.

The names you select for your survey (perhaps 1000 names from the total million or so) should also be: 52% girls, 20% 0–3, etc. This will then be a suitably representative sample of the whole.

10 step guide to sampling

quantifiable chance of being selected. This is not true of a non-probability sample where the researcher may not know the probability of any one subject being selected – and some may have no chance at all. It is a subjective approach.

RANDOM (PROBABILITY) SAMPLING METHODS

Just as the name suggests, the people or things selected for a random sample all had an equal chance of being chosen. Just like the numbers on a roulette wheel, each was equally likely to come up. Before they can be selected, however, the researcher must have a complete list of the entire research population (a **sampling frame**). If someone is missing, then clearly they cannot be chosen and the sample will not be entirely random.

SAMPLING FRAME

The sampling frame might be a telephone directory, an electoral register, a list of members of a club, or any other list that represents the research population as a whole. The list should contain accurate records of the **entire** research population and it needs to include contact details. It is usually very difficult to obtain a complete and accurate sampling frame but, without it, probability sampling is not possible. Consequently most researchers find they have to use a non-probability sampling method such as **purposive sampling** (see overleaf).

There are a number of different types of random sampling including:

- simple random sampling
- stratified random sampling
- systematic random sampling
- area or cluster sampling.

sampling frame
a list of the actual members of a population from which a sample is then chosen

purposive sampling
a non-probability sampling method, which means that every member of the research population does **not** have an equal chance of being picked. The researcher uses their judgement to choose the units to be studied

Simple random sampling

For **simple random sampling**, every member of the population should have an equal chance of being selected. This complete randomness can be quite difficult to achieve in larger populations and so there is a useful variant on this pure simple random sampling: **systematic random sampling**.

Systematic random sampling

For systematic random sampling, each individual in the sampling frame is identified by means of a number and then regularly spaced numbers are chosen until the sample has been filled. The **first** name should always be drawn by simple random sampling (see above) and after that, names are chosen at regular intervals, e.g. every seventh name on the list, to make up the desired sample size.

Stratified random sampling

Stratified random sampling divides the population into mutually exclusive groups and draws random samples **from each group**. For example, the population could be sorted according to social grades and respondents drawn randomly from each group. (Be aware, though, that classifying people according to their social grade has always been one of the most dubious areas of market research investigation, even though it is still one of the most widely used classification systems.)

Area or cluster sampling

The research population is divided into mutually exclusive groups (e.g. geographical region: perhaps by postcode) so that a random sample **of the groups** can be selected. For example, in a survey of inner-city residents' attitudes to supermarkets, the researcher may have identified all cities of a suitable size and then randomly selected a smaller group (sample) to survey. This process can have several stages: selecting further subsets of the groups.

NON-PROBABILITY SAMPLING METHODS

Random samples are expensive, time-consuming and risky. An inaccurate sampling frame or too many non-responses can invalidate the research. Consequently most researchers use non-probability sampling methods. Commonly used methods include:

- purposive sampling
- convenience sampling
- quota sampling.

Purposive (judgemental) sampling

This is a non-probability sampling method, which means that every member of the research population does **not** have an equal chance of being picked. For example, if the experts within a particular industry are well-known, the researcher can simply choose from these people to represent the expertise of the industry. Knowledge gleaned from these experts would be more useful than knowledge from a larger sample of people who are less expert in the particular field. In another example, we know that there are a vast number of retail outlets selling food in Britain, but there are only a few national supermarket chains (e.g. Tesco, Wal-mart/ASDA, Sainsbury's, Morrison's and Waitrose). So a purposive sample of large retail firms would include these stores.

Convenience sampling

A **convenience sample** is picked on the basis of convenience to the researcher. Organisations sometimes use their own employees to evaluate new products or prototypes that their research and development departments have come up with. Universities and colleges carry out market research surveys based on convenience samples of students and visitors to their campuses.

Convenience sampling lends itself to qualitative research, where consumer information can be obtained fairly quickly, inexpensively and effectively from convenient respondents who are close to hand. The rationale is to select the most accessible members of the population from which to conveniently draw the sample. Unless the members of the population are reasonably uniform (e.g. in expectations, socio-demographic make-up, etc.), there can be problems as the sample may not be representative of the population. In such a case a quota sample (see below) would be a better method.

convenience sample a sample picked on the basis of convenience to the researcher, e.g. work colleagues

Quota sampling

In marketing research it is common practice to use **quota samples**. The population is divided into relevant categories, e.g. train travellers, car drivers, bus passengers, etc. Researchers then question a set number of people from each category. That number should be set to reflect the proportions of the total research population. This sampling method is often used in street surveys where each researcher will be given a quota of respondents, e.g. asked to find 30 train travellers, 15 male and 15 female, to take part and, of these, 10 should be from each of three income brackets.

As another example, a survey of the manufacturers of paints should include a selected number or quota of the large companies, such as Dulux. In consumer studies, quotas can be set based upon socio-economic and demographic characteristics such as age, race, gender and education attained.

quota samples picks respondents in proportion to the population's profile, e.g. if 25% of the population are under 25 and female, then researchers set a quota of 25% females under 25 for the sample

SECONDARY (DESK) RESEARCH

The terms 'desk research' and 'secondary research' have become interchangeable so, for the purposes of this chapter, the term 'secondary research' will be used to embrace 'desk research' as well. Secondary research is the search for good-quality secondary data that have been validated and are already published in some form. Secondary data sources may be internal (i.e. the organisation's own records) or external. Companies, government institutions and international bodies such as the Organisation for Economic Cooperation and Development (OECD) and the World Trade Organisation (WTO) maintain databases of current information useful for trade. Firms like Mintel, Keynote and the British Market Research Bureau collect data on markets, products and customers which they sell on to other interested organisations. Exhibit 5.3 shows internal and external sources of secondary and primary data.

Whenever data from another source is used, researchers have to be careful to acknowledge that source, and to get permission from publishers or data owners.

Secondary research is important in establishing what is already known so that researchers can build on that information rather than just rediscover it. Information about past events, and the dates they occurred, can be helpful in establishing the background of significant product and market developments. This information

e-focus: Drowning in data

There's a story popular with marketers that, when it first introduced its now familiar Clubcard, Tesco produced so much more data than envisaged, it just didn't know what to do with it. This may, of course, not really be true of Tesco, but it has surely happened somewhere to some unsuspecting but enthusiastic loyalty schemer.

Over 70% of Tesco's customers now have a Clubcard. Every time they use it they provide Tesco with a breakdown of their shopping. Nectar cards are accepted by an even wider range of retailers and so build an even more complete picture. Combine this data with the demographic information supplied on the card application form, and you can build a detailed profile of shoppers.

The possibilities are enormous. A well-managed loyalty scheme can help a company do so much more than just promote repeat sales (important though that is). Armed with that kind of information, firms can manage the way they interact with their customers and so increase customer satisfaction and long-term profitability. For example, if Tesco has a regular customer who has the right profile for Internet shopping but who does not do it, it might want to find out why. If it can fix the issue, then it can encourage them into a better shopping pattern and, as it is unlikely that this issue is unique, it will probably pick up other new online shoppers too.

They know us so well.

can also be used to help forecast future patterns or trends (assuming past and current assumptions hold). The volume of secondary data available increases year on year and modern technology, e.g. databases and the Internet, makes it widely available and easier to access.

The starting point for secondary research is usually the organisation's own records. If there is insufficient relevant information available internally, then researchers will look for alternative, external data sources.

The advantages of secondary data collection include:

- it is non-reactive – i.e. it can be carried out without alerting any other organisation or business
- it is unobtrusive because it only seeks out what is already available
- the issue of confidentiality in the use of materials is not usually a problem (so long as copyright permission has been obtained)
- accountability is rarely a problem because such published data have been vetted by previous research and reviewers, so the data collected can be used

to back up one's own opinions and statements about what is known about the research problem at hand

- it is an economical method whose costs (e.g. database access or the price of a market research report) are usually known very quickly
- it is a speedy research method as the data have already been collected.

In any research project, secondary data should be collected first, i.e. before any **primary research** is undertaken. Secondary research is usually much cheaper and if the data you want already exists, why collect it again? Researchers use primary research methods to fill in gaps; to find out things that secondary research could not tell them.

However, there are limitations to secondary data. The data has been compiled for the original publisher's own purposes. So the data collected is relevant to that organisation and might not be applicable to studies currently being conducted by others. It might be biased or have left out things that were not relevant to the original research project. The secondary data might also be out of date, depending on how many years ago it was collected. It may just be wrong: sloppily collected or collated. Always check data against multiple sources.

COMMERCIALLY AVAILABLE RESEARCH

There are a number of commercial organisations (such as Mintel, Nielsen, TNS and Keynote) which conduct research and publish substantial reports which other researchers and client companies can then purchase. For example, Kantar Media's *Target Group Index* (TGI) is derived from a questionnaire of over 45 pages, sent out to representative consumers (**consumer panels**). The selected consumers, usually in their own homes, answer questions or perform small tasks and return their responses to the research agency. In this way information is obtained about respondents' general purchasing habits, lifestyles and needs. The surveys cover a comprehensive range of topics, such as brands consumed, levels of income and expenditure. Information collected in this way can be sold to businesses that are interested in any of these consumer topics. More information on TGI can be found on Kantar Media's website (**http://kantarmedia-tgigb.com**).

Mass media advertising can be very expensive: usually accounting for the largest part of the campaign budget. Accurate intelligence on consumers' media habits is therefore important and worth paying for. There are a number of commercial organisations who provide these insights to their clients, e.g. Nielsen (**www.nielsen.com/uk/en/measurement.html**), Kantar (**www.kantarmedi-auk.com**) and Forrester Research (**www.forrester.com**). Media owners, e.g. television companies, social media sites and newspapers, are eager to publicise their viewing statistics and audience profiles. The Broadcasters' Audience Research Board (BARB) collects information on a regular basis on what television programmes are watched. These data are used to compile the 'most popular programme' lists often published in magazines.

Nielsen, and other research agencies, provide data about the total sales of retailers' and manufacturers' brands in many product categories. A product's barcode

Discovering Customer Needs Through Research

primary research (field research) research carried out specifically for the research task in question

consumer panels a primary research technique that seeks the views, attitudes, behaviour or buying habits of a group of consumers

contains information such as contents, manufacturer, price and country of origin. Each product is scanned at the store's checkout and this information can then be used by marketing research agencies to compile **retail audits**.

Exhibit 5.3　Examples of secondary and primary data sources

	Internal sources	External sources
Secondary data collection	Customer records Sales reports Retail outlet/dealer's feedback Financial figures about customers, suppliers and dealers Research and development studies Production and technical records Management reviews Marketing intelligence assessments	Trade and consumer press Periodicals and journals Commercial and industrial reports Government publications Trade association reports Other companies' reports Directories Market reports Retail audits
Primary data collection	Current customer feedback Current customer complaints Sales interviews and daily feedback Current delivery situation Current state of stock turnover Current feedback from marketing, discounts and promotional activity State of current production levels to keep pace with dealer and customer demand Current research and development activity to give competitive edge	Observing behaviour: • watching customers and situations • surveillance by electronic means Questioning respondents: • asking questions in personal interviews • asking questions by telephone • using mailed questionnaires • using computer-assisted interviewing • using video links to ask questions Carrying out experiments: • carrying out product trials in a laboratory setting • carrying out consumer tests, e.g. eye tracking • carrying out trials in the field, e.g. a sample of respondents trying a product at home or in a public place within a specified period

EXPAND YOUR KNOWLEDGE

Classic article

Montgomery, D.B. and Weinberg, C.B. (1979) 'Toward strategic intelligence systems', *Journal of Marketing,* 43: 41–52.

The paper argues that as strategic planning tools become more sophisticated, the quality of information inputted into the planning process becomes more important such that increased attention should be paid to the range of information used and to the systematic development of strategic intelligence systems to deal with this information. An intelligence cycle is introduced emphasising information, sources of intelligence and analysis and processing considerations.

PRIMARY RESEARCH

When relevant secondary data are not available, information has to be gathered directly from individuals and the market. This is known as primary research. Researchers always begin with secondary research as this is cheaper and usually quicker. Primary research is then used to fill in the gaps or examine findings in greater detail.

External primary research may involve dealers, suppliers, customers, consumers, trade associations, industry groups and government institutions. This **primary data** is useful in building up pictures of levels of satisfaction with the products and services and of general attitudes towards an organisation and its activities.

Advances in computing have made gathering, recording and analysing information much easier and quicker. Researchers can involve substantially greater numbers of respondents, or respondents who might be difficult to reach by other means. Computer-based research can also have the advantage of providing a record of what was said (see *interviews* and the *e-focus* box 'e-questions' below for more on computer-assisted personal interviewing (CAPI)). There are a number of websites, e.g. survey monkey and smart-survey, which automate questionnaire production and distribute questionnaires online. Although the basic service may be free, they charge for the more sophisticated features that are usually required by professional or academic researchers (including students).

There are two broad approaches to primary research: quantitative and qualitative, which should be seen as mutually supportive. Each has its advantages and both can be of benefit to research clients in terms of problem-solving and decision-making. **Quantitative research** is numerical, **measures** market phenomena and usually involves statistical analysis. By contrast, **qualitative research** deals in words and does not attempt to count things; instead it provides an understanding of how and why things are as they are.

primary data
first-hand data gathered to solve a particular problem or to exploit a current opportunity

quantitative research
seeks numerical answers, e.g. how many people have similar characteristics and views

qualitative research
investigates people's feelings, opinions and attitudes, often using unstructured, in-depth methods

exploratory (research)
initial research to
see whether a more
comprehensive study
is needed

biographical research
an individual's story or
experiences told to a
researcher or found in
other materials

**phenomenological
research**
describes the
experiences of
individuals concerning
some specific
phenomena or
occurrence

in-depth interviews
one-to-one research
interviews; commonly
used in qualitative
research

focus groups
a qualitative research
technique using a
group discussion
overseen by a
moderator, used
to explore views,
attitudes and
behaviour with
regard to a marketing
issue; common in
advertising research

CONTRASTING QUANTITATIVE AND QUALITATIVE RESEARCH

Quantitative research has the reliability of numbers and statistically proven large-scale results while qualitative studies help to understand respondents' attitudes, motivations and behaviour. For example, quantitative research might be used to find out how much of a product is bought, when it is bought and where. This information shows marketing managers how and what customers have purchased, from which they can deduce what customers are likely to consume in the near future. However, should the marketing team want to know *why* people buy what they do, numbers alone will not suffice. A qualitative approach is better at discovering such customers' purchase intentions. The customers would need to be interviewed and probed for in-depth answers.

Qualitative and quantitative research should be seen as mutually supportive. For instance, as quantitative surveys taking in large numbers of people are expensive to conduct, a smaller-scale exploratory qualitative study is often conducted first to see whether a quantitative survey might be worthwhile and to assist with the design of that survey. For example, if the exploratory study unearths only very limited demand for a new product, then the need for an expensive quantitative survey is questionable.

QUALITATIVE RESEARCH

Qualitative research helps researchers to find new or different ways of looking at problems. Unlike quantitative research, qualitative research techniques 'do not attempt to make measurements, [but] seek insights through a less structured, more flexible approach' (Birn et al., 1990). It is used to 'increase understanding, expand knowledge, clarify the real issues, identify distinct behavioural groups' (Gordon and Langmaid, 1988). Qualitative research is about finding out what people think and feel and it is often used as a means of developing the design of a quantitative research programme, e.g. by helping to design the questions for a survey. It can be **exploratory**, i.e. a small-scale attempt to find out the particular circumstances of a market and its customers. It can be relatively unstructured, e.g. an interview where the interviewees are encouraged to discuss answers freely and so unearth a greater wealth of information for the researchers. It can be descriptive, as in the narratives offered in **biographical** or **phenomenological research**. It can be explanatory in nature, trying to discover why people do particular things, unearthing their attitudes and motivations. It may cover a broad range of companies or consumer types or it may look at one or two particular instances in depth.

The most common qualitative research methods are **in-depth interviews** and **focus groups** both of which are covered in more detail later in this chapter.

EXPAND YOUR KNOWLEDGE

Rose, G.M., Merchant, A. and Bakir, A. (2012) 'Fantasy in food advertising targeted at children', *Journal of Advertising*, 31 (3): 75–90.

This study used content analysis research techniques to look at the responses of children to fantasy in food advertisements.

customer focus: At home with your research subjects

Stacy Graika
Ethnographic
research

Ethnography may be described as a research approach in which time is spent with consumers in their own environment. Bruce Davies, an ethnographic researcher, explained: 'Rather than bringing consumers into companies, it's about bringing a company to consumers … It's good at finding new perspectives from old topics and unmet needs in mature markets'. His ethnographic research has helped develop two new brands in established markets: Zopa, an online financial exchange based on the eBay approach, which connects a community of users who want to borrow and lend money to each other; and Monkey Shoulder, a whisky brand from William Grant and Sons, aimed at appealing to younger (but of legal age) whisky drinkers. For Zopa, ethnography identified a community of entrepreneurs who were willing to exchange funds with each other rather than using the traditional channels of banks or financial institutions. The ethnographic research led Davies to recognise that the brand needed to be about exchange relationships that were social rather than just economic.

According to Fiona Jack, Chair of the Association of Qualitative Research, ethnography can sometimes be more effective than focus groups because it allows consumers to show how they do things in context rather than talking about what they do: 'Often consumers can't remember what they do until they're stood in front of something. Don't tell me but show me. It could involve anything from observing a consumer cleaning their toilet to accompanying them on a shopping trip for mascara.'

Pampers realised the benefits of this approach over ten years ago when their marketing team spent a week with different consumers in their own homes. They realised that the nappy itself was not the only important part of the experience of being a new mum, but that mums really cared about information and knowledge. Based on their consumer insight, the brand launched Pampers.com, an online community for mothers, and the website now has 650,000 unique users across Europe.

Ewan Jones, partner at Lippincott Mercer, a brand strategy and design consultancy, emphasises that ethnographic techniques can be especially useful for brands in the service sector that need to understand consumers' unmet needs: 'It helps brand positioning in a fact-based way. Should an airline invest in cabin seating or in-flight entertainment or staff? It helps to define the "touchpoints" in an experience'.

SOURCES: Lewis, 2005: 19–21.

© iStockPhoto.com/quavondo

EXPAND YOUR KNOWLEDGE

Levy, S.J. (2012) 'Marketing management and marketing research', *Journal of Marketing Management*, 28 (1–2): 8–13.

As a practitioner and an advocate of the use of qualitative methods of research, the author notes specific instances of their applications and sums up the awareness he has gained about marketing management and the use of marketing research.

QUANTITATIVE RESEARCH

Quantitative research requires much larger numbers of respondents than qualitative research. Its aim is to find out how many people have similar or specific characteristics and views. If there are large numbers of respondents, a quantitative survey is used to collect the data. It would be too time-consuming and costly to cover a large number of respondents with a qualitative approach. Use of questionnaires is a popular technique adopted, and these can be cost-effective in reaching many people when posted, faxed, emailed or completed online. The answers are then subjected to analyses using statistical computing software (e.g. SPSS or Microsoft Excel).

The largest type of quantitative study, and the most complete way of collecting data, is to conduct a full-scale CENSUS of the entire population within a country. Full-scale census surveys are used by governments all over the world as aids to planning and forecasting. Each census provides a large amount of information that gives reliable statistical data about population characteristics. The heads of households, or chief income earners, in each household have to fill in the census questionnaire. The process is expensive and time-consuming so population censuses are only conducted every ten years in the UK.

It is impossible for market research organisations to draw data from every member of the country's population in the way a census does. Respondents do not have to cooperate and, anyway, the costs involved would be huge. Therefore, they question a sample of the population. Each member of that sample group may represent hundreds, or even thousands, of people. It is therefore vital to choose your sample carefully to ensure you have the same balance of characteristics (sex, age, background, etc.) that are representative of the statistical population that is being studied. Sampling is considered later in this chapter as it is such an important part of the survey process. However, before leaving the issue of the use of census data, it is worth noting here that researchers use the term 'population' in a particular way and this does not necessarily mean the whole population of a country. Marketing researchers are concerned with the research population. If the research only needs to be focused on a particular group of people, such as attendees at a specific concert, then this would be the relevant research population. While it may still be inappropriate to survey all of them for cost and time reasons, a census would be a survey of all of these people, not of everybody in the population at large. From a research perspective, the important consideration is the definition of the research population which might be used for a census or from which a sample can be drawn.

SPSS
(Statistical Package for the Social Sciences) a software program for statistical analysis

census
a survey that includes all members of a population

The strength of quantitative research lies in the way statistical analysis is used to explain marketing phenomena. Marketers can base their decisions on statistically proven facts with known margins of error. The development of computer-aided simulations and database applications has greatly enhanced the ability of marketing researchers to build customer characteristics from geo-demographic data (see Chapter 4 for more information on market segmentation and geo-demographics) and purchasing records to build up more accurate customer profiles.

ACTIVITY

Go to the library and find examples of recent market research reports and company directories. Look for company directories such as Kompas and Dunn and Bradstreet, and market research reports such as Mintel and Keynote. What information do they provide? What other examples containing useful marketing information can you find and what do they cover?

EXPAND YOUR KNOWLEDGE

Stewart, D.W. and Hess, M. (2011) 'How relevancy, use, and impact can inform decision making: the uses of quantitative research', *Journal of Advertising Research*, 51 (1): 195–206.

This paper reviews the current state of use (and value) of quantitative research in advertising. It concludes that the value of quantitative research is well established but its use is less than might be expected. The authors discuss the reasons for this.

PRIMARY RESEARCH METHODS AND TECHNIQUES

Primary research is original research, i.e. it is not reliant on previously published information. There are two major forms of primary research:

- asking questions (surveys and interviews)
- watching how people behave (observation).

QUANTITATIVE SURVEYS

Quantitative surveys are what most people think of when they think of market research. Surveys involve asking respondents questions and recording their responses. There are a number of different ways to administer a survey and a range of techniques available to the researcher. Respondents may complete the survey forms themselves (e.g. if it is sent by post or emailed or is online) or they may be asked questions by a researcher (e.g. on the phone or face to face), who

Exhibit 5.4 Comparison of some of the primary research methods

	Advantages	Disadvantages
Email survey (quantitative)	Cheaper than offline methods Good for international surveys Versatile and very quick Can link to website	Poor email lists can make it hard to reach a representative sample Brevity of responses May be seen as spam
Website surveys and studies (quantitative or qualitative)	**Intranet** sites are low cost and easily accessible to **within** an organisation **Internet sites** have similar advantages to email surveys Easily accessed Social networking groups contain lots of information and can facilitate extensive discussion	Respondents select themselves Little control over sample Reliance on people to find the website Vested interests may distort the findings
Postal survey (quantitative)	Self-administered so lower cost A large number can be surveyed Possibility of enclosures	Limited to short questionnaire (otherwise people will not fill it in) Hard to ask follow-up questions or probe deeper Low response rates
Telephone survey (quantitative or qualitative)	Allows follow-up questions Avoids cost of travel Can choose time to call Computer-assisted telephone interviewing (CATI) for automated data collection	Intrusive Hang-ups Time-consuming CATI is more expensive to set up than using phone
Face-to-face interviews (quantitative or qualitative)	Flexibility; questions can be flexed Visual materials and other aids can be used Allows follow-up questions and probing: greater depth Personal relationship: builds trust Computer-assisted personal interviewing (CAPI) is faster and more accurate	May be expensive (e.g. travel, time) Time-consuming Interviewees may cancel appointments at short notice CAPI is more expensive to set up and more staff training is required
Focus groups (qualitative)	Flexibility: 'moderator' can encourage conversational directions Visual materials and other aids can be used Allows follow-up questions and probing: greater depth Discussion encourages more ideas	Needs good control by the 'moderator' otherwise group dynamics can cause a loss of direction Can be problematic to get a truly representative sample of individuals Time-consuming to set up

Exhibit 5.4 *Continued*

	Advantages	Disadvantages
Consumer panels (usually quantitative – but may be qualitative)	Consumer can do product testing or give responses from home Regular panels: good response rates Automate response through Internet links	Expensive and time-consuming to set up Can be problematic in getting a truly representative sample of individuals
Use of observational equipment and recorders (e.g. cameras/CCTV) (quantitative)	Can be always-on Captures actual behaviour Useful in everyday and test situations Less intrusive than human observer	Much information is irrelevant Time-consuming to review Requires monitoring of respondents in test situations (more researcher time)
Autonomic response measurement (e.g. eye tracking, galvanic response, pupilometer, tachistoscope, neuro-measurement – see page 220) (qualitative)	Measures natural, unconscious responses Can be used before market release Alternative materials and treatments can be tested	Laboratory situations Needs specialised equipment Limits number of respondents

then completes the questionnaire on their behalf. The following are some of the more popular methods:

- email surveys
- postal surveys
- telephone surveys
- face-to-face surveys
- web surveys
- omnibus surveys
- panels
- syndicated surveys.

Most surveys employ some form of questionnaire answered individually or, less commonly, in pairs (duos) or small groups. The last three on the list above have some special characteristics which are explained below.

Omnibus surveys

In an omnibus survey research agencies collect information on behalf of a number of their business clients at the same time and on a regular basis. A new sample of respondents is recruited each time (one of the key differences between this and a 'panel' – see below). Typically, clients pay to have one or a series of questions

omnibus survey a large questionnaire that provides data for multiple clients

put into a larger questionnaire. Such a questionnaire might contain different sections relating to lifestyles, consumption habits, financial circumstances, ownership of motor vehicles, etc. In the motor car and financial services industries, where manufacturers and institutions are very protective of their corporate reputations, omnibus surveys are useful in helping to hide from the respondents the purposes for which the answers to the questionnaire are required. When reporting the findings, the research agency will just report back the responses to the specific questions asked by the client and not the full questionnaire results.

Panels

Panels are most often thought of as 'consumer panels' but can equally be industrial or b2b. Groups of people are recruited to respond to a specific survey over a period of time, and some are set up permanently by research agencies who only have to recruit new members if existing ones drop out or if they choose to increase the size of the panel. They can be expensive to set up but relatively cheap to run and maintain. A big advantage is that once recruited, high response rates can be assured and the same group of people are available throughout the research process. Consumer panels are frequently used for surveying buying habits and usage behaviour of grocery goods and for researching media habits such as watching TV, listening to the radio and reading the press.

Syndicated surveys

Syndicated surveys are similar to omnibus studies in that they are undertaken on behalf of a range of clients who pay into the syndicate. The difference here, however, is that where omnibus research involves a questionnaire composed of questions from different clients and each client only sees the responses to its question(s), syndicated research is designed by the research agency as a complete piece of research which is sold to each of the clients with full results from the research made available at a cost. For example, an organisation with a small research budget may buy into a syndicated advertising tracking study along with other organisations as a cost-effective way of finding out how its and others advertising is being received by the target market.

QUESTIONNAIRE DESIGN

questionnaire
a set of questions for
use during a survey

Questionnaires are possibly the most common research tool and are especially used in quantitative surveys. The questionnaire is a flexible tool for the market researcher who can use it to obtain important information about consumer behaviour, attitudes to products, shopping habits, media habits and many other marketing-related issues. Quantitative researchers often use standardised questionnaires with samples of several hundreds or even thousands of respondents. Such questionnaires often consist of highly structured questions for ease of coding and statistical analysis. Designing questionnaires looks easy but designing **good** questionnaires is a highly skilled task. Questionnaires should always be pilot tested with typical respondents for whom the questionnaire was constructed. Such testing invariably shows ways to make the questionnaire more effective.

A questionnaire should be easily understood by the people who have to answer the questions, otherwise they are likely to give incorrect or misleading answers. It is therefore usually better to use everyday language and simple wording.

Guidelines for the wording of questionnaires:

- use complete sentences
- avoid abbreviations and acronyms
- avoid slang and colloquialisms
- take care with jargon and technical expressions (will the respondent understand?)
- ask an expert researcher to review the questionnaire
- test the questionnaire on a typical respondent
- avoid two-edged questions, e.g. 'do you buy milk and eggs?' – these may be hard to answer accurately
- avoid introducing bias or strongly emotive language, e.g. 'do you think that the way supermarkets encourage food waste is criminal?'
- avoid negative phrasing as these questions are harder to answer and may be misinterpreted, e.g. 'did you enjoy the film?', not 'did you not enjoy the film?'

(based on Fink, 1995)

10 steps to questionnaire design

Keeping language simple and making the questionnaire easy to complete is especially important for self-administered questionnaires (i.e. questionnaires that will be completed without a researcher present to provide guidance). Generally speaking, the less trouble a questionnaire is to fill in, the higher the response rate is likely to be.

e-focus: e-questions

Researchers often use email, or links to websites, to administer their questionnaires. This means that information can be collected much faster and that physical distance is no obstacle. Through email and the Web it is no more expensive to contact people on the other side of the world than it is to talk to people in the next office.

Computerised questionnaires have other significant advantages over their old-fashioned paper counterparts. The computer does away with that tedious (and confusing) business of 'if you ticked yes, now go to question 44b, otherwise go to question 16'. Each answer can determine what the next question will be.

The information collected from all the respondents is then downloaded, collated, statistically analysed, cross-related and systematically grouped into the types of categories that will allow researchers to make meaningful statements to their clients about the findings. This type of computer-assisted personal interviewing (CAPI) is cost-effective and saves a lot of time. Computer-assisted telephone interviewing (CATI) works on the same principle, by allowing responses on the telephone to be recorded on to the computer and computer-generated analyses to be carried out speedily and impartially. Further examples of electronic assistance include small, digital, handheld cameras, traffic sensor devices and closed-circuit television (CCTV) equipment, often used in stores and shopping precincts to observe and record the behaviour of customers.

Exhibit 5.5   Examples of ways of asking questions

Closed questions:

'What is your age?'	16–25	26–35
'Do you have a bank account?'	Yes	No
'Do you own a car?'	Own	Don't own

Scale questions:

Likert scale

Superdry is a fashionable brand

1	2	3	4	5
Strongly agree	Slightly agree	Neither agree nor disagree	Slightly disagree	Strongly disagree

Comments:_____

_____

_____

Osgood's semantic differential scale

Was Rosannica Restaurant's service:

Reliable   _ _ _ _ _ _   Unreliable
Friendly   _ _ _ _ _ _   Unfriendly
Expensive   _ _ _ _ _ _   Inexpensive

Comments:_____

_____

_____

Rank order scale

Please rank in order of preference each of the following university facilities:

Sports facilities   ☐
Medical centre facilities   ☐
Library facilities   ☐
Parking facilities   ☐
Restaurant facilities   ☐

Comments:_____

_____

_____

Open-ended questions:

'What did you enjoy about the play last night?'

_____

_____

'Describe your feelings concerning the news about brand X'

_____

_____

'What do you think the level of competition will be like in the next five years?'

_____

_____

OPEN OR CLOSED?

Closed questions can be answered in a single word (often yes or no). They are useful for getting a definitive answer or pinning things down and are easier to code and analyse than open-ended questions. An open-ended question gives the respondent more freedom to answer the question in their own way. Open-ended questions are useful for opening up a subject and discovering more about it. They are much used in qualitative research.

Although they are easier to analyse, closed questions can seem more difficult to write because the researcher has to know the possible answers in advance: not such a problem for 'yes' or 'no' questions, or for categorical data such as which gender a person is or where they live, but trickier if a scale of answers is required, for example, the question 'How often have you visited this place?' requires the researcher to have a good idea of what might be the maximum number of visits. If the questionnaire allows for possible answers of '1–2; 3–4; 5–6; 7–8; more than 8' and in fact lots of people have visited 20 or more times, the resulting data will be of poor quality.

OBSERVATION TECHNIQUES

Observation, as the name suggests, is about watching how people behave rather than asking them questions about their behaviour. Simple observation involves watching and recording people and their activities: perhaps using products or doing their shopping. A 'pantry audit' is an example of simple observation. Researchers list all the products or brands that are kept in someone's home. A useful observation for a toy manufacturer is watching children play with their toys to see exactly how they behave and enjoy themselves. For a restaurant owner, watching people use their services can be highly insightful. Participant observation, which is a variant, requires the researcher to become involved in the activity or task being observed, e.g. the researcher might accompany the respondent on a shopping trip.

An advantage of using observation as the research approach is that there should be no researcher or response bias in the observation process, although the recording of the observed behaviour may cause problems. Technology helps to overcome this problem. Observees can be filmed or sound-recorded unobtrusively (though this should always be done with their permission, of course). For example, television viewing habits can be monitored electronically as the television is turned on and channels changed.

Other recording devices include:

- eye movement camera – used for such things as assessing advertisement designs by electronically tracking exactly what the eye is looking at (see Exhibit 5.6)
- tachistoscope – used to show images very quickly which can be used, for example, to measure brand image awareness
- pupilometer – used to measure pupil dilation (the size of the pupil in the eye); the larger the pupil, the more it indicates how much the image being viewed is liked
- psycho-galvanometer – used to measure changes on the surface of the skin when the respondent is viewing images or answering questions or performing a task
- neuro-research – this is a growing area of research which involves the measurement of brainwave patterns as respondents are presented with different messages or images and using different media.

The immense advantage all these techniques share is that they measure autonomic responses in respondents. These are biological changes that are automatic and well documented for their reliability.

closed questions
questions that expect a one-word (usually yes or no) answer

open-ended questions
questions that invite the respondent to comment rather than just give a one-word answer

categorical data
also known as 'nominal' data, data that has no numerical value and so cannot be statistically analysed although each category may be counted, e.g. gender, star sign, hair colour

observation
a primary research technique that involves watching how subjects behave in their normal environment

Exhibit 5.6   Example of a stationary eye-tracking system; alternative systems are smaller and can be more conveniently head mounted. The latest systems use small cameras placed unobtrusively (and unobserved) in front of viewers

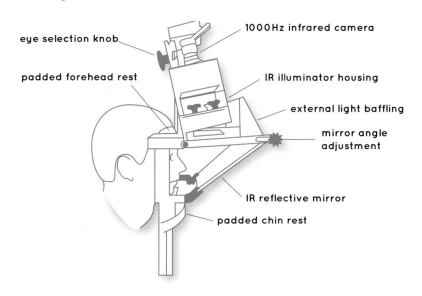

How to use Google Analytics

marketing metrics
'measurements that help with the quantification of marketing performace, such as market share, advertising spend, and response rates elicited by advertising and direct marketing' (Chartered Insitute of Marketing)

data mining
using specialist software to analyse large amounts of data (held in a database) to idenitfy patterns or relationships in that data

WEB ANALYTICS

Thanks to the Web, it is easier now than ever before to collect up-to-date, detailed, data on customer behaviour. Organisations have access to masses of data; sometimes more than they know how to deal with.

In order to make the most of this wonderful potential information, it is important to plan the data collection carefully. Key questions to be answered when planning include:

- what **marketing metrics** are needed?
- how might the necessary data be collected?
- which of those methods will be most effective in terms of cost, accuracy and time?
- who will be responsible for the data collection (e.g. in-house or agency)?
- how will the data be stored?
- how will it be analysed (**data mining**)?
- what reports should be produced to assist managers in their decision-making?

Ryan and Jones (2012) suggest seven key performance indicators (KPIs) for websites:

- conversion rate; the number of visitors who make a purchase, or book an appointment etc.
- page views

- absolute unique visitors
- new vs. returning visitors
- bounce rate: the number of visitors who leave the site immediately, having only looked at the first page (the 'landing page')
- abandonment rate: the number of visitors who do not complete an action, typically leaving without checking-out the items in their basket
- cost per conversion, including advertising.

Website visitors and email recipients leave digital footprints that can be tracked and analysed, making online marketing communications much easier to measure than offline (Charlesworth, 2009) although it is still hard to tie online promotional activity directly to offline sales (see Chapter 8, 'Promotion'). The two most common ways to collect information about website visitors are through web access logs, which are created and held by the organisation's own web server, and page tags (embedded code) which send data to the organisation's analytics service provider. There are a number of commercial organisations which provide analysis services, e.g. Google (**www.google.com/analytics**) and Yahoo (**http://help.yahoo.com/l/us/yahoo/ywa/**). The information may be supplemented through 'cookies' (see e-focus).

Web analytics tagging & tracking explained

e-focus: Do you like cookies?

The main point of the World Wide Web is that it's user friendly. We surf at will, tracking down interesting clips and articles, looking for information on our favourite things (shows, people, brands, etc), playing good games, finding the best product deals. Cookies help this to happen.

Cookies are small files which are stored on your hard drive and are available to the browser (e.g. Internet Explorer or Firefox). They are used to tailor your experience of the Internet and personalise it to you. It's how sites are able to greet you by name and show you what's new since your last visit. This sounds good, so why are they controversial and why has the EU passed a law restricting their use?

Most cookies are harmless and enhance your online experience. The problem cookies are called 'persistent third party cookies'. They come from a different site: one that you may not even know about. They can be used by advertisers and trackers to record your browsing habits, following you wherever you go, even when you've moved off the site where you encountered the cookie. They arrive in various forms, e.g. through adverts, widgets or embedded content (often videos).

The EU Directive on Privacy and Electronic Communications came into force in May 2012 and it requires users' explicit consent before data can be stored on their computers. That's what's behind all those pop-ups telling you that a site uses cookies. Do you click and read the details of **how** they are used?

By these means, organisations can find out: where in the world the person browsing is located, how they came to the site (e.g. directly or through an advert or via a search engine – in which case they can also see the search terms entered) and their journey through the site (Ryan and Jones, 2012).

This information is, of course, very helpful for improving the website design, making it stickier (so people stay longer), placing links appropriately to help them to the right pages and identifying any page that commonly causes them to leave the site, but it can be used more strategically to improve overall business performance. According to a recent IBM Executive Report, an effective customer analytics strategy can help drive top-line growth, avoid unnecessary costs and increase customer satisfaction (Teerlink and Haydock, 2011). The Internet can provide masses of information on customers but, too often, the insights gleaned from web analytics stay in the IT department instead of being used more widely to help grow the business.

Google4
Entrpreneurs:
Using Web
Analytics

QUALITATIVE STUDIES

Qualitative techniques include:

- interviews
- focus groups
- projective techniques.

IN-DEPTH INTERVIEWS

Interviews (in-depth interviews) are ideal for gaining detailed information on a topic from a limited number of people. The decision about who to interview clearly depends on the objectives and nature of the study. Sometimes it is appropriate to interview loyal customers or fans and sometimes the researcher may want to talk to people who never buy the brand. Expert interviews can be very useful in getting in-depth information and an industry view. For example, students often want to interview marketing managers or advertising agencies for their projects.

Denscombe (2000) suggests two questions to be answered before choosing interviews as a research technique:

- Does the research really require the kind of *detailed information* that interviews supply?
- Is it reasonable to reply on information gathered from a small number of informants?

Interviews provide depth of information, but not usually breadth.

Interviewers usually start by asking a few general questions or putting up a problem situation or case scenario for the interviewee to respond to. Although interviewers vary in approach and style, they should always create a situation where the respondent feels at ease and can talk freely about the subject, thereby

Face-to-face interviewing.

global focus: Elusive data

Marketing research in less developed countries (LDCs) can present particular problems. Often, there is very little secondary data available, and what there is may be out of date or unreliable. Population censuses are expensive and so poorer countries are unlikely to do these often, if at all. Few houses, especially in rural areas, may have phones and so the telephone directory will be a slim volume. (In many LDCs, people in remote areas are more likely to have mobile phones than landline telephones.)

This lack of secondary data also affects primary research as it is hard to obtain an accurate sampling frame. As a consequence, convenience samples are often used.

The very collection of primary data can also be difficult in itself. In some countries, women still play a subservient role to their men and would not be permitted to talk to a man – certainly not alone. So who do you send to do the interview? The obvious answer would be a woman. But how will you find a trained female market researcher in a country where women do not work outside the family? In such countries, people can also be reluctant to talk to strangers at all, especially about personal matters.

On the other hand, countries that have not always enjoyed the privilege of free speech may prove a researcher's dream. Response rates to surveys can be very high – though whether this is because people are accustomed to cooperating with official enquiries, or just because they find being asked their opinion on consumer products a novelty, is as yet unclear.

generating more information and insights for the interviewer. The aim is to encourage the respondent to freely express her or his opinions, attitudes, experiences, interpretations and motivations. Interviews are time-consuming and can take from one to several hours. A voice or video recorder can be helpful if its use is agreed with the respondent. Analytical software such as NVivo can be useful when analysing interview transcripts.

FOCUS GROUPS

A focus group comprises a number of respondents (usually 6–12 people) led by a professional researcher who is called the facilitator or moderator. The researcher starts by asking questions or prompting the group members to respond to the words, sights, sounds and touch of visual images, or the actual products themselves in order to get the group discussion flowing freely about the subjects or objects. By observing the interactions and recording the discussions, the researcher can gain useful insights about the groups' intentions and feelings towards the subjects or objects.

Focus groups talking about TV sponsorship

Focus Group Smartphone Testing

Focus groups can give useful insights into people's views and feelings.

PROJECTIVE TECHNIQUES

Projective techniques use indirect questions to understand respondents' perspectives better. Examples of projective techniques include word associations – one word is said and the respondent supplies her/his own immediate associated word in response; picture associations – respondents are shown a range of pictures and asked to choose those that best represent the item being researched, e.g. the pictures that best represent a particular brand; sentence completion – respondents are asked to complete incomplete sentences; cartoon test or thought bubbles – a cartoon or picture is shown and the respondent has to fill in the captions or thought bubbles; third-person techniques – the respondent is asked what they imagine a specified other person, e.g. a friendly Martian, might say about something; personalisation of objects – e.g. respondents are asked to imagine if the brand was a celebrity who it would be; collages – respondents are asked to create a collage representing the research item from a pile of pictures.

ethical focus: Reaching out

Recruiting the right people to interview is a crucial, but can be a difficult, part of the research process, especially if the people you need to interview are hard to find or unlikely to want to talk to you. This is often the case with vulnerable people like the homeless or mentally ill.

One answer to this is a technique known as 'snowballing'. It lets the participants recruit each other.

Ipsos MORI's Participation Unit explored various approaches as part of a methodological trial assessing the impact of different interviewee recruitment methods on a particularly hard-to-reach group: occasional drug users. Thanks to the snowballing technique, peer interviewers were able to interview a wide spectrum and diversity of drug users in locations most researchers could not usually reach. In contrast, interviewees recruited by professional market research agency staff were all participants in rehabilitation programmes. Of course, there are drawbacks to using peer interviewers and appropriate training has to be provided to ensure that there is no bias in the way the interviews are conducted.

It does seem that snowballing can get answers from places that more traditional approaches would never reach.

b2b focus: A primary research illustration

Simply Software is considering selling hardware maintenance services. Initially, they send an email to their entire salesforce asking how many customers have enquired about such services. Next they ask the sales team to sound out their customers at their next visit. Additionally, they could write to members of organisations such as the Computer Users' Association. While waiting for responses, they check their own records of customer usage and complaints and assess competitive offerings via a web-search.

If there is sufficient interest in the new service, the company will need to design it to fit with customer needs. To find out what would appeal to customers, it could invite groups to come in and talk about their current hardware service arrangements: what's good and what's not; what extra services they would like; and what they would be prepared to pay. Again they could consult the salesforce and other key employee groups. They could send a questionnaire to current customers.

This scenario makes use of a variety of research techniques and approaches: internal data analysis, web-searching, salesforce information, trade association information, focus groups, face-to-face interviews and a survey. This use of multiple methods is sometimes called 'triangulation': gathering the information that the company needs from a variety of sources and perspectives to ensure that it is as full, and as accurate, as possible.

PRE-TESTING, TRACKING AND POST-TESTING

Marketing communications, especially advertising campaigns, can be expensive to implement. While a planned programme of pre-testing, tracking and post-testing can also be expensive, it is usually a lot less expensive than a failed campaign and the results can help ensure maximum effectiveness for the campaign.

Pre-testing is a way of assessing the likely effectiveness of marketing communications campaigns before the firm commits to the expense of running them. Respondents are asked for their responses to different advertisements – most usually in a focus group convened by the agency. Alternatively, they may be asked about brand names or promotional offers). Direct marketers pre-test a number of different offers and creative treatments to assess which ones different types of people are most likely to respond positively to. Post-testing (i.e. afterwards) can provide further observations about the marketing communications effects. For example, the firm can pre-test the effects of marketing communications by showing advertising material in advance of a new advertising campaign and post-test the effects after the campaign has been run to see if it worked as they expected.

Tracking is simply the testing process that measures what is going on over a period of time. Such testing is commonplace in the marketing communications industry where pre-testing may be used to evaluate and select advertising concepts, tracking is used to measure changes in recognition and recall of the advertising, branding and attitudes, and post-testing is used to assess the overall effect of a campaign.

TEST MARKETING

test market
a subset of a market in which a product offering can be sold for a short period of time in order to predict demand and to try out and refine the marketing mix

A **test market** is a mini-market – a smaller version of the whole market, in which changes to any or all elements of the marketing mix can be tried out, e.g. new products, promotions, distribution, retail display, pricing, etc. If the testing is successful in the test market, then it can be rolled out to the real market with more confidence; there is less risk of it proving an expensive failure. In the UK, television advertising campaigns are sometimes tested in one of the television regions before going national. However, not all countries have regionalised television (e.g. Germany, for instance, does not), so TV adverts are more difficult to test.

The use of test marketing is a recognition of the difficulties of researching matters, as a scientist might, by controlling conditions in order to test one particular variable (e.g. the price, or the communications medium). In the world of marketing and social research, variables cannot be controlled in the field. The test market therefore needs to be as close as is reasonable (or variations accounted for) to the whole of the market. While the variables cannot be controlled, they are at least presumed to have approximately the same effect in the test market as they would in the full market. Test marketing may be particularly useful when launching a new product or significantly changing or experimenting with changes to the marketing mix.

QUALITY OF MARKETING INFORMATION

Wrong information or missing information is no use at all. Sound marketing decisions can only be made on the basis of good quality information. The data must be:

- timely
- accurate
- reliable
- valid.

TIMELINESS

It is important that research is finished on time. If it is late, then it may be too late to be of any use. For example, the management problem may have become acute or the marketing environment may have changed. Out-of-date data is worthless.

ACCURACY

Accuracy is about correctness or precision. Clearly it is desirable to have absolutely accurate data. However, this is not always possible (complete accuracy is rare) and comes at a high cost. Frequently, researchers have to make estimates and it is important that they make it clear when this is the case. Relying on inaccurate data can lead to poor decisions, but if we know how inaccurate a figure may be, then we can make allowances. For example, if a thermometer consistently shows boiling water to be 91°C, instead of 100°C, then we know it is inaccurate and by how much.

RELIABILITY

Reliability refers to the consistency of results. If a piece of research is repeated with an identically composed sample, would it produce the same results? In the example above, does the thermometer read 91°C each time? Even though the measurement is inaccurate, if it returns the same result, it is reliable.

VALIDITY

Validity is a key concept in assessing the quality of research. Research should deliver evidence that can be used to answer the research problem. 'Internal validity' is an indicator of whether the research measures what it claims to measure. It is no use using a barometer (which measures pressure) if you want to measure temperature. That requires a thermometer. If research has 'external validity' it means that generalisations can be made from the research carried out on a sample to the wider population from which the sample is drawn.

Researchers have ways to deal with issues of validity which are beyond the scope of this book. Just remember the importance of taking care over research design to ensure that the research outcomes are valid.

EXPAND YOUR KNOWLEDGE

LaPointe, P. (2012) 'The dog ate my analysis: the hitchhiker's guide to marketing analytics', *Journal of Advertising Research,* 52 (4): 395–6.

While the age of big data allows for more in-depth insight into consumer behaviour and enables more sophisticated targeting, it is also important to be aware that this is just a small portion of consumers' shopping and buying behaviour. Using marketing analytics as a predictive tool is complex and over-analysis can lead to skewed results. When applying marketing analytics it is vital to be mindful of scale, relevance, validity and reliability and to not forget that gut instinct still goes a long way.

SUMMARY

Marketing research is a crucial aspect of marketing. It provides the basis for all marketing decisions.

Good marketing research is essential to the objectives and successes of both profit and not-for-profit organisations. The procedures used are well-established forms of collecting, analysing and conveying information about people and markets. Markets can be described and analysed in detail so that opportunities can be taken, the performances of organisations assessed and competitors' activities tracked. Marketing research is, therefore, indispensable for the marketing intelligence purposes of organisations and in helping them to develop their marketing strategies.

Marketing research starts with secondary data which should be collected before any primary research is undertaken. The broad categories of qualitative and quantitative research have been described along with the many and varied primary research methods that fit into these categories. The decision of which method or methods to use is a direct function of the information needed which, in turn, is a function of the marketing management problem the researcher is trying to solve.

CHALLENGES REVIEWED

Now that you have finished reading the chapter, look back at the challenges you were set at the beginning. Do you have a clearer idea of what's involved?

HINTS
- Sources of secondary information, internal records, primary research approaches
- Objectives of research
- Appropriate qualitative research methods
- Sampling.

READING AROUND

JOURNAL ARTICLES

Barker, M. (2003) 'Assessing the "quality" in qualitative research: the case of text-audience relations', *European Journal of Communication*, 18 (3): 315–35.

Brien, R. and Stafford, J. (1968) 'Marketing information systems: a new dimension for marketing research', *Journal of Marketing*, 32 (Jul): 19–23.

Earls, M. (2003) 'Advertising to the herd', *International Journal of Market Research*, 45 (3): 311–36.

LaPointe,P. (2012) 'The dog ate my analysis: the hitchhiker's guide to marketing analytics', *Journal of Advertising Research,* 52 (4): 395–6.

Levy, S. (2012) 'Marketing management and marketing research', *Journal of Marketing Management*, 28 (1–2): 8–13.

Lukas, B., Whitwell, G. and Heide, J. (2013) 'Why do customers get more than they need? How organizational culture shapes product capability decisions', *Journal of Marketing*, 77 (1): 1–12.

Montgomery, D. and Weinberg, C. (1979) 'Toward strategic intelligence systems', *Journal of Marketing,* 43: 41–52.

Rose, G., Merchant, A. and Bakir, A. (2012) 'Fantasy in food advertising targeted at children', *Journal of Advertising,* 31 (3): 75–90.

Stewart, D.W. and Hess, M. (2011) 'How relevancy, use, and impact can inform decision making: the uses of quantitative research', *Journal of Advertising Research*, 51 (1): 195–206.

Tarran, B. (2003) 'The birth of an idea', *Research* (the magazine of the Market Research Society), August: 22–4.

MAGAZINE ARTICLES

Noble, T. (2013) 'Neuroscience in practice', *Admap*, March, London: WARC.

BOOKS AND BOOK CHAPTERS

Belk, R., Fischer, E. and Kozinets, R.V. (2013) *Qualitative Consumer and Marketing Research*. London: Sage.

Burcher, N. (2012) 'Listening', in *Paid Owned Earned: Maximizing Marketing Returns in a Socially Connected World*. London: Kogan Page, Chapter 2.

Clow, K.E. and James, K.E. (2013) *Essentials of Marketing Research*. London: Sage.

Parsons, E. (2009) 'New technologies of marketing research', in E. Parsons and P. Maclaran, *Contemporary Issues in Marketing and Consumer Behaviour*. Oxford: Butterworth Heinemann, Chapter 11.

WEBSITES

www.barb.co.uk – Broadcasters Audience Research Board, e.g. market research applications.

www.cia.gov/library/publications/the-world-factbook – the CIA's world factbook, for country information.

www.mrs.org.uk – home of the Market Research Society.

Market research reports

Mintel, Keynote and *Euromonitor* are commonly found in university libraries or can be accessed online by subscription.

SELF-REVIEW QUESTIONS

1. Why is marketing research sometimes referred to as market research? (See pp. 192–3)
2. If marketing managers know about their customers from past purchases, why do they need to conduct marketing research? (See p. 193)
3. What are retail audits and consumer panels? (See pp. 199–200 and 207)
4. What is meant by defining a research problem? (See p. 195)
5. Define random sampling. (See p. 203)
6. What are the advantages of secondary data over primary data? (See p. 209)
7. What is qualitative research? (See pp. 209–10)
8. What is the difference between simple random sampling and stratified random sampling? (See p. 204)
9. List three qualitative research techniques. (See p. 210)
10. Name three commercial market research organisations. (See p. 207)

 Mini case study: Holidaying at home

Your company is considering developing a small, UK-based chain of bed and breakfast (b&b) accommodation but first you need to do some market research to see if this is likely to be a good investment.

1 Start with some secondary research. Check the latest relevant market reports (e.g. Mintel and Keynote), specialist travel sites and the travel sections of newspapers. What trends might be relevant?

2 Check out the competition. What are the key differences between a b&b and a hotel? What do they offer to guests? (Tip: you can use the Internet for this but do not just rely on a search engine such as Google – this will mainly be trying to sell you holidays, so think it through and check a variety of sites, e.g. tourist boards.)

3 Develop three research objectives for a small primary research project to help you to assess the b&b's potential.

4 Which primary research method(s) would you use and why?

Millions of Britons go abroad each year – largely to escape the British weather. For many people, holiday sunshine has become an essential that only the gravest of crises would persuade them to forego. However in 2009, about 60% of Britons took their holidays in the UK. It wasn't global warming that changed their minds, but the recession and the weakness of the pound which together made trips abroad unaffordable.

Britain offers a wide variety of holiday options: from posh hotels to b&bs and camping sites, from seaside resorts to stunning countryside to cosmopolitan cities, from ancient to modern. One of the newer accommodation trends was the emergence of boutique hotels such as those owned by Hotel du Vin: relatively small, luxurious and decidedly chic. Such treats were beyond the budget of many holidaymakers though and so there seemed to be an opportunity for something with the same kind of feel but cheaper rates: perhaps an ultra-comfortable, fashionably decorated budget hotel or b&b.

REFERENCES

American Marketing Association (2004) 'Definition of marketing'. Available at: **http://www.marketingpower.com/AboutAMA/Pages/DefinitionofMarketing.aspx** (accessed 20/02/14).

Birn, R., Hayne, P. and Vangelder, P. (1990) *A Handbook of Market Research Techniques*. London: Kogan Page.

Brien, R.H. and Stafford, J.E. (1968) 'Marketing information systems: a new dimension for marketing research', *Journal of Marketing*, 32 (Jul): 19–23.

Charlesworth, A. (2009) *Internet Marketing: A Practical Approach*, Oxford: Butterworth Heinemann.

Denscombe, M. (2000) *The Good Research Guide*. Buckingham: Open University Press.

Dichter, E. (1947) 'Psychology in marketing research', *Harvard Business Review*, 25 (Summer): 432–43.

ESOMAR (2008) Global Market Research 2008 Report, September. Available at: **http://www.esomar.org/** (accessed 09/03/10).

Fink, A. (1995) *How to Ask Survey Questions*. London: Sage Publications.

Gordon, W. and Langmaid, R. (1988) *Qualitative Research: A Practitioner's and Buyer's Guide*. Aldershot: Gower.

Kotler, P., Keller, K., Brady, M., Goodman, M. and Hansen, T. (2012) *Marketing Management*, 2nd edn. Harlow: Pearson.

Krugman, H.E. (1965) 'The impact of television advertising: learning without involvement', *Public Opinion Quarterly*, 29 (Fall): 349–56.

LaPointe, P. (2012) 'The dog ate my analysis: the hitchhiker's guide to marketing analytics', *Journal of Advertising Research*, 52 (4): 395–6.

Levy, S.J. (2012) 'Marketing management and marketing research', *Journal of Marketing Management*, 28 (1–2): 8–13.

Lewis, E. (2005) 'Getting involved', *The Marketer*, September: 19–21.

Lukas, B.A., Whitwell, G.J. and Heide, J.B. (2013) 'Why do customers get more than they need? How organizational culture shapes product capability decisions', *Journal of Marketing*, 77 (1): 1–12.

McLuhan, R. (2006) 'Informed decisions', *Marketing*, 13 December.

Market Research Society (n.d.) 'Standards and guidelines'. Available at: **www.mrs.org.uk/ standards/revised_code_definitions.htm** (accessed 06/03/10).

Montgomery, D.B. and Weinberg, C.B. (1979) 'Toward strategic intelligence systems', *Journal of Marketing*, 43: 41–52.

Oppenheim, A.N. (1992) *Questionnaire Design, Interviewing and Attitude Measurement*. London: Pinter Publications.

Rose, G.M., Merchant, A. and Bakir, A. (2012) 'Fantasy in food advertising targeted at children', *Journal of Advertising*, 31 (3): 75–90.

Ryan, D. and Jones, C. (2012) *Understanding Digital Marketing*, 2nd edn. London: Kogan Page.

Sainsbury's (2002) 'Nectar launches today', J Sainsbury plc (10 September). Available at: **www.j-sainsbury.co.uk/cr/index.asp?PageID=115&subsection=&Year=2002&New sID=291** (accessed 13/07/07).

Stewart, D.W. and Hess, M. (2011) 'How relevancy, use, and impact can inform decision making: the uses of quantitative research', *Journal of Advertising Research*, 51 (1): 195–206.

Teerlink, M. and Haydock, M. (2011) *Customer Analytics Pay Off*. IBM Institute for Business Value.

Thomas, J. (2010) 'Sainsbury claims biggest UK loyalty scheme with Nectar', Marketing. Available at: **http://www.marketingmagazine.co.uk/article/982407/sainsburys-claims-biggest-uk-loyalty-scheme-nectar** (accessed 20/02/2014).

Visit the companion website on your computer at **www.sagepub.co.uk/masterson3e** or MobileStudy on your Smart phone or tablet by scanning this QR code and gain access to:

- **Videos** to get a better understanding of key concepts and provoke in-class discussion.
- Links to useful **websites and templates** to help guide your study.
- Access **SAGE Marketing Pins (www.pinterest.com/sagepins/)**. SAGE's regularly updated **Pinterest** page, giving you access to regularly updated resources on everything from Branding to Consumer Behaviour.
- **Daily Grind podcast series** to learn more about the day-to-day life of a marketing **professional**.
- Interactive **Practice questions** to test your understanding.
- A **bonus chapter on Marketing Careers** to not only support your study, but your job search and future career.
- **PowerPoints** prompting key points for revision.

The Marketing Mix

WHAT THIS PART IS ABOUT

When they have completed their research and analysis, and so have developed an in-depth understanding of their marketing environment and of their customers, marketers make plans to satisfy those customers' needs. At the heart of these plans is a set of tools known as the marketing mix. The marketing mix is traditionally referred to as the 4Ps: product, promotion, place and price. The 4Ps are not enough for today's more complex product offerings though, so three more have been added to take account of the nature of services (see Chapter 7). The 7Ps add physical evidence, people and process to the original four. All the marketing mix elements must be blended together to produce an integrated plan of action to build brands and deliver long-term profits.

The marketing mix sounds deceptively simple, but a product is so much more than the item you buy. The product that is offered to customers includes its packaging, its brand and its supporting services and the decision to buy it may have more to do with those things than with the make-up of the item itself. Promotion is so much more than just advertising and is much more subtle than simply saying 'buy this'. Place is about getting the right products to the right people at the right time and about making it easier for customers to buy our products. Without a price, a product is a gift. Set the wrong price (either too high or too low) and products may not sell at all. The success of a service product may be largely reliant on the people that provide that service or the process that delivers it. Some services, e.g. restaurants, are heavily reliant on other products (peripheral products) such as the food served or on the décor of the restaurant. Both of these would be considered physical evidence.

Decisions about the marketing mix elements should not be made in isolation. The Ps need to fit with each other. An exclusive product, such as a designer suit or a Bang and Olufsen stereo, commands a high price, is sold in upmarket shops, or delivered to your door in a smart van, and should be high quality. An everyday product, such as shampoo or cat litter, should do its job reliably, be inexpensive and be widely available. If just one of the Ps is out of sync, then the whole of the product offering will be devalued.

Product 6

CHAPTER CONTENTS

PRODUCT CHALLENGES

The following are illustrations of the types of decision that marketers have to take or issues they face. *You aren't expected to know how to deal with the challenges now*; just bear them in mind as you read the chapter and see what you can find that helps.

- You are a manager in a large confectionery company which has just taken over another company. You now have too many chocolate products which are proving to be complex to manage. You have been asked to recommend which should be kept and which dropped. How will you decide?
- You are the marketing director of a large car company. The finance director wants to cut the product development budget. She cannot see why you need to keep launching new models so often. Can you convince her that this is necessary?
- You are given the task of managing a well-known and long-established brand of jeans. The brand is showing its age and sales are slowly falling year on year. What might you do to halt the decline and revitalise the brand?
- You are a salesperson at an electronics retailer. You stock the same PCs as everyone else and cannot change the basic products themselves. How can you make it more attractive for customers to come to your store rather than go to your rivals?
- You have recently been appointed marketing manager for a manufacturer of kitchen appliances (fridges, microwaves, dishwashers, etc.) and have just discovered that your products have built-in obsolescence, i.e. they are made to last five years only and then they have to be replaced. It would be easy to make them so that they lasted longer, but then you would not make the replacement sales. What is your position on this?

INTRODUCTION

marketing mix
the basics of
marketing plan
implementation,
usually product,
promotion, place and
price

Product is one of the 4Ps of the **marketing mix**: the central elements of a marketing plan. The other 3Ps are promotion, place and price, and these 4Ps together are the basic tools marketers use. (Services marketers extend these 4Ps to 7Ps – see Chapter 7). They must be carefully planned out so that they all work together in order to meet companies' targets for sales and profit.

Product
Promotion
Place
Price

positioning
the place a product
(brand) is perceived
to occupy in the
minds of customers/
consumers of the
relevant target
market relative to
other competing
brands

All commercial enterprises have products to sell and these products are both the result of, and the reason for, marketing activities. Products are developed to meet customer needs and so those needs must be researched and understood. The product can then be targeted at a specific market segment and a marketing mix developed to support its desired **positioning**. Product managers, or brand managers, have to design marketing programmes for their products and develop good customer relationships to ensure their brands' ongoing success.

The ways in which research into new products can be carried out was discussed in Chapter 5. Targeting and positioning were covered in Chapter 4 and customer needs in Chapter 3. Chapters 8–10 are on the other major marketing mix elements and how they can be blended to support each other in an integrated marketing programme.

goods
tangible products, i.e.
those with physical
substance

Some products are tangible (i.e. they have physical substance, they can be touched) and some are intangible (without physical substance, they cannot be touched), such as insurance or a dental check-up. The tangible products are often referred to as **goods**, while the intangible products are referred to as services. However, no product is completely physical; all have service elements to them, e.g. after-sales service, warranties, guarantees, installation assistance. Equally, very few services are pure service; most have a physical element to them. When you have your car cleaned, the cleaner uses detergent, wax, etc. When you eat in a restaurant, you are served food. Goods providers often use the service aspects of their products to differentiate them from the competition, whereas service providers may try to use the products associated with their services to do this.

This chapter will concentrate on tangible products, or goods (i.e. the ones you can actually touch), leaving services to be dealt with in more depth in the next chapter. It will consider what makes a new product a success in the marketplace and why so many fail. Most companies sell more than one product and the entire range must be managed so that individual products contribute to the success of the brand. Product managers use a number of analysis tools and these will be considered here, along with the strategies they feed into.

Branding is one of modern marketing's most popular tools and much has been written about the power of the brand. Branding was perhaps the primary competitive weapon of the 1990s, and in the twenty-first century it has become almost ubiquitous – everyone wants a brand. In this chapter, we will look at branding as a part of the product offering. Chapter 11 will revisit branding and its place in the whole of the marketing mix and in marketing strategy.

WHAT IS A PRODUCT?

A product can be described as a bundle of attributes or characteristics. A loaf of bread may be large, sliced and wholemeal, or it may be small, white and unsliced. These are its physical attributes and they provide benefits to the person who buys and/or eats the loaf. For example, the loaf may be good value for money, good for your health or convenient for sandwich making. Products exist to satisfy people's needs. The primary purpose of bread is to satisfy hunger whereas a watch satisfies our need to know the time, a car satisfies the need to travel from one place to another and washing powder cleans clothes. The product's attributes (or characteristics) must satisfy the customer's needs.

Essentials of product design

Customers judge the value of a product by weighing up all its aspects – the **total product offering**. The total product may have to satisfy a range of needs, e.g. Diet Pepsi has to quench thirst, taste good, be low calorie, be convenient to drink and convey a suitable image. Needs range from the simple (e.g. quench thirst) to the elaborate (e.g. convey suitable image). Some of these are fulfilled by basic product characteristics, e.g. the water in Diet Pepsi satisfies thirst, but some needs require more than just product ingredients. For instance, Pepsi's image is largely created by its advertising and the convenience of drinking is down to the size and design of the can or bottle. Whether or not an exchange (see Chapter 1) will take place, i.e. a sale be made, depends upon the customer's judgement of the total product's value. The customer's perception of a product's value may differ greatly from the company's perception, and is dependent upon all the elements of the marketing mix, i.e. the 4Ps (product, promotion, place and price). Customers have expectations of products that go beyond product performance. They may expect helpful product support, clear instructions and a fair price. They may also want their purchases to be ethically sound: non-exploitative, safe to use and environmentally friendly, perhaps. The marketing mix must therefore be well planned and integrated to create a total product offering that matches, or exceeds, the customer's expectations and needs.

total product offering
the total package that makes up and surrounds the product, including all supporting features, such as branding, packaging, servicing and warranties

TYPICAL REASONS PRODUCTS FAIL TO MEET CUSTOMER EXPECTATIONS

Ways in which products may fail to live up to consumer expectations include the following:

- **Non-performance**: the product may not deliver the core benefit required. It may not meet the basic need for which it is being bought (i.e. it may not work). The car may not start, the CD may not play. There are degrees of non-performance. The product may meet the core benefit but not deliver all the additional benefits anticipated (e.g. the car works but there is a strange squeak coming from somewhere), or it may be too complicated (e.g. the car radio has more functions than required) or, at the extreme, it may turn out to be physically dangerous (e.g. the car's brakes do not work).
- **Not for me**: the product may not suit the customer after all. They get it home and do not feel good about it. A skirt may be unflattering; paint can turn out to be the wrong colour after all; pizzas sometimes have too little or too much topping.
- **Social disapproval**: the customer's friends and family may not like the product.

- **Poor value**: there are several elements to this. A customer may wonder whether he or she could have got the product cheaper, or it may turn out to be of lower quality or a lower specification than anticipated. Alternatively, it may take up too much time, either in the purchasing or in the installation, in learning how to use it or in its ongoing use.
- **Non-delivery**: the product may never arrive. This is a common fear of Internet shoppers.

THE TOTAL PRODUCT OFFERING

Thanks to modern manufacturing techniques, most products can be copied by competitors with relative ease – and often made more cheaply than the originals. Firms rarely compete on the basis of their products' physical features alone; they offer their customers much more than that. A product may enhance the customer's image, it may offer better value than others, or better after-sales service, or come in a handier packet, or it may be a preferred brand. Mass-produced products are usually differentiated from each other by their additional characteristics rather than by their fundamentals and so marketers must design a complete package, a total product offering.

CORE BENEFITS (OR THE CORE PRODUCT)

core benefit (core product) the minimum benefits a product should confer, e.g. a pen must write, a car must go

A product's main reason for existence is called its **core benefit**. It is the simplest possible answer to an expressed need: no frills, no branding or packaging, no warranties or service promises, just the most basic reason why that product would be needed. The core benefit of a food product is to provide nutrition or satisfy

Exhibit 6.1   The total product offering

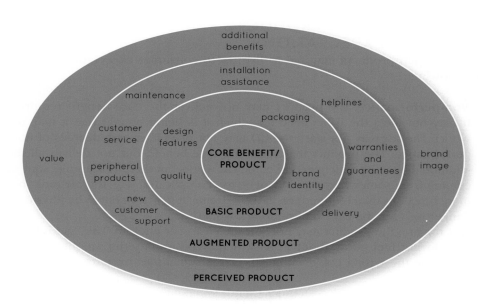

hunger. A coat is needed to keep a person warm. Medicine is meant to cure or relieve an illness.

Surprisingly, perhaps, there is no such thing as a new need; just new or different ways of solving a problem, i.e. satisfying that need. For example, riding horses was an improvement over walking from one place to another, trains replaced the horses, cars have largely supplanted trains and aeroplanes have, in many types of journey, replaced trains and boats. The transport problem is being solved in new and different ways. Electric light replaced gas for lighting, which in turn had replaced paraffin and candles, which in turn had replaced tallow wicks. The core benefit of all these things is to light the dark.

It is dangerous to lose sight of this important concept. Marketers must be sure that their products satisfy a need in its most basic sense. Products that do not offer a sound core benefit will usually fail. For example, it would be an uphill task for Rolex to attempt to sell watches that are not accurate timekeepers. No matter how precious the metals they are made of, or how many jewels are used to decorate them, watches must keep good time. Likewise, no matter how cheap it is, a washing powder that fails to get clothes clean has little chance of success since it does not deliver the core benefit it was bought for.

Marketing managers have to keep focused on the basic problems to be solved: understand them well, address them precisely and directly and place these solutions at the core of their products. This satisfaction of needs may be upfront or concealed within the complete product, but it must be there as it is central to the customer's perception of the product's value. The next stage is to consider how the product offering can be improved so that it will appeal to more customers. This requires a thorough understanding of what customers want from this type of product (see Chapter 5), as well as awareness of what is already being offered by the competition.

ACTIVITY

There are a number of coffee shops in most shopping areas (e.g. Starbucks, Costa Coffee, Caffè Nero) and they generally sell very similar products: lattes, cappuccinos, etc. Visit two, or more, of them and observe how they try to differentiate themselves from their competitors. It may be by service, quality, product range, surroundings and so on. How well do they do it?

In a monopoly situation, where there is only one provider of the means to satisfy needs, that provider can get away with offering just the bare minimum. If there is no choice, customers have to satisfy their requirements as best they can with whatever is available, however poor the product. When there are multiple providers of a product, they have to compete with each other for customers. There will therefore be a variety of products available, all designed to meet the same basic needs. Customers have choices as to what to eat or wear, which hamburger or trainers to buy. With choice comes the opportunity for customers to express their individuality in the way they make this choice. They will choose the products and

monopoly
a market in which there is only one supplier

These products all share the same core benefit, though they differ in other ways.

© Dave Pickton

services that have the most value to them. An understanding of how customers see value gives the organisation a chance to make a product offer that matches their preferences better than the competition's products do.

Most products on sale will meet customers' basic need for that product, i.e. they all offer the same core benefit, and so the choice is often made on the basis of what else the products offer; on their points of difference. It may be the flavour of the burger, the type of bun it comes in, the restaurant where it is served, the extras, the way it is packaged. These things all form part of the total product and are illustrated in Exhibit 6.1 above.

BASIC PRODUCT

basic product
a bundle of essential characteristics; a product described in terms of the features that deliver its core benefit (e.g. the ingredients of a soft drink – fizzy orange) without reference to service or other more sophisticated elements

The **basic product** is just what it sounds like – the product stripped down to its essentials. These include its features (for a car, these would be the engine, the gear box, the braking system, the available colours, etc.), quality level, brand name and logo, and packaging. These things are the means by which the core benefit is delivered and, to the customer's thinking, they add up to the product itself. These product attributes attract the customer's attention, and are often the first things used to judge the product against the competitors' offerings.

AUGMENTED PRODUCT

The next level of the total product model contains supporting features. Among these are guarantees, service network, delivery, after-sales service and credit facilities. These can be an important source of differentiation from the competition. They enhance the product offering and can be used to counter objections or resolve doubts in a customer's mind. For example, a guarantee reassures a customer who is worried about quality and a credit agreement helps convince a customer who is concerned about the price.

As such extras are not physically part of the product, they can often be changed without modifying the basic product itself. For example, Fiat offered a 12-year anti-perforation warranty on the bodywork of its cars. The cars were the same as in previous years, so the basic product was the same, there was no change in production, only the augmented product changed – and could easily be changed again. Despite there being no change in the way the cars were produced, there may have been some actual costs incurred in this augmentation process (especially, for example, if someone claimed under the warranty) that must be borne by someone, either by the supplier or by the customer, or both. A balance always needs to be struck between increased cost and increased perceived value.

PERCEIVED PRODUCT

The outer ring of the total product model (see Exhibit 6.1) is the perceived product. Customers' perceptions of a product vary, e.g. different customers have different views on what a product is worth or how fashionable it is. Perception involves the way in which we interpret our world and is built from our life experiences and our personalities. We have different likes and dislikes, different tastes – that is largely why suppliers offer us a choice of products.

One of the big challenges of marketing is to ensure that customers perceive a product in the way that is intended. If there is a mismatch of customer perception and supplier intention, then there is a problem. For example, when Sunny Delight was launched, it was positioned as a healthy drink for children – as one that children would like the taste of and parents would feel was doing them good. Children did like the taste but parents did not share Procter and Gamble's view of the product's healthy qualities. There was a rethink, a redesign and a relaunch.

ACTIVITY

Ask some friends to describe a well-known branded product – for example, the Big Mac, Marks & Spencer underwear, Nike shoes, Bounty chocolate bars. It is likely that they will have different views, i.e. they will each perceive that product differently.

global focus: I'll have the usual please

Unfortunately, you may not be able to get your usual product abroad. There is an ever-increasing number of global brands available but, although they may look the same as the ones at home, there are sometimes subtle differences.

Take Coca-Cola, for example. The US drink is not quite the same as the one you can buy in parts of Asia, where it has more sugar added. McDonald's? Well, you can hardly sell hamburgers in India where the cow is sacred, so those burgers are made of lamb instead. Then there's the strange story of the Mars bar. Mars was founded in the USA – and Britain. The first company was the US one, and it was

so successful that its founder could see no reason to change. However, as is the way of the world, his son wanted to make improvements. Frustrated by his father's blocking his ambitions, the son emigrated to England where he set up his own company.

Mr Mars Senior's bestselling line in the USA was Milky Way. The new British company started with the same product but called it the Mars bar instead. Eventually father and son, and the two companies, were reunited. However, the Mars bar and Milky Way are still confused – if you know someone who is going to the USA, ask them to bring you a Mars bar and see what you get.

Google's driverless car

Products deliver benefits other than the core ones. A car's core benefit may be flexible travel – there is no need to go to specific departure or arrival points, such as bus stations or airports, at specific times, and they also carry one or several people, with luggage if required. All cars provide this benefit and so a customer's choice of car will depend upon the other rings in the total product model (see Exhibit 6.1) and upon individual preference. Some people want fast cars, some want safe cars, some want cars that keep them cool, some want enough room for the whole family and others want cars that are easy to park. In a competitive market, the customer's perception of the total product (is it fast, safe, roomy, etc.?) is the main determinant of their choice.

A NOTE ON BRANDING

Branding spans two levels in the total product model. As brand identity, it is a part of the basic product, giving it a name and signalling its level of quality. Brand image is also an important part of the customer's perception of the product and so fits into the model's outer ring (see below and Chapter 11 for further explanation of branding).

PRODUCT TYPES

Products differ in the way they do things, the way they are used, the way they are distributed and who they are aimed at. The successful management of a product, brand or group of products and brands, depends to a great extent on an understanding of the types of products and brands to be managed. This is essential in order to select the most appropriate way in which to design and communicate a properly integrated and focused set of images, messages and customer relationship activities. Products can be grouped with others which satisfy broadly the same needs (Exhibit 6.2).

CONSUMER PRODUCTS

The following are some common categorisations of products. There is overlap and some products may fit more than one category. For example, shampoo is both a non-durable good and a convenience good – and it is usually categorised as FMCG.

DURABLE GOODS

These products are expected to last a considerable length of time. They are not used up all at once but can be used repeatedly. A washing machine, for example, is expected to perform a large number of washes, a car a large number of journeys.

NON-DURABLE GOODS

These products are used up in the process of consumption. They do not last. Fruit is eaten. Soap dissolves.

SERVICE PRODUCTS

Services cannot be stored at all. Normally they are used there and then. You watch a film and are left with only a memory (and possibly a ticket stub). You get off the bus and have no further claim on it. Services present marketers with particular challenges and will be discussed in more depth in the next chapter.

---

brand identity
all the outward trappings of the brand, e.g. logo, name, colours, strap line and packaging

brand image
people's perception of the brand

FMCG
(fast-moving consumer goods) low-value items that are bought regularly (the shelves empty quickly), e.g. toothpaste

Exhibit 6.2   Product types

Consumer products	Examples
Durable goods	Fridges, bicycles
Non-durable goods	Fresh food, toiletries
Services	Theatre seats, haircuts
Convenience goods:	
Impulse buys	Snacks, flowers
Staples	Bread, washing-up liquid
Emergency	Headache pills, tissues
Shopping goods	Stereos, cars
Speciality goods	Antiques, sports cars
B2B/industrial products	
Capital goods	Fork-lift trucks, computers
Accessories	Screwdrivers, hard hats
Raw materials	Flour, steel
Sub-assemblies/components	Engines, wheels
Supplies	Stationery, paper cups
Services	Cleaning, accountancy

CONVENIENCE GOODS

These are products that customers buy frequently and think little about. They are of little value and have many close substitutes so they need strong branding and eye-catching colours and designs to make them stand out from the rest. There are a number of subcategories of convenience good:

- **Impulse goods**: spur-of-the-moment purchases that have no advance planning, e.g. an ice cream bought while queuing to get in somewhere or flowers bought at the station on the way home. Customers are not usually prepared to pay a high price for such purchases.
- **Staple goods** (essential goods): staple goods are purchased regularly, perhaps always kept in the cupboard or fridge (e.g. coffee, milk, shampoo). Customers usually look for good value.
- **Emergency goods**: emergency goods are infrequently purchased but needed at short notice (e.g. rain capes, sun hats, plasters). Such products may be location-specific (rain capes sell well at Disney World and Wimbledon) and have a high value to customers at that time, so their prices can be higher.

ACTIVITY

Classify the products in the photo. Are they:

- impulse goods?

- staples?

- emergency purchases?

Items shown: loaf of bread, bottle of milk, bag of tea bags, bar of chocolate, box of throat lozenges, bag of rice, can of cola drink, box of mouth fresheners, tube of antiseptic cream

© Dave Pickton

Fast-moving consumer goods (FMCG) are a form of convenience good, but in this case looked at from the retailer's point of view. They are the products that move off the shelves quickly and so need frequent restocking, e.g. toothpaste, washing-up liquid, instant coffee.

SHOPPING GOODS

Shopping goods carry a higher associated risk for a customer than convenience products do. They may be set at a higher price or it may be that the cost of product failure is high.

Customers usually shop around to find the right car, stereo, furniture, necklace or lawn mower (hence the name shopping goods). For many, shopping for such things is an enjoyable leisure activity in its own right. Customers are likely to spend some time over the decision-making process, assessing the options, seeking information and opinions, trying things out. These products are therefore sometimes referred to as high-involvement purchases, i.e. the customer gets very involved in the decision-making. For more on decision-making processes, see Chapter 3.

SPECIALITY GOODS

Speciality goods are unusual, and often quite expensive, products which are commonly sold in niche markets. They may be high-risk products and so customers may need extensive emotional support and encouragement from the supplier before they buy. This often means that they are sold through limited outlets (see 'exclusive distribution' in Chapter 9) by highly trained staff. Examples of speciality goods include model aeroplanes, health foods, wedding clothes, horses and classic cars.

EXPAND YOUR KNOWLEDGE

Classic article

Bucklin, L.P. (1963) 'Retail strategy and the classification of consumer goods', *Journal of Marketing*, 27 (Jan): 51–6.

This article takes as its starting point Copeland's classification of consumer goods: convenience, shopping and speciality, and develops the concept and classification extending it to apply to retail strategy formulation.

B2B AND INDUSTRIAL PRODUCTS

Capital goods

Capital goods are durable products (i.e. they are designed to last for a number of years), such as machinery and buildings. They are usually high cost, bought infrequently and carry high potential risk. Consequently, great care is normally taken over these purchases.

Accessories

These are smaller capital items, e.g. chairs, shelving, hand tools such as screwdrivers. They support the production process. As they are lower cost, they represent a lower financial risk to a company. However, some accessories are essential and their failure may have far-reaching consequences so not all are low risk. For example, a hand tool that breaks may cause serious injury. The total product still plays a part in the differentiation of such products.

Raw materials

Raw materials are goods that will be processed, and added to, by the manufacturing process. Together they become the finished article. For example, cotton is knitted into socks; crude oil is refined and becomes petrol (and a number of other products); water, hops and yeast are brewed into beer. At this level it may be difficult to distinguish one supplier's products from another since, by their nature, raw materials may be similar. They are often **generic products**; however, service, delivery terms, technical assistance, financial arrangements and many other aspects can be exploited to make the organisation different and thus the preferred supplier (see Exhibit 6.1).

generic products physical products that have no discernible difference from each other; often used to mean unbranded products

Sub-assemblies, components and parts

These products have already been manufactured but are not finished goods. They are bought by businesses to incorporate into their own products. For example, Levi's buys denim fabric to make into jeans, Nokia buys microchips for its mobile phones and Siemens buys condensers to put into its fridges.

Supplies

Numerous minor items are used in the production process; and they are important in the smooth running of the whole process. Companies depend on such things as soap, stationery, pens, copier paper and cleaning materials. These are not capital goods as they are non-durable (i.e. they are used up relatively quickly rather than being reused over and over).

Services

Manufacturing businesses rely on efficient machinery so maintenance and repair services are important to them. All workplaces need regular cleaning. Buildings must be painted and repaired. In addition, there are a large number of business services, such as consultancy, accountancy, legal advice and IT support. The special nature of services is discussed in the next chapter.

There are many different ways to categorise products and different markets have their own preferred descriptors. Many products are bought both by businesses and by consumers (though the specifications may be different). For example, envelopes may be b2b supplies and bought in bulk, or a consumer staple good bought in smaller packs.

These product types refer to basic products. However, most of the products we buy today are not generic products – they are branded.

BRANDING

Branding is a strategy used 'to differentiate products and companies, and to build economic value for both the consumer and the brand owner' (Pickton and Broderick, 2004: 242). This section will discuss branding as part of the total product offering, whereas the strategic nature of branding, along with the building of strong brands, will be considered in Chapter 11.

WHAT IS A BRAND?

From the earliest times, people have marked their possessions in order to differentiate them from other people's. The term 'branding' seems to originate with American ranchers, who branded their cattle to advertise their ownership. Each branding iron was unique and formed an indelible, identifying mark. That mark was an assurance that the animal in question was from that particular ranch and also came to be used as a guide to the quality of the beef. However, modern brands are:

> much more than just logos or names. They are the culmination of a user's total experience with the product … over many years. That experience is made of a multitude of good, neutral and bad encounters such as the way a product performs, an advertising message, a press report, a telephone call, or a rapport with a sales assistant. (CIM, n.d.)

Business branding's origins lie with craftsmen who made especially good tools or leather, and later with manufacturers who could provide consistent quality. They realised that they could attract more customers and could charge a higher price than their rivals if they could label their products to make them easily recognisable. Through the latter part of the twentieth century, branding developed alongside marketing as a managerial process, although some of today's well-known brand names existed as company names long before they became part of a branding strategy, e.g. Sunlight Soap, Swan Vesta matches, Daimler motor cars, His Master's

global focus: What's in a name?

Increasingly, manufacturers are trying to use the same name for their products worldwide. In Britain, Jif cleaning cream became Cif to match the rest of Europe. Marathon bars became Snickers, and Oil of Ulay, rather oddly, became Oil of Olay. The UK won on Twix, though; that used to be called Raider elsewhere, but now it's Twix to everyone.

Those name changes were made as part of global branding exercises. Having the same name helps to standardise brand positioning, promotes global recognition and, of course, it's cheaper in terms of packaging, support literature and promotion. Sometimes, though, the name changes because it has to. The existing name just will not do in other languages. For example, Vauxhall used to make a car called the Nova. Ask someone who speaks Spanish what '*no va*' means and you'll see why they changed it. In China, Coca-Cola translated as 'bite the wax tadpole'. The Jolly Green Giant turned into 'Intimidating Green Ogre' in its Arabic translation.

Here are some products that never made it in English-speaking countries:

- Pocari Sweat and Mucos (soft drinks, Japan)
- Pipi (orangeade, Yugoslavia)
- Pschitt (soft drink, France)
- Skinababe (baby cleanser, Japan)
- Polio (detergent, Czechoslovakia)
- Shitto (hot pepper sauce, Ghana)
- Krapp (toilet paper, Sweden)

SOURCES: Dennis, 2010; Paliwoda and Thomas, 1999.

Voice records (HMV), Boots the Chemists. Today a strong brand brings with it a wealth of quality, value and high performance cues and can even be an intrinsic part of its customers' lifestyles.

With the growth of branding has come a change in emphasis within organisations. Companies used to be centred on the production of goods or services. The emphasis was very much on quality and efficiency (see Chapter 1 for production and product orientation). The importance of marketing has long been well accepted in most organisations, although unfortunately rivalries do still exist between the marketing, finance and production functions. Customer satisfaction is now seen as being at the heart of success rather than excellence in production or selling, largely as a result of increased competition making it harder to attract and keep customers.

Brands are differentiated by their unique names, logos and packaging. This makes up their brand identity. That identity is designed to represent the brand's values and to signal them to potential customers. The way they see values then helps the customers to form a brand image in their minds (see Chapter 11).

THE ADVANTAGES OF BRANDING PRODUCTS

Companies invest millions in the development and protection of their brands. A strong brand is seen as key to commercial success, providing the following advantages (and more):

brand equity
the monetary value
of a brand

- high **brand equity**
- increased product awareness levels
- the ability to charge a premium price
- reduced susceptibility to price wars
- competitive edge
- a sound basis for building strong customer relationships
- higher likelihood of repeat purchases
- retail leverage
- the fact that new products have a better chance of success thanks to the brand name.

Brands must be built in order to become strong and benefit from the advantages listed above. It is not enough just to attach a name and a logo to a product. Nor do brands automatically maintain their strength. They must be nurtured and carefully managed (see Chapters 8 and 11 for more on building brands).

HIGH BRAND EQUITY

A well-known brand adds value to a product both from the customer perspective and from the company's. Brands may be the most valuable assets that a company has. For more on brand equity, see Chapter 11.

INCREASED PRODUCT AWARENESS

Clearly, it is crucial that potential customers should be aware of a product. It is the first stage on their journey to buying it (see sequential models in Chapter 8). One of the key roles of advertising is to build that awareness and an easily recognised brand makes that task much easier. Product and packaging design play key roles here as well, by making the product more visible and reinforcing the brand's values.

PREMIUM PRICING AND REDUCED SUSCEPTIBILITY TO PRICE WARS

A good brand name helps a firm achieve a premium price for its products. Think of the differences in the prices of trainers. The well-known brands, e.g. Nike and Reebok, can charge much more for their products than lesser-known brands. It is not just a question of having a well-known name. The strength of the brand depends upon the values associated with it in that particular market. Marks & Spencer is a well-known brand but they cannot get away with charging Nike prices for their trainers, even if the quality is comparable.

Without a brand, a firm will have to settle for a commodity position in the market where low prices alone drive sales. Some firms actively choose this position, e.g. the makers of generic pharmaceuticals, but it does not sit well with the concept of marketing as a series of complex management tasks leading to greater success for the organisation. In very price-conscious markets, e.g. children's shoes and clothing, or in economic downturns, marketers can come under great pressure to compete on price but this might devalue their brand (assuming it already has a reputation). Aaker (2002) argues that pressure to compete on prices can even undermine attempts to build up a brand as one of the main impetuses for branding, i.e. the differentiation from the competition that allows a firm to charge premium prices, is removed.

COMPETITIVE EDGE

A branded product simplifies shopping by assisting with a customer's **product adoption process** (see Chapter 4). If the marketing communications have worked well, then the potential customer will already have built up a set of associations with the brand, short-circuiting a lot of the information searching that they might otherwise have to do. This is good for customers as they save time and effort (this assumes that their image of the brand is correct) and is certainly an advantage to the branded product as it is likely to be preferred to other unknown or less well thought of products.

product adoption process
the stages a buyer goes through before purchasing a product

ACTIVITY

What do these car marques say to you? What values do you associate with each of the brands?

How does Porsche's logo compare to that of Jaguar or Mini? What do the differences say about each brand's personality?

The Porshe, Jaguar, Mini Cooper, and Mercedes logos are the registered trademarks of each respective corporation. Use of the logos here does not imply endorsement of the organisations.

BUILDING RELATIONSHIPS

The strength of the customer's relationship with a brand is central to that brand's growth. The relationship is normally between the customer and the brand, rather than between the customer and the brand's owner, which may even be a company that the customer has never heard of. There are many big companies which own many brands that do not bear their owner's name. For example, Diageo is the owner of a large number of drinks brands (Smirnoff, Bailey's, Guinness, Johnny Walker, Captain Morgan) and yet 'I'll have a Diageo please' is never heard in bars (see 'Brand types' in Chapter 11).

The importance of this brand relationship has prompted companies to develop various relationship-building activities which establish a two-way flow of communication with their customers and encourage them to integrate brands into their lives. Examples of these activities include club memberships, loyalty card schemes,

brand communities
a group of people, usually consumers, formed on the basis of their sharedadmiration for a particular branded product or range of products, e.g. the BMW owners' group

Celebrity brands

registration of warranties, other products such as T-shirts and bags with the brand name and logo on, and website activities.

The number of brand communities is increasing rapidly, thanks in part to the World Wide Web, and they form a significant part of a growing number of people's social lives. Muniz and O'Guinn (2001: 412) first coined the term 'brand community' and they defined it as 'a specialised, non-geographically bound community, based on a structured set of social relations among admirers of a brand'. Brand communities are characterised by a set of shared attitudes towards, and beliefs about, the brand (shared consciousness), rituals and traditions connected with the brand and a sense of moral guardianship for the brand. A brand that is liked well enough to inspire a community to grow around it clearly has a number of loyal consumers and therefore this is generally held to be a positive thing for the brand – though members of brand communities can be the brand's greatest critics as well as its greatest fans. Brand communities can be very possessive towards brands and the importance of understanding their views is illustrated by the reaction of loyal customers to the introduction of a new recipe for Coca-Cola. They boycotted the product and sales slumped so badly that the original recipe had to be reinstated. New Coke lasted about three months (see customer focus box).

EXPAND YOUR KNOWLEDGE

Hewer, P. and Hamilton, K. (2012) 'Exhibitions and the role of fashion in the sustenance of the Kylie Brand mythology: unpacking the spatial logic of celebrity culture', *Marketing Theory,* 12 (4): 411–25. Available at: **http://mtq. sagepub.com/content/12/4/411** (accessed 25/07/13).

'Celebrity demands a stage, or better, an exhibition space.' This paper considers how the appeal of celebrity works beyond advertising to engage audiences and build intimacy with brands.

REPEAT PURCHASES

Most human beings instinctively avoid unnecessary risk. Buying things represents at least a financial risk in that money may be wasted if the product is not fit for purpose. There are other possible risks too. For example, there is ego risk if the product is unflattering (e.g. clothes) or ridiculed by others (e.g. an unpopular scent), or physical risk if the product turns out to be unsafe (e.g. faulty machinery). A brand that has been bought before and found to be satisfactory reduces these risks and so people are more likely to buy that trusted brand again.

A good experience of a brand results in a happy customer who continues to purchase. Conversely, a bad experience can lead to an unhappy customer who may very well reject future offerings bearing this brand, no matter how attractive the offering appears to be. Worse still, they may tell their friends, family and acquaintances of their bad experience, influencing them against the brand. Attraction and retention are the key words when thinking about the development of a brand.

customer focus: Brand new love

Coca-Cola is one of the most successful products ever but even the Coca-Cola company makes product mistakes sometimes. In 1985, they changed the tried-and-tested secret formula and introduced New Coke. They did this in response to Pepsi's repositioning as a youth brand and its much publicised triumph in blind taste tests – people generally preferred its sweeter taste. Sure enough, the taste of New Coke was popular in all the trials. However, Coke had underestimated the power of its brand and its customers' loyalty to the original Coca-Cola. When the new replaced the old on the shelves, there was a storm of protest across the USA. A part of American history had been devalued, replaced. According to its advertising, Coca-Cola was *the real thing* and yet now it seemed there was a new real thing – a contradiction in terms. Within three months, New Coke was withdrawn and the old favourite was back on the shelves.

SOURCES: Haig, 2003.

RETAIL LEVERAGE

In many countries, notably in the UK, large retailers have enormous power when it comes to setting prices and dictating terms of purchase and sale. Tesco, for example, is one of the largest companies in the world, much larger than many of the manufacturers who supply it. Tesco therefore has a great deal of buying power (see Chapter 9). However, there are some branded products that are so popular that even a retailer as powerful as Tesco is unlikely to leave them off its shelves, e.g. Heinz Tomato Ketchup, Heinz Baked Beans, Kellogg's cereals, Coca-Cola, Kleenex tissues.

NEW PRODUCT SUCCESS

Even the most innovative and high-quality new products struggle to make headway in today's markets. Many entrepreneurs have launched seemingly superb products only to watch them fail. A strong brand gives that vulnerable new product a much better chance of success. The customers can call on their experience of previous products of the same brand, and transfer those brand values to the new product.

This reduces the risk associated with trying something new and so the new product is more likely to make it into their **evoked set** of products, and therefore they are more likely to try it. Take the BBC iPlayer, for example. It was launched into a market that was struggling to gain consumer acceptance. ITV and Channel 4's catch-up TV services were not attracting sufficient viewers but the BBC's new product changed the market profile completely by reassuring reluctant viewers and encouraging them to try the catch-up service. Now all three services are doing well and others, e.g. Sky, have joined them. The market has continued to grow further with new product development facilitating recording and catch-up viewing on numerous devices from set-top boxes and TV to Internet-linked smartphones and Wii.

evoked set
the products or brands from which a person will make their purchase choice

For more on branding, including brand components, types of brand, branding strategies and brand equity, see Chapter 11.

EXPAND YOUR KNOWLEDGE

Belén del Rio, A., Vazquez, R. and Iglesia, V. (2001) 'The effects of brand associations on consumer response', *Journal of Consumer Marketing*, 18 (5): 410–25.

This paper studies the dimensions of brand image by focusing on the value of the brand as perceived by consumers. Four categories of functions are identified: guarantee, personal identification, social identification and status. These functions are shown to have a positive influence on the consumer's willingness to recommend the brand, pay a price premium and accept brand extensions.

PRODUCT DEVELOPMENT

New products are the lifeblood of a company. Competitors improve their product offerings all the time and customers usually prefer to buy the latest products. They want this year's fashions, the technology with the latest features, the most convenient household products, the healthier version or the greener version or just the more economical one. This philosophy of constant innovation, especially in consumer goods markets, has been adhered to by leading companies for many years. However, it is important

---

 ethical focus: What do you do with old products?

How will products be disposed of when they are obsolete? Britain has a mountain of old fridges awaiting safe disposal. Products such as washing machines used to be designed with built-in obsolescence – they would not last more than about ten years. This was a marketing idea, not a technological limitation. Is this a responsible use of resources? The late twentieth century was a throwaway society: convenience was all.

Things were not mended as it was cheaper to buy new ones. However, is it really cheaper? It may cost an individual less in the short term to buy a new vacuum cleaner rather than to get the old one fixed, but the new one is using valuable resources in its manufacture, while the old one may be adding to a landfill site somewhere. In the very long term, it could cost us the ability to make such things at all.

to plan and to manage the process carefully. Too much innovation too quickly can be disruptive and make product lines too complicated to manage effectively. As the complexity of the management task increases, so the organisation's costs rise and its profit margins shrink. To maximise its profit potential, the company needs to be sure that any additional products add more value than the costs they create.

It is a key marketing task to deliver products that meet needs. If those needs change, e.g. there is now a need for green fuels that will not harm the atmosphere, then marketers must find new ways to satisfy those needs – and this often means that they must develop new products. The better a product offering matches customer needs, the more likely it is to achieve customer satisfaction, and consequent success in the marketplace.

Innovation is expensive and requires the support of top management and an organisational culture that encourages new ideas. The new product development process can take a number of forms. It may be an informal exercise in encouraging ideas or a formal, structured approach with its own staff and facilities dedicated to the research of changing customer needs and the development of new ways to fulfil them.

New products do not have to be totally new inventions. In fact, truly new products are very rare. Even those that seem to be so innovative, e.g. iPods, iPads, tablets and other multimedia devices, are really advancements on previous products that played music (gramophones, CD players, tape machines) or made calls (landlines and telephones). Most new products are modifications of previous offerings rather than new-to-the-world products. So the PC manufacturers make their laptops lighter and with better screens, mobile phones have more features, skirt lengths go up (or down), food has less fat, etc.

THE IMPORTANCE OF INNOVATION

Some industries compete largely on the strength of their new ideas (e.g. computer games, mobile phones, convenience foods), and for firms in these industries it is particularly important to invest in research and development. They need original, well-researched product ideas in order to stay competitive. Just how innovative an organisation and its products are depends on a number of things, including:

James Dyson explains bladeless fan

- how old the product, or the technology the product is based on, is – the older the technology, the more likely it is to be replaced; younger technologies may be able to be refined
- the size of the organisation – small firms are often more inventive, it is easier for new ideas to get heard; unfortunately, they often lack the resources to develop an idea fully and so may lose out to a larger firm
- how competitive the market is – lots of competitors may drive a firm to innovate; however, monopolies are more likely to have the money, if they see the need
- how quickly consumer tastes change – anything that could be considered a fashion item will change frequently; anything that customers will tire of (films?) will be replaced regularly.

New products can be used to:

Innovation and success

- increase or defend market share by offering more choice within the range or by updating older products (e.g. Ford has developed people-carrier versions of most of its models; Stella Artois has introduced Cidre)

- appeal to a different market segment (e.g. Guinness bitter, Häagen-Dazs frozen yoghurt)
- maintain reputation as a leading-edge company (e.g. Apple iPhones, iPads and iPods)
- diversify into new markets and thereby spread risk (e.g. Dyson hand dryers)
- improve relationships within distribution channels (e.g. Allied Domecq offering its Baskin-Robbins franchisees further franchise opportunities in Dunkin' Donuts and Togo's)
- make better use of resources such as production capacity (e.g. some chocolate bars can be made on the same production machinery as others)
- even out peaks and troughs in demand (e.g. ice cream parlours selling baked potatoes; Father's Day was invented by greetings card companies).

TYPES OF NEW PRODUCT

Most new products' newness stems from innovation in the basic, augmented or perceived product rather than from true innovation in the product's core (see total product offering). Very few are designed for an entirely new purpose, i.e. to meet a new need or one that was not met by any product before. New products can be classified as follows:

- ***Innovative product***: this is likely to be a technological or medical breakthrough, e.g. Biodiesel (a vegetable oil-based fuel), the Internet, text messaging, laser eye surgery. There are relatively few of these types of new-to-the-market products and services. Innovative new products may be protected by a patent, requiring imitators to obtain a licence to produce their version or risk being sued.
- ***Replacement product***: these are more common than innovative ones. The customer need has been satisfied by a previous product but the replacement product does it better (or at least differently), e.g. multimedia devices are replacing CD players just as they (more or less) replaced record players and tape decks; the Ford Focus replaced the Ford Escort.
- ***Variant product***: many companies frequently introduce new, related products to their ranges. These may be temporary or more permanent additions, e.g. Kit Kat Chunky (long term), Ford Fiesta Flame (special edition).
- ***Me-too product***: these are imitations of products already on the market, e.g. Wrigley's Extramints, Trebor 24/7 chewing gum or the many tablets and other multimedia devices that followed the iPad and Kindle on to the market. It makes sense to let others do the costly market research and development first – to let them take the risks.
- ***Relaunched product***: this is not really a new product at all. Rather, the physical characteristics of the basic product may not be altered (or only slightly) but the total product offering has changed. There will be a different marketing strategy, perhaps changing the emphasis on product benefits, e.g. the magazine *Inside Soap* was relaunched as a weekly, rather than a fortnightly, publication.

Breakthrough designs

THE NEW PRODUCT DEVELOPMENT PROCESS

New products are evaluated at each stage in their development process. If an idea is not going to make it to launch, then it is better if it is eliminated as early in the process as possible. The product's development costs mount up as it moves further through the development process and as these costs increase, failure results in greater financial (and possibly reputational) loss.

e-focus: Clockwork power

As the pace of technological change gathers speed, there are, apparently, fewer and fewer areas where customers might be surprised by new-to-the-world ideas. New and wonderful electronic gizmos, both for entertainment and for more serious applications, are everywhere and have become the norm. Yet it is still possible to be surprised. Take, for example, the Bayliss wind-up radio, which exploited old clockwork technology, applied modern techniques and produced a fully portable power source that is now being exploited elsewhere – e.g. in powering laptop computers, satellite navigation systems and even for recharging mobile phones by use of a device included in a pair of hiking boots (every step generates power for the user's phone).

Initially, Trevor Bayliss found it next to impossible to find a manufacturer prepared to back him. They were unable to envisage the potential of his radical, old idea.

Producers should not always rely on customers to judge the merits of a new-to-the-world product idea. Sometimes new products fulfil a need that it had not occurred to customers *could* be met, and so it is not really possible to assess customer reaction accurately before they see the finished item. Take, for example, electric light. It is taken for granted now, but 100 years ago people were quite happy with gaslight and it didn't occur to them that a better, clearer artificial light source might be possible. They liked the greenish glow gas lighting gave and appreciated the extra warmth in winter. Thomas Edison knew that electric light would sweep civilisation but he was greeted with scepticism at first and had to give many demonstrations and use his own money to pay for generators to light the streets of New York before he got his point across. In the early days of domestic electricity, the electricity companies had to offer to wire up houses free of charge to encourage use – rather like modern-day digital television services. Of course, it may not take long before such new products are taken for granted. Mobile phones are a relatively recent phenomenon as are the smartphones that are replacing them yet almost everyone has one and many would not be without them. Tablet computers have only recently been introduced with Apple leading the way. They have become so popular in such a short period of time (in the first year of launch in spring 2010 it was estimated by some that 10.3 million units had been sold) (O'Dell, 2011) and are becoming so commonplace with many other competing models being made available that it seems as though they have always been around. On the other side of the coin, the Sinclair C5 car is an example of a new product development failure. Sir Clive Sinclair was a notable innovative entrepreneur, well recognised for introducing many new products over his career from one of the first pocket calculators to one of the first home computers to his well-renowned C5. He was also well recognised as someone who did not believe very strongly in market research on the grounds that his inventions were so ground-breaking that potential customers would simply not know how they would respond. The C5 car was a small, single-person, battery-driven vehicle that was an ecological and economical breakthrough; a truly innovative product well in advance of the vehicles available now. Sinclair developed his car in the belief that it would meet market demand. While he did test the technology, customer and market evaluation was limited. The car was developed and put onto the market but very few were sold. The concept was sound but the technology was still in its early days and was, perhaps, too under-developed. It had major limitations such as how far the car would be able to travel before running out of power. Significantly, the car was very small with a very low profile. Potential customers thought the vehicle seemed dangerous and worried that drivers of other larger vehicles might not be able to see the C5. There was also concern over running out of power and breaking down. Ironically, Sinclair's car might have had success if it were launched for use on closed road systems such as in leisure parks but he was insistent that the car be launched into the general car market. Perhaps as costs escalated, Sinclair felt forced to aim for mass market appeal and more sales in order to break even. The result, however, was financial catastrophe.

Exhibit 6.3   New product development process

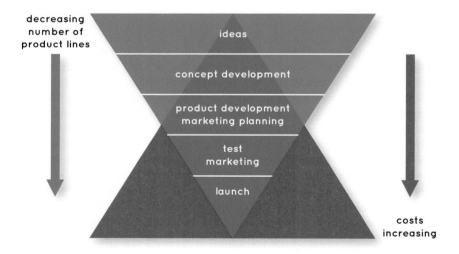

The model in Exhibit 6.3 shows the stages of the product development process. Product development should not be seen as a one-off or ad hoc activity but as a continuous process. That way, there will be a fairly consistent stream of new product ideas available to be taken to the next stage and ready to replace older products when their time comes.

Constant monitoring and evaluation are essential in this product development process. The aim is that only the right products should progress while those with little chance of commercial success are deleted as early as possible. The number of products in development reduces at each stage as some are rejected. However, the costs associated with the development of each product mount as it goes through the stages. So the costs associated with the product development process escalate, and the number of viable product ideas reduce, as time passes.

IDEA STAGE (GENERATION AND INITIAL SCREENING OF IDEAS)

Ideas for new products may be generated internally or externally. Some companies are technology led, e.g. Dyson and Apple, and get the inspiration for most of their new products from their own product research. They have substantial research and development departments whose job it is to design technologically advanced products. Other companies, particularly the more market-orientated ones, take their lead from their customers and look to develop products that match explicitly stated customer needs. Others may employ a marketing agency which specialises in new product ideas.

Market research seems a sound way to find ideas for new products and it will certainly help establish customers' views on the firm's existing product offering and, by establishing what is wrong with it, suggesting new ideas. It is better at uncovering customer needs than at finding specific product solutions, as customers are rarely able to imagine the design of a product that does not exist.

Product innovation with the iPhone 5c

ACTIVITY

Be a market researcher briefly. Ask some of your friends, family or classmates what new communications products they would like. Do not lead or prompt them. Then ask them what is wrong with the products they already own (computers, mobile phones, telephones, etc.) and if they can think of any improvements to them.

How many new product possibilities have you discovered? Which technique generated more?

There are many ways to generate new product ideas: from brainstorming (a lively group session where ideas spark other ideas and all are captured, none discounted or disparaged), to analysing customer complaints and competitive products, to establishing original research facilities. 3M (the makers of Scotch Tape and Post-it Notes) deliberately encourages a culture of creativity and allows its employees to spend some of their time on personal projects that may, or may not, produce ideas the company can use. The company expects all of its employees to devote some of their time to thinking up new ideas, but also has sophisticated research facilities. Any source of new ideas is acceptable although many ideas will be discarded, sometimes very early in the process of monitoring and evaluation.

At the start of the process, the focus is on generating as many ideas as possible. The impractical ones are then quickly discarded while the possibles will progress to the next stage.

CONCEPT STAGE (DEVELOPMENT AND TESTING OF THE PRODUCT CONCEPT)

A product concept is much more than just an idea. The product has to be thought through from both technical and consumer, or end-user, points of view. This may involve the production of drawings, detailed descriptions and theoretical models – all of them aim to assess whether the idea works. As well as testing the product design and consumer reactions, at this stage the concept should be examined to see whether or not it fits in with the organisation's marketing strategy. Is it a product that will add to and complement the company's existing range of products?

In the motor industry many ideas are floated but get rejected quickly. Those that have potential are passed to the design studio where the proposed car is mocked up, perhaps even as a full-size model that can be seen in three dimensions. Individuals, both inside and outside the organisation, are then shown the model and asked for their opinions.

The product concept is tested both for its viability as a product and as a business proposition. Business analysis involves reviewing costs and sales projections in order to arrive at a profit forecast and to assess the likelihood of this product meeting the company's objectives for it. Products that meet the company's criteria move on to the next stage: product development.

PRODUCT DEVELOPMENT STAGE (PROTOTYPING AND PILOT PRODUCTION)

Prototyping and/or pilot production of a product is very costly and so only products with good potential are allowed to get this far. Such products have passed concept tests and are now ready for production, but first the company may make a prototype (or prototypes) in order to conduct further tests. These tests check the safety of the product, its durability, usability, etc. Car manufacturers such as Volvo use crash test dummies to see what happens when the car crashes at various speeds. Toy manufacturers call children in to play with the new toy to see how well it stands up to their misuse. Computer games companies employ people to play and test their prototypes to ensure good gameplay and eliminate bugs and crashes. Many organisations use computer simulations for this stage, especially if the prototype would be expensive to make and/or would require an actual production facility. The results from these tests are used to refine the design before production starts.

Full-scale production is very expensive and so most companies start by making one, or a small number, of the products so that they can test their production plans and make any necessary changes before committing to large-scale manufacture. These initial pilot runs may involve making the product entirely by hand as setting up a working production line is expensive and time-consuming and may be a waste if the product does not make it to the next stage of the development process. Critical evaluation now takes place, assessing the product in its approximate final form.

Computer-aided design is widely used in product development.

MARKETING PLANNING

The marketing planning process will have already begun – sometimes these stages overlap at least a little. The marketing department have to work out what price to charge, how much advertising and other communication will be required and where and how the product will be sold. They will develop a formal product marketing plan that sets out the product's proposed positioning, their sales targets and other formal marketing objectives. See Chapter 12 for more on the drawing up of marketing plans.

TEST MARKETING STAGE

Concepts will only progress this far if the company believes that those products will sell. They may now be made in small quantities and sold to a small, selected market, usually a geographic region, in order to obtain information about customer reactions. A test market is the market in miniature. The area chosen should represent the whole market as closely as possible in all its key characteristics, e.g. demographics, lifestyles, media, outlets, competition. Not only the product itself, but also all the related marketing mix activities are tested. If the mix works well, then the product may be launched immediately afterwards. Alternatively, the test-marketing exercise may suggest modifications to the mix, or that the product should not be launched at all.

Test marketing is expensive and time-consuming and also has the disadvantage of allowing the competition to assess the new product. Competitors may even attempt to spoil a test market, perhaps by deliberately lowering the price of their own products in that area, or launching their own, local promotional campaign. Some have even been known to launch special, limited edition versions of their own products in order to spoil the sales and market research data from the test market.

Test marketing is not essential, only desirable, and in any one case the drawbacks may outweigh the benefits. If the new product is a simple modification of an existing one, the market is well known and understood, and the data is therefore likely to suggest only minimal changes, then the product may be launched without exposure to a test market.

LAUNCH (COMMERCIALISATION)

This is the final stage in the product development process. The company is now committed to full-scale manufacture and distribution, and has many decisions to make before the product is ready to be shipped out. All marketing mix elements must be finalised: prices set, promotion booked, packaging arranged, the distribution chain set up and all the operational issues involved in supplying the product to the market resolved. The company's personnel will need to be trained on the new product and enthused about it. Timing is crucial to a successful product launch and therefore there must be a detailed project plan. Companies trading internationally will have to decide where to launch as well as when. Very few will roll out a new product in all their markets at the same time as that would place too great a burden on even a multinational's resources.

The launch of a new-to-the-world product (or even a major innovation on an old one) is a time for the company to celebrate. They might host an event for customers, staff and journalists with the intention of gaining publicity for the new product. The launch of a new consumer product needs to be well publicised as its initial reception and the speed with which early sales build up are often crucial to its long-term success.

New products are launched regularly. The continued existence of many large high-tech corporations relies upon the successful launch of their next product. The producers of computer games frequently battle to be the first to launch the

complementary product
one that is required by another product, e.g. a printer needs paper, a DVD player needs DVDs

latest technology. Sega used to be a major player in this market, producing its own consoles and equipment, but now they have to be content to produce software for other manufacturers' platforms. Fall behind on the technology and billions of pounds' worth of sales can slip into the hands of competitors. So much depends on the effectiveness with which target markets have been researched, and expectations matched, when the new product is launched.

 ## b2b focus: Getting the drinks in

Consumers of premium spirit brands, such as Bacardi light rum and Gordon's Gin, can be fierce champions of their favourite brand, claiming it has superior taste and that they can always pick it out. Such spirits are rarely drunk neat though – they are mixed with something else and that something else is usually a larger measure than the alcohol. Take gin and tonic or rum and coke, for example – in both cases there is more mixer than spirit in the drink. How can the superiority of the chosen spirit be best preserved? The answer clearly lies in a premium quality mixer. Mixers are **complementary products**. They are most commonly bought to go with another product, gin or rum for example.

The Fever-Tree range of mixer drinks was developed to fill this perceived gap in the market. There was a clear need for the product: consumers wanted more natural drinks and most existing mixers were highly artificial and stuffed with additives. Fever-Tree used only the best, exotic natural ingredients, even producing the world's first naturally low-calorie tonic water (no artificial sweeteners; just a blend of fruit sugars, citrus, aromatic botanicals, natural quinine and spring water).

However, it is one thing to come up with a great idea, but quite another to make it

into a success. The challenge was to get it to the consumers. To do that, Fever-Tree needed to convince retailers to stock it. They began with sales calls to upmarket hotels and restaurants, including The Ritz and Claridges, but they needed a supermarket stockist if they were to make significant inroads into this market. Positive media coverage in papers such as the *Sunday Times* helped convince Waitrose to stock Fever-Tree and the brand's market share soon increased by a percentage point (a significant amount in a market as large as this one).

Fever-Tree is now available from Tesco, Sainsbury's, Harrods, Fortnum and Mason and many smaller retailers, cafes and bars. It is served in six out of the top 10 restaurants in the world (as voted for by *Restaurant* magazine in 2008). World-renowned chef Ferran Adria of Spain's El Bulli restaurant has turned Fever-Tree Premium Indian Tonic Water into a course in itself: 'Sopa de Fever-Tree tonica'. In the USA, the world's largest mixers market, Fever-Tree was awarded 'Best New Product' at the 2008 Tales of the Cocktail awards. Fever-Tree also won the new brand (SME) award at the Marketing Society's Golden Jubilee Awards 2009.

New products are launched to replace old ones that no longer have significant markets. Most new products will, unfortunately, fail despite companies' best efforts in their development. The time in between their launch and their deletion can be viewed as the life of that product and one of the tools available to aid managers with their product planning is the product life cycle.

THE PRODUCT LIFE CYCLE

The **product life cycle** concept is one that has many opponents and many supporters. On the one hand, it has limited usefulness as a management tool since it provides no absolute answers. On the other hand, it does help analyse the market for the product and so can be a helpful decision-making aid. The position of a product in its life cycle can indicate whether there are likely to be further significant increases in sales or not – and provide pointers on what to do in order to maximise those sales.

The model in Exhibit 6.4 illustrates how products move through a series of stages in their progress from introduction to a market to their final replacement with another product – i.e. another way to deliver the core benefit that the old product delivered or another solution to a particular customer need. The product's progress is mapped out in a similar way to a human being's progress through life: birth, growing up, reaching maturity, declining into old age and ultimately death – or, in the product's case, deletion. The duration of each of the stages will vary considerably from product to product; some will take a long time to be accepted and so the first, introduction stage may be extensive; some will have long, slow growth, others very rapid and short-lived growth, etc. High fashion products may display a life cycle with very rapid progress through introduction, growth and maturity and equally rapid, if not more rapid, decline and deletion.

> **product life cycle**
> a product analysis tool based on the idea that a product has life stages: introduction, growth, maturity, decline, deletion

THE STAGES OF THE PRODUCT LIFE CYCLE

Introduction
At the introduction stage, sales are low (initially zero) and the product is usually making a loss. The challenge is to get people to try the product. The people most likely to try it are the **innovators** (see the section on the product adoption process in Chapter 3) and so marketing efforts are usually directed at them.

> **innovators**
> people who are most receptive to new ideas and are first to try out new products

Growth
Sales increase during the growth stage, as does customer understanding and appreciation of the product. This stage is critical to the product's long-term survival as it is now that customers decide whether to make the product one of their regular purchases (in the case of FMCG) or not. For shopping goods such as DVD players, the decision is more whether to buy a second one or to replace worn-out products as clearly these goods are not regular, repeat purchases. Aggressive pricing and intensive promotional campaigns are often used during this stage as competitors fight to capture, and retain, customers.

The product should be settling down during the growth stage and any teething problems should have been dealt with. This is the time to introduce new members of the product range and add features. A more heavily featured product may attract

Exhibit 6.4   Product life cycle

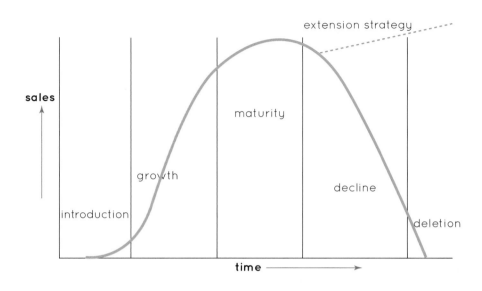

early majority
a substantial group
of customers
who follow early
adopters in buying
a new product or
service

more customers. The **early majority** (see Chapter 3) should be displaying an interest by now and they are likely to be tempted by a lower price.

Maturity

Sales peak during the maturity stage of the life cycle although their growth rate slows as this is now a relatively stable market. This is the stage at which the greatest profit may be made as development and launch costs should have been covered. Competition hots up in the maturity stage. The market is likely to have been split into numerous segments. For example, when chocolate was first introduced into the UK market, it was sold as cocoa to be made into drinks. In today's mature confectionery market, just think how many different types of product, aimed at different types of people, are chocolate-based?

Mature products are likely to be more standardised, although they may be more sophisticated than the original basic ones. This makes manufacturing easier and cheaper. However, there may still be a number of variations. For example, kitchen furniture may have a standard, modular design but come in a choice of colours, finishes, handles, etc. There may also be special editions available for limited time periods.

This is the time to look for an extension strategy in order to delay decline.

Extension strategies

The
Magners
Effect

It may be possible to extend the profitable life of a product which is starting to decline. The product might do better in another market, e.g. in another country or aimed at a different age group. Guinness is a classic example of how successful re-targeting can extend the life of a product. Many years ago, Guinness was regarded as an old person's drink, with its slogan 'Guinness is good for you'. There was a distinct problem: its market was dying – literally. Award-winning advertising helped to make the drink trendy and more appealing to a younger market segment, and so it lives on today.

The product may need to be repositioned in order to bring in new customers. Lucozade, for example, was known for many years as a drink for invalids to 'aid recovery'. The product's owners then repositioned the drink as an energy boost for sports people and it assumed a much more youthful, isotonic personality. The brand personality has been changed yet again to become a mixture of a health drink and an energy drink. Each change has been to target different market segments.

Product sales may be increased by persuading existing customers to use more of it, e.g. by finding new uses for it, perhaps in different combinations with other products, or by using the product in a different way (100 uses for WD40, or Rice Crispies made into a dessert for children's parties).

There are numerous strategies to try but they need to be planned and implemented before the product goes too far into decline. Despite marketing departments' best efforts, sadly most products do eventually decline and die.

Decline

The decline stage, which companies try to delay for as long as possible, is characterised by falling sales. This may not be as catastrophic as it at first appears, as there are numerous examples of products being well managed in their decline and producing very satisfactory profits. This time can also be used to prepare the market for the successful introduction of the old product's replacement.

In the decline stage, everything starts to wind down. Product ranges and features are cut to a minimum, with unprofitable products and less popular features being phased out and so the customer has a lot less choice. Unless an extension strategy can be found quickly, or the product gains cult or classic status (as some music or fashion products might), it is headed for deletion.

Deletion

The final stage in a product's life cycle is its end – the deletion stage, when the decision is taken to withdraw the product from sale. The product may be costing more to maintain and support than it brings in. The market is shrinking, as evidenced by falling sales, declining profits and the existence of new, alternative ways of satisfying customer needs and wants.

Kellogg's
case study

Pony traps, hula-hoops (the plastic toys, not the snack), yo-yos and typewriters have one thing in common: they are all products that were introduced, grew, matured and declined, and no longer hold any significant commercial value (apart from occasional reappearances as novelty items). They were all replaced by other products that better satisfied customers' needs.

Deleting a product is a big decision and there a number of things to consider before it is reached:

- Is the company prepared to risk losing other business because of this?
- What effect will the deletion have on the rest of the product range? Would it leave a gap that would drive customers to competitors? For example, if a restaurant stopped offering a salad bar, customers might go elsewhere for the sake of the one salad eater in their group.
- Will the products' disappearance upset loyal customers?
- What residual problems may the company be left with? Previously sold products may still have outstanding warranties and will require support.

Take, for example, an airline that has decided to delete a service. Frequent users of this service may have accumulated a substantial number of Air Miles, which they are now no longer able to use. These will continue to show as a debt on the airline's books until the customers use them and yet these customers can no longer use them as there are no flights. There is a serious customer relations issue here. Since the Air Miles have no expiry date, this debt can apparently exist forever. The airline can solve the problem by converting the value of the Air Miles into shopping vouchers, which the customers can spend at home. Microsoft and most other software companies give notice before discontinuing support for their obsolete products. Many users do not upgrade to the latest versions of the software and they must be supported for a reasonable time. Eventually products enter the 'limited support phase' and the company makes renewed attempts to get them to upgrade to the newer products.

EXPAND YOUR KNOWLEDGE

Classic articles

Levitt, T. (1965) 'Exploit the product life cycle', *Harvard Business Review*, 43 (Nov–Dec): 81–94.

Levitt reviews the product life cycle and suggests ways of turning it into an effective instrument of completive power.

Enis, B.M., LaGarce, R. and Prell, A.E. (1977) 'Extending the product life cycle', *Business Horizons,* 20 (Jun): 46–56.

The paper questions the concept of the product life cycle, particularly in accepting inevitable decline, and proposes that the product life cycle can be extended further. It proposes strategies for each stage of the life cycle and for its extension.

USING THE PRODUCT LIFE CYCLE AS AN INPUT TO PLANNING

It is difficult to determine exactly where a product is in its life cycle. Any management action the life stage suggests will be an opinion based on past experience. The product life-cycle model is just one of many inputs into the decision-making process.

BIC
case study

The product's life stage can be helpful when making marketing plans. Should new features or even new models be introduced? Should the price be changed? Is it time to step up promotional activity? Should the emphasis of that activity be changed from informational to persuasive? Would the product benefit from being offered more widely or perhaps distribution should be cut down?

A product's life is governed by the market forces it is subjected to and the decisions that its managers make. Its life can be terminated or extended. Aspects of the product can be changed to help it adjust to changing market conditions, e.g. new competition, changing customer tastes or reduced incomes. The product life-cycle

customer focus: New life for an old product

People get tired of even the best products. Competitive pressures, different environmental circumstances, demands for increased profitability and customers' changing requirements all mean that products that were once successful eventually reach the end of their useful lives. Companies need to maintain or increase sales and so they need to act. However, introducing new products is not always the answer, as those old products may still have life left in them. Perhaps the market has room for new, improved versions? Customers may want products that wash whiter, last longer, perform better or are lighter, brighter, faster, bigger than ever before. Listen to the advertising, look around the retailer shelves and you will see examples of this. Marketers are always on the look-out for ways to inject new life into their products.

Potato crisps (or chips as they are known in many countries) may seem a mundane product but not for PepsiCo who are by far the world's leader in the savoury snacks market. Lays, their principal potato chips brand, is probably the world's best known. However, they use the brand name Walkers in the UK and Ireland, Chipsy in Egypt, Poca in Vietnam, Tapuchips in Israel, Elma in Brazil and Sabritas in Mexico.

Potato chips/crisps started their life as plain, unsalted and unflavoured. If you wanted a salted version you could rummage around the crisp bag, find the small blue pouch of salt, untwist the blue wrapper, sprinkle the salt and shake the bag. Ready-salted crisps were the first improvement and then different flavours were introduced starting with BBQ in the late 1950s. It was not until the early 1990s that the idea of new flavours really took off: a highly successful product life-cycle extension strategy. Potato chips/crisps are now tailored to local tastes; Marmite for the UK, Bolognese for the Netherlands, Red Caviar for Russia, Tzatziki for Greece and Cyprus, Paprika for Germany, Beef Carpaccio and Parmeggiano for South America, Ketchup for Canada, Sour Cream and Onion for the USA, Salmon Teriyaki for Japan, Greek Feta and Herb for Australia, Magic Masala for India, Pakistan and Bangladesh.

Introducing new flavours was not the only way companies improved on the potato crisp formula, as the early 1990s also saw the introduction of the new, improved 'stays fresher longer' crisps in better packaging. Lower fats, lower salt, lower calorie and fat-free versions were added to the product line. There are hand-cooked and kettle-cooked lines. Crisps may be ridged or uniformly disk-shaped (Pringles) or made of other vegetables. There are now hundreds of varieties of these mashed, reformed and fried potato products. Where next for the crisp?

model is an aid to understanding products and their markets, and a useful tool for helping to manage product portfolios. A company with too many products in the decline stage would need to think of ways to extend some of those products' lives rapidly or to hurry the introduction of some new ones. If they had paid more attention to the mapping of their products' life cycles earlier, then they might have avoided the problem by ensuring that new products were in the pipeline ready to replace these older ones. Equally, a company with most of its products in the growth stage would be in a high-risk category because of the high expenditure needed to support them in what is likely to be a competitive marketplace.

The product life-cycle model was originally devised for generic products, i.e. the product type, not the individual branded item (shoes, not Clarks shoes). It is often, however, applied to products, product classes or specific brands. The idea behind the product life cycle is that products have an inbuilt life that can be mapped and so its application to a specific branded product can be difficult. One brand may be out of step with the rest of the products in its class, i.e. it is following a differently timed life cycle. The reason for that is likely to lie with its marketing mix, i.e. it is likely to be an internal cause rather than an external one which would affect other similar products as well. For this reason, as well as to ensure that you are comparing like with like, it is always important to be clear what you are analysing. Is it hatchbacks, cars or Volkswagens?

This model can also be related (though not precisely) to the stages of product adoption (see Chapter 3). In the early stages of a product's life, its buyers will largely be innovators, i.e. the risk takers who are happy to try a new product and who like to own the latest thing. In the growth stages of the product life cycle, customers may be early adopters or the early majority. These people may have a special interest in, or knowledge of, such products and are quite adventurous in their product choices. The majority of customers will buy the product during its maturity phase – this is when sales peak. In the early stages of decline, most customers will be from the late majority and the laggards categories. These are people who prefer to wait until a product is tried and tested (by other people) before they buy it and may even wait until it is a product that other people will be surprised that they do not have.

It is often claimed that product life cycles are getting shorter. Certainly, high technology products, such as computers, have noticeably short lives as newer, improved models seem to come out almost immediately after purchase. Some products have always had short lives, such as fashion items, but others seem to live on forever. There is no sign of a significant decline in the demand for bread, for example, and that has been around for thousands of years. The belief in shorter product life cycles can become a self-fulfilling prophecy if decisions on product development and management are based on it. This might lead companies to withdraw or sell off products before their time. Equally, this perception that products have shorter lives can encourage companies to step up research and development and so decrease the time between innovations, and to introduce more and more new products as quickly as possible (Rifkin, 1994) which, given the expense of development and the frequency with which new products fail, may be a costly exercise.

CRITIQUE

The product life-cycle model is not without its critics. Its simplicity leads many to say it cannot possibly represent the situation in a complex and dynamic marketplace accurately. Not all products follow this pattern, of course. Some just never seem to die. For example, gin, cutlery and bread have been with us for centuries, if not millennia. They have been adapted, e.g. the gin may be purer, the cutlery

e-focus: Something new to read

New technology can create new opportunities to satisfy old wants and needs in new ways. There is no better example of this than the product development of the e-reader. Reading has been one of the most popular pastimes for centuries and is apparently becoming even more popular thanks to e-readers.

E-readers are dedicated book-sized hand-held devices whose screens have been developed to replicate the printed page through the use of e-ink technology. Market adoption has been very rapid despite some early technical difficulties. Amazon launched its Kindle e-reader in 2007 in the USA since which time e-readers have become a worldwide phenomenon. Although the States are said to hold some 60% of the global market, it is predicted that Chinese e-reader sales will equal those of the USA by 2014 in a worldwide market that it is estimated will be worth over US$6billion by the end of 2014. Recognising the potential of this market opportunity, competitors have developed their own e-readers which, unlike the operating platforms adopted by Amazon's Kindle (ADZ and KF8), permit more convenient sharing and library loan using the more widely distributed e-pub and Adobe pdf formats. Although Amazon has been notoriously reluctant to release its sales figures, the Kindle brand is recognised as market leader with over 40% market share. It is being chased by Pandigital (Novel) and Barnes and Noble (Nook), Sony and the Chinese brand Hanvon. Together they make up the bulk of the global market (around 90% collectively in 2013).

In a rapidly expanding market which also faces competition from non-dedicated e-reader devices such as tablets and smartphones, product development has been rapid with new models being introduced all the time to extend product ranges or replace deleted models. Screen sizes have changed, button functions have been replaced with rapidly improving touchscreen technology which has also improved reading clarity, Wi-Fi connectivity has been included, 'glo-light' has been added to make it easier to read in dim light, colour has been introduced, graphics improved – all over a period of less than 6 years.

In 2012, Amazon built on the equity of the Kindle brand to extend the range to include the Kindle Fire, a tablet designed to compete with the already established Apple iPad and challenger brands such as Samsung's Galaxy Tab.

According to research, the initial purchasers (innovators) of e-readers were mainly young, male and affluent. The market has now moved into the early adopter phase with other purchasers from a wider demographic range joining the customer group. Nearly a quarter of US households with two or more children living at home own at least one e-reader. In the UK, an Amazon spokeswoman reported: 'As soon as we started selling Kindles it became our best selling product on Amazon.co.uk so there was a very quick adoption.' British Kindle users buy four times more books than they did before. According to unaudited figures released by Amazon in August 2012, since the start of that year, for every 100 hardback and paperback books sold on its site, customers downloaded 114 e-books. Fears over the death of the printed book seem exaggerated though as print sales have increased too and still represent over 90% of the total market. But how long will that last?

Think about how this relates to the concepts introduced in this chapter: new product development, product launch, product adoption, total product offering, product range, product life cycle and branding.

SOURCES: IDC, 2011; Malik, 2012; O'Dell, 2011; Renub Research, 2011.

may now be dishwasher-proof and the bread now has E numbers, but those product classes live on. Others, of course, never actually grow to maturity. It is estimated that at least 50% of new products fail within a year of their launch: they die before they have lived. So the product life cycle is a model of a successful product, not a failure.

Product life cycles vary in the time they take to run their course. The lives of some highly successful products are so short that they cannot be mapped before they are over. High fashion products fall into this category.

Dhalla and Yuspeh (1976) claimed that the product life cycle was dangerously misleading and often caused companies to delete products that could have been profitable for many more years with the right adjustments to their marketing mix. They found that the concept was even less helpful in assessing the potential of brands where the brand's apparent decline could be reversed. A product can defy the rules of the product life cycle through clever repositioning, perhaps even taking up a position outside its current category, as the Fox network did in the USA when it aired a cartoon aimed at adults in a prime time television slot normally reserved for family sitcoms. When a breakaway position such as this works, the product redefines its competition. *The Simpsons* cartoon is the longest-running sitcom ever in the USA (Moon, 2005).

PRODUCT PORTFOLIO MANAGEMENT

product line
a product and all its variants (models, colours, styles, sizes, etc.)

product breadth
the number of product lines a company supports

product depth
the number of items within a product line

Few companies sell just one product; some sell thousands. Their products are collectively referred to as their product portfolio, and this needs careful management.

The number of **product lines** a company sells is referred to as **product breadth**. Within each line, there will be several products (**product depth**). For example, the Ford Fiesta is one product line, while the Ford Focus is another. The Fiesta line has a number of models (Finesse, LX, Zetec, Ghia, etc.), which may have different engines and other features. That is its depth. The product manager lays down guidelines for the consistency required within each line, both in terms of product features and in terms of marketing activities. Products may be introduced, dropped, modified, replaced. Sufficient resources must be allocated (e.g. budgets for advertising, research, customer support). The manager must also agree what contribution to profits the product ought to make and this will become a target or sales objective. The company must have enough cash-generating products to support the cash eaters.

A number of management tools have been developed to help managers to manage their product portfolios. These help to judge how individual products and brands, or ranges of products and brands, or **strategic business units (SBUs)** are performing. Then decisions can be taken on the various products' futures.

Although these **product portfolio analysis** tools may appear simple, they require considerable research, calculation and analysis if they are to be a useful management tool. The Boston Consulting Group matrix (BCG matrix) considers the growth of the market and the size of the product's share of that market relative to the market leader's share (see Exhibit 6.5). The GE-McKinsey matrix uses market attractiveness and competitive position (see Exhibit 6.6).

BOSTON CONSULTING GROUP (BCG) PORTFOLIO MATRIX

The **Boston Consulting Group (BCG) portfolio matrix** shows the relationship between cash-generating products and cash-eaters. This model plots products, or SBUs, in a matrix formed by two axes: market growth rate and relative market share. It is important to note that this is the growth rate of the *whole* market and so it takes into account all sales within that category, including competitors' sales. So, if, for example, the matrix was being drawn up for Nestlé's chocolate products, then the market would be chocolate generally and Cadbury's, Mars and many other brands would be added in when working out its size and growth rate. The market needs to be carefully defined and this may not be easy. For example, are Green and Black's chocolate bars part of the chocolate bar (countline) market, or a general chocolate market, or confectionery, or snacks, or organic foods? Once the market has been defined, the market growth rate is calculated by working out the percentage increase (or decrease) in sales from the previous year.

For example:

current market sales	£ 2 200 000
minus last year's sales	£ 2 000 000
equals sales increase	£ 200 000
as a percentage of last year's sales	$\frac{£\ \ \ 200\ 000}{£\ 2\ 000\ 000} \times 100$

market growth rate = 10%

High growth markets are attractive to companies as they offer a better chance to increase sales; the company's sales just have to move with the market's and they will go up. Exactly what constitutes high growth for a market, and what is low, is uncertain. Traditionally, the mid-point is often taken as 10% and so it can be construed that anything over that may be high and anything below it may be low (Doyle, 2002). However, different markets are likely to vary considerably and so a judgement must be made.

The other axis is labelled 'relative market share' and measures the product's success (in terms of sales) against the market leader in its field. The dividing line between high and low is where the product has equal share with the market leader.

JD Sports' product portfolio management

Exhibit 6.5   Boston Consulting Group portfolio matrix

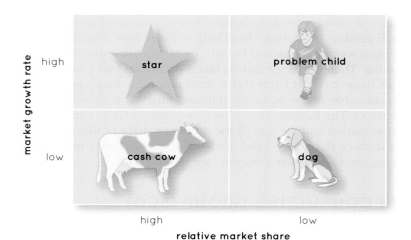

To the left of the line (high), the product is the leader in the market. The further left it is, the greater its relative share and so its leadership. To the right of the line represents a relative market share lower than the market leader. The further it is to the right, the smaller its relative share and the weaker its relative position. The company's product(s) are placed in one of the four boxes of the model and thereby categorised as stars, problem children (sometimes referred to as question marks or wild cats), cash cows or dogs. The boxes are not absolutes. The products do not always have to be in the middle of a box. For example, a product in the medium growth market may be categorised as a dog but placed towards the top of the box, or as a problem child but near the bottom of the box.

It may be more profitable to have a small share of a large market than it is to have a large share of a small market (so a problem child in a large market can be more valuable than a star in a smaller one), and so the BCG portfolio matrix should also be refined by careful definition of the appropriate market and to reflect market size.

STAR

stars
a category within the Boston Consulting Group matrix; products or SBUs (strategic business units) with high market share in a high-growth market

Products in rapidly growing markets in which the company has a high relative market share are called **stars** (e.g. Apple's iPad, Amazon's Kindle). They generate a large amount of cash but are also expensive to support. They are good investments as they have high earning potential both at the present time and in the future. That investment is likely to be needed if the company wants to retain its market position, as competitors such as Samsung with its Galaxy tablet and Barnes and Noble with its Nook e-reader will be trying to emulate stars.

Stars therefore often require high promotional expenditure and perhaps additional product development in order to keep their competitive edge. If this is managed successfully, then when the market's growth rate slows down (as markets inevitably do), these stars will become cash cows.

CASH COW

Products in slow growth, or even static, markets in which they have relatively high market share are called cash cows. They require little promotion although under-investment can turn them into dogs (see below) so they should not be taken for granted. The company's objective is likely to be to hold this position in order to obtain maximum return on investment (ROI). The profits from cash cows can be used to invest in stars, which are high maintenance, or problem children (who need help).

PROBLEM CHILD

Products in this quadrant are in a rapidly growing market but hold a relatively low market share. They are also called question marks or wild cats. The market looks attractive (as long as it keeps growing) and just maintaining current market share will increase sales as the company would then have the same percentage of a bigger market. However, the company may be unsure how the market will develop or whether it can acquire enough customers to make further investment here worthwhile. Small companies often suffer by having too many problem children in their portfolios.

Problem children will require heavy investment in a successful marketing mix if they are to develop into stars. Left alone, they will almost certainly go to the dogs as the market growth rate declines over time. If they prove to be too much of a drain on resources, it may be prudent to sell them off, if possible.

DOG

Dogs are in stagnant or slow-growing markets and have relatively low market share. When a dog gets old it may be kindest to put it to sleep but, from a company's perspective, there may be sound reasons to keep it alive. It might be an effective loss leader or barrier to market entry by competitors or it might still be generating profits. It can be quite difficult to judge just when a product has reached the end of its useful life and, ideally, rather than just phase it out, it is often worth trying to sell it on to another company. One company's dog can become another's cash cow or even a star if they are operating in different markets or market segments.

Attempts are sometimes made to relate the BCG portfolio matrix to the product life cycle. Problem children may be in the introduction phase, stars are in the growth stage, cash cows are generally mature products and dogs are in old age (decline). However, this is not necessarily the case and to characterise a problem child as being in the introductory phase may be unhelpful if the product has in fact been around for some time. Additionally, the match is of limited help in analysing the product portfolio.

> Here is a saying that may help you to remember the BCG matrix: milk the cow to feed the problem child, in the hope that it will grow up to be a star. And shoot the old dog. (Although you may, of course, find reasons not to do that last bit!)

GE-MCKINSEY MATRIX

This is another classic portfolio analysis tool which is also known as the market attractiveness, market strength matrix. This nine-box matrix is a systematic approach to determining which products or SBUs (strategic business units) are the best ones

cash cows
a category within the Boston Consulting Group matrix, products or SBUs (strategic business units) with relatively high market share in low-growth markets

dogs
a category within the Boston Consulting Group matrix, products or SBUs (strategic business units) with relatively low market share in low-growth markets

problem children
a category within the Boston Consulting Group portfolio matrix; products or SBUs (strategic business units) with relatively low market share in high-growth markets

Exhibit 6.6   GE-McKinsey 9-box matrix

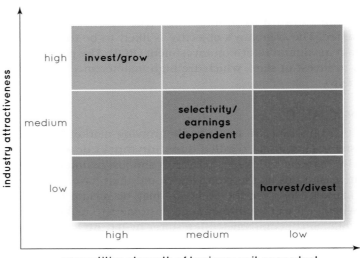

for investment. Rather than rely on managers' forecasts, the company judges how well a product may do in the future on the basis of two, currently known factors: the attractiveness of the industry or market it is in and its competitive strength within that industry or market.

Attractiveness can be defined in a number of ways depending on the particular circumstances of the company, for example:

- market size
- market growth rate
- ease of market entry
- competition
- profitability
- social and environmental impact
- technological requirements
- legal implications
- energy and other resource requirements.

The business's competitive position may be calculated by assessing its:

- market share
- market share growth rate
- management team's skills and competences
- product quality
- brand strength
- distribution channels
- promotional effectiveness
- production capacity
- production efficiency

- unit costs
- research and development success.

These criteria are then weighted according to their relative importance to the company and the market.

Boston matrix

Products that fall into the three boxes in the top left-hand corner of Exhibit 6.6 would appear to have the growth potential to be worth investing in. Those in the three boxes on the diagonal are borderline. The company may invest in them if it has sufficient funds, or it may let them go (divest). Those below the diagonal, i.e. in the bottom right-hand corner are likely to be sold off (divested) or kept in the portfolio only if they can generate sufficient short-term cash (harvested). Their long-term potential is poor.

Placing products or SBUs in these three categories is a good starting point for strategic analysis, but sound managerial judgement is still needed to ensure the right decisions are made. For example, a strong brand that dominates an unattractive market, perhaps a slow-growing one, may still be a far better prospect than a weak brand in a highly attractive market and yet they both fall into the selective investment section of the matrix (Coyne, 2008).

There are many different portfolio analysis tools and organisations will have their favourites – even their own variants. The BCG Portfolio Matrix (see above) and the GE-McKinsey matrix are, however, the basis for many of these more modern techniques.

EXPAND YOUR KNOWLEDGE

Gluck, F.W., Kaufman, S.P., Walleck, A.S., McLeod, K. and Stuckey, J. (2000) 'Thinking strategically', *McKinsey Quarterly*, June. Available at: www.mckinsey.com/insights/strategy/thinking_strategically (accessed 14/05/13).

The Boston Consulting Group portfolio and the GE-McKinsey matrices were radical innovations of their time. They are included here as they formed the basis for many other portfolio analysis tools, e.g. MACS (Market Activated Corporate Strategy) and the Portfolio of Initiatives.

For further information on the Portfolio of Initiatives, see:

Bryan, L.L. (2002) 'Just-in-time strategy for a turbulent world', *McKinsey Quarterly*, June. Available at: www.mckinsey.com/insights/strategy/just-in-time_strategy_for_a_turbulent_world (accessed 14/05/13).

CRITIQUE

It has been argued that portfolio analysis tools over-simplify what are actually complex situations. Ironically, some of these tools have now grown so complex that they cannot meaningfully be applied in real life. Some of the criticisms are briefly outlined below.

First, they merely provide a snapshot of the company's portfolio at a single point in time. The next day, things may have changed. Also, they ignore products in development that have yet to be launched into the market.

Second, consider how market share is calculated. At best, it is a guesstimate, often based on knowledge of one's own business and estimates of competitors' sales, sometimes informed by industry analysts (usually only when the stock market has a keen interest). How, then, is it possible to calculate market share accurately or to compare the relative growth of one market to another in order to map the company's portfolio? Furthermore, is market growth the best criterion for analysis? Perhaps profitability is more important?

Third, these tools fail to recognise any interdependencies between elements of the company's product portfolio. For example, a dog may be essential to the sales of a cash cow if they are complementary products such as an inkjet printer and print cartridges.

This is not to say these tools are not useful as a systematic approach to portfolio analysis. They are a sound base for further exploration of issues and subsequent management decisions. Also, these product portfolio tools can be useful when allocating resources, but it is important to recognise their general limitations and not follow them blindly.

SUMMARY

In this chapter we have attempted to look at products from all angles. There are many different types of product and each has particular characteristics that influence its marketing, but all must be designed to deliver a core benefit. Competitive advantage often comes through differentiating aspects of the total product, rather than just the basic product, and the service elements of a product can be a key selling point (as can the product elements of a service). Branding is today a key differentiator and this is often at the heart of the customer's choice of product and may even inspire loyalty to a particular product.

Management of a product portfolio is a huge marketing challenge. Products are launched, build sales and eventually die. There are a number of portfolio analysis tools which can help managers to judge a product's contribution to the company and to decide what course of action to take next. In this chapter we have briefly considered two of them: the Boston Consulting Group portfolio matrix and the GE-McKinsey matrix. There are criticisms to be made of these tools, as there are of the product life-cycle concept, but they all provide useful insights to help manage the product offering.

CHALLENGES REVIEWED

Now that you have finished reading the chapter, look back at the challenges you were set at the beginning. Do you have a clearer idea of what's involved?

HINTS

- Product portfolio management
- Importance of innovation
- Product life cycle – extension strategies
- Total product offering – augmented and perceived product, particularly service aspects
- Is this right? Can preserving our environment be compatible with making products? Would customers pay more perhaps for products that lasted longer? Would they choose your company over others if it had a more responsible attitude? Bear in mind that there are likely to be laws about manufacturers' responsibilities for disposal of old products soon.

READING AROUND

JOURNAL ARTICLES

Belén del Río, A., Vázquez, R. and Iglesias, V. (2001) 'The effects of brand associations on consumer response', *Journal of Consumer Marketing*, 18 (5): 410–25.

Bryan, L. (2002) 'Just-in-time strategy for a turbulent world', *McKinsey Quarterly*, June. Available at: **www.mckinsey.com/insights** (accessed 14/05/13).

Bucklin, L. (1963) 'Retail strategy and the classification of consumer goods', *Journal of Marketing*, 27 (Jan): 51–6.

Enis, B., LaGarce, R. and Prell, A. (1977) 'Extending the product life cycle', *Business Horizons,* 20 (Jun): 46–56.

Gluck, F., Kaufman, S., Walleck, S., McLeod, K. and Stuckey, J. (2000) 'Thinking strategically', *McKinsey Quarterly*, June. Available at: **www.mckinsey.com/insights** (accessed 14/05/13).

Gottfredson, M. and Aspinall, K. (2005) 'Innovation vs. complexity', *Harvard Business Review*, 83 (12): 62–71.

Hewer, P. and Hamilton, K. (2012) 'Exhibitions and the role of fashion in the sustenance of the Kylie Brand mythology: unpacking the spatial logic of celebrity culture', *Marketing Theory,* 12 (4): 411–25.

Levitt, T. (1965) 'Exploit the product life cycle', *Harvard Business Review*, Nov–Dec: 81–94.

Rubinstein, H. (1996) '"Brand first" management', *Journal of Marketing Management,* 12 (4): 269–80.

BOOKS AND BOOK CHAPTERS

Haig, M. (2011) *Brand Failures: The Truth about the 100 Biggest Branding Mistakes of All Time*, 2nd edn. London: Kogan Page.

Haig, M. (2011) *Brand Success: How the World's Top 100 Brands Thrive and Survive*, 2nd edn. London: Kogan Page.

Hart, S. (2008) 'New product development', in M.J. Baker and S. Hart (eds), *The Marketing Book*, 6th edn. Oxford: Butterworth Heinemann, Chapter 13.

Hartley, R.F. (1995) 'A giant fails to cope', in R.F. Hartley, *Marketing Mistakes*, 6th edn. New York: John Wiley, pp. 57–73.

WEBSITES

www.cim.co.uk – the Chartered Institute of Marketing.

www.designcouncil.org.uk – the Design Council, includes articles on product design.

SELF-REVIEW QUESTIONS

1. Define a product. (See p. 237)
2. What is meant by the term core product? (See p. 238)
3. How can products be differentiated? (See pp. 240–2)
4. Which usually attracts higher customer involvement – convenience goods or shopping goods? (See pp. 243–4)
5. What does FMCG mean? (See p. 244)
6. Why are good brands so important to companies? (See p. 248)
7. Draw the product life cycle diagram. (See p. 262)
8. What is an extension strategy? Give two examples. (See p. 262)
9. Is the product life cycle universally applicable? If not, why not? (See p. 266)
10. Draw the BCG matrix. (See p. 270)
11. What should you do with a dog? (See p. 271)
12. Why is innovation important? (See pp. 253–54)

Mini case study: Piège à Souris – 'SuperCat', the better mousetrap

Read the questions, then the case material, and then answer the questions.

Questions

1 What do you think the marketing professor meant when he said, 'the aim of marketing is to make selling superfluous'?

2 What stage in the product life cycle (PLC) are mousetraps in, in general? Why would a company think it a good idea to introduce a new mousetrap when they are generally in this stage of the PLC? Would the new product be in the same stage or could such a product innovation be said to be in a different PLC stage? If so, which?

3 Consider the description of the mousetrap and draw a total product offering (TPO) diagram to highlight its main elements. Can the TPO be helpful in understanding why the SuperCat has been successful in European markets? Do you think the launch of the product is likely to be successful in Britain, Ireland and Scandinavia?

Are there specific elements in the TPO that you would highlight to which particular attention should be given to increase the chances of success in launching the product in new markets?

It has been said that if you build a better mousetrap, the world will beat a path to your door. But what does this mean? The mousetrap has been around for a long time and sales of mousetraps in general are in decline. The mousetrap, a device for catching and killing mice and other small rodents that may infest a home, is a pretty basic product. Yet it is one that many householders value for those times when they need to eradicate that nuisance mouse or family of mice that have made the householder's home their own. The traditional mousetrap is a small wooden device with a spring-loaded clip. Cheese, which mice are said to love, is used as bait and the mousetrap is set in a place that the mouse is expected to visit. One nibble of the cheese and the spring clip flips down across the neck of the mouse, catching it and killing it. Sometimes this works, sometimes it does

© Dave Pickton

The better mousetrap.

(Continued)

(Continued)

not. If a better, more effective mousetrap could be designed, then, as the saying goes, the world will beat a path to your door – or, in other words, the product will be in high demand. Indeed, the idea is that the product will be so good that marketing will almost be unnecessary – it will practically sell itself. As one eminent marketing professor has said, 'the aim of marketing is to make selling superfluous'.

So entering into the marketplace is a new and more effective mousetrap. A Swiss-based company, which prides itself on developing and marketing innovative products, launched its better mousetrap originally in Germany, Switzerland and Austria in 1999. In 2000, it extended its international distribution to France, Italy, Holland and Spain. It is now looking to improve sales in those countries as well as launching in Britain, Ireland and Scandinavia. The mousetrap is called 'SuperCat'. It is new and it comes with its own permanent, non-toxic, more enticing bait. The company claims it has four innovations that make it better than other traps: it can be used immediately (it does not need to be baited); it is efficient and hygienic; it is easy to use; and it does not cause harm to children or domestic pets (presumably this assumes you do not have a pet mouse or hamster). It carries a 100% guarantee. It is packed for sale in pairs. To operate the trap, the rear clip is pushed down. It is ready to use. When a mouse is caught, it can be disposed of without having to touch the mouse. You simply carry the trap to a bin and push the rear clip down again, and the mouse falls out. The trap is once again ready for use. The bait lasts a long time although refills can be bought. In fact the trap is so cheap, it could be thrown away and a new one purchased.

Since 2002, the company has extended its product range and entered into collaboration with other companies in international markets. Its own-designed and own-produced devices now include other pest control products (rat traps, mole traps and fly traps) and household products (paint brushes and firelighter sticks). It distributes these itself and through its collaborative partners, and also distributes other garden and household goods. But the SuperCat remains its central focus.

REFERENCES

Aaker, D.A. (2002) *Building Strong Brands*. Sydney: Simon & Schuster.

Anon (n.d.) *Vodka: History, Development and Origin*, Gin and Vodka Association. Available at: **www.ginvodka.org/history/vodkaHistory.asp** (accessed 17/07/09).

Belén del Rio, A., Vazquez, R. and Iglesia, V. (2001) 'The effects of brand associations on consumer response', *Journal of Consumer Marketing*, 18 (5): 410–25.

Bryan, L.L. (2002) 'Just-in-time strategy for a turbulent world', *McKinsey Quarterly*, June.

Bucklin, L.P. (1963) 'Retail strategy and the classification of consumer goods', *Journal of Marketing*, 27 (Jan): 51–6.

Coyne, K. (2008) 'Enduring ideas: the GE–McKinsey nine-box matrix', *McKinsey Quarterly Strategic Thinking*, September. Available at: **http://www.mckinsey.com/insights/ strategy/enduring_ideas_the_ge_and_mckinsey_nine-box_matrix** (accessed 20/02/14).

Dennis (2010) 'Life's bloopers, foreign brand names', *True North Strong and Free*, Canada. Available at: **http://tnsf.ca/bloopers/index.php?Page=FB** (accessed 03/08/13).

Dhalla, N.K. and Yuspeh, S. (1976) 'Forget the product life cycle concept!', *Harvard Business Review*, 54 (1): 102–12.

Doyle, P. (2002) *Marketing Management and Strategy*. Harlow: FT/Prentice Hall.

Enis, B.M., LaGarce, R. and Prell, A.E. (1977) 'Extending the product life cycle', *Business Horizons*, 20 (Jun): 46–56.

Euromonitor (2010) cited in **www.gurufocus.com/news/168723/pepsico--hidden- potato-chip-dominance** (accessed 12/02/13).

Gluck, F.W., Kaufman, S.P., Walleck, A.S., McLeod, K. and Stuckey, J. (2000) 'Thinking strategically', *McKinsey Quarterly*, June. Available at: **http://www.mckinsey.com/ insights/strategy/thinking_strategically** (accessed 14/05/13).

Haig, M. (2003) *Brand Failures: The Truth about the 100 Biggest Branding Mistakes of all Time*. London: Kogan Page.

Hewer, P. and Hamilton, K. (2012) 'Exhibitions and the role of fashion in the sustenance of the Kylie Brand mythology: unpacking the spatial logic of celebrity culture', *Marketing Theory*, 12 (4): 411–25. Available at: **http://mtq.sagepub.com/content/12/4/411** (accessed 25/07/13).

IDC (2011) *Worldwide Quarterly Media Tablet and eReader Tracker*, 18 Jan.; available at: **http://www.idc.com/about/viewpressrelease.jsp?containerId=prUS22660011** (accessed 05/01/13)

Levitt, T. (1965) 'Exploit the product life cycle', *Harvard Business Review*, 43 (Nov/Dec): 81–94.

Malik, S. (2012) 'Kindle ebook sales have overtaken Amazon print sales, says bookseller', *The Guardian*, 6 Aug., available at: **http://www.theguardian.com/books/2012/aug/06/ amazon-kindle-ebook-sales-overtake-print** (accessed 05/01/13).

Mintel (2009) *Vodka UK Market Report March 2009*. London: Mintel.

Moon, Y. (2005) 'Break free from the product life cycle', *Harvard Business Review*, 83 (5): 86–94.

Muniz Jr, A.M. and O'Guinn, T.C. (2001) 'Brand community', *The Journal of Consumer Research*, 27 (4): 412–32.

O'Dell, J. (2011) *The State of the Tablet and eReader Market*, 27 July; available at: **mashable. com/2011/07/27/tablets-ereaders** (accessed 05/01/13).

Paliwoda, S.J. and Thomas, M.J. (1999) *International Marketing*, 3rd edn. Oxford: Butterworth Heinemann.

Pickton, D. and Broderick, A. (2004) *Integrated Marketing Communications* (2nd edn). Harlow: FT/Prentice Hall.

Renub Research (2011) *E-reader Market and Future Forecast Worldwide 2010–2014*, April. Available at: **www.researchandmarkets.com/reports/1595756/ereader_market_ and_future_forecast_worldwide** (accessed 05/01/13).

Rifkin, G. (1994) 'The myth of short life cycles', *Harvard Business Review*, 72 (11): 11.

Visit the companion website on your computer at **www.sagepub.co.uk/masterson3e** or MobileStudy on your Smart phone or tablet by scanning this QR code and gain access to:

- **Videos** to get a better understanding of key concepts and provoke in-class discussion.
- Links to useful **websites and templates** to help guide your study.
- Access **SAGE Marketing Pins (www.pinterest.com/sagepins/)**. SAGE's regularly updated **Pinterest** page, giving you access to regularly updated resources on everything from Branding to Consumer Behaviour.
- **Daily Grind podcast series** to learn more about the day-to-day life of a marketing **professional**.
- Interactive **Practice questions** to test your understanding.
- A **bonus chapter on Marketing Careers** to not only support your study, but your job search and future career.
- **PowerPoints** prompting key points for revision.

Service products

7

CHAPTER CONTENTS

SERVICE PRODUCTS CHALLENGES

The following are illustrations of the types of decision that marketers have to take or issues they face. *You aren't expected to know how to deal with the challenges now*; just bear them in mind as you read the chapter and see what you can find that helps.

- You are at the bank asking for a loan to help your chauffeuring service through a slump. If you are refused the loan, then you will have to sell off some of your limousines at a fraction of their value to you. It is unlikely that you will ever be able to afford to buy such cars again. The bank manager is not impressed with your business. He says it can never be a source of real wealth as it does not make anything. What could you say to convince him that the business is worthwhile?
- You manage the check-in operation for a major airline. You are visiting your staff at Gatwick airport when ten of your planes have to be withdrawn from service for safety checks. The queues of angry passengers are building up and you can see staff at a competitor's check-in looking smug and preparing to lure some of your customers away. What are you going to do? How can you come out of this with an even better reputation for great service?
- You are the marketing manager for a company that makes office furniture. Despite being one of the best recognised brands in your home business-to-business market, you have recently lost a couple of big orders to a foreign rival whose prices are much lower. To make matters worse, their furniture is just as well designed and as good quality as yours. Their brand name is as well recognised too. The production manager has shown that there is no way your company can match their low prices. You need a way to make customers value your products more highly. What are the possibilities?

- You used to sell cars but now you are a travel agent and you have two, difficult, potential customers in front of you: a bride and groom who want to fly an entire wedding party to a Caribbean island and put them up in a smart hotel. This would be a major sale but they are nervous about signing the agreements and want to be reassured that everything will be just perfect. When you were a car salesperson, you would have shown them the car and taken them for a test drive in it, but your budget does not stretch to flying the couple to the Caribbean – and anyway it is currently the monsoon season. How will you reassure them and make the sale?

INTRODUCTION

Products come in many forms, from ice creams to consultancy, from photocopiers to physiotherapy. Many products have no substantial physical form: we cannot pick them up, put them away in a cupboard, sell them on to someone else. Hairdressing, cleaning, insurance, maintenance, teaching – these are all service products and they are just as real, and potentially just as profitable, as the products that you can touch.

The study of services marketing encroaches into other disciplines rather more than most marketing topics do, incorporating aspects of design, human resource management and operations. Europeans sometimes use the term 'service management' instead as a more accurate, and less restricting, description (Grove et al., 2003). There is no clear defining line between the sale of a service, its production and its use. These aspects of a service product are often inseparable.

Take hand car washing as an example. A motorist pulls into a petrol station, or parks in a car park, and is approached by a young man who asks if she would like her car washed. She says 'yes' and the same young man produces bucket and sponge and gets to work. That young man has sold the service and delivered the service and his customer has used the service all within a very short space of time. In fact the provision of the service (the young man wielding bucket and sponge), and the use of the service (the car becoming clean) happen simultaneously. It is possible to build in a delay between sale and consumption, if, for example, there had been a queue for car washes, but often the whole process happens all together.

So service products are indeed rather different from the goods we studied in the last chapter, although they still have to be priced, delivered and promoted. This chapter will explore those differences, the challenges they present and the recognised ways of overcoming them. It will also show why service products are so important to all businesses today – to goods manufacturers as well as to service companies.

DEFINITIONS

total product offering the total package that makes up, and surrounds, the product, including all supporting features such as branding, packaging, servicing and warranties

A defining feature of service products is that they are intangible (they cannot be touched) as opposed to goods, or physical products, that are tangible. Unfortunately life, and business, is rarely that straightforward. Few products are exclusively tangible or intangible. A car is a solid object but it comes with a warranty which is not. The car needs insurance and will need servicing in the future. It may be wise to have a roadside recovery package such as that offered by the AA in the UK or ANWB in Holland. The availability, price and quality of these additional services are often important factors in a customer's decision to buy a car and are all part of the **total product offering**.

Similarly, many things that are classed as services have substantial physical products at their heart.

services
intangible products

Take the restaurant business, for example. A key determinant of the diner's satisfaction will be the food itself. The surroundings and the service are important, but if the food is no good then the restaurant is no good either. So although marketers, and governments and other interested parties, like to distinguish between goods and services, there are significant overlaps between the two.

There are a number of definitions of services, most of them having at their heart this idea of intangibility. According to Palmer, services are:

> The production of an essentially intangible benefit, either in its own right or as a significant element of a tangible product, which through some form of exchange, satisfies an identified need. (Palmer, 2005: 2–3)

Another defining feature of a service is that the customer does not actually own anything as a direct result of receiving the service:

> Any activity or benefit that one party can offer to another which is essentially intangible and does not result in the ownership of anything. Its production may or may not be tied to a physical product. (Kotler et al., 2001: 535)

Here is an alternative definition:

> A service is an activity which benefits recipients even though they own nothing extra as a result.

This simple definition encapsulates the key ideas of conferring a product benefit, no rights of ownership and of services being processes, or activities, rather than material things.

global focus: World services

Services create a high proportion of many countries' GDP (Gross Domestic Product) and the bulk of their working populations may be employed in service industries.

Exhibit 7.1 shows the approximate proportion of GDP that services contribute, and the approximate percentage of workers in service industries in a selection of countries/regions.

China, possibly the fastest developing, major economy today, is still focused on agriculture and manufacturing, but there are signs of a fast-developing service sector there too. The box also illustrates the difficulty of collecting reliable data in many countries; most of these figures are estimates and some are quite out of date – yet these are the most reliable figures the Central Intelligence Agency (CIA) can find to publish.

Exhibit 7.1 Contribution of service industries to selected countries/regions

Country	Services GDP (as % of total GDP)	Services jobs (as % of all jobs)
European Union	73.5% (2012 estimated)	71.8% (2011 estimated)
France	79.8% (2012 estimated)	71.8% (2005)
USA	79.7% (2012 estimated)	81.1%
UK	78.2% (2012 estimated)	80.4% (2006 estimated)
Denmark	76.6% (2012 estimated)	77.1% (2011 estimated)
Japan	71.4% (2012 estimated)	69.8% (2010 estimated)
India	65% (2011 estimated)	28% (2011 estimated)
China	44.6% (2012 estimated)	35.7% (2011 estimated)
Nigeria	26% (2012 estimated)	20% (1999 estimated)

(CIA, n.d.)

THE IMPORTANCE OF SERVICES

M&S white glove delivery service

M&S in-store purchasing

Services are becoming more and more important to both businesses and consumers. The majority of business start-ups are service businesses, although admittedly many of them are very small.

Some countries are said to have service economies, i.e. they rely on service businesses for the bulk of their wealth. Service businesses are sometimes criticised on the grounds that, unlike manufacturing businesses, they do not produce any increase in wealth. Restaurant or hotel customers spend their money and are poorer – they have nothing of ongoing value in exchange. Food has been eaten, sleep has been had, but customers own nothing new that they can sell on. This idea dates back to Adam Smith, an eighteenth-century economist who argued that intangible products did not create anything of real value unlike the products of manufacturing or agriculture (Palmer, 2005). As we can see from Exhibit 7.1 though, service customers contribute significantly to the income of a country. One of Britain's main foreign currency earners is the City of London, where banks, insurance companies and other financial institutions carry out their business. However, hotels and restaurants also bring huge amounts of money into most European capitals, largely thanks to visiting tourists. The more traditional services still have their part to play – even highly paid city bankers have to eat.

outsourcing
the subcontracting of a business process, e.g. delivery or maintenance, to another organisation

KNOWLEDGE-BASED ECONOMIES

The trend towards service industries is at its most advanced in the MDCs (most developed countries), but it is notable worldwide. The MDCs could be said now to have moved beyond services and into a new era of knowledge-based activities where expertise is prized above all else. These are nations of consultants, financiers and lawyers, who **outsource** more basic services such as call centres and computer programming to other countries which possess skilled workforces (particularly in IT).

So Europe has become a continent of knowledge-based workers who are paid for their expertise while other countries, with cheaper labour costs, do the manufacturing. Current thinking is that it is a company's intellectual capital that is its most valuable asset, rather than the more tangible things it owns. This, as Handy (2002) points out, can cause a problem because companies do not actually *own* their employees. They are not slaves. They are free to leave and take their expertise with them. Handy quotes a story about the world-renowned advertising agency Saatchi & Saatchi. The board fired Maurice Saatchi, one of the agency's founders, who duly left, taking major clients and some of the agency's best staff with him. These things did not belong to the company or its shareholders.

REASONS FOR THE GROWTH IN THE SERVICES SECTOR

There are a number of reasons behind this rise in the popularity of service businesses, including:

- more employment in knowledge-based industries
- increased consumer leisure time and consequent demand for leisure services
- the popularity of outsourcing services as a cost-cutting and efficiency measure
- displaced workers setting up their own small businesses, notably consultancy, training and coaching
- complex modern products requiring support services
- the fact that the service element is now often the key (if not only) way to differentiate a goods item (physical product).

First, the knowledge workers and other highly skilled service staff, who are the backbones of advanced economies, have to keep their knowledge and skills up to date. ('Knowledge worker' is a term first used by Peter Drucker to describe people who work with information rather than in more traditional industries. Knowledge workers may be thought of as the ultimate service industry employees.) Such personnel need ready access to detailed information banks as they are insatiable users of information services and they also need training, even coaching and mentoring. Corporate coaching is a service that has taken off in the last few years. Experienced business people, with specific coaching training, help hard-pressed executives to make the most of their talents and their time.

Second, people in the more developed nations have larger incomes and a lot more free time to spend it in. This means that the demand for leisure activities, largely services, has gone up. Hotels, restaurants, cafés, bars and health clubs have been the main beneficiaries of this new-found wealth, closely followed by retailing. So many people love to shop! This increase in disposable income also means that many people can afford to pay others to do things that most of their grandparents would have done themselves: mending pipes, fixing windows, cleaning, gardening, laying patios, decorating, etc. However, many services are considered luxuries, e.g. restaurants and travel, and these suffer badly during hard times such as recession.

Growth of the Service Sector

The increased popularity of outsourcing has also encouraged new service businesses to start up. Company profits are under closer scrutiny as more businesses are publicly quoted or are registered as limited liability companies – meaning they have shareholders who demand higher profits. Consequently, today's businesses are

ethical focus: Playing with lives

Channel 4 transmitted a stunt featuring the illusionist Derren Brown. The stunt was Russian roulette – with a real bullet. The programme was billed as going out live but, in actual fact, there was a slight delay in the transmission just in case something went wrong and he actually did kill himself.

On the night there was indeed a hitch, but fortunately only in that Derren mistook a blank bullet for a live one, and fired it into the waiting sandbag rather than his head.

The show was not universally popular. Parents' groups and police criticised it on the grounds that it might inspire youngsters to copy it. There were also complaints that, in a week when there had been a number of shootings and gun crime was a hot topic in all the newspapers, the programme was in bad taste. Channel 4 defended the show by pointing out that it contained a number of warnings of the dangers, and explanations that the game was enacted within a controlled environment and under the supervision of firearms experts.

Was this programme an ethically sound product?

always looking for ways to cut costs and one of the recommended routes to lower cost operations is to focus on the core business and outsource as much of the rest as possible. Many businesses employ other companies to perform key tasks such as delivery, installation, maintenance, call centres, even new product development, as well as more peripheral, but nonetheless important, activities such as cleaning, vehicle fleet management and staff training. All the above-mentioned examples are services and this outsourcing has created a lot of new businesses whose core business is to provide these services.

Outsourcing is not without its drawbacks, however. Although costs may be saved up front, there may be further expense incurred if the outsourcing goes wrong. Firms who outsource customer contact activities, such as call centres or Internet order taking, are handing over a significant part of their customer relationship to another company. They are trusting the outsource partner to care for their company's image and reputation, and not to set up a rival business and poach their customers.

The outsourcing of work to other countries where land and labour costs are cheaper boosts those countries' economies and helps to turn them into viable markets for the home country's products. However, outsourcing to other countries can sometimes create a level of dissatisfaction in the home country. In the UK, for example, some banks and insurance companies are endeavouring to create competitive advantage by making a virtue of returning all of their call centres to the UK.

This trend towards setting up operations in lower-cost countries has meant that the displaced workers of Western Europe, North America, Japan and other post-industrial nations have had to seek alternative employment. Many have turned to self-employment, either in a new industry or as consultants or trainers to their old one. Service businesses are often relatively cheap to set up as many require little in the way of heavy machinery, land or premises. A cleaning service needs mops, buckets, brushes, polish, etc., and maybe a small van to travel from place to place, but little else. A consultant may only need an office, a car and communications equipment. Many service businesses are small and so the investment needed to start one up is also small. It is actually an advantage to be small in some types of service, particularly where personal service is prized (e.g. decorators). Recent years have seen a huge increase in the number of self-employed workers and small business owners, many of whom are offering services.

Another reason for the increase in service products can be found in the world of physical products. Modern technology has created ever more complex products, such as laptops, MP3 players, hard disk recorders, intelligent cars and all the technical paraphernalia (routers, Bluetooth devices, scanners, etc.) that surround computers. Such complex products can be prone to breakdowns and so they need maintenance and repair services. Some, such as heavy industrial plant or highly technical products, need training courses for users before they can even be started up.

As advanced production techniques have made products more standardised, it is often the service aspects (the support: helpdesks, training, service engineers, etc.) that are the means of differentiating one product from another. Customers frequently choose a more expensive supplier on the grounds that they believe the installation or the ongoing service will be better. They are wise enough to recognise that the cost of their new central heating boiler, car or PC does not end at the point of purchase. They take account of the ongoing service costs and the hassle factor when deciding what to buy and from whom (see Chapter 3 for more on how customers make purchase decisions).

Exhibit 7.2   Circle of service creation

a service is provided, e.g accountancy

it creates opportunities for supporting services, e.g. training, cleaning

those businesses also need services, e.g. accountancy

Training and support is another major growth area. Services are people-intensive and rely on the skills of those who provide them. All these lawyers, accountants, nurses, IT technicians, plumbers, consultants and trainers need to be trained and supported themselves and so we have a self-perpetuating cycle of service (see Exhibit 7.2).

Most of today's products have a strong service element, which may be the source of their competitive advantage. Equally, many services have a physical product element and this may be the source of theirs, although skills are a more common determinant of the quality of a service. Service products can use physical elements within the offering, and physical products can use service elements, to add to the satisfaction provided by the product.

THE NATURE OF SERVICES

A cut and blow dry needs shampoo. A car service needs filters. A consultancy project produces a report. A night's sleep in a hotel room means there must be a bed. There are very few pure services (i.e. with no physical element at all) in existence, just as there are increasingly few pure goods (i.e. with no service element). Whether a product is primarily a good or a service makes a great deal of difference to the way in which it will be marketed.

Exhibit 7.3 presents a continuum upon which example products are placed according to their degree of physicality.

Exhibit 7.3   A product continuum, tangible to intangible

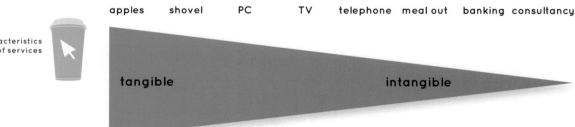

Apples bought in a shop have the benefit of all the retail and distribution services that got them there. However, apples picked on a pick-your-own farm or from your own garden have no service element. A shovel will probably be bought from a shop but requires no maintenance or other services, unlike a PC where the warranty and back-up service may be important. Televisions may well be chosen for their features: widescreen, digital, surround sound, portable, etc., but they are of no use without a signal from one of the television broadcasters – unless you just want to use them as a monitor for playing DVDs of course. Telephones usually have fewer features than televisions but their whole point is to receive telephone calls. Restaurants are selected for their standards of service and their ambience as much as for their food. Traditional banking provides us with little of substance: bank notes, cheque books, cards. Online banking is even less tangible.

The ultimate intangible product is perhaps consultancy. Although consultants usually provide a written report at the end of their work, it is not the writing down that clients are really paying for but the ideas contained within the report – the consultant's expertise.

The overlap between goods and services is so large and yet so difficult to pinpoint that some marketers have expressed doubts as to whether services marketing is a distinct marketing area at all.

EXPAND YOUR KNOWLEDGE

Classic article

Shostack, G.L. (1984) 'Designing services that deliver', *Harvard Business Review*, 62 (Jan–Feb): 133–9.

The author notes that despite the importance of the services sector, little effort is exerted to apply the sort of rational management techniques so common in the goods-producing sector. The article reviews this position and presents a systematic management process that can be applied to services.

CHARACTERISTICS OF SERVICES

Throughout much of this book, goods and services are treated similarly. A service is a product and it needs pricing and promoting just as any product does. As Theodore Levitt said, 'There are no such things as service industries. There are only industries whose service components are greater or less than those of other industries. Everybody is in service' (cited in Kotler, 2003: 167). However, the provision of and marketing of services presents some additional challenges. Many of these arise from the nature of services – the way they differ from goods.

Services have a number of defining characteristics which set them apart from goods. The following are typical service characteristics and will be discussed in the section that follows:

- services confer benefits
- services are intangible – they have no (or little) physical form and so cannot be touched
- services are time and place dependent – they cannot be stored or moved
- the service provider is part of the service
- the consumer is part of the service
- services are inconsistent
- services cannot be owned.

Some academics believe that the distinctions between goods and services have become so blurred that even these key characteristics are unreliable and should be revised (Grove et al., 2003). It is certainly true that technology has made a difference. Some Internet services can, in a way, be stored. Purchases can be left in a shopping basket and paid for later, downloads can be bought and then watched later. The Internet has also meant that the service provider and customer do not always have to be together. Think of Internet banking, for example. So it may be best to consider these as typical characteristics of traditional services, some of which can be mediated by technology.

SERVICES CONFER BENEFITS

Just like goods, services are designed to meet customer needs and so services also have core benefits. The core benefit from having your car serviced is the prevention of a breakdown. The core benefit from a haircut is to look better. The core benefit from most medical services is to feel better. There may be additional benefits, e.g. the car being worth more, but marketers must ensure that the service provides the core benefit well, or customers will not return. Once you have had a bad haircut, you do not usually go back to that hairdresser no matter how good the coffee was, unless the service recovery was really good, of course. (Service recovery will be examined later in the chapter.)

This does not mean, however, that service products can be analysed in the same way as physical products. Chapter 6 presented a total product offering model, with outer rings comprising largely service elements or other intangibles. While the idea of a core benefit from services is useful, much of the rest of the total product offering model needs modification when applied to services.

The concept of the total service product offering is illustrated in Exhibit 7.4 using the example of a concert.

Music fans go to concerts in the hope of being entertained, maybe leaving the venue feeling exhilarated or even inspired. Those are the benefits that they are looking to the concert to provide. The second ring shows the things that may contribute to that core benefit. Clearly, the band itself is a major factor, along with what they play (features) and how well they play it (quality). The sound system will also contribute to the quality of the event and technicians (people) will be important to ensure that sound and lighting work properly. The thrill of the concert may be spoilt if the audience has to queue for hours to get out of car parks or on to buses at the end (accessibility) or if crowd control is too aggressive (processes). The idea of branding a band is not novel. Bands can effectively be considered as brands – some even have logos and merchandising (the sale of branded goods such as T-shirts and posters) is typically a key part of concert activity. The experience will be enhanced if the desired refreshments are available (tangibles) and these tangibles are represented in the third ring of the model.

SERVICES ARE INTANGIBLE

Services are, at their core, intangible. You cannot smell them, touch them or throw them at anyone. However, some services are more intangible than others (see Exhibit 7.3). For example, a dental check-up is almost completely intangible. There may be no products involved beyond the dentist's instruments. The essence of the service lies in the dentist's skill and that has to be taken on trust. On the other hand, a meal in a restaurant has a lot of tangible things associated with it, especially the food. This intangibility makes services harder to market than goods. Potential customers feel more confident buying something that they can see and feel – and take back if necessary. So one of the key challenges for marketers is to

Complaints after Justin Bieber concert

Exhibit 7.4 Total service offering for a concert

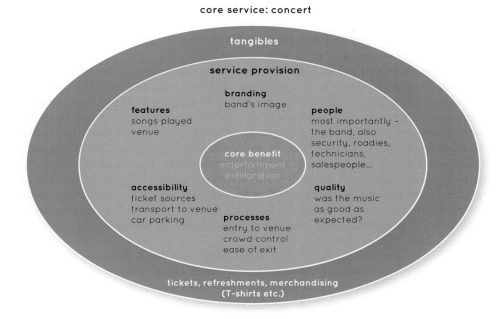

core service: concert

tangibles

service provision

branding
band's image

features
songs played
venue

people
most importantly –
the band, also
security, roadies,
technicians,
salespeople...

core benefit
entertainment
exhilaration

accessibility
ticket sources
transport to venue
car parking

quality
was the music
as good as
expected?

processes
entry to venue
crowd control
ease of exit

tickets, refreshments, merchandising
(T-shirts etc.)

reduce the perceived risk involved in buying a service by making it appear more tangible, often by emphasising the **peripheral products** used in carrying out the service. Restaurants usually try to convince potential diners that the food is really good. Beauticians stress the properties of the face masks and moisturisers they use.

This intangibility presents marketers with an additional competitive headache. It is more difficult to protect a service from imitation. The inventors of physical products can apply for **patents** to safeguard the product in its early years while they recoup their development investments. Patent laws, and the rigour with which they are enforced, vary from country to country but few, if any, allow for the patenting of service products. Other intellectual property laws, such as copyright and trade mark registration, afford some protection but are even harder to enforce, and recent efforts to extend UK patent laws to include business processes and software have failed (Patents Office, n.d.).

peripheral products
a secondary product often provided as part of a service, e.g. the complementary mints at the end of a meal, shampoo at the hairdressers

patent
a legal protection for inventions that prohibits unauthorised copying

SERVICES ARE TIME AND PLACE DEPENDENT (THEY CANNOT BE STORED OR MOVED)

Services are transient. They happen at a particular time and cannot be stored for later sale or use. You cannot buy a service to keep in the cupboard

Promotional merchandise is one of the tangibles at a rock concert.

and use at your convenience like you might a tin of soup or a bottle of shampoo. Planes and trains leave at specific times and customers have to be on board if they want to take advantage of the service. The train or plane operator has to sell seat tickets before departure. If seats remain unsold, they have lost potential income. This perishability of services, as some writers refer to it, greatly complicates the planning of service operations.

The management of peaks and troughs of demand is more difficult for service providers. Whereas a retailer or a manufacturer has a stock room in which to keep surplus products until demand picks up again, service providers just lose business if they do not have enough products. The retailer or manufacturer can stockpile in anticipation of a future peak in demand, fans for the summer perhaps, and so keep their workforce employed, but a hairdresser cannot get ahead by doing extra haircuts and keeping them for later. Service providers may need to employ seasonal staff and lay them off again when demand is low – a reason why so many students find jobs in the holiday industry. Another way that service providers can manage these peaks and troughs is through changing the price (see price discrimination in Chapter 10) to attract extra customers when business is slack or to increase profits in times of high demand.

Additionally, for most services, the number of customers that can be accommodated at any one time is limited and so services often involve appointments, e.g. for the dentist, or queuing, and service customers are more often turned away than are customers for goods. There are a limited number of tickets for a concert. There are a limited number of seats on the plane.

Service products cannot be moved like physical products which can be bought in one place and then transported to another location. Few services can be delivered long distance (though modern electronic technologies do facilitate this for some services). A hotel room cannot be moved; you must sleep in the hotel. A play is not performed whenever and wherever you want; it must be at the theatre and at a scheduled performance time.

The time dependency of many services has major implications for the service supplier, who must be a master of demand forecasting if they are not to be left with time on their hands or unsold seats. Late customers cause significant problems. If a customer misses an appointment or is late for it, then this can cause serious scheduling problems. The person who was to perform the service (the hairdresser, the dentist, the bank manager) will be left with extra time that they could have used more profitably while any revised scheduling may impact on the quality of service for subsequent customers.

THE SERVICE PROVIDER IS PART OF THE SERVICE

A service provider is an intrinsic part of the service. It is rarely possible to disassociate the person or organisation that performs the service from the service itself. This is often referred to as the inseparability of services and it is a key difference between services and physical products. Customers frequently buy products with no knowledge at all about how and where they were produced and by whom. Do you know which company made the bread for your sandwich? Have you visited their factory? Do you know the name of the baker?

Case study:
Bank of
Scotland

In the case of personal services, such as dentistry, the service provider must actually be physically present at the point that the service is consumed, e.g. the tooth is filled. This is not true for all services. The less personal the service, the more likely it is that it can be performed remotely. For example, an Internet user may shop in the middle of the night, while all the online retailer's staff are asleep. Technology is often the facilitator of remote services. We no longer need telephonists to make connections for us; we can dial the numbers ourselves. We do not always need computer programmers to search databases for us, nor do we need a salesperson to place an order online.

Technology also allows service providers to cut costs. Traditionally, services have been very staff intensive, much more so than manufacturing, and this is expensive, especially in the more developed nations where wages are high. Thanks to advanced telecommunications, organisations can move their customer service operations to other countries where staff costs are lower and often employment law is less stringent. A number of British companies have call centres in India, for example.

Thanks to the Internet, organisations can get their customers to do some of the work for themselves, e.g. placing orders online or filing tax returns electronically. This offloading of work on to the customer is not a particularly new idea and it is not solely due to technological advance. Self-service in supermarkets and cafés has the same cost-cutting motivation.

THE CONSUMER IS PART OF THE SERVICE

The consumer of the service is part of the experience whether or not they perform a part of the service themselves, e.g. by serving themselves in a petrol station. Because the production and consumption of services cannot be separated, the consumer has to be considered as an element of the production process and their actions, reactions or inaction need to be taken into account in the service offering's design. This brings into sharp focus the emphasis that is now placed on customer relationship management (CRM). Not only has the importance of customer loyalty been recognised in successful marketing, but also the way in which building relationships is a fundamental part of the service offering. Early work in recognising the shift of marketing emphasis from goods to services and the roles of relationship marketing can be found in the publications of such authors as Grönroos and Gummesson in the late 1970s and 1980s.

For most service customers, ease of use of a service will be important. They do not want to be over-involved in the service delivery. If an investment service is too complicated or there are too many forms to fill in, then the potential customer may be put off. Most people shop at the supermarket that is the closest to them or has good parking. Consumers value **service convenience** which they measure in terms of the time and effort they have to expend on the service. Berry, Seiders and Grewal (2002) have proposed five categories of service convenience:

service convenience
a measure of how much time and effort consumers need to expend to use the service offered

- decision convenience
- access convenience
- transaction convenience
- benefit convenience
- post-benefit convenience.

First, there is the question of the ease of decision-making. People are more likely to consider performing a service themselves (e.g. DIY) than they are to consider making a physical product. Service providers must ensure that there is enough information available, and in the right form, to inform this decision as well as the choice of supplier.

Second, the customer may consider how easy it will be to ask for the service, e.g. do they have to go to the restaurant or can they order by phone and have their food delivered? Is the website easy to navigate or is it disjointed and slow?

The third category is transaction convenience: how long will it take to pay and how secure is the payment? Often you have to pay for services before you actually receive them, e.g. you have to buy a ticket for a play. If it takes too long to pay (perhaps there is a queue) people may give up. E-tailers suffer particularly from this as many shoppers abandon their baskets before the check-out.

e-tailers
online retailers

service encounter
the time during which a customer is the recipient of a service, e.g. the duration of a meal in a restaurant

Next is benefit convenience: the time and effort that the consumer has to expend in order to actually receive the core benefit of the service while the service is happening, i.e. during the service encounter. For example, the benefit of a taxi ride would be considerably reduced if the customer had to walk the last mile of their journey.

This is the one point of the service process where customers do not always mind spending extra time. If the service is a hedonistic one, e.g. a holiday, then customers may well be happy to prolong the experience.

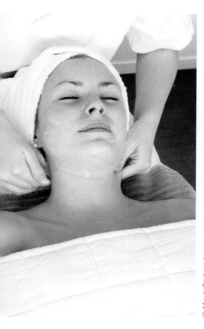

Most personal services, such as beauty treatments, require both people to be present.

Some services have been delegated to customers so that the service provider does not need to be present.

Non-personal services are less likely to require the presence of both people, e.g. windows are often cleaned in the householder's absence.

Finally, there is post-benefit convenience. Customers want hassle-free ongoing benefits from the service provided and not to have to return to complain or to have the fillings replaced in their teeth too quickly (see service recovery later in this chapter).

e-focus: Internet banking

New technologies have overcome some of the difficulties normally found in the marketing of services. In particular, technology has helped address the issues of inconsistency and inseparability (the service provider having to be there to deliver the service).

In the virtual world, consumption can take place without both provider and customer being in the same place at the same time. Automation also improves service consistency, although the differences in consumers and their skills may make them experience the service differently. This has a major advantage in terms of opening hours. Internet banking, for example, is available 24/7 without staff having to be there.

First Direct, now a division of HSBC, was a pioneer of telephone banking and was also among the first to move into Internet banking. Customers can manage most aspects of their accounts online: view balances and statements, transfer money, pay bills and set up direct debits. First Direct has no branches, which means it makes considerable cost savings.

The website helps First Direct in other ways too: the technology provides a more consistent service delivery than a person would; imagery and branding are more tightly controlled; and a record of transactions is created automatically. On the other hand, customers are at the mercy of the unpredictability of the Internet service itself and this may affect their perception of the service. Also, an Internet service is quite easy to mimic, making it harder for brands to differentiate themselves from the competition.

EXPAND YOUR KNOWLEDGE

Farquhar, J.D. and Rowley, J. (2009) 'Convenience: a services perspective', *Marketing Theory*, 9 (4): 425–38.

Farquhar and Rowley argue: 'The concept and construct of convenience is at the forefront of customer and user evaluation of services experiences and should therefore play a much more pivotal role in marketing theory than it does at present.' (2009: 425)

OTHER PEOPLE MAY ALSO BE PART OF THE SERVICE

Consumers' enjoyment of a service is also affected by other people, particularly other consumers, and especially if the service is one that is offered to a group rather than just to individuals. For example, a play can be spoilt by someone else's mobile phone. A train journey can be turned into a distressing rather than relaxing experience by the bad behaviour of fellow passengers. Equally, a holiday may be made so much more fun thanks to good company. It can be hard for service providers to control the behaviour of their customers and sometimes their very attempts at control cause a problem for others, e.g. the puzzled old ladies who are no longer allowed to take their nail scissors on to aeroplanes because of increased security measures.

ACTIVITY

Imagine you are a holiday rep at a Mediterranean beach resort. You are based in a large hotel that is popular with both young people, who want to go out clubbing, stay out late and then stay in bed until the afternoon, and with families. What problems might you anticipate and what can you do to resolve them?

Local people have complained about the behaviour of both groups of customers. Is that your concern? What can you do about it?

SERVICES ARE INCONSISTENT

Physical products aim for consistency in quality, packaging and features and many can rely on advanced manufacturing equipment to help them deliver it. Even physical products are not infallibly the same though. Flaws in ingredients or components may have an adverse effect on manufactured goods. Nature is not always as bothered about consistency as some fussy humans are either – fruit and vegetables come in various shapes and sizes, and often with blemishes despite farmers' best efforts with pesticides. The EU has rules about the shape of some produce, there was a media fuss about the requirement for straight cucumbers not long ago, and supermarkets demand standard sizes and shapes and have had a major influence on which varieties are grown and sold. Sometimes inconsistencies are viewed positively, as in home-baked goods, where the slightly irregular shapes are proof that they are genuinely hand prepared, but usually standardisation is preferred.

The issue of consistency is even more pronounced for service products. Variability is inherently part of services. They are difficult to standardise. The intangibility of services means that we cannot know exactly what we are getting until it is too late. We can try on clothes to see if they fit. However, if we ask a plumber to mend a leak for us, we will not know whether we are going to receive a good service until after it has been performed. Only then can we tell if the leak is fixed. This is so much more risky and one of the ways that customers reduce the risk is by relying on past performance as a guide to the future (something that the financial services adverts point out that you should never do). If the plumber did a good job last time, we assume that this job will also be good. If our expectations are not met, if the standard of work is inconsistent, then we will be unhappy with it, and possibly protracted and bitter arguments and negotiations will ensue. It is not a question of just putting the trousers back on the rail and trying another pair, the quality of the work is often a matter of judgement.

ethical focus: Free-(down)loaders

If you cannot see it, touch it or smell it, can you steal it? Police in West London arrested a man for stealing a wireless broadband connection. He was sitting on a garden wall outside a house (not his own), using his laptop and the house owner's broadband. Many people would claim that this was a victimless crime. The broadband subscriber did not have to pay more because of the extra use that was made of his connection, and his service was not affected in any way.

The first person to be prosecuted for this crime was another West London man who was fined £500 and given a 12-month conditional discharge in 2005. The number of arrests in the UK, under the Communications Act 2003, for dishonestly obtaining free access to networks has risen steadily. However, it may prove difficult, if not totally impractical, to arrest all the perpetrators of this crime.

Critics argue that it is not difficult to password-protect a connection and so, if people want to prevent others from using their broadband, then they should secure the connection. In a further blow to attempts to police these connections, some Internet Service Providers are encouraging their users to make the connections available to others and so build up national wireless access. They advertise 'hot spots' where any of their broadband customers can access the Internet by piggybacking on someone else's connection.

The police, and consumer groups, maintain that it is unacceptable to use services without the subscriber's permission. They argue that the freeloaders, by getting services without paying, increase the costs for those who do pay – and someone has to pay or there will be no service provided.

What do you think? Is it acceptable to use another's service or not?

SOURCES: Topping, 2007.

Service products are dependent upon humans, and humans are not always consistent. It is rare that two haircuts would be exactly the same. In a restaurant, you might order the same food as before but it is unlikely that it will be prepared and served by the same staff – and, even if it was, it could still be a little different.

Consistency is something that many services strive for, but few deliver. It is more important for some services, e.g. financial ones, than it is for others. Lawyers and accountants rely upon documentation to try to provide consistent services. The Internet has been of great assistance here. Services provided online are made more consistent by the constraints of the technology. However, it could be argued that with this consistency comes an inflexibility that does not always provide the service that customers actually want.

Another way to provide consistent service is by following strict procedures. Service owners devise a plan for their employees to follow so that each service encounter will be as similar to the previous one as possible. Fast-food chains have tight controls over what their staff do. Kitchen staff walk along set paths from fryer to sink to serving hatch. Bells ring when it is time to turn the burger or take the chips out of the fat. Nothing is left to chance. This heavily proscribed way of working has the added advantage of meaning that trained chefs are not required. The work, however, is repetitive and can soon become boring. Staff turnover is often high in such restaurants.

Flow charts are often used to work out how best to provide a consistent, quality service (see Exhibit 7.6 on p. 306) or there may be a service **blueprint**. These tried-and-tested procedures are part of what a franchisee is paying for when they buy their business idea from the **franchiser**.

The best service providers go to great lengths to ensure that they provide a high-quality service, one that customers can rely on – and still they will receive some complaints. Customers are no more consistent than staff. Some will like their burgers overcooked, others will not. One customer will love their haircut, but it will not suit her friend. There are diners who like loud music in restaurants and there are those who complain that they cannot hear their companions talk – and those may actually be the same people but at different times, or with different companions. Services are often inconsistent in their reception as well as in their delivery and so all service businesses must be adept at handling complaints if they are to be successful (see service recovery later in this chapter).

SERVICES CANNOT BE OWNED

This is largely a function of the intangibility of the service. There is nothing to actually own. A client pays for the beautician's skill (and the lotions and potions applied) but at the end of the treatment has nothing more than a good feeling (and possibly better skin) to take home. Service clients are paying for expertise, experience, advice, skills, knowledge and the benefits these bring. The benefits may last, but the service itself is of limited duration. Of course, it is possible to augment the service offering with additional items (peripheral products), some of which may be physical goods. For example, in the case of hairdressing or beauty treatments, the client may be able to purchase hair care and beauty goods for use at home.

DIFFERENT TYPES OF SERVICE

The services sector is a very large one and so it is easier to study if it is broken down into smaller groupings or subcategories. Traditionally, similar activities have been grouped together, e.g. the UK government grouped together 'retail, hire and repair', 'media and creative services', 'health and social care services', 'personal services', 'IT and telecommunications services'. While this is easy to do, it is a business-based categorisation rather than a customer-based one and therefore not **market-orientated**. A marketer would prefer to see the groupings based on customer needs and the way the services are used rather than the type of skills and resources needed to provide them. However, classifying activities in this way can lead to some very broad categories which are not particularly useful for marketing. Palmer (2005: 52) suggests that it would be better to group them along the lines of 'processes by which customers make decisions, methods of pricing and promotional strategies'.

blueprint
an original plan or set of instructions for how something should operate

franchiser
owner of a business idea or product who grants a licence to someone else to market it

market-orientation
provision of customer value determines an organisation's direction

Additionally, there are problems when classifying some large and diverse organisations. For example, Tesco would be classed as a retailer even though it also offers banking services. That category of retail is so broad anyway, incorporating organisations as diverse as Tesco, Holland & Barrett (health food chain) and individually owned corner shops – all, incidentally, food retailers but with very little in common in terms of their business operations.

Academics tend to place services on a continuum according to their nature – most commonly their degree of intangibility. Dibb et al. (2006) also propose a five-category classification scheme:

1   Type of market.
2   Degree of labour intensiveness.
3   Degree of customer contact.
4   Skill of the service provider.
5   Goal of the service provider.

retail
selling goods to customers for their own use, i.e. not for resale

In this schema, type of market would typically be 'consumer' or 'business' and a description of the core activity, e.g. consumer legal advice. The degree of labour intensiveness would be classed as either high or low depending on how automated it was. The degree of customer contact would also be classed as high or low, with healthcare being an example of a service with a high degree of customer contact and the postal service being an example of a low level of customer contact. Dibb et al. (2006) consider the skill of the service provider in terms of professional or non-professional. Accountancy is a professional skill whereas dry cleaning is not. The rationale behind this is that professional services are more complex and their practitioners have to be sure to comply with more regulations than non-professionals do. Clearly, there is a cross-over area here as it is not only the traditional professions, such as lawyers, doctors, accountants, who are highly regulated, as anyone who works with children in the UK will vouch. The final classification category, the goal of the service provider, refers to whether they are a profit or non-profit organisation (e.g. charities, the National Health Service).

There is no general agreement on a useful classification system for services and it may well be that service products are so diverse that any system will be flawed. It is important to remember that these categorisations are meant to assist the study and marketing of services and, if they do not do so, then there is little point to them. Choose a category or system that fits the service you are considering, and do not be afraid to choose a different one in a different situation.

Another consideration in categorising services as an aid to marketing them well is to think about the degree of involvement of both the service provider and the consumers. In considering the nature of services in the section above, it was identified that both the service provider and the consumer are integral parts of service provision but the extent of their involvement in the process will vary: some services require high levels of direct involvement by the provider (e.g. dentistry) and some low levels (e.g. online ordering). Similarly, this is the case with the level of involvement by the consumer. It is possible to consider the marketing implications of each in defining the service provision.

ACTIVITY

The following services vary in terms of how reliant they are on goods. Try placing them on a scale from pure service to high use of (peripheral) products. Then try and categorise them using any of the systems mentioned above:

- banks
- insurance companies
- hotels
- casinos
- bookmakers
- restaurants
- travel agencies
- airlines
- educational establishments
- crèches
- debt collectors
- beauticians
- doctors' surgeries
- plumbers
- management consultancies
- cleaners
- stockbrokers
- garages
- personal trainers
- life coaches.

Gymbox: standing out

Inside Amazon

personal selling
an oral presentation, in a conversation with one or more prospective purchasers, for the purpose of making sales

distribution channel
a chain of organisations through which products pass on their way to a target market

RETAILING AND E-TAILING

In many of the more developed countries, shopping is a major pastime. This is a relatively new phenomenon. Shopping used to be considered a chore rather than a leisure activity. This change in shopping's status has significant implications for retailers and for retailing's place in marketing. Is it a service or is it a form of **personal selling** or is it the final stage in the **distribution channel**? (See Chapter 9.) So which P of the marketing mix (see below) should we put it in: product, promotion or place? The answer is, of course, that there are aspects of retailing which fit into all of these categories. Here in the service products chapter, we are mainly concerned with retail as a service to the consumer: a provider of goods and services and a leisure activity.

As the main source of goods, retailing has a special place in the services spectrum. Its *raison d'être* is to provide other products and it is difficult to separate it out from those products. So we have two issues of inseparability here: the service provider (in this case the efforts of the retailer, including shop staff) is an integral part of the service and so are the goods sold. Retailers will be judged on the quality of both.

ACTIVITY

Refer back to Exhibit 7.4 of the total service offering. Re-draw the diagram for a retailer of your choice.

Whereas traditional retailers are tied to a particular place, a high street or out-of-town shopping centre perhaps, there are other retailers who are not. Mail order (or catalogue) companies have sold their goods and services through the post for many years. Their business is based upon the convenience of bringing the shop to the shopper's own home. A modern variant of home shopping is provided by the Internet. A large proportion of books and CDs are now sold online and a greater variety of goods are being bought there, from groceries to concert tickets to financial services. High street retailing and Internet retailing are becoming blurred. Tesco's, for example, extol the virtue of 'You shop, we drop' as customers order online while Tesco's deliver to your door.

As the Internet becomes a mass marketplace, ease of use becomes more and more important: high quality and service convenience are demanded by e-shoppers too. The early Internet shoppers were computer-skilled bargain hunters, but this is no longer true. Today's online shoppers are motivated by the convenience of shopping from home at any time of the day or night, and having products delivered to their door. Ease of use is paramount and numerous customers give up and abandon their shopping baskets before they make it all the way through to the check-out pages (Jayawardhena et al., 2003). If the process takes too long, it may not only negate the service convenience advantage, but also anger the customer to the point that they never return.

THE SERVICES MARKETING MIX

THE OTHER 3PS

The traditional marketing mix of 4Ps (product, promotion, place and price) needs some expanding in order to cope with the distinctive qualities of services. In 1981, Bernard Booms and Mary Jo Bitner proposed the addition of a further 3Ps: **physical evidence**, participants (people) and **process** (cited in Bitner, 1990).

Service companies have an even greater need to build customers' trust in the products they offer than do goods providers. They need to reassure customers that the service will be a quality experience, especially as most of the time the service is bought untried. One obvious strategy to overcome fears associated with the service product's intangibility is to turn it into something more tangible. It is

Case study: ASOS

BA people and planes

physical evidence
the tangible aspects of a service, e.g. a bus ticket, shampoo (at the hairdressers); one of the 7Ps of services marketing

process
one of the 7Ps of the services marketing mix; the way in which a service is provided

e-focus: Going shopping

Why were Primark so slow to sell online? They didn't start trading online until summer 2013, by which time most of their competitors were well established on the Internet.

There are massive advantages to selling online: reaching new markets, saving money on expensive high street properties, employing fewer staff, centralising warehousing and improving stock control. A website is so much cheaper and easier to manage than a chain of shops. Primark's high-street rivals had both: they were bricks and clicks operations, not pure plays. Next's online sales were growing substantially while their offline sales stayed fairly level. Were Primark being admirably cautious or were they missing out?

Primark's sales performance had been remarkable. Their sales grew by nearly 25% in six just months in 2013. The clothes were flying off the shelves – and perhaps that was the issue. Primark's business model was based on cheap, disposable high fashion. Customers went back again and again because they wanted the latest thing – not things that would last. The store changed its ranges many times in a season. You got the look, wore it until you were tired of it, then went back to the store and got something else. Stock turnover was high – and that can be a nightmare for an online retailer.

One of the common complaints made about websites is that they often display items that are out of stock or, even worse, they send substitute products that customers just don't want. How could Primark keep a website up to date while continuing to constantly offer new clothes? They would have to change item listings hourly – and still they would be running the risk of upsetting their loyal customers. Perhaps it was better to have those customers come to the shop and browse. Let them see how cheap and lovely the clothes were – and buy multiple items because they couldn't decide which one they liked best.

In 2013, Primark asked Asos to trial an online store for them. Check the news and their website – who's running the show now?

generally recognised that the surroundings in which a service is delivered are a key part of customer satisfaction. The ambience of the restaurant, the plates, the music, the state of the toilets – all these things contribute as much to a meal out as does the quality of the food. These more tangible aspects of services are called physical evidence and they are important contributors to customer satisfaction. These things are largely within the control of the staff and so, if they are not pleasing to the customers, then it is often the fault of the staff. However, if the service environment is good, and seems well organised, customers are less likely to blame the staff for service failures, even when it is really their fault (Bitner, 1990).

The second P of this extended marketing mix is more commonly referred to as 'people' rather than as 'participants' (the original term). Delivery of a service is

Exhibit 7.5 The 7Ps of services marketing

P	Description	Examples
Product	The core service offering	Haircut
Promotion	Advertising and other tools	Student discount, press advertisement, business cards
Place	Where the service is delivered Intermediaries involved in service delivery	The salon franchises (e.g. Toni and Guy)
Price	The money part of the exchange	May be scaled according to stylist's experience
People	Who deliver the service and who receive it	Hair stylist, junior, receptionist, service consumer
Process	How the service is delivered	From booking the appointment to leaving the salon – and beyond
Physical evidence	The tangible aspects of the service	Shampoo

usually reliant on staff and so they are important, but the customers and consumers are also important factors affecting the delivery of the service and so they are included in the mix too.

Then there is the question of the actual provision of the service: the process. When a customer buys a product, such as a DVD, it is put in a bag, taken home and watched whenever the new owner feels like watching it. They do not actually see the product being made, they just buy the end result. However, a service only exists while it is being delivered. When a customer has a haircut, the only thing that gets taken home is a new look – and if it is a bad look, then little can be done about it. The actual process of hair cutting is the chargeable thing. Exhibit 7.5 illustrates the 7Ps of the service marketing mix.

The first 4Ps of the marketing mix were introduced in Chapter 6 and have their own individual chapters in this book. The extra 3Ps of services marketing are discussed individually below.

PEOPLE

It is the organisation's people who deliver the service, and their attitudes, skills and efficiency often determine how satisfied customers are. It is therefore important that customer-facing staff should be well trained, appropriately turned out and courteous. It is often people that build relationships rather than companies. (In some industries, employees have to sign a contract preventing them from working in the same area for a specified time period in an attempt to prevent them from taking customers with them when they leave.)

BA future pilot programme

If the service personnel are on the end of a telephone line, then it is a good telephone manner that is essential. If they are communicating by email, it is their written communication and efficiency that are important.

ethical focus: Google.cn (censored)

The world's favourite search engine has never thought of itself as a mainstream company. More traditional businesses have watched and waited for the company to come crashing down. Analysts thought its stock market floatation would fail but it was a success. IT gurus thought that search engines had a limited life and that eventually people would go straight to their favourite sites without searching, but they don't. Google has been a phenomenal success and, through it all, maintained that quirky, alternative image that made it so popular in the first place. That was until they expanded into China. Initially, they offered a Chinese language version of the site but, in 2005, they launched a Chinese site – censored by Google itself. The idea was that the new address would make the search engine easier and quicker to use. The company argued that, while removing search results was inconsistent with Google's mission, cutting the Chinese people off from information was even worse.

The Chinese government kept a tight rein on the Internet and on what users could access. The BBC news site was inaccessible and a search for the banned Falun Gong spiritual movement directed users to a string of negative articles. Initially, Google, whose motto is 'Do no evil', modified the version of its search engine in China to exclude these and other controversial topics such as the Tiananmen Square massacre, freedom for Tibet and independence for Taiwan. Later, a compromise was reached with Google posting a warning to Chinese users that the search they had entered was politically sensitive – but still the Chinese government cut them off.

This latest dispute comes amid a wider crackdown on Internet use in China including blockades on the use of 'virtual private networks', which help people access the web anonymously. The ruling Communist party wants to force Internet users to fully identify themselves to service providers, raising fresh concerns about freedom of speech in the country. Email, chat room and blogging services were not made available on the Chinese Google site because of concerns that the government might demand users' personal information. The US government had tried something similar but Google refused to pass data on. Not long before, Yahoo had been accused of supplying data to the Chinese authorities that was used as evidence to jail a journalist for ten years.

The censorship of the Chinese site provoked a backlash in Google's core Western markets. Google is now often compared to Microsoft because of its dominant position and power, and many people feel the company's values have been undermined. In its defence, Google says that much of this is based on misperceptions caused by inflammatory newspaper headlines. Asked whether he regretted the decision, Sergey Brin, one of Google's founders, admitted: 'On a business level, that decision to censor … was a net negative.'

What do you think? Given that Google could not have operated in China uncensored, should they have given up that market?

SOURCES: Halliday, 2013; Martinson, 2007.

Technology does not replace people completely in the delivery of most services, it just makes them more remote (and means that the company needs fewer of them). The loss of the personal touch means that it is even harder to build customer relationships. The Internet has the potential to remove all human interaction from transactions, reducing them to mere routines (Pincott and Branthwaite, 2000). Amazon and other online booksellers work really hard to build relationships with their customers. They personalise web pages and greet their returning visitors by name. However, there is growing evidence that too much personalisation is unpopular with some customers, who find it intrusive and who do not want so close a relationship with their bookseller (O'Connor and Galvin, 2001).

The quality of a service is largely dependent upon the skills of the people who provide it, and so the quality of the people who provide a service is even more important than the quality and skills of those who make products. Good, up-to-date training is important. Faulty products may be caught by quality control before they leave the factory, but there are no second chances with services. It is not possible to rewind and start again.

EXPAND YOUR KNOWLEDGE

Echeverri, P., Salomonson, N. and Åberg, A. (2012) 'Dealing with customer misbehaviour: employees' tactics, practical judgement and implicit knowledge', *Marketing Theory*, 12 (4): 427–49. Available from **http://mtq.sagepub.com/content/12/4/427** (accessed 25/07/13).

The 'People' element of the marketing mix refers to both customers and service providers. This paper looks at the range of ways in which frontline staff deal with difficult customers.

PROCESS

Process is the way in which the service is provided. Burger King is self-service whereas Pizza Express offers waiter service. The processes involved are different, although each scenario is capable of providing competitive advantage.

Boarding a BA flight at London City airport

How bookings are made and how customer enquiries are handled is part of the service process. This is an aspect of service management that is becoming increasingly outsourced and automated through ticket agents, and Internet and telephone sales. This outsourcing is potentially damaging for the customer relationship. Customers may actually build relationships with the firm's subcontractor rather than the firm itself. This makes the customers harder to retain in the future. Even worse, it has been known for companies that started as subcontractors to expand and take on the whole business themselves (e.g. plumbers contracted to a home services company could decide to take on the customers themselves).

The service encounter, which determines the perceived quality of the service, should be carefully thought through. Flow charts may help us to understand the process better (see Exhibit 7.6 below for an example).

History
of British
Airway
uniforms

PHYSICAL EVIDENCE

Although fundamentally intangible, most services do have a tangible element (just as goods, physical products, frequently have intangible service elements). Even dentists give you appointment cards and occasionally free toothpaste, and they certainly have instruments and a chair, and reception and waiting areas designed to look pleasant and comfortable.

ACTIVITY

Next time you use a service provider, whether it is a dentist, a hairdresser, a bar, a library or any other, note down all the items of physical evidence you can spot. What is their role in the service's marketing? What changes and improvements would you suggest?

These tangible aspects are known as physical evidence and are key in shaping the customers' perception of the quality of the service. Physical evidence takes many forms. It may be a peripheral product, e.g. the oil used in a car service or the soap provided in a hotel. It may be the surroundings in which the service is delivered – the ambience. This comprises décor, music, colour scheme, etc., which is particularly important in places of entertainment such as bars and restaurants (see servicescapes below for more on the environment in which a service is delivered). It may be a ticket or a contract, the physical proof that you have paid for the service. Tickets may sound trivial but they play a vital role in reassuring customers that their flight, theatre seat or concert is booked. There is no real need for an airline to issue a ticket, indeed some Internet-based airlines do not, but the ticket tells the customer where to go to catch the plane and is a chance to check that the flight is correctly booked. Even when booking on the Internet, airlines usually

Exhibit 7.6   Simple flowchart for a hairdressing service encounter

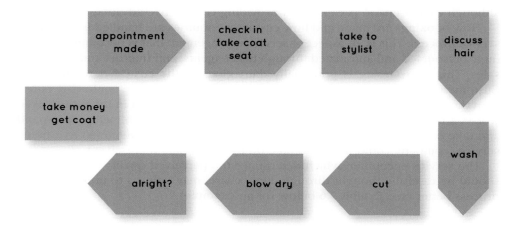

send a confirming email as, increasingly, do online retailers seeking to reassure customers that their order has been registered and will be dispatched.

Taking a visit to the hairdresser, for example (see Exhibit 7.6), the experience starts with the booking of the appointment. What impression is created by the person who answers the phone? Their courtesy and helpfulness, along with the availability of appointments, will be the first point at which the experience could go bad. When the customer arrives at the salon, the welcome they receive is important. This is the start of the service encounter and sets the tone for the rest of the experience. Each stage in the process must be carefully managed so as to meet customer expectations.

EXPAND YOUR KNOWLEDGE

Classic article

Grönroos, C. (1984) 'A service quality model and its marketing implications', *European Journal of Marketing*, 18 (4): 36–44.

This is one of the early articles highlighting the need to add issues of service quality to marketing thinking. A model of service quality is introduced which identifies perceived and expected service as important contributions to customers' overall perception of a service's quality.

Servicescapes

The environment in which the service is provided and experienced plays a significant part in the overall effect and assessment of the service. Consumers do not typically go to too much trouble in analysing individual components (unless prompted to do so), but rather experience a totality. Booms and Bitner (1981) proposed the concept of the **servicescape** to describe the total (and frequently complex) environment in which the service encounter takes place. They defined servicescape as:

Servicescapes

servicescape
the total environment in which a service is experienced

> The environment in which the service is assembled and in which the seller and customer interact, combined with tangible commodities that facilitate performance or communication of the service. (Booms and Bitner, 1981: 56)

The ambiance, décor, staffing, layout, accessories, and so on contribute to the total experience of the service encounter of a theatre or bar or other service offering. The environment is one that helps to define the service, distinguish it from competitor offerings and ultimately generate customer satisfaction or dissatisfaction. Take Abercrombie and Fitch, for example. This is not just any shop. Customers go there for the experience as much as for the clothes. The ultra trendy décor is inspired. Lighting is dim (apart from strategically placed spots so that shoppers can see the clothes on offer), music is loud (check their website for playlists), the assistants are all young and good-looking (they are 'cast' rather than hired), and bare-chested male models often adorn the entrance. There are queues both outside the shop and inside for the tills where people queue for up to an hour just to pay.

In a virtual or online situation, the environment becomes the website and the situation surrounding the computer in which the Internet is being viewed. Servicescapes thus become composites of what the service provider offers and what

Upmarket servicescape: a luxury service such as a trip on the Orient Express demands luxury surroundings.

the consumer brings to the service encounter. Again, this emphasises the potential for inconsistency in the service offering as different customers interact in different ways and at different times with the service being offered.

SERVICE QUALITY

Service companies need to build the customer's trust in the services they offer. They need to reassure the customer that the service will be a quality experience. Given that services are intangible and inconsistent (see the 'Characteristics of services' section on p. 289), it is all the more important to pay particular attention to the quality of service offered. Many papers and articles have been written on customer expectations and perceptions of service quality. Perhaps the most famous model used to measure service quality is SERVQUAL (Parasuraman et al., 1988), which employs five dimensions that contribute to service quality:

1   Tangibles (see physical evidence above)
2   Reliability (how dependable is the service, can its performance be relied upon?)
3   Responsiveness (speed of response and helpfulness of staff)
4   Assurance (confidence in the service offering, credibility and consistency)
5   Empathy (good customer understanding).

Customers are asked to complete a questionnaire that uses a series of questions related to the five dimensions listed above. Importantly, SERVQUAL has two parts: the first asks about the service in general and the second part asks the same questions about the specific service received. For example, if the service was a restaurant, Part A would be about restaurants of a similar type more generally and Part B would ask about the specific restaurant whose service quality was being measured. The reason why this is significant is that Part A gives an indication, a benchmark, against which the service being evaluated can be assessed. Gaps between expectations in general and the perception of the service offered in particular can be highlighted and improvements made where relevant. It is important to assess service quality against the right benchmarks. There would be little point in trying to assess the service quality of a small, local restaurant against what may be expected of a particularly high-class, expensive restaurant of the type run by celebrity chefs.

Customers and consumers do not expect perfection. Typically, they have a tolerance range and are willing to accept anything that falls within it. Things can and do go wrong. What is usually important is what the service provider is able to do about it and this is where service recovery comes in (see below).

Eurostar serves Michelin quality food

EXPAND YOUR KNOWLEDGE

Classic article

Parasuraman, A., Zeithaml, V.A. and Berry, L.B. (1988) 'SERVQUAL: a multiple-item scale for measuring consumer perceptions of service quality', *Journal of Retailing*, 64 (1): 12–40.

In the first article, the authors, experts and key researchers in the field of service quality, develop a scale for measuring service quality.

Parasuraman, A., Zeithaml, V.A. and Malhotra, A. (2005) 'E-S-QUAL: a multiple-item scale for assessing electronic service quality', *Journal of Service Research*, 7 (3): 213–33.

In this second article, the authors modify the scale to assess service quality on the web, which they use to measure service quality delivered on e-tailing sites.

BRANDING SERVICES

The idea of branding a service is a relatively new one, although there are a few notable exceptions that have been around for a while. Branding started in the world of the physical product, at a time when manufacturing processes had advanced to the stage at which consistency and quality could pretty much be assured. Services tend to be inconsistent, which makes them harder to brand. However, there are lots of famous service brands today: British Airways, Avis rent a car, HSBC, NHS (National Health Service), McDonald's, J. Walter Thomson, Wetherspoons, etc. Brands are seen as a badge of quality. Consumers have been educated by the physical products companies to understand this and so, in our age of the brand, service companies are able to switch things around and create brands that confer quality – rather than products of quality that therefore deserve brands.

ACTIVITY

Identify ten major service brands. It may help if you look at advertising in the press to jog your memory. Try to identify examples from a range of different sectors, such as travel/tourism, financial services, high street and online retailing, telephony and communications, etc. Consider the ways in which the companies have created and promoted their brands and what you think those brands represent. What message do they convey to customers?

A good brand not only reduces the customer's perceived risk, but actually enables a company to charge a higher price for its services.

customer focus: McLibel

McDonald's is one of the largest and best-known brands in the world. The company's revenues exceed those of a number of smaller, less well-off countries. There are over 25,000 McDonald's restaurants in the world and about 40 million people eat there every day. But not everyone loves McDonald's. Towards the end of the twentieth century, protests against their products, and the means of producing them, were growing steadily. Still, McDonald's fans outweighed the critics massively and so the company seemed secure.

Then, one day in a flat in North London, a postman and a gardener wrote a little pamphlet lambasting McDonald's for its unethical products, employment practices and means of production. They handed it out to passers-by on the local streets and got vegetarian restaurants to display it. The pamphlet was fairly innocuous, a little out of date and, according to Naomi Klein, clearly the product of a 'meat is murder' vegetarian attitude. It was therefore unlikely to worry the core McDonald's customer. McDonald's really should have let it go, but they didn't, they sued.

The two activists, Helen Steel and Dave Morris, had little money and were denied legal aid. In court, these two quite ordinary-looking people had to face a battery of top lawyers on the other side. The trial was the longest in the history of English law – and the newspapers gleefully reported on it every day. Helen and Dave's views, previously only communicated to the few Londoners who had bothered to read the pamphlet, were now written up with commentary by leading journalists and posted on the Web for the world to see and blog about. As for the original pamphlet, that had become a collector's item. More recently, in 2005, a documentary film was made about the McLibel two. Who won and who lost the case is largely irrelevant. This was one of the biggest corporate PR disasters of all time and its effects are still being felt – and seen – in McDonald's current marketing strategies.

For the full story of the McLibel trial, visit www.mcspotlight.org/case.

SOURCES: BBC News, 1999; Haig, 2003.

Dave Carroll on How United Airlines broke his guitar

SERVICE RECOVERY

Nobody can guarantee that all service encounters will run smoothly or as intended. Things go wrong. Trains, boats and planes run late and are delayed. A financial transaction may contain errors. The food may not taste as it should in a restaurant. The plumber may not fix a leak or an electrician may charge more than expected. These things may occur despite the best efforts of the service provider and may be simple but unfortunate mistakes.

One bad service encounter is a serious thing that may lead to a significant loss of custom, not only from the person directly affected but also from others if that person tells family and friends of the bad experience. Bad news travels fast! Consequently, service recovery is very important. If the service does go wrong, then the customer's complaint must be handled with great care. Good customer relationships are even more important to service businesses.

A complaint should be looked at as an opportunity to provide great service. It is often possible to turn the situation around and impress the customer after all. Bars and clubs may apologise profusely and take things off the bill or offer free drinks. Airlines may upgrade seats to first class or offer free tickets for another flight. The result can be a more satisfied customer than the one who received good service in the first place.

While poor service encounters need to be avoided, service recovery provides opportunities for greater customer satisfaction if dealt with well. Encouraging customers to state their complaints may seem counter-productive but analysis of complaints can be an important research activity that can avoid customer disappointment at the time of the service delivery and can be built into overall improvement plans to avoid future complaints by other customers.

Service recovery

EXPAND YOUR KNOWLEDGE

Hocutt, M.A., Bowers, M.R. and Donavan, D.T. (2006) 'The art of service recovery: fact or fiction', *Journal of Services Marketing*, 20 (3): 199–207.

As it is impossible to ensure all customer experiences are positive, it becomes all the more relevant to understand the importance of what companies do about poor customer experiences. Bad experiences may be spread to others through word-of-mouth, creating even lower levels of customer satisfaction and loyalty. Service recovery is, therefore, a critical concept. If handled well, service recovery can lead to greater levels of customer satisfaction.

SUMMARY

Services are aspects of the total product offering. While it is convenient to think of physical products and service products as different, in reality they are part of the same product continuum (Exhibit 7.3), in which services have greater intangibility than physical goods. From a marketing perspective, it is always wise to consider what services may be added to enhance physical products and what physical products can be used to enhance the service offering.

In most developed countries (MDCs) there has been a significant economic shift from manufacturing output to service provision. For this reason, the economies of MDCs place great reliance on services and on those companies that provide them. In marketing, therefore, it is important to recognise the distinctiveness, and key characteristics, of services. This chapter has highlighted the nature of services and identified seven particular characteristics: the customer gains some benefit from them; they are mostly intangible; they are time and place dependent (they cannot be stored); the service provider is an intrinsic part of the service itself; the consumer is also an intrinsic part of the service itself; services are inconsistent; and there is no resulting ownership of anything significant.

The interest in services marketing has led to an expansion of the traditional marketing mix from 4Ps to 7Ps by the inclusion of physical evidence, people and process. While the 7Ps clearly relate to services, many physical products also contain elements of services and therefore the 7Ps can be used for all types of products.

This chapter also highlighted a number of other key concepts, such as service convenience, service encounter, service quality, servicescape and service recovery as important considerations when marketing services. Branding is a strategy that evolved in the world of physical goods, but it has lately been successfully applied to services. Branding is covered in greater depth in Chapters 6 and 11.

CHALLENGES REVIEWED

Now that you have finished reading the chapter, look back at the challenges you were set at the beginning. Do you have a clearer idea of what's involved?

HINTS

- The UK and most other highly developed countries are service economies so talk about how much income service businesses generate, the jobs they create and how they facilitate other businesses.
- Service recovery – remember that people often think more highly of a company that treats them really well after a mistake has been made than they do of companies who have never made mistakes.
- There are a number of answers to this problem – an obvious one relies on offering a better service; think about peripheral products, processes and how to exploit the skills of your people (who have the advantage of being more local).
- This is about the intangibility of services and how that makes them high-risk purchases. You need to reduce the perceived risk somehow, e.g. by emphasising the tangible aspects of the service being offered (such as the hotel's facilities)

and the brand values of the airline, and/or by reference to previous satisfied customers. Do not forget about what guarantees and assurances you can offer.

READING AROUND

JOURNAL ARTICLES

Berry, L. (1980) 'Services marketing is different', *Business*, 30 (3): 52–6.

Echeverri, P., Salomonson, N. and Åberg, A. (2012) 'Dealing with customer misbehaviour: employees' tactics, practical judgement and implicit knowledge', *Marketing Theory*, 12 (4): 427–49. Available at: http://mtq.sagepub.com/content/12/4/427 (accessed 25/07/13).

Farquhar, J. and Rowley, J. (2009) 'Convenience: a services perspective', *Marketing Theory*, 9 (4): 425–38.

Grönroos, C. (1984) 'A service quality model and its marketing implications', *European Journal of Marketing*, 18 (4): 36–44.

Grönroos, C. (1997) 'From marketing mix to relationship marketing: towards a paradigm shift in marketing', *Management Decision*, 35 (4): 322–39.

Grove, S.J., Fisk, R.P. and Joby, J. (2003) 'The future of services marketing: forecasts from ten services experts', *Journal of Services Marketing*, 17 (2): 107–21. (A journal article that gave insights into the future of services marketing that you can read and compare with your knowledge of what has actually happened.)

Hocutt, M.A., Bowers, M.R. and Donavan, D.T. (2006) 'The art of service recovery: fact or fiction', *Journal of Services Marketing*, 20 (3): 199–207.

Parasuraman, A., Zeithaml, V. and Berry, L. (1988) 'SERVQUAL: a multiple-item scale for measuring consumer perceptions of service quality', *Journal of Retailing*, 64 (1): 12–40.

Parasuraman, A., Zeithaml, V. and Malhotra, A. (2005) 'E-S-QUAL: a multiple-item scale for assessing electronic service quality', *Journal of Service Research*, 7 (3): 213–33.

Shostack, G.L. (1984) 'Designing services that deliver', *Harvard Business Review*, 62 (Jan–Feb): 133–9.

BOOKS AND BOOK CHAPTERS

Chaffey, D. and Smith, P. (2012) 'Remix', in *Emarketing Excellence: Planning and Optimising Your Digital Marketing (Emarketing Essentials)*, 4th edn. Oxford: Routledge, Chapter 2.

Gummesson, E. (2008a) 'Exit services marketing – enter service marketing', in M.J. Baker and S. Hart (eds), *The Marketing Book*, 6th edn. Oxford: Butterworth Heinemann, Chapter 23.

Gummesson, E. (2008b) *Total Relationship Marketing*, 3rd edn. Oxford: Butterworth Heinemann.

WEBSITES

www.hospitalityassured.com – a website for an organisation (Hospitality Assured) dedicated to raising standards in the hospitality industry. Check out *The Standard* with its ten key steps to achieving service and business excellence.

SELF-REVIEW QUESTIONS

1. Define services. (See p. 282–3)
2. Why should marketers be more concerned in today's economies with the marketing of services? (See pp. 284–8)
3. What does the product continuum describe? (See p. 288)
4. Identify the seven characteristics that describe the nature of services. (See p. 289)
5. What is meant when we say that services are inconstant? (See pp. 296–8)
6. Dibb et al. propose a way of classifying services based on five criteria. What are they? (See p. 299)
7. What is meant by the consumer being part of the service? (See pp. 293–6)
8. What is 'service convenience'? (See p. 293)
9. What are the 7Ps? (See pp. 301–7)
10. Why is physical evidence important to the marketing of services? (See p. 306)
11. Why is it important to assess service quality and what is SERVQUAL? (See p. 308)
12. Why is service recovery an important concept? (See pp. 310–11)

Mini case study: Rock Planet

Read the questions, then the case material, and then answer the questions.

Questions

1 Identify and explain examples of the 7Ps at work in the case study.

2 What is Rock Planet doing well? Where does it fall down?

3 Using the 7Ps to guide you, recommend three improvements the restaurant can make. You should explain and justify your ideas.

The Rock Planet restaurant opened with a burst of publicity and a celebrity launch party just over a year ago. For the first few months it was the place to eat, although even then there were mutterings about slow service and rude waiters. Now it's a familiar London landmark, particularly popular with tourists who like the inexpensive set lunch menu. Its reasonable prices and rock star connections also attract the young for celebrations such as birthdays and leaving parties. The bouncers look formidable, but they've never been known to refuse anyone entrance unreasonably.

The restaurant is usually full, so diners wait in the bar, which is loud and crowded. A 1960s-style jukebox adds to the din. Customers get a Rock Planet buzzer, one of five designs (each a model of an artist), which lights up and sings when their table is ready. Flamboyant waiters shake cocktails in dramatic style against a backdrop of rock memorabilia. Electric guitars adorn the walls alongside pictures of their famous former owners. One of Jimi Hendrix's guitars has pride of place above the bar. To its right, under thick glass, is a scrap of paper on which John Lennon jotted some of the words to 'She Loves You'. On the left is Badly Drawn Boy's hat.

The rock décor is carried through to the restaurant, as is the music. All the waiters are young and dressed up. There are the teddy boy suits and the flared skirts and short socks of the 1950s, glam rock, grunge and some of the latest club styles. The restaurant serves fast food American style: hamburgers (and a veggie burger), fries, salads, chicken and ribs. It also does take-aways and delivers within a five-mile radius.

The biggest complaint is that food doesn't come to the table fast enough – something that is rubbed in by the lights that flash on a neon map of the USA to tell the waiters when an order is ready for collection. However, many diners find the friendly service makes up for their building hunger. And they tend to order more drinks. Home-delivery customers have to order at least two hours before they want the food.

Rock Planet is a place where people like to celebrate their birthdays and so the staff have a birthday routine. They dance through the restaurant carrying sparklers and then, when they reach the birthday table, they sing 'Happy Birthday' and encourage the rest of the diners to join in. The birthday boy or girl is presented with a cupcake with an everlasting candle on it and a small bag of inexpensive Rock Planet merchandise.

Further entertainment comes from the Rock Planet Moments. Each day, the manager chooses three dishes to be the special recommendations of the day. When the 20th order for that dish is delivered to a table, there is a fanfare and lights flash. The lucky diner gets the featured dish on the house and a complementary cocktail (alcoholic or non-alcoholic) of their choice. For the 50th order, the diner gets their whole meal free.

Very lucky diners may get to sit at a table next to the stars. The restaurant is owned by a group of well-known musicians who make a point of eating there as often as possible. Sometimes, you might even get 'Happy Birthday' sung by a megastar.

One of the biggest challenges for the management is keeping the place clean. It's a large, busy restaurant and lots of children eat there. Inevitably this means that there are spills and it can be hard to get them cleaned up while people are eating. The toilets are checked every hour but they still sometimes run out of towels or soap. The floor seems always in need of a clean. The problem in the bar is even worse. Staff have trouble fighting their way to tables to collect glasses and wipe down tabletops. A dropped tray of glasses means dangerous glass on the floor, so staff are reluctant to collect too many at once. Frequently the bar staff run out of clean glasses altogether.

Rock Planet has had some bad reviews recently. Critics say the food is unimaginative and of low quality, the restaurant too loud and too dirty, the service too slow and the waiters often get the orders, or the bill, wrong. But apparently the diners disagree – it's still packed out every night.

NOTE: Rock Planet and this case study are entirely fictional.

REFERENCES

BBC News (1999) *McLibel Duo Gain Part Victory*. Available at: **news.bbc.co.uk/1/hi/uk/308453.stm** (accessed 20/05/13).

Berry, L.L., Seiders, K. and Grewal, D. (2002) 'Understanding service convenience', *Journal of Marketing*, 66 (3): 1–17.

Bitner, M.J. (1990) 'Evaluating service encounters: the effects of physical surroundings and employee responses', *Journal of Marketing*, 54 (2): 69–82.

Booms, B.H. and Bitner, M.J. (1981) 'Marketing strategies and organization structures for service firms', in J.H. Donnelly and W.R. George (eds), *Marketing of Services*. Chicago: American Marketing Association, pp. 51–67.

Central Intelligence Agency (CIA) (n.d.) *The World Factbook*. Available at: **https://www.cia.gov/library/publications/the-world-factbook/index.html** (accessed 28/04/13).

Dibb, S., Simkin, L., Pride, W.M. and Ferrell, O.C. (2006) *Marketing Concepts and Strategies*, 5th edn. Boston: Houghton Mifflin.

Echeverri, P., Salomonson, N. and Åberg, A. (2012) 'Dealing with customer misbehaviour: employees' tactics, practical judgement and implicit knowledge', *Marketing Theory*, 12 (4): 427–49.

Farquhar, J.D. and Rowley, J. (2009) 'Convenience: a services perspective', *Marketing Theory*, 9 (4): 425–38.

Grönroos, C. (1984) 'A service quality model and its marketing implications', *European Journal of Marketing*, 18 (4): 36–44.

Grove, S.J., Fisk, R.P. and Joby, J. (2003) 'The future of services marketing: forecasts from ten services experts', *Journal of Services Marketing*, 17 (2): 107–21.

Haig, M. (2003) *Brand Failures: The Truth about the 100 Biggest Branding Mistakes of All Time*. London: Kogan Page.

Handy, C. (2002) *The Elephant and the Flea*. London: Arrow.

Hocutt, M.A., Bowers, M.R. and Donavan, D.T. (2006) 'The art of service recovery: fact or fiction', *Journal of Services Marketing*, 20 (3): 199–207.

Jayawardhena, C., Wright, L.T. and Masterson, R. (2003) 'An investigation of online consumer purchasing', *Qualitative Market Research: An International Journal*, 6 (1): 58–65.

Kotler, P. (2003) *Marketing Insights from A to Z: 80 Concepts Every Manager Needs to Know*. New York: John Wiley & Sons.

Kotler, P., Armstrong, G., Saunders, J. and Wong, V. (2001) *Principles of Marketing* (European edn). Harlow: Pearson Education.

Martinson, J. (2007) 'China censorship damaged us, Google founders admit', *The Guardian*, 27 January.

O'Connor, J. and Galvin, E. (2001) *Marketing in the Digital Age*. Harlow: FT/Prentice Hall.

Palmer, A. (2005) *Principles of Services Marketing*, 4th edn. Maidenhead: McGraw Hill.

Parasuraman, A., Zeithaml, V.A. and Berry, L.B. (1988) 'SERVQUAL: a multiple-item scale for measuring consumer perceptions of service quality', *Journal of Retailing*, 64 (1): 12–40.

Parasuraman, A., Zeithaml, V.A. and Malhotra, A. (2005) 'E-S-QUAL: a multiple-item scale for assessing electronic service quality', *Journal of Service Research*, 7 (3): 213–33.

Patents Office (n.d.) *Media Centre: Journalists' Guide to Intellectual Property*, UK government. Available at: **http://www.ipo.gov.uk/** (accessed 19/07/06).

Pincott, G. and Branthwaite, A. (2000) 'Nothing new under the sun?', *International Journal of Market Research*, 42 (2): 137–55.

Shostack, G.L. (1984) 'Designing services that deliver', *Harvard Business Review,* 62 (Jan–Feb): 133–9.

Topping, A. (2007) 'Man using laptop on garden wall charged with wireless theft', *The Guardian,* 23 August, p. 3.

Visit the companion website on your computer at **www.sagepub.co.uk/masterson3e** or MobileStudy on your Smart phone or tablet by scanning this QR code and gain access to:

- **Videos** to get a better understanding of key concepts and provoke in-class discussion.
- Links to useful **websites and templates** to help guide your study.
- Access **SAGE Marketing Pins (www.pinterest.com/sagepins/)**. SAGE's regularly updated **Pinterest** page, giving you access to regularly updated resources on everything from Branding to Consumer Behaviour.
- **Daily Grind podcast series** to learn more about the day-to-day life of a marketing **professional**.
- Interactive **Practice questions** to test your understanding.
- A **bonus chapter on Marketing Careers** to not only support your study, but your job search and future career.
- **PowerPoints** prompting key points for revision.

3rd edition

Rosalind Masterson & David Pickton

MARKETING
an introduction

Promotion (marketing communications)

8

PROMOTION CHALLENGES

The following are illustrations of the types of decision that marketers have to take or issues they face. *You aren't expected to know how to deal with the challenges now*; just bear them in mind as you read the chapter and see what you can find that helps.

- You are a marketing manager responsible for a new range of chilled fruit drinks. What budget would be appropriate for the launch?
- You run a small, specialist soft drinks firm. Your marketing budget is a tiny fraction of that of your major competitor and you certainly cannot afford television advertising. How will you get your brand noticed by potential customers?
- Disaster! You are the public relations manager for a major airline. The check-in staff and baggage handlers have gone on strike, leaving thousands of passengers stranded at an international airport. They are angry and frustrated. What will you do now? What will you do later when the crisis has passed?
- You are an advertising account manager and one of your clients is a multinational snack food manufacturer whose account is worth £30 million per year to your agency. In the past, most of that money has been spent on advertising during children's television programmes but recently there has been a consumer backlash against adverts, and junk foods, which target young children. You need to advise your client on their future marketing communications strategy.

Working as an Account Manager

INTRODUCTION

Promotion is one of the 4Ps of the marketing mix and an essential part of the total product offering. No matter how good your product is, if people do not *know* it is good, then they will not buy it. Equally, no matter how good your promotion is, if your product is poor, then people will not continue to buy it. Some form of promotion, or marketing communication, is necessary to make customers aware of the existence of the product, help create its brand identity, and persuade them to try it and even to incorporate it into their life.

To be effective, promotional activity must be based on a sound understanding of how and why products are bought, consumed or used and of current market trends. Clearly, this involves in-depth research as well as an understanding of the principles of buyer behaviour (see Chapters 5 and 3 respectively). Marketers segment their potential audiences (using the techniques discussed in Chapter 4) in order to select the best group(s) at which to aim their communications.

DEFINITIONS

In marketing, promotion, another term for marketing communications, refers to communication designed to persuade others to accept ideas, concepts or things; to motivate customers and consumers to take action. It rarely results in an immediate sale. Promotion's role is to move people closer to a purchase decision.

This chapter will examine the reasons why it is necessary for organisations to communicate, who they communicate with and how they can get their message across. It will also consider the regulatory environment within which marketers operate (with particular reference to UK regulatory bodies). The chapter concludes with a brief section on setting marketing budgets.

THE PROMOTION MIX

There are many promotional tools or activities and the traditional way of categorising all of them is as the **promotion mix**, which (traditionally and at its most basic level) comprises:

- advertising
- public relations (PR)
- sales promotions
- personal selling.

Just as there are 4Ps in the marketing mix, product, promotion, place and price, there are also four main elements to the promotional mix (although unfortunately they do not all start with the letter P).

Although it is sometimes used as yet another alternative term for promotion or marketing communications, in its stricter sense the term advertising describes any **paid** form of **non-personal** presentation of ideas, goods and services by an **identified** advertiser. Most advertising consists of paid-for promotional messages carried by the mass media (TV, radio, press, cinema, posters, Internet).

Public relations (PR) uses different activities designed to promote goodwill and enhance and protect reputations. These activities may include providing news and feature stories for the media, running events, sponsorship, or building relationships with influential individuals and groups. PR may use the same media (e.g. television, radio, the Internet) as advertising but in a very different way. While advertisers buy space or airtime and control (within the regulations) what goes into it, PROs (Public Relations Officers) have to persuade journalists to include stories about their brands and cannot control what those journalists say.

Sales promotions are short-term, special offers and other added-value activities intended to induce buyers to buy, or try, a product. Such offers include two for the price of one, money-off coupons and instant wins.

Personal selling, as the name suggests, is the most personal of the promotional tools. It involves persuading customers of the benefits of products and services, usually on a one-to-one basis. Such personal communication is costly – imagine sending a salesperson out to sell single bottles of shampoo to individuals. Consequently, it is an approach favoured in business-to business (b2b) sales where the order quantities are higher. Similarly, it would be a waste of television advertising if it was used to sell ball bearings as the vast majority of those who saw the ad would not be interested, so it would be more efficient to send sales representatives to the few companies that might want to buy them.

Different techniques are needed in different markets, in different situations and to achieve different ends. This chapter will examine those techniques and their effective use.

MARKETING COMMUNICATIONS OR PROMOTION?

The terms, 'marketing communications' and 'promotion' mean the same thing. Promotion is the older name and fits within the mnemonic the 4Ps. In this chapter (as in life), the two terms will be used interchangeably.

Each tool in the promotion mix has certain strengths that will be outlined below. Some organisations – e.g. Nike, Cadbury and Volkswagen – emphasise advertising and public relations efforts in their promotional mixes. Others, especially those engaged in b2b marketing, choose personal selling as a significant promotion mix ingredient. Smith & Nephew, Johnson & Johnson and 3M sell healthcare products to hospitals and all tend to favour personal selling in these situations. This is, in part, because of the more complex nature of the decision-making (see Chapter 3) and the need to identify and nurture different stakeholders.

MANAGING PROMOTION

A key part of a marketing communications manager's job is to plan and coordinate the promotional mix elements:

- setting objectives for what the elements are intended to accomplish
- setting budgets that are sufficient to support the objectives
- designing campaigns that will achieve those objectives
- checking the results of the campaign regularly to ensure that it is on track to achieve the marketing communications objectives (evaluation and control).

CAMPAIGNS

A campaign is a series of coordinated marketing activities designed to achieve specific objectives, e.g. to reposition a product or to educate people about its correct use or to raise a brand's awareness levels. Each of these objectives needs a different set of promotional activities. Educating people about products' use is quite different

Mars
re-launch
campaign

from raising brand awareness: different messages, different techniques. Managers must decide what emphasis to put on interpersonal versus mass communication, whether to select a push strategy or a pull strategy, and how much importance to place on each of the different promotion mix elements.

As well as being internally coordinated, all a company's campaigns should fit with each other. Managers need to be able to think in a joined-up way. It is counter-productive to have one campaign's message or feel contradicting another one's. Consequently, the design of campaigns starts higher up. It starts with the development of overall **marketing communications objectives** and a promotional strategy.

MARKETING COMMUNICATIONS OBJECTIVES

An objective is something that an organisation wants to achieve: a target to aim for. Well-chosen marketing communications techniques are capable of achieving many positive things for a company, but clearly it makes sense to think through exactly what the organisation wants to achieve before designing, and then spending money on, a campaign. The objectives of a Ryvita campaign were to 'reposition crispbread from diet to delicious healthy food whilst normalising the product and the user' (White, 2013). Heinz's Classic Soup campaign won a silver award in the Design Business Association's (DBA) 2009 Design Effectiveness Awards. The campaign's objectives were to:

- reinvigorate the brand
- 'remind consumers that Heinz provides good, nourishing food made with wholesome ingredients'
- 'make the range feel relevant to a contemporary audience and get consumers to "fall in love" with Heinz again'
- get people to eat more soup.
  (DBA, 2009)

Without clear-cut objectives it is impossible to know whether a campaign was a success or not. It really is not enough to produce an attractive campaign that people like, or even one that wins awards. Companies expect their advertising to help their business. They expect it to achieve something worthwhile.

THE IMPORTANCE OF TARGETED OBJECTIVES

A strategy is the means by which a firm tries to achieve its objectives. Objectives are fundamental in providing direction for an organisation and can only do this if they are clearly stated, compatible with each other, known, understood and followed (Pickton and Broderick, 2004). A marketing manager must set the promotion objectives before deciding on the best promotion mix.

In order to set realistic promotional objectives, the firm needs a clear statement of its target market. However, a promotional campaign may not be aimed at the entire market; it may even be aimed at people who are not part of the market at all. Promotional campaigns reach out to **target audiences**.

TARGET AUDIENCE OR TARGET MARKET?

Target markets are customers (i.e. the people who buy goods and services). The term is also used to refer to consumers or users (who may or may not have

target audience
the people, or organisations, that are selected to receive communications

bought the product themselves). However, in marketing communications, everyone involved in the purchase decision, however indirectly, needs to be understood and addressed. The people that organisations want to *talk* to are target *audiences* and may include potential agents, distributors, retailers, opinion leaders and formers, journalists, employees, the government, present and potential shareholders – anybody who is important to the organisation. So the term 'audience' is potentially much broader and may, or may not, include the market. Markets are places where things are bought and sold, while audiences are the people that communicators want to listen to them.

For example, Domino Pizza's target market is broad and encompasses families, singles and students, but the target *audience* for a very successful campaign was:

- customers of competitor stores (specifically Pizza Hut)
- lapsed or occasional pizza eaters who have (through experience) low expectations of home delivered pizza.
  (Makin, 2002)

The target audience is often more specific and narrower than the target market and closely targeted communications tend to be more effective:

Adidas'
target
audience

> Products are sold to target **markets**.
> Marketing communications are addressed to target **audiences**.

A good deal of marketing has international dimensions. Although not all organisations are global, many audiences are worldwide and major brands try to maintain consistency in their worldwide positioning. How disappointing to visit a foreign country and find that your favourite designer is considered downmarket, or that your beer is thought to be poor quality. Marketers have to take a varied international audience into account when designing their marketing communications strategies.

PROMOTIONAL STRATEGY

There is no one clear definition of the term 'strategy'. Over the years strategy has acquired a number of meanings, and academics and practitioners are not in total agreement. Broadly speaking, Engel et al. (1994) used the term 'promotional strategy' to refer to a controlled, integrated programme of communication methods designed to present an organisation and its products or services to prospective customers, to communicate need-satisfying attributes, to facilitate sales, and thus to contribute to long-term profit performance. Pickton and Broderick (2004) emphasised the need to consider a range of target audiences when determining strategy and not just to focus on customers.

PUSH AND PULL STRATEGIES

One way of understanding the different promotional emphases of various organisations is to think of them as push or pull. Who are the target audiences? If the campaign is directed towards consumers or end-users, then it is hoped that by demanding the product, they will pull it through the supply chain. If, on the other hand, the campaign is directed at intermediaries, e.g. retailers, then its purpose is to persuade them to push the products.

push strategy
a promotional
strategy aimed
at distribution
channels

pull strategy
a promotional
strategy aimed at
end customers or
consumers

In some companies, marketing efforts and tactics are aimed primarily at the trade, such as wholesalers, distributors and retailers. In this case, advertising and sales promotion, selling effort, as well as pricing strategies, are aimed at generating trade interest and demand for the company's products. This promotional focus is designed to push a product into, and through, the distribution channel. **Push strategies** are common in the industrial sector and also the field of medicine. Medical sales representatives from companies such as Astra-Zenica promote (push) products very strongly to general practitioners and support this push with promotional material from the marketing department. This promotional material may include brochures and branded merchandise. Next time you visit your doctor, observe the different promotional materials in the surgery, such as posters, post-its, pens and mouse mats.

Conversely, a **pull strategy** focuses a company's marketing efforts on the final customer or consumer. The objective of this strategy is to generate sufficient consumer interest and demand for the company's products to be pulled through the distribution channels. The goal is to generate demand at the retail level in the belief that such demand will encourage retailers and wholesalers to stock the product.

Although we see push and pull as distinctive strategies, it is usually not a case of deciding between one or the other, but more of determining where the balance should be. An effective marketing communications strategy often uses a combination of push and pull.

The strategy is implemented through the marketing communications mix, which is considered in more detail later.

THE MARKETING COMMUNICATIONS PROCESS

An understanding of the communications theory that underpins the marketing communications process is helpful in ensuring that messages arrive safely. Schramm (1955) is attributed with first modelling the communications process and the model presented in Exhibit 8.1 is based on his initial, simple model.

There are two principal participants (or sets of participants) in the communications process:

1   The sender is the originator or source of the message. This is the company which is doing the advertising, such as BT or Coca-Cola. Although in practice, agents or consultants may actually do a lot of the work on behalf of the sender.
2   Receivers are the people to whom the message is sent, the target audience(s).

Exhibit 8.1   Simple communications model – after Schramm (1955)

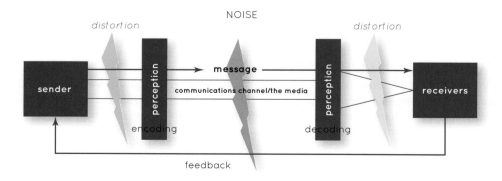

Advertising will be used for the purposes of this explanation; however, the model is applicable to all forms of marketing communications. The advertiser wishes to communicate with a chosen target audience. The message is the actual information and impressions it wishes to send. This message is coded into an advert by the agency's creative team (they make the ad). It can then be sent. The 'media/channels' are the means used to carry the message, e.g. in the case of advertising this may be by television, radio, cinema, etc.

The challenge of marketing communications is to ensure that this process communicates the right message, in the right way, to the right people, in the right place, at the right time. Communication only actually takes place when the receiver understands the message and, ideally, acts upon it. This may not be a physical action – it may be a change of attitude (a frequent objective of advertising) – but something happens to the receiver as a result of receiving the message – even if it is only an increase in knowledge.

Senders are not usually telepathic. They cannot transmit pure thought so they have to put the message across through a commonly understood code, such as words, pictures, symbols and/or actions. Senders *encode* messages, using their skills and resources (e.g. film studios or printers). Encoding is the first step in the communications process. Ideally, the sender's intended message is transmitted, although in reality this does not always occur. Have you ever tried, unsuccessfully, to express an idea? You know what you intended to say, but the words that came out of your mouth failed to reflect your thoughts? Media advertising is an expensive business. An advert that does not come across well to its target audience is a major waste of time and money. That is why agencies, and their clients, put so much into getting them right.

Messages that are encoded badly get distorted and are not received correctly: distortion is a coding problem, a lack of skill, or care, either on the part of the sender (who encodes) or the receiver (who decodes).

The message may get distorted at either end of the channel. For example, the press release may be badly written, the prize for the sales promotion poorly selected, the salesperson might be disagreeable that day or the problem may lie with the poor language skills of the receiver or their lack of attention. In marketing communications, it is up to the sender to try to ensure that the way the message is coded is suitable for the intended target audience.

Distortion is not the only barrier to communication. There are a number of other things that may get in the message's way: poor television reception, graffiti on a poster, a computer going down, crackle on a telephone line, the receiver having a headache – this is all noise.

There is no excuse for poor coding by professional communicators such as advertising agencies. However, decoding happens at the other end of the channel as well and the receivers' decoding skills are less certain. Whether or not the message is correctly received depends upon the receivers' receipt and interpretation of the message transmitted. The sender hopes that the message received is identical to the one transmitted, but this is not always the case.

Levels of coding skill and external noise are easier to deal with than the distortion that comes from perceptual problems. Perception is how we see the world. Our perception is built up over the years through all of our experiences. Without it, we would be unable to interpret the world around us. Think of a newborn baby. It knows nothing and may well misinterpret its world. How puzzling those new shiny toys must be – especially the ones that make its mother shout when it reaches

distortion
a barrier to communication; poor coding skills, e.g. a badly devised ad or a badly worded sales promotion, that prevent the message from being received correctly

noise
a barrier to communication, usually from an external source

for them. There is no understanding, no ability to interpret external stimuli, without learning and experience. As no two people's lives are exactly the same, then their perceptions will not be the same either, and this can cause communication problems. The person whose experience includes severe seasickness may view a boat sailing out to sea with dread, while others might see that as an invitation to relaxation or adventure. So be careful what images you use in your advertisements.

Individual perceptions are influenced by selective attention and selective distortion (see Chapter 3).

After the decoding process, the receiver responds to the message. The receiver may show interest in the message and may accept everything that is communicated without question. However, the receiver may also react unfavourably to the communication or may totally ignore it. From the marketer's perspective, the message will not be effective unless it elicits the desired response. This may be covert, such as a favourable attitude change towards a product or increased awareness or knowledge of a product. Sometimes the response is overt, such as redeeming a coupon, or returning a form to order a product or to receive more information. The sender needs to know that the message has been understood: **feedback** is the response from a receiver back to the sender.

feedback
a part of the two-way communications process whereby the receiver sends a message back to the original sender

Feedback can sometimes, especially with advertising, be hard to pick up. The change in the receiver may be slight, e.g. an increased awareness of the shampoo on offer. The original Schramm model portrayed one-way communications, where there was no feedback. This is no longer accepted as correct. Communication must be two-way. It should be a dialogue, not a monologue.

This two-way communication may be asymmetric or symmetric. In two-way asymmetric communication, there is communication from a sender to a receiver with little or delayed feedback, producing a non-direct dialogue, such as in most mass media advertising. In two-way symmetric communication, there is a direct dialogue between the sender and the audience who play equal parts in the communication. Two-way symmetric communication has been the goal of PR since Grunig and Hunt first proposed their highly influential four models of public relations in 1984. Traditionally, personal selling activities have provided this major benefit. Today, new technologies are creating new opportunities for better interactivity and near immediate response. Interactive digital television, the Internet and telephone call centres are aiding this process. While this improved two-way communication can clearly aid better understanding, it is still questionable just how equal and balanced any form of persuasive communication, even PR, can really be. Will one party always have more say than the other?

The more comprehensive models of the communications process regard communication as an exchange process in which thoughts or ideas are the things exchanged.

INFLUENCING CUSTOMERS

Influencing and encouraging buyers to accept or adopt goods, services and ideas are among the key objectives of marketing communications. In fact, some argue that the ultimate effectiveness of promotion is determined by its impact upon product adoption among new buyers or increases in the frequency of current buyers' purchases. A single promotional activity rarely causes an individual to buy a previously unfamiliar product and so, to have realistic expectations about what promotion can do, product adoption should be viewed not as a one-stop process, but as a multi-stage process.

EXPAND YOUR KNOWLEDGE

Classic book

Grunig, J. and Hunt, T. (1984) *Managing Public Relations*. London: Thomson Learning.

Still considered by many PR people to be the foundation for PR theory, this book sets out four models of PR:

- Press agency/publicity (one-way communications)
- Public information (one-way communications)
- Two-way asymmetric communications
- Two-way symmetric communications.

In Chapter 3, the six stages of the consumer buying process were identified as:

1   Need or problem recognition
2   Information search
3   Evaluation of alternatives
4   Purchase decision
5   Purchase
6   Post-purchase evaluation.

Throughout this process the consumer deliberately, or unconsciously, adopts various attitudes, or has various mind-states, in relation to the product/service offer. The nature and objectives of marketing communications need to alter to take account of these in order to encourage the correct purchase, or re-purchase, decision.

Several models, known as hierarchy of effects models, have been developed to illustrate the activities required to take a consumer from the state of unaware-ness about the product to one of willingness to purchase the product or service.

AIDA is a simple model commonly used by marketing professionals. According to this model, potential buyers go through a psychological or behavioural process before purchasing a product. AIDA is an acronym for:

Attention
Interest
Desire
Action

hierarchy of effects models describe the stages individuals go through when making a purchase or consumption decision

AIDA a sequential model showing the steps that marketing communications should lead potential buyers through: attention, interest, desire, action

It incorporates various psychological processes. Attention (or awareness) is a cognitive process. It relates to how and what we think and believe. Interest and desire are affective processes; they relate to our emotions, how we feel about something. Finally, action takes the form of manifest behaviour (i.e. actually doing something) – we buy the product or tell others about it.

AIDA AND SETTING PROMOTIONAL OBJECTIVES

Although a simple model, AIDA is very helpful when setting promotional objectives and is a good way to demonstrate how these sequential models work.

AIDA Model

Attention

In the initial stage, say for a new product, the promotion objective is to get the product seen and, ideally, talked about by the target audience. For example, an effective advertisement must grab attention from the very first viewing or hearing. If the target audience's attention has not been caught, then whatever follows will be of little use.

Interest

After the audience's attention has been gained, their interest in the product must be aroused. This may be achieved by creating an understanding of the benefits of the product in relation to the personal need(s) of customers, and focusing the message on how the product or service being advertised actually meets these needs. Much modern advertising tries hard to be entertaining and to generate interest in the product behind the advert in that way. The main objective of the interest stage is to motivate individuals to want information about the product: its features, uses, advantages, disadvantages, price and location, etc.

Desire

At this stage, a company tries to appeal to the target audience's wish to fulfil some need. While it is usually best to aim advertisements (or other promotional material) at moving the audience from one stage to the next, interest in, and desire for, the product can often be established simultaneously.

Action

As the name suggests, the action stage aims to get individuals to do something such as purchase the product or service. This is often helped by making it easier for the potential customer to take action. This can be done by giving a phone number, an Internet address or closing with a note saying that credit cards are accepted. Personal selling and sales promotion are particularly effective at closing sales, the latter by offering an additional incentive to buy, e.g. money off or a free gift with purchase.

AIDA AND THE PROMOTION MIX

Think for a moment about the sequential nature of AIDA. It comprises a number of stages that follow on, one from the other. However, it is not always necessary for organisations to start promotional campaigns at the top of the hierarchy, at the attention or awareness stage. The product may have been around for a while and everyone has already heard of it.

The choice of promotion mix will depend on where in the response hierarchy the organisation wishes to direct its promotional effort. For example, if the firm's primary objective is to catch the audience's attention, then advertising is often the most effective promotional tool. Advertising can also be very effective at creating and holding interest, and at reinforcing positive aspects of the product to develop post-purchase satisfaction. PR is also extensively used to raise interest levels in a product. Personal selling tends to be effective at creating desire and motivating purchase. Sales promotion is good at closing the sale, for example by making a time-limited offer: 'half price this week only'.

Exhibit 8.2 illustrates the uses of the various promotional tools. Hierarchical models such as AIDA describe the step-by-step process through which individuals move when exposed to marketing communications; these encompass the cognitive (thinking), affective (feeling) and conative (doing) steps.

Russell Colley (1961) developed a hierarchy of effects model known as **DAGMAR** (Define Advertising Goals for Measured Advertising Results). In this he stressed the importance of setting objectives against each element within the hierarchy (or at least those that were relevant to the promotional campaign being devised). Although his focus was on advertising objectives, his ideas are equally appropriate for consideration across all marketing communication tools (see Exhibit 8.3).

DAGMAR
acronym for Defining Advertising Goals for Measured Advertising Results, a hierarchy of effects model describing the stages individuals go through when making a purchase, or consumption, decision

Exhibit 8.2   AIDA and the promotion mix

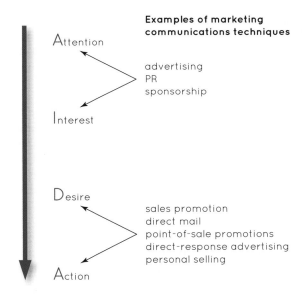

Exhibit 8.3   DAGMAR: a hierarchical model

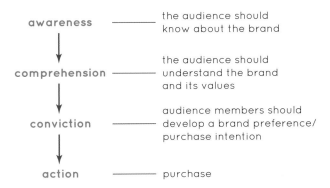

Making of Old
Spice Man
commercial

Behind
the Old
Spice Man
Advert

paid media
channels of
communication in
which advertisers buy
space, e.g. television,
magazines, social
media sites

owned media
channels of
communication
which belong to the
client company, e.g. a
company website or
in-house newsletter

earned media
channels of
communication
outside marketers'
direct control that
are used to talk
about brands, issues,
organisations;
traditionally PR
media, e.g. newspaper
columns/editorials
(**not** advert space),
an individual's blogs,
individual social media
pages

reach
the number (or
percentage) of the
target audience
exposed to an advert
or other promotion
during a campaign;
also referred to
as coverage or
penetration

viral marketing
an electronic form
of word-of-mouth
marketing

EXPAND YOUR KNOWLEDGE

Classic article

Colley, R. (1961) *Defining Advertising Goals for Measured Advertising Results.* New York: Association of National Advertisers.

Colley introduced DAGMAR to the world in this article. He argued that advertising outcomes can be improved by firstly recognising that a hierarchical process of communications is involved, then setting appropriate advertising goals related to this process. (Others have criticised Colley's specific hierarchy and, even, whether any specific hierarchy exists that covers all eventualities.)

MARKETING COMMUNICATIONS MEDIA

Over the last few decades, massive technological change has changed our media habits dramatically. Mass media had barely come of age when it was fragmented by the introduction of hundreds of TV channels, radio stations and magazines. Then the Internet took hold and even the traditional notions of publisher and reader were challenged.

There are a number of ways of classifying modern media but perhaps one of the most useful, and marketing-oriented, is POEM: **P**aid, **O**wned or **E**arned **M**edia.

The term paid media refers to channels for which the brand has to pay a fee to the media owner, e.g. TV or press. This includes traditional mass-media advertising where there is a charge for ad space and some hybrid marketing communications techniques ('hybrid' here refers to a blend of advertising and PR) such as sponsorship. The sponsor pays a fee for the privilege of being associated with the thing being sponsored (the sponsorship 'vehicle') such as a sports team or an event. (For more on sponsorship, see below.)

The main advantages of paid media lie in its access to a large audience, its broad creative scope and its relatively good control over how and when the brand is presented to its target audience. The main disadvantage is that these paid media have become increasingly cluttered with brands and messages, making it hard to stand out from the crowd and be heard above all the noise.

Owned media are owned and controlled by the brand owners themselves, e.g. corporate websites, blogs, newsletters and brochures. Clearly brand owners have almost absolute control over how the brand appears and what is said about it in these media, but they may not have the reach or gain the attention that paid media can.

The content of earned media is controlled by individuals or organisations who may be customers, consumers or critics. Brands have always tried to get customers to recommend their products to friends and to talk about them enthusiastically. More recently, they have aimed for greater brand engagement by trying to ensure consumers see brands as intrinsic parts of their lives or essential to their lifestyle. Word of mouth (WOM) and viral marketing have been valuable techniques for a long time but the advent of social media, such as Facebook and YouTube, has opened up new opportunities for brands to reach farther, faster. WOM and viral have to be **earned**, they do not happen automatically. (See below for word of mouth and viral marketing examples.)

The main disadvantage of earned media lies in the brand's lack of control over what is said about it. This has been a major worry for many brand owners who fear that the brand's image will be hijacked by bloggers and social media networkers who may poke fun at it or show it in a bad light. In practice, this rarely happens. Most of the tribute adverts on sites like YouTube really are tributes. One of the most popular examples is the Cadbury's gorilla advert which sparked numerous copies showing the gorilla playing to different music and even inspired a sketch on *The Sunday Night Project* TV show in which Lily Allen and Alan Carr mimicked the Cadbury's eyebrow-dancing ad before co-host Justin Lee-Collins, in a partial gorilla suit, started that famous drum roll: plugs for two Cadbury's ads in one show. Even when people do poke fun at an ad, or lambast it, as they did with Brad Pitt's ad for Chanel No. 5, the resultant publicity may not be harmful.

Media planners aim to blend these three types of media to broaden the campaign's reach, create a buzz and deepen audience engagement. One of the most successful examples of this is the Old Spice Man campaign starring Isaiah Mustafa. The Old Spice Man started life in **paid** media as a TV advert (first aired during the Superbowl in the USA). On YouTube, the original ad generated nearly 45 million views (and still rising) and the shorter follow-up ads also gained millions of views. However, it was the buzz that this advert created that really set it apart. A coordinated social media campaign included the opportunity to ask the Old Spice Man questions such as 'Do you have any experience in taming wild whales?' and get a personal, videoed response from him on YouTube. Additionally, the advert sparked numerous tribute adverts as fans cast themselves, or others, in the role. Some of these also gained millions of views (see YouTube for examples). This is **earned** media. Finally, the company's own YouTube Channel and website carried the ads and related materials. Those would be classed as **owned** media.

An important point to understand about this classification of paid, owned and earned media is that the classification is dependent upon how the medium is used rather than the medium itself. A TV advert is using paid media, a TV interview on a chat show is using earned media and, if the company has its own TV channel, that is owned media. An advert placed on someone else's website or on a search engine such as Google is using paid media, a brand communication on the brand's own website or social media page is using owned media, while a mention in someone else's blog or an online review, or a sharing on social media, e.g. a re-tweet, is classified as earned media.

POEM is not the only way to classify media. Changes in technology keep changing the media landscape and marketers look for new ways to make sense of it and plan their communications. For example, in 2012 the IPA (Institute of Practitioners in Advertising) and the Future Foundation proposed other ways to differentiate between media:

```
named     --------------  not-named
screen    --------------  non-screen
two-way   --------------  one-way
```

Named or not-named refers to whether or not the communication is personal or impersonal. Direct marketing communications are addressed to an individual by name. TV, outdoor digital screens, websites, cinema, etc. are all screen, whereas print, flyers, mail are not-named.

Screen and non-screen puts TV with the Internet, which may be useful given the increasing convergence between the two (watching TV on your laptop or tablet, accessing the Internet via the TV). Screen would also include cinema and outdoor digital. Content may be similar for all these screens. Non-screen would be everything else which may be rather too broad as a category. The usefulness of this seems to lie more with looking at all the screen technologies together.

Two-way and one-way is an interesting classification. It has long been accepted that the most effective communication is two-way, i.e. there is a response from the audience. Mass media advertising has frequently been criticised for being one-way communication. Modern technology makes audience response so much easier and these response mechanisms are built in to some media, e.g. Internet sites, digital TV and mobile marketing, while they are harder or impossible on others, e.g. cinema, radio.

MEDIA CLASSES

A media class is a type of media, e.g. television or press. Media classes can be broken down into different media vehicles, e.g. specific programmes or titles. Exhibit 8.4 lists examples of the media currently available – although new ones appear all the time. Of the traditional advertising mass media, press takes in the most money despite being a less expensive medium than TV – there is just so much more of it. The picture is constantly changing, though. New digital TV channels keep appearing. These are cheaper vehicles than terrestrial television and can be targeted more closely as many channels are very specialist and so appeal to clearly defined audiences, e.g. a home improvement channel is clearly a good place to advertise DIY equipment.

The Internet, along with other digital technologies such as iTV and mobile phones, is still often referred to as the new media – although digital media or e-media is becoming a more accepted term as the newness wears off. The technology behind digital media has a number of advantages:

- interactivity
- faster response times
- more direct communications
- greater possibilities for interaction between audience members and user-generated content
- the ability to put the message across in a more sophisticated way.

ambient media
unusual out-of-home (OOH) media, e.g. lasers, tickets, promotional clothing, tattoos, pavements

The term **ambient media** was originally applied to unusual outdoor media. It is becoming more widely used now to describe any outdoor media, although some ambient media may actually be indoors. Used in this broader way, the original, and still the biggest, ambient media are poster sites. Advertising is getting everywhere and the discovery of new media possibilities is a great source of differentiation and a way to cut through the noise created by communications overload. More unusual ambient media include cars, laser light shows, people, tickets, stairs, postcards, balloons and skywriting.

ACTIVITY

Take a walk around your local high street or shopping centre. Note down the different types of ambient media you find.

Exhibit 8.4   Examples of promotional media

TV	Posters	Underground stations
Newspapers	Magazines	Video games
Cinema	Buses	Trains
Video	Taxis	Telephones
CD/DVD	Search engines	Mobile phones
Radio	Websites	Cars/vans/lorries
Email	Directories	DOOH screens (Digital Out Of Home)
Shop fronts	Escalator steps	Beer mats
Pavements	Post-it notes	Promotional gifts
Sides of buildings	Packaging	Clothing, e.g. T-shirts
Skywriting	Blimps	Road signs
Tickets	Notice boards	Blogs and wikis
Outdoor screens	Windows	Bar optics
Social networking sites	Rubbish bins	Bus shelters
Laser projection	Students' heads (transfers or shaved into hair)	Anything else that could carry a promotional or persuasive message

e-focus: Zipping and zapping

Television advertising just isn't as effective as it used to be. There are so many adverts that audiences just tune out – sometimes literally. If viewing a programme as it is aired, they use the remote control to zap and channel hop to a station where there are no ads. When watching recorded programmes, they zip through the adverts and watch only the programme.

There is a silver lining here for advertisers and it comes in the form of TV sponsorship.

Think about it. When you're zipping through the ads, what are you looking out for so that you know when to stop? Is it the sponsor's message (ident) perhaps?

Another way the TV companies are fighting back is by placing ads at the beginning of the playback on their online catch-up services. These can't be fast-forwarded, and viewers have to watch them before the programme will start.

WORD OF MOUTH AND VIRAL MARKETING

One of the most powerful ways to transmit a message is through word of mouth/ viral marketing. When friends and relatives talk positively about a product or service, it sounds so much more convincing than when the words come from an actor on television who has been paid. Some adverts are deliberately designed to stimulate word of mouth, to get people talking, tweeting, blogging and posting on social media sites. T-Mobile have been particularly good at this in recent years. It started with a flashmob on Liverpool station (**www.youtube.com/ watch?v=VQ3d3KigPQM**) and progressed to Josh's band (**www.youtube. com/watch?v=jzRF10wwdvo**) and the Royal wedding (**www.youtube.com/ watch?v=Kav0FEhtLug**) and beyond. These brand experiences are designed to showcase brand values and build consumer relationships with the brand, however their ability to stimulate word of mouth or to go viral broadens their reach and makes them so very much more effective as marketing tools.

Electronic media, such as email and texting, lend themselves well to word-of-mouth advertising as they make it easy to pass a message on. Electronic word of mouth is referred to as viral marketing and is becoming increasingly important. Advertisers look for ways to engage their audience and encourage them to pass the message on. They hope to create a buzz. This encouragement may involve some financial reward (e.g. by offering customers money-off vouchers for passing messages on to their friends), or may just be based on entertainment value.

e-focus: Is that a real gorilla?

Cadbury's gorilla was the star of a TV advert that got everyone talking. The ad won numerous awards and generated massive media coverage. It showed a gorilla playing the drums on Phil Collins's song, 'In the Air Tonight'. It was a long ad (90 seconds) with a slow build-up and the gorilla was perfect. Chocolate sales rose and so did sales of the song. Within a week of the ad being aired, 'In the Air Tonight' went to number 14 in the UK singles chart and 9 in the downloads chart. Many of the younger purchasers had never heard of Phil Collins before.

The gorilla rapidly became an Internet sensation. Over 4 million people have viewed the advert on YouTube and the gorilla has several Facebook pages, the most popular of which has over 2600 members. Fans made their own versions, dubbing in different songs. Some of those became YouTube sensations too.

The buzz surrounding this ad centred on what the ad was about. The majority found it puzzling and couldn't see what it had to do with chocolate – but they didn't care, they loved it anyway. The sharper-eyed viewer spotted the purple background and linked that to Cadbury's. The cynical declared that it wasn't actually made as a Cadbury's ad, but was meant to promote the new Phil Collins greatest hits album. Gradually a YouTube consensus formed. The advert was about joy: the joy of playing the drums, the joy of eating the chocolate. Despite that glorious opening drum roll, the song itself isn't joyful though. After its release in 1981, the talk was of its dark side.

The other major topic of speculation was who was in the gorilla suit? Was it actually Phil Collins? Was it a real gorilla? People expressing this view were quickly laughed down – but either would have been great!

ACTIVITY

Check YouTube for tribute adverts and other user-generated advertising content. Try Cadbury's, Lynx, Sony and McDonald's as starting points and then see what's new.

THE MARKETING COMMUNICATIONS MIX

Marketers have a large number of promotional tools which they can use to achieve their communications objectives. Historically these tools, or techniques, have been organised into four broad categories: advertising, public relations, sales promotion and personal selling. This is known as the promotion mix (or marketing communications mix). However, increasingly, other categories are being added that either do not fit neatly into these four or that some people feel deserve their own category heading. Examples include **direct marketing**, sponsorship and packaging. Whichever classification is used, what is most important is to recognise the vast array of promotional activities that is available to marketers.

These promotional tools involve either direct (i.e. personal) communication, usually on a face-to-face basis or on the telephone (and, perhaps, through video-conferencing and email), or indirect (i.e. non-personal) communication via a medium such as television, magazines or radio, or through packaging, leaflets, etc. It is the responsibility of the marketer to determine which approach is best for each situation.

Whichever element, or elements, of the promotion mix organisations choose, the purpose is to communicate a message to an appropriate target audience in order to elicit a favourable response, such as purchasing a product or changing an attitude. The term 'integrated marketing communication' is used to emphasise that all elements of the promotion mix should be coordinated and systematically planned to complement each other.

direct marketing
'all activities that make it possible to offer goods or services or to transmit other messages to a segment of the population by post, telephone, email or other direct means' (Chartered Institute of Marketing)

ACTIVITY

Collect or identify as many examples of promotional material from one organisation as you can. How do they differ? Why do you think they differ? Who are the audiences?

The separate elements of the promotion mix will now be discussed in more depth under each of the four basic headings that were introduced at the start of this chapter, namely:

- advertising
- public relations (PR)
- sales promotions
- personal selling.

b2b focus: Talking shop

Although much of marketing and marketing communications theory focuses on consumer goods, particularly fast-moving consumer goods (FMCG), a significant amount of marketing communications is conducted between businesses. Interestingly, the big FMCG manufacturers' primary contact is with trade, not end customers. Managing trade contacts (e.g. wholesalers and retailers) is quite different from dealing with end customers and consumers. For example, whereas a consumer might want one bottle of wine, a retailer may want many cases of different types.

Such major sales warrant a different approach. The supplier may well send a sales representative cold-calling or use techniques such as telesales, direct mail (post, fax or email) or trade exhibitions, either to make sales or to set up appointments for the rep to call.

Audi's award winning advertising

ADVERTISING

Advertising is a broad term for any **paid form** (i.e. paid for by the advertiser) of **non-personal** presentation of ideas, goods and services by an **identified** advertiser. Communication by advertising is transmitted to a target audience through various forms of media, which include television, radio, cinema, press, posters and the Internet. Other marketing communication tools also use these media (notably PR) and so it becomes even more important to coordinate promotional activities through integrated marketing communications planning.

The major benefit of mass media advertising (e.g. television) is its ability to communicate to a large number of people all at once, e.g. all the existing and potential consumers for McDonald's fast food.

Traditional mass media advertising is indirect and non-personal (i.e. not individually addressed). It allows marketers to send a uniform message with great frequency. However, it does have several disadvantages. Even though, for example, the cost per person reached by the advertising may be relatively low, the total financial outlay can be extremely high – especially for commercials shown during popular television programmes such as Coronation Street or The X Factor. These high costs can limit, and sometimes prevent, the use of this type of advertising in an organisation's promotional mix. It should be remembered that not all companies have huge marketing communications budgets like Nike or Coca-Cola (and that even these aim for effectiveness and efficiency in using their companies' budgets). However, television advertising is now within the reach of those with a smaller budget thanks to the many digital channels available. Costs can also be kept down by focusing on specific ITV regions.

Additionally, the non-personal nature of the advert makes it harder to measure, or even receive, a response from the audience, making this effectively a one-way means of communication. Technology is helping to overcome this limitation.

Interactive television, mobile and Internet advertising all make two-way communication so much easier.

HOW DOES ADVERTISING WORK?

Over the years, researchers have designed a number of models to investigate how advertising and other marketing communication tools work. Two of the more popular ones, AIDA and DAGMAR, are outlined above. The truth is that we still do not know exactly how advertising works – but we do know that good advertising *can* have positive effects on customers and on sales. Many of these explanatory models are sequential, showing the customer moving through stages beginning by becoming aware of a product and ending with a sale or some form of post-purchase re-evaluation. Such models are essentially about persuasion, about moving people on to the next stage. Although these sequential models have been much criticised in recent years, they are still helpful to marketing communicators seeking to understand their customers and to help them to make the right decisions.

T Mobile: life's for sharing

EXPAND YOUR KNOWLEDGE

Classic article

Jones, J.P. (1990) 'Advertising: strong or weak force? Two views oceans apart', *International Journal of Advertising*, 9 (3): 233–46.

This article reviews the conventional view of advertising – the strong theory – which is all but universally believed in the USA and which sees advertising as a dynamic force operating as an engine for brand innovation and other types of change in the marketplace. Andrew Ehrenberg's theory sees advertising as a weak force. This paper argues that a good deal of confusion has been caused by an uncritical belief that the strong theory operates in all circumstances. As a result, advertising has been associated too much with over-promise and under-delivery.

ADVERTISING OBJECTIVES

Marketers use advertising in a number of ways. Most consumer advertising is product (or brand) advertising, however there are other forms, for example corporate, that communicate the values and ideas of organisations.

Advertising is rarely the best tool for closing a deal, so advertising objectives tend to relate to the early stages of sequential models like AIDA. Advertising can create awareness of a brand, ensure improved knowledge of that brand and its attributes, create a more favourable image, stimulate positive attitudes and achieve many other things, but product advertising's underlying objective is usually sales and its ultimate function is to sustain a brand and make it profitable.

Advertising Association

The problem with trying to measure advertising's effectiveness on sales alone is that it is hard to prove that the advert really did cause the increase in sales. Of course, there is a lot of anecdotal evidence to suggest that advertising has a positive

Exhibit 8.5   Typical categories of advertising objectives

Awareness or attention	Usually of a new product
Recognition (or prompted recall)	A form of awareness – particularly important for a new product, where the purchase decision is made at the point of purchase, e.g. anything sold in a supermarket
Recall	Another form of awareness – the ability to remember the product rather than just to recognise it; useful where decisions are made in advance of purchase, e.g. seeing a film at the cinema
Reminder	For established products that may be being overlooked
Repositioning	Altering the way the brand is viewed by the target audience, e.g. Baileys is an anytime drink, not just an after-dinner liqueur
Differentiation	Making the brand stand out from the competition
Information	Telling the audience something about the brand, e.g. that it has new features
Build brand image	Associating desired qualities with the brand, e.g. that it is innovative or youthful
Image change	A form of repositioning, altering the market's perception of the brand, e.g. Old Spice is for young, sexy men
Education	Telling the audience what the product is for or how to use it – especially new products
Stimulate word of mouth – or create a buzz	Getting people talking about the brand
Go viral	Enticing people to pass the ad on, or to comment on it, electronically, e.g. re-tweet or share on Facebook
Information gathering	For example, direct-response advertising gives audience information back to the advertiser
Attitude change	Changing a negative to a positive, e.g. 'Volvos are not for me' to 'That's a cool car'
Attitude reinforcement	Encouraging positive attitudes, e.g. 'I like brand X'
Correction of a misconception	Giving the audience a new angle, e.g. 'I can't afford a new car' to 'That's cheaper than I thought'
Trial stimulation	If a person never tries your product, then they can never become a regular purchaser
Sales	Purchase of the new product

effect on sales. Sales do tend to rise during an advertising campaign – and then to fall off soon after. However, that is not conclusive proof. There could be any number of other reasons why the sales rose, e.g. a competitor was short of stock, there was a price reduction at major retailers, a journalist wrote a good review. Conversely, it might be unfair to judge the advertising as bad just because sales do not rise. It may not be the advertising's fault. Many companies today advertise just to keep up. It is not so much a question of trying to increase sales, but of protecting their market share. If they stop advertising, they hand an advantage to the competition.

THE ESSENTIALS OF ADVERTISING

A way of simplifying our study of advertising (and of marketing communications as a whole) is to consider its four essential elements, as identified in Exhibit 8.6 and discussed in turn in the section that follows.

Exhibit 8.6   Advertising essentials

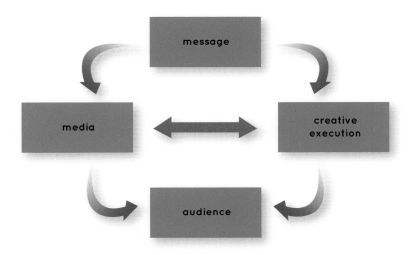

Rubicon hits sales targets

AUDIENCE

Get the right message to the right audience and you have a good ad. It sounds simple, but unfortunately it is not. Advertising agencies put a lot of time and effort into understanding audiences and into developing **audience profiles**. If you want to communicate effectively with someone, it helps to know them well. (See Exhibit 8.7 for an example of an audience profile.)

Remember that a target audience is not the same as a target market. The audience for an advert is the people at whom the message of the ad is aimed. They may be part, or all, of the target market, or they may not. Sometimes adverts are deliberately aimed at influencers rather than actual purchasers, e.g. many toy ads are (rather controversially) aimed at toy consumers (children) rather than customers (parents). In the past, anti-smoking campaigners have also aimed at children, urging them to nag their parents into giving up. Trade audiences are often wider. Take, for example, an advert in a trade magazine for cars. It could be aimed at the fleet manager (who manages the company's car fleet), professional buyers (who negotiate terms of purchase), the company owner or the finance director (who may make the ultimate decision), the people who have cars (who may push for new ones) or the PR department (which guards the company's image) – in fact at any member of the decision-making unit (see Chapter 3).

audience profile a detailed description of audience characteristics used by communicators to tailor their promotional efforts

b2b focus: *Sun* readers

T his is an example of an audience profile. 'Cover (%)' refers to the people in that category as a percentage of the population who read the newspaper, e.g. 19.2% of 25–34-year-olds read the *Sun*. 'Profile (%)' refers to the percentage of the overall *Sun* readership that falls into that category, e.g. 19% of *Sun* readers are DE men. Advertisers and PR agents use these newspaper profiles when planning their media strategies.

Exhibit 8.7   Audience profile of the *Sun*

Circulation
Circulation refers to the number of sold, reduced price and free copies of a title distributed on an average day (excluding Sundays) over the stated period of time.

Print: **2,279,492** (25 Feb. 2013 – 31 Mar. 2013)

Online (daily average unique browsers): **1,785,821** (1 Feb. 2013 – 28 Feb. 2013)

Source: NRS, 2013

Estimated readership
Estimated readership refers to the number of people reading a title on an average day (excluding Sundays) over the stated time period.

July–Dec. 2012: **6,713,000**

Demographic profile

Source: NRS July-Dec 2012	Estimated readership (000s)	Cover (%)	Profile (%)
All adults	6712	13.26	100.00
Men	3804	15.37	56.67
Women	2908	11.42	43.32
Age			
15–24	997	12.62	14.85
25–34	1299	15.67	19.35
35–44	1132	13.80	16.86
45–54	1119	13.00	16.67
55–64	874	12.40	13.02
65+	1292	12.22	19.25
Social class			
AB Adults	673	5.01	10.03
ABC1 Adults	2323	8.51	34.60

Source: NRS July–Dec 2012	Estimated readership (000s)	Cover (%)	Profile (%)
ABC1C2 Adults	4477	11.69	66.69
C1 Adults	1650	11.88	24.58
C2 Adults	2154	19.61	32.09
DE Adults	2236	18.15	33.31
AB Men	447	6.43	6.66
ABC1 Men	1384	10.38	20.62
ABC1C2 Men	2700	14.01	40.22
C1 Men	937	14.69	13.96
C2 Men	1316	22.16	19.60
DE Men	1104	20.13	16.45
AB Women	227	3.51	3.38
ABC1 Women	940	6.72	14.00
ABC1C2 Women	1778	9.34	26.49
C1 Women	713	9.50	10.62
C2 Women	838	16.60	12.48
DE Women	1132	16.55	16.86
Region			
London	1797	14.47	26.77
Midlands	1467	14.79	21.85
North West	531	8.60	7.91
Yorkshire	876	13.67	13.05
South and South East	573	10.56	8.54
East of England	700	15.05	10.43
Wales and West	543	11.25	8.09
Central Scotland	603	18.59	8.98
North East	394	13.69	5.87

SOURCE: NRS July–Dec. 2012.
Reproduced with kind permission of the National Readership Survey.

MESSAGE

Once the advertisers have established exactly who it is they want to talk to, they can develop the correct message to achieve their advertising objectives. They develop an **advertising proposition**: what the advertising should say and the impression it should create, but not necessarily phrased in the way that the ad will say it. For

Ryvita
minis
Big taste
Mini waist

**advertising
proposition**
what the overall
advert should say to
the target audience,
the impression that
should be left in
their minds (this
is not theslogan;
the whole of the
advert should
communicate the
proposition)

example, the message that this is a fun beer that enhances sociability while also providing refreshment might result in the slogan 'refreshes the parts other beers cannot reach'. The slogan is the clever, catchy form of words that goes into the actual ad. It is part of the creative work and is written by a copywriter (copy just means text, i.e. the words in an ad).

EXPAND YOUR KNOWLEDGE

van Kuilenburg, P., de Jong, M.D.T. and van Rompay, T.J.L. (2011) '"That was funny, but what was the brand again?": Humorous television commercials and brand linkage', *International Journal of Advertising*, 30 (5): 795–814.

This study examined the effects that humour complexity and humour relatedness in humorous television commercials have on brand linkage.

Specsavers
Spoof Ad

creative execution
the way an advert
is designed in order
to put the message
across

CREATIVE EXECUTION

The message is not normally put across through words alone. There are visual elements to most advertising that assist its transmission: a picture, a scene, colours, designs. There may also be music, other sound effects, acting – all of these form part of the **creative execution**. This is the heart of the advert. Advertisers appeal to our emotions (e.g. through humour or sex) and/or to our rational side (e.g. through value for money or product features), in order to interest us in their products.

There are a number of common execution approaches including those below. Look out for these and others as you see and listen to advertisements. Think of them as movie genres, as types of advertising – although adverts may well combine aspects of a number of these executions and some, e.g. music, are not standalone. These are presented here as advertising executions, but some are also useful to other marketing communication tools, such as PR, to get messages across.

Slice of life: a real, everyday situation shows the product in normal use, e.g. a little boy plays his separated parents off against each other and persuades them both to take him to McDonald's.

Animation and CGI: cartoon characters can liven up a dull product, deal with an embarrassing subject, e.g. cartoon bears and toilet rolls, meerkats and insurance.

Endorsement: uses supposed experts, or past users, to verify the merits of the product, e.g. 'my washing has never been so white'. Testimonials are commonly used in Internet advertising. There is more space to print endorsing statements, making them more credible. Testimonials are reassuring in a medium where lack of trust is a problem. References in blogs are even more reassuring as they have the impartiality of word-of-mouth advertising, which is perhaps why less scrupulous advertisers sometimes write these themselves.

Celebrity: attracts attention, gives the product credibility. Sometimes celebrities are endorsing the product, e.g. Cheryl Cole seems to be 'worth it' for L'Oreal, but sometimes their involvement in the ad is more peripheral, e.g. Jenson Button, Rory McIlroy and Jessica Ennis are seen in adverts for Santander, but are we meant to believe they actually bank there? Beyonce is the face of H&M but does she shop there?

News style: common in press adverts, makes the advert look more like part of the publication.

Fantasy: catches the imagination, particularly useful when the product cannot be shown in use, e.g. Smirnoff vodka ads. Advanced CGI has made many fantasy executions even more fantastical, e.g. a Coca-Cola advert had someone disappear into a vending machine and emerge in a completely different world.

Spoof or parody: catches attention through humour, e.g. Specsavers parodied the Lynx ads; the original Gary Lineker Walker's crisps ads played on his good guy reputation.

Demonstration: shows how the product works, e.g. how Flash can clean up a floor so quickly. These can be more imaginative than a straight demonstration and may be combined with a fantastical element, e.g. in a mini convertible ad, a man was surrounded by threatening hoodies every time he tried to close the roof, but they disappeared when he desisted. Eventually we got the message: 'leave it open'.

Comedy: engages the audience – so long as they get the joke. Humour can be very effective and entertaining but it must be used carefully to ensure it does not offend. Also, jokes are not as funny the second, third, fourth time around so these ads may have limited lives. There are numerous examples. Try Volkswagen's Darth Vader ad with its follow up 'The Dog Strikes Back', or any of the Lynx ads.

Audience participation: advertising is no longer content with actors on a screen; some adverts invite the actual participation of target audiences or are mini films of events. T-Mobile staged a flashmob at Liverpool Street Station but the main point was that it would be filmed, not only by their agency for use as an advert, but also by commuters (on their phones) for sharing. Coca-Cola's Coke Chase advert invites the audience to decide who wins the race. This kind of active audience engagement reinforces messages and creates a buzz.

Music: often a key part of the creative execution, it creates mood, attracts attention, reinforces a message, inspires word of mouth and makes the ad more memorable. Music is not a stand-alone execution, of course – it is most commonly in the background – but it can be a major element as in the Cadbury's gorilla ad (Phil Collins, 'In the Air Tonight'), John Lewis's 2011 'never knowingly undersold' ad (Paloma Faith, 'Never Tear Us Apart'), or Xbox 360's ad (Lily Allen, 'The Fear') which made more of the music by featuring Lily Allen singing along with hundreds of Xboxers (so there was a celebrity element too).

Lily Allen
for Xbox

EXPAND YOUR KNOWLEDGE

Garretson Folse, J.A., Netemeyer, R.G. and Burton, S. (2012) 'Spokescharacters: how the personality traits of sincerity, excitement, and competence help to build equity', *Journal of Advertising,* 31 (1): 17–32.

Spokescharacters are 'humanlike visual images that can symbolically convey a brand's attributes, benefits, or personality'; they are usually cartoon-like characters such as Tony the Tiger or the Honey Monster.

media vehicle
the newspaper,
magazine, poster site,
etc. where adverts
appear

**media class or media
category**
type of media, e.g.
television, press,
posters, cinema

ADVERTISING MEDIA

The final essential of advertising is the media: the carriers of the message. Without media, no one will ever hear or see it. The right choice of media is essential to the effectiveness of a campaign. It has to be appropriate to the target audience and to the message.

There is little point in advertising in *Cosmopolitan* if you are trying to reach elderly men (though there may be some point if you are trying to reach younger men as, apparently, a large number of them read it; they do not buy it, they just read their girlfriends' copies). It is important to establish the readership/viewership profile of media vehicles and match this to your audience profile. Newspapers, TV channels, etc., provide guides to assist with this and to help sell their advertising space.

The choice of media also affects how the message comes across. If your message is a complex, informative one, perhaps explaining the technical advantages of a new computer system, then a 30-second TV ad just will not do. You need the space and copy possibilities of the press. However, if you want your new jeans to catch the eye of the younger generation, then the creative scope offered by a cinema ad may be the best thing (and then you can cut it down to show on TV as well).

Posters can have great impact.

Advertisers must choose a media class (the inter-media decision, e.g. television or Internet or press) and then a media vehicle (the intra-media decision, i.e. the actual TV programmes or websites or magazine titles). This decision is based on the creative scope a medium offers and its audience profile. For example, a TV advert aired during *Big Brother* would allow the advertisers to use colour, sound and movement (actors, props and/or animation) to create an impact on a young audience. An ad or a page on Facebook could use interactivity to engage a sociable, IT-literate audience.

The traditional mass media is still commonly used, although other media types are becoming increasingly popular, particularly digital media and ambient media.

PUBLIC RELATIONS (PR)

Traditionally, PR was perceived to be a corporate function. Today, there are a number of types of PR, and marketing communications has embraced and adapted the various elements of the discipline. Creating and maintaining goodwill and a good reputation is just as relevant to product brands as it is to corporations as a whole.

Raising the visibility of organisations and encouraging interest in them is an important function of marketing communications. In recent times, public relations has assumed a greater significance at both the corporate level and within the promotion mix.

WHAT IS PUBLIC RELATIONS?

According to the Chartered Institute of Public Relations:

> Public relations is the planned and sustained effort to establish and maintain goodwill and mutual understanding between an organisation and its publics.

The gnome experiment

Reflecting on this definition, the words *planning*, *sustained effort* and *mutual understanding* need emphasising. Good public relations involves conducting planned programmes with clear objectives, so that results can be assessed and understood. Good public relations involves sustained activity over time. The objectives of creating and maintaining goodwill are not achieved by short-term activities alone. Finally, good public relations requires mutual understanding between the organisation and its various publics. In public relations, the organisation receives as well as transmits information, listens as well as speaks (Jefkins, 1989).

THE SCOPE OF PUBLIC RELATIONS

Public relations can raise awareness, inform, interest, excite, educate, generate understanding, build trust, encourage loyalty and even help generate sales (Pickton and Broderick, 2004). PR can raise visibility and also help develop corporate and product credibility in ways that other promotional tools cannot. It can also be used to enhance the effectiveness of advertising.

Any solid management planning relies on research and analysis and PR is no exception. The planning and management of PR is a systematic process of identifying PR tasks, setting objectives, defining PR **publics**, integrating PR within the promotion or marketing communications mix, scheduling, managing the implementation of PR techniques and assessing their effectiveness.

publics
the groups of people with whom the organisation communicates

PR TECHNIQUES

Media relations/publicity

Publicity can stimulate demand for goods or services by generating news about them in the mass media. This is done by means of news releases, press conferences and events or publicity stunts (e.g. Richard Branson flying across the Atlantic in a hot-air balloon to get the Virgin name in the news).

Good media relations encourage media coverage and favourable, positive publicity. Equally valuably, they also discourage negative coverage. This is an important function of professional public relations specialists and involves developing strong personal relationships with editors and journalists. Media releases contain information about the organisation and its products or brands in the hope of obtaining positive editorial coverage and are sent to journalists who may, or may not, use all (or more usually part) of the content. Publicity may use the same mass media as advertising. However, unlike advertising, the media costs are not paid for directly by the company, nor does publicity identify itself as coming directly from the company; it can therefore have greater impact as it has the appearance of coming from an impartial source.

What is PR?

ACTIVITY

Press releases are often written as articles suitable for publication. Time-strapped editors sometimes print them with little or no amendment. Browse through a newspaper or magazine and try to find stories that may have been placed by a commercial company (the weekend glossies or special interest magazines are often the best source). What's the objective behind the story?

Publicity can be an impressive and effective promotional tool. However, as it involves a third party, such as a newspaper reporter or editor, who has the power to determine the nature of the message, a firm has little control over its timing and content. An extreme example of this is the publicity – good, bad or indifferent – a company's products get in *Which?* consumer magazine. *Which?* regularly evaluates products and publishes the results of the tests. Companies have no control over the tests or the resultant publicity. Visit **www.which.co.uk** for examples.

Publications

The PR department or agency is usually responsible for this important task, although advertising agencies and others also offer the service. Organisations produce a variety of publications, e.g. employee newsletters, financial reports, consumer magazines, brochures and media packs. Such publications are a major tool of much organisational PR.

Websites and social media sites

When customers want to find information about a product, they most commonly Google it. Websites are really important sources of information. Brand owners provide information, entertainment and incentives through their own websites and through social media sites. These sites may be managed by an in-house team or by an agency, which may be PR, advertising or digital. Constant monitoring and updating is vital if the site is to stay accurate and prove valuable to potential customers.

Corporate communications

Aspects of corporate communications that fall into the category of PR include corporate identity programmes, corporate image management, corporate advertising, some internal communications and some communications with other publics or stakeholder groups.

Public affairs and community relations

This involves contact with the government and government agencies, special interest and professional groups, as well as the local community, with a view to building and maintaining local, national and international relations.

Lobbying

An approach associated with public affairs and media relations. It aims to build and maintain positive relations with, for example, group leaders, legislators and officials, through negotiation and persuasion.

ethical focus: Sponsorship: saviour or villain?

Should the Notting Hill Carnival or school lessons or sport be sponsored? These, and many similar questions, are being hotly debated by various publics worried about the sponsor's influence on the event or person sponsored. So if sponsorship can be controversial, why does it have such an important role in marketing communications?

Sponsorship is an effective and valuable marketing communications tool. The sponsorship of events, activities and organisations will continue to grow because it provides access to specific target audiences and enhances the sponsor's image.

The key reasons for sponsorship's increase in popularity are: national and European policies on tobacco and alcohol, which prevent them being advertised, a greater focus on promotional cost-effectiveness, the proven ability of sponsorship to deliver good results in terms of brand awareness and image change, new opportunities for sponsorship as people have more leisure time, greater media coverage of events resulting in a wider reach for the sponsorship, and a recognition of the inefficiencies associated with more traditional media. At the same time, sponsorship has become recognised as a good way to raise money for any vaguely worthy or socially popular activity. Most football clubs have sponsors, as do most athletes. Exhibitions look for sponsorship funds from the outset. Concerts and plays rely on sponsors to subsidise the revenues from ticket sales.

Certain activities have attracted sponsorship more than others: sports, programmes and broadcasts, the arts and other areas that encompass socially responsible activities such as wildlife conservation and education. Without sponsorship, many of our favourite pastimes and pet projects just wouldn't happen.

© Pascal Guyot/AFP/Getty Images

Formula 1 has always provided attractive sponsorship vehicles.

Sponsorship

Sponsorship is a business relationship in which one organisation provides funds or other resources/services to another organisation (or an individual) and gains commercial advantage through being linked to them. It may be on a relatively small scale directed at a local activity, or involve millions of pounds. Typical

Vodafone sponsorship

sponsorship vehicles include sports (events, teams, individuals), television programmes and the arts.

Xbox
innovative
product
placement

PRODUCT PLACEMENT

This is another promotional tool that is growing in importance. How many times
have you downloaded a film or watched a recorded TV programme and zapped
through the adverts to the start of the film itself? The marketing communications
industry is aware that adverts, whether on television or in other media, can irritate
some of the audience. This, as well as clutter in the marketplace, was the impetus
behind product placement. Today, a wide variety of brands is directly placed in
television programmes and films. The brands become props and are seen being
used (and thus, by implication, endorsed), although the audience is not always
fully aware that this is effectively advertising. The communications process is
quite subtle.

EXPAND YOUR KNOWLEDGE

Dens, N., De Pelsmacker, P., Wouters, M. and Purnawirawan, N. (2012) 'Do
you like what you recognize? The effects of brand placement prominence
and movie plot connection on brand attitude as mediated by recognition',
Journal of Advertising, 31 (3): 35–53.

This paper examines the relative effectiveness of different forms of brand
placement in movies.

BRANDED CONTENT

A natural progression from media sponsorship and product placement, branded
content is more common in the USA than in Europe, where it has been slow to
take off. It is still in the early enough stages of development to have a number of
different names. In the USA, it is more likely to be called 'branded entertainment'
and it is also sometimes called 'advertiser-funded programming'. Branded content
is a logical progression from sponsorship. Instead of selecting a suitable event to
sponsor, the advertiser creates one. For example, Heinz, having discovered that
their products were most often consumed by families eating together, created a
family cooking television programme.

Product
placement
in TV

EVENTS MANAGEMENT

This is the staging of events such as conferences or festivals. They may be one-
offs or something that occurs regularly. If a new product is to be launched, there
may be internal announcement meetings. External events may be staged to attract,
hopefully, favourable publicity and extensive media coverage.

ACTIVITY

Visit an exhibition. Observe and evaluate all the activities that are going on. Consider the organisation of the exhibition as a whole – the number of stands, layout, visitor attendance, exhibitor attendance, promotional/informational materials, atmosphere and all the supporting services.

- Evaluate the whole event from a visitor's perspective.
- Evaluate the event from an exhibitor's perspective.
- What recommendations would you make for future exhibitions?

CRISIS MANAGEMENT

Dealing with unforeseen events is an important facet of PR and is often referred to as damage limitation. It may involve product recall, such as in the now famous Perrier case, or dealing with major ecological disasters, such as the *Exxon Valdez* oil spillage, or a scandal such as a football manager being overheard insulting his club's fans.

EXPAND YOUR KNOWLEDGE

Cleeren, K., van Heerde, H.J. and Dekimpe, M.G. (2013) 'Rising from the ashes: how brands and categories can overcome product-harm crises', *Journal of Marketing,* 77 (2): 58–77.

This is an examination of how different marketing actions mitigated the negative effects of having to recall an entire line of faulty products.

Carrillat, F.A., d'Astous, A. and Lazure, J. (2013) 'For better, for worse? What to do when celebrity endorsements go bad', *Journal of Advertising Research,* 53 (1): 15–30.

This experimental study examined what is the optimal decision for a company whose brand is endorsed by a celebrity immersed in a scandal.

SALES PROMOTION

Organisations spend more of their marketing budgets on sales promotion than they do on advertising. Clearly, then, this is a very important promotional weapon, so what exactly is it? The Institute of Promotional Marketing (IPM), the professional body that represents all the major sales promotion practitioners in the UK, gives this definition of sales promotion:

Sales promotion comprises that range of techniques used to attain sales/ marketing objectives in a cost-effective manner by adding value to a product or service, either to intermediaries or end-users, normally, but not exclusively, within a defined time period. (ISP 2010)

'Adding value' has been emphasised in the definition above because this is the single most important thing about sales promotion. It works by making a product into a better deal. It offers something extra for free or money off or the chance to win something else and most people, it seems, like to think that they have got something for nothing. It could perhaps be free conditioner with your shampoo, or money off a badly wanted computer game or an instant-win competition. Sales promotions are intended to induce buyers to purchase, or try, a product, or to improve the effectiveness of marketing channel members (e.g. retailers or wholesalers).

Advantages of sales promotion as a marketing communications technique include:

- It has been shown to work. Sales promotion campaigns usually produce notable increases in sales, or trial of a product.
- This effectiveness can be measured, and therefore proved, quite easily. A sales promotion's impact on sales is more directly attributable to the promotion (rather than other activities) because it is a short-term offer and because there is usually some easy means to collect data, e.g. counting money-off coupons handed in, or counting competition entries.
- It can be closely targeted. Thanks to computer databases, a special offer can be directed at specific groups of people within particular market segments, e.g. online retailers might send out incentives to people who have registered but never bought.
- It is manageable within a smaller budget. By managing the length of time the promotion is available, and the number of winning entries or coupons or free products available, sales promotion can maximise the effectiveness of a limited budget. This is a very important aspect of sales promotion, although it must be managed carefully or the costs can get out of hand.
- It has an almost immediate effect. The fortunes of brands and companies are increasingly volatile. Sales promotions can be devised, implemented and take effect far more quickly than other forms of promotion.
- It creates interest. Sales promotion brings in an element of novelty and excitement, which customers enjoy and to which, more importantly, they respond.

SALES PROMOTION OBJECTIVES

Sales promotion is usually used to achieve short-term objectives such as to:

mobile sales promotion campaigns

- introduce a new product
- encourage greater usage
- combat or offset competitors' marketing efforts
- stimulate product trial.

It should be fully integrated with other promotional tools to form a cohesive plan that supports the organisation's long-term objectives. Many sales promotions are seen as downmarket and therefore unsuited to campaigns that are promoting an upmarket image. Also, some types of promotion would be too expensive to fund if extended to high-priced goods, and so BOGOF promotions, for example, tend to be found on low-priced products such as toiletries, food and drinks. Sales promotion is at its most effective in the latter stages of the buying process. Promotions are good at prompting action.

There are three categories of sales promotion: consumer, trade and salesforce.

CONSUMER PROMOTIONS

Trial is regarded as the most important action objective for almost every brand. In FMCG, getting a customer to buy for the first time is harder than getting repeat purchases. Customers making high-involvement purchases may also want to try them out, e.g. test driving a car. Sales promotions are a good way to stimulate trial, to add value and to reassure.

Consumer promotions are generally one of three types: save, win or free. For example:

- samples – standard or trial-size giveaways
- coupons, e.g. 25p off your next purchase
- premiums – an extra, free item, e.g. BOGOF
- special offers, e.g. half price this week
- bonus packs – extra quantity or larger product, e.g. 25% bigger bar
- multipacks – cheaper than buying separately
- competitions, e.g. answer the following questions ...
- prize draws, e.g. check the number by ringing/writing in
- instant wins, e.g. Kit Kat's 'Win a Million' promotion
- points to collect, e.g. Air Miles or Nectar card points
- tie-ins – giving a different product away, e.g. cereal gifts
- cause-related promotions – the seller gives a donation to a worthy cause for every product sold, e.g. Pizza Express donates to the Venice in Peril Fund every time one of its Veneziana pizzas is sold
- **self-liquidating special offers**, e.g. a cereal company offering a set of breakfast bowls in return for £10 and four tokens.

Consumer sales promotion programmes may be paid for by the retailer but are commonly financed by the manufacturer. They are often supported by advertising, **point-of-sale (POS) promotions** (also known as point-of-purchase (POP)) and **merchandising** activities within retail outlets.

TRADE PROMOTIONS

Consumer goods suppliers spend a great deal on trade promotions to distributors, including retailers, as part of their push strategy.

Promotions by manufacturers to their distributors, generally called trade promotions, are often some form of price promotion because the main factor motivating distributors is their reseller profit margin.

© Dave Pickton

Supermarkets use a lot of sales promotions.

self-liquidating special offer
a sales promotion that pays for itself (usually because the company making the offer has bought the promotional items in vast quantities and so obtained a substantial discount)

point-of-sale (POS) promotion
the general term for any type of promotion found where the sale takes place; most usually associated with retail outlets

merchandising
selection and display of products within a retail environment

Eye-catching point-of-sale displays can boost sales.

© Dave Pickton

Price promotion is often used to stimulate trial, i.e. persuading the distributor to stock a product for the first time. There are three main types of trade trial promotion:

1   New line fees (slotting allowances): these are cash payments or a proportion of the shipment (consignment of goods) donated free, which amounts to a price inducement, in return for stocking a new product or offering a new service for a specified period of time.
2   Price-offs: these are straight reductions in the selling price to the distributor and are sometimes called off-invoice promotions.
3   Returns: the manufacturer agrees to buy back unsold quantities of the product. Distributing on consignment is an extreme form of this. The distributor pays nothing to the manufacturer until the product is sold (also known as sale or return).

Price promotions are also important in encouraging repeat purchase by distributors. There are four types:

1   Price-offs: as described above, but on the understanding that part of the discount will be passed to the end customer or consumer, or that the distributor will provide extra display, advertising or both.
2   Joint promotions: these are agreements by which the manufacturer and distributor both contribute funds towards promotional expenditure. The proportion of contribution may vary.
3   Sales contests: competitions in which retailers or other trade partners can win attractive prizes.
4   Sales education: this is applicable mainly to industrial products and services, or to the more technical types of consumer durable. Manufacturers train the retailer's or wholesaler's staff and all parties benefit from the increased sales.

SALESFORCE PROMOTIONS

Manufacturers have a salesforce to motivate. Salesforce promotions include monetary rewards, such as bonuses, and non-monetary rewards, such as prizes, training programmes, motivational meetings and selling aids.

WHAT CAN GO WRONG?

Sales promotions must be very carefully planned. There is a code of practice to abide by, and laws on gambling and competitions to be obeyed. For example, if someone has to pay to enter, then that is gambling and, in the UK, a licence is required to run gambling games. Hence that familiar phrase 'no purchase necessary'. There is a thriving sales promotion industry in the UK and, as the details of promotions can get quite complex, it is usually advisable to enlist expert help for anything but the simplest of offers. Some of the scenarios that might arise are outlined below.

- Over-redemption:
  - bad promotion design, e.g. the classic case of the Hoover flights promotion. Hoover offered a free flight to New York with every vacuum cleaner purchase. Unfortunately, the vacuum cleaner was cheaper than the flight and people flocked to electrical appliance stores instead of to travel agents. That promotion is reported to have cost £48 million.
  - error in administration, e.g. Pepsi's Philippine subsidiary promised one million pesos (about £25,000) for bottle caps bearing the winning number 349. When Pepsi had paid out £8 million, it realised something was amiss – there were far too many winners. The withdrawal of the offer provoked riots.
- Misredemption: one of the advantages of sales promotion is the accuracy of its targeting. You can send a coupon to precisely the person you want to redeem it, but can you prevent it from being passed on to someone else?
- Malredemption: the likely number of winners for any promotion is carefully worked out and budgets are set. Lottery syndicates are encouraged but, if a promotion requires the collecting of a set of something, beware: joint efforts (and swaps arranged through newspaper columns or on the Internet) could blow the budget.
- Faulty pack design: some sales promotions require a special pack design to disguise which one is the winning pack. This packaging must be designed with great care. If someone swallows a prize notification ticket when upending a packet of crisps into their mouth (as has happened), then trouble will ensue.
- Pilfering: if the pack design is not good enough to disguise a winner, the chances are it will never make it out of the shop. Bored sales assistants enjoy trying to spot a winning pack.
- Lost in the post: many samples fail to reach the right target. They may arrive but be picked up by another member of the household. Recently, there have been complaints that some of the promotional items that land on doormats are dangerous to young children who may think that they are toys or sweets, when they are not.

Sales promotions need careful, worst-case scenario planning – and professional indemnity insurance.

PERSONAL SELLING

Avon personal selling

There is talk of outlawing door-to-door selling in the UK. This will be good news for many people, who feel threatened and coerced by such salespeople, and bad news for the unprofessional sales organisations whose behaviour has prompted the ban. Putting to one side the ethical problems associated with extreme forms of personal selling, it has a major role to play in the promotion mix of many companies. Personal selling is an oral presentation, in a conversation with one or more prospective purchasers, for the purpose of making sales.

Personal selling involves informing customers of the benefits of products, and persuading them to buy through personal communication in a potential exchange situation. It includes such things as a salesperson explaining a product's features, a technician demonstrating a new MRI scanner to relevant hospital personnel, and even the person at the supermarket who gives you a free sample of a new luxury ice-cream while telling you something about it.

Personal selling differs from other forms of communication in that messages flow from a sender to a receiver directly (often face to face). This direct and interpersonal communication lets the sender receive and evaluate feedback from the receiver immediately. This communications process, known as dyadic communication (between two people or groups), allows the message to be tailored more specifically to the needs of the sender and receiver than do many of the other media.

global focus: Doing business abroad

Company representatives and salespeople have to learn the business conventions of other countries in order to do business there. Failure to do so can leave an impatient North American hanging around for hours in a South American office wondering what has happened to the meeting or a disappointed European waiting for a contract that they believe has been promised by a Japanese firm but which never materialises.

Many Latin Americans have a different attitude to time than do their North American counterparts. In the USA, meetings should start on time. Further south, they can see no point in starting before everyone is ready. The Japanese dislike saying an outright no, as it seems rude, and are also concerned not to lose face by admitting that they do not have the authority to say yes. Either or both of these situations can leave a European with the false impression that they have made a sale.

In many countries business is a much more personal thing than it is in the West. Arabs prefer to do business with people they know. The Japanese too spend time getting to know people and building trust before they commit to any business dealings. Much time may be spent on the golf course before business is even mentioned.

Conducting business in some countries is particularly awkward for women. There are many countries, notably Arab and African ones, where women are still not accepted as equals in the workplace. On a positive note here, Western women tend to be treated as representatives of their companies first, their countries second – and their sex third. So they do get on rather better than local women do and it is by no means impossible for women to strike deals in such countries. Some Western companies refuse to bow to local custom and send their female employees as trailblazers.

Reaching a limited number of people through personal selling efforts costs, proportionately, a considerable amount more than it does through advertising. However, in many situations it is thought to be worth it because of the immediate feedback and its greater persuasive impact on customers.

SALESPEOPLE

To develop a salesforce, a marketing manager needs to decide what kind of salesperson will sell the firm's products most effectively. Various authors classify sales roles in different ways. Some classify sales jobs into two broad categories: service selling, which concentrates on getting sales from the existing customer base, and developmental selling, which aims to convert prospects into customers. Others refer to three basic roles: order taking, order supporting and order getting. From reading the above, you will understand that there are many sales roles and, in reality, these roles may not be discrete. Salespeople now have to perform many tasks and activities daily (not just selling), which involve numerous skills, such as:

- buyer/seller team coordinator
- customer service provider
- buyer behaviour expert
- information gatherer
- market analyst and planner
- sales forecaster
- market cost analyst
- technologist.

EXPAND YOUR KNOWLEDGE

Storbacka, K., Ryals, L., Davies, I.A. and Nenonen, S. (2009) 'The changing role of sales: viewing sales as a strategic, cross-functional process', *The European Journal of Marketing*, 43 (7–8): 890–906.

The role of sales within the promotional mix is constantly changing. A study by Storbacka, Ryals, Davies and Nenonen revealed that the twenty-first-century sales function is changing in three interrelated aspects: from a function to a process; from an isolated activity to an integrated one; and from operational to strategic.

STAGES OF SELLING

A number of sequential steps go into making a sale. These are illustrated in Exhibit 8.8.

Prospecting is about finding potential customers. Exhibitions are good sources of prospects, as are direct-response promotions. Websites are often used to identify people who are interested in a brand or product category. It is important that a salesperson should prepare before approaching a prospect. They need to know what kind of person they are dealing with, why they might want the product and what their likely hot buttons are. The next step is to get the appointment. This

prospecting
looking for prospective customers

Exhibit 8.8 Personal selling

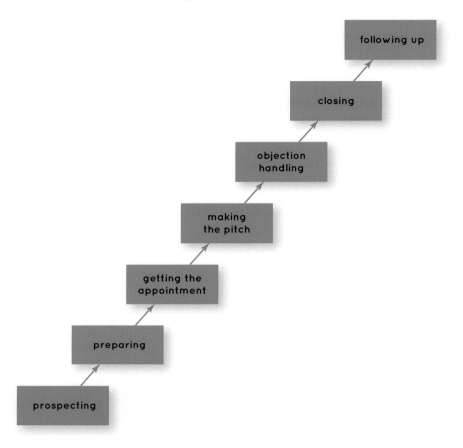

cold call
when a
salesperson calls
on a prospect
without an
appointment

may be arranged in advance (e.g. over the phone) or the salesperson may **cold call**. The next step is a big one. Although, in Exhibit 8.8, it is labelled 'making the pitch', there is more to it than that. First, the salesperson should find out what the customer wants, then he or she can draw attention to the most appropriate products and their benefits. The best salespeople are good listeners. It is unlikely that the product will fit the customer's needs perfectly – there will be some objections raised (e.g. it is too expensive, it is the wrong colour, it has no cover). The salesperson must address these concerns honestly, and perhaps convince the customer that the things the product lacks are unimportant. Now comes the close. This is the part that many salespeople find the hardest: they just have to ask for the order. Finally, there is the follow-up: making sure the product is delivered, that it works properly and, of course, checking if the customer needs anything else. This could be the start of a long and profitable relationship.

Not all steps are used in all sales situations. The retail sales assistant, for example, will be in a very different situation from a key accounts salesperson who works for a manufacturer of heavy industrial equipment.

customer focus: Closing techniques

Salespeople employ a number of closing techniques to persuade customers to place orders. Some are more effective than others and some are less ethical than others. Good salespeople are honest and straightforward. If customers like and trust them, they are far more likely to buy from them.

Some examples of closing techniques are:

- the straight close, e.g. 'So would you like one?' followed by silence

- the deadline close, e.g. 'There is only the one left in stock and I don't know when we'll be able to get more'

- the assumptive close, e.g. 'So I'll get it delivered next week then'

- the alternative close, e.g. 'Would you like the blue or the green?'

- the no problem close, e.g. 'Order it now and you can cancel it later if you change your mind'

- the sympathy close, e.g. 'I just need one more order to make my sales quota this month.'

Look out for these next time you're out shopping. You may even be able to add to the list.

DIRECT MARKETING

It is not always easy to fit all the elements of the marketing communications mix into four broad categories. Where to put direct marketing (or more accurately in the context of promotion, **direct marketing communication**) is one such problem, as it can make use of advertising as well as sales promotions and personal selling.

Most promotional tools are aimed at mass audiences but there are weaknesses with the mass approach and so many companies have adopted a more direct approach to their markets. They are motivated not just by cost advantages but also by opportunities to improve quality and service provision.

Direct marketing establishes personal contact with prospects and customers to encourage a direct response. Early direct marketing focused on providing a telephone number or a response card in advertisements (i.e. direct-response advertising). Today, **direct mail**, telemarketing, door-to-door, email and interactive website forms are among the main response media used.

Direct marketing has outgrown its early roots and has become a sophisticated marketing tool used for building relationships with customers. **Direct-response advertising** is now only a part of the huge direct marketing industry. The Institute of Direct and Digital Marketing's (IDM) definition emphasises the importance of building customer relationships through direct marketing efforts: 'planned recording, analysis and tracking of individual customers' responses and transactions for the purpose of developing and prolonging mutually profitable customer relationships' (IDM, 2010). The primary objectives of direct marketing are to build and

direct marketing communication promotional material designed to prompt a direct response from the recipient to the sender

direct mail promotional material delivered by post

direct-response advertising 'advertising, or selling, through any medium inviting the consumer to respond to the advertiser' (IDM Direct Marketing Guide)

IDM

sustain a mutually rewarding relationship with individual customers, to reduce media cost and to improve the effectiveness of marketing communications and the measurement of results.

Undoubtedly, direct marketing has grown and developed because of rapid advances in computing and communications technology, transportation and changing market conditions. Technology has facilitated the collection, storage, analysis and retrieval of customer data. It has increased opportunities for direct communication even on an individual basis to millions of people. It offers a solution to the fragmentation of the marketplace. It can also create problems of unwanted communications.

DATABASE MARKETING

Database marketing is a sophisticated tool that owes everything to technology. Customer (and potential customer) data is held in a database, which is really an electronic filing system with extensive cross-referencing and processing capabilities (see Exhibit 8.9 for examples of the kind of data that would be held). This data is used to identify prospects for a company's products. These prospects are then targeted for marketing and sales activities, usually by being placed on specific mailing lists. Take the example of a department store. It may have lists for men, women, parents, customers of specific cosmetics companies, people who buy designer clothes, people who have its store card, people who do not have its store card, people who purchased electrical goods such as televisions or household appliances. This information is gathered from purchases made in store, data provided by customers when they fill in forms (such as applications for store cards, credit agreements, competition entries) and bought in from other sources (there are companies that specialise in buying in data and selling it on).

The targeted customers may be sent mailings, telephoned, emailed or just added to a list to receive regular newsletters, updates, etc.

Databases have been used for years to analyse customer buying patterns and identify prospects for other products and services. The technology has, of course, got more sophisticated and powerful, and so have the uses to which it can be put. Today, many companies have data warehouses and use data mining software to sift through the enormous amounts of data stored in them and make the connections between the data. For example, a company can match up customer profiles in different parts of the country with past sales at specific times of year and use this link to identify new ranges that might sell well. There is almost no limit to the connections data mining might make – as long as the data exists in the database, of course.

ACTIVITY

When you get home after your next shopping trip, take a look at what you've bought. What could a company work out about you from your purchases?

These sophisticated computer systems are at the heart of customer relationship management (CRM). Organisations have more information on customers than they ever had before, as well as the technology and techniques to use it to understand and serve their customers better. There really is very little excuse for poor customer service today and yet it does still exist in some places. Have you ever received a standard response to a query that really just did not answer it? It can be a mistake for an organisation to become over-reliant on automation.

ACTIVITY

Gather together all the promotional items that you receive in a week (through the post and by text, email or through your social media pages). Then sort them according to their relevance to you.

How many did you receive? Whose mailing lists are you on? How did you get there?

DIRECT-RESPONSE ADVERTISING

Direct-response advertising is, according to the IDM (2010), 'advertising or selling through any medium inviting the consumer to respond to the advertiser'. As with all advertising, it requires good audience profiling, creativity and wise media choice. Direct marketers make good use of database technology to build up information on customers and prospects. Using this, they can compile mailing lists, or lists suitable for other media, and so reach their target audiences.

Exhibit 8.9 Examples of customer database information

Type of information	Possible source(s) include
Customer contact details	Order forms, sales team
Customer sales history	Past orders, loyalty cards
Customer demographics	Order forms, credit applications, market research reports
Customer psychographics	Customer surveys, sales team
Customer preferences	Customer correspondence, enquiries, sales team
Customer business details	Annual report and other publicly available documents, company website, sales team

Exhibit 8.10   Direct-response media

Press: display advertising, classified advertising, inserts in magazines/newspapers	Flyers
Mail and door-drops	Internet: websites (e.g. banner ads), pop-ups and instant messages, search engines, email
Telephone and text messages	iTV

MEDIA CHOICE

Most media can be used for direct communications. The key thing is that the media should be able to provide a specific response mechanism, e.g. a phone number, a link to click or an email address. Exhibit 8.10 outlines the main media choices open to direct marketers.

FACTORS AFFECTING MEDIA CHOICE IN DIRECT MARKETING COMMUNICATIONS

No one medium always achieves the highest response at the lowest cost, and it is generally true that those media that elicit a higher response also tend to be the most expensive. For example, telephone responses are potentially the highest of any media, but the costs are also the highest.

To assess the media for a direct marketing campaign, the framework AIMRITE can be used as a decision-making aid (Pickton and Broderick, 2004).

- **Audience**: does the media reach the desired target audience?
- **Impact**: does the media have sufficient impact to ensure the message has a chance of getting through the clutter?
- **Message**: does it help ensure the message is clearly communicated?
- **Response**: does it make responding easy?
- **Internal management**: does it enhance the efficient management of the campaign?
- **The end result**: what are the costs and projected likely revenues? Taking the above into account, and looking at the average response rates for the chosen media, how likely are you to hit target for the campaign?

ACTIVITY

Obtain a direct-response press or magazine advertisement or a piece of direct mail. Critically appraise the media choice made, using the AIMRITE framework (although you are not likely to be able to assess the end result).

REGULATIONS

Throughout Europe and elsewhere, marketing communications are subject to constraints and regulations. Some controls are set by law and others are self-imposed voluntarily by the marketing communications industry itself. The balance of legal and self-regulations varies from country to country. Collectively, the UK regulations seek to uphold four guiding principles. Promotions should be:

- legal
- decent
- honest
- truthful.

ethical focus: Breaking the code

It's in the nature of human beings to push boundaries to see how far they'll stretch, and advertisers are no different. The ASA and OFCOM are there to maintain standards.

The UK's most complained about ad to date is a KFC Zinger Crunch ad showing workers at an emergency helpline talking with their mouths full of chicken. The main cause for complaint was their appalling table manners and the example they set to children. There were 1679 complaints but the ASA decided it was all right: complaint not upheld.

A Carphone Warehouse ad attracted complaints from 145 people including some of its competitors. Ads in a range of media, including TV, press and on a CD, promoted a new TalkTalk telephone package with 'free broadband forever'. The complaint was that it was misleading to suggest that the broadband was free when it involved an 18-month contractual commitment to the calls package, a connection charge of £29.99, ongoing costs of £9.99 per month plus line rental (£20.99 in total) and a disconnection fee of £70. The complaints were upheld.

Ninety-six viewers complained about a Kellogg's Crunchy Nut Cornflakes ad which showed a man riding a large dog in order to get home quicker to eat his cornflakes. Despite an on-screen warning of 'Don't try this with your dog at home', viewers felt that it might encourage cruelty to animals. The ASA considered the ad obvious fantasy and so did not agree.

John Lewis fell foul of animal lovers with its 2010 Christmas advert, a hugely popular advert which showed a little boy pinning a Christmas stocking to his dog's kennel on a windy, snowy day. Many thought this endorsed leaving animals out in the cold and was unacceptable but the ASA did not uphold the complaints.

To find out more about the advertising codes, and for examples of complaints, visit www.asa.org.uk.

These principles are used to produce a series of codes of practice covering different media and types of promotion. These codes can be seen on the web at **www.asa.org.uk**.

Despite attempts to ensure that these principles are maintained, there are examples of some dubious practices. Regulatory bodies police the industry and, where necessary, require that promotions are withdrawn if they contravene the principles above. Legal action can be taken in extreme cases.

In general, it is up to the media owners (TV, radio, cinema, newspaper and magazine owners, etc.) to decide whether or not an item is likely to contravene the codes of practice, and to refuse to run the promotion where this may happen. In the case of TV and radio, any advertising should be pre-vetted – that is, checked before transmission, but in the case of most other promotions, such pre-vetting is impossible because of the volume of advertisements involved and so checks are made after the promotions have been circulated. Members of the public are encouraged to make complaints, which are subsequently investigated. In the case of the UK, a great deal of voluntary self-regulation is relied on to enhance the legal controls. The Advertising Standards Authority (ASA) is responsible for regulating advertising, sales promotions and direct marketing (including the Internet). There are also numerous other professional bodies representing the different elements of marketing communications, which also have their own codes of professional practice. Most other countries have similar arrangements although the extent, and nature, of the control exerted varies significantly.

SETTING THE MARKETING COMMUNICATIONS BUDGET

Marketing communications should be seen as an investment. It can, however, be quite expensive and so attention should be paid to getting the budget right. Setting the promotional budget is not an exact science. Various techniques are used by organisations, the five most popular ones being:

- arbitrary method
- affordable method
- competitive parity method
- objective and task method
- percentage of sales method.

Budgeting methods between organisations vary in popularity. While the percentage of sales method is reputed to be a favoured approach in larger organisations, small businesses are more likely to use arbitrary or affordable approaches.

ARBITRARY METHOD

Rather than a method, this is an approach to arriving at a budget figure. It is more a judgement that seems right at the time. It is unlikely to be based on any significant criteria and is more likely to be based on gut feeling or intuition. It is an educated guess – but, remember, it may have been made by a very experienced marketing director.

AFFORDABLE METHOD

In essence, this means that the company will spend on promotion what it thinks is reasonable and can afford. Organisations using this approach, like the arbitrary approach, are more likely to reflect a view that marketing communications are an expense rather than an investment.

The affordable method causes problems with long-range planning. The company cannot guess the funds that will be available in the future to spend on promotion. Also, in times of recession or hardship, very little will be spent on promotion, and yet this is most likely to be the time when extra spending would be of benefit.

COMPETITIVE PARITY METHOD

A budget is set that matches, exceeds or is in proportion to competitors' budgets. Care has to be taken in applying this method. For example, not all companies have the same objectives. Some may want to become the market leader (market share objective), while others may wish to become more profitable (profitability objective). A company's nearest competitor may be much bigger or much smaller than it is. Simply matching expenditure in this situation would not be sensible. Setting the budget as an appropriate proportion would be a better approach.

OBJECTIVE AND TASK METHOD

The objective and task method determines a budget based on what the various communications activities need to achieve. In essence, objectives are set and then the marketing communications tasks to achieve the objectives are decided upon. By calculating the costs of those tasks, a budget is set.

Although this method may appear to be the best, it is a method that is rarely applied in its entirety. Difficulties in implementing this approach include:

- the company may not be able to afford the budget arrived at
- it is time-consuming (and therefore expensive to prepare)
- the task may not actually achieve the objective anyway, e.g. the planned PR campaign may not raise the company's credibility as intended.

PERCENTAGE OF SALES METHOD

The percentage of sales method is probably the most popular method. It is the classical approach partly because it is easy to calculate. It links marketing communications expenditure directly to levels of sales by allocating a fixed percentage of turnover to marketing communications.

However, there are difficulties. What percentage should be used and how should the turnover be determined? The percentage may be based on previous practice, on competitor allocations or on industry averages. Turnover could be based on historic sales, last year's sales or sales averaged over a number of years. It could be based on current sales levels, or it could be based on forecast sales (which may, of course, be wrong).

Perhaps unsurprisingly, in practice, most organisations use a combination of all these approaches to set their budgets.

SUMMARY

This chapter has introduced some basic concepts and models that support marketing communications decisions. The key model to understand is the communications process, since marketing communications, or promotion, is a communication process. This involves an understanding of the sender, the message, the media and the receivers.

Organisations can use a variety of promotional tools to communicate with potential customers, whether consumer or organisational. The major promotional tools are advertising, PR, sales promotion and personal selling. To these can be added direct marketing and sponsorship, together with many other activities such as packaging and events. Collectively, these are known as the promotion or marketing communications mix.

The organisation can use its promotion mix to develop both push and pull strategies. With a push strategy, the organisation directs its promotional efforts at marketing channel members. These then push the product forwards to the final buyer. With a pull strategy, the organisation directs its promotional efforts at the final buyer to develop a strong demand for the product that is used to pull a product through the marketing channel. Most organisations use a combination of push and pull.

The purpose of all marketing communications is to create a response from potential buyers. One response model, also known as a hierarchy of effects model, is AIDA (Awareness, Interest, Desire and Action). Each promotional tool has different degrees of effectiveness in eliciting these different responses.

One approach does not fit all. There is no single optimal promotion mix and no one accepted scientific approach to determining the promotion mix. Many factors need to be considered, such as: the objectives of the marketing plan; the size and characteristics of the target market/audience and their buying decision process; the type of products being promoted; the objectives of the promotional efforts; and competitors' promotional efforts.

CHALLENGES REVIEWED

Now that you have finished reading the chapter, look back at the challenges you were set at the beginning. Do you have a clearer idea of what's involved?

HINTS

- See 'setting the marketing communications budget'.
- Think beyond mass media advertising to other promotional tools and more targeted media.
- Time for crisis management – see 'publics' and 'media relations'.
- Think about repositioning and take great care not to be misleading in your approach – check the advertising code carefully.

READING AROUND

JOURNAL ARTICLES

Carrillat, F.A., d'Astous, A. and Lazure, J. (2013) 'For better, for worse? What to do when celebrity endorsements go bad', *Journal of Advertising Research,* 53 (1): 15–30.

Cleeren, K., van Heerde, H. and Dekimpe, M. (2013) 'Rising from the ashes: how brands and categories can overcome product-harm crises', *Journal of Marketing,* 77 (2): 58–77.

Colley, R. (1961) *Defining Advertising Goals for Measured Advertising Results.* New York: Association of National Advertisers.

Dens, N., De Pelsmacker, P., Wouters, M. and Purnawirawan, N. (2012) 'Do you like what you recognize? The effects of brand placement prominence and movie plot connection on brand attitude as mediated by recognition', *Journal of Advertising,* 31 (3): 35–53.

Garretson Folse, J.A., Netemeyer, R. and Burton, S. (2012) 'Spokescharacters: how the personality traits of sincerity, excitement, and competence help to build equity', *Journal of Advertising,* 31 (1): 17–32.

Jones, J.P. (1990) 'Advertising: strong or weak force? Two views oceans apart', *International Journal of Advertising,* 9 (3): 233–46.

van Kuilenburg, P., de Jong, M. and van Rompay, T. (2011) '"That was funny, but what was the brand again?" Humorous television commercials and brand linkage', *International Journal of Advertising,* 30 (5): 795–814.

Storbacka, K., Ryals, L., Davies, I. and Nenonen, S. (2009) 'The changing role of sales: viewing sales as a strategic, cross-functional process', *The European Journal of Marketing,* 43 (7–8): 890–906.

MAGAZINE ARTICLES

Carter, S. (2013) 'A creative legend's lesson to planners', *Admap,* February, London: WARC.

Cooper, A. (2013) 'Keep sponsorship local', *Admap,* March, London: WARC.

BOOKS AND BOOK CHAPTERS

Abilasha, M. (1999) 'Celebrities in advertising', in J.P. Jones (ed.), *The Advertising Business.* London: Sage, Chapter 17.

Barry, A. (with a foreword by Sir Richard Branson) (2005) *PR Power: Inside Secrets from the World of Spin.* London: Virgin Books.

Burcher, N. (2012) *Paid Owned Earned: Maximizing Marketing Returns in a Socially Connected World.* London: Kogan Page.

Grunig, J. and Hunt, T. (1984) *Managing Public Relations.* London: Thomson Learning.

Hackley, C. (2010) *Advertising and Promotion,* 2nd edn. London: Sage.

L'Etang, J. (2007) 'Public relations in promotional culture and in everyday life', in *Public Relations Concepts: Practice and Critique.* London: Sage, Chapter 10.

Levinson, J.C., Meyerson, M. and Scarborough, M.E. (2008) *Guerrilla Marketing on the Internet: The Definitive Guide from the Father of Guerrilla Marketing.* Irvine, CA: Entrepreneur Press.

Springer, P. (2007) 'Rethinking mass media', in *Ads to Icons.* London: Kogan Page, Chapter 1.

WEBSITES

www.asa.org.uk – the website for the Advertising Standards Authority; check out the complaints and adjudications.

www.brandrepublic.com – access to news stories and feature articles.

www.creativeclub.co.uk – subscription-only site; excellent source for current advertising.

www.nmauk.co.uk – the Newspaper Marketing Agency; check out its 'breaking ads' page.

http://www.theidm.com/ – the Institute of Direct and Digital Marketing; go to the knowledge centre and browse.

www.warc.com – the World Advertising Research Centre: journals, case studies, papers on best practice and much more.

JOURNALS

International Journal of Advertising
Journal of Advertising
Journal of Marketing Communications

MAGAZINES

Admap
Campaign
Marketing
Marketing Week
PR Week

VIDEO

AMC TV, *Madmen* – TV series, available on DVD.

BBC4 (2008) *Hard Sell programmes 1–6* – Phil Jupitus narrates a series exploring 50 years of British TV advertising.

Sky Atlantic (2012) 'Admen' extracts and write-up available from **http://skyatlantic.sky.com/shows/ad-men** (accessed 20/05/13). A review of British advertising from the 1960s to date.

SELF-REVIEW QUESTIONS

1. List and explain the key elements in the communications process model. (See pp. 324–6)
2. Identify sources of noise in the communications process. (See p. 325)
3. What are the main elements, or tools, of the promotion mix? (See pp. 320–1)
4. What are the advantages and disadvantages of mass communication and interpersonal communication? (See pp. 330–4)
5. Define push and pull strategies. (See p. 324)
6. What are the problems with using 'increase sales' as a promotional objective? (See pp. 337–9)
7. How is advertising controlled or regulated in the UK? (See pp. 361–2)
8. What is the AIDA model and how can it be used to set promotional objectives? (See pp. 327–9)
9. Explain how personal selling is a two-way communications process. (See p. 354)
10. Explain and give examples of the major types of consumer sales promotion. (See p. 351)
11. What is direct-response advertising? (See pp. 357–8)
12. Discuss the strengths and limitations of each budgeting method. (See pp. 362–3)

Mini case study: A fly-away success story: Red Bull gives you wings

Read the questions, then the case material, and then answer the questions.

Questions

1 Analyse Red Bull's marketing communications strategy in terms of: objectives, target audience and brand positioning.

2 Red Bull make excellent use of paid, owned and earned media. Identify examples of each and discuss how they support each other to maximise audience reach.

3 How well integrated are Red Bull's marketing communications activities? What pulls them together?

How do you become a market leader? One way is to create a whole new category and then launch your brand into it with a bang. That's what Red Bull did back in 1987 and they are still leading the energy drinks market that they created. In 2012 they sold 5.2 billion cans.

Strong brands like Red Bull don't happen by accident. The company has invested a lot into its marketing: a lot of thought and effort, although not really such a lot of money. Compared to companies like Coca-Cola and Pepsi, their marketing budget is tiny, yet a can of Red Bull can cost over twice as much as a can of cola.

It all started in the 1980s when Austrian entrepreneur Dietrich Mateschitz visited Thailand and was impressed and energised by a local drink. He adapted the ingredients to better suit Western tastes and launched it in 1987 as Red Bull, Europe's first energy drink. The first press ad claimed that it was so awesome polka dots would fly off your tie.

1988 saw Red Bull's first sponsorship deal: the Red Bull Dolomitenmann: 'one of the toughest extreme sport relays on the planet', a marathon event combining mountain running, paragliding, kayaking and mountain biking. More extreme sport sponsorships followed: snowboarding, mountain biking and cliff diving but this wasn't enough for Red Bull. The brand wanted to be even more involved in the exciting lifestyle represented by these high-risk challenges, and so they began creating their own events. They became an integral part of the action rather than just standing at the sidelines.

Red Bull run a number of different contests and events such as a soapbox race and the Red Bull Flugtag. Flugtags challenge contestants to build flight machines which are then launched (or crashed) off a 30 foot platform into water. The flight record for one of these amateur machines is 207 feet, their crashes are spectacular and prizes are awarded not just for length of flight but also for imaginative design and humour. Flugtags have been held all round the world and attract huge crowds at the actual event – though the bulk of the audience watch online via Facebook or YouTube. Two years on, that record-breaking flight in Minneapolis had over half a million views on YouTube.

Red Bull Flugtag

(Continued)

Red Bull
space
jump

(Continued)

In 2012, Red Bull launched a man into space – and then threw him out. Felix Baumgartner set the world record for skydiving when he fell approximately 39 kilometres, reaching an estimated speed of 1357.64 km/h (843.6 mph), or Mach 1.25. He was the first person to break the sound barrier without being inside any form of vehicle. The event was watched live around the world – and then watched again and again on YouTube. The space dive made sense both for daredevil Felix and for Red Bull. It was a logical progression from what they had done before. Over the years, Red Bull's association with daring stunts and extreme sports had successfully created an independent, edgy image that has served it well. More recently, the brand has added creativity to its image with its involvement in contemporary culture through events such as Word Clash street poems and Art of Can which invited would-be artists to create sculptures using Red Bull cans – inspired recycling! (http://www.redbull.com/en/stories/1331580470607/red-bull-art-of-can-inspired-recycling).

Through these events Red Bull carries on an intense conversation with its youthful and independent-minded target audience. The brand is part of their lives, providing entertainment, excitement, challenge. The buzz around Red Bull is regularly stoked by another high-risk brand experience but it is the audience and their engagement that has really built that brand strength.

Red Bull has extended its do-it-yourself approach to events into media. Now they have an online TV channel (www.redbull.tv/Redbulltv) where you can watch sports and entertainment programmes and listen to music. It's all free – but it's also all heavily branded. The Red Bull Media House provides web clips, documentaries and photos for other publishers. The official Red Bull website looks more like a sports site with tabs for motorsports, biking snowboarding and surfing. It also has games and music. The emphasis is clearly on what Red Bull does as a brand, not on the product itself. This is lifestyle branding at its best.

Red Bull's promotional activities are so well integrated that they seem like one long, continuous campaign. While their focus is on events and branded content, they do also make use of paid media. The famous tag line, 'Red Bull gives you wings', is frequently seen on television, in the press and on other web pages. They use the different promotional tools for different purposes. The adverts create awareness and build brand image through their humour and consistency. Sponsorship of sports like Formula 1 builds credibility by association and the Red Bull branded events and online content, e.g. the Red Bull Air Race and Last Man Standing 48-hour Motocross, differentiate the product and engage the audience.

Red Bull promises to deliver energy. It will wake you up, enhance your performance. The universal appeal of this brand promise helps the brand to cross international boundaries. The drink may have started in Austria, inspired by a Thai tonic, but now it is boosting energy levels all over the world.

REFERENCES

Buttle, F. (1984) 'Merchandising', *European Journal of Marketing*, 18 (6/7): 104–23.

The Chartered Institute of Public Relations (2013) 'What is PR?,' available at: **www.cipr.co.uk/content/careers-cpd/careers-pr/what-pr**.

Colley, R. (1961) *Defining Advertising Goals for Measured Advertising Results*. New York: Association of National Advertisers.

DBA (2009) *Heinz Classic Soups*, Design Business Association Effectiveness Awards 2009. Available at: **www.warc.com** (accessed 13/12/09).

Dens, N., De Pelsmacker, P., Wouters, M. and Purnawirawan, N. (2012) 'Do you like what you recognize? The effects of brand placement prominence and movie plot connection on brand attitude as mediated by recognition', *Journal of Advertising*, 31(3): 35–53.

Engel, J.F., Warshaw, M.R. and Kinnear, T.C. (1994) *Promotional Strategy*, 8th edn. New York: Irwin.

Garretson Folse, J.A., Netemeyer, R.G. and Burton, S. (2012) 'Spokes characters: how the personality traits of sincerity, excitement, and competence help to build equity,' *Journal of Advertising*, 31(1): 17–32.

Grunig, J. and Hunt, T. (1984) *Managing Public Relations*. London: Thomson Learning.

IDM (2010) Institute of Direct Marketing website. Available at: **www.theidm.com/resources/jargon-ouster** (accessed 15/05/10).

IPA and the Future Foundation (2012) 'The future of advertising and agencies – a 10 year perspective', available at: **www.futurefoundation.net/page/view/the_future_of_advertising_and_agencies_-_a_10_year_perspective** (accessed 15/11/12).

Jefkins, F. (1989) *Public Relations Techniques*. London: Heinemann.

Jones, J.P. (1990) 'Advertising: strong or weak force? Two views oceans apart', *International Journal of Advertising*, 9 (3): 233–46.

Makin, C. (2002) *Domino's Pizza: Building a High Street Brand through a Change in Media Strategy*, IPA Effectiveness Awards, Best Interactive. Available at: **www.warc.com** (accessed 01/09/03).

National Readership Survey (NRS) (2007) London: NRS.

Pickton, D.W. and Broderick, A. (2004) *Integrated Marketing Communications*, 2nd edn. Harlow: FT/Prentice Hall.

Schramm, W. (1955) 'How communication works', in W. Schramm (ed.), *The Process and Effects of Mass Communications*. Champaign, IL: University of Illinois Press, pp. 3–26.

Storbacka, K., Ryals, L., Davies, I.A. and Nenonen, S. (2009) 'The changing role of sales: viewing sales as a strategic, cross-functional process', *The European Journal of Marketing*, 43 (7–8): 890–906.

White, T. (2013) 'Ryvita crisp bread: ladies that crunch', IPA Effectiveness Awards 2012, available at: **www.warc.com/Content/ContentViewer.aspx?MasterContentRef=03ed9049-99e0-420e-a5f1-24dd648b8d0c&q=objectives** (accessed 23/02/13).

Visit the companion website on your computer at **www.sagepub.co.uk/masterson3e** or MobileStudy on your Smart phone or tablet by scanning this QR code and gain access to:

- **Videos** to get a better understanding of key concepts and provoke in-class discussion.
- Links to useful **websites and templates** to help guide your study.
- Access **SAGE Marketing Pins (www.pinterest.com/sagepins/)**. SAGE's regularly updated **Pinterest** page, giving you access to regularly updated resources on everything from Branding to Consumer Behaviour.
- **Daily Grind podcast series** to learn more about the day-to-day life of a marketing **professional**.
- Interactive **Practice questions** to test your understanding.
- A **bonus chapter on Marketing Careers** to not only support your study, but your job search and future career.
- **PowerPoints** prompting key points for revision.

PLACE CHALLENGES

The following are illustrations of the types of decision that marketers have to take or issues they face. *You aren't expected to know how to deal with the challenges now*; just bear them in mind as you read the chapter and see what you can find that helps.

- Imagine that you work for Reebok. Your objectives are to increase the number of sales made in your home market and to maintain the relative exclusivity of the brand. How can you use the stores to achieve your objectives?
- A journalist you know is writing a story about the increase in direct marketing and has come to you, as a marketing consultant, for some advice. You have told her that getting the right product to the customer on time is critically important. In reply, she has asked you to explain why, if it is so important, all manufacturers do not take responsibility for every aspect of deliveries themselves.
- You are working for a French wine company. You know that Australian and American wine producers are seen as more technologically advanced and better value. How can you compete?
- Your small furniture company is located in a small industrial estate in Cornwall. You know that your products have great potential if only consumers could see them. Unfortunately the major retailers tell you that you cannot make enough furniture to be worth their while working with you. How can you develop to get around this?
- You are the headteacher of a large secondary school which is always in need of cash. A snack food manufacturer wants to install vending machines in the school to sell crisps, chocolate and biscuits. They will stock and maintain the machines and give the school 15% of the takings. What do you need to consider before accepting or rejecting the deal?

Case study:
direct selling

INTRODUCTION

Where did you buy your last T-shirt? Do you know where it was made and how it got from there to you? Billions are spent on products every year but few people look beyond the places where they buy things. They do not think about the plantation that their bananas came from or the factory in which their television was made. For a marketer, place includes *all* the activities and all the organisations involved in getting goods from their point of origin to their point of sale.

Place is one of the elements of the marketing mix and is really more accurately referred to as distribution, but then the marketing mix would not be the 4Ps; it would be 3Ps and a D which would be far less memorable.

Many of the activities involved in managing product distribution are crucial to effective targeting and positioning (see Chapter 4). For example, placement in an upmarket store sends an upmarket message that helps build a brand image in customers' minds. The timely arrival of goods is seen as good customer service. Contrarily, late arrival of goods, or the arrival of the wrong goods, or of goods in poor condition can undermine all the good work of the product managers and marketing communications managers and cause customers to reject a brand completely. There is a significant management challenge here: a challenge requiring the management of both time and space.

This chapter looks at some key elements of the exchange relationship (see Exhibit 9.1), in particular how this idea of place brings together sellers and buyers, products and the needs they are designed to fulfil. We will discuss the importance of time, space, information, bargaining power and what sellers have to do to match buyers' expectations. By the end of the chapter, you will begin to realise just how much work has been done to put those trainers in your local sports shop or to make your next dream holiday a reality.

EXPAND YOUR KNOWLEDGE

Classic article

Pearson, M.M. (1981) 'Ten distribution myths', *Business Horizons*, 24 (3): 17–23.

Michael Pearson goes through ten myths in turn, explaining that these myths exist due to our lack of understanding of the true nature of distribution.

THE IMPORTANCE OF DISTRIBUTION

marketing
opportunity
a chance to reach
a particular group
of customers with a
product offer

All businesses depend on marketing opportunities to meet potential customers' needs. Opportunities, whether taken or missed, are what shape the future of the enterprise.

Changes that affect place frequently bring new **marketing opportunities**. These may be technological changes. For example, the Internet has changed the way in which many products are delivered to customers. Newspapers are able to meet their customers' demand for continuously updated and instantly accessible news and information, for instance. They may be changes in the competitive environment, such as a company withdrawing from a market and so freeing up its channels of distribution. Changes in the political and regulatory environments can affect how and when companies get products to customers, e.g. the relaxation

Exhibit 9.1 The exchange relationship system

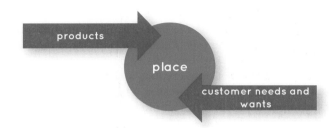

 b2b focus: An opportunity to become one of the most successful companies in the world

Most of today's PCs are based on IBM's architecture which was originally developed for the IBM PC launched in 1981 (the only sizeable alternative architecture is Apple), but IBM was not the first to make a personal computer. Towards the end of the 1970s, the market leader for large business computers realised that it had to get into the growing market for small home and personal computers quickly or it would miss out on a huge opportunity. That meant, unusually for IBM, contracting out some of the development. IBM was one of the largest companies in the world and many companies did not want to get involved in a project where the power was so one-sided. However, IBM's decision to work with others presented major, and unusual, marketing opportunities for smaller firms who were prepared to develop components and software for the new PC.

This proved a golden opportunity for two little known companies: Intel and Microsoft. Microsoft produced the original PC Disk Operating System. DOS has, of course, long since been replaced by Windows. Microsoft was handed a new product development contract but the real value lay in the chance to have a Microsoft operating system sold with every IBM PC globally. So this was really a distribution (or place) opportunity.

IBM no longer make PCs, having sold that part of its business to Lenovo, but a large number of other companies (e.g. Dell, Toshiba, Sony, Acer, Fujitsu, Siemens, Hewlett Packard) do make computers which use Microsoft's operating system and they hugely outsell the IBM-branded ones – just as Microsoft's profits far exceed IBM's.

SOURCES: Bellis, 2007; IBM, n.d.

'Working for IBM'

of Sunday trading laws or the granting of new casino licences. All of these things provide marketing opportunities.

In a competitive environment, the customer can shop around. It is not generally desirable to be second choice. The tension between consumer needs and business capabilities creates a constant dynamic for change. One of the key roles for marketing management is the creation of attractive opportunities for exchange and that means monitoring the changes carefully and getting the place right.

CHANNEL MEMBERS

supply chain
the network of businesses and organisations involved in distributing goods and services to their final destination

A **supply chain** is a network of businesses and organisations through which goods pass to get to their final destination (see Exhibit 9.2). In most developed markets, these networks will be extensive and have many participant businesses. A global business, such as the Ford Motor Company, has a supply chain that runs through a number of countries. Each of the businesses within that chain is likely to have further international suppliers so that the whole network spans the world. So, Ford buys raw materials and parts from a number of other businesses and sends cars on to a number of resellers.

As companies have got larger, and marketing has become global, so warehouses and distribution networks have grown. It may appear to be cheaper (thanks to economies of scale) to put one huge warehouse in the Netherlands and use it to send goods all over Europe, but this will use more petrol (a scarce resource) and cause more pollution. Bigger is not always better.

A distribution channel (sometimes called a marketing channel) is a product's route through the supply chain. The distribution channel is a specific product's path through the supply chain. Its shape is determined by the product's manufacturer in order to meet their marketing objectives. For example, Rolex watches target quite a small customer group (the relatively affluent), offer high-quality service and want to project a quality image. Consequently, Rolex generally uses upmarket retail partners with comparatively few stores. This is called selective distribution (see 'Designing the supply chain' on pp. 390).

To summarise, a supply chain includes all of the channel members but a specific distribution channel is limited to just one group of channel members chosen to deliver a particular product to a particular market.

Exhibit 9.2   Example of a supply chain: suppliers, intermediaries, customers

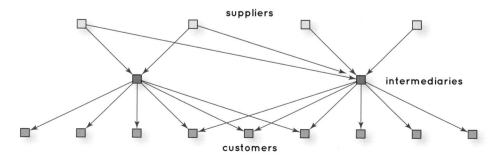

BUYERS – CONSUMERS, BUSINESSES AND OTHER ORGANISATIONS

This group is at the end of a supply chain. Its members do not sell the product on but buy it to be used by themselves or their organisations. (For more on customer types see Chapters 1 and 3.)

SELLERS – MANUFACTURERS, RETAILERS, WHOLESALERS, RESELLERS

Manufacturers and producers are the major group of sellers. Many of the largest manufacturers achieve global recognition for their products. For example, Hewlett Packard is considered to be one of the world's leading computer printer

Magna Park in Leicestershire is Europe's largest distribution park.

manufacturers. Its products are sold to customers in different markets through a global network of outlets, some of which are **retailers** selling to end-user customers, and some of which are **resellers** selling the products on. Coca-Cola is known globally as a producer of soft drinks, although in many countries the drinks are produced by another company under licence rather than by Coca-Cola itself.

Products are transformed as they move through the supply chain, i.e. each company that receives products uses its expertise and resources to change them in some way before passing them on. For example, FAG buys steel and then transforms it into ball bearings, which it then sells to motor manufacturers across the world. The motor manufacturers sell their motors to quarry plant manufacturers, who make equipment to extract material from the earth. At each stage, value is added to the bought-in product, i.e. it is transformed into something more desirable or useful and can command a higher price (e.g. steel into ball bearings or fresh peas into frozen ones). The length of a product's supply chain is determined by the complexity of the final product and its user's needs.

Intermediaries within the part of the supply chain that makes up the distribution channel (or marketing channel) also add value to the product. They deal in finished products, in bars of soap and televisions rather than ingredients or sub-assemblies such as vegetable fat and electrical components. Marketing channel members may, for example, re-package goods, take them to more convenient places for sale or offer extra services such as delivery, installation or advice on the product's use.

The seller that most consumers buy from is the retailer. The retailer is usually the last member of the supply chain before the end customer. Retailers may operate from a shop, a catalogue, a phone line, a direct-response advert in the press or on television, or a website (sometimes a combination, as is the case with Argos, for example). The retailer uses their market knowledge to select goods and services that their customers will want to buy. When this is done well, the retailer thrives; when it is done poorly, the retailer does poorly too.

Retail organisations come in all sizes. The biggest retailers, such as Wal-Mart and IKEA, are global household names and can offer consumers products from around the world. The smallest are corner shops or even businesses run from home.

Retailers buy goods in and sell them on, transforming them and adding value to them (partly through providing a more convenient way to buy them) in the process.

retailers
sales outlets that deal with end customers, e.g. a shop

resellers
businesses that buy the product from the manufacturer with the purpose of selling it on to another business further down the chain

intermediaries
businesses that form part of the distribution channel, passing goods on towards the end customer

The Rational Consumer goes Shopping

In-store innovation at Tesco

It is this transformation that turns the buying business into a selling business. An illustration of this is Sainsbury's transformation of Heinz beans. Sainsbury's buy millions of cans of beans which arrive at its distribution depots packed in cartons and on pallets. These pallet loads are then broken down into individual cans that can be stacked on the supermarket's shelves. Sainsbury's sell the individual cans of beans to the final customer. In an IKEA store it may be the customer who has to take the product from the stack of products in the warehouse, which directly passes the cost of the work to the customer.

breaking down
the process of
reducing the quantity
of product to be
moved

Wholesalers are one step further away from the final customer than retailers are. They usually buy products to sell on to other members of the supply chain and they support smaller retailers by holding stock in a more convenient location, thus reducing the delivery time from the manufacturers. Most retail wholesalers (e.g. cash and carries) also transform the products by breaking down the quantities supplied by the manufacturer. In this respect they are quite similar to the retailer.

This type of business is often found in clothing and food markets because the volume of transactions is high and that helps reduce the risk in holding quantities of stock available for other channel members to buy.

economies of scale
unit costs fall as
larger quantities
are produced; a
cost advantage
associated with large
organisations

Wholesalers are currently in decline and the main reason for this is the growth of large retail businesses, such as the big supermarkets and high street multiples, which generate significant economies of scale by buying in bulk direct from the manufacturers. This makes it more difficult for the wholesaler to sell their products at prices that earn sufficient profit.

In business-to-business (b2b) markets, many businesses carry out the breakdown of bulk function. They are called resellers, i.e. businesses that buy the product from the manufacturer with the purpose of selling it on to another business further down the chain.

FACILITATORS – AGENTS AND LOGISTICS SERVICES

This group of businesses smoothes the flow of products through the supply chain. Members of this group usually have specific expertise in a market, or other specialist resources that enable them to undertake distribution tasks more efficiently.

Agents are businesses that represent other businesses in a particular market. Smaller businesses often use locally based agents as a means of entering new or distant markets because the agent has knowledge of the market and access to local facilities. The agent can thus reduce the costs and risks associated with entering the new market. These businesses do not usually buy the products from the manufacturer so they cannot be classed as resellers. They take orders and are paid a commission.

Robots
in the
workplace
(Wired)

The UK housing market provides a good example of how agents work. In this market, the buyers and sellers tend to be individuals or families with just one house to sell. The estate agency does not take ownership of the house at any point; it brings buyers and sellers together by communicating the property's details to potential buyers and showing them around the house. The agency then charges the seller a commission for any subsequent sale of the property.

logistics
the flow of goods and
services through the
supply chain

The final category of participants is that of the businesses that transport and store products for the various members of the supply chain. They are known as logistics services, and include warehouses, distribution depots and transport services.

Exhibit 9.3   Types of retailer

Type of retailer	Description	Examples
Market traders	Stall in open or covered market, low rent, few facilities, may move location regularly, specialist or variety; markets are traditional across the world but have fallen out of favour in the UK; some have been repositioned upmarket and there is also an upsurge in farmers' markets	Leicester market (traditional), Borough market (more upmarket), Columbia Road market (flowers and plants)
Independents	The majority of shops are independent but, in the UK and many other industrialised nations, they account for only a small proportion of sales; they have fewer resources and usually less expertise than the large high street multiples	One-off newsagents, restaurants, hairdressers
Multiples and chains	Have a standardised image; they may specialise in a specific range of goods (e.g. women's fashion) or may stock a wider range or be service providers	Topshop, Marks & Spencer, Toni and Guy, Starbucks, Slug and Lettuce, Shell
Supermarkets, superstores and hypermarkets	Usually multiples, common in food but also found in specialist categories such as golf or hardware; hypermarkets are usually out of town	Tesco, Aldi, PC World
Convenience stores	Smaller than supermarkets and with more limited stock but easier for shoppers to pop in to; local shops and garage forecourt shops	Spar, Londis, Tesco Metro, BP Connect
Department stores	A collection of shops or departments under one roof; the store is centrally owned although parts may be rented out	House of Fraser, Debenhams, El Corte Inglés, Printemps, Vendex
Discount stores	Traditionally large, warehouse-like shops with cheap prices; their cost savings come from: lower rents (they are often out of town), minimum service levels, rudimentary display and bulk purchase; increasingly moving online for further cost savings and wider reach	Lidl, Mountain Warehouse
Warehouse clubs	Large stores offering wholesale prices to members only; members may be individual and/or trade; a cross between a cash and carry and a discount store (see above)	Costco, Sam's Club (USA)

(Continued)

Exhibit 9.3 *(Continued)*

Type of retailer	Description	Examples
Voluntary chains	A network of individually owned shops which club together to benefit from economies of scale and to gain marketing advantages	Mace, Spar
Franchises	A type of multiple, the outlets are individually owned but licensed by a larger company to sell their products	Body Shop, Domino's Pizza, Merry Maids (cleaning service)
Factory outlets	May be large and out of town (and grouped into a factory outlet or shopping village) or smaller and more central; originally sold seconds but are now also used to get rid of excess stock; paradise for bargain hunters	Bicester Outlet Village, Cheshire Oaks, The Galleria Outlet Centre
E-tailers	Primarily sell online; many offline retailers also sell online (bricks and clicks), few are pure Internet businesses (pure plays)	Amazon, Ocado

© Dave Pickton

Eddie Stobart is a well-known logistics contractor.

The simplest form of transportation is the postal service. For bigger items, courier services or small transport companies may be used. If there are vast quantities of products to be moved around, then the logistics business will also need to be a big company. These businesses have specialist facilities and knowledge. Some, e.g. UPS, have grown to a global scale and can take products to market anywhere in the world. The vast majority of logistics businesses, however, are much smaller.

Companies who use specialist logistics companies do so primarily to reduce costs. By concentrating on just this one specialist function, logistics businesses benefit from economies of scale (e.g. they can use larger lorries and so make fewer trips) and so are able to deliver goods more cheaply than most manufacturers can. They also transport a large enough volume of products frequently enough to make it worthwhile investing in specialist storage and transport. For example, Christian Salvesen operates a number of cold-storage depots across the country. Manufacturers and retailers that need special conditions to store chilled food products use these depots rather than buying and maintaining these facilities for themselves.

There are drawbacks to contracting out deliveries. For a mail-order company, the only face-to-face contact with the customer may come at the point of delivery and then that is not with one of its own employees. The customer service provided by the logistics company is therefore a major determinant of customer satisfaction, but it is not in the seller's control. Apart from the impact this has on customer relationships, there are a number of marketing opportunities lost here. For example, the lorries and packaging may not bear the seller's name. To get around this, many major retailers who contract out their distribution insist that the transportation company paints its vehicles in the retailer's corporate colours. Those Marks & Spencer lorries you see on the motorway actually belong to Exel Logistics and are driven by that company's staff.

EXPAND YOUR KNOWLEDGE

Classic article

Hollander, S.C. (1960) 'The wheel of retailing', *Journal of Marketing*, 25 (Jul): 37–42.

The 'wheel of retailing' was a term coined by McNair. It describes the process by which new retailers enter the market and over time change and grow and by so doing create opportunities for new entrants. Hollander explains the wheel and examines examples that conform and some that do not conform to the wheel.

THE RIGHT SPACE AND TIME

Customers choose where and when to buy something. For example, if they want farm-fresh fruit and vegetables, they may go to the farm on the day they want these things. If they want designer clothes, they go to an appropriate upmarket store at a time that is convenient to them. These are fixed, geographic spaces – geography is the simplest idea of place. Whether you can buy the food that you want also depends on the growing season of the product (or it used to – now food is flown in from around the world all year round). Whether you can buy the jacket you want depends on the season and what is fashionable at that time. It also depends on the opening times of the outlets and whether you have time to get there. So another fixed point, a point in time, can be added to the concept of place.

Experian: consumer classification

In our increasingly technology-driven world, these concepts of space and time have become more flexible. Thanks to the Internet, customers can shop at any time of day or night. They can stay at home and have everything delivered to them.

Place, or distribution, is often summed up as *getting the right product to the right place at the right time*. No matter how good the product, if it is not available when and where the customer wants it, then there will be no sale. So if the shop is closed, or too far away, or if the salesperson calls at a bad time, customers are likely to make their purchases elsewhere. The time and place and manner of the sale are important parts of the product offer.

RIGHT SPACE

There is an old saying, which has been attributed to a number of famous retailers, that there are three secrets to business success: 'location, location, location.' So how do businesses, not just shops but all the other members of the supply chain too, choose their locations?

According to McGoldrick (2003), the most important consideration is the firm's target market. Who are they, where are they, and where do they want to buy things? Other considerations include the competition and costs.

There are several questions businesses need to ask when choosing the right location for retail premises:

- Are there enough of the right type of customers there?
- Where do they go now? What would make them become your customers instead?
- Is it easy to get to? Is there good public transport? Car parking?
- Will staff be able to travel there at a price they can afford (this can be a problem with some of the more exclusive areas)?
- What are the costs involved?
- How many competitive outlets are there? Is there enough business to support a newcomer?
- Are there complementary businesses nearby? For example, customers of a real meat butcher may be good prospects for an organic vegetable shop or a good bakery.
- Is there a suitable building available in the right timescale?
- Do you need planning permission? Is it likely to be granted? If the premises were used for another purpose before, then you are likely to need permission for 'change of use'.
- Has there been a similar business in the area? How did it do? Many people take over a failing business, e.g. a restaurant, and then fail too. It is important to analyse why the previous business failed *before* starting up.
- What other legal restrictions are there? For example, some areas are conservation areas, making it difficult to alter premises, others are residential only areas, and still others may prohibit certain types of business, e.g. pubs.
- For chains, what impact will the new outlet have on existing ones? Is it too close? Will it take away trade?
- What does the location say about your business? Does it project the right image?

Sometimes a retailer spots a marketing opportunity – a high street with no food store, a vacant shop near a school, a residential area with no bars or restaurants, an out-of-town site large enough to take a superstore with parking. These are places where there is little or no competition and where the retailer could reasonably expect to make good profits.

If a clothing retailer wants to attract the rich and fashionable, then its stores will need to be in exclusive locations, such as Bond Street in London or the Quadrilatero della Moda in Milan. The image of an area, its surroundings (e.g. residential or business), is a good indicator of the type of customer likely to be found there. If, however, the retailer depends on high sales volumes, then they will need to be somewhere busy, such as London's Oxford Street or in a popular shopping mall. Here they are also more likely to get passing trade (i.e. people who are just passing on their way somewhere else but who might pop in).

EXPAND YOUR KNOWLEDGE

Teller, C. and Dennis, C. (2012) 'The effect of ambient scent on consumers' perception, emotions and behaviour: a critical review', *Journal of Marketing Management*, 28 (1–2): 14–36.

Based on a critical literature review and a field experiment in a regional shopping mall, the researchers investigate the effectiveness of ambient scent. Interestingly, the researchers cast doubt on previous studies and the impact scent has on shoppers in a shopping centre environment.

ACTIVITY

Think about something important that you bought recently. How did you choose the place that you bought it from? Did you just go somewhere you'd been before, or did something else affect your choice?

A busy location with lots of passing trade is a popular place for many retailers of low-value goods – they need a high volume of sales in order to make profits. There is usually a newsagent and a café near a railway station. People want things to read and eat on train journeys. When they miss their train (or it is delayed), then they want a drink and a snack to while away the time. In the early days, McDonald's used to snap up sites near highway intersections – often in the middle of nowhere. It had realised that the bulk of its customers came by car, usually on their way somewhere else, and could be tempted to take a break by the sight of those famous golden arches. Other fast-food retailers sometimes set up shop anywhere McDonald's did – just because McDonald's was so good at picking locations.

Clusters of similar businesses are quite common. Some areas become known for certain types of shop. For example, London's Tottenham Court Road is full of PC dealers, the Lanes in Brighton is known for antiques, Hatton Garden is the place for jewellery. Clearly, these retailers are not trying to avoid the competition, rather they seem to revel in it. So why do they do it? Again, it is about volume of customers. If an area is known for a product type (e.g. PCs), then customers will flock there and not bother to go anywhere else. They know that they have a wide choice in that one place.

ethical focus: The death of the high street

Channel 4
Death of
the High
Street
report

In the UK, the trend recently has been towards bigger and bigger stores. These superstores are too big to fit into the centre of town and so out-of-town shopping centres have become commonplace. These are clearly popular with many consumers, as hordes of people drive out to them every day. However, there are those who object to the building of these retail parks.

The only way to get to many of these out-of-town stores is by car, so people who do not have cars cannot shop there. This does not seem to be too much of a problem. After all, they can just carry on shopping on the high street, can't they? Well no, not for everything. So much business has gone out of town that many high street shops have had to pack up.

Not all of them, of course. Walk through any UK city or town centre and you will see a lot of familiar names: WH Smith, Boots, Marks & Spencer, Topshop, Starbucks, Caffè Nero, Pizza Express. In fact, there are so many familiar names on every big shopping street that it has given rise to another complaint – that everywhere looks the same. Not so long ago, every shopping street was different – each had its own character largely thanks to the shops, restaurants and cafés there. There used to be many one-off coffee and tea shops in Britain. They were owner-run places and they were all different. There were butchers and bakers and fishmongers and hardware stores. Does your high street still have those?

Nowadays almost all regular purchases are made in the big supermarkets and they have put a lot of effort into brand building. Those brands are a guarantee of quality – and of uniformity. You can buy the same products in ASDA anywhere in the country. By being different, the old one-off shops offered choices. In their quest for standardisation and economies of scale, the big chains have actually reduced choice. This affects the whole supply chain. Farmers will only grow what they can sell and if the supermarkets want Braeburn and Red Delicious apples, then that is what is grown – and orchards of more unusual apples, such as the Bloody Ploughman or the Knobby Russet, are destroyed to make way for them.

Some smaller shops have survived, notably the corner shop whose demise was widely predicted. Corner shops cannot compete with the big supermarkets on price, but they offer convenience – they are local to the customers. Some are now part of chains, notably Spar, and their success has attracted the big supermarkets back into town. Sales are growing faster in London's neighbourhood shops than they are in the big stores and both Tesco and Sainsbury's now have a number of smaller stores. It remains to be seen whether local shops have built sufficiently strong relationships with their customers to survive this strong competition.

Where do you prefer to shop? And why?

ACTIVITY

Find a map of your local area. Where would you want to open the following types of retail outlet:

- an upmarket restaurant
- a bar
- a clothing store
- a DIY store
- a sweet shop?

What problems might you face, i.e. what are the constraints?

Any retail business has to decide whether its strategy will be to take its stores to the customers or to try to attract customers to its stores. Desirable as it may be to set up shop in a busy area with lots of the right type of customer, it is not always possible to find suitable premises there and so it may be necessary to attract customers away from their usual haunts. This was the idea behind the first of the out-of-town superstores in the UK. There were no sites big enough to house the vast stores that the retailers had in mind in the town centres, and so they went out of town – making sure there were good roads and ample parking, of course.

Intermediaries further up the supply chain (e.g. wholesalers, agents, distributors) may deliver goods to their customers and that makes a big difference to how they choose their location. In fact they may choose to be nearer their suppliers. It is unlikely that they will be reliant on passing trade and so they can afford to be in a more out of the way place. Good transport links are important, as is cost-effectiveness of course.

Many businesses now choose to locate themselves on the Internet. This is a wonderful way to be close to the customers – right in their homes. It is important not to forget that any goods ordered will need to be delivered, though, so the location of warehouses, or suppliers if goods are coming direct, still needs to be thought through carefully.

RIGHT TIME

To deliver what the customers want exactly when they want it requires flexibility in the supply chain and that usually results in higher operating costs. Think about how food is sold. For millions of people, the superstore has become part of everyday life. These huge buildings frequently offer over 20,000 different products. Millions are spent weekly on food and drink. Some of these stores are open 24 hours a day, six days out of seven. This creates the impression that you can get anything you want at any time. Stores have to live up to this expectation by trying to ensure that their whole range is always in stock. Clearly, stock costs money and so accountants will always try to minimise stock levels and the capital that is tied up in that stock. Overstocks (stock that cannot be sold) are expensive as they have to be sold off cheaply or binned. This is especially a problem with perishable goods such as food. There is therefore a tricky balancing act with stock: stores need enough to meet demand without running out, but not so much that there is a lot of waste. Stock, or inventory, management is a very difficult thing.

The only thing that stops some shops being permanently open is government legislation, i.e. the UK laws limiting the hours of trading on Sundays, and even this last hurdle can be overcome thanks to modern technology. The large grocery businesses, such as Tesco and Sainsbury's, provide Internet ordering services so that shoppers can order their food and drink at any time to suit their own needs. For a small fee, these products are then taken to the location specified by the shopper at the time specified by the shopper. However, this still will not get you a pint of milk in the middle of the night. Available delivery slots are limited to more sociable hours.

Making sure that goods are always available requires good logistics planning. This is a complex process with lots of scope for mistakes which may lead to **stock outs** or overstocks. An empty space on a shelf inevitably means lost sales – missed opportunities for both retailer and manufacturer. If customer demand was constant, then logistics would be much easier, but unfortunately demand fluctuates with people's changing tastes, the weather, changes in competitive offerings, items on the news, new campaigns – the list is endless. Imagine buying food for a small seaside café early in an English summer. How would you know how much ice cream to get in? How much soup and other warming dishes? Will the demand be for iced lattés or for hot chocolate? Alternatively, take pity on department store buyers at Christmas. If they buy too many Christmas goods, they are left with stock nobody wants in January. If they buy too few, they have missed valuable sales and gained frustrated customers.

Fernie and Sparks (2004) identified five key aspects of logistics management:

- suitable storage facilities for stock
- keeping the right amount of stock – not too much or too little
- good communications throughout the distribution channel so that suppliers can respond quickly to requests for products
- transport that is capable of carrying the required quantities of products safely to their destinations
- packaging that will protect the product in transit and storage while being easily handled – so boxes should not be too big or heavy, or too small as small packages take longer to pack.

Some products need specialist storage facilities, e.g. refrigeration or a dust-free atmosphere. All need to be located conveniently, to be secure and to be accessible for onward transportation. Retailers used to keep their stock on the premises so that they could refill shelves quickly, but only the smallest do this today. Retail space is expensive and so is better used for displaying goods rather than storing them. Large retailers have their own distribution centres situated close to clusters of stores so that they can restock easily. Some manage these themselves but others contract out to logistics specialists. For example, Exel manages seven of Marks & Spencer's 11 UK distribution centres as part of a range of activities that Exel is responsible for across Marks & Spencer's entire supply chain. These functions include imports, in-store logistics, home delivery, systems design and transportation (*Logistics Today*, 2003).

---

stock out
when a supplier
runs out of a
particular product

Keeping the right amount of stock requires good sales forecasting. Most retailers and wholesalers use computerised stock control programs fed with data from **electronic point of sale systems (EPOS)**. Bar-coded products are scanned at checkouts, or by hand-held scanners in warehouses, and stock figures are adjusted automatically. This information can then be communicated, either by the Internet or the company's own system (Intranet), to other members of the supply chain. Replacement stock may be ordered with no further human intervention at all.

Transporting goods may sound straightforward but it is not. Some town centre shops are difficult to access and deliveries may only be permitted at certain times (usually out of hours) so as to prevent traffic hold-ups. There are restrictions on lorry size and how long drivers can drive. The thoughtless driving of lorries with the company's logo emblazoned on the side is a PR problem. There are environmental considerations. Trains and boats are considered less polluting than road or air, but boats are slow and so are unsuitable for the shipment of perishable goods from a distance. In the UK, there is a growing consumer preference for local products. Not only are they perceived as fresher, but their purchase is seen as supporting the local economy and as less polluting because they have travelled a shorter distance. Marks & Spencer tries to fill any spare space in its lorries by making it available to other companies with goods to ship. With the help of the Strategic Rail Authority, the company has also set up a rail system to deliver wine from France directly to its Midlands distribution centre (Marks & Spencer, n.d.).

Packaging has a number of functions within the supply chain. It may have a promotional role (see Chapter 8) and even be an intrinsic part of the product, e.g. an individual ice cream tub, a toothpaste tube or a bottle for shower gel. Its logistics role is protecting the goods during transit, storage and handling, and making them easier to handle, stack and secure.

EPOS (electronic point of sale)
a computerised system that collects sales data at a retail checkout

DIFFERING VIEWS OF PLACE

THE CONSUMERS' VIEW

Generally speaking, shoppers do not think very much about place or the management of the supply chain. Shoppers are usually more concerned with the availability of the goods and services that they want. Shoppers' perceptions are thus largely focused on the last link in the supply chain, usually the retailer (Piercy, 2002). Just take a moment to think about your daily newspaper. Millions of people take it for granted that their preferred title will be available in a local shop each morning. They don't think about how it gets there or how its components have been brought together. They want the information or entertainment it contains and they will be frustrated if it is not there when they want it. Similarly, when was the last time that you thought about where your trousers came from and the activities that made it possible for you to buy them from the outlet you did? The key management task is to ensure that the right goods are there when and where the customer wants them.

Sometimes shoppers will be very concerned about the source of the goods, usually on health or ethical grounds. Shoppers who want organic food will seek reassurance from the retailer that the original source is reliable and truly organic. This is fairly easy for a major grocer to do as the reassurance comes from their own brand and the trust that the shopper has in that reputation. You can see from this example that the provision of relevant information to help the decision-makers is critical to completing the buying process. (For more on branding, see Chapters 6, 8 and 11.)

Shoppers may be concerned about ethical issues. For example, there have been numerous instances of child labour being used to produce goods and many shoppers in developed countries do not approve of this, considering it to be the exploitation of vulnerable children. Sellers can respond by collectively organising to reassure shoppers that their products are ethically produced. The Rugmark label is an example of one such scheme. Retailers subscribe to a neutral third-party organisation that checks the product's source to ensure that it does not use child labour. Only products that meet the specification can bear the label.

Clearly, the design, and ongoing management, of the distribution channel is extremely important. The specific design will vary from product to product and will be discussed later in this chapter. Shoppers need more than just quality goods and services; they also need a reassuring purchase experience so that they feel they can trust their suppliers and are comfortable with their purchases.

Organisations buy more things than consumers do and, just like consumers, they want to know where their goods and services come from and to buy them from suppliers they can trust.

ethical focus: FAIRTRADE

What is
FAIRTRADE?

The FAIRTRADE Foundation, which awards the FAIRTRADE Mark in the UK, is made up of different organisations, such as Oxfam, the World Development Movement and Christian Aid. The FAIRTRADE Foundation is a member of the standard-setting umbrella organisation FAIRTRADE Labelling Organization International (FLO). The FAIRTRADE Mark shows consumers that the farmers and workers who produced the products received a fair and stable price. They also have safe working conditions, stronger rights and treat their environment with care.

FAIRTRADE products include cocoa, coffee, tea, sugar, bananas, orange juice, honey and cotton. Any end product that is awarded the FAIRTRADE Mark must meet strict conditions of production and the Foundation has independent assessors to check that these conditions are being met.

Through such third-party schemes, the concerns of the consumers are passed up through the supply chain to the original source of the products. The customer can be satisfied that the farmers and workers who grew the products are getting a better deal. In this way, the FAIRTRADE Mark meets consumers' need to avoid exploiting poorer workers in the developing world.

THE ORGANISATION'S VIEW

Does a business see the supply chain in the same way as the shopper? The answer is that it depends on the business, what it is buying (or selling) and what it intends to do with that purchase. A local newsagent selling pick 'n' mix sweets needs small paper bags which will have to be bought in. How much effort should the newsagent put in to finding the cheapest source? After all, these are low-value items with limited impact upon the business. This is a tactical, not a strategic, decision. It is likely that the newsagent will simply add the bags to its shopping list for the next visit to the **cash and carry** (a form of wholesaler). In this respect, the business is acting like a typical **consumer** and will be just as frustrated if the bags are not in stock.

On the other hand, a multinational buying electrical components to build into its products is likely to see the supply chain in a very different way from an individual shopper. The buyer for such a company will have to answer to others for their purchase decision and so will seek a different level of reassurance about the goods and the buying situation – quite likely in writing. They will also be treated differently. Organisational buyers rarely go to the shops. Instead, salespeople visit them at the buyer's convenience.

Organisations have a view both up and down the supply chain. They may be at its end for some purchases, in its middle (as intermediaries) for others, and, if they are manufacturers, at the start of it for some. At times they are buyers, at others they are sellers.

To ensure that potential suppliers are able to meet the organisation's needs, many large organisations engage in a process of **vendor rating**, which involves evaluating sellers' performances against a set of predetermined measures. These measures usually include reviews of product range (both the current offerings and potential new ones), product quality, production capability and capacity. For example, Daimler Chrysler, the car manufacturer, uses a vendor rating system that has four broad headings, each with its own importance weighting:

vendor rating
a vetting process to help buyers identify where there may be potential benefits or difficulties associated with a particular supplier

- quality (40%)
- delivery (25%)
- price (25%)
- technology (10%).

Each of these broad headings has four further measures within it so the overall vendor rating system considers 16 elements of the supply relationship. Such systems can be used to assess not just potential sellers, but also existing sellers to ensure that they are still the best choice. The organisation's purpose in using a vendor rating system is to ensure that they identify and select the best suppliers for each item that they buy. In this way the company tries to make its supply chain as effective and efficient as possible (Lysons and Gillingham, 2003). It is interesting that the growth in the use of the Internet for consumer products has led to similar vendor ratings in the form of customer reviews, star ratings and 'likes' on social network sites such as Facebook and Twitter.

Its supply chain can make or break a business and so its design is a strategic decision which requires the best information available to ensure that it is right. Vendor rating data is a key input to the decision. When things go wrong in the supply chain, the impact is often felt throughout it; all the companies involved in the production and delivery of the goods suffer. This is one reason why it is considered good practice to view other channel members as partners rather than merely suppliers or customers. Sometimes the damage can be permanent. The BSE crisis in the early 1990s is still affecting sales of British beef across the world.

THE PARTNERSHIP VIEW

It has become normal practice for businesses to organise partnerships both upwards and downwards in the supply chain. This is most evident in the retail field. It is now common for the tills in a store to be linked to a head-office computer. This machine checks stock quantities against predetermined levels and produces an order that is transmitted electronically to the seller's computer. The seller then takes responsibility for delivering the order to the store. There is a considerable degree of trust built into such relationships. The retailer benefits from reduced stock risks but pays a higher price for the flexibility that this gives. The seller has to be more flexible in production but receives a higher unit price to cover the increased costs. Thus, with the improved flow of information between the buyer and seller, both can benefit.

A seller that always delivers quality goods on time, with no subsequent problems, at a price that is acceptable to the market develops a reputation as a good company to do business with and is therefore more likely to be a successful operation. This can help it to develop its business beyond its existing set of customers or to strengthen its defences against possible newcomers to the market, providing they disseminate this information widely enough and well, perhaps through the media or, even better, word of mouth. Good suppliers help make the buyer's business better too. Additionally, if a business treats its sellers well, then they may be offered support in the development of new products or in helping to establish new ways of trading.

PLACE MANAGEMENT

In its simplest form, place management is only concerned with the moment at which an exchange of value happens. In reality, although the moment may be simple, there is usually some preparation needed to make the exchange possible. For example, you might go into a corner shop and buy a bar of chocolate. If the owner of the shop had not previously been out and bought it (usually from a wholesaler), then your visit would have been a waste of time. This also holds true for the wholesaler, who would have had to purchase the bars from the manufacturer. From this simple example you can see that the supply chain extends away from the final exchange by a series of prior exchanges. If this chain is broken at any stage, then the final exchange is at risk. Ensuring that the chain is in place and delivering the expectations of all businesses involved is an important part of the management function.

In a small business, the buying and selling tasks are likely to be only part of a manager's job. In a larger organisation, these functions are likely to be carried out by specialists in dedicated departments. In such departments there are likely to be individuals with significant amounts of product expertise. There will often be a group of people focused on selling the organisation's products: the sales team or sales department. This group has a crucial role in the relationship with customers and potential customers. Having taken the orders and made the delivery promises, it is also usual for sales departments to organise the physical delivery of the product to the customer. There may also be a buying department, or a merchandising department, with specialist personnel who buy particular types of product, e.g. homewares, children's fashion, men's grooming products.

Finding, and keeping, the right place for the exchange usually requires the development of successful long-term business partnerships within the distribution

Institute of Place Management (IPM)

merchandising
(1) selection and display of products within a retail environment; (2) a form of licensing spin-off products often inspired by entertainments (e.g. T-shirts at a concert)

channel. Only rarely will it benefit a business to change sellers regularly. There is usually much more to be gained from working together.

THE SUPPLY CHAIN AS A NETWORK OF PARTNERS

Substantial networks, both horizontal and vertical, may be developed in pursuit of the right place design. Consider the linkages necessary for a pick-your-own (PYO) fruit farm to reach its market. Initially it might seem that there could not be a simpler form of exchange. After all, customers just take the food from the ground and pay for it. However, if we look backwards up the supply chain, there are a considerable number of other participants in the process. For a crop such as strawberries, most PYO farms will buy in the plants from a dedicated nursery that has grown the plants from seeds. The growth of the plants can be further encouraged by the use of fertilisers bought from agricultural merchants. Next the potential customer has to be told about the opportunity to pick fruit, and so another relationship is needed to develop the promotional aspects of the business. This may be with a local printer or the local newspaper. The place where the exchange happens affects all other aspects of marketing function (Michel et al., 2003).

 b2b focus: Petrol crisis

Motorists were dismayed by a spate of reports about car engines unexpectedly seizing up. Many of the broken down cars were taken to garages who suspected a problem with the fuel. It took a while to track down the source of the problem as the motorists had filled their cars at a number of different places – but all the pumps used were at either Tesco's or Morrison's stores. One immediate effect of this discovery was a surge in demand for petrol from competitive outlets – some of which ran out.

The two supermarket chains accused of supplying faulty fuel then had the task of tracing the suspect petrol back up through their distribution channels. The common source of the contaminated petrol proved to be the Royal Vopak oil terminal in Essex. This storage facility was used by a number of companies, including Greenergy, a blender and wholesaler of fuels and both Tesco's and Morrison's supplier. The source of the contamination appeared to have been a component product bought for the production of unleaded fuel by yet another company which shared the Royal Vopak storage tanks, Harvest Energy.

All the supply chain members involved had to work together to solve this problem. The supermarket managers at the retail end of the supply chain had little chance of preventing this crisis, but they had to bear the brunt of consumers' anger and their companies had to make apologies and offer compensation.

Then petrol prices went up a little.

SOURCES: Anon, 2007; Greenergy, 2007; Harvest Energy, 2007.

customer focus: Professional purchasers – what we see is what they get

Most large retail chains have teams of buyers and merchandisers who choose and source the goods that we see in store. The entry point for these careers is usually trainee assistant buyer or merchandiser, from where you can work your way up to buyer or merchandiser for your own designated ranges. The department store Debenhams describes these roles as follows.

Buyers take control for the overall style and direction of their department and work closely with merchandisers and designers so that all elements of the product make them irresistible to the customer. They must be numerate – as it's all about making money for Debenhams – as well as having outstanding people management and negotiating skills, along with an instinctive fashion sense.

Merchandisers run their own departments as independent profit centres and, by working with the buyer, make all the key decisions relating to the product positioning, price and quantity. With the potential to manage large teams and a worldwide supply base, their strong people management and negotiation skills are tested daily.

SOURCES: Debenhams, n.d.

A shop floor showcases the work of buyers and merchandisers throughout the supply chain.

Photo courtesy of Debenhams and www.prshots.com

FAIRTRADE
Ugandan
coffee

DESIGNING THE SUPPLY CHAIN

The design of the supply chain is a strategic management function. Its consequences are long-term and far-reaching. A well-designed supply chain can reduce costs by minimising overlaps between channel members and cutting out redundant parts of the network. It can also increase companies' responsiveness to market conditions, enabling them to restock or deliver more quickly, for example.

No one channel member can control the entire supply chain. Until relatively recently, marketers focused exclusively on the chain downwards (towards the final customer) from them, i.e. their distribution channel. However, all the sellers in the supply chain have an impact upon each other and so the network does need to be considered as a whole – despite its sometimes awesome complexity. Chain is perhaps a misnomer as it suggests linearity, a set of links with a beginning and an end. A supply chain is really more of a network (see Exhibit 9.2 on p. 374). There are many different branches and routes through. Each of the network's members has something to offer and something to gain. In addition, the businesses in a network all have customers to whom they address their efforts and for whom they design a product offering. These customers may become sellers in their turn. The supply chain is built upon a succession of negotiated agreements between buyers and sellers.

There are three key words in supply chain design: effectiveness, economy and efficiency. These three words shape the objectives for the operation of any supply chain. If the goods are not in the right place at the right time, then the exchange is not likely to take place and the supply chain is not effective. If there are too

e-focus: Showrooming

Times are hard for high street stores. As if it wasn't bad enough trying to sell to price-conscious, recession-hit consumers, they also have to deal with new competitors and new ways to shop.

'The staff at Jessop's would like to thank you for shopping with Amazon', read a sign in the window of a newly closed Jessop's store. The specialist camera retailer had gone into liquidation and clearly blamed the online competition. They weren't the only multiple to blame technological advancement for their demise. DVD rental firm Blockbuster found it couldn't compete with video on-demand services and HMV lost out to downloaded music. Their shops were often full so how could this happen? Well, there may have been people in the shops, but they weren't all customers; many were just showroomers.

A showroomer is someone who goes into a shop to browse and try out the merchandise, then checks for the prices online and buys it cheaper from somewhere else, usually an online retailer. Sometimes, they even make the purchase on their mobile while still in the store. Research by design agency Foolproof found that 24% of people showroomed while Christmas shopping and 40% of them took their business elsewhere. Online retailers can afford to charge less for the same products because they don't have to pay those expensive high street rents nor the staff salaries.

So how can high street shops fight back? Some have tried charging a browsing fee but even genuine shoppers are understandably reluctant to pay. Others, e.g. specialist sports stores, make sure they offer valuable expertise and excellent service. You have to have a really thick skin to walk out of a shop to find a cheaper price if an assistant has measured your feet, watched you run to assess your gait, asked you about your exercise programme, advised you on it and then recommended the perfect running shoes for you. Though probably some die-hard showroomers still will.

There is an interesting twist to this tale. Online retailers and the physical stores have a symbiotic relationship. The online stores sell more if shoppers have been able to see, feel and try out the goods. Amazon recognise this and have considered setting up in-town showrooms of their own: a pure play moving into bricks and clicks. It is unlikely that you would be able to buy goods actually in store – but at least you could order them on your mobile without having to hide in the corner.

SOURCES: Campbell, 2013.

The peril of "showrooming"

many costs being added to the basic product by the various players, then the final product will be too expensive and not economical and the customer may choose to buy from another source. Lack of efficiency at any stage will add to these costs and thus put the whole exchange process at risk. It takes a coordinated effort from all channel members to create an effective, economical and efficient supply chain.

The choice of supply chain members depends on the product, the market and the tasks to be undertaken. If there are many stages in the process of manufacturing a product, the supply chain is likely to have many members. It does not stop there. Many other companies may become involved before the final customer takes delivery of their product.

Take aeroplane manufacture as an example. There can be hundreds of companies involved in the production of these large and complex products which the manufacturer, e.g. Airbus, sells to airlines or governments. To make the planes into passenger carriers, these organisational customers need other products, e.g. catering, cleaning, refuelling, airport, services, films. The providers of all these purchases form part of the airline's supply chain. The tasks of partner selection and the maintenance of the relationships are now critical issues for management (Gattorna and Walters, 1996). To further complicate the issue, companies may need to find different partners, and design different channels, in different countries as distribution infrastructures are not the same the world over.

Some products might have specific requirements for their handling from manufacturer to final customer, and this can have an influence on the choice of partner. Take ice cream, for example. Many customers have this product at home, but how did it get there? Just as customers need freezers to store the product, so does every business involved in moving the product from the manufacturer to the retailer's store. There has to be a transport system capable of moving the product in its frozen condition. Not every transport business has such resources and this limits the potential number of partners. The same idea applies to other types of product. For example, specialist transport companies transport industrial gasses in specially designed bulk tankers. The specific needs of the supply chain can thus create niche business opportunities.

ACTIVITY

You are planning a 21st birthday party for 400 guests. Identify the different businesses that you will need to work with to make the event a success. How will you choose each of the businesses?

MASS MARKETING OR SELECTIVE MARKETING?

The next thing to think about is the nature of the market that the company is trying to reach (Hutt and Speh, 2001); the wider the range of potential customers, the wider the supply chain. If there is only one customer, then the relationship between manufacturer and customer is likely to be very direct. The distribution channel will be exclusive, i.e. there will only be one outlet. Exhibit 9.4 illustrates this connection.

Exhibit 9.4   Exclusive distribution

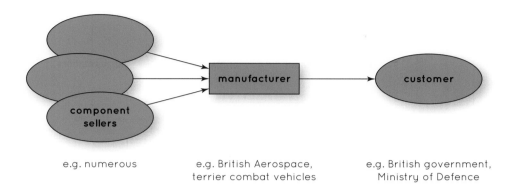

e.g. numerous   e.g. British Aerospace,   e.g. British government,
                       terrier combat vehicles   Ministry of Defence

Exclusive, luxury goods, such as designer clothing, would normally have the most restricted distribution channels, i.e. **exclusive distribution**. In extreme cases, the designers may only support one or two outlets for their products, often those directly owned by the designer. This allows them to keep very close control over their distribution.

Where there are many different types of customer, perhaps in different locations, then the pattern of connections becomes more complicated. Such situations call for **intensive distribution**, in which numerous outlets are used. In between these two extremes, there are products that are available in a number of places, but not all. This is termed **selective distribution**.

A company like Nike could not have become as large as it has by using selective or exclusive channels – it had to be intensive. Nike operates its own stores and has a large number of major retail partners, both specialist sportswear outlets (such as JJB Sports) and clothing stores. The range offered in the general clothing stores is limited so as not to challenge the specialist sports sector. This use of different types of channel to reach the same potential target group is also known as **multichannel distribution** (see Exhibit 9.5).

exclusive distribution the distribution channel has only one or two outlets

intensive distribution products are available at numerous outlets

selective distribution the distribution channel is restricted to a few outlets

multichannel distribution the use of different types of channel to reach the same target market

EXPAND YOUR KNOWLEDGE

Kabadayi, S., Eyuboglu, N. and Thomas, G.P. (2007) 'The performance implications of designing multiple channels to fit with strategy and environment,' *Journal of Marketing*, 71 (4): 195–211.

This paper investigates whether multiple channel systems make their greatest contributions to firm performance when their structures are properly aligned with their firms' business-level strategies and with environmental conditions.

Exhibit 9.5   Multichannel distribution

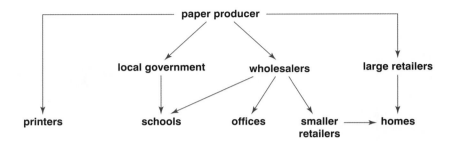

NOTE: Each member of the supply network will have numerous contacts with other businesses.

SHORT, SIMPLE CHAINS OR LONG, COMPLICATED CHAINS?

Exclusive, selective and intensive distribution are to do with the breadth of the distribution channel, i.e. how many members it has at each level in the channel. When designing a channel, it is also important to think carefully about its depth, i.e. how many levels (or intermediaries) there will be *between* the producer and the final customer (see Exhibit 9.6).

Exhibit 9.6   Distribution channels: simple

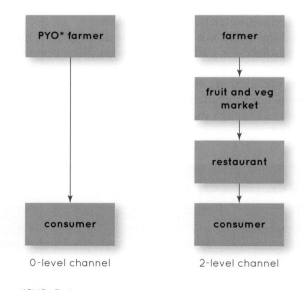

*PYO: Pick your own

The simplest distribution channel is the one that connects the producer directly to the consumer. Contrast this with the multiple channels design between a paper manufacturer and its customers in Exhibit 9.7.

Exhibit 9.7 Distribution channels: multiple

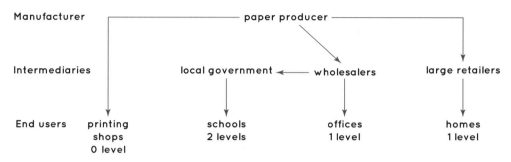

NOTE: To achieve the broadest market coverage some suppliers use many intermediaries while smaller, or more specialist, suppliers will use only some of the intermediaries available. Each member of the supply network will have numerous contacts with other businesses.

The shortest channel has no intermediaries at all. The producer sells direct to the end customer. This is called a 0-level channel or direct selling (direct sales). If there is one intermediary between the producer and the end customer, we call that a 1-level channel, while two intermediaries make a 2-level channel, etc. The longer the channel, the less control the producer has over how its products are presented to consumers (or to the final customer organisations in the case of b2b markets). You will have in your home products made by companies that you have never heard of. Do you know who made the components in your television? What about the zips in your jeans? Or who grew, or cooked, the food with a supermarket label on it in your fridge? Many producers advertise to consumers even though they do not deal directly with them. This is part of building a brand name and thereby making their goods more attractive to the intermediaries so that they stock them. A company such as Heinz is entirely dependent upon retailers to make sales. It redresses the power imbalance through marketing communications campaigns designed to persuade end customers to ask for its products when they go to the shop. In the UK, even the largest of supermarkets would not want to be without Heinz baked beans and ketchup.

© Dave Pickton

A zero-level supply chain, straight from farmer to customer.

ACTIVITY

Visit the Heinz website at **www.heinz.com**. What is its business purpose? How does it try to achieve this?

global focus: Delivery terms

Different countries have different trading practices. In some it may be customary for the buyer to arrange delivery of the goods, while in others it is the seller who does this. In some countries it is common practice to pay for the goods up front, whereas in others this might be considered sharp practice. It is therefore hardly surprising that this is an area where misunderstandings frequently arise.

To minimise such misunderstandings, in 1936 the International Chamber of Commerce devised a set of rules for the interpretation of international terms and conditions. These became known as **incoterms** (international commercial terms) and although they have been revised many times since, incoterms are still helping to simplify international trade today. They set out how activities, costs and risks are to be split between the buyer and seller and range from everything being the responsibility of the buyer to the other extreme, where everything is the responsibility of the seller.

The chosen incoterm appears as a three-letter code in the contract followed by the relevant place, e.g. EXW London ('ex works') means that the buyer is collecting the goods from the seller's premises in London and is responsible for transportation costs, taxes and duties from that point onwards. In contrast, DDP Paris ('delivered duty paid') makes the seller responsible for costs and delivery to the buyer at their address in Paris.

The latest revision was in 2010 and so the set of rules now in force are known as Incoterms 2010. There are 11 terms grouped into two categories based on the method of transport. Seven of the terms apply to all forms of transport and the remaining four terms apply only to sales that only involve transportation over water.

For a more detailed explanation of what they mean, see www.bdpinternational.com/wp/wp-content/uploads/Incoterms-2010-EU.pdf

SOURCES: UK Government, 2012.

---

incoterms
a set of rules governing the delivery terms for international sales

There are a number of different ways to create the potential for exchange between customer and business. All channels depend on a number of participants of different types who are called channel members. Some of the channel members are manufacturing businesses, others may be retailers and some businesses exist to provide supporting services, e.g. transport companies (see 'Channel members' on p. 374).

OVERSEAS OPERATIONS AND MARKET ENTRY OPTIONS

Most marketing textbooks include a substantial section on market entry options, but it is important to remember that marketing efforts do not finish once a market has been successfully entered. Very few organisations enter international markets with a short-term involvement in mind. Breaking into a new market is a complicated and costly business and most who take on the challenge will be hoping that they are setting up a long-term, profitable part of their business.

The first choice facing any seller who wishes to trade internationally is whether to:

Boosting
trade via
supply
chains

- make the products at home and export them, or
- make the products abroad.

Many firms start by exporting. This is an easier route, with lower financial risks. Manufacturers can continue to use their existing facilities (perhaps expanded) and suppliers, just as they have always done for their domestic markets. They find an agent or distributor with knowledge of the target market and use them to sell, arrange delivery of, and service products overseas. This is known as **indirect export**. Larger, or more experienced, firms may handle the export themselves (**direct export**), sending personnel overseas as required. As business builds and becomes more profitable, and as the firm's knowledge of the market grows, it may set up facilities overseas – perhaps a sales or servicing office, an assembly plant, even a fully-fledged factory. (See Exhibit 9.8.)

How to enter an overseas market becomes a more complex choice for service marketers who, because of the nature of services (which are intangible and

indirect export
using a third party
(e.g. an export
management
company), based
in the firm's home
country, to sell
products abroad

direct export
when a company
makes products in
its home country for
sale abroad and then
manages the overseas
sales and marketing of
them itself

Exhibit 9.8 Market entry and operational options

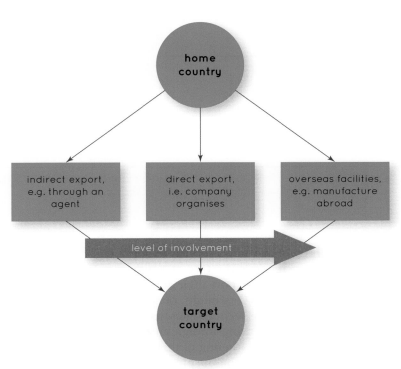

cannot be stored – see Chapter 7), can rarely make the product at home and export it. Electronic services, such as banking and credit card transactions, can indeed be hosted in one country while sold and used elsewhere, but services which require the personal touch, e.g. medical care or maintenance, generally cannot. So the choices for service marketers depend upon the nature of the service. Most service companies will have to set up operations overseas if they wish to sell their product there (see 'Services' below).

In global markets expansion is often crucial to long-term business success. A larger organisation can reduce its overall costs thanks to economies of scale. These cost reductions can then be used to increase the business's competitiveness (usually by lowering prices, although there are other ways, e.g. increasing advertising) and/or its profit margins. The world's biggest retailer, Wal-Mart, has cost reduction as a key objective and although it has not always been successful in its overseas developments, it is globally feared by all of its competitors.

To become a global business a company needs to consider carefully the extension of its supply chain and the development of the new distribution channels needed. In order to grow, it will need suitable partners to help provide the benefits that new customers seek.

Exhibit 9.9   Comparison of direct and indirect export

Indirect export	Direct export
The least effort for the exporter, as long as the trading partner performs well	Requires more effort, finance and resources from exporter, e.g. logistics management
Lowest risk option	Higher risk than indirect export as more investment is required, but still low risk compared to setting up more substantial overseas operations
Usually the easiest exit strategy (can cancel agreements, depending upon terms of contracts, and withdraw from market)	Ease of market exit depends on the degree of involvement, i.e. how much the firm has invested in the operation
Little or no customer contact	Owns the customer relationship, but has to manage customer-facing staff from a distance
Gains no market experience and is reliant upon agents to feed back data	Builds up market experience within the exporting organisation

SERVICES

Many developed countries have huge service exports, e.g. one of the UK's biggest earners of foreign currency is the City of London with its financial services products. Service providers can export their services either by sending personnel abroad, as consultants or lawyers might, or through direct marketing via the Internet or other communications technologies, as insurance providers or bankers might. Another alternative is to bring foreign customers to the service provider, as hospitals sometimes do. The marketing of this service happens abroad, though the service encounter would be in the hospital's home country.

Clearly, service providers do not need factories, but they may well need bases of operations. Franchising is particularly popular with retailers and restaurant chains. Both Marks & Spencer and McDonald's franchise many of their overseas outlets. At the same time, both companies also own and manage some of the stores or restaurants themselves.

Just as it is for manufacturing firms, ownership of overseas facilities represents the riskiest option for service providers because of the financial investment involved and because there is no local partner to provide the needed skills and market knowledge. This risky strategy has claimed many high-profile victims, such as British Airways which failed in its attempt to break into the US market by purchasing US Air. The American staff objected to the imposition of British working practices and BA were unable to maintain standards or to turn a profit. Sainsbury's failed in Egypt, but Tesco has done well in Ireland, the Far East and Eastern Europe. Also, the Carphone Warehouse has been hugely successful in pursuing its overseas expansion plans and can now be found in France, Spain, Germany, Sweden and the Netherlands where the less-limiting name 'The Phone House' is used (Palmer, 2005).

franchise
a type of multiple, the outlets are individually owned but licensed by a larger company to sell their products

British Franchise Association (bfa)

SOURCES OF POWER AND CONFLICT IN THE SUPPLY CHAIN

The different routes through the supply chain to the final customer are known as distribution channels. Each business involved is known as a channel member. Any supply chain is dependent for its success on the individual contributions of its members, which are selected for their resources and skills. Each member has some power in the particular distribution channel of which it is a part (see Exhibit 9.10). Businesses with greater power have significant advantages. An extreme example is provided by Marks & Spencer. By 1996 Marks & Spencer had grown to be the world's fifth largest retailer and was making profits of £1 billion (€1.4 billion) per year. Under the chairmanship of Sir Richard Greenbury, the company was proud to announce that the vast majority of its products came from British sources. Unfortunately, the company's financial performance stalled and then collapsed. As profits slumped, Sir Richard was replaced and the management of Marks & Spencer's operations was severely overhauled. One result of these changes was a new approach to buying products. The old 'Buy British' strategy went and, as a result, several of Marks & Spencer's old suppliers collapsed. In this channel, Marks & Spencer was the dominant player and even had the power to close down other members' businesses. This example is related here because it illustrates the importance of the relationships between channel members. In most cases businesses recognise that being too dependent on another business is potentially dangerous (in fact, Marks & Spencer did, at one time, have a policy of never allowing a supplier to become dependent upon its orders so as to avoid this situation). Most businesses aim to have a variety of different customers, which spreads the risks and reduces the chance of collapse if one partner fails.

In the example above, Marks & Spencer had power because of its size and consequent financial strength. Most businesses do not have sufficient resources to control the whole supply chain. There are, however, other sources of power that channel members can use to gain advantage in their relationships. The main source of power, outside that of financial influence, is knowledge or expertise. This is known as referent power.

referent power
influence over others gained through superior knowledge or expertise

Exhibit 9.10   Factors influencing the relationship between buyers and sellers

Businesses that are expanding into new areas look for partners that have knowledge of that particular market. This knowledge will help to reduce mistakes and to build relationships that may lead to further profitable developments. Customers expect shops in specialist stores to be well informed. This is the basis of specialist retailing across the globe: from fashion shops, where the merchandisers are expected to be aware of trends and details, to delicatessens, where staff should know a Serrano from a Parma.

A third source of power in the supply chain comes from specific regulations or laws that are used to regulate markets. This is also known as **legitimate power**. This form of power can be used to increase control over the other channel members. This is definitely the case when one partner owns a patent on the required item. This type of power is commonly found in pharmaceutical markets where drug companies can legally protect their investment in new products for a number of years. No competitor can make Viagra until its legal protection runs out, unless its inventor, Pfizer, decides to allow other businesses to buy production licences. The e-focus box below, 'Video wars', contains another illustration of how control of a specific technology can bring about market power.

Creating a brand is another way of gaining legal support for your products. Millions are spent on creating images that position the brands in the market. A brand needs to be able to protect its image if it is to be able to charge a premium price for the products it offers. The law can be used to protect a brand in a number of ways. There have been cases of retailers virtually copying a manufacturer's branded product and selling it as if it were the retailer's own product. ASDA was found guilty of this when it copied the McVitie's Penguin biscuit bar. The court took the view that such activities were intended to mislead the customer as to the origin of the product, and were therefore unacceptable. This case illustrates the problems that can arise between channel members when one challenges the power of another's brand. (For more on branding, see Chapters 6 and 11.)

A well-designed supply chain should limit the potential for conflict between the channel members. Any conflict reduces effectiveness in the supply chain and may ultimately lead to channels being closed off. Failure to resolve conflict between members, without the use of the law courts, should be seen as a failure of the management of the buyer–seller relationship.

legitimate power influence over others conferred by law or regulations

e-focus: Video wars

One of Japanese electronics company JVC's claims to fame is that it invented VHS, one of the earliest, and most successful, systems for recording TV pictures. A few years before JVC patented its invention, Sony had launched its own TV recording system, which was known as Betamax. Although the two companies had an agreement to share each other's technologies, both of them wanted to create the dominant system. The stage was set for a global battle between these two Japanese companies. There were other recording systems, such as those invented by Philips and Grundig (two European companies), and RCA in America, but only the two Japanese giants invested in the business support and global marketing needed – so the other products swiftly disappeared.

Sony had the technically superior system but wanted to maintain control over its distribution and restricted production to a small number of manufacturing sites. JVC, recognising the technical inferiority of the VHS system, decided to allow many other companies to make VHS-based video recorders. The company now had partners across the world and could thus reduce the costs of manufacture, reducing prices for consumers. These two advantages, of price and availability, sped up consumer acceptance of the JVC system. Then Hollywood decided to give VHS a starring role. More people had VHS than Betamax so, to reach this wider audience, the Hollywood studios made more videos in VHS format than in Betamax format, and this gave JVC even greater advantage in the market. Developing supply chain relationships and allowing its technology to be used widely did not weaken JVC. Far from it, it gave the company a winning advantage over its rival.

Some years later a similar format war arose between Sony's Blu-ray and Toshiba's and NEC's HDD DVD technologies.

MARKETING FUNCTIONS IN THE SUPPLY CHAIN

As a product passes along the supply chain, its costs rise, partly because the activities carried out at each stage (e.g. transport, storage, re-packaging) have to be paid for, but also because each intermediary needs to make a profit. This is why the shorter the channel, generally speaking, the lower the final price. There would be no point to this if each stage in the chain did not also add value to the product. Both parties to an exchange want good value and so customers must value the product more highly than the retailer did and so be prepared to pay more for it (see Chapters 1 and 10 for exchanges and customer value). The members of the supply chain make their contributions to the eventual product experience in a number of ways.

STOCK HOLDING

For a retailer, having stock available is critical to success because usually no stock means no sales. Stock that does not sell is a waste of the retailer's money, so every effort is made to minimise this. This often means putting pressure on sellers to hold stocks away from the retailer's stores but ready to be called in at short notice if required. This just-in-time (JIT) or quick response (QR) approach reduces the retailer's waste but increases the seller's financial risk if the products do not sell.

just-in-time (JIT)
a lean manufacturing and stocking approach where little or no stock is held

TRANSPORTATION

Clearly, there must be a means to get the product to the customer. Consumers often visit stores themselves and so they take care of the transport of their purchases themselves. Businesses are likely to require delivery. Transportation is often contracted out to logistics services who are outside the buyer–seller relationship (see 'Channel members' above) or companies may use couriers, or even the post office. Online bookseller Amazon may now have its own warehouse (it did not originally, but relied on others to fulfil orders), but they outsource their deliveries.

For some products the task of transportation is complicated by the nature of the product itself (e.g. moving natural gas from the North Sea to homes). The transportation system for this example includes production platforms, pumping stations and thousands of miles of pipeline. Without that specialist transportation system this market could not exist.

INFORMATION GATHERING

This is a function that is undertaken by all participants. Information gathering does not necessarily require a formal market research project as all businesses obtain information on the markets that they serve as the result of their day-to-day operations. Many small businesses fail to recognise the value of this by-product of their work and therefore lose out on numerous marketing opportunities. Successful businesses, however, will analyse the information to shape the ways in which they approach their customers, both current and potential.

In some cases, the information is shared with other members of the supply chain. This sharing activity helps to improve the efficiency and effectiveness of the chain as a whole, and is evidence of healthy relationships between the participants.

COMMUNICATING

This function helps to develop efficiency in the supply chain. If information can be shared quickly, then the costs of operation can be reduced. Most major retail businesses use EPOS (electronic point of sale) systems to capture information from their stores. Such systems use the barcodes on products to identify the items and quantities that have been sold. This data is then sent to a head-office computer that adds up all of the individual stores' information. If more stock is needed, the central computer can place an order with the seller's computer using an EDI (electronic data interchange) system. Replacement products can thus be ordered without any human effort. These systems can work 24 hours a day, seven days a week and are a major force in the globalisation of retailing.

Constantly swapping business partners is inefficient. It leads to additional costs in selecting and evaluating prospective candidates. The development of long-term relationships helps to create trust and facilitates the exchange of information between the partners. In the longer term, this reduces the costs in the supply chain and brings financial benefits to all members.

global focus: Cheap sources of supply

Everybody likes a bargain and retailers try really hard to deliver good ones. The combination of customers wanting cheap prices and retailers wanting to beat their competitors' prices puts severe pressure on manufacturers to keep costs down. Gone are the days when Marks & Spencer proudly proclaimed that it used only British suppliers. M&S, like almost every other chain-store, looks abroad for lower cost items.

So why are those imported skirts and T-shirts so cheap? How can that be when the transportation costs must be so much higher? Partly it's due to differences in currency values and living standards, but often the main differences are that labour is cheaper and there are fewer, costly regulations to be complied with. A garment factory in Bangladesh that made clothes for European high street brands, including Primark, Benetton, Bonmarche and Matalan, collapsed killing at least 80 people and injuring up to 800 more. This prompted calls for these multimillion-pound Western businesses to take more responsibility for the way their clothes were produced.

It isn't just clothing manufacturers that can be criticised for cutting costs to the point where supply chain members cut corners. In 2013, Britons were shocked to find that much of the beef they had bought in supermarkets was in fact horse – something not commonly eaten in Britain. To the media's apparent surprise, the British public's main issue with this was that they had been missold rather than that they had inadvertently eaten an animal usually considered a pet rather than a source of food. The supermarkets' defence was that their supply chains were so long and complicated, and crossed so many borders, that they hadn't known where this meat originated, relying on the next business up the chain to do the checking.

How much responsibility do you think retailers should take for what goes on further up the supply chain? How much responsibility should we as consumers take? Should we think rather harder about why those clothes (or those ready meals) are so cheap and perhaps just refuse to buy them?

PROMOTING

All buyers and sellers in the supply chain will promote their goods and services to each other. The final consumer does not see the majority of such promotional efforts, but they are vital to the development of the various relationships in the supply chain.

Promotional activities can be very sophisticated and behind the scenes, such as a manufacturer giving the retailer a retrospective discount dependent on the volume of product sold in a particular period of time. Alternatively, the effort can be blatant, such as Debenhams' Blue Cross Sale advertisements that announce 20% discounts on specific days (often on Tuesdays to boost sales in the quieter part of the week). Some retailers combine the two forms, such as KwikSave's '£1 off Beefeater Gin' promotion. In this case, the product is a brand of Allied Domecq, a wine and spirit distribution company. This company sees it as in its own interests to support the retailer in promoting its product in preference to those of its competitors.

The possible objectives and the various methods for these promotional activities are discussed more fully in Chapter 8.

E-CHANNELS

ELECTRONIC DISTRIBUTION

One of the biggest changes the Internet has brought to our lives is through electronic distribution. Anyone who has played a game through their Smartphone or listened to music on an MP3 player has probably downloaded some software from a website. Computers' anti-virus protection can be automatically updated online at a time that is convenient to the customer – even in the middle of the night.

The possibilities are growing almost daily. You can download a complete movie through the Internet or watch missed television programmes on a PC. With the spread of new technologies such as 4G, download speeds are constantly increasing and the quality of transmission is improving. The Internet offers 24/7 access to services delivered directly to the receiver's PC. This level of convenience is something that store-based retailers cannot match and gives e-tailers (using e-distribution) a distinct market advantage.

Jack White: Record Store Day

EXPAND YOUR KNOWLEDGE

Xing, Y., Grant, D.B., McKinnon, A.C. and Fernie, J. (2011) 'The interface between retailers and logistics service providers in the online market', *European Journal of Marketing*, 45 (3): 334–57.

The growth in online shopping has presented challenges for physical distribution service quality provided by retailers and logistics service providers. Through interviews with retailers, logistics service providers and experts, this paper examines issues regarding electronic physical distribution service quality.

BUSINESS TO BUSINESS (B2B)

Over the last decade, the revolution in communications technology has affected almost all businesses. As defined in this chapter, the concept of place has two major components: time and space. The Internet has affected both of these.

In the b2b sector, some small businesses still use paper-based ordering systems. Salespeople may collect orders personally and forward them to a central sales office. However, handheld computers and other electronic devices are rapidly replacing the old systems. The Internet creates opportunities for customers to send in their orders without any such visits from salespeople. Online customers can choose the time when the ordering will take place and can be shown a much wider variety of products than any sales representative is able to carry.

It is this capacity for carrying information, and for transmitting it so speedily, that makes the Internet so effective as a channel for communication. Buyers can surf the net looking for potential suppliers from anywhere in the world. Similarly, suppliers can also use the Internet to find potential customers anywhere in the world. Some facilitating businesses exist simply as portals, allowing sellers to post their products on the host site (for a fee, of course). This saves the buyers search time and the sellers gain access to a worldwide marketplace. One such business is click2procure, which has over 1000 supplier businesses listed, each paying around €3000 for the privilege. This may seem expensive but the payback comes from the €1 billion worth of contracts that have been arranged via the online trading system. One estimate is that this system has reduced buying costs by up to 25% for some contracts.

For example, the German electronics giant Siemens has set up an EDI system that allows it to communicate directly with its suppliers for a quarter of all its procurement. Although this represents a significant advance, there are still some major drawbacks associated with EDI systems. Most importantly, the initial development costs are high. Then there is a requirement for the suppliers to buy in to the system. Also, not all members of the distribution channel will have the same systems which can cause compatibility problems. The Internet helps here as it provides a common communications platform. Siemens recognised the benefits of this type of structure for its operations and set a target of 50% of all products to be sourced via the Internet. For Siemens, this means that products worth around €20 billion will be traded annually over the Internet. As the software available develops into mass-market applications, so the number of smaller companies able to take advantage of electronic trading will also grow dramatically, and the shape of the exchange relationship will alter accordingly.

BUSINESS TO CUSTOMER (B2C)

The bulk of commercial electronic transactions are b2b, but consumers are catching up as e-shopping becomes more popular. Many retailers who never used direct marketing techniques, such as catalogues or telesales, are now online – albeit reluctantly in some cases. In the UK, it is now unheard of for any major retailer not to have a web presence.

Initially, customers were reluctant to shop online as they did not trust the technology. They were worried about credit card fraud, whether the goods would ever turn up, whether they would be in good condition, what they could do if they wanted to return something. Advances in security, the experience of others, and the appearance of known and trusted companies and brands online have reassured them, and now books, music and flowers are commonplace online purchases while the more adventurous customers also buy such products as groceries, electronics, household goods and clothing. Convenience has won shoppers over and, far from being the bargain hunters that the early e-shoppers were, today's time-starved consumers are prepared to pay extra for their groceries, in the form of delivery charges, so that they can shop from home (Huang and Oppewal, 2006).

The willingness of consumers to shop online has had a knock-on effect in b2b markets. Previously, it was necessary to have shops, often large ones and often chains of them, if you wanted to sell to consumers. Now products can be sold from a website without the need for such expensive investment. This has changed the competitive nature of many markets (e.g. booksellers). It is easier for new competitors to enter markets and it is easier for producers to sell direct. Internet retailers are judged by the impression their website makes. It is much cheaper to build an impressive website than an impressive shop, and so smaller companies can compete much more easily with larger ones.

There are snags, of course. Manufacturers have little or no experience of dealing with consumers. They still need to break down bulk as consumers will not want to buy a case of mayonnaise, just a jar. Then there is delivery. This is where many of the direct sellers fall down and where they lose the trust of their customers. In the early days, Internet-ordered goods were frequently late, wrong, damaged or 'no-shows'. It is still vital to get the right goods to the right customer at the right time – and that is not such an easy task.

CUSTOMER TO CUSTOMER (C2C)

One of the most radical changes that the Internet has made to supply chains is the introduction of another channel member – the consumers themselves. Some consumers have always passed on goods in a small way, usually secondhand goods, maybe some unwanted gifts (or more dubiously acquired items), but this activity was so small-scale that it barely registered in the commercial world. The World Wide Web has provided the means for individuals to access thousands, even millions, of other individuals and so has opened the way for a host of small-scale exchanges and facilitated the birth of numerous businesses.

Some businesses tap into this potential by offering services for individual sellers. For example, Amazon marketplace is a forum where individuals can offer books and other items for sale, either through a listing or by auction, but without the risks inherent in running an Internet business as Amazon manage the site and collect the payments for them (for a commission of course). Another, even bigger, example is eBay, which claimed a global customer base of 233 million in 37 markets worldwide in 2012 (eBay, n.d.). Their phenomenal reach is often cited as the reason for the collapse of a number of small antiques and collectibles shops – they are just no longer competitive.

So supply chains become ever more complex, ever harder to manage. New members join, although sometimes they are uninvited. Others leave. The concept of place is a dynamic one and it is one of management's major challenges to keep up with it.

For the marketer, new technology allows new services to be created and these will need to be distributed to customers. These new opportunities also bring potential dangers. In a digital world, it is very difficult to control the distribution of a digital product. If you have an MP3 player, then you may be using pirated recordings. Services such as Napster grew from individuals illegally copying CD-based music and making it available through the Internet. With physical products a counterfeiter has to create a manufacturing facility, and that takes resources. With digital products the copying and distribution can be done at the press of a button. In the future, marketers will have to pay more attention to protecting the distribution of their digital products if they are to secure the maximum return on their investments.

SUMMARY

Throughout this chapter we have seen that effective place management is vitally important to the marketing function. The elements of space and time are combined to create opportunities in which buyers and sellers can come together. A clear understanding of the buyer's needs, not just from the product but from the exchange itself, helps the seller to shape an offer that maximises the chances of an exchange.

Most exchanges will use existing supply chain networks. These are formed from different types of business that are connected by their own exchange relationships. These networks have many forms, from the simple (farmer direct to consumer) to the complex (Boeing building a 787 Dreamliner). As the networks become more sophisticated, so there is more likelihood that the members will begin to operate as business partners. These partnerships may be for a particular project or on a long-term basis.

Each business in the supply chain has its own skills and capabilities. These are a source of business power in its relationship with the other members of the network. In most cases there is little open conflict, but there is usually some tension because of the opposing profit objectives.

In the twenty-first century, business exchange relationships are increasingly global. We have seen how changes in communications and physical distribution have made this growth possible. As the geographical distances between buyers and sellers have increased, the management of the physical movement of goods has become progressively more important and more complex. In recent times there has been massive technological changes, and these changes in communication and transportation technologies have had a massive impact on our ideas of place. As technology continues its rapid development, marketers will need to be open to change if they are to maintain their business's effectiveness.

Successful management of place also requires an understanding of its role in the marketing function. Place offers opportunities for information gathering, for testing new products, for trying out promotional techniques and for getting feedback on pricing strategies.

A manager's ability to create, sustain and develop relationships is a fundamental skill in generating business success. To manage place well requires that you manage relationships well. These relationships will be both internal (with other departments that affect the flow of products through the business) and external (with customers and suppliers) (Gadde and Håkansson, 2001).

Getting all the activities that come under the heading 'Place' right will set the scene for a successful exchange. For that to happen, marketers must ensure that the right goods get to the right customer in the right time and space.

physical distribution
the process of moving goods and services between businesses and consumers

CHALLENGES REVIEWED

Now that you have finished reading the chapter, look back at the challenges you were set at the beginning. Do you have a clearer idea of what's involved?

HINTS

- Breadth of distribution coverage and merchandising support – see also 'Marketing functions in the supply chain'
- Marketing functions in the supply chain
- How do the members of the supply chain add value? (Also branding)
- The importance of building relationships through the supply chain
- Junk food and child obesity problems – what responsibilities do schools have to the children in their care?

READING AROUND

JOURNAL ARTICLES

Drucker, P. (1962) 'The economy's dark continent', *Fortune*, April: 265–70.

Hollander, S. (1960) 'The wheel of retailing', *Journal of Marketing*, 25 (Jul): 37–42.

Kabadayi, S., Eyuboglu, N. and Thomas, G. (2007) 'The performance implications of designing multiple channels to fit with strategy and environment,' *Journal of Marketing*, 71 (4): 195–211.

Pearson, M.M. (1981) 'Ten distribution myths', *Business Horizons*, 24 (3): 17–23.

Teller, C. and Dennis, C. (2012) 'The effect of ambient scent on consumers' perception, emotions and behaviour: a critical review', *Journal of Marketing Management*, 28 (1–2): 14–36.

Xing, Y., Grant, D., McKinnon, A. and Fernie, J. (2011) 'The interface between retailers and logistics service providers in the online market', *European Journal of Marketing*, 45 (3): 334–57.

WEBSITES

www.bdpinternational.com/wp/wp-content/uploads/Incoterms-2010-EU.pdf – this site provides a useful simple summary of Incoterms with explanatory diagrams highlighting buyers and sellers' risks and costs.

www.ethicaltrade.org/ – Ethical Trading Initiative – *respect for workers worldwide*.

www.experian.co.uk/assets/business-strategies/brochures/mosaic-uk-2009-brochure-jun10.pdf – this is a guide to Experian's MOSAIC geodemographic neighbourhood profiling system which retailers and other service providers can use to locate and target customer groups. It is an approach that has many uses including help in siting new stores and operations. You can even download an interactive iPhone app which you can use to view different postcode locations and house types. You can also check out the application of MOSAIC in different countries.

http://acorn.caci.co.uk/ – view videos and see the guide book for CACI's system of classifying neighbourhoods. Compare how CACI's ACORN goes about this process with Experian's MOSAIC (see the reference above).

DIRECTORY

Yellow Pages – to see the variety of businesses, and the range of different suppliers that they can use.

BOOKS

Harvard Business School (2011) *Harvard Business School on Managing Supply Chains*. Boston: HBR Press.

VIDEO

BBC *Mary Queen of Shops* – retailing insights.

MAGAZINE

Retail Week, UK

SELF-REVIEW QUESTIONS

1. What is a supply chain and what is its purpose? (See p. 374)
2. How can a manufacturing business be both a buyer and a seller? (See p. 375)
3. What is the main function of an agent? (See p. 376)
4. Why do major supermarkets, such as Tesco and Sainsbury's, have Internet stores when they have invested so much in physical supermarkets? (See pp. 379–85)
5. How can a firm use the concept of place to help it position its business against its competitors? (See pp. 380–3)
6. Heinz engages in direct marketing communications to the final consumers of its products. Why it is unlikely to engage in direct delivery of its products to those customers? (See pp. 375–6)
7. Why would businesses want to create long-term relationships with their suppliers? (See pp. 387–92)
8. Why is it important that the supply chain should be responsive to customers' needs? (See pp. 385–6)
9. What is vendor rating and in what kind of business would you be most likely to find it? (See p. 387)
10. Why is product expertise important to businesses? (See p. 392)
11. What is the difference between direct export and indirect export? (See p. 397)
12. Why does the physical nature of the product sometimes affect the choice of supply chain participants? (See pp. 392–5)

Mini case study: Honest, tasty and real: Dorset Cereals

Read the questions, then the case material, and then answer the questions.

Questions

1 How would you categorise Dorset Cereal's distribution strategy before and after the re-positioning exercise? Why?

2 Discuss the advantages and drawbacks of a brand like Dorset Cereals being stocked by large supermarkets such as Tesco and Sainsbury's.

3 Revisit the section headed 'Marketing functions in the supply chain' above. How can Dorset Cereals and its retail partners manage these marketing activities to the best, mutual advantage? What would you expect them to do?

Muesli has gone through a rejuvenation of late and Dorset Cereals is largely responsible. Back in the early 2000s, muesli was worthy but rather dull. Everyone knew it was good for them but not everyone wanted to eat it.

(Continued)

(Continued)

Supermarkets stocked the big brand names, such as Alpen, and their own-label products. Health food stores stocked the real deal but it was often compared to sawdust or cat litter.

Dorset Cereals had been around since 1985 and was sold in most of the specialist health food shops such as Holland and Barrett. However, their sales figures were flat even though healthy cereals were the only category in the cereal market showing a healthy growth. The breakfast cereal market generally was saturated. Cereals had been so well marketed that it was hard to find new customers or ways to grow the business. Also, it was dominated by large multinationals like Kellogg's and Nestlé who filled whatever space remained on supermarket shelves once their own-label products had been displayed.

According to Mintel (2008), grocery multiples like the well-known supermarkets account for 94% of all breakfast cereal sales. There are a number of niche players who sell through health food shops or even, like Mymuesli, online but If they wanted to make any serious inroads into the market at all, Dorset Cereals needed to be on the supermarket shelves. To achieve that they needed a radical brand makeover.

They researched the market and interrogated their own brand, establishing its values clearly. They realised that the supermarket's shelves were already full of cereals that claimed to have natural qualities and healthy ingredients but none of them claimed to taste good! Dorset Cereals repositioned itself as 'honest, tasty and real'. This new positioning was encapsulated in a radical new brand identity.

A simple, eye-catching leaf icon adorned the improved packaging. The leaf symbolised the natural ingredients of the muesli and was easily recognisable even when re-coloured for different recipes, or turned into a cellophane window on the pack through which the product could be seen. It soon came to represent Dorset Cereals in the minds of both consumers and trade.

Previously, the muesli had been packaged in basic plastic bags that:

- faded into the background on shelves and so were rarely noticed

- would not stay upright on display stands and so looked a mess in store and irritated shopkeepers

- failed to protect the product well enough in transit causing wastage

- regularly spilt cereal across kitchen tables to the intense annoyance of consumers.

The new packs were bigger and made from recyclable card. They stood out, stood up and kept the cereal in good condition whilst being transported, stored and displayed in store. They also featured the kind of quirky copy that makes a good breakfast time read.

Armed with this new look, the company approached the major supermarket chains,

some of whom (notably Waitrose) took the brand on trial. With its more appealing brand identity, it flew off the shelves and further orders were placed. Soon it stopped being the preserve of upmarket stores like Waitrose, and became a staple on the shelves of Tesco, Sainsbury's, Morrison's and the rest. At the same time, the Dorset Cereals sales team persuaded a number of high-end, independent retailers to stock the brand and so they kept up the muesli's luxury image. In a later development, the company launched individual portion catering packs for hotels and restaurants and so broke into yet another new market thanks to imaginative packaging.

As a result of the improved distribution, Dorset Cereals' market share more than doubled, outstripping competitors' mueslis and even growing the breakfast cereal category overall.

By making their cereal look more exciting, Dorset had got people more excited about breakfast.

SOURCES: Mintel, 2008; WARC, 2007.

REFERENCES

Anon (2007) 'Tesco petrol "back to normal"', *The Independent* (online), 6 March. Available at: **news.independent.co.uk/uk/transport/article2332263.ece** (accessed 21/04/07).

Bellis, M. (2007) *The Unusual History of MS DOS the Microsoft Operating System*, about.com, part of the New York Times Company. Available at: **inventors.about.com/library/weekly/aa033099.htm** (accessed 18/04/07).

Campbell, A. (2013) 'The peril of showrooming', *BBC News Magazine*, 21 April. Available at: **www.bbc.co.uk/news/magazine** (accessed 08/05/13).

Debenhams (n.d.) *Buying and Merchandising*, Debenhams. Available at: **www.debenhamsweddings.com/site_services/article_summary. jsp?FOLDER%3C%3Efolder_id= 4112323& bmUID= 1177242009406** (accessed 22/04/07).

eBay (n.d.) *Business Centre*, eBay. Available at: **pages.ebay.co.uk/aboutebay/thecompany/companyoverview.html** (accessed 19/03/13).

Fernie, J. and Sparks, L. (2004) 'Retail logistics: changes and challenges', in J. Fernie and L. Sparks (eds), *Logistics and Retail Management: Insights into Current Practice and Trends from Leading Experts* (2nd edn). London: Kogan Page, pp. 1–25.

Gadde, L.E. and Håkansson, H. (2001) *Supply Network Strategies*. London: Wiley.

Gattorna, J. and Walters, D. (1996) *Managing the Supply Chain: A Strategic Perspective*. Basingstoke: Macmillan.

Greenergy (2007) *Fuel Quality Statement*, Greenergy, 2 March. Available at: **www. greenergy.com/company/news_media/current_releases.html#Feb_statement** (accessed 21/04/07).

Harvest Energy (2007) S*tatement by Harvest Energy on South East of England Fuel Supply Issues*, Harvest Energy, 4 March. Available at: **www.harvestenergy.co.uk/news_story. php?articleID= 20** (accessed 21/04/07).

Hollander, S.C. (1960) 'The wheel of retailing', *Journal of Marketing*, 25 (Jul): 37–42.

Huang, Y. and Oppewal, H. (2006) 'Why consumers hesitate to shop online: an experimental choice analysis of grocery shopping and the role of delivery fees', *International Journal of Retail and Distribution Management*, 34 (4/5): 334–53.

Hutt, M. and Speh, T. (2001) *Business Marketing Management*. New York: Harcourt.

IBM (n.d.) *IBM Archives 1981*. Available at: **www-03.ibm.com/ibm/history/history/ year_1981.html** (accessed 18/04/07).

Kabadayi, S., Eyuboglu, N. and Thomas, G.P. (2007) 'The performance implications of designing multiple channels to fit with strategy and environment,' *Journal of Marketing*, 71 (4): 195–211.

Logistics Today (staff reporter) (2003) 'Exel and Marks and Spencer announce supply chain partnership', *Logistics Today*, 31 March. Available at: **http://logistics today.com/mag/ outlog-story-5000/**.

Lysons, K. and Gillingham, M. (2003) *Purchasing and Supply Chain Management*. Harlow: FT/Prentice Hall.

Marks & Spencer (n.d.) *The Company, Our Responsibilities, Environment, Transport*, Marks & Spencer. Available at: **www.marksandspencer.com/gp/node/ n/45941031?ie= UTF8&mnSBrand= core** (accessed 21/04/07).

McGoldrick, P. (2003) *Retail Marketing*. Maidenhead: McGraw-Hill.

Michel, D., Naudé, P., Salle, R. and Valla, J.P. (2003) *Business-to-Business Marketing*. Basingstoke: Palgrave Macmillan.

Mintel (2008) *UK Breakfast Cereals Market Report*. London: Mintel.

Mintel (2010) *e-commerce – UK February 2010*. London: Mintel.

Ocado (n.d.) 'Our awards', available at: **www.ocado.com/theocadoway/ awardwinning%20service/our-awards.html** (accessed 29/07/10).

Ocado (n.d.) 'About as', available at: **www.ocadogroup.com/about-us/** (accessed 29/07/10).

Palmer, A. (2005) *Principles of Services Marketing* (4th edn). Maidenhead: McGraw Hill.

Pearson, M.M. (1981) 'Ten distribution myths', *Business Horizons*, 24 (3): 17–23.

Piercy, N. (2002) *Market-led Strategic Change*. Oxford: Butterworth Heinemann.

Teller, C. and Dennis, C. (2012) 'The effect of ambient scent on consumers' perception, emotions and behaviour: a critical review', *Journal of Marketing Management*, 28 (1–2): 14–36.

UK Government (2012) 'Guide: Incoterms', available at: www.gov.uk/incoterms-international-commercial-terms/what-the-terms-mean (accessed 05/04/13).

WARC (2007) 'Design Effectiveness Awards', Design Business Association. Available at: **www. warc.com/ArticleCenter/Default.asp?CType= A&AID= HomeEC90615&Tab= A** (accessed 30/12/09).

Xing, Y., Grant, D.B., McKinnon, A.C. and Fernie, J. (2011) 'The interface between retailers and logistics service providers in the online market', *European Journal of Marketing*, 45 (3): 334–57.

Visit the companion website on your computer at **www.sagepub.co.uk/masterson3e** or MobileStudy on your Smart phone or tablet by scanning this QR code and gain access to:

- **Videos** to get a better understanding of key concepts and provoke in-class discussion.
- Links to useful **websites and templates** to help guide your study.
- Access **SAGE Marketing Pins (www.pinterest.com/sagepins/)**. SAGE's regularly updated **Pinterest** page, giving you access to regularly updated resources on everything from Branding to Consumer Behaviour.
- **Daily Grind podcast series** to learn more about the day-to-day life of a marketing **professional**.
- Interactive **Practice questions** to test your understanding.
- A **bonus chapter on Marketing Careers** to not only support your study, but your job search and future career.
- **PowerPoints** prompting key points for revision.

Price 10

PRICE CHALLENGES

The following are illustrations of the types of decision that marketers have to take or issues they face. *You aren't expected to know how to deal with the challenges now*; just bear them in mind as you read the chapter and see what you can find that helps.

- You run a medium-sized business, a secondhand car dealership: A competitor, the showroom on the other side of town, reduces its prices. Should you do the same? What will happen if you don't and if you do?
- You have decided that it is a good time for your business to grow. The business is fashion design and is just getting known. You need to make more money to fund that growth: to make sample garments for the shows and to give away to celebrities. Could changing prices help at all? Should you put them down, or up?
- You have developed a new product. It is brand new, a technological breakthrough: a teleporter. It will make most other forms of transport redundant. How do you know how much to charge for it?
- You work for a large chain of furniture stores. Business is slack and competition for the few customers buying furniture is fierce. Your boss suggests offering credit deals to low-income households who would find it hard to borrow money from a bank as they are too great a risk. What are the potential drawbacks to this idea?
- Yours is a multinational company with branches in most countries. Incomes and currencies vary. How can you set prices for your televisions that will maximise profits in the richer countries without losing business in the poorer markets?

Aldi Price
Comparison

INTRODUCTION

Price is often a seriously undervalued part of the marketing mix. On the one hand, this is a great shame as many companies miss out on the competitive edge that the creative use of pricing brings. On the other hand, it is a good thing for the marketers who do appreciate the finer points of pricing. Pricing can be a devastating competitive weapon.

While some notable retailers such as Sainsbury, Asda and Tesco clearly take continuous pricing research seriously, very few companies base their pricing decisions on serious pricing research or revise their prices often enough, most thinking that it is good enough to set them once a year, along with the budgets (Cox, 2001). Other common mistakes include not taking into account the rest of the marketing mix and focusing too much on costs.

Price is the odd one out in the 4Ps of the marketing mix. The other three elements can be perceived as costs but the price of the goods and services a firm sells is a direct determinant of its profit – and most businesses' primary aim is to make high profits. Pricing strategy, therefore, is a key part of a firm's overall marketing strategy and one that has a direct effect on the bottom line.

As an alternative to, or in combination with, other marketing mix elements, a company can use pricing to improve the customer's perception of the product's value. Lowering the price is not the only way to do this; in fact, it might be counterproductive, making the product seem cheap. This is where creativity and judgement come in. This chapter will attempt to show how that works.

Through most of this chapter, price will be used in the simpler sense of the money charged for a product (unless otherwise stated). However, there is more to price than the price tag. The price to the customer is everything they have to give up to obtain the product. This includes time, effort and alternative purchases. The chapter will begin by considering the implications of the price of a product and how it affects a business. It will move on to look at the different influences on price setting and how prices can be used to help achieve marketing objectives. Pricing strategies and tactics for both new and existing products will be covered alongside some of the additional complexities of pricing in multiple countries. Prices are not fixed once and for ever more, so it is important to understand the implications of changing prices. The chapter then makes a brief excursion into economics for price elasticity of demand – an important concept for marketers as it helps them to forecast sales at different price levels. It finishes with a brief look at the special case of pricing on the Internet.

WHY IT IS SO IMPORTANT TO GET THE PRICE RIGHT

profit
the difference between what something costs to make and the price for which it is sold

costs
what an organisation pays for the goods and services it receives; see also direct costs, indirect costs; variable costs and fixed costs

The price of the goods and services a firm sells is a major determinant of its **profit** – and most businesses' primary aim is to make high profits. Pricing strategy, therefore, is a key part of a firm's overall marketing strategy. Even not-for-profit organisations usually need to cover their **costs** if they want to continue their existence, and so their costs must be covered too. In hard times, companies may be focused on survival rather than on profits, but then too, they need to pay careful attention to their pricing strategies. As the one part of the marketing mix that delivers money to the firm, rather than takes it out, price is always important.

The prices an organisation charges have a direct bearing on key corporate and marketing **objectives**, as described below.

objective
a goal or target

WHAT IS PROFIT?

Profit is what's left over when all the bills have been paid.

sales revenue – costs = profit

So to make the most profit, you need to get in as much money as possible (revenue):

sales revenue = sales volume × selling price

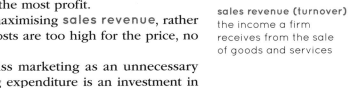

Price-quality
relationship

... and pay out as little as possible (costs).
Here's an example of how to work out profit:

Kidzone clothing sells 100 T-shirts at £5.00 each. Each T-shirt costs £1.00 to make, distribute and sell. Sales revenue from the T-shirts is:

100 (volume) × £5 (price) = £500

The company's profit is:

£500 (sales revenue) – £100 (total costs) = <u>£400</u>

PROFIT AND REVENUE

It is easy enough to sell a lot of something – just sell it really cheaply. Firms that use this technique will lose out on profit, of course. So why not set the price really high? Now the firm will not sell anything at all. This much is obvious, but what is not so easy is finding the spot in the middle: the highest price at which the most people will buy. This is the price that will earn the most profit.

Generally speaking, marketing focuses on maximising **sales revenue**, rather than on keeping costs down. However, if the costs are too high for the price, no amount of clever marketing can make up for it.

sales revenue (turnover)
the income a firm
receives from the sale
of goods and services

Finance people have been known to dismiss marketing as an unnecessary cost. The marketers' response is that marketing expenditure is an investment in the firm's future. It is true, however, that pricing is the only part of the marketing mix that does not involve financial outlay.

IMAGE

'Pile it high, sell it cheap' is a motto that has been attributed to various supermarkets. Is this a strategy designed to promote an upmarket or downmarket image? The strategy of reducing price, and so selling large volumes, appears a downmarket ploy. Price affects image.

SURVIVAL

A sure way to go out of business is to set prices lower than costs. Firms may get away with this in the short term (see

Pile it high, sell it cheap.

© iStockphoto.com/Juanmonino

'Contribution pricing' and 'Loss leaders' later in this chapter), but keeping prices too low for too long is a recipe for disaster.

MARKET SHARE

If a company wants to increase sales, this is likely to mean taking customers away from a competitor (unless the overall market is growing in which case all companies may be able to grow). Any increase in one firm's market share means a decrease in another's. One of the most common ways to do this is by undercutting competitors' prices (see 'Market penetration' and 'Predatory pricing' below).

PRICING VIEWPOINTS

WHAT IS A PRICE?

A basic definition of price is:

> ***The money charged for a product or service.***

That does sound obvious and there is more to it than that. Think about what you *really* pay for a product, say a computer. There is the price of the PC itself, but then there are other things too: peripherals, software, maybe service agreements. The customer and the salesperson may see the price differently. The customer may have gone into the store to buy a PC and have a price in mind for that. The salesperson may see the PC as the starting point of a deal that will include numerous extras, and over a much longer period. They will try and sell extended warranties and service agreements as well as additional software and a higher specification PC.

A more comprehensive definition of price is:

> ***Everything that a customer has to give up in order to acquire a product or service.***

This second definition takes account of the added costs associated with the purchase. For example, buying a new pair of shoes takes time: going to the shop, trying them on, maybe taking them back. It costs additional money for transport, maybe for lunch too. Then there may be accessories to buy, such as cleaner, protector, a handbag. It takes effort. It involves giving up alternatives that the money could have bought (opportunity cost). It takes an investment of brain power and judgement to ensure you get the right pair. There is also the actual money paid for the shoes.

To illustrate the complexities of pricing decisions, Lancaster et al. (2007) consider three differing perspectives on pricing: the economist's, the accountant's and the marketer's. There is also the customer's view, of course.

opportunity cost
alternatives that could have been had/done instead, e.g. the opportunity cost of a lunchtime sandwich may be a pre-packed salad, and an evening at the cinema costs a night's study

THE ECONOMIST'S VIEW OF PRICING

In a free market, a product's price would be set by the forces of demand and supply (see Chapter 1). The idea is that the price goes up, and down, until it settles at the point where buyers are prepared to buy just exactly the same amount as sellers are prepared to sell (see Exhibit 10.1).

If there are more buyers than products, the price goes up until enough buyers fall out of the market and demand equals supply again. If there are more products than customers, the price falls until more customers are attracted into the market.

Take the example of a fruit and vegetable stall in a market towards the end of the day. The trader shouts out his or her prices, gradually reducing them until

Exhibit 10.1   Price in the balance

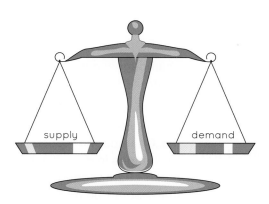

he or she attracts customers. At an auction, the potential buyers bid against each other, pushing the price up: the more buyers there are, the higher the price goes. If there is only one potential buyer, then the price stays low.

However, that is not the way business is done in shopping malls. The economist's view is more theoretical than the real world. In practice, shops and suppliers cannot change prices so dynamically; their prices are largely fixed in advance. The concept of supply and demand remains useful, though. Clearly, the higher the price of a product, the fewer people will be prepared to buy it, and so if a firm wants to clear out old stock, then it will usually reduce the price. The consequent increase in sales is evidence of the law of supply and demand.

Drawbacks in the economist's view of pricing include the following:

- It assumes that the firm's main objective is to maximise short-term profit. This is not always true, as they may want to break into a new market, or they may be a not-for-profit organisation, or in an industry where excess profits are unacceptable (e.g. electricity supply). There are many reasons why a firm may choose to make less profit than it could.
- It assumes all companies have perfect information concerning competitor prices.
- Price is not the only thing that influences demand, and it is complicated to work out a demand function using all of the possible variables, e.g. marketing communications, competitors' prices. Therefore, demand forecasts are never 100% accurate.

THE ACCOUNTANT'S VIEW OF PRICING

Accountants want to make sure that the price of a product or service covers all its costs, so that a profit can be shown (see 'Cost-based pricing' below). Drawbacks in the accountant's view of pricing include:

- It can be hard to work out all the costs involved.
- Focusing solely on the firm's own costs means ignoring the market and the power of the rest of the marketing mix. People may be prepared to pay more, especially if the brand is strong, or there has been a good advertising campaign, or a firm has shops in better locations, or all the competitive products are twice that price. This could be a missed opportunity for profit.

ethical focus: Cheap cheers!

Christmas 2009 had even more sparkle than usual thanks to the availability of bargain bottles of champagne. Supermarkets cut prices of top brands such as Bollinger and Veuve Clicquot by as much as £15 per bottle. However, drinkers were warned not to get used to the high life as prices were unlikely to remain so low for long.

So why the unusually low prices? It was mainly because of the worldwide recession which meant fewer people could afford champagne, or at least not so often. Regular champagne drinkers traded down to Italian Prosecco and Spanish Cava and only went for the real French champagne for special occasions or when there was a need to impress.

Champagne growers had come to rely on the steadily increasing demand from countries such as Britain (the Brits are second only to France in champagne consumption), India, Russia and China. Sales had been so good that they had even extended the prestigious Champagne region so that nearly 40 new growing areas were able to call their products

champagne: a privilege reserved for a strictly controlled area of France.

It takes two years to turn a grape harvest into market-ready champagne and so it is hard for the Champagne Houses to respond quickly to changes in demand. In 2009 there was too much champagne but it was predicted that there would be a shortage a couple of years later. Concerned that the drop in prices would harm their product's reputation and make it harder to command premium prices in the future, the champagne producers tried to reduce supply. Capping the volume of grapes that growers could legitimately produce would mean fewer bottles of champagne in the future. The consequent shortage would then push prices back up. Although, if consumers have developed a taste for sparkling wines from other regions, the Champagne Houses may find that they have overstocks once again.

Is it ethical to create a shortage deliberately in order to keep prices high? Is it good business? Does it encourage over-consumption?

THE CUSTOMER'S VIEW OF PRICING

Customers usually want the best quality at the lowest price. For a customer, the price has to represent good value:

perceived value = perceived benefits – price

Drawbacks in the customer's view of pricing include:

- Quality costs money – there has to be a trade-off between the two; the highest-quality products cannot be sold at the lowest prices.
- People's perception of the value of a product differs – e.g. some people will pay a lot more for branded goods such as Nike, while others will not.

THE MARKETER'S VIEW OF PRICING

Marketers see pricing as an opportunity to gain competitive advantage. It is vital to take account of what the market can bear: how much people are prepared to pay, and how much competitors are charging. Drawbacks in the marketer's view of pricing include:

- Marketers may set a price that does not actually cover the costs of making a product. Clearly, this can only be sustained in the short term or the firm will make a loss (see 'Loss leaders' and 'Contribution pricing' later in this chapter).

A concept that is gaining in popularity is that of 'shared value'. In their *Harvard Business Review* article, Porter and Kramer (2011) emphasise that by adopting the concept of shared value, the competitiveness of a company can be enhanced while simultaneously benefitting the economic and social conditions in the communities in which it operates, i.e. a win–win situation for the company, customers and the wider community. They believe that shared value is not social responsibility, philanthropy, or even sustainability, but a new way to achieve economic success that may well give rise to the next major transformation of business thinking.

EXPAND YOUR KNOWLEDGE

Bertini, M. and Gourville, J. (2012) 'Pricing to create shared value', *Harvard Business Review*, 90 (6): 96–104.

In this article, the authors highlight that most companies 'use pricing to extract what they can from every transaction' and provide examples to illustrate their point. They consider this antagonistic, destructive and a dated approach in an environment where today's consumers are not passive price-takers and will abandon companies who take advantage. They contend that 'value neither originates with nor belongs solely to the firm. Without a willing customer, there is no value. Therefore, value must be shared by a firm and its customers.'

PRICING IN THE MIX

Clearly, it is important to have a good product, but a product without a price is a gift. So, marketers must set a price. The key question is how much and the answer must take account of the rest of the mix. The price sends a message, just as the promotion, distribution channels, product and its packaging do. People do not expect Harrods to be cheap, but what about PriceRite? Which is likely to sell the highest-quality goods? The price sends a message about quality. Customers associate a high price, sometimes mistakenly, with high quality.

ACTIVITY

Visit a local department store (such as John Lewis, Fenwick, Rackhams or House of Fraser), go into the fashion, sport or perfumery department and find examples of expensive, and cheaper, products in the same category (e.g. tennis racquets, football boots, perfume, trainers, shirts). What are the differences in terms of packaging, materials used, presentation? Could you tell which was cheaper before you looked at the price tag?

Now go to a discount store or a chain store (such as Littlewoods, Matalan or BHS) and see if you can find the same brands. If you cannot find them, find the most similar thing you can and compare that with your impression of the more expensive department store brands.

Certain styles of promotion are associated with cheaper or more expensive products. When prices are rock bottom, the advertisers often shout – literally or through their choice of bold colours. There is more sales promotion (money-off coupons, two for the price of one, etc.) at the lower end of the market. Marks & Spencer used to think that advertising and sales promotion were too downmarket and unnecessary for such a well-known brand. Top fashion brands only advertise in glossy high-fashion magazines such as *Vogue* (if they advertise at all – public relations is more their forte).

PRICING OBJECTIVES

Pricing objectives can be grouped under two main headings:

- financial return, e.g. maximising revenue, recovering an investment made (usually in developing the product)
- market orientated, e.g. positioning, maintaining brand image, building market share, enticing customers to the store, rewarding customers for loyalty.

The financial objectives are largely inward-looking, while the market-orientated ones look to the external environment. Some of these objectives are really short term, e.g. 'enticing the customer into the store', and some should normally be long term, e.g. 'maximising revenue'. There may also be an ethical element to the setting of prices, e.g. governments may make services affordable to target social groups, such as the low paid, even pricing on a sliding scale to encourage those on low incomes to take advantage of services such as school dinners or education. Some companies also deliberately keep prices low for specific groups, e.g. IKEA's flatpack houses were only made available to people with combined incomes of under £35 000.

There are numerous pricing techniques that are used to meet these objectives.

PRICING TECHNIQUES

STRATEGIES, TACTICS AND METHODS

Textbooks and commentators cannot seem to agree on which of the various ways of setting prices are strategies, tactics or methods. Some have apparently given up on categorisation altogether.

In this book, a pricing strategy is defined as being medium to long term and having a significant impact on the company's overall marketing strategy, or even corporate strategy. A pricing tactic is defined as a short-term action, or one with limited impact beyond the product being priced. Pricing methods are mechanical ways to set prices. They are a good starting point, or a good way to check that the price arrived at is sane, but, marketers would argue, not a way to set prices in isolation. It is also important to check out the ways price can be used to greater effect via a specific strategy or tactic. Some pricing techniques, e.g. market skimming (see later in this chapter), could be used as strategies (longer term) or tactics (shorter term).

Pricing strategy

PRICING METHODS

There are three key elements to price setting: competitors' prices, customers' perceptions of the product's value, and costs.

A business's costs must be covered, but too great an emphasis on costs in a pricing strategy leads to missed opportunities. It is vital to take account of what is going on in the market. What are competitors charging? How much do customers want to pay? Exhibit 10.2 shows the key influencers on the pricing decisions.

Exhibit 10.2   Price setting

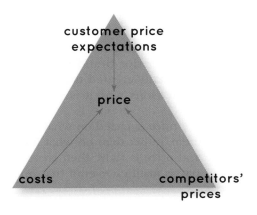

In the case of a car manufacturer, there would be substantial costs in buying the materials required to make the cars. In the long run, these must be covered by the pricing of the car or the company will be out of business. Costs of supplies are an important consideration. The company buys in engine parts, sheets of metal, mirrors, etc., and then adds value to them by turning them into a functional car. They have to pay wages, rents and other bills in order to do this. So additional cost is incurred here. But then there is the question of value. Is the car only worth the sum of its parts? Of course not, otherwise why bother to put it together at all? It is worth more as a car than as a pile of materials and sub-assemblies, but how much more?

Competitors and customers have a key role to play in determining how much value has been added by turning the parts into a car. Is it a better or worse car than the competition's? How much are customers prepared to give up for it?

Most methods of pricing can be classified as either:

- market-based pricing (taking account of competitors and/or customers), or
- cost-based pricing.

Pricing
the
product

MARKET-BASED PRICING

There are a large number of different market-based pricing methods, including:

- customer value pricing
- psychological price barriers
- auctions
- going-rate pricing
- tenders
- cartels.

Customer value pricing

A product is only worth what someone will pay for it. The price is the company's estimate of the product's value. The customer may place a different value on the product. The trick is to make these two concepts of value balance, so that the firm is paid a fair price and the customer gets a good deal. This is a difficult balancing act. The seller will have invested a great deal of time, money, effort and creativity into its offerings. They have great value. The customer has many choices as to what to buy, and will consider their relative values. The seller can increase the value of its offering in a number of ways, e.g. through added features, better quality, a superior brand image, better service, home delivery. Increases in value are usually created through the other elements of the marketing mix – one of the reasons why it is so important to coordinate all marketing mix elements.

In customer value pricing, the price is based on what customers value a product at, i.e. what it is worth to them, rather than on what it cost the firm to make. If the balance between value and price is right, then customers will see that the price they are being asked to pay is justified even if that price is higher than the competition's.

Psychological price barriers

Many people have a budget in mind before they go out to buy something. They may exceed the budget by a little, but there will be a price beyond which they will not go. That is their psychological price barrier. Some marketers set prices by conducting research to establish just where that barrier is. Then they set prices just below it.

ACTIVITY

How much are you prepared to pay for:

- lunch
- a CD
- a jacket
- a pair of shoes
- a concert ticket?

Work out your own psychological price barriers. Then, the next time you buy such things, see how well the products available match up to your budget.

You are likely to find a range of prices, e.g. lunch can cost anything from a sandwich at less than £2 to a fancy restaurant meal at £50 plus. Where do you fit in this range and what affects the price barriers you have identified? (See also 'Product line pricing' later in this chapter.)

Psychological pricing is a related concept (see 'Pricing tactics' below).

Auctions

Auctions used to be the preserve of art galleries and antique dealers, but the advent of the Internet has changed all that. Now auctions are a way to get products cheaper – online. Bandyopadhyay et al. (2001) attribute the success of auctions on the Internet to simplicity, real-time price negotiation and the large number of participants. There are a number of variants on the traditional auction, in which buyers keep bidding until only one is left in, e.g. some goods are sold by 'reverse auction'. At a reverse auction, suppliers make the bids, undercutting each other, and the customer takes the final offer and so gets the best price. (For a full explanation of Internet auctions, see **www.ebay.co.uk**.)

Going-rate pricing

Competitors' prices have to be taken into account when setting prices. Charge twice as much as the competition and the firm will make no sales; charge half as much and it is missing an opportunity for profit (as well as possibly sending the wrong message about quality).

Some established firms are considered to be **price leaders** or **price makers**. They set the prices that the others, the **price followers** or **price takers**, follow. Price leaders are often the largest competitors in the market but sometimes a smaller company is recognised as having particular expertise, and even larger firms will follow its lead. This happens quite often in the financial services industry.

price leaders
set prices for a market; other firms follow their lead

price makers
another term for price leaders

price followers
firms that set their prices in accordance with others in the market, notably a price leader

price takers
another name for price followers

Going-rate pricing is one of the most common ways of choosing a price. It is especially favoured by new entrants to a market who need to make sure that they set their prices at a realistic level in comparison to the competition, and who have no track record to guide them.

Advantages of going-rate pricing are that it:

- avoids **price wars** (see below)
- makes use of the expertise of more established firms.

Disadvantages are that it:

- assumes that competitors got their sums right and set the best price – they may not have
- firms have different cost bases; it is quite possible that Coca-Cola can charge 23p (€0.32) per can and still make a profit whereas it may cost a new competitor 25p (€0.35) just to make the drink and can it.

TENDERS

There are numerous types of **tender**, but the basic premise of all of them is that a number of firms bid for a contract. The contract is usually awarded to the lowest bidder although this is not always the case non-price criteria may be taken into account. This type of pricing is common in government, particularly for public works contracts such as road or bridge building, where the tender system is seen as being open and above reproach.

Tenders may be by sealed bid (when a firm does not know what the others are bidding) or open.

Cartels

A **cartel** is a group of companies that get together and fix prices between them. Cartels are most common in **oligopolistic** markets where they justify their joint price setting by saying that it avoids price wars. When companies get together and choose a mutually acceptable price, it tends to be higher than it would have been had they had to compete with one another. So it is cosy and safe for business, but not always good news for consumers.

Probably the most famous cartel is OPEC (the Organisation of the Petroleum Exporting Countries). In the 1970s and 1980s, OPEC set the prices for the world's crude oil. Now there are other countries involved, but the 12 OPEC members (Saudi Arabia, Iraq, Kuwait, Venezuela, Nigeria, Algeria, Libya, Iran, Ecuador, the United Arab Emirates, Angola and Qatar) still 'ensure the stabilization of oil markets in order to secure an efficient, economic and regular supply of petroleum to consumers, a steady income to producers and a fair return on capital for those investing in the petroleum industry' (OPEC, n.d.).

Cartels are considered an anti-competitive practice and are illegal in the EU. However, that did not stop eight European drugs companies colluding to fix the price of vitamins. In 2001, they were fined €855.2 million (£529.5 million) for what the EU anti-trust chief, Mario Monti, described as the 'most damaging series of cartels the Commission has ever investigated' (Anon, 2001).

---

price war
two or more firms keep undercutting each other in an attempt to build market share until one or the other backs off or goes out of business

tender (tendering)
where firms bid for a contract and, usually, the lowest-priced bid wins

cartel
a group of companies that get together and fix prices between them

oligopoly
a situation where the market is dominated by a small number of very large companies

EXPAND YOUR KNOWLEDGE

Jobber, D. and Shipley, D. (2012) 'Marketing-orientated pricing: understanding and applying factors that discriminate between successful high and low price strategies', *European Journal of Marketing*, 46 (11/12): 1647–70.

The paper aims to test seven marketing-orientated factors that have the potential to discriminate between the setting of successful high and low prices. The study supports a marketing-orientated theory of price determination based on market, customer and competitor factors.

COST-BASED PRICING

Many marketers warn against placing too great an emphasis on costs when setting prices. However, they are important. If a firm does not cover its costs, then, sooner or later, it will go out of business. The downside of focusing on covering costs is that the firm may miss out on profit, but determining the cost of a product may not be straightforward. There are different types of cost as shown below.

TYPES OF COSTS

- total costs – the sum of all costs
- direct costs – costs that are clearly due to the making of a particular product, e.g. cocoa and sugar are direct costs of Cadbury's Dairy Milk
- indirect costs – costs that cannot be attributed to one particular product as they are not directly associated with any one product's production or sale, e.g. the running costs of the chief executive's car
- variable costs – costs that go up as production increases, e.g. electricity bills
- fixed costs – costs that do not vary with production, e.g. insurance premiums.

Costs are either fixed or variable *and* either direct or indirect. Examples include:

- electricity is usually a variable, indirect cost – it costs more as production increases, but it is hard to work out just how much electricity went into the making of a particular product
- raw materials are variable, direct costs – you need more flour to make more cakes, and you still know just how much flour it takes to make a cake
- rent is usually a fixed, indirect cost – it does not vary month on month, and contributes to a number of different products
- highly specialised machinery may be a fixed, direct cost – the nozzle that pipes the perfect star on top of the coffee creams in the chocolate factory, perhaps.

Cost plus pricing

Cost and price are different. Costs are monies that a firm has to pay to its suppliers. Prices are what they charge customers for the products/services they sell. The 50p a customer pays for a chocolate bar is a cost to him or her, but a price to the shop that sells it. Clearly, prices should be higher than costs – at least most of the time.

There are a number of pricing methods that take the costs of making the goods, or of delivering the service, and then add an amount on to arrive at a price. It is therefore now necessary to take a slight detour into accounting, to see briefly how cost plus pricing is used in making decisions.

Cost plus pricing methods include:

- mark-up pricing
- full-cost pricing
- contribution pricing.

Mark-up pricing

This pricing method is common in retail as it is a relatively straightforward way for a shop to set prices: calculate the **direct cost** of the product, then add on an amount to cover **indirect costs** and provide a profit. For example, a boutique buys in dresses for £50 each. The £50 is the direct cost, but there are other costs involved in running the shop (heating, lighting, rent, wages, etc.). To price the dresses, it uses a simple formula, perhaps adding on 300% of the direct cost. This should mean that each dress sold covers *all* costs, and makes a profit.

direct cost	£ 50.00
mark-up	£150.00
selling price	£200.00

direct costs
costs that are clearly due to the making of a particular product, e.g. cocoa and sugar are direct costs of Cadbury's Dairy Milk

indirect costs
costs that cannot be attributed to a particular product as they are not directly associated with its production or sale, e.g. the running costs of the chief executive's car

Advantages of mark-up pricing are that:

- it is a relatively simple way for retailers (and some other businesses) to set their prices
- unlike full-cost pricing (see below), mark-up takes account of demand. Retailers do not apply the same mark-up to all products – they are usually adept at varying prices to take account of the popularity of products.

Disadvantages are that:

- the mark-up may not be high enough to cover all the indirect costs, especially if some products remain unsold
- a retailer knows the (direct) cost of products but it is not always so simple; direct cost per unit varies depending upon the level produced, e.g. there may be a discount available for buying a larger quantity, so costs come down (economies of scale).

Exhibit 10.3   The vicious circle of price setting

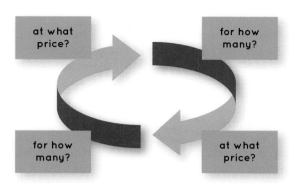

So we need to know the demand for the product before we can set the price, and demand is largely determined by price. What output level shall we pick to get our cost base? It is a vicious circle (see Exhibit 10.3).

Full-cost pricing
This is also known as absorption costing.

Full-cost pricing is as it sounds: work out the total unit cost (i.e. the **total** cost per product) of making the product, then add a further amount, and that's the price. For example, the local pizzeria adds up the costs of all the ingredients on its four seasons pizza, adds in an amount for wages and the running costs of the restaurant, then adds 100% – for profit.

full-cost pricing
prices are set
by adding an
amount (usually a
percentage) to the
full (i.e. total) costs
of making and selling
the product

per pizza	direct costs	= £0.75
	indirect costs	= £1.25
	total cost	= £2.00
	+100%	= £4.00, so that's the price

ACTIVITY

Using the full-cost pricing method, work out the price for a box of chocolates when:

fixed costs (rent, etc.)	= £40,000 per month
variable costs (ingredients, etc.)	= £1 per box
sales volume	= 100,000 per month

The accounts department has set 25% as the profit margin.

(The answer is at the end of the chapter, on p. 457.)

Advantages of full-cost pricing are:

- All production costs are covered by the price.
- Cost increases get passed on to the customer in the form of a price increase, so profit margins (in percentage terms) remain the same.
- It may be the only way to price a job for which the amount of work cannot be predicted, i.e. the price is set retroactively, when all the costs are known, e.g. for a research and development project.

Disadvantages are as follows:

- Direct costs, such as ingredients, are easy enough to allocate to a product (a baker knows how much flour was used in each loaf), but if a salesperson sells a range of products, of differing values, how much of his or her salary, company car costs, etc. should be added to the cost of each item? And just imagine how complicated that would be to work out for each of a thousand products sold by a hundred salespeople, all on different salaries. Then there's the other staff, buildings costs, etc. This allocation of indirect costs to a product is often quite arbitrary – what percentage of the chief executive's car costs should be allocated to each Dream bar?
- It ignores the market forces of demand and supply (although changing the profit margin can help to account for this) and the price sensitivity of customers – they may be prepared to pay more, or they may not be prepared to pay that price at all, in which case a way would have to be found to reduce the costs.
- If a firm gets more efficient (i.e. fixed costs per unit go down – perhaps because you have installed more modern equipment), then their price goes down too, but if the product was selling well at a higher price, why lower it? In practice, a firm might not lower prices in this circumstance, but that would mean that it was no longer naively adhering to the firm's cost plus pricing policy and had allowed some market awareness to creep into its price setting by adjusting its profit margins.

Contribution pricing

Mark-up pricing uses direct costs as a basis on which to set the price. Full-cost pricing uses the total cost as a basis. Contribution pricing is based on variable costs.

It is being included here with the other cost-based pricing methods, but this one is rather different. Really, within the classifications given earlier in the chapter, contribution pricing is usually used as a pricing tactic. It is something that can only be used in the short term – usually just for one order. Try to use it all the time, on all products, and the company will rack up the losses and go under. However, it is also a way to price loss leaders (see below).

The idea behind contribution pricing is that, as long as the product is sold for more than its variable cost, it is making a contribution towards the fixed costs and profits.

Contribution pricing is often used for one-off orders. For example, the Alpha Company's monthly fixed costs (FC) are £3,000 and variable costs (VC) are £3 per product. It regularly sells 2000 alarm clocks each month.

---

profit margin
the difference between cost and price, expressed as a percentage

total cost
all product costs, i.e. direct + indirect, or fixed + variable

contribution pricing
pricing method based on variable costs

variable costs
costs that go up as production increases and down when it decreases, e.g. electricity bills

loss leader
a product that is sold at a loss, usually to tempt shoppers to make other purchases

contribution
the amount of money remaining from the sale, when the variable costs have been paid

fixed costs
costs that do not vary with production levels, e.g. insurance premiums

So:

fixed cost per product, i.e. average fixed cost (AFC) = the fixed costs divided by the sales volume, i.e.

$$= \frac{£3000}{2000} = £1.50$$

total cost per unit   = AFC + VC

= £1.50 + £3.00 = £4.50

A new customer, Beta Holdings Ltd, wants to buy 500 clocks, but is only prepared to pay £4.00 per clock. This will not cover the total cost of making the clock, but it will cover the variable costs – anything over £3.00 makes a contribution. Should Alpha accept the order? It depends on:

- whether the fixed costs are actually already covered by other orders
- whether they have enough capacity to make the new order
- how much goodwill the acceptance of this order will generate – will Beta Holdings turn into a regular customer, maybe at a better price?
- how much bad feeling may be created if other, regular, customers find out and feel over-charged.

This is similar to the technique that economists call **marginal cost pricing**. Marginal cost is the cost of making additional units. So, in the example above, Alpha would work out what *additional* cost was involved in making the extra 500 clocks – it would need components, use more electricity, and perhaps would have to pay some overtime. Often, these additional costs will be the same as the variable costs of the order.

However, it is possible that Alpha would have to buy more machinery and, in that case, the additional cost (marginal cost) would be more than just the variable cost as additional fixed costs would be incurred too.

Advantages of contribution pricing are that:

- in a highly competitive business, a company may have the opportunity to achieve significant extra business by putting in a low bid
- it may mean keeping workers on, when otherwise they would have been laid off causing hardship for them and their families
- it keeps workers' skills honed – if they spend time idle, or doing other work, they are likely to get out of practice and will not be so efficient in the future
- if you let workers go, your competitors may snap up the best of them
- idle machinery sometimes seizes up and may require more maintenance in the future
- idle machinery is a wasted investment and still costs money in service agreements, etc.

A related concept is that of loss leaders (see below).

Target profit pricing

It would be useful for the firm to know how much, i.e. what sales volume, it has to sell in order to cover its costs. Then it can see if it is likely that the product will sell

marginal cost pricing similar to contribution pricing, a margin is added to the marginal cost (the cost of making an additional product) to arrive at a price

Exhibit 10.4 Breakeven

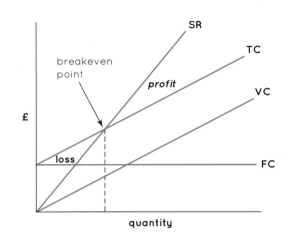

Key

SR = sales revenue
TC = total cost
VC = variable cost
FC = fixed cost

that many, and so if it is worthwhile. Clearly, price is one of the main determinants of how many products people will buy. The law of supply and demand (as well as common sense) tells us that higher prices result in lower sales, and vice versa.

breakeven point
the amount of goods a firm needs to sell in order to cover its costs

The firm can work out the required sales volume, *at a given price*, that will cover costs. This is called the **breakeven point**.

Breakeven analysis

Breakeven analysis can be done graphically (see Exhibit 10.4) or as a calculation.

A breakeven chart is a clear, visual way of analysing a firm's profit at various levels of output, and a set price. By drawing a new chart, managers can see the impact of a change in price on the firm's profits, breakeven point and margin of safety. If costs change, a new chart will also show the impact of that. Increases in costs will push the breakeven point higher; increases in price will result in a lower breakeven point.

At any given price, the firm will break even at the point where total cost (TC) = total sales revenue (SR). Further graphs can be drawn to work out the breakeven points at different prices.

If it sells a larger quantity than the breakeven point, it makes a profit. If sales fall below breakeven, it makes a loss.

If you would like to try drawing a breakeven chart, have a go at the additional activity at the end of this chapter (Appendix: Additional cost-based pricing activity).

Margin of safety

If a firm sells more than is required to break even, then that extra quantity is referred to as its 'margin of safety'. In Exhibit 10.5, a firm sells 100,000 products, but breaks even when it sells 75,000. The margin of safety is 25,000. The significance of this is that the firm knows how many sales it can afford to lose before it hits crisis point.

Setting a target profit

When firms use target profit pricing, they want to set a price that will result in a defined overall profit. This method of price setting is popular with the privatised

Exhibit 10.5   Margin of safety

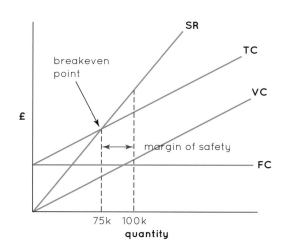

Key

SR = sales revenue
TC = total cost
VC = variable cost
FC = fixed cost

Exhibit 10.6   Roadrunner Co. target profit chart

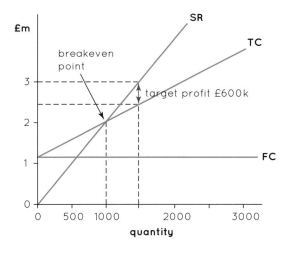

utilities, which have a duty to provide fair prices and not to make excess profits. On a normal breakeven chart, firms set a target profit by finding the point at which the difference between sales revenue and total cost equals the target profit. Then they simply draw a line down to the quantity axis and read off the sales volume required to achieve that target profit (see Exhibit 10.6).

Target profit pricing can also be calculated. The formula for this is:

fixed cost + profit target
contribution per item
= required level of output

Exhibit 10.7   Stepped breakeven chart

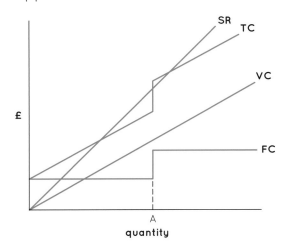

For example, the Roadrunner Co. wants to make £600,000 profit on its bicycles. Fixed costs total £1.2 million, while variable costs are £800 per bike. The bike is priced at £2000.

contribution	= selling price – variable cost
	= £2000 – £800 = £1200
$\dfrac{1{,}200{,}000 + £600{,}000}{£1{,}200}$	= 1500 bicycles

So it knows that if it sells 1500 bicycles at a price of £2000 each, then it will make £600,000 profit (see Exhibit 10.7). Alternatively, it could read this figure off a breakeven chart by finding the point at which the SR and the TC lines are £600,000 apart.

Remember that a breakeven chart works for one price only – you need to draw a new chart to try out the profit target at a new price.

Drawbacks to breakeven analysis include:

- it assumes that all the products made will be sold
- it is a static model – if costs change, then a new chart has to be drawn
- as with all analysis tools, its effectiveness depends upon the quality of the figures it uses: rubbish in = rubbish out
- it is actually more complicated than the example in Exhibit 10.6 shows because fixed costs are not always linear. They can increase (e.g. when the capacity of a machine is reached and a new one has to be bought) (see Exhibit 10.7).

PRICING STRATEGIES

Price cut!
Blackberry
Z10

NEW PRODUCT PRICING STRATEGIES

The price is one of the most difficult things to get right for a new product. Many products fail because they are either too expensive, and therefore do not sell, or too cheap and so the company is unable to meet its costs. Small businesses often charge too little for their products and it is one of the reasons that so many of them fail. It is much harder to explain a price increase to customers than it is to explain a decrease. It is often difficult to raise a price once a product has been launched on to the market as customers by then have a view of the right price and are reluctant to pay more. This is why so many new products declare that they have an introductory price. This leads customers to expect a price rise in the near future.

1 The two major new pricing strategies are:
2 market penetration
3 market skimming.

Market penetration

When a company first enters a market, it needs to build market share. A low price should tempt people to try the new product. If they like it, they will buy it again. So product trial may lead to product adoption. The main objective of a penetration pricing strategy is to establish the product in the market: to build a customer base.
   Advantages of **market penetration pricing** are that:

- it encourages people to try a product
- it encourages retailers to build up stocks – then they will not have room for competitors' products.

Disadvantages are that:

- it may provoke retaliation from existing companies
- it is not suitable for products with a short product life cycle as there may not be enough time to recover from the initial, low revenue.

The big disadvantage to the consumer is, of course, that the price does not stay low forever. New credit cards offer low, or no, interest. Then, when they are established, the 'introductory offer' disappears and they hope that their cardholders will not bother to change cards again. Many of the broadband service companies (such as BT and TalkTalk) and TV subscription companies (such as Virgin Media and Sky) also offer introductory prices for the first few months with a price increase specified thereafter.

Market skimming

This is really the opposite of penetration pricing. Firms following a skimming strategy set their prices higher than they need to, in order to maximise profits. The key to the success of a **market skimming** strategy is that there should be no significant competition – otherwise people will just buy the cheaper alternative. The company may be launching an entirely new product or entering a new market.
   This strategy works well where:

- there is insufficient market capacity and competitors cannot make more of the product
- there are no competitors (either because they do not exist at all or, perhaps, they have no distribution in that particular geographic area)
- demand for the goods in question is relatively **price inelastic**
- a high price is seen as an indicator of high quality.

market penetration pricing
pricing a product lower than competitors in order to gain market share

market skimming
setting a relatively high price to take advantage of limited competition

price inelastic demand
product sales are not very sensitive to price changes (see also inelasticity)

Advantages of market skimming are:

- early cash recovery – this is particularly important if this is a new product and the firm has made a significant investment in its development; it needs to get its money back before other firms copy the invention and the market becomes more crowded. This is something that pharmaceutical companies are particularly keen to take advantage of before their patent protection runs out.

Disadvantages are that:

- there is a high danger of encouraging other firms to enter the market – they see high profits being made and they want to make them too
- depending upon the type of product and the market in question, there may be an ethical issue over charging high prices, e.g. for prescription drugs, or in less-developed countries.

EXPAND YOUR KNOWLEDGE

Classic article

Dean, J. (1976) 'Pricing policies for new products', *Harvard Business Review,* 1 November. Part of the HBR Classic Articles series.

Joel Dean was an economist and one of the writers to influence early marketing thinking concerning the important issues of pricing. Determining the price level of a new product or service is one of the most important and most difficult marketing problems faced by a manager.

GENERAL PRICING STRATEGIES

General pricing strategies are:

- prestige pricing
- pre-emptive pricing
- product line pricing
- price discrimination.

Prestige pricing

prestige pricing
pricing a product high in order to enhance its status

Prestige pricing sets a high price for a product. Unlike price skimming, this is an ongoing strategy – the product stays expensive throughout its life. The high price is designed to associate an image of quality and high status with the product. This high price is itself an important motivator for consumers. Customers with higher incomes are less price-sensitive and more interested in buying high-quality, prestigious products that enhance their image. Promotional strategies revolve around these aspects of the product, helping to justify the high price in the customer's mind. Typical prestige brands include Chanel, IBM, Bang & Olufsen, Cartier and BMW.

Pre-emptive pricing

A company following a **pre-emptive pricing** strategy sets low prices to deter new entrants to the market. This is especially suitable in markets where there are few other barriers to entry, e.g. the company does not hold a patent and/or entry costs are low. (For more on barriers to entry, see Chapter 12.)

© Dave Pickton

Pre-emptive pricing should not be confused with **predatory pricing** (see 'Pricing tactics' below). Pre-emptive pricing is a perfectly legitimate strategy, whereas predatory pricing, which sets prices below costs in order to drive another firm out of business, is illegal in many countries including Britain. The calculation and allocation of costs to particular products is not always straight forward and a company accused of predatory pricing may have a defence against such accusations. The use of loss leader pricing (again, see 'Pricing tactics') also complicates the issue.

Rolls-Royce: a prestige product sold at a prestige price and here being used to provide a special service.

Product line pricing

Many companies develop product lines, rather than just single products, and these lines may be named and branded distinctly. A company's product range may contain a number of product lines, e.g. Ford produces the Ka, Fiesta, Focus, Fusion, Mondeo, Galaxy, Maverick ... and all of these lines have a number of models with different engine sizes, different finishes and different features.

The product manager has to set price steps within the product lines. How much more will a customer pay for a Focus with a 1.6-litre engine rather than a 1.4? How much extra should be charged for a Zetec? There will be some overlap between the top of one line and the bottom of the next one up, but how much can they overlap without the top of the line losing business?

Some sellers use well-established price points for the products in their line: so a restaurant's main courses may be premier price (for a particularly special dish, such as lobster), top price (for more expensive ingredients such as entrecote steak), mid-price (for most dishes) and low price (perhaps for vegetarian options).

Price discrimination

Price discrimination can be dangerous, but can also be very profitable. It relies heavily upon market segmentation (see Chapter 4). Price discriminators charge different prices *for the same products* to different market segments. The most common segments used are time, geography and age. Some examples are outlined below.

Time-based discrimination:

- many train services are more expensive if you want to travel before 9.30 am
- British Airways' return economy air fare from London to Sydney is approximately £1700 over Christmas, but only £820 in June (BA, n.d.)
- many entertainment venues give a discount if you book in advance.

Geographic discrimination:

- CDs are cheaper in the USA than they are in many European countries
- cars are cheaper on mainland Europe than they are in Britain (see e-focus box below)
- African countries are (at last) being allowed to buy AIDS drugs for a fraction of their normal price.

---

pre-emptive pricing
setting prices relatively low in order to deter others from entering a market

predatory pricing
also known as destroyer pricing or extinction pricing, it is when a dominant company sells products at a loss with the intention of driving a rival firm out of the market

price discrimination
charging different prices for the same products/services to different market segments, e.g. off-peak fares

Google's 'predatory pricing'

Age discrimination:

- children travel on public transport at reduced prices
- OAPs get discounts on cinema and theatre tickets
- if you are under 26, you can get a one-month Inter-rail ticket, valid for trains in 30 European countries, for about two-thirds of the price that over-26s pay (InterRail, n.d.).

The key to successful price discrimination is that customers should not be able to move between segments. It is surprising how many teenagers will happily take a couple of years off their age in order to get a cheaper bus fare. If people can move themselves into a cheaper segment, they will.

ACTIVITY

Search the World Wide Web. What's the best price you can find for a current top-10 CD?

 e-focus: The great British rip-off

For years, British consumers paid far more than their European counterparts for cars. The car companies gave a number of reasons for this, including the additional manufacturing costs incurred by putting the steering wheel on the other side and the additional distribution costs caused by having to cross the Channel.

They got away with it for so long largely because not enough people knew about it, but once customers found out there was a stream of car buyers catching ferries or the Eurostar across to France and Belgium and bringing their new cars home. They saved several thousand on the deal. So what changed?

One of the main reasons for the change was the advent of the Internet. It is so easy now to do price comparisons across the world. The Internet gives customers almost perfect pricing information, making it far harder for sellers to get away with high prices. Internet comparison shopping agents (programs such as Price Grabber and Kelkoo that automatically search a number of websites for the best price for a particular product) make it even easier for customers to get a better deal.

global focus: Cheap imports

Where do they come from, those piles of branded goods in the local supermarket? How can Superdrug afford to sell perfume so cheaply? Sometimes the goods are legitimate supplies – perhaps excess stock or the end of lines that the manufacturers are selling off. Sometimes their route to market is murkier – grey in fact. Grey importing is when someone outside the official supply chain buys goods, often in another country, for sale back home. Some of these products come from less-developed countries where prices have to be lower (otherwise people could not afford to buy them). This price discrimination tempts buyers from the more expensive markets who know they can then substantially undercut the manufacturer's recommended price and still make a profit.

In the European Union, borders are easy to cross, and there is no duty on goods brought in for personal use. Europeans frequently visit neighbouring countries to get a better deal – on a car, on alcohol and cigarettes, on Christmas presents. It gets harder to maintain different prices in different countries when people are able to travel freely.

The Internet has been a major blow to the price discriminators. Now, consumers can surf the World Wide Web looking for bargains. They can check out prices all over the world and either buy online or use their superior pricing knowledge to drive down high-street prices.

INTERNATIONAL PRICING

All the pricing methods, tactics and strategies covered in this chapter are valid in international marketing too, but here they are overlaid with all the difficulties of competing in a foreign environment. Goods and services sold in another country normally have to be priced in that country's currency. However, in business-to-business (b2b) deals, there may be arguments for pricing a contract in either the buyer's or the seller's currency – or even in a third-party currency such as the US dollar. Rates of exchange fluctuate and so it can be difficult for a company to maintain consistency in its pricing across countries: €120 may equate to £80 one day and £75 the next. Clearly, if the price has been set at the level that represents a fair exchange, then such fluctuations are not desirable.

PARALLEL IMPORTING (THE GREY MARKET)

Adapting prices to suit local income levels may sound like good business practice but it does have a downside. If a product is cheaper in one country than in others, then there is a danger that people will buy it in the cheaper country and then export it themselves to the more expensive one. Companies sometimes find themselves

parallel importing
when someone
outside of the official
supply chain sells
goods that were
bought abroad
(usually more
cheaply)

competing against their own products. In order to prevent this, either the product must be varied or the price must be pitched at a level that makes **parallel import-ing** (also called grey importing) unattractive. Different prices can still be charged so long as the difference is small enough that the additional cost of exporting means that it is not worthwhile. Many companies go to the courts to try and stop parallel importers but this is often unsuccessful and always time-consuming and expensive. It is better to avoid the problem entirely through judicious use of the marketing mix.

Sometimes companies set different prices in different countries deliberately in order to maximise profits (see 'Price discrimination' above) and sometimes prices differ as a result of exchange rate changes or the actions of third parties, such as retailers. Varying prices across the world, and particularly across regions, such as the EU, can cause significant problems for a company. For example, they may have a negative effect on the product's image or they may provide the opportunity for parallel importing, i.e. when trade customers buy in a cheaper country and then import the goods themselves, thus undercutting the manufacturer and undermining their positioning strategies.

There are further complexities to setting prices in foreign currencies:

- it may be harder to get reliable market information as the company is less familiar with this foreign market or because the information does not exist in the form that the company is used to (many third-world countries do not collect the market data that more developed countries do)
- prices in different currencies, and in multiple markets, require a lot of management time to monitor and to compare to competitive prices
- pricing laws vary from country to country (e.g. many Muslim countries do not allow credit, some governments will not allow foreign companies to undercut local ones).

PRICING TACTICS

Shorter-term, limited impact or special situation pricing options include:

- predatory pricing
- psychological pricing
- loss leaders
- promotional pricing and discounts.

PREDATORY PRICING (DESTROYER PRICING, EXTINCTION PRICING)

This pricing tactic is considered an anti-competitive practice in a number of countries, including the UK (i.e. it is against the law, but it is notoriously hard to prove).

> Predatory pricing occurs when a dominant undertaking incurs losses with the intention of removing a rival and/or deterring other potential competitors.
> (Office of Fair Trading, 2002)

The larger firm can carry this because it benefits from economies of scale. There have been some notorious examples of predatory pricing in the airline business and also in publishing.

The Times newspaper was accused of this back in 1998, when it reduced its cover price from 35p to 20p (€0.49 to €0.28), seriously undercutting its broadsheet rivals.

However, the allegation was never proven. In 2002, Aberdeen Journals Ltd was fined £1.328 million (€1.86 million) for abusing a dominant market position. The Office of Fair Trading (OFT) decision followed a Competition Act investigation into allegations of predatory pricing by Aberdeen Journals, a sister paper of the *Daily Mail* (Office of Fair Trading, 2002). In the USA, American Airlines was renowned for behaviour that seemed to many clearly to be predatory. For example, every time a fledgling airline tried to get a foothold in the Dallas market, American Airlines met its fares and added flights. As soon as the rival retreated, American Airlines hiked up its fares again. When a court case was brought against American Airlines, the judge ruled that it had to be proven that the company sold its products or services for less that its average **variable** cost. The lawyers realised that this would be almost impossible within the airline industry. Like high tech, they have high fixed costs and low marginal costs. Once a flight is scheduled, the marginal cost of providing a seat for an additional passenger is peanuts – plus a Coke, maybe. The ruling means that it will be very difficult to prove predatory pricing in industries with low variable costs such as airlines, pharmaceuticals and computing software and hardware companies, as much of the costs are in equipment and research and development and are therefore fixed (Carney, 2001).

PSYCHOLOGICAL PRICING

A surprisingly large number of products are priced at X number of pounds and 99p: £4.99 and £9.99 are particularly popular prices. The idea, of course, is to fool the customer into thinking that the item is cheaper than it really is: £1000 sounds so much more than £999 – or so the theory goes.

 ethical focus: Microsoft vs. Netscape

In 1996 Microsoft started giving away Internet Explorer, its web browser. In fact, it was argued that in some cases Microsoft effectively paid people to use Internet Explorer in preference to their existing browser, by giving them free software and marketing assistance. The strategy was crucial to the company's success in taking the market leadership away from arch-rival Netscape, which was, up until then, the most popular web browser. 'Even though Netscape constantly revised its pricing structure, it was impossible to stay competitive with "better than free"', testified Netscape CEO James L. Barksdale in the Justice Department's anti-trust suit against Microsoft (France and Hamm, 1998).

Advantages are that:

- the lower price provides a competitive advantage
- this can build the brand if people associate the company with value for money
- there may be opportunities to sell complementary products, upgrades or follow-on goods/services, e.g. a maintenance agreement
- it stimulates word-of-mouth promotion.

How can businesses afford to do this? Well, as with contribution pricing this is not a tactic that can be employed for everything, or all the time. Profits from the other items on sale have to cover the losses of the loss leader. Some retailers even put their other prices up in order to compensate, so watch out.

This links to psychological price barriers (see above). If a customer's top price for a bunch of supermarket flowers is £3.00, then it makes sense to price some at £2.99. The customer feels he or she got a good deal and the supermarket has only lost out on a penny.

LOSS LEADERS

loss leader
a product that is sold at a loss, usually to tempt shoppers to make other purchases

This tactic is often employed by retailers as a means of getting customers into a shop. Getting customers into the shop is a major retail objective as, once inside, they are more susceptible to the in-store promotional displays and impulse buys. A **loss leader** is a product, prominently displayed and advertised, that is priced well below its normal price, even below its cost to the seller. It is a lure.

PROMOTIONAL PRICING AND DISCOUNTS

© Dave Pickton

Seasonal sales and special offers are types of sales promotion.

Short-term special offers are really sales promotions rather than price reductions, so see Chapter 8, which covers marketing communications, for discussion of those. Discounts are often part of the pricing policy, especially if offered as a matter of course, for a reason. For example, many firms give a discount for bulk purchase.

A number of supermarkets give a fixed percentage reduction to customers who buy six bottles of wine or offer six bottles for the price of five. Clearly, this is to encourage people to buy more, and, if they do buy more, then the supermarkets can afford to charge a little less and still make a good profit.

Many restaurants have a table d'hôte menu: two, three or even four courses for a fixed price. The restaurant can afford to offer diners

ethical focus: Not so happy hour

‘The binge drinking girl who suffered liver failure at just 14' (*Daily Mail*)

‘Italian children's binge drinking blamed on Britain' (*Daily Telegraph*).

It's not something the UK really wants to be known for, but some British youngsters are notorious for their binge drinking. Doctors worry that youthful drinkers are heading for long-term health problems. Local communities and police see

them as troublemakers or potential victims of unscrupulous attackers. Pubs and clubs see a lucrative business opportunity. So what can, or should, be done?

A number of government-funded promotional campaigns have tried to reach youngsters with messages about health risks, about personal danger when drink makes them vulnerable, and even about making them see how ridiculous drunks look. One ad showed a night out in reverse. A young woman with messed up hair and smudged make-up, wearing ripped clothes covered in drink and vomit stains, staggers out of her front door on broken heels. A young man pours curry down his chest, rips his clothes and beats himself up. The strap line reads: 'You wouldn't start a night like this so why end it that way?'

Taxes on alcohol are high, making prices higher. This is partly to make it less affordable and partly because the taxes on alcohol sales raise valuable revenue for the government. If people drank less, the Treasury would actually suffer. Even so, there is talk of raising prices further to discourage excess drinking.

There are rules governing the sale of alcohol. In the UK you have to have a licence to sell it. Only over-18s can buy it. It can only be drunk in designated places such as bars and restaurants. Some councils have now banned drinking in the street, for example. In Sweden, the rules are even stricter.

The UK has regulations governing alcohol advertising, e.g. advertising cannot suggest that having a drink makes you more attractive or more capable. It must not target young people and so all the actors or models must look over 25. The ads mustn't plug into youth culture – as some alcopops advertising used to do. In France, mass media alcohol advertising is banned altogether.

Drinks manufacturers have pledged to encourage more moderate drinking. Some cans and bottles carry advice to 'enjoy this drink sensibly'. Diageo, who makes brands such as Guinness and Smirnoff, has run sensible drinking campaigns (though with a rather smaller budget than their brand advertising campaigns). At the same time, pubs are running sales promotions designed to get young people to drink more: happy hours where drinks are half price, buy one get one free promotions, reduced prices, loyalty cards – you can probably think of others.

The government has tried several times to introduce stricter rules on alcohol sales promotions but most are resisted by the powerful drinks lobby. One such initiative involved setting a minimum price per unit of alcohol but, although a minimum pricing law was passed by the Scottish Parliament, they struggled to introduce it in the face of strong objections from the Scottish Whisky Association among others. Legislation was rejected for the rest of the UK.

So what is the answer? Who is responsible? Should we rely on the drinks trade to police itself and on young people to take care of themselves? Should these promotions be banned? Should alcohol advertising be banned? Should the sale of alcohol be further restricted?

Would higher prices make young people drink less?

a good deal because this helps with its ordering and planning. If it knows that a lot of people will order the same dish, then there is less waste, and so less cost.

CHANGING THE PRICE

For many businesses, changing prices is expensive and time-consuming, so it is not something they want to do frequently. They have to rework the figures, recalculate VAT, redraw breakeven charts and work out new profit forecasts. Mail-order companies have to reprint their catalogues (the larger, glossier ones can cost as much as £5 or more each). Restaurants have to reprint their menus. Shops have to change price labels and tills have to be reprogrammed.

So, given the trouble and expense involved, why would a firm change its prices? There are a number of possible, pressing reasons:

- a substantial change in business costs, perhaps because raw materials have become cheaper or new production techniques have become more efficient (a lower price can be charged), or materials or wages have become more expensive (an increase in prices is needed to compensate)
- an imbalance between supply and demand, i.e. customers want to buy more than the company has to sell; if there's a shortage, then prices may rise – possible causes include production hold-ups, such as strikes, shortages in materials, machine breakdowns, and the product suddenly becoming fashionable (the latest craze)
- an imbalance between supply and demand, i.e. customers do not want to buy as much as the company has to sell; if there's a surplus, then prices may fall – possible causes include a bumper harvest, a better product hitting the market, a health or safety scare (e.g. news stories about red meat being bad for you caused a massive drop in the sales of beef, pork and lamb)
- a change in competitors' marketing, e.g. a price decrease, a major advertising campaign, new stores opening up
- a changed economic situation, e.g. inflation
- new laws, new taxes or other government pressure, e.g. government-appointed regulators review the prices charged by privatised utilities (BT, water companies, gas and electricity providers)
- as a result of a change in the firm's marketing strategy, e.g. as part of a repositioning exercise.

EXPAND YOUR KNOWLEDGE

Classic article

Guiltinan, J.P. (1976) 'Risk-aversive pricing policies: problems and alternatives', *Journal of Marketing*, 40 (1): 10–15.

Joseph Guiltinan reports on the increasingly important role of pricing for marketing. Current pricing responses to economic uncertainties are reviewed and key problems are identified. Alternative responses are developed.

PRICE WARS

A price war is a destructive spiral of reducing prices. It starts with one seller trying to undercut competitors by reducing prices. Others follow suit, meaning that the first firm has to reduce prices again in order to maintain its competitive advantage. So it goes on, sometimes until the weaker competitors (those with fewer financial resources) go out of business (see Exhibit 10.8).

Exhibit 10.8   Price wars

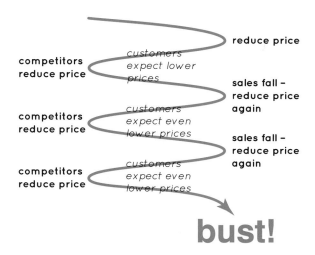

bust!

In the short term, a price war is popular with consumers, but it is bad for business and, in the longer term, it is bad for consumers too.

Businesses lose profits – they are cutting prices and, because others are matching their price cuts, they are not gaining market share. So they are just selling the same amount but at a reduced price. Eventually, either firms will go out of business, thus reducing consumer choice, or the firms involved will call a truce. Then they may have to put prices back even higher to recoup the profits they lost during the price war.

customer focus: Egg wars

The Easter weekend holiday is traditionally a happy time for many reasons. For food retailers it is second only to Christmas as a time of high sales, but lately those sales volumes have come at a price – a low price.

Easter is a time for eggs – chocolate eggs. The variety available has spiralled ever upwards but now the prices are spiralling downwards. This seems good news for the egg eaters, but it is not necessarily so good for the retailers. While the luxury end of the market is expanding, as discerning consumers trade up to organic and high cocoa content chocolate, the cheaper end of the market has contracted and a price war is being waged.

In 2002, a basic chocolate egg, such as those mass-produced by Cadbury, Mars and Nestlé, cost about £3. In 2006, they were priced at three for £5. In 2007, Woolworths were selling them at three for £3 – so you could get three for the price that just one would have cost four years back. Tesco went further. They were selling the eggs at two for £1.49, i.e. 75p each. Why did the price of Easter eggs drop so far so

(Continued)

(Continued)

rapidly? It happened because some supermarkets slashed the prices to attract customers in to do their Easter shopping, and then the others felt they had to follow suit or miss out on sales. Then the smaller retailers, even newsagents, also had to slash the price of the chocolate eggs or they would not sell any at all.

According to Tony Page, Woolworths' commercial and marketing director, the Easter eggs were being used as loss leaders by the big chains, i.e. the prices were designed purely to attract customers into the stores and bore little or no relation to the costs of the eggs and produced little or no profit for the stores involved: 'The price deflation is driven by competition in the market. It does not reflect cost deflation. And it does not reflect the value of the product.' He also expressed concern that this downward pressure on prices was

devaluing Easter eggs in the eyes of consumers. They were no longer seen as a special treat and children were buying them instead of a normal chocolate bar. In some cases, it was cheaper to buy an egg with a chocolate bar included than it was to buy the chocolate bar on its own.

It is interesting to see what has happened seven years later in 2013. Woolworths are no longer in business on the high street (although the low price of Easter eggs cannot be held solely responsible for their demise) and the major supermarket chains are still using low-priced Easter eggs to attract their customers. Of course, if they are all doing the same, what is the advantage? This is a case of ensuring you are not out of step with your competitors' prices.

SOURCES: Finch, 2007.

Price Elasticity of Demand

PRICE ELASTICITY OF DEMAND

Price elasticity of demand is a measure of price sensitivity, i.e. it measures how many more, or fewer, products are sold when the price changes (see Exhibit 10.9).

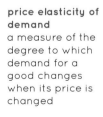
price elasticity of demand
a measure of the degree to which demand for a good changes when its price is changed

Exhibit 10.9   Price elasticity of demand

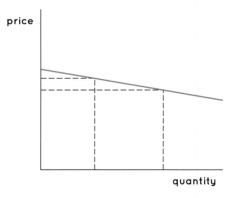

We know from basic demand theory (and from common sense) that if the price of a product goes up, then fewer people will want to buy it, and vice versa. If a product's demand is very sensitive to a change in price, i.e. when the price goes up just a little, then far fewer products are sold and it is said to be **price elastic**. If the product's sales do not vary by much when price changes, then its demand is said to be **price inelastic** (see Exhibit 10.10).

price inelastic the percentage change in demand is less than the percentage change in price, e.g. price goes up by 10%, but the demand is unaffected or is effected to a lesser extent

Exhibit 10.10   Price inelasticity of demand

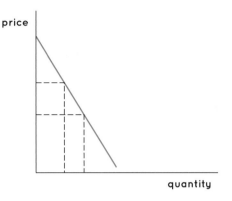

e-focus: Price matching, price beating

Listen to the TV ads, check out what's happening at the checkout. Shop in major supermarkets, online or in-store, and you will see how improved pricing research, technology and developments in EPOS (electronic point of sale) are affecting the price you pay at the till. Asda maintains that baskets of goods bought there are consistently cheaper than its rivals. This claim is based on continuous independent market research. Sainsbury offers price matching on leading brands by being able to check precisely, on a daily basis, what Tesco charges for the same brands. If others are cheaper, Sainsbury provides you with a till offer to the value of the price difference on your next shop. Tesco has responded with similar offers extended to non-leading brands as well. Many try to tempt you back to shop with them next time by printing out a whole variety of money-off coupons at the same time as your receipt; offers personalised to you based on your shopping habits and how much you have spent.

By contrast, Aldi have embarked on a TV campaign in which they directly compare their own brands to brand leaders on a range of products. Rather than claiming they can offer the same brand at a lower price, they are saying, why buy the leading brand when the Aldi versions are as good if not better and will cost you less?

Such price comparisons, of course, are not confined to the high street and shopping centres. E-tailers can show price comparisons and offer deals even more easily. Shopping search engines and price comparison sites such as Kelkoo, Megashopbot, comparethemarket.com, moneysupermarket.com and pricerunner.com can search out the best prices for your chosen product. Go on to the Amazon website and a comprehensive listing of prices from different suppliers available through Amazon will be listed for you to choose between. Looking for a bargain? Try out the 'coupon' sites such as Groupon, Vouchercloud and Dealcloud.

Sainsbury's
Brand Match

The steep curve is a price inelastic demand curve for a product such as cigarettes. As they are addictive, few people give up, even after a significant price increase.

Calculating elasticity

In order to calculate elasticity, the price *change* and the quantity *change* first need to be expressed as *percentages* of the *original price and quantity*:

Price elasticity   = % change in quantity demanded
                             % change in price

The bigger the answer, the greater the elasticity. For example, Le Café is considering increasing the price of its café latte. It wants to know whether this price increase will achieve the aim of increasing revenue. This depends on how many customers stop buying the lattes because they are too expensive. Last time it increased the price, it went from £1.50 to £1.65, and Le Café sold 480 cups a week instead of 600. Price elasticity can help.

Step 1: work out price change

£1.65 – £1.50
= 15p

Step 2: to express the price change as a percentage, divide the change in price by the original price then multiply by 100

15p/150p × 100
= 10%

Step 3: work out quantity change
480 – 600
= –120
–20/600 × 100
= –20% (don't worry about the minus – it will be explained later)

Step 4: to express the quantity drop as a percentage, divide the change in quantity by the original quantity then multiply by 100
–120/600 × 100
= –20% (don't worry about the minus – it will be explained later)

Step 5: now substitute the figures into the elasticity equation

% change in quantity demanded
        % change in price
20/10
= –2

If the answer is higher than 1 (ignore the minus sign), the product's demand is elastic. The product is significantly sensitive to price changes and raising the price will lead to a large fall in sales. This is the case with the café lattes.

So, if you are the marketing manager of Le Café, you need to be wary of increasing the price. A better way to increase revenue would be to *decrease* the price, then a lot more people will buy the product, and the increase in the volume of lattes sold will outweigh the price decrease per latte.

If the answer is below 1, then the product in question has an inelastic demand curve. Raising the price will not put many people off and revenue should increase.

The minus sign just means that when price rises, demand falls, i.e. they have a negative relationship. If demand rose with price (as in the case of some antiques, works of art, shares), then there would be no minus sign.

FACTORS AFFECTING THE PRICE ELASTICITY OF DEMAND

- Necessity or luxury? To an economist, a luxury is anything inessential: chocolate, bubble bath, ready-made meals, DVDs, etc. Really luxurious products, such as diamonds, sports cars, top designer clothes, etc., are termed **prestige goods**. Generally, necessities and prestige goods have inelastic demand, while luxuries have elastic demand.

  prestige goods high-status goods, e.g. Rolls-Royce, Rolex

- Close substitutes: if there are many alternative products available, then the demand will tend to be elastic. A substitute is something that a customer could buy instead, e.g. there are lots of different makes of ballpoint pen or pencils.
- Habit forming? If it is, then the demand will tend to be inelastic, e.g. cigarettes.
- Time period: many products are more responsive to changes in price (i.e. more elastic) in the long term. It takes a while for people to find an alternative, although they eventually will. Also, higher prices will encourage new competitors into the market, and so more choice will be available.
- Frequency of purchase: the more often customers buy the product, the more impact a price increase has on their budget, and therefore the more price elastic the demand is, e.g. a student may have a favourite brand of beer, but if the price goes up, he or she may have to switch to a cheaper one.
- Customer loyalty: if a brand is well established, then it may have loyal customers who are reluctant to change. The demand will be inelastic.
- Price level: elasticity varies along the demand curve. When something is already very cheap (e.g. matches), making it cheaper may have little effect. Similarly, if something is too expensive for most people (e.g. a Rolls-Royce), making it even more expensive may have little effect on demand. So very expensive goods may have price inelastic demand above a certain level, but elastic below a certain level. Imagine £20 off trips to Australia – it is not enough to make a difference, but £200 off might. Necessities are usually price inelastic at lower price levels, but may become elastic at higher levels as more alternative products become economically viable, e.g. cakes instead of bread, or would people take a bus to work if it cost the same as a taxi?
- Stage of the product life cycle: a new product may have price inelastic demand on introduction (little competition), be more price elastic during the growth phase, less elastic during maturity (assuming brand loyalty has been built up) and have a high level of price elasticity in its decline.

It is important for a company to know how demand for its product will react to a change in circumstances. This chapter has only considered elasticity in terms of price, but the concept can be applied to all marketing variables.

OTHER ELASTICITIES OF DEMAND

There are numerous different kinds of elasticity that can be calculated: advertising elasticity of demand measures how responsive sales are to a change in the advertising budget; income elasticity measures the response to a change in people's earnings. Of particular significance is cross-elasticity of demand. This measures the change in one company's sales in response to the change in price of a competitive product. For example, Coca-Cola would expect to sell more if Pepsi raised its price. Calculating the cross-elasticity would help Coca-Cola to know how many more cans to produce.

EXPAND YOUR KNOWLEDGE

Bezawada, R. and Pauwels, K. (2012) 'What is special about marketing organic products? How organic assortment, price, and promotions drive retailer performance', *Journal of Marketing,* 77 (1): 31–51.

This paper investigates the demand elasticities of marketing mix elements in the sale of organic foods.

Customer focus: Price rise or price cut?

Although few marketing managers work out the exact elasticity of their products' demand curves, this is a concept that everyone involved in setting prices needs to be aware of. It is a vital consideration when changing prices as it determines whether lowering, or raising, prices is most likely to result in a revenue increase.

If a product has a price inelastic demand, then putting prices up will result in increased total sales revenue. Very few customers will stop buying the product, and their loss will be amply covered by the higher price that remaining customers pay.

If a product has a price elastic demand, then to increase revenue, the price should be lowered. Many more people will buy the product. So many that they will compensate for the lower price. Of course, competitor activities need to be taken into account as well.

Most essential goods (bread, petrol, power, etc.) are not particularly price sensitive (inelastic). Whereas inessentials (cream cakes, bubble bath, meals in restaurants, etc.) are usually more sensitive to price changes (elastic).

This can be seen from the demand curves in Exhibits 10.9 and 10.10. The shallow curve is for a product with a price elastic demand, i.e. it is very sensitive to a change in price. A small price change results in a large change in the quantity of the product demanded.

PRICING ON THE INTERNET

What makes pricing on the Internet unusual is the ready availability of information and the degree to which customers can participate in price setting – and turn into sellers themselves. eBay has been a phenomenal success, attracting many more customers than offline auctions do and even becoming a way of life for some devotees (and destroying the businesses of some others, e.g. sellers of collectibles). The Internet empowers bargain hunters who can more easily search out the best offers available (Wright and Jayawardhena, 2001) and at the same time provides a more convenient shopping experience for the time-starved.

Online pricing strategies

There are a number of factors that combine to make Internet prices lower than their offline equivalents. Strauss et al.'s (2008) suggestions include:

- shopping agents (see below)
- reverse auctions, where sellers bid for the buyer's business
- venture capitalists, who are prepared to take a long-term view of their investment, meaning that the Internet company can charge less and sustain a loss for some time
- competition, which is fierce and worldwide
- lower costs, due to cutting out intermediaries (e.g. retailers), getting customers to do some of the administration (e.g. filling in order forms), cutting staff (automation), reduced printing requirements
- high price elasticity, i.e. price sensitivity (see above for a more detailed explanation) – online markets appear more price-sensitive than their offline equivalents
- frequent price changes – e-tailers can respond more quickly and easily to changes in competitive prices or in other market conditions.

To these can be added tax avoidance, as very few people pay the import duties on products bought over the Internet and shipped in from abroad.

In the early days of the Internet, economists gleefully anticipated the realisation of something that had, until then, been only a theory: an **efficient market**. In an efficient market, buyers have ready access to pricing information for all their choices of products to buy. The Internet provides this thanks to the ease of searching numerous possible suppliers, its interactivity (which enables real-time auctions), the ease with which prices can be changed and the availability of shopping agents. Shopping agents are software programs which search the Internet and then display a table of comparative prices for a specified item, e.g. PriceSCAN or Kelkoo. Interestingly, despite the opportunities to shop around, not all Internet shoppers choose the lowest possible price. One of the reasons for this is the trust issue. Although e-shopping is now widely accepted, many consumers prefer to buy from known and trusted sites rather than risk their credit card details to less well-known ones – and they are prepared to pay a price premium for that privilege.

efficient market
a market in which prices adjust quickly, and frequently, in response to new information (in economic theory)

There is much debate as to whether the Internet is really a different marketplace or just a different marketing channel. Does it reach a new set of customers or just reach the same ones in a different way? Whether it is a new market or not, most of the old rules still apply to it – and that includes the pricing strategies, tactics and methods discussed elsewhere in this chapter. Sometimes, however, it does provide a new way to implement the old ideas. Take price discrimination, for example.

Price comparison websites

The Internet has provided companies with additional segmentation tools and price discrimination possibilities. Information about customers gained through cookies and registration forms can be used to segment customers and charge them different prices. Companies need to exercise care here, though, as consumers are likely to perceive the charging of different prices on this basis as unfair and therefore to trust the suppliers less in the future (Grewal et al., 2004). The music industry has come in for a lot of criticism because of its pricing policies, both on- and offline. For example, Apple iTunes customers are charged differently for downloads according to the country revealed by their email address – a practice which has resulted in an EU investigation of the record companies responsible for the differing charges (Jacoby, 2007).

SUMMARY

Pricing is a much neglected marketing tool. Too many firms take a mechanical approach to the setting of prices, often purely on the basis of costs. Far too few organisations review their prices regularly enough and so they miss marketing opportunities.

Pricing is a competitive weapon that should be deployed alongside the rest of the marketing mix. A product's price sends a message – of quality, of desirability, of status, of a good buy. It has to vary according to place of purchase – wholesale, retail, Internet. It is a key part of the brand.

Common pricing objectives include maximising revenue, maintaining brand image, building market share, recovering an investment made (usually in developing the product), enticing customers to the store, and rewarding customers for loyalty.

Pricing methods are largely either cost-based or market-based. Too great an emphasis on cost can lead to missed profit. Market-based methods take account of what the market can bear, but the price must always be high enough to cover costs in the long run.

Pricing strategies and tactics overlap. There are specific strategies for new product pricing. Firms following a market penetration strategy set their prices low. A market skimming strategy employs high prices. General pricing strategies include: prestige pricing, where a high price is set to confer status; pre-emptive pricing, where a lower price is set to discourage competition; product line pricing, where related products are sold at a variety of prices; and price discrimination, which charges different prices for the same product to different market segments.

Pricing tactics include psychological pricing, which sets a price that sounds cheaper (e.g. £999) and loss leaders, which are products sold very cheaply but made up for by the profits of others.

Elasticity is a key concept when changing prices. Products with price inelastic demand will earn more revenue if the price is increased. Prices for products with price elastic demand should be lowered if the firm wants to increase its sales revenue.

CHALLENGES REVIEWED

Now that you have finished reading the chapter, look back at the challenges you were set at the beginning. Do you have a clearer idea of what's involved?

HINTS

- Profit margins and price wars
- Price elasticity of demand and the impact of price on image
- New product pricing strategies – skimming
- Think about why the banks will not make the loans – can these people afford to pay them back? What will happen if they cannot make the payments?
- Remember parallel importing. The product may need simplifying in order to reduce costs.

READING AROUND

JOURNAL ARTICLES

Bertini, M. and Gourville, J. (2012) 'Pricing to create shared value', *Harvard Business Review*, 90 (6): 96–104.

Bezawada, R. and Pauwels, K. (2012) 'What is special about marketing organic products? How organic assortment, price, and promotions drive retailer performance', *Journal of Marketing*, 77 (1): 31–51.

Bray, J.P. and Harris, C. (2006) 'The effect of 9-ending prices on retail sales: a quantitative UK-based field study', *Journal of Marketing Management*, 22 (5/6): 601–17.

Dean, J. (1976) 'Pricing policies for new products', *Harvard Business Review*, 1 November. Part of the HBR Classic Articles series.

Guiltinan, J. (1976) 'Risk-aversive pricing policies: problems and alternatives', *Journal of Marketing*, 40 (1): 10–15.

Jobber, D. and Shipley, D. (2012) 'Marketing-orientated pricing: understanding and applying factors that discriminate between successful high and low price strategies', *European Journal of Marketing*, 46 (11/12): 1647–70.

Kumar, N. (2006) 'Strategies to fight low cost rivals', *Harvard Business Review*, 84 (12): 104–12.

Mitchell, V-W. and Ka Lun Chan, J. (2002) 'Investigating UK consumers' unethical attitudes and behaviours', *Journal of Marketing Management*, 18 (1/2): 5–26.

Porter, M. and Kramer, M. (2011) 'Creating shared value', *Harvard Business Review*, Jan.–Feb., 89 (1/2): 62–77.

WEBSITES

There are numerous websites that you can go to for price comparisons to find cheaper prices. For example:

www.comparethemarket.com
www.kelkoo.co.uk

SELF-REVIEW QUESTIONS

1. How does price affect a product's brand image? (See p. 415)
2. How do the forces of supply and demand affect prices? (See pp. 416–7)
3. Complete this formula: perceived value = perceived benefits ... (See p. 418)
4. List three possible objectives of a pricing strategy. (See p. 420)
5. List the three key influencers on pricing decisions. (See p. 421)
6. What is a psychological price barrier? (See p. 422)
7. Whose prices are taken into account in 'going-rate pricing'? (See p. 423)
8. Which type of cost is mark-up pricing based on? (See p. 426)
9. If a new customer wanted to place a large order but would only accept a low price, what would you take into account when deciding whether or not to take the order? (See pp. 429–30)
10. What are the drawbacks to breakeven analysis? (See p. 432)
11. Briefly describe two major new product pricing strategies. (See p. 433)
12. Define price elasticity of demand. (See p. 444)

Mini case study: Levi's vs. Tesco

Read the questions, then the case material, then answer the questions.

Questions

1 Why was Levi's so reluctant to sell its jeans to Tesco?

2 How was Tesco able to sell the jeans so cheaply?

3 If large food retailers are able to sell designer brands at cheap prices, what are the long-term implications for branding?

The world's biggest brands have spent a fortune building their names and they protect their image jealously. Large retail chains have enormous amounts of marketing power and are used to being able to dictate terms to their suppliers. A clash seemed inevitable. The court case involving Levi Strauss and British supermarket chain Tesco was part of a power struggle between these two camps.

Britons spend an estimated £20 billion a year on branded fashion goods, and Tesco wants the right to sell those designer brands cheaply, but if it wins, then the brands' exclusivity is lost. Sourcing the goods was not easy. Tesco had to buy them through the grey market. Levi's would not sell to the supermarket directly and bona fide Levi's distributors were worried about selling the jeans on to supermarkets.

Christine Cross, head of Tesco's non-food sales, felt that consumers should not have to pay such high prices: 'Consumers today are very well travelled, they see prices all over the world . . . why should Levi's be one price in America, another in France and a third price in the UK?' However, Levi's was concerned for the future of its business: 'Our brand is our most important asset. It is more valuable than all the other assets on our balance sheet. It's more valuable than our factories, our buildings, our warehouses and our inventory,' explained Joe Middleton, Levi's European president. 'The true cost of making this jean is not just the factory element. It is much more than that.'

Many were unconvinced by the brand's arguments. If the superstores gained the right to stock anything they wanted to, then Brits could buy cheaper jeans – either with their groceries or through traditional channels forced to reduce prices or lose sales. Of course, the longer-term casualty would be brand value, which would be unlikely to survive the shame of jeans being sold alongside baked beans.

The court decided that a manufacturer had a right to oversee the distribution of its products. Levi's won and its brand image was saved – until next time.

SOURCE: Datar, n.d.

REFERENCES

Anon (2001) 'Vitamin cartel fined for price fixing', *The Guardian*, 21 November.

Bandyopadhyay, S., Lin, G.B. and Zhong, Y. (2001) 'Under the gavel', *Marketing Management*, 10 (4): 24–8.

BA (n.d.) *Buy Travel*, British Airways. Available at: **www.britishairways.com/travel/fx/public/** (accessed 04/04/13).

Bertini, M. and Gourville, J. (2012), 'Pricing to create shared value', *Harvard Business Review*, 90 (6): 96–104.

Bezawada, R. and Pauwels, K. (2012) 'What is special about marketing organic products? How organic assortment, price, and promotions drive retailer performance', *Journal of Marketing*, 77 (1): 31–51.

Carney, D. (2001) 'Predatory pricing: cleared for takeoff', *Business Week Magazine*, 13 May. Available at: **www.businessweek.com/stories/2001-05-13/commentary-predatory-pricing-cleared-for-takeoff** (accessed 03/04/13).

Cox, J. (2001) 'Pricing practices that endanger profits', *Marketing Management*, 10 (3): 42–6.

Datar, R. (n.d.) 'Battle of the brands', *The Money Programme*, BBC TV. Available at: **news.bbc.co.uk/1/hi/programmes/the_money_programme/archive/1604636.stm** (accessed 03/04/13).

Dean, J. (1976) 'Pricing policies for new products', *Harvard Business Review*, 1 November. Part of the HBR Classic Articles series.

Finch, J. (2007) 'Supermarkets wage Easter egg price war', *The Guardian*, 7 April, p. 35.

France, M. and Hamm, S. (1998) 'Does predatory pricing make Microsoft a predator?', *Business Week*, 23 November. Available at: **www.businessweek.com** (accessed 03/04/13).

Grewal, D., Hardesty, D.M. and Gopalkrishnan, R.I. (2004) 'The effects of buyer identification and purchase timing on consumers' perceptions of trust, price fairness, and repurchase intentions', *Journal of Interactive Marketing*, 18 (4): 87–101.

Guiltinan, J.P. (1976) 'Risk-aversive pricing policies: problems and alternatives', *Journal of Marketing*, 40 (1): 10–15.

InterRail (n.d.) Untitled. Available at: **www.interrail.eu** (accessed 03/04/13).

Jacoby, M. (2007) 'EU music complaint focuses on record firms: Apple's iTunes store isn't getting scrutiny in price investigation', *Wall Street Journal* (Eastern Edition) Technology, 4 April, p. B5.

Lancaster, G., Withey, F. and Ashford, R. (2007) *Marketing Fundamentals*. CIM Workbook. Oxford: Butterworth-Heinemann.

Office of Fair Trading (2002) 'OFT fines Scottish newspaper publisher for predatory pricing'. Available at: **www.oft.gov.uk/news-and-updates/press/2002/pn_58-02#.UfzqZ5LVCSo** (accessed 03/08/13).

OPEC (n.d.) Mission statement, Organisation of the Petroleum Exporting Countries. Available at: **www.opec.org** (accessed 08/04/13).

Oxenfeldt, A.R. (1973) 'A decision-making structure for price decisions', *Journal of Marketing*, Jan: 48–53.

Porter, M.E. and Kramer, M.R. (2011) 'Creating shared value', *Harvard Business Review*, Jan–Feb 89 (1/2): 62–77.

Strauss, J., Frost, R. and El-Ansary, A. (2008) *e-marketing*, 5th international edn. Harlow: Pearson Prentice Hall.

Wainwright, M. (2007) 'Ikealand: where an Englishman's home is his Bo Klok', *The Guardian*, 31 January.

Wright, L. and Jayawardhena, C. (2001) 'Netting the consumer: the e-direct marketing imperative', *Proceedings of the Marketing Science Conference*. Cardiff: University of Cardiff.

APPENDIX: ADDITIONAL COST-BASED PRICING ACTIVITY

ACTIVITY: DRAWING A BREAKEVEN CHART

You will need proper graph paper, a ruler, pencil, rubber and calculator for this.

The Roadrunner Co. produces racing bicycles:

fixed costs (FC) total £1.2 million

variable costs (VC) are £800 per bike

the bike sells for £2000

1 The first challenge is to decide on the scale for the graph. In real life, you would know current output levels and could use that as a guide. Otherwise, it is really trial and error. Draw the y (vertical) axis along the short side of your paper. For our Roadrunner example, let's label the (vertical) y axis £m, and take it up to £4m, and the (horizontal) x axis (quantity of bicycles) to 3500.

2 Now, plot the fixed costs. This is the easy one – fixed costs do not change so we draw a straight, horizontal line across from the y axis at £1.2 million. Label this line 'FC'.

3 Next, draw the variable costs (VC) line. VC are £800 per bike, so pick a number (any number between 1 and 3500) and work out the VC at that level of output.

For example, 500 × £800 = £400,000.

Now make a small mark at the point where 500 on the x axis meets £400,000 on the y axis. Repeat for another random point, say 2000:

2000 × £800 = £1,600,000.

Next, taking 0 (bottom left corner of the graph) as your starting point, just join the dots to make a variable cost line (it should be a straight, diagonal line; if it is not, then check the two calculations). Label this line 'VC'.

Why use 0 as a starting point? It is because if you don't make any products, then there will be no variable costs – they are ingredients and raw materials, remember.

4   The next line to draw is the total cost (TC) line and there's a cheat's way to do this.

Take a ruler and lay it along the VC line, then carefully move it up, keeping the angle the same, until it crosses the *y* axis at the start of the FC line. Then draw a straight diagonal line, starting at the *y* axis. This line should be parallel to the VC line. Label this line 'TC'.

Why does the total cost line start at the FC line? Because total cost = fixed cost + variable cost, so it can never be *less* than fixed cost.

Exhibit 10.11   Roadrunner Co. breakeven chart

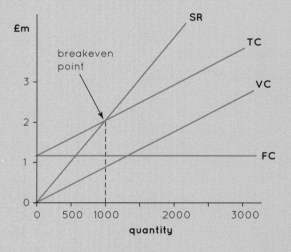

5   The sales revenue (SR) line is drawn in a similar way to the VC line. Pick two numbers (any two numbers within the scale of the graph). Work out the revenue at those sales volumes (quantity × price), then, using 0 as a starting point, plot a straight diagonal line that joins all three points. Label this line 'SR'.

6   Now you're ready to read off the breakeven point. X marks the spot, i.e. it is where the sales revenue and total cost lines cross. Draw a line down to the quantity axis – the answer should be 1000.

Of course, if the company wants to know what happens if the price is increased to £2100, it will have to draw a new line for sales revenue.

As an alternative to the graphical method, the firm might calculate breakeven points using this formula:

Fixed costs

Contribution **per item**

Let's revisit the Roadrunner Co. figures:

fixed costs total £1.2 million

variable costs are £800 per bike

price is £2000

contribution	= selling price – variable cost
	= £2000 – £800 = £1200
$\dfrac{1,200,000}{1200}$	= 1000

So, it needs to sell 1000 bicycles at £2000 in order to cover all its costs, i.e. to break even.

ACTIVITY: ANSWER TO FULL-COST PRICING ACTIVITY (SEE PAGE 427)

total cost	= fixed costs + variable costs
fixed cost per unit (box)	= $\dfrac{£40,000}{100,000}$ = 40p
total cost per unit (box)	= 40p + £1 = £1.40
price, i.e. total cost + 25%	
	= £1.40 + (£1.40 × 25%)
	= £1.75

Visit the companion website on your computer at **www.sagepub.co.uk/masterson3e** or MobileStudy on your Smart phone or tablet by scanning this QR code and gain access to:

- **Videos** to get a better understanding of key concepts and provoke in-class discussion.
- Links to useful **websites and templates** to help guide your study.
- Access **SAGE Marketing Pins (www.pinterest.com/sagepins/)**. SAGE's regularly updated **Pinterest** page, giving you access to regularly updated resources on everything from Branding to Consumer Behaviour.
- **Daily Grind podcast series** to learn more about the day-to-day life of a marketing **professional**.
- Interactive **Practice questions** to test your understanding.
- A **bonus chapter on Marketing Careers** to not only support your study, but your job search and future career.
- **PowerPoints** prompting key points for revision.

PART
FOUR

Managing Marketing

WHAT THIS PART IS ABOUT

The final section of this book draws together all the previous areas and shows what marketers actually do with the resources at their disposal. Branding is a major weapon in a marketer's armoury and so Chapter 11 looks back at previous chapters on the marketing mix and shows how the marketing mix elements combine to build brands. Chapter 12 explains the marketing planning process and how it is used to manage marketing activities and to achieve marketing goals.

Modern organisations are highly reliant upon marketing and successful marketing is dependent upon the skills of marketers. There is a wide range of different roles within marketing: research and analysis, logistics planning and management, account handling, brand management, new product development, price setting – it would take too much space to list them all here. However, we do want you to share our enthusiasm for marketing and to find your ideal marketing role. So we have put an extra, bonus, section on this book's companion website that explains what marketers do in more detail and how your career might develop.

Go to **www.sagepub.co.uk/masterson3e**

We wish you good luck in your future marketing career!

Building brands using the international marketing mix

11

BRAND-BUILDING CHALLENGES

The following are illustrations of the types of decision that marketers have to take or issues they face. *You aren't expected to know how to deal with the challenges now*; just bear them in mind as you read the chapter and see what you can find that helps.

- Aphrodite is a small, well-known confectionery brand that wants to change its image to that of a supplier of high-quality, special-occasion sweets. The marketing director has asked you to review current marketing activities to ensure that they support this new market position. What do you need to check?
- You are the marketing manager for a well-known designer fashion brand. A chain store has approached your company with a view to placing a large order. The finance manager is delighted and is prepared to discount the price. However, the managing director has some concerns. Do you think this order should be accepted? Do you want to impose any special terms and conditions?
- A friend owns two coffee bars, one in Leicester and one in Edinburgh. She now works in Edinburgh as that coffee bar is new and has no manager yet. Since she left, takings at the Leicester restaurant have dropped right down and she doesn't know why. She has asked you to help her find the problem. Do you know what to do?
- You are the brand manager for a range of jams that are one of the oldest brands in the world. The range has distinctive and well-recognised packaging. However, the packaging is not recyclable and you are under pressure to change it. You are worried about losing your brand's competitive advantage. What do you need to consider? What can you do?

INTRODUCTION

The marketing mix is at the core of any marketing plan. The most commonly used schematic for the marketing mix is the 4Ps and this has the advantage of being both widely recognised and easy to remember.

The marketing mix is a set of tools and should be treated as such. No one element can stand alone; they must all support each other. If they conflict, target markets will be confused, objectives will not be met and the brand's image will be diluted. Marketing managers blend their marketing mixes to make an integrated plan that will achieve their marketing objectives.

This chapter is a round-up of the marketing mix, summarising the techniques, demonstrating how they fit together and showing how they can be integrated to build brands. The idea of branding as an integral part of a modern product was introduced in Chapter 6. It will be considered here as a strategy that employs all elements of the marketing mix.

MARKETING MIX OBJECTIVES

Before any decisions are taken on what to do with the marketing mix, it is important to know what you are trying to achieve. If you just get into your car and drive, without first deciding where you want to go, then you will just drive around aimlessly. To reach a destination, you have to know where you want to be and plan a route to get there. The marketing mix is the organisation's route to its marketing objectives (see Exhibit 11.1).

Exhibit 11.1   Planning to meet objectives

where are we now?
(the situation)

where are we going?
(the objectives)

how will we get there?
(strategy and planning)

what exact route shall we take?
(marketing programmes)

how will we know when we get there?
(monitoring and control)

Exhibit 11.2   Hierarchy of objectives

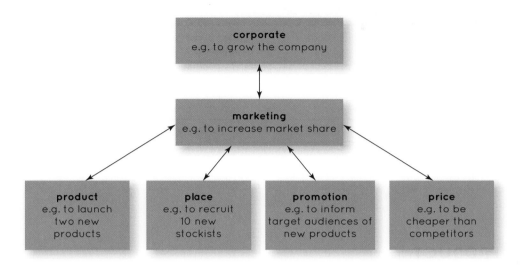

An organisation's objectives work in a hierarchy. At the top level are the corporate objectives. All other objectives, including marketing, should be designed to contribute to those overall, corporate objectives.

The objectives illustrated in Exhibit 11.2 are insufficiently detailed for the real world – more precision and explanation is required

The meeting of customer needs is at the heart of good marketing. Marketers have to get inside their customers' heads and see the offering through their eyes. If the offering is noticeably better than that of the competition, then competitive advantage will be created. For example, it may be better quality, or cheaper, have a better image or be more readily available. The marketing mix will be more effective if it is well integrated, i.e. each element fits with the others so that there are no contradictory signals (see 'Mixing it' below). Resources are always a constraint on marketing activities. There is no point in designing a mix that the company does not have the resources (finance, expertise, time or a suitable infrastructure) to implement.

THE MARKETING MIX: A REPRISE

The Marketing Mix

FIRST THERE WERE 4PS: THE TRADITIONAL MARKETING MIX

Each of the 4Ps is covered in more depth in its own chapter (Chapters 6–10). This chapter focuses on integrating the elements of the marketing mix to build brands and also introduces some of the additional complexities associated with international marketing and the marketing of service products. Exhibit 11.3 summarises the 4Ps and shows how they can fit together.

Exhibit 11.3　The 4Ps: key variables

Product	Price	Place	Promotion
Features (characteristics, attributes)	Price range	Intermediaries (retailers, wholesalers, etc.)	Advertising
Range	Discounts	Coverage	Personal selling
Support services	Allowances	Order processing	Public relations
Brand	Negotiation policy	Stock control	Sales promotion
Design	Credit policy	Delivery	Direct marketing
Packaging	Price changes	Transport	Sponsorship

PRODUCT

It may seem obvious just what a product is (a pen, a car, a ring, a bar of chocolate, etc.), but there is rather more to it than that.

Products of the same type, e.g. cars, and even produced by the same manufacturer, e.g. Ford, are differentiated by features, quality, size, speed, shape and colour. They have different features (engine size, braking system, colour, interior trim, etc.) and come in different sizes for different drivers (small car, small family car, family car, executive, limousine, van, minibus, people carrier, etc.). All these things are characteristics (or attributes) of a particular car and so a product could be said to be a bundle of characteristics. It is the quality of these features, coupled with the workmanship that goes into the product, that determines its quality. Quality is something that most customers look for in a product, even though they cannot always afford to buy the best. This is an example of how the marketing mix integrates. The best components, such as those that go into a Rolls-Royce (e.g. walnut veneer dashboards), cost more than others (e.g. plastic dashboards). This means that a higher price will have to be set for the products that have the higher-quality components. Some customers will be willing and able to pay that price (so long as the quality really is better), some will not. Those who do buy a Rolls-Royce will be buying not just a car but an exclusive image. They will therefore expect impeccable service, both before and after the sale.

Companies provide a range of products, of differing quality, with different features, different images and different levels of support, to match the prices that different customers are prepared to pay for that product type.

So a product is a bundle of characteristics but, of course, that is not what customers really want to buy. What the customer really wants is the **benefit** that the product brings. People do not just buy cars, they buy means of transport or status symbols. They do not really buy rings because they want small bands of metal, they want tokens of affection, gifts, decorated fingers, symbols of their engagement. Marketers must concentrate on the benefits their products bring to their purchasers – the product features and quality are really just the means by which those benefits are delivered.

ACTIVITY

Choose a pair of products from the list below. What are their features? What are the benefits that those features are designed to deliver?

- Kindle Fire and Kindle Paperwhite
- a tub of Häagen-Dazs ice cream and a Unilever Cornetto
- a pair of trainers and a pair of walking boots
- sleeping bags and duvets (think of all the possible variances)
- music downloads and CDs.

Products have a number of levels, which together make up the total product offering. Customers may decide between two products on the basis of any of the attributes listed in Exhibit 11.4, e.g. customer support, but they will not buy a product that does not deliver the core benefit required. A pen must write, chocolate must taste good, a car must go.

The basic product is the product itself and includes features, components and quality level. Remember that this may be a physical product or a service product. Service products also have features, components, quality levels, etc. Take a dry cleaning service, for example. It may be local (a feature), include ironing (a component), be standard or gold service (quality), and be given back to the customer in a plastic

Exhibit 11.4 The total product offering

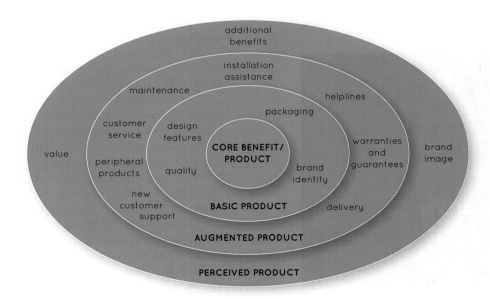

bag or a strong clothes carrier (packaging). The perceived product is the product as the customer actually sees it, which may not be in quite the way the supplier intended. For example, a restaurant may wish to be thought of as upmarket, but its target market may just think it is over-priced. The augmented product is the surrounding support for the product, including all support services, delivery and installation.

Take a shirt as an example. Its core benefits are that it covers nakedness and provides some warmth. As a basic product, the shirt is blue, fashionably styled, available in most sizes and made of 100% cotton of the highest quality. The supplier offers a no-quibble, money-back guarantee if the shirt fails to live up to expectations. This augments (adds to) the product. If the shirt in question also happens to be made by Armani, how does that affect your perception of it?

Previously, firms tried to differentiate themselves from their competition through tangible product advantages: their products might be better quality, come in more colours, have additional features, etc. Competitive strategies centred upon developing a product that was demonstrably superior to competitors' products and then updating it regularly in order to maintain that superior position. However, as markets have become more competitive, tangible product differences are harder to maintain and so the augmented product has become the main source of competitive edge for many companies – providing their **unique selling propositions (USPs)**.

unique selling proposition (USP) a clear point of differentiation for a product/service

The term USP originally stood for 'unique selling point' and was first used by Rosser Reeves, whose idea was that advertising worked best when it made one clear point. Unfortunately, the phrase was picked up and reinterpreted as meaning that a product must have a unique feature, something that it is increasingly hard to maintain (Pickton and Broderick, 2004). The word 'point' caused confusion and consequently 'unique selling proposition' is the definition now generally preferred. The USPs of today are most likely to be derived from additional services or from branding. (For more on services, see Chapter 7.)

Virgin

Branding is part of the augmented product and is one of the best ways to differentiate a product from its competition. Towards the end of the twentieth century, branding came to be seen as the main contributor to a company's competitive edge. The emphasis was on brand value. Leading brands battled for the loyalty of consumers: few more fiercely than the big sportswear companies, Nike, Reebok and Adidas, who spent millions on promoting their brands. They competed as fiercely to sponsor the best, or in some cases the most photogenic, sports stars as those athletes competed themselves.

Some highly successful organisations are just brands – they don't actually make anything and may franchise the selling operation too. For example, Virgin has lent its name to a number of products (vodka, cola, cosmetics) that it has very little to do with. At the beginning of the twenty-first century, the brand's power looks less sure. Customers seem to want more value than a brand alone can give. Customer service may be a key source of competitive edge over the next few years.

© Matthew Peters/Getty Images

Famous faces can help make brands famous too.

International product decisions

Most consumer products are adapted in some way to suit the needs of different countries although there is some convergence of global tastes and preferences, largely due to improved communications and the efforts of multinational and global companies. This allows manufacturers to standardise products in certain categories. For example, Gillette's Mach 3 was developed as a world product. It is a standard shaving system designed to meet the needs of men who want a quicker, closer shave – whatever their nationality.

ACTIVITY

This exercise is perhaps best done in class, or at least with a group. List as many products as you can that are absolutely standard in all their features and characteristics, the world over. Then compare lists and see if you agree with the products that others have listed.

There are some products that look the same and are assumed to be the same, but even Coca-Cola is not the same in all countries, e.g. it has more sugar in India than it does in Europe. There are many more standardised products in b2b and industrial markets. Raw ingredients such as vegetables, commodities such as salt, metals, minerals and gemstones are all more likely to be standard, as are many office and computer supplies. Analysis tools such as the product life cycle and the Boston Consulting Group Portfolio Matrix (BCG matrix) are used in international marketing as well as in domestic marketing. Products may be at different stages in their life cycles in different countries, although these differences are reducing as the forces of globalisation gather force. Exporting has long been seen as a means of extending a product's life cycle but, with the convergence of life cycles internationally, the general shortening of product lives and the trend for global brands to launch new products simultaneously in multiple countries, this is becoming less common. In terms of the BCG matrix, at the simplest level the 'market' referred to on the axes can be taken as the country in question, although it should be remembered that few countries are really just one big uniform market segment. (See Chapter 6 for more on the product life cycle and the BCG matrix.)

PROMOTION (MARKETING COMMUNICATIONS)

Consumers have a wide choice of products on which to spend their money. Sellers try to influence that choice through the use of promotion. This is the part of the marketing mix that is primarily concerned with communication, which is why it is now more commonly known as marketing communications. Marketing communications is thought to be a better term as it is a more accurate description and because there was always the possibility of confusion between promotion and sales promotion. Marketing communications and promotion are interchangeable terms and this book uses both.

The promotional mix traditionally comprises:

Tata
Nano

global focus: Cars for the people

A car is often the single most valuable item that a person owns. Great thought and effort goes into the selection and purchase of a car: it is not just transport, it is a statement, a status symbol, an outward representation of its owner's inner self. In the developed world, the make and style of a car says a lot about its driver, especially about their wealth. Then again, in some other parts of the world, just owning a car, any car, speaks of affluence. Imagine the joy of buying your first, brand new car in a society where fewer than eight people in a thousand own one.

This is the dream that the Tata motor company hoped to make come true for thousands of Indians when it proudly launched the world's cheapest car. With a price of just 100,000 rupees (which was less than £1450/€1600), the Nano was less than half the price of the next cheapest car already available in India and only slightly more expensive than an upmarket motor bike. It was aimed at those who wanted quick and convenient transport but could not afford any of the cars then on the market.

The idea for this radical new product came from observing whole families piled on to one motorbike (quite a common sight on Indian roads), father driving with a child standing between his knees while mother sits behind with the smallest child on her lap. Tata's designers felt that the practice demonstrated a clear customer need for safer, more comfortable transport.

The Nano was promoted as the latest in a distinguished tradition of people's cars that started with the Model T Ford and included the Volkswagen Beetle and the Mini. The Nano had no radio, no boot, no airbag, no passenger side mirror and only one windscreen wiper. It was light and simple, held five adults (just), had more plastic than steel and was held together by hi-tech glue. Questions were raised about its ability to pass the stringent safety tests required by markets such as the European Union (EU) but Tata claimed that the design allowed for further strengthening with metal plates should they decide to sell it in such markets – at a cost of course.

Analysts were predicting that India would soon be the fastest-growing car market in the world but still not everyone wanted to celebrate the launch of this new wonder car. Environmental campaigners were concerned about the pollutant effect of so many extra cars on the road. They made the point that if just 10% of Indian motorcyclists bought Nanos instead, there would be an extra 1 million cars in the country. Many major Indian cities already suffered from smog and the traffic in Delhi crawled along at an average of nine miles an hour. Delhi's Centre for Science and Environment argued that people needed better public transport rather than more affordable private cars.

The Indian motoring lobby remained positive in the face of the criticism and pointed out that Indians owned very few cars compared to Western consumers who had been able to afford cars for many years. Would the highly affordable Nano be able to do for the Indian car market what Ford's Model T did for the USA?

- advertising
- public relations (PR)
- sales promotion
- personal selling.

Direct marketing communication and sponsorship can be added to these.

Advertising uses paid media (advertisers buy space or air time in which to show their adverts), e.g. television, radio, cinema, Internet, leaflets. Media relations is a large part of public relations (PR) and this uses earned media, mainly through media releases, the placing or seeding of stories, press conferences or briefings, and publicity stunts. Although PR does not use paid-for space or air time, it would be a mistake to describe PR as free. PR agencies do not work for free and there are printing and other costs to account for as well. Organisations use a range of PR activities, including exhibitions, hospitality, sponsorship and product placement. All of these are designed to build relationships with audiences and promote understanding of the organisation and its activities. Short-term special offers (money-off coupons, multibuys, competitions, free trials, etc.) are called sales promotions and are a popular choice, especially among FMCG retailers. Personal selling ranges from sales assistants in shops, through door-to-door salespeople and telesales, to the high-level account managers who sell large capital items (such as bridges and mainframe computers) to governments and the boards of multinational clients.

All these activities must be integrated so that they support, rather than contradict, each other. The same message and tone should come through from each activity. This is an important part of building brand image. As well as being integrated with each other, marketing communications activities must also fit with the rest of the marketing mix as the message comes through from all of the mix, not just from explicit communications. Harrods sells quality products at premium prices, and we expect its communications to be similarly upmarket. A gaudy advert in a downmarket magazine offering a BOGOF would detract from its carefully cultivated image. (For more on marketing communications, see Chapter 8.)

Walls ice cream displays from around the world.

© Dave Pickton

hospitality
hosting clients (e.g. providing refreshments in a private room) at events

BOGOF
buy one get one free

INTERNATIONAL PROMOTION (MARKETING COMMUNICATIONS) DECISIONS

While promotional strategies may be global, differences of language and environment mean that they can rarely be absolutely standard in their detail. Adverts, packaging and promotions will all have to be translated. Different images, and

b2b focus: Marketing communications

The biggest promotional tool in b2b is personal selling. Firms who operate in b2b markets, rather than consumer markets, usually have fewer customers who buy more. This makes the expense of salespeople worthwhile. Salespeople can explain complex products and build relationships with their customers. They are an important source of competitive edge and repeat business.

Trade shows and exhibitions are important in business markets. Most industries have these (e.g. Internet World, the Motor Show, the Boat Show). They are good for networking, product demonstrations, identifying prospects, building contact databases, entertaining customers and checking out the competition.

Businesses do use advertising to market to other businesses, but they use different media. Television would be overkill. Most adverts appear in the specialist trade press, such as *The Grocer, Computing, Accountancy Age, Environmental Engineering* and *The Hat* magazine. Sometimes businesses will do some consumer marketing to help their trade customers sell products on. So diamond miners might promote jewellery to increase the derived demand for diamonds.

actors, may need to be used if locals are to relate to them. Some countries insist on local actors appearing in all adverts and there are numerous other regulations that affect what promoters can and cannot do, country by country. There are a number of ways around these problems. Television and cinema adverts may be dubbed (although this does not help overcome the foreign looks of the actors). Some companies develop pattern adverts. These have a consistent look and tone, although some images and the slogan may be written for a specific audience.

Advertising media varies in its availability and quality. Some countries have no national press, some have no local press. In remote parts, television reception may be poor. The Internet is still banned in parts of the world (although this is hard to enforce in practice). In recent years, many companies have made their first foray abroad via the Internet which is an excellent direct sales medium provided that the product in question does not require too much personal support.

Trade fairs and exhibitions are often important to firms who are trying to get established in an overseas market. These provide the perfect place to demonstrate products, meet potential buyers and agents, and check out the competition.

PLACE (DISTRIBUTION AND LOGISTICS)

Place is perhaps the least descriptive of the marketing mix titles and therefore the most likely to cause confusion. Place refers to the whole distribution process – from customer enquiry to after-sales service. In consumer marketing, the place where the actual sale happens is part of that, but it is not the whole story. In b2b, the sale often takes place on the customer's premises, where a salesperson has called.

The **marketing channel**, or distribution channel illustrated in Exhibit 11.5, is a three-level channel (i.e. there are three links in the chain between the manufacturer of the product and the eventual customer).

marketing channel
another term for distribution channel

Exhibit 11.5   Example marketing channel for clothing

fabric and trims suppliers ➡ manufacturer ➡ import agent ➡ wholesaler ➡ fashion stores ➡ customer

An important task of marketing management is to design the marketing channel. The longer the channel, the more removed the producer of the product is from its customers and the more opportunity there is for things to go wrong. Most manufacturers have little or no customer contact; it is the retailer who builds a relationship with the customer. This lack of contact makes it harder for manufacturers to get to know what their customers think of the products, what they would like to see changed, what new products they might like. It also means they have to work harder to build **brand loyalty**.

The shortest channel is a zero-level (0-level) channel. This means direct sales – there are no intermediaries. The product's producers deal with the customer themselves.

brand loyalty
the attachment that a customer or consumer feels to a favourite product

ACTIVITY

Given the availability of the Internet, its relatively low cost and the fact that most households now have access to it, why don't all manufacturers sell directly to customers? Why do they let their products be sold through traditional marketing channels at all? What is it that they may not be able to do, or not do as well as wholesalers and/or retailers?

Think this problem through from the point of view of:

- a PC manufacturer such as Hewlett Packard
- an FMCG manufacturer such as Kellogg's
- a car manufacturer such as Renault
- a shoe manufacturer such as Clarks.

Marketing managers not only have to work out the length of a channel, but its breadth. How many retailers, distributors, etc. will handle the product? The answer will partly depend on whether this is an exclusive or a **mass-market** product. Is it cheap or expensive? Again, the mix intermingles. The nature of the product helps to determine the nature of the channel.

Channel design is only the beginning. The supply chain for a product may be complex and will require careful ongoing management. Good relationships throughout the chain are essential for long-term success. Distributors need support and encouragement if they are to choose to push the right product forward.

Place is about getting the right product to the right customer at the right time. A lot goes on behind the scenes to ensure that this happens.

mass market
a homogeneous market, i.e. there is no distinction between segments

e-focus: Channel conflict

The Internet opens up new markets for all members of the supply chain, from raw materials suppliers through to retailers. This freer market access brings new competition with it, both from companies at the same level in the supply chain and from those at different levels who were not previously seen as competitors at all. Organisations can reach previously inaccessible markets, e.g. overseas markets, and at the same time the distinction between levels is blurring as wholesalers and manufacturers sell directly to consumers.

For example, a number of sportswear retailers have set up Internet sites to offer their customers an alternative way to buy sporting goods. In the world of e-commerce, these retailers may have to deal with competition from retailers in other countries (although in practice, many retailers cannot cope with supplying overseas orders and so only deliver to specific locations). Most of these retailers get their stocks from wholesalers, who can also now sell sports goods directly to consumers.

Wholesalers do not operate from smart high-street stores and so, in the past, were not equipped to deal with end customers. Now they can. With an Internet site, the wholesalers can cut out the retailers and sell direct. It doesn't stop there. If the wholesalers can do this, why not the manufacturers themselves?

This merging of customer bases is a cause of channel conflict. Supply chain members are able to compete with other members higher up, or lower down, the chain. Some manufacturers choose not to compete. They may offer products direct to customers but make sure that the deal is not as good as can be obtained at online retail sites. There is sound reasoning behind this strategy, and it is often to do with order administration and the problems of dealing with thousands of customers when you are only used to dealing with tens of customers.

International place decisions

indirect export using a third party (e.g. an export management company), based in the firm's home country, to sell products abroad

Indirect exporters leave the job of getting goods to customers to someone else, but companies with a more direct involvement have to organise distribution themselves. This can be a difficult task as distribution channels, and the nature of the intermediaries available, can vary enormously. The Japanese distribution infrastructure used to be so fiendishly complicated that some would-be exporters claimed it was an unofficial barrier to trade. (For more on place, see Chapter 9.)

PRICE

Price is the one element of the marketing mix that does not need a budget. The other three Ps all cost significant amounts. Price brings the money in.

At one level, the price is what a business charges its customer for the goods and services it provides. However, the product that the customer is buying may actually cost more than the price suggests. This may be because of hidden costs, such as a computer upgrade required before the software will run, or it may be more subtle, like the time it will take the customer to install the new software (time is money), or the loss of the benefits they would have got if they had bought a different package. So the organisation needs to bear these other things in mind when setting the actual price.

The price of a product is usually the most significant part of the value that a customer hands over in exchange for a product. Therefore, the perceived value of the product must be at least equal to the price. Other elements of the mix can be used to increase the perceived value and therefore allow the charging of a higher price, e.g. attractive or useful packaging, a free gift or an additional feature such as the bonus disks that come with some DVDs.

The price of a product sends a message to potential customers: high quality, cheap and cheerful, bargain, or somewhere in between. It is important that this message accords with the actual product. If Rolls-Royce halved its prices, people would be likely to think that the quality had dropped significantly. If Toshiba drops the price of its computers because a new model will be out soon, people may see this as a bargain and snap them up. The price and the product must match up if marketing is to work successfully.

Prices must also be in accord with place. If a restaurant wants to charge high prices, it usually needs not just good food, but also to be in a prime location. Perhaps then the restaurant critics will give it good write-ups (which is good PR). (For more on price, see Chapter 10.)

customer focus: Now with added extra!

Some organisations add new features to their products in an attempt to make them seem better value. However, if customers see no benefit to the additions, this ploy will only add to the firm's costs, eventually necessitating a higher price that customers may be unhappy to pay. For example, an online retailer offered a reduced-price DVD player in its clearance sale. As an added incentive, the player came with 50 free films. They were not well-known films and spanned a variety of genres – they looked like the titles that usually appear in the bargain tub.

Does this seem like a good deal?

International pricing decisions

Organisations with trading partners or customers overseas, have to choose a currency in which to price contracts for sale. Given that marketing is about meeting customer needs, it would seem to be good marketing practice to price in the customer's currency. However, this has some disadvantages for the seller in terms of costs and practicalities of converting the customer's currency into their own. In practice, many contracts are priced in a well-accepted, stable, easily convertible currency, such as the US dollar – whether or not one of the parties is American.

Goods and services that are sold directly to end-users or consumers, rather than through marketing channels, will normally have to be priced in the local currency.

Lovely Packaging

PACKAGING – THE FIFTH P?

Whether or not we grant packaging the status of a fifth P, it is certainly a very important part of the product offering. Packaging transcends the traditional 4Ps, playing a part in each and every one.

It is part of the product. Many products have to be packed or they cannot be sold. For example, the product may be liquid (e.g. cough syrup), dangerous (e.g. acid), potentially damaging (e.g. hair dye), delicate (e.g. contact lenses) or perishable (e.g. foodstuffs). As well as protecting the product, the packaging may be there to protect consumers. Childproof tops protect the young from accidental ingestion of harmful medicines. Tamper-proof packs prevent the malicious from poisoning, or otherwise spoiling, products.

Sometimes the packaging is more than a means to contain the product; it is an integral part. Products such as toothpaste turn packaging into a feature: pump or tube? Food can be packaged in different ways and this turns it into different products. For example, peas may be sold in tins, jars, packets, vacuum packs or their original pods. Individual drinks cartons have straws attached to make them easier to drink on the go.

Some packs are deliberately made attractive so that people will use them rather than put the product into something else (e.g. some of Marks & Spencer's desserts come in glass bowls). This can be good promotion too if the pack has the product's name on it. How many people, even in cafés, bother to decant ketchup out of the bottle rather than have it sitting on the table advertising Heinz?

ACTIVITY

Next time you go grocery shopping, look carefully at the different types of packaging used. Who are they designed to appeal to? Are you influenced in your choice of product by the packaging?

Packaging can be a key consumer decision criterion, especially for commodity products. Take milk as an example. Milk can be packaged in a number of ways: glass bottle, plastic bottle, paper carton, tin or packet (for dried milk). Some customers may choose the milk with the carton that is easiest to open, or the one that pours best, or keeps the milk freshest longest, or survives freezing.

Innovative packaging can confer competitive advantage. A supplier who invents a new and better way of packaging has an advantage over its competitors – at least until they catch up. Imagine having been the first to put fruit juice into a small carton with a straw, milk in an easy-pour carton, shampoo in a sachet or tissues in a pocket-sized pack.

The packaging is a key part of the brand identity and so is jealously guarded by brand owners. Coca-Cola watches competitors carefully and is quick to object if any rival product looks too similar to its own (e.g. the first can design for Sainsbury's Cola bore too close a resemblance). Distinctive packaging becomes associated with the product and is the means by which the product is recognised: Jif's lemon juice is packed in a yellow plastic lemon. Perrier has a distinctive green bottle.

Packaging is sometimes referred to as the silent salesman because of its marketing communications role. Packaging sends a message about the product inside. This may be explicit (i.e. it may be a slogan or on-pack promotion) or it may be implied through the packaging's style. Advertisements often contain a **pack shot**, usually at the end of the ad. It is hoped that this image of the pack will stay with the consumer and then, when they see it in the shop, they will remember the message of the advert. This is particularly useful for products that rely on recognition, i.e. when customers may browse shelves looking for a suitable product to buy (this applies to most FMCG).

pack shot
a picture of the product, in its packaging, used in an advert to aid recognition

Packaging is also informative. It states country of origin, lists ingredients, gives instructions for use and carries warnings (e.g. not suitable for children under 3).

The packaging can also be used to persuade people to use more of the product. Allegedly, Domestos increased its sales substantially by changing the instruction 'use sparingly' to 'use liberally'. Foodstuffs regularly carry recipes designed to encourage cooks to see how else the product can be used. Imaginative packaging can help to sell the firm's other products, e.g. by including other products in the recipes, attaching a trial-size packet of biscuits to the coffee (or vice versa). There are many possibilities.

Packaging can be varied to give a company more pricing options. Refill packs are cheaper than original products. Larger sizes are often better value.

Good packaging is essential to protect products during distribution. Secondary packaging (large cartons and palettes) may be needed here to make sure goods are easy to handle, can be stacked safely, and arrive at their destination in good condition. Sometimes this secondary packaging can be turned to good promotional advantage. Packets of crisps, which are notoriously hard to keep on the shelves (they sell fast and so run out, and they also slip about), are normally supplied to retailers in large brown boxes. One innovative crisp company decided to use these boxes to give their crisps an edge. They perforated a hole in one side of the box so that, when the hole was punched in, customers could reach into the box and pull out the crisps. The boxes had become display stands (all bearing the crisp manufacturer's name and logo, of course). Shops no longer had to unpack the crisps and restock the shelves. When a box was empty they just brought in the next box.

INTERNATIONAL PACKAGING

Packaging is an important part of the mix and must be carefully designed for overseas markets. The following should be taken into account:

- any laws and regulations governing its composition, recycling, the languages used
- cultural issues that may affect the size of the packet, the colours used – and the languages used
- education and literacy levels in the country – how should the instructions be written? Perhaps they should be diagrammatic? Dangerous products (e.g. pharmaceuticals) must be especially carefully explained
- transport – one of packaging's main functions is to protect the goods during transit. How rough is the handling likely to be?

Internationally consistent packaging has the advantage of being recognisable to travellers and so is especially important for products that might be bought by visitors to a country: camera film, headache pills, toiletries, suntan lotion, etc. They may not speak the language well enough to ask and so the sight of a familiar package will reassure them and give that product a competitive edge over others.

Lookalikes

ethical focus: The lookalikes

A number of manufacturers have taken retailers to court over own-label brands that just look too much like the real thing. The complaint may be about the make-up of the product itself or it may be about the packaging – an infringement of the brand is potentially even more damaging than a rip-off of the product itself.

Tesco, Marmite and Asda's own brand yeast spread – packaged inspiration.

© Dave Pickton

- United Biscuits, makers of the much-loved Penguin, sued ASDA over its Puffin bars.

- Coca-Cola's objection to Sainsbury's Classic Cola can resulted in a redesign.

- Kellogg's has complained about the package design of Tesco's breakfast cereals.

- ASDA was in trouble over the appearance of its own-label versions of popular spirits such as Archers and Malibu.

The original manufacturers have put millions into brand development and don't see why these retailers should cash in. It is difficult to decide where to draw the line – when is it a product inspired by the original and when is it a cheap imitation?

THE EXTENDED MARKETING MIX: 7PS

The 4Ps do not provide enough scope for the support of modern products, many of which have a strong service element. The 7Ps were developed as a marketing mix for services, but are really more appropriate than four for all but the simplest products today. Exhibit 11.6 shows examples of the use of the additional 3Ps.

The first three products in Exhibit 11.6 are services, while the last one is a physical product, a PC, but it still has a number of service elements that are important to the customer. Retailing is itself a service and so the shopper is a service user. With a product like a PC, there may be more service elements involved: helplines, installation assistance, maintenance, etc. Contrast this with an FMCG purchase, such as soap powder. There is no installation help or maintenance required for this product, but there is still a retail service to be provided. Also, check the side of the box. Many

FMCG products do offer advice lines or similar services – all are designed to try to establish a relationship with the customer and offer a better service.

These additional 3Ps must also be integrated into marketing plans. They too should support the rest of the mix, not clash with it.

Exhibit 11.6   Examples of use of the additional 3Ps

Example products	Examples of physical evidence: the tangible aspects of the service	Examples of people: who deliver the service	Examples of process: how the service is delivered
Car cleaning	Car shampoo, sponges	The cleaners	While you shop
Restaurant meal	Food, tables, cutlery	Cooks, toilet cleaners	Self-service
Car hire	The car, maps	Receptionist, mechanics	Car delivered to home address
Personal computer	Retail environment	Shop assistants, helpline operators	Assistants' approach to customers in store, call-queuing systems

PHYSICAL EVIDENCE

Physical evidence includes peripheral products, such as free peanuts on a bar, products that are part of the service, such as ice in a drink, the décor of the place where the service is provided – and anything else that is tangible, but not the actual physical product itself.

The physical evidence may be the key thing in setting customer expectations. A smart, trendy bar with genuine art on the walls, expensive-looking furniture and waiters in tuxedos sets the expectation of superior service, a good wine list, high prices and a classy clientele. Contrast that with a typical local pub or bar, with posters and a wide-screen TV on the walls, a footrest around the base of the bar, hard-back chairs, a juke box and the bar staff in T-shirts. Quite a different customer expectation is set. Customer expectations are extremely important in marketing, and particularly in services marketing. A customer who has been let down, i.e. has received a service that does not meet their expectations, is an unhappy customer. They are liable to complain and to say unflattering things about the product to their friends. Often, if they had received the same service but had known what to expect beforehand and chosen it anyway, then they will be quite content with that situation.

So physical evidence is an important aspect of customer service and must match the rest of the mix if expectations are to be met.

© Dave Pickton

Carrier bags: carrying the message home.

PEOPLE

Most services require people to deliver them and to receive them. Although there are an increasing number of services delivered electronically, e.g. Internet messaging, where people's involvement is limited to the original set-up and maintenance of the service and dealing with queries and complaints, people remain an important asset for most service providers. The quality of the service is liable to be largely dependent upon the quality of the people involved in its delivery and so, once again, the people must match the rest of the mix. A high-class restaurant needs silver service waiters; a burger joint does not.

The people who deliver the service are an integral part of its marketing mix, as are the people who receive that service. Customers are part of the interaction and influence the way a service operates. For example, it is quite possible for two people to eat the same meal in the same restaurant and experience the same service but one will love it and one hate it. This is equally true of concerts, haircuts and service from shop assistants.

PROCESS

Process starts long before a service is actually experienced. It starts with the prospect's very first contact with the service-providing organisation. This may be reading a brochure, visiting a website, making a phone call or calling into an office or shop. The process of service delivery is key to customer satisfaction and therefore to the stimulation of positive word of mouth and repeat business. The restaurant can be the smartest in the world, the staff the best trained and friendliest, but if customers find their booking has been lost, or if the food takes hours to arrive, they will not be happy. In a pizza restaurant, however, there may be no advance bookings and customers may be expected to queue. Customers may be happy to do this, especially if they are able to sit in the bar and have a drink, listen to music, read the menu. That is all part of the process.

Once again, the process has to be right, and fit with the rest of the marketing mix, if the product is to be a success. (For more on the 7Ps, see Chapter 7.)

MIXING IT (INTEGRATING THE MARKETING MIX)

Each element of the marketing mix should support the others. They should build to a consistent whole that accords with the organisation's brand values and so builds the brand's image. For example, an upmarket, exclusive fashion brand would:

- require high-quality products, made with top-class fabrics, that are well styled and well made, perhaps finished by hand (product)
- command premium prices (price)
- be sold in more exclusive, fabulously done-up stores (place, physical evidence)
- be sold by smart, fashionably dressed staff (people)
- provide an alteration service to achieve a perfect fit (process)
- be promoted in a tasteful, creative way, perhaps with adverts placed in fashion and lifestyle magazines, and with suitably upmarket celebrities wearing the clothes (promotion).

However, a mass-market clothing brand might:

- use cheaper fabrics and mass-production techniques while keeping fancy trims to a minimum

- undercut competitors' prices
- be sold everywhere
- be carried home in cheap plastic bags
- be promoted extensively, in newspapers and magazines that the customers read, on billboards, even on flyers.

These mixes send clear, but very different, messages about the company's offering. If the messages are contradictory, then customers will become confused. You cannot charge a high price but use cheap materials (at least not for long). If your products are on sale everywhere, they lose their exclusive image (this is why Levi's was so keen to stop Tesco selling its jeans, and why perfumers such as Calvin Klein do not want their products sold in high-street stores such as Superdrug).

The marketing mix is used to implement marketing strategies and plans. It is the marketer's toolkit, and deciding how to use each tool is a key part of the marketer's job. Those decisions are made in the light of the organisation's objectives and its overall strategy to meet those objectives. Look back at the above example: if a brand wants to maintain its upmarket position, then clearly it must be in the best shops and be made of high-quality materials. The desired market position informs the choice of how to use marketing tools. With the marketing purpose firmly in mind, marketing managers are able to design effective marketing programmes, which must be based on a well-coordinated marketing mix.

VARYING THE MIX THROUGH A PRODUCT'S LIFE

Marketers do not decide on the best marketing mix for a new product and leave it at that forever. The mix has to be varied over time in response to, or in anticipation of, the changing marketing environment (see Chapter 2) and the brand's circumstances. The product life cycle (which was introduced in Chapter 6) provides an illustration of how the optimal marketing mix may change over time (see Exhibit 11.7).

Exhibit 11.7   Mixing it through the product life cycle

Nestle:
Long term
maintenance

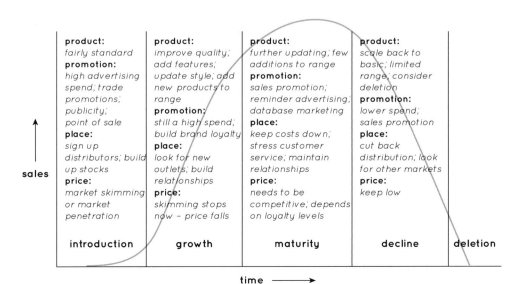

introduction	growth	maturity	decline	deletion
product: fairly standard **promotion:** high advertising spend; trade promotions; publicity; point of sale **place:** sign up distributors; build up stocks **price:** market skimming or market penetration	**product:** improve quality; add features; update style; add new products to range **promotion:** still a high spend; build brand loyalty **place:** look for new outlets; build relationships **price:** skimming stops now – price falls	**product:** further updating; few additions to range **promotion:** sales promotion; reminder advertising; database marketing **place:** keep costs down; stress customer service; maintain relationships **price:** needs to be competitive; depends on loyalty levels	**product:** scale back to basic; limited range; consider deletion **promotion:** lower spend; sales promotion **place:** cut back distribution; look for other markets **price:** keep low	

sales

time ⟶

The product life cycle model was originally devised for generic products, i.e. the product type not the individual branded item (e.g. shoes, not Clark's shoes). It can, however, be applied to individual, branded products as well.

INTRODUCTION

Products are often very expensive to launch. The research and development that goes into a new product can cost hundreds of thousands or even millions, and will have to be recouped in the early life of the product. Initially, the promotion budget will be at its highest. People do not know about this new product and so they must be told. There may be no distribution channels and so those need to be built up. If the product is a new invention (e.g. 3D films, space flights or domestic robots), then the company may be able to use a price-skimming strategy to help recover some of its costs more quickly (see Chapter 10). However, the prospect of large profits will encourage competitors into the market (unless the new product is protected by patents – though often even these are not enough).

GROWTH

During the product's growth stage, organisations should be focusing on building brand loyalty and encouraging repeat purchases. They might introduce new products or lines and add more advanced features to existing products. A lower price may attract new customers or encourage existing ones to buy more. However, if the initial strategy was penetration pricing, perhaps for a me-too product, then prices may now be put up. Distribution coverage is vital to build up sales. A good push strategy (i.e. promoting the product to members of the distribution channel) may encourage retailers and other intermediaries to stock the product.

MATURITY

By this stage there are likely to be a larger number of competitors in the market and so competition for customers is fierce. Promotion strategies will be geared towards maintaining market share and extending this profitable maturity stage for as long as possible. Good customer service and the rewarding of loyal customers will help to retain them. Generally, the price of a mature product needs to be competitive, but if the firm has done a good job of building brand loyalty, then demand may now be more price inelastic. If its customers are truly loyal, truly committed to the brand, then the firm may actually be able to charge a slightly higher price than its competitors.

DECLINE

When a product is in decline, ranges and features are cut to a minimum. Unprofitable products, and less popular features, are phased out. Expensive promotion is unlikely to be worthwhile and so the marketing communications budget is cut. If there is no immediate replacement on the way, then some distributors may be dropped. Demand for the product is likely to be very price elastic and so prices need to stay low in order to make sales. The exception to this is when a product has built a highly loyal following (perhaps it has gained the status of a cult product), where a few people may be prepared to pay high prices to obtain their beloved product before it disappears forever.

EXPAND YOUR KNOWLEDGE

Classic article

Levitt, T. (1965) 'Exploit the product life cycle', *Harvard Business Review*, 43 (Nov/Dec): 81–94.

The product life cycle is a well accepted concept in marketing although it needs to be applied wisely. In this article, the author demonstrates the significance of product life cycle to marketing planning in each of the stages of the cycle.

CRITICISMS OF THE MARKETING MIX

The mix has been at the heart of marketing since the 1960s, but it is not universally acclaimed. There are those who find the 4Ps too limiting and so add further elements to the list. Some authors feel the fifth P should be packaging, others that it should be people. The element of people is formally included in the 7Ps of services marketing but packaging still moves around.

Jones and Vignali (1994) added an S, for service. It is today recognised that all products have a service element and that this is key to their acceptance and success. Customer service must be at the heart of a market-orientated organisation and the responsibility of everyone in the company, not just the marketing team. Grönroos (1997) considered that to view service as a separate element of the marketing mix would be disastrous for an organisation as it would isolate customer service as a distinct function apart from the rest of the organisation rather than being fully integrated at its core. This would downgrade its importance.

Modern marketing stresses the importance of building good relationships with customers and intermediaries, and so one problem with the marketing mix is that it emphasises techniques rather than customers and their needs. We could see relationship building as part of promotion, but this brings a danger of inducing customer cynicism. Card-based loyalty schemes are viewed by many as mere sales promotion – and customers are likely to have cards, and collect points, from all competitors.

The marketing mix has occasionally evolved into other letters. For example, Lauterborn (1990) proposed the 4Cs:

- customer needs and wants
- cost to the customer
- convenience
- communication.

The 4Cs have the advantage of being more customer focused. However, the 4Ps are indelibly lodged in the minds of several generations of marketers and are likely to be the preferred model for some time to come.

The development of faster and better methods of manufacture has led to the vastly increased level of choice being offered to the customer. This change from a supply-dominated marketplace to one where customers demand certain things, and are prepared to look for what they want, comes from the certain knowledge that those things will be available from one of the many possible sources now competing for their business. Increased distribution of goods and services nationally, internationally and globally, presents vast choice to customers. The challenge in such a world is to find customers in the first place, and to hang on to them in the future. This is one of the objectives of branding.

Brand strength is important and so maintaining and building this strength is an essential part of managing a brand. Strong brands sell more easily, both initially and to loyal customers and are therefore valuable organisational assets.

Exhibit 11.8   The world's top brands

According to Interbrand, a leading global brand consultancy, the top ten brands (with values ranging from Coca-Cola's US$77,839 million to Toyota's $30,280 million) of 2012 were:

1. Coca-Cola 77,839 ($m)
2. Apple 76,568($m)
3. IBM 75,532 ($m)
4. Google 69,726 ($m)
5. Microsoft 57,853 ($m)
6. GE 43,682 ($m)
7. McDonald's 40,062 ($m)
8. Intel 39,385 ($m)
9. Samsung 32,893 ($m)
10. Toyota 30,280 ($M)

IT and electronics companies continued to dominate the listings, with another four technology companies in the next ten (Cisco, Hewlett Packard, Oracle and Nokia). Coca-Cola has maintained its first-placed position while Apple has pushed IBM into third place. Only two of the top ten are from outside of the USA: South Korean Samsung and Japanese Toyota.

See **www.interbrand.com** for the full report.

SOURCE: Interbrand, 2013.

Apple: Our
Signature

BRANDING

Brands are important assets for many companies, and building and maintaining their strength is a key marketing task that involves all of the marketing mix. A brand is more than a design or a concept. It is a combination of values which together promise customers the solution to their problems or the answer to their needs. The brand is greater than the products it encompasses and adds value to it. Modern branding has seemed to be the saviour of mass-produced products which often have little or no other means of differentiation. However, it has now become a victim of its own success. The credit for the success of many modern products has been attributed to their branding, but now it is often thought to be the brand that can cause a product to fail (Haig, 2003). If a brand's image deteriorates, then its sales will suffer as Levi's found to their cost when their jeans were no longer perceived as fashionable, nor even as a youth brand, in the late 1990s.

Exhibit 11.9   Brand view

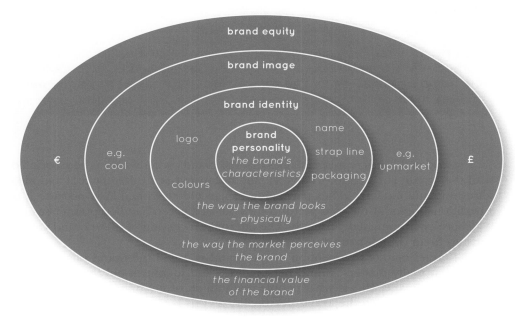

brand equity

brand image

brand identity

€   e.g.
cool

logo

name

brand
personality
*the brand's
characteristics*

strap line

packaging

colours

e.g.
upmarket   £

*the way the brand looks
– physically*

*the way the market perceives
the brand*

*the financial value
of the brand*

brand personality
the heart of the
brand, the sum of its
values, its character
traits, e.g. bubbly,
elegant, friendly

brand identity
all the outward
trappings of the
brand, e.g. logo,
name, colours, strap
line and packaging

BEHIND THE BRAND

Branding has given rise to a host of terms that are often used slightly differently in different texts and by different people. At the heart of a brand is its **brand personality** (see Exhibit 11.9). A brand can be described in a similar way to a person. Brands may be young (e.g. FCUK), mature (e.g. Epicure), rebellious (e.g. Virgin), understated (e.g. Liberty), classy (e.g. Aston Martin), forceful (e.g. Nike), caring (e.g. Body Shop) – any personality descriptor that can be applied to a person, can be (and probably has been) applied to a brand. Marketers develop their brands' personalities, which may be articulated in a brand personality statement, e.g. 'This is a chocolate bar that bites back. It's edgy and assertive whilst being absolutely dependable – a bar you want on your side.' This is not meant as a slogan for an advertising campaign, although it might help inspire one. This is the way the brand team see their product, and it is what they want their customers to see too. Their next challenge, therefore, is to find a way to express their chocolate bar's personality clearly to others.

Brand personality is encapsulated in **brand identity**. A brand's identity is a set of cues which help people to form their impressions of the brand, e.g. logo, name, colours, strap line and packaging. However, messages are not always received as intended (see Chapter 8). The target audience's perception of the brand may be different from its intended personality.

© Dave Pickton

Cadbury has a strong brand identity.

brand image
people's
perception of the
brand

Who
Controls
the Brand

Those identity cues represent values that the brand owner wants to be associated with the brand. For example, Pepsi is blue because it is a different cola and also refreshing and modern. Hovis packaging has an old-fashioned look because it is a traditional brand. Unleaded petrol comes out of a green-handled pump because it is more environmentally friendly. The internal processing of these brand values adds up to an overall **brand image**.

The target market's perception of the brand is called the brand image and it is this that really matters. Brand personalities and identities only exist in order to create an image. This is what people really think of the brand and, in an ideal world, it would match the brand personality as this is the image the brand team wanted people to have. A brand's power stems from the collective nature of these perceptions. One person's perception cannot create a powerful brand; it takes numerous people accepting the brand truth and reinforcing it in their everyday lives (Holt, 2004). Whether or not personality and image match will depend upon how well the brand team have constructed their brand's identity, and upon what else people hear about the brand. Brands exist independently of their owners. Brand owners cannot control everything that is said about them or how they are used. A person forms a brand image on the basis of all their experience with the brand – not just the official brand communications.

EXPAND YOUR KNOWLEDGE

Cleeren, K., van Heerde, H.J. and Dekimpe, M.G. (2013) 'Rising from the ashes: how brands and categories can overcome product-harm crises', *Journal of Marketing*, 77 (2): 58–77.

Product-harm crises can cause major revenue and market-share losses, lead to costly product recalls, and destroy carefully nurtured brand equity. The authors analyse 60 fast-moving consumer goods (FMCG) crises that occurred in the United Kingdom and the Netherlands to assess the effects of post-crisis advertising and price adjustments on the change in consumers' brand share and category purchases, the extent of negative publicity surrounding the event and whether the affected brand had to publicly acknowledge blame. The authors provide context-specific managerial recommendations on how to overcome a product-harm crisis.

ethical focus: Sweet and innocent

The Innocent brand is one of the big success stories of the 2000s. It has grown from a virtually unknown fruit drink found in just a few stores to a must-have for every food shop and sandwich store of note. The makers of Innocent smoothies take great care to ensure that the product is as high quality as it can be – pure fruit, no additives and no concentrates – but that is only part of their appeal.

Their strong brand identity has played a key role in building the Innocent brand. Their distinctive, apparently hand-sketched, fruits or shapes with halos logo have a childlike quality and are reassuringly simple looking. The brand personality seems to be good quality, good for you, pure, fun and ethical. The fun aspects come out through their advertising and most strongly through the packaging, which also showcases their ethical stance. Take the time to read an Innocent pack and you will not only find out exactly what's in your drink, but also what isn't, e.g.

- No concentrates
- No stabilisers
- No flavourings
- No GM stuff
- No preservatives
- No added sugar
- No e numbers
- No funny business

You may also find such things as a picture of a fireman's hat (drawn by Kat, aged 26 ½) alongside a little story about energy entitled *smoky bacon*.

A brand personality such as Innocent's demands environmental friendliness. The individual-size smoothie bottles are made of 100% recycled plastic: 'greener than your seasick Auntie Sue on a cross-channel ferry after a big night out at Wetherspoons' (www. innocentdrinks.co.uk). Their green credentials are further strengthened by sourcing all their bananas from plantations certified by the Rainforest Alliance ('We love them') and by donating 10% of their profits to charities working in the countries where their fruits come from.

A Fruity
Success
Story

© innocent. Picture courtesy of innocent

Exhibit 11.10   Creating brand image

To sum up, the brand personality is put across through symbols known as the brand identity and these create, alongside other cues such as the advertising, a brand image in the minds of the target market.

BRAND EQUITY

A good brand image has a value. Branded goods usually carry higher prices than unbranded ones. Compare the prices of lesser-known brands of sportswear with those of Nike and Adidas. This value is known as brand equity and it is a difficult thing to calculate even though it is often one of the company's most valuable assets.

High brand equity is clearly a desirable thing and the brand's marketing mix should be designed with this in mind. For example, frequent price promotions, such as discounts or sales, indicate low brand equity and will do nothing to build it up, whereas brands that have a high price, high distribution intensity, pleasant shopping environment and large advertising budget are likely also to enjoy significant brand equity (Yoo et al., 2000).

One way to value brands is to examine takeover bids. Companies usually have to pay more than the value of a firm's physical assets in order to buy it. They pay for goodwill (ongoing business prospects) and they pay for brands. In the early 1990s, Nestlé paid £2.5 billion ($3.6 billion) for Rowntree's, which was much more than the company was apparently worth (Smith, 2006), in a deal that gave it rights to one of the biggest-selling chocolate snacks of all time: Kit Kat. Unfortunately, this technique does not help put a value on the balance sheet of a company that is not subject to a takeover bid.

An alternative way to value a brand is to ascertain how much extra customers are prepared to pay for the branded good rather than an unbranded one. So, how much more would you pay for a Kit Kat than for an unheard-of chocolate wafer biscuit? That price premium can then be multiplied by the number of bars sold (say in a year) to arrive at the brand equity. Neither these, nor the many other valuation methods tried, are entirely satisfactory. However, it is generally agreed that strong brands do have value – we are just not sure how much.

EXPAND YOUR KNOWLEDGE

Hennig-Thurau, T., Houston, M. and Heitjans, T. (2009) 'Conceptualizing and measuring the monetary value of brand extensions: the case of motion pictures', *Journal of Marketing*, 73 (6): 167–83.

Valuing brands is complicated; valuing brand extension potential is even more so but Thorsten et al. have developed a means to measure the monetary value of brand extension rights in the context of motion pictures (i.e. movie sequel rights) and to calculate the effect of variations of key product attributes, such as the continued participation of stars, on this value.

BRAND TYPES

There are a number of different types of brand in the marketplace today (see Exhibit 11.11) each of which has advantages and disadvantages. Most of Cadbury's products have an individual brand name as well as the corporate name. Cadbury's name is the badge of quality, while the individual name is an identifier for a particular recipe of confectionery. A purely descriptive name for Cadbury's Flake would be too long and would not differentiate the product from the competition. Heinz, however, traditionally sticks to straightforward descriptions of its products alongside its corporate brand name, e.g. Heinz baked beans, Heinz tomato ketchup. The company relies on its own name to help establish the desired brand image. Even Heinz, who traditionally used their corporate brand name only, have now caught the brand name fever, though, by introducing, or acquiring, some range brands (e.g. Weight Watchers and Linda McCartney).

Exhibit 11.11   Brand types

Corporate umbrella brands	The products use the corporate name	e.g. Heinz, Next
Range brands	Groups of related products share a brand name	e.g. Taste the Difference (Sainsbury's), Lean Cuisine (Nestlé)
Individual brands	Each product has its own brand name	e.g. Twix (Mars), Bold (Procter & Gamble)
Own-label (private) brands	Products bear the retailer's (or wholesaler's) name	e.g. Tesco, Marks & Spencer
Generic brands	A product descriptor with no brand or owners' name	e.g. Ibuprofen

Own-label brands are a big success story. Once the poor relation of branding, seen as inferior to manufacturer brands, they now take up the bulk of supermarket shoppers' trolleys. They are popular with retailers (and some wholesalers) because they enable them to earn better profits. These products are not manufactured by the retailers, just badged by them. The advantage to the manufacturer is that it can use up spare capacity this way. However, these brands can be the cause of friction in the supply chain if the manufacturer believes that the own-label product is too similar to its own (see ethical focus box 'The lookalikes' on p. 476).

Generic brands are less common in FMCG than they used to be. Nowadays, they are more likely to be pharmaceuticals and they can be controversial. Many life-saving drugs, e.g. for cancer or for AIDS, are very expensive and well beyond the reach of third-world countries. Some companies, notably in India, ignore **patents** and make copies of these drugs and sell them for a fraction of the normal price. Is this a crime or a public service?

BRAND NAMES

There are historical reasons behind most corporate **brand names**. Companies often start out with the owner's name (e.g. Mars, Cadbury, Sainsbury, Guinness, Ford, Mercedes, Marks & Spencer, Dior). This remains the corporate brand name as it is well known and people make associations with it. In the 1990s, however, there was a management craze for renaming organisations, i.e. changing their brand names. There were a number of reasons behind this, including:

- a more attractive name that either described the organisation better or enhanced the brand identity
- a name that was more acceptable (or just easier to pronounce) in international markets (e.g. Jif household cleaner became Cif)
- distancing the organisation from its past (e.g. Andersen Consulting became Accenture after a scandal).

Not all of these renamings were successful. Take Consignia, for example. This was the new name chosen, after extensive consultation and market research, for the Royal Mail service. There were good reasons for wanting to change the name. The business had changed and was no longer merely a mail service. They operated call centres, courier services and logistics services and so the name no longer described the business that well. It was limiting their ability to add new services. Also, the organisation wanted to grow its business in overseas markets, beyond the rule of Queen Elizabeth II, where there might even be other 'Royals' and 'Royal Mails' to cause confusion. Finally, it wanted to revamp its image and be seen as a modern business rather than one stuck in the nineteenth century. Consignia was chosen because it does not actually mean anything in any language, but it sounds attractive and relevant.

It was a disaster. The organisation and its branding consultants severely underestimated the British public's attachment to the old name, and the media's will to sink the new one. Within about three years, the old name was back.

People do not like change. They get used to a brand and its look, and can react surprisingly strongly to management improvements. Such updates therefore need to be handled very carefully.

patent
a legal protection for inventions that prohibits unauthorised copying

brand name
the product's, or product line's, given name

BRANDING STRATEGIES

The types of brands a company uses, and the way they relate to each other and to the corporate brand, is often referred to as their **brand architecture**. There are a number of brand architectures in use today but the best known are the **branded house** and the **house of brands** (Abraham and Taylor, 2011). According to the World Advertising Research Centre's best practice briefing (WARC, 2012), a house of brands comprises a set of stand-alone brands, e.g. Mars owns Dolmio, Pedigree Petfoods and Uncle Ben's. This architecture helps firms to position different products clearly and to maximise their impact in their target markets. It is also useful for a diverse portfolio where the company needs to distance some brands from each other. For example, customers may not be happy to buy the same brand of chocolate and dog food. A branded house (which is sometimes known as monolithic) uses a single master brand to span a set of products, known as sub-brands. This master brand reassures potential purchasers while the sub-brand serves as a descriptor, e.g. Virgin (master brand): Virgin Trains, Virgin Atlantic, Virgin Mobile, Virgin Media, Virgin Money (sub-brands).

The choice of brand type can almost be said to be a strategy in itself. It certainly has far-reaching consequences for the company's marketing. However, there are some specific strategies that relate to branding.

Branding strategies are used 'to differentiate products and companies, and to build economic value for both the consumer and the brand owner' (Pickton and Broderick, 2004: 242). The following are some of the more commonly used strategies.

Co-branding is when two companies' brand names appear together, as on PCs when the brand name of the chip manufacturer appears alongside the PC maker (e.g. 'Intel inside'). Either or both brands should benefit from this as the good reputation of one rubs off on the other.

Multibranding is a strategy employed by companies that have multiple products within the same category. This gives the customer the illusion of choice. They can switch brand but still be buying from the same supplier. For example, Procter & Gamble has many different brands of washing powder: Ace, Dreft, Bold (Bolt), Ariel, Dash, Fairy, Daz, Bonus, Vizir and Tide. These are not all available in all countries, and each lays claim to slightly different properties, but they all clean clothes.

The above are ongoing strategies. However, one of the great advantages of a strong brand is that it can be used to launch new products with a far greater chance of success. According to Kotler (2003), there are three ways to introduce more products under the auspices of an existing brand:

- line extension – introducing product variants under the same brand name, e.g. a new flavour or colour
- brand extension – using the brand name on products in a new category but within the same, broadly defined market, e.g. a biscuit company starting to produce cakes
- brand stretching – using the name on products in a different market, e.g. a cigarette company making clothes.

For example, when Robinsons launched a new summer fruits drink flavour, that was a line extension. When Mars started making ice cream bars, that was a brand extension. The king of brand stretching is Richard Branson of Virgin, taking a brand

brand architecture
the structure of an organisation's brand portfolio which shows how their brands relate to one another; it typically includes master and sub-brands

branded house
a form of brand architecture which uses a single master brand to span a set of products, known as sub-brands

Virgin Hot
Air Balloons

house of brands
a form of brand architecture which comprises a set of stand-alone brands with their own names and identities, although there may be a reference to the owning brand

Marmite

e-focus: Making angry birds fly further

Rovio was founded in Finland in 2003 and had just two employees. Now the company employs more than 500 staff and has offices in China, USA and Sweden. How did that happen? Rovio is the company that made those birds angry – and let them fly!

Angry Birds is one of the most successful paid-for apps ever. It is available on numerous platforms and in numerous versions; from Brazilian birds to Star Wars. According to Michele Tobin, the company's vice president, brand ad partnerships and advertising in the Americas, its success was based on 'a lot of science, a lot of trial and error and a little bit of magic'.

The existence of over 260 million Angry Birds players across the globe suggests that there may be substantial opportunities for Rovio to expand into other sectors. The company is pursuing brand stretches into theme parks and films. It already sells books and consumer products such as clothing, toys and accessories and has an online store as well as a bricks and mortar store in Helsinki.

Rovio has an impressive animation studio where it produces a weekly cartoon series called Angry Birds Toons. The cartoon is available on a range of media: there is a dedicated channel on Rovio's website, a new button within its games and smart TV apps for appliances made by firms like Samsung and Roku. MTV, the Cartoon Network and Comcast Xfinity on demand have also signed up to broadcast the series, which will be aired in nations from Brazil and India to Germany and the USA.

Each new Rovio game now contains customised, integrated adverts. They favour brands that add value to the games, for example by offering rewards or additional content:

> 'For us, it is all about how to deliver a better experience that will benefit both the advertiser and our fan base', said Tobin. 'Because we're a multi-faceted media company, we can do some pretty interesting things not only in the game, but outside the game.'

One example of this was an initiative undertaken with McDonald's in China. In a twist on the premise of Angry Birds, the idea was that pigs had stolen food from McDonald's. Television adverts told this story, and giant, empty burger boxes and packs of French fries began to appear in Beijing and Shanghai. The fast-food chain's famous golden arches were turned into slingshots, and limited-edition merchandise was available in branches. This multimedia campaign also used geo-location technology on smartphones to tell fans who were near a McDonald's store that they would receive special in-game rewards and content if they just went inside.

The Rovio company was built on just one game, one idea but Angry Birds has been an amazing success and prompted huge brand love. One good brand can launch many popular products.

SOURCES: Whiteside, 2013.

name originally chosen for the music industry and launching it into airlines, drinks, trains, radio, cosmetics, mobile phones, etc. – that is really stretching a brand!

These new product strategies carry different levels of risk. The lowest risk would appear to be the line extension. It can be anticipated that existing, loyal customers will try a new variant of a product they already buy. However, all that is happening here is that they are substituting the new version for the old. There is no overall increase in sales. Line extension does have a role to play, though. It is essential to many brands that new versions be introduced or the line will become boring. Chocolate manufacturers launch new bars. Perfumiers introduce new scents or packaging. Drinks companies try out new flavours. New versions of products replace those that have reached the end of their lives and no longer sell well. A good **brand manager** anticipates that decline, and has the new variant ready in advance of it (refer to the section on the product life cycle in Chapter 6 and above).

brand manager responsible for marketing a particular set of branded products

customer focus: Overstretched?

Some brands are so strong that they have their own mythologies. It is a brand manager's dream to work on such a brand or, even better, to raise their brand to that status. Harley Davidson is one such brand. Its customers are more than loyal – they are in love with those bikes. Many Harley owners are tattooed with the brand name and imagery. Other motorcycles may be technologically superior or a better ride, but Harleys are more macho and they just belong on the road to freedom.

The temptation to capitalise on such a strong brand proved irresistible. The company opened a chain of shops with a wide range of Harley-branded merchandise: T-shirts, socks, lighters, ornaments, even aftershave and perfume. It didn't go down well with the core market of bikers.

Harley had failed to remain true to its heritage and had ignored the nature of those loyal bikers. In the past, the company was had been fussier about what was badged 'Harley

Davidson', understanding the importance of focusing on motorbikes and so preserving the Harley mystique. Toiletries were too great a stretch for the bikers and therefore for the company. Fortunately, the error was recognised in time and the unsuitable merchandise has been withdrawn. So it's back to leather jackets and motor oil – and the open road.

SOURCES: Haig, 2003.

© John Albano/Corbis

Harley riders.

Brand extension carries a higher risk of failure. People loved Mars ice cream. It was such a success that other chocolate manufacturers followed suit. So would you buy any kind of food from Mars? How about frozen ready meals? Baked beans? Breakfast cereal?

Unilever successfully extended its Lynx brand. The original Lynx was just a deodorant, but now a wide range of grooming products are available under that brand name. Sometimes a brand carries with it associations that would be unhelpful to the new product. Companies may then actively try to disassociate the two. So Levi's did not call its cotton trouser 'Levi's' but Dockers instead. Sometimes, a company opts for a new range brand name, perhaps coupled with the corporate brand (e.g. Tesco Finest).

The riskiest of these three strategies is brand stretching. Often, the stretched brand breaks. Xerox computers were never as popular as the company's copiers and printers. *Cosmopolitan*'s move into the health food sector (with a range of low-fat dairy products) did not work, nor did its Cosmo Spirit Cafés (Anon, 2003). The strategy does work for some, however, even without a new range brand name. Yamaha successfully added musical instruments, home audio/video equipment, computer peripherals and sports equipment to its motorcycle range. Many retailers have successfully moved into financial services, offering credit cards, loans and insurance. Usually they do not run these services themselves, of course, but license others to do so, lending their name to the enterprise.

EXPAND YOUR KNOWLEDGE

Eckhardt, G.M. and Bengtsson, A. (2010) 'A brief history of branding in China', *Journal of Macromarketing,* 30 (September): 210–21.

In this article, the authors trace branding practices in China from 2700 BC to contemporary times and demonstrate that China has had a sophisticated brand infrastructure with a continuous history. They chronicle the consumer culture of the time in China, and how brands developed out of it, demonstrating that brands can develop in varying ways.

No Logo &
Corporate
Brands

GLOBAL BRANDING

Although it is rare to find globally standardised products, there are a number of global brands. A global brand may not have (in fact, almost certainly will not have) a completely standardised marketing mix, but it will have the same brand personality the world over and that personality will be expressed through a brand identity that is standard in its essential design, even though there may be some variance in packaging, languages used, etc.

Take McDonald's, for example. The golden arches are a well-recognised symbol throughout the world. Ronald McDonald has clowned his way through restaurant openings from New York to Shanghai. The writing beneath the arches may be in another language, or even another alphabet, but the brand identity is nonetheless the same. The products are not exactly the same though, and nor is the marketing mix. In India, Hindus do not eat beef products and so the burgers have to be made of something else, originally mutton but now the Maharaja burgers are chicken. Veggie burgers are also available in India, where the staff who make them wear a different uniform and prepare them separately from the meat (this is an example of a different process). The veggie burgers are also sold in other countries where there is a significant demand for vegetarian foods (e.g. some European countries), but are not generally available in the USA. In predominantly Muslim countries, the burgers are called beefburgers rather than hamburgers because Muslims do not eat pig products and the word 'ham' is therefore off-putting (even though there is no ham in the burger – the name comes from Hamburg where the recipe originated). In Australia, you can get a McOz: a quarter pounder with beetroot, tomato, lettuce and onions.

McDonald's, Beijing.

Prices vary according to local costs, ingredients and income levels. Promotions have to be in the right language and suited to local audiences. In some countries, McDonald's own their own restaurants; elsewhere they are franchised. Some outlets, e.g. in Japan, sell ranges of branded toys and other products; others do not. Yet McDonald's is held, quite rightly, to be the epitome of a global brand. Its image is consistent, as is its positioning.

EXPAND YOUR KNOWLEDGE

Classic articles

Levitt, T. (1983) 'The globalisation of markets', *Harvard Business Review*, 61 (May–Jun): 92–102.

Ohmae, K. (1989) 'Managing in a borderless world', *Harvard Business Review*, 67 (May–Jun): 152–61.

These classic papers address the challenges of marketing worldwide in interlinked economies. The papers have at their hearts the inescapable view that marketing should no longer be thought of at a local level alone and suggest how to handle marketing across borders.

BRAND LOYALTY

A company's loyal customers consistently choose that brand over any other. This brand loyalty has to be earned by the company and can be destroyed much more quickly and easily than it can be established. Loyalty is important because loyal

02: Revolves Around You

customers make the best brand ambassadors, spreading positive word of mouth and so encouraging others to buy the product, and because repeat purchases mean a steadier, more reliable volume of sales for the company in question. Quality is crucial, both in the product itself, and in any supporting service. Poor service will lead to disappointment in the purchase and a reluctance, if not downright refusal, to ever buy that brand again.

A customer who repeatedly purchases the same brand may, or may not, be loyal to it. True loyalty comes from an ongoing relationship, not from convenience. So a customer who shops in their local supermarket every week may do so out of convenience rather than loyalty. It may sound like this does not matter, as the sales are made anyway, but what happens when another store opens nearby? Does that supposedly loyal customer stay with the shop they have always used or do they switch? Also, where do they shop when they are away from home? Truly loyal customers will stick with their store and that makes them valuable.

Brand loyalty is based on an emotional bond between the customer and the brand. It can be very personal and powerful, and is usually formed on the basis of past experience, past brand encounters. When Coca-Cola launched New Coke in the USA in the 1980s, the reaction from customers was phenomenal. The product had been extensively blind taste-tested in the marketplace and had been almost universally described as having a superior taste to original Coke. However, when the new version replaced the old, public reaction was violent. Street protests took place to demand that the old recipe be reinstated. Customers were so emotionally involved with the brand, it meant so much to them, that the change was felt as a personal blow. They felt betrayed and so their loyalty was tested to the limit. Wisely, just 79 days after the launch, Coca-Cola changed back – and apologised.

It is far more expensive to win a new customer than to keep an existing one and so it is cost-effective (as well as nice) to build these emotional linkages, and hence brand loyalty. Wise companies calculate the customer lifetime values (the net present value of all their purchases of the brand, past and future), rather than just looking at short-term sales. This approach is not without its drawbacks, however. The very act of calculation tends to reduce exchanges to transactions rather than relationships (Peelen, 2005), and without a good relationship with customers it is unlikely that the company will retain customers for a lifetime anyway.

ACTIVITY

Pick a favourite product – one that you are loyal to (a chocolate bar, drink, restaurant, brand of sports equipment, TV programme). Make a list of what might cause you to buy, watch or consume something else instead.

A strong brand is a good starting point for building brand loyalty, but the loyalty does not happen automatically. Loyalty comes out of a good, mutually beneficial relationship and its foundation is trust. This trust must go both ways. Clearly, customers must trust the brand. They must feel comfortable with it, secure that products will do what they are supposed to, that the quality will be maintained, that their brand experience will be the same as it was the last time they made a purchase, and the time before, and the time before that. Equally, the company must display some trust in its customers. A company that treats customers as if they are trying to con it will never build a relationship with those customers, will never gain their loyalty. This demonstration of trust can be an explicit part of the offer, or it may be demonstrated on an individual basis as part of the brand's customer service. For example, Virgin Wines will leave a delivery of 12 bottles of wine on a customer's doorstep if they are out when the delivery driver calls. If the wine is stolen, they replace it with no questions asked. Similarly, they encourage their customers to try wines by offering to refund any bottles that the customer does not like. Clearly, it would be easy to take advantage of this but, as the company has been making those offers for a large number of years now, it would seem that Virgin customers are generally honest and so the company's trust is not misplaced.

Customer satisfaction is a key contributor to loyalty, but not all satisfied customers will be loyal. For example, you may have really enjoyed the last holiday you took – the flight, hotel, resort and value were all great – but you will probably want to go somewhere else next time. Satisfied customers will have a positive attitude towards the company and will probably intend to buy from it again. This, however, may not be enough to clinch the actual sale. A positive attitude is only a predisposition to behaviour; other things often get in the way and cause a person to do something else. They may even go out with the intention of buying one thing but come home with another. (For more on attitudes and their relationship to behaviour, see Chapter 3.)

Customers remain loyal because they value what they get from a firm (Reichfeld, 1994). This value mainly comes from product quality, functionality and style, service and support. These things are not all within the control of the marketing department, so if a company wants to build loyalty, it needs all departments to work together to achieve this. There needs to be an integration of customer-related activities across the whole organisation. This is easier for companies with a customer focus (see Chapter 1).

EXPAND YOUR KNOWLEDGE

Matzler, K., Pichler, E., Füller, J. and Mooradian, T.A. (2011) 'Personality, person–brand fit, and brand community: an investigation of individuals, brands, and brand communities', *Journal of Marketing Management*, 27 (9–10): 874–90.

This paper, based on research with car enthusiasts attending a 'brandfest', investigates the links between personality traits, product attachment, brand trust and loyalty, and wishes to be part of a brand community.

LOYALTY SCHEMES (CARDS)

The term **loyalty scheme** is really a misnomer. You cannot buy true loyalty; it has to be earned through excellence in products and customer care. The loyalty cards available from so many large retailers today are, more accurately, reward cards, and they are a sophisticated form of sales promotion and a source of customer data. Customers earn points on their bill, which they can exchange for money off

loyalty schemes ways in which companies try to retain customers and encourage repeat purchases, often accomplished by awarding points (e.g. Tesco Clubcard, Air Miles)

the next bill or other treats, such as days out or tickets for the cinema or other entertainment venues. The Boots Advantage Card is one of the largest, and most generous, reward schemes in the UK, with nearly 15 million cards in circulation (Boots, n.d.). Advantage Card holders earn four points for every pound spent. Each point is worth a penny off future purchases. In-store machines give out points balances, vouchers and details of special offers.

Most of the people who have a supermarket reward card have at least two. One of the UK's biggest supermarket chains, Asda, ditched its reward card scheme for a while, claiming that research shows that its customers prefer lower prices. Asda's sales figures suggested that this strategy can work well. Later they offered customers a store card with 1% cashback on Asda shopping and 0.5% on other purchases – with an introductory bonus of 0% interest on the credit. Is that different to collecting points? It may be more attractive to customers who can spend the cash wherever they like.

These reward card schemes cost millions. Tesco issued vouchers worth £320 million (approximately €470 million) in 2005 (Tesco, 2006). On top of that, there is the cost of mailshots, the administration of the scheme, the customer support. Why are these companies prepared to spend all this money? Mainly, they do it for market research and improved target marketing. Every time a customer uses their card at the checkout, a computer records all their purchases. This information, combined with the personal information the cardholder gave when they filled out the application form, helps companies build up a detailed customer profile of shoppers. They then use this information to improve their marketing by stocking the products such customers are most likely to buy and by tailoring offers to suit them.

Customer data can highlight a marketing opportunity that sales data would not. For example, according to sales data, the market for birdseed and feeders was

customer focus: Punishing loyalty

There has been a finance battle going on in the UK. Credit cards have been employing some highly destructive weapons in their fight for new customers. The bait they offer is 0% interest on balances transferred from other cards. This free offer has a time limit, of course – often six months. After that, the customer has to pay a standard interest rate. The offer is not usually available to existing customers, only to new ones when they first take out a card.

Many customers play a lucrative game with this, taking out a new card with a new company at the end of the honeymoon six-month period, transferring their outstanding balance on again and so still getting their 0% finance. Some forget and so have to pay some interest at least some of the time. Are the credit card companies actively encouraging disloyalty? It seems hard to believe that this is their intention.

How would you feel as a long-standing customer who isn't getting such a good deal?

very small. However, by analysing its customer data, Tesco found that people who bought bird feeders were also likely to buy organic foods. So it stocked a wider range of bird feeders, told its organic food customers about them – and watched the sales rocket (Shabi, 2003).

The information that stores gain from their reward card schemes is worth a lot to them. Market research can be expensive, yet here the stores have customers volunteering their information, electronically, every time they present their card at the till. The set-up costs are high but the research information pours in.

EXPAND YOUR KNOWLEDGE

Hollebeek, L.D. (2011) 'Demystifying customer brand engagement: exploring the loyalty nexus', *Journal of Marketing Management,* 27 (7–8): 785–807.

Hollebeek explores the emerging concept of 'engaged customers' and its relationship to brands.

SUMMARY

Most marketing plans rely heavily on the marketing mix for their implementation. The 4Ps has been the most commonly used framework for many years but this is always extended to 7Ps when considering services marketing. As so many products now have service elements to them (warranties, guarantees, after-sales service, retailing, etc.), the 7Ps framework has become generally preferred for all products – tangible and intangible ones. Packaging is another important marketing tool and is often proposed as the fifth P.

Although they remain the most popular frameworks, the 4Ps and 7Ps models are not without their critics, mainly on the grounds that they are insufficiently customer-focused.

A brand's marketing mix should be integrated, each element working with the others to present a united front and support the organisation's marketing objectives. An uncoordinated mix sends conflicting messages to target customers and is much less effective in terms of building brand values and achieving marketing goals.

CHALLENGES REVIEWED

Now that you have finished reading the chapter, look back at the challenges you were set at the beginning. Do you have a clearer idea of what's involved?

HINTS

- The marketing mix must be integrated so all elements should support the organisation's desired position in its market.
- See 'Contribution pricing' in Chapter 10 but also remember that price is seen as a determinant of quality.
- The 7Ps of services marketing are key determinants of the attractiveness of services to customers.
- This is an ethical question – how important is the environment to your firm? Are there ways to maintain the brand identity even when changing packaging (Nestlé managed it with Kit Kat, for example)?

READING AROUND

JOURNAL ARTICLES

Borden, N. (1964) 'The concept of the marketing mix', *Journal of Advertising Research,* June: 7–12.

Cleeren, K., van Heerde, H. and Dekimpe, M. (2013) 'Rising from the ashes: how brands and categories can overcome product-harm crises', *Journal of Marketing,* 77 (2): 58–77.

Eckhardt, G. and Bengtsson, A. (2010) 'A brief history of branding in China', *Journal of Macromarketing,* 30 (September): 210–21.

Grönroos, C. (1997) 'From marketing mix to relationship marketing – towards a paradigm shift in marketing', *Management Decision,* 32 (2): 4–20.

Hennig-Thurau, T., Houston, M. and Heitjans, T. (2009) 'Conceptualizing and measuring the monetary value of brand extensions: the case of motion pictures', *Journal of Marketing,* 73 (6): 167–83.

Hollebeek, L. (2011) 'Demystifying customer brand engagement: exploring the loyalty nexus', *Journal of Marketing Management,* 27 (7–8): 785–807.

Levitt, T. (1965) 'Exploit the product life cycle', *Harvard Business Review*, 43 (Nov./Dec.): 81–94.

Levitt, T. (1983) 'The globalisation of markets', *Harvard Business Review*, 61 (May–June): 92–102.

Matzler, K., Pichler, E., Füller, J. and Mooradian, T. (2011) 'Personality, person–brand fit, and brand community: an investigation of individuals, brands, and brand communities', *Journal of Marketing Management* 27 (9–10): 874–90.

Ohmae, K. (1989) 'Managing in a borderless world', *Harvard Business Review*, 67 (May–June): 152–61.

BOOKS AND BOOK CHAPTERS

Baker, M. (2008) 'The marketing mix', in M.J. Baker and S.J. Hart (eds), *The Marketing Book*. Oxford: Butterworth Heinemann, Chapter 12.

de Chernatony, L. (2010) *From Brand Vision to Brand Evaluation,* 3rd edn. Oxford: Butterworth Heinemann.

Haig, M. (2006) *Brand Royalty: How the World's Top 100 Brands Thrive and Survive*. London: Kogan Page.

Holt, D. (2004) *How Brands Become Icons: The Principles of Cultural Branding*. Boston: Harvard Business Review Press.

Klein, N. (2000) *No Logo*. London: Flamingo.

Slater, J.S. (1999) 'Product packaging: the silent salesman', in J.P. Jones (ed.), *The Advertising Business*. London: Sage, Chapter 42.

WEBSITES

www.cim.co.uk – the Chartered Institute of Marketing.
www.interbrand.com – Interbrand.

SELF-REVIEW QUESTIONS

1. What are the 7Ps? (See pp. 476–8)
2. Where does packaging fit in the marketing mix model? (See pp. 474–6)
3. What are the characteristics of a well-designed marketing mix? (See p. 463)
4. Name and describe the levels of the total product offering. (See pp. 465–6)
5. What are the main tools of the promotional mix? (See p. 469)
6. What is another name for 'promotion'? (See p. 467)
7. How can packaging give a product a competitive advantage? (See pp. 474–6)
8. What is the relationship between brand personality and brand image? (See p. 483–4)
9. Why is it important that all elements of the marketing mix match and support each other? (See pp. 478–9)
10. What faults can you find with the marketing mix as a framework for marketing activity? (See p. 481)

 Mini case study: Small objects of desire

Read the questions, then the case material, and then answer the questions.

Questions

1 Identify the elements of Apple's brand identity.

2 Was the launch of the iPhone a line extension, a brand extension or a brand stretch? Explain your answer and then discuss the advantages of this strategy.

3 What evidence is there that Apple enjoys a high level of brand loyalty? What advantages does this bring the company?

4 Is Apple a lifestyle brand? Give reasons for your answer. (You may want to refer back to the section on lifestyle branding in Chapter 1.)

5 Should electronics manufacturers take responsibility for the impact of their products on the environment? What could they do to make their businesses more environmentally friendly?

Why would anyone queue for over 24 hours to buy an (arguably) over-priced phone? Especially when they could buy it from a shop around the corner for the same price and without queuing at all? Questions like these were puzzling passers-by on the day that the Apple iPhone went on sale in London for the first time.

The queues outside Apple's flagship store in Regent Street started two days before the iPhone's much publicised arrival. It was November.

It was cold and wet. Even the people queuing seemed bemused as to why they were doing it. 'I'm a commercial director. This is ridiculous behaviour for someone like me', said one member of the queue, while a civil servant near the front offered at least a partial explanation for why he wanted to be one of the first to own the iPhone: 'Several of my colleagues have tried to arrange meetings with me on Monday just to have a look at it.'

The Apple iPhone combines a phone with a fully featured web browser, advanced camera and music player. Even at the time of its launch, it was by no means the only device on the market to do all of these things. There were a number of cheaper rivals but none of them inspired the adulation given to Apple's new product. Fans of the iPhone raved over the deceptive simplicity of the design and were especially enthusiastic about the minimalist touchscreen. The iPhone is beyond such restraints as a conventional keypad. Lucky iPhone owners just brush their fingertips over the sleek, full-colour display. *Time Magazine* called it 'the invention of the year'.

Over half a million iPhones were sold over the weekend of its launch in the USA. This extraordinary level of sales made the company's first-year sales target of 10 million look easily achievable. With that sales volume, Apple would achieve 1% global mobile market share which, while impressive for a new entrant in such a short space of time, would still be a long way short of market domination – in volume terms at least.

Apple has a reputation for leading-edge technology and attention to detail, particularly style detail. Very few other brands generate such interest and inspire the number of brand ambassadors that Apple does. Apple customers believe that the company really cares about the way they use the technology – and about the way people look while using the technology. As a web designer in the iPhone queue on that wet November morning in London said: '…the point is the attention to detail. I'm actually going to enjoy using my phone, and Apple are the only company that I know in most of consumer electronics who care about this stuff.'

The Apple Mac pioneered an icon-based operating system (the source of a long-running dispute with Microsoft over the Windows design) which was the starting point for Apple devotion. Mac users would not dream of trading in their computers for mere PCs and, years after the Mac revolution, Apple's entry into the MP3 market inspired a similar response. The iPod dominates that market, not least in terms of brand awareness and desired purchase. Apple products are recognised as style icons by a wide demographic: their appeal crosses divides of age, income, gender and taste – although approximately 93% of the queue for the new phone were male.

The phone's launch price was a hefty £269 (€399) but there was speculation that the price might come down. In the USA, Apple cut the original price of the iPhone by $200 (£100, €135) and then had to offer refunds to early customers who complained vociferously.

Price was not the only off-putting feature of the iPhone. In the UK, broadband Internet access was available through Edge but, at the time of the launch, Edge only covered 30% of Britain, so in most places iPhoners would not be able to use that feature. Additionally, in an attempt to maximise revenues, Apple had negotiated exclusive contracts with specific network providers. All iPhones bought in the UK were tied into the O2 network for 18 months. These network deals had already broken down in France and Germany, where local anti-competition laws had forced Apple to unbundle the iPhones and offer them with a free choice of network. This freedom of choice came at an even higher price, of course. In Germany, the unbundled iPhones were on sale at €999 (about £720), while it cost €399 (the same as in the UK) to buy an iPhone with a contract with Apple's German partner, T-Mobile.

Among all the Apple-inspired hype came a burst of bad publicity too. Green lobbyists took advantage of the interest in the iPhone's launch to make their own attack on the mobile phone market. Greenpeace claimed that mobile phones were significant polluters and that mobile companies needed to do far more to minimise their impact on the environment. Zeina Alhajj, Campaign Coordinator for Greenpeace, said: 'Over the life cycle of a phone there is massive pollution. The phone companies are making big changes – transparency and reporting is far ahead of what it was four years ago, for example – but it is still far away from being a really green industry.'

A recent Greenpeace report claimed to have found evidence of widespread, hazardous chemical contamination of rivers and underground wells in countries where electronics goods are manufactured. Greenpeace also complains that consumers are wasteful, replacing phones more often than is necessary and so artificially inflating the demand for new phones. Western consumers

(Continued)

(Continued)

in particular frequently replace working phones with the latest models, keeping phones on average for only 18 months when they are designed to last for ten years.

Only a small proportion of these thousands of discarded phones are recycled. Nokia, the world's biggest mobile handset manufacturer, believes that about 48% of old handsets are abandoned or forgotten by their owners – many of them are just lying at the bottom of drawers.

SOURCES: Burkeman, 2007; Judge, 2007a, 2007b.

REFERENCES

Abraham, M. and Taylor, A. (2011) 'Brand Housing', *Admap*, February 2011, London: WARC.

Anon (2003) 'Cosmo forced to scrap branded cafe project', *Marketing Week*, 7 August.

Boots (n.d.) *About Boots*, Boots the Chemist, Nottingham. Available at: **www.boots-the-chemists.co.uk/main.asp?pid=1673** (accessed 13/07/2007).

Burkeman, O. (2007) 'At 6.02pm the worshippers got their reward', *The Guardian*, 10 November, p. 3.

Cleeren, K., van Heerde, H.J. and Dekimpe, M.G. (2013) 'Rising from the ashes: how brands and categories can overcome product-harm crises', *Journal of Marketing*, 77 (2): 58–77.

Eckhardt, G.M. and Bengtsson, A. (2010) 'A brief history of branding in China', *Journal of Macromarketing*, 30 (September): 210–21.

Grönroos, C. (1997) 'From marketing mix to relationship marketing: towards a paradigm shift in marketing', *Management Decision*, 35 (4): 322–39.

Haig, M. (2003) *Brand Failures: The Truth about the 100 Biggest Branding Mistakes of All Time*. London: Kogan Page.

Hennig-Thurau, T., Houston, M. and Heitjans, T. (2009) 'Conceptualizing and measuring the monetary value of brand extensions: the case of motion pictures', *Journal of Marketing*, 73 (6): 167–83.

Hollebeek, L.D. (2011) 'Demystifying customer brand engagement: exploring the loyalty nexus', *Journal of Marketing Management*, 27 (7–8): 785–807.

Holt, D.B. (2004) *How Brands Become Icons: The Principles of Cultural Branding*. Boston: Harvard Business Review Press.

Interbrand (2013) 'Best global brands 2012 rankings'. Available at: **www.interbrand.com/en/best-global-brands/2012/Best-Global-Brands-2012-Brand-View.aspx** (accessed 04/04/13).

Jones, P. and Vignali, C. (1994) 'Commercial education', *Journal of Retail Education*, cited in C. Vignali and B.J. Davies (1994) 'The marketing mix redefined and mapped', *Management Decision*, 32 (8): 11–17.

Judge, E. (2007a) 'Green group shines light on safety of the Apple iPhone', *Times online*, 5 November. Available at: **business.timesonline.co.uk/tol/business/industry_sectors/technology/article2806228.ece** (accessed 27/11/07).

Judge, E. (2007b) 'Fresh blow for exclusive Apple iPhone strategy', *Times online*, 21 November. Available at: **business.timesonline.co.uk/tol/business/industry_sectors/telecoms/article2914903.ece** (accessed 27/11/07).

Kotler, P. (2003) *Marketing Insights from A to Z: 80 Concepts Every Manager Needs to Know.* New York: John Wiley & Sons.

Lauterborn, R. (1990) 'New marketing litany: four Ps passé; C-words take over', *Advertising Age,* 61 (41): 26.

Levitt, T. (1965) 'Exploit the product life cycle', *Harvard Business Review,* 43 (Nov/Dec): 81–94.

Levitt, T. (1983) 'The globalisation of markets', *Harvard Business Review,* 61 (May–June): 92–102.

Matzler, K., Pichler, E., Füller, J. and Mooradian, T.A. (2011) 'Personality, person–brand fit, and brand community: an investigation of individuals, brands, and brand communities', *Journal of Marketing Management,* 27 (9–10): 874–90.

McCarthy, J.C. (1960) *Basic Marketing: A Managerial Approach.* Toronto: Irwin.

Ohmae, K. (1989) 'Managing in a borderless world', *Harvard Business Review,* 67 (May–June): 152–61.

Peelen, E. (2005) *Customer Relationship Management.* Harlow: FT/Prentice Hall.

Pickton, D. and Broderick, A. (2004) *Integrated Marketing Communications,* 2nd edn. Harlow: FT/Prentice Hall.

Reichfeld, F.F. (1994) 'Loyalty and the renaissance of marketing', *Journal of Marketing Management,* 2 (4): 10–21.

Shabi, R. (2003) 'The card up their sleeve', *The Guardian Weekend,* 19 July, pp. 15–23.

Smith, S. (2006) 'The evil that men do lives after them...', *Marketing Week,* 9 March.

Tesco (2006) *Annual Review and Summary Financial Statements.* Tesco plc. Available at: **www.tescocorporate.com/annualreview06/index.html** (accessed 13/07/07).

WARC (2012) 'WARC Briefing: Brand Architecture', available at: **www.warc.com** (accessed 02/01/13).

Whiteside, S. (2013) 'Rovio takes flight with Angry Birds: leveraging growth from a mobile gaming phenomenon', Event Reports: MMA (Mobile Marketing Association) Forum, May. Available at: **www.warc.com** (accessed 17/05/13).

Yoo, B., Donthu, N. and Lee, S. (2000) 'An examination of selected marketing mix elements and brand equity', *Academy of Marketing Science,* 28 (2): 195–211.

Visit the companion website on your computer at **www.sagepub.co.uk/masterson3e** or MobileStudy on your Smart phone or tablet by scanning this QR code and gain access to:

- **Videos** to get a better understanding of key concepts and provoke in-class discussion.
- Links to useful **websites and templates** to help guide your study.
- Access **SAGE Marketing Pins (www.pinterest.com/sagepins/)**. SAGE's regularly updated **Pinterest** page, giving you access to regularly updated resources on everything from Branding to Consumer Behaviour.
- **Daily Grind podcast series** to learn more about the day-to-day life of a marketing **professional**.
- Interactive **Practice questions** to test your understanding.
- A **bonus chapter on Marketing Careers** to not only support your study, but your job search and future career.
- **PowerPoints** prompting key points for revision.

Marketing planning 12

CHAPTER CONTENTS

MARKETING PLANNING CHALLENGES

The following are illustrations of the types of decision that marketers have to take or issues they face. *You aren't expected to know how to deal with the challenges now*; just bear them in mind as you read the chapter and see what you can find that helps.

- Your uncle runs a shoe factory that is struggling to compete with cheaper manufacturers from the developing world. He knows you've done a business course so he invites you to a management meeting to discuss the way forward. Do you have anything to contribute?
- A friend wants to start up her own company and needs a bank loan. The bank won't give her the loan without a marketing plan. She doesn't know how to write one. Can you help her?
- You run a medium-sized import/export agency. The international environment is turbulent and you are concerned that some of your markets and sources of supply will dry up. What should you be doing?
- You are the marketing director of a successful UK chain of restaurants. The company has money to put into expansion and you have been asked to present the options to the board.
- You work for a major British bank that is thinking of moving into the insurance market. You have to assess how well your bank is likely to be able to compete with the other insurance companies. How will you do this?

INTRODUCTION

Marketing decisions are key drivers to success in the modern marketplace. Marketing has the power to influence every part of the business and affect how organisations meet the needs of their customers, how they respond to competitors, deal with suppliers and financiers, as well as how they treat their employees. In turn, marketing outcomes and performance are influenced by a wide variety of individuals within the organisation and even many people outside the organisation who have associations with it. Even if an organisation has a marketing department, it is wrong to presume that they are the only ones who are involved in marketing activities. Other departments exert a strong influence and have significant effects on how well marketing is carried out.

How organisations manage their marketing activities is affected by many factors, not least the extent to which they are market-orientated or adopt an alternative orientation stance (see Chapter 1), what management style they choose to adopt, what preferences they have for organisational structure and the extent to which they carry out their planning as a **top-down approach** or a **bottom-up approach** (these are considered in more detail shortly).

This chapter will consider marketing's place in the company's overall plan and how marketing can help the organisation achieve its goals. It will cover the basic planning process and marketing analysis tools. It will introduce you to a wide variety of key strategic and management aspects of marketing. The chapter will first consider organisational structures before moving on to some of the challenges faced in planning and implementing marketing (as well as other management functions): the approach to planning, barriers to planning, reasons for planning failure and organisational approaches to marketing. Having completed this overview, the rest of the chapter is structured in a way that mirrors the marketing planning process, taking each of the elements or stages in turn and introducing the more important concepts at each stage. The material covered in Chapters 6 and 11 is also relevant to marketing planning and these chapters should be read in conjunction with this chapter, especially the sections on branding, product development, the product life cycle and product portfolio management in Chapter 6 and marketing mix objectives, varying the mix through the product's life and branding strategies in Chapter 11.

top-down approach senior managers specify objectives, budgets, strategies and plans that are passed down to functions and departments to put into action

bottom-up approach functions and departments recommend objectives, budgets, strategies and plans to senior management

ORGANISING FOR MARKETING

An organisation's structure will give clues as to how customer-focused it is and, therefore, its likely attitude towards marketing. Although many companies have a marketing department, roles within this department will vary depending on the type of business conducted or types of customer it serves. For example, the marketing department in a b2b company, i.e. one that does not have direct contact with end-users or consumers, may primarily be a sales team, while a company managing a number of brands is likely to have product, brand and category managers.

The following are examples of different types of typical organisational structure:

Types of organisational structure

- functional, based on the different management functions that run the business, e.g. marketing, human resources, finance, manufacturing
- geographic, based on the regions where the company operates, e.g. Europe
- product, based on the products, groups of products or brands the company manages
- market/customer groups, based on the markets or customer groupings in which the company operates, e.g. Dell operates in both customer and b2b markets, which includes education, and small and medium-sized businesses; particularly important customers, i.e. those that are strategically important to the company, may be dealt with as key accounts
- matrix, a hybrid-type structure where the company incorporates all functions into teams supporting different products or brands
- network, a highly versatile and relatively new approach that is, in essence, a coalition between a number of independent specialist firms, coordinated by a 'control centre' organisation. Specialist firms may be product designers, component manufacturers or distributors.

A company may choose a mix of the structure types and structures may change over time. There is no single best solution. Exhibit 12.1 gives some examples of the different types of structure that can be adopted.

The structure a company adopts depends on its core values and the strategies of the management team and should be in line with organisational aims and objectives. It is important to recognise that structure is evolutionary since companies operate in a dynamic environment and, in order to retain position, will evolve to

Exhibit 12.1   Illustration of organisational structures

(a) Marketing organisation – functional management structure

(b) Marketing organisation – hybrid of product, geographical and functional

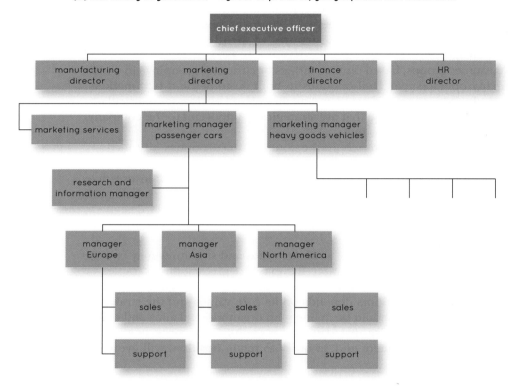

(c) Marketing organisation – product/brand management structure (FMCG)

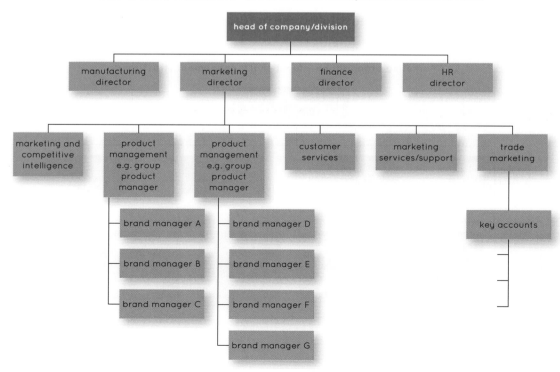

(d) Marketing organisation – market/customer management structure

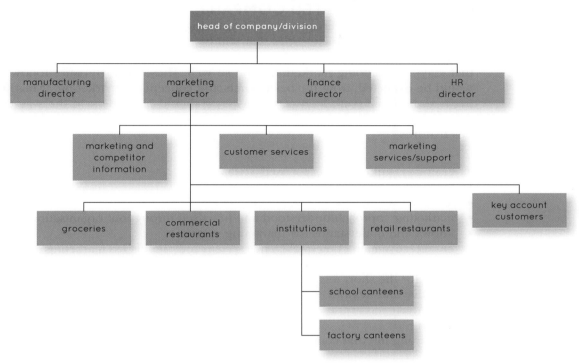

(e) Marketing organisation – matrix structure (product/market matrix)

		MARKET MANAGERS			
		Menswear	Womenswear	Furnishings	Industrial
PRODUCT MANAGERS	Rayon				
	Nylon				
	Orlon				
	Dacron				

ensure they remain at the forefront of their customers' minds. Such changes must be managed particularly well in order to ensure that the company's stakeholders are not alienated. It is why, yet again, we need to appreciate that internal marketing is an important part of the process in aligning the business to meet the needs of customers.

SOME OF THE CHARACTERISTICS OF A MARKET-ORIENTATED COMPANY

Although there are different ways of organising companies, there are said to be certain features or characteristics that will be evident in a marketing-orientated company that may not be present at all or to only a limited extent in companies that may not be doing marketing quite so well. These characteristics follow, as would be expected, from the basic tenets and concepts of marketing. If marketing is to be done well, then certain aspects should be evident in the way that the organisation is structured and managed. Here are a few of the more obvious features:

- customer and consumer focused
- market led
- identifies and balances stakeholder needs
- marketing approach understood and practised throughout organisation
- knows and understands the marketing system
- has effective marketing intelligence system and established marketing database
- sensitive to market trends
- plans for the short term and long term
- adaptive and flexible
- proactive
- creative
- has strong internal communication.

TOP-DOWN OR BOTTOM-UP PLANNING?

The top-down process refers to the senior managers specifying objectives, budgets, strategies and plans that are then passed down to operating functions to put into action. The bottom-up approach works in reverse. Objectives, budgets and plans are set at operational level and are passed up to senior management for approval and consolidation into the company's overall plans (see Exhibit 12.2). Both processes have their advantages and disadvantages but they do not need to be mutually exclusive. It is often advisable to use both approaches together. Involving more people in the planning process makes it more likely that they will agree with and adhere to the plans developed.

outside-in approach
the organisation looks outwards to focus on the needs of the marketplace to determine appropriate courses of marketing action

inside-out approach
focuses on the needs of the organisation first, and customers and the marketplace second

Another consideration is the extent to which companies adopt an **outside-in approach** (Schultz, 1993a) to their management and planning, in contrast to an **inside-out approach**. An organisation with an outside-in approach looks outwards, focusing on the needs of the marketplace to determine appropriate courses of marketing action. Customer perspectives are adopted and so this approach corresponds with a strong marketing orientation (see Chapter 1). The inside-out approach is inner-directed and focuses on the needs of the organisation first, and customers and the marketplace second. Clearly, a balance of the two is required if the basic outcomes of marketing are to be achieved, as identified in the Chartered Institute of Marketing's definition:

Marketing is a management process which identifies, anticipates and satisfies customer requirements profitably.

Exhibit 12.2 Focus of planning and management

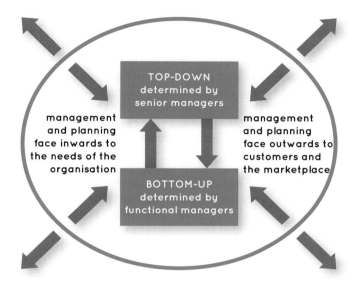

Carrying out marketing well is not an easy task. The structure of organisations may make it difficult to coordinate and manage the different departments and specialisms as one entity. Management's response when faced with large, many-faceted tasks has been to divide them into sub-units (departments) in order to cope with the magnitude of operations and to outsource activities by commissioning specialists to undertake certain tasks (e.g. advertising and promotion agencies, market research agencies, call centres, etc.). While project teams and cross-functional assignments can help to improve working arrangements, organisational barriers remain that may impede the smooth implementation of marketing plans. Schultz (1993b) has identified these barriers as:

- hierarchical management structures
- vertical communications
- horizontal communications
- turf battles
- power struggles
- functional silos.

When faced with these barriers, individuals and groups may conflict as they protect their own specialisation and interests. These stakeholders may be within the organisation or outside it, and their vested interests can vary significantly.

hierarchical management structure
each manager has a set place within a vertical chain of command

vertical communications
communications happen up and down the hierarchical organisation structure, e.g. sales manager to salesperson and vice versa

horizontal communications
communications happen sideways within an organisation, e.g. between workgroups or departments

turf battle
when individual managers or departments fight for their own interests at the expense of those of other managers or departments

functional silo
when departments or work groups act as independent entities rather than as components of a much larger system despite having many overlapping activities and information needs

Shareholders will be looking for profits and returns on investment. Suppliers will be looking for continuity of custom. Employees will want security, a good working environment and good wages. They will be concerned with fulfilling their own departmental objectives, which will differ between departments even though they may share the same organisational objectives, and so on.

Somehow, the organisation as a whole needs to balance these interests to achieve a level of satisfaction for all. An added complexity is that marketing departments frequently make use of a wide variety of external agencies which may, in turn, experience barriers and conflict not only with the organisation itself but also between themselves. Where distribution channels are used, such as wholesalers, retailers and physical distributors companies, these channel members also add to the complexity of interrelationships. Thus, from a marketing point of view, the complete and extended marketing organisation is a family of interrelated departments and organisations, many of which lie outside the direct control of marketing managers but which nevertheless have to be managed.

McKinsey's 7S framework helps with understanding the interaction between these different elements (both inside and outside the company) in implementing marketing strategies and programmes (see Exhibit 12.3).

A company uses the particular *skills* of many different *staff* who require organising (*structuring*) in a way that maximises their benefit to the company. The company uses different *systems* in order to operate, e.g. computer systems, decision-making systems, work processing systems. It adopts a distinct *style* based on its leaders and organisational culture, and all individuals must *share values* that are similar in order to meet the *strategic* goals.

Richard
Branson:
Losing my
virginity

Exhibit 12.3   McKinsey's 7S framework

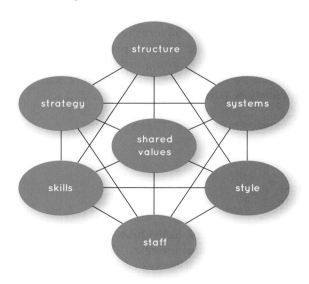

SOURCE: Peters and
Waterman, 2004.

Making strategy happen, however, presents a distinct set of problems to many managers as, by its nature, it involves change, which is invariably resisted to some extent or another. Change within the marketplace is to be expected and welcomed and the organisation has to respond appropriately. Change is also initiated within the organisation, not only as a response to market changes but also in a proactive way as managers seek to improve their performance, their effectiveness and efficiency, and plan for anticipated future events.

Addressing issues such as these requires **internal marketing**. The purpose of internal marketing is to address the concerns, and therefore needs, of different groups or segments of employees. For some, concerns may come from a lack of information on the changes, while others may not possess the know-how or skills to act upon the changes proposed. Others may have both the knowledge and the know-how but lack the willpower or may hold different vested interests.

internal marketing also called internal PR, it addresses the needs (particularly information needs) of employees

For each of these internal segments, management must inform, develop through appropriate training and incentivise appropriately. Needless to say, failure to implement successfully the changes proposed may ultimately result in the failure of the company or, at least, a swift change in position for those responsible for the failure. Failure may, however, be due to reasons other than a lack of support from employees. Quite simply, it may be the wrong strategic choice (see Exhibit 12.4 for possible reasons for failure).

Exhibit 12.4 Reasons for failure in strategic planning

Lack of chief executive officer (CEO or MD) support	Failure to take account of individuals within the company
Too narrow an outlook	Using the wrong measures of success
Irreversible decline of the company or market	Managerial conflict
Emphasis on *where* to complete, rather than *how* to compete	Lack of information or wrong information or information withheld from key decision-makers
'Me-too' instinct	Results of planning ignored
Not enough emphasis on *when* to complete	

Internal marketing is an important activity that will enable a company to remain focused on the needs of its customers.

Firms that do not or will not embrace the issues of internal marketing and incorporate those ingredients into their strategic marketing plan will see their market share and profit base erode. Internal promotion can create a positive and/or superior image of the firm and its products in the mind of the customer. (Greene et al., 1994: 10)

THE MARKETING PLANNING PROCESS

Marketing management and planning are parts of a wider activity that involve the whole organisation. The output of the total planning process is the production of a series of plans covering the various functional areas of the business. Such plans, while having a longer-term focus, usually cover a 12-month duration to coincide with the financial planning period. Although a great deal has been written about how plans should be developed, organisations and their managers tend to adopt processes with which they feel most comfortable. Sometimes this results in plans not always being fully documented and objectives and strategies left vague.

At its highest level, the organisation has to set its corporate (business) mission and goals that act as an overall direction for the business. To achieve these goals, each of the functional areas within each of the **strategic business units (SBUs)** (if an organisation has them) needs to set their own plans, involving objectives, strategies and tactics. In the VW/Audi global focus box presented earlier, each of the VW/Audi Group brands makes up a different SBU for the Group: one for VW, one for Audi, one for Seat and one for Skoda. The approach can be top-down or bottom-up, or a combination of the two. For this reason, the arrows shown in Exhibit 12.5 point in both directions. Collectively, the plans for production, finance, marketing, human resource management, and so on, form the composite that becomes the plan for the SBU. The plans for the SBUs come together to create the corporate plan for the organisation as a whole. For companies that do not have SBUs, the functional plans simply form the basis of the corporate plan, as illustrated in Exhibit 12.5. It is important to recognise that marketing planning does not take place in isolation from the rest of the organisation, but is an integral part of it.

The process for setting each plan within the overall corporate plan is similar but we will concentrate solely on the marketing management and planning process.

Chapter 2 (Marketing environment) introduced the basic questions that need to be answered in marketing planning (see page 84) and these were revisited in Chapter 11. Here the model is extended by adding extra questions to make a total of seven key planning questions. These three extra questions are important additions because they emphasise the need to explore not only 'where are we now?' but highlight the danger of not considering trends in performance. By only

strategic business unit (SBU)
a distinct part of an organisation that has an external market for its products and services

BT strategic planning

Exhibit 12.5 How functional plans combine into the corporate plan

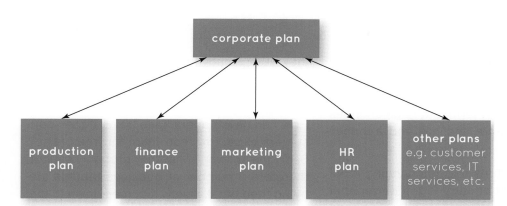

asking 'where are we now?', we are only invited to consider the situation at a single moment in time. We need to know what we have done previously that has given rise to our current situation and also to consider if we continue to follow the same path of activities, where this will lead. Companies, unless just starting out, are continuing businesses that have a track record of performance in the marketplace that has to be recognised and understood in order to plan best for the future. A company's past, present and future form integral parts of the planning process. The first three questions then become part of what is generally referred to as a situation analysis, and this provides an insight into the organisation's past and present, as shown in Exhibit 12.6.

Exhibit 12.6 The strategic gap

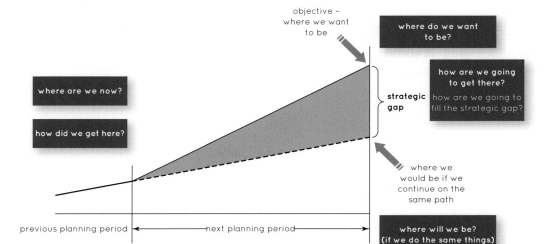

e-focus: Making the news

Managers continually update their product plans to keep up with changes in the marketing environment. Small changes may be made in the short term, but large changes usually require more analysis and a longer-term plan.

One of the industries that is changing most in the twenty-first century is the newspaper business. This really is a question of change or die. Newspapers have known they were under threat for a decade or more. So have they stayed the same and waited for the inevitable end? No, of course not. Just look how they've changed.

Newspapers have always relied heavily on technology. The invention of the printing press made the newssheets possible in the first place. Advances in printing technology made their large-scale production possible. Now the demise of printed paper in our Internet age is forcing another major change.

Most newspaper readers still read the printed version but national newspapers are now available in a number of formats. They can be read on PCs, tablets, e-readers and mobiles. The formats aren't perfect representations of the printed copy (for example, some of them can't cope with the crossword puzzle), but they have the advantages of being accessible on the move, and of being cheaper or free.

Is it a product if it has no price? Or is it a gift? How can newspapers keep going if their consumers expect to read them for free online? Sadly the answer is that they probably cannot, therefore a number of business models are being tried out. Largely, it comes down to the newspapers being either funded by advertising or charging their readers a subscription. Only those with the largest circulations online, e.g. the *Daily Mail* and the *Guardian*, are likely to be able to make enough from advertising, so subscriptions would seem to be the way forward, but will readers accept this and pay for online content? In 2010 *The Times* started charging for its online edition and there was an outcry. Online readership plummeted and negative word of mouth soared.

Some readers do pay for downloadable content but the attitudes of the majority will have to change if newspapers are to survive. And that means that newspaper groups' marketing plans will need to take this threat seriously, set objectives for online versions, devote suitable resources to them and work out how to compete in the digital future. Those with the best plans are most likely to be the survivors.

The seven key planning questions, then, are:

Writing a marketing plan

1 Where are we now?
2 How did we get here?
3 Where will we be? (by the end of the planning period if we continue to do the same things)
4 Where do we want to be? (by the end of the planning period)

5 How are we going to get there?
6 Are we getting there?
7 Have we arrived?

By answering the first three questions and then posing the fourth, we can complete a strategic gap analysis. This is an important contribution to the marketing planning process. By knowing what we have done in the past and evaluating those activities (question 2), we can then forecast what would happen if we continued on our current path (question 3). Armed with this understanding and specifying where we would wish to be by the end of the planning period (question 4), we can determine what course of action would be necessary for us to make the shift from where we would be based on the current course to where we want to be based on our new objectives. It is rather like a boat changing tack and correcting its course so that it might reach its final destination. The answer to question 6 allows this change of tack to occur within a single planning period and the strategic gap analysis allows a change of tack as we move from one planning period to the next. Exhibit 12.6 shows this process and the strategic gap that needs to be filled as the organisation moves into its new planning period.

While there are a variety of marketing planning process models, there is general agreement on the sequence and stages involved. They relate directly to the seven basic questions above. Marketing planning and implementation thus require marketers to:

How to get your ideas to spread

1 **Analyse** the current situation. This has implications for the use of databases, management/marketing information systems, and market research activities that have to be organised to deliver information in a timely fashion for the analysis to be undertaken. Data from previous planning periods can provide a basis for the analysis. It is important to consider trends in this process and not just what is happening at one point in time.
2 **Understand** markets, customers and competitors.
3 **Establish** segmentation, targeting and positioning.
4 **Determine** objectives and direction in line with corporate objectives and strategies.
5 **Develop** marketing strategies and programmes (and contingencies), including resource/budget implications. This has implications for collaboration with other departments within the organisation, with outsourced agencies and with members of the distribution channel(s).
6 **Identify** control approaches to evaluate progress and activities.
7 **Implement** the plan.
8 **Track** progress.
9 **Adjust** activities as necessary.
10 **Evaluate** outcomes at the end of the planning period.
11 **Use** findings from tracking and final evaluation as part of the analysis of the current situation for the next planning period.

Exhibit 12.7 shows the planning process in a diagrammatic form, linking the seven questions to the analysis and decision-making process. The stages enable marketers to produce plans that form the basis of how the company will approach and operate in the marketplace.

Exhibit 12.7   A model of the marketing planning process

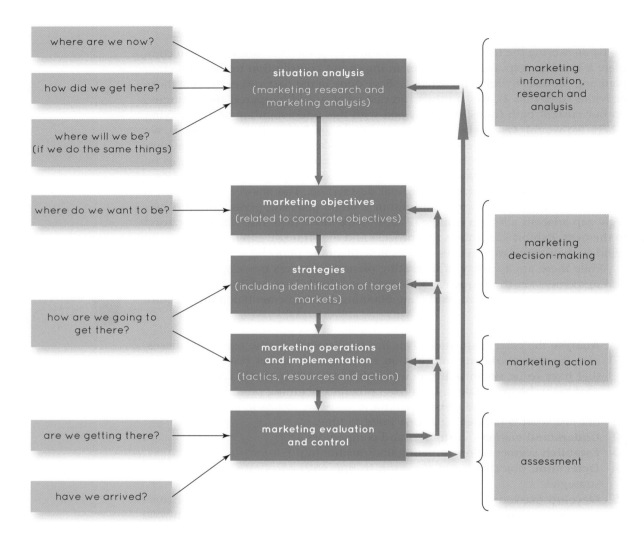

Exhibit 12.7 illustrates how the situation analysis forms the first stage of the planning process. Based on an understanding of the situation (past, present and future forecasts), new marketing objectives are set and strategies are determined to achieve the position the company wishes to be in by the end of the planning period. The strategies which are of a general nature, indicating the direction that the marketing activities will take, are then made more detailed in terms of the tactics (operational activities) that will be implemented. Exhibit 12.7 also illustrates how the evaluation and control of marketing activities feeds back into the rest of the planning process to check that current plans are being achieved on an ongoing basis and whether or not they have been achieved at the end of the planning period. These final evaluations provide a basis for the

development of future plans. The feedback process (frequently known as tracking) allows plans to be modified as necessary throughout the planning period. It is important to understand what works and why. If there have been changes in the marketing environment – perhaps competitor activity has increased – then the plans need to take account of these changes and the marketing activities need to be modified accordingly. This is the process of changing tack that was referred to earlier, as the marketing activities are modified in the light of the tracking evaluations so that the final outcome is reached as intended. Changes to plans may be at the strategic level or at the operational, tactical level. The tactical level of marketing is often thought of as the use of the marketing mix elements. Aspects of marketing strategy that are broad-level decisions are considered later in this chapter.

Within the overall framework of the planning process model, there are a number of marketing management tools that can be used at the different stages in order to aid analysis and managerial decision-making. They help us achieve what is, basically, a systematic approach to identifying and analysing competitive advantage in the marketplace for our products, i.e. goods and services, thus helping to achieve long-term benefits for companies. A summary of examples of these tools is shown in Exhibit 12.8.

What has been described above is a systematic, deliberate and prescriptive approach to planning and management. This is consistent with most texts and descriptions of the planning process (e.g. see McDonald, 2008). However, planning and management in practice tend to be a much less tidy business, in which ambiguity, inaccuracy, conflict and confusion can and do arise.

The main output from these planning activities is the marketing plan. The marketing plan is a document that summarises the key points of planning and highlights the marketing activities that will take place throughout the period of the plan. In reality, there may actually be a collection of marketing plans that together cover all products, markets and marketing functions rather than a single plan that covers everything. There may be separate plans for each brand or each main marketing function (e.g. advertising plan, sales plan, distribution plan, etc., covering all the elements of the marketing mix) or each target market or each market by area, region or country.

Marketing plans can appear in a range of different formats and structures but they should contain a basic minimum range of information. The planning period needs to be specified as part of the plan. This may be over a total of 3–5 years in outline, but the detail is likely to be over a single year to coincide with the organisation's financial planning periods – it may be broken down into quarter-year periods. The main sections of a plan are shown in Exhibit 12.9.

SITUATION ANALYSIS

Measuring marketing (McKinsey & Co)

Marketing analysis involves an understanding of how the company is operating in its marketing environment. The marketing environment comprises a complex set of factors that affect marketing decisions and plans, and ultimately affect business performance. It is important that the company monitors itself and its environment in order to prepare for future activities and, particularly, to build and maintain competitive advantage. This type of analysis is not just a one-off,

Exhibit 12.8 The marketing planning process and useful tools for analysis and decision-making

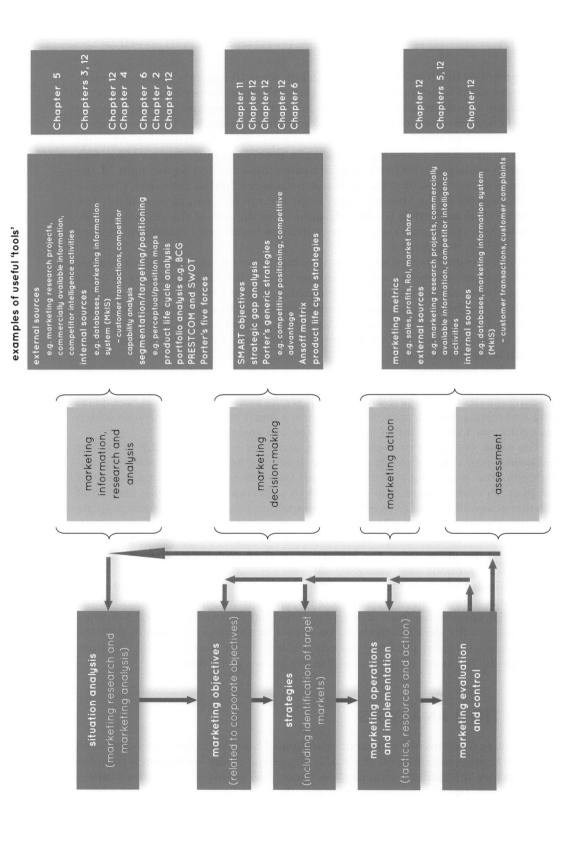

examples of useful 'tools'

external sources
e.g. marketing research projects,
commercially available information,
competitor intelligence activities
internal sources
e.g. databases, marketing information
system (MkIS)
 – customer transactions, competitor
    capability analysis
segmentation/targeting/positioning
e.g. perceptual/position maps
product life cycle analysis
portfolio analysis e.g. BCG
PRESTCOM and SWOT
Porter's five forces

Chapter 5
Chapters 3, 12

Chapter 12
Chapter 4

Chapter 6
Chapter 2
Chapter 12

SMART objectives
strategic gap analysis
Porter's generic strategies
e.g. competitive positioning, competitive
advantage
Ansoff matrix
product life cycle strategies

Chapter 11
Chapter 12
Chapter 12
Chapter 12
Chapter 6

marketing metrics
e.g. sales, profits, RoI, market share
external sources
e.g. marketing research projects, commercially
available information, competitor intelligence
activities
internal sources
e.g. databases, marketing information system
(MkIS)
 – customer transactions, customer complaints

Chapter 12
Chapters 5, 12

Chapter 12

marketing
information,
research and
analysis

marketing
decision-making

marketing action

assessment

situation analysis
(marketing research and
marketing analysis)

marketing objectives
(related to corporate objectives)

strategies
(including identification of target
markets)

marketing operations
and implementation
(tactics, resources and action)

marketing evaluation
and control

Exhibit 12.9   Outline marketing plan

Section	Description
1 Executive summary	A brief overview of the main points of the plan highlighting the main objectives/intended outcomes, activities and resource requirements.
2 Current marketing situation	Summarises the environmental situation *and* trends: analysis of both internal and external factors including PRESTCOM and SWOT. Subheadings might include: 2.1 Key macro environmental influences (PREST factors) 2.2 Competitor analysis, e.g. industry structure and trends, direct and indirect competitors and their activities, competing brands and distinctions between them (position map), expectations of competitive activity, assessment of competitors and their brands' strengths, weaknesses and positions 2.3 Organisation analysis, e.g. sales and profits, mission and objectives, strengths and weaknesses 2.4 Product analysis, e.g. product portfolio, branding issues, product market analysis (Ansoff matrix), assessment of brand performances 2.5 Market analysis, e.g. marketing channel issues, customer/consumer analysis, e.g. identification of segments and targets, motivations, brand perceptions, buying habits, etc.
3 Objectives	What the plan should achieve. Objectives should be SMART (see later in this chapter). This section may contain a reiteration of the corporate objectives as well as the overall marketing objectives. Objectives are set for each of the elements of the marketing mix though these may be presented in section 6 below.
4 Target markets	Segmentation, targeting and positioning.
5 Marketing strategies	A broad statement of how the marketing objectives will be achieved. This section builds on the previous section on targeting, which itself is an aspect of the marketing strategy.
6 Marketing programmes	The details of marketing to be undertaken. These are specific activities, schedules, costings and responsibilities. There will be subheadings for each key marketing mix element, for example: 6.1 Product (e.g. details of product portfolio, branding issues, product development, new product launch, etc.) 6.2 Promotion/marketing communications: advertising, sales promotions, public relations, direct marketing, salesforce, other (such as events, merchandising). (Digital marketing may be shown under this subheading or separately – although it is important that all promotional activity is planned together.) These may be organised as push (aimed at trade customers) and pull (aimed at consumers or end users) promotional strategies (see Chapter 8)

(Continued)

Working in digital marketing

Exhibit 12.9   *(Continued)*

Section	Description
	6.3 Place: distribution channels, logistics, etc. (see Chapter 9)
	6.4 Price: e.g. trade pricing, recommended retail pricing, discount arrangements, etc. (see Chapter 10)
	6.5 Service: e.g. after-sales service, installation service; this might also include the remaining 3Ps of the 7Ps
	6.6 Other elements might include issues of brand and corporate identity and image.
7 Resources and financial aspects (budgets)	Statements of required financial budgets and human resources needed. These may have implications for recruitment, possibly upsizing or downsizing the marketing department or other related departments (e.g. customer services department) and salesforce, and for outsourcing, e.g. the use of promotional agencies, call centres, fulfilment companies, research agencies, etc.
8 Implementation controls	Evaluation and assessment of the plan *on an ongoing basis* and *not just* at the end of the plan. Contingencies may be identified at key points if the expected plan outcomes are not being achieved. It is important to consider possible changes to the plan over the period of the plan, rather than waiting to the end before seeing if things have worked. This section would highlight the research and assessment that would be carried out and the metrics (measurements) that would be used. By undertaking evaluation by tracking performance against the plan's objectives, it is possible to adjust the plan and corresponding activities to keep the programmes on track.

marketing metrics
'measurements that help with the quantification of marketing performance, such as market share, advertising spend, and response rates elicited by advertising and direct marketing' (Chartered Institute of Marketing)

never to be repeated activity, but something that successful businesses do on an ongoing basis. Environmental analysis was covered in detail in Chapter 2 where situation analysis was also introduced. Some overview points are restated here to show how and why marketing analysis fits into the marketing management and planning process.

With the advent of sophisticated databases and the growth in readily available marketing research data, there is a wealth of information available to marketers, who are increasingly being required to assess their performance and measure the effectiveness and efficiency of marketing activities. This has been called **marketing metrics**. Marketing is an expense to any organisation – a necessary one, but an expense nonetheless. It is important that measurement systems are in place to analyse the value of marketing and to use those systems to improve marketing performance in the future. This information is fed into the analysis process from the marketing evaluation and control mechanisms that form part of the total marketing planning process. Where extra information is needed, such as other secondary or primary research, this needs to be budgeted for and carried out.

There are a variety of tools and approaches that can be used in marketing analysis. Some of the more important ones are outlined below. You should also re-read Chapter 6, 'Product portfolio management', for further information.

PRESTCOM AND SWOT ANALYSIS

PRESTCOM was first introduced in Chapter 2 as a tool that can be systematically applied to analyse an organisation's internal and external environment. External factors are usually outside the control of an organisation or they may have only limited control over them. Internal factors are completely under the control of the organisation. PRESTCOM is a mnemonic to remind us of the main areas that should be analysed by organisations. It stands for Political, Regulatory, Economic, Social, Technological, Competitor, Organisational and Market factors.

SWOT analysis template

Having identified the key factors impinging on an organisation, a SWOT analysis can then be undertaken to identify which of the factors represent the organisation's strengths and weaknesses as part of the internal environment and which of the factors represent external opportunities and threats to the organisation. Opportunity and threat analysis can be made more meaningful by using opportunity and threat matrices in which the likelihood of the factor occurring and the potential impact it might have can be assessed. For example, if a threat is not likely to occur, or if it does, its impact is assessed as minimal, then this can probably be ignored or relegated as being of low concern. If an opportunity has low-cost implications, is within the capabilities of the organisation and is likely to be very profitable with limited competitive interference, then it might be a good opportunity to pursue. Please re-read Chapter 2 for more details on PRESTCOM and SWOT.

COMPETITOR ANALYSIS

Capability analysis and marketing information systems

It is particularly important to understand how the company's products and brands compare with those of the competition. Competitor analysis is important in determining whether or not the products marketed by a company have a sustainable advantage in the marketplace. This is not something that should be done just once at the launch of a new product or service, but should be undertaken on a continuous basis throughout the life of the brand.

The process of competitor analysis must involve an analysis of the strengths and weaknesses of competitive products/brands and the basic capabilities of the competition. It may involve some form of benchmarking. This is where companies compare themselves to the best-in-class companies in their industry, typically the market leader. The purpose is to identify areas for potential improvement. A useful tool for this is highlighted by Hooley, Piercy and Nicoulaud (2011) (see Exhibit 12.10).

Companies compete in the market using the elements of the marketing mix (the 4Ps or 7Ps). It is important to understand not only how competitors succeed in the market but also how they fail. You can learn from their mistakes just as

competitor analysis
the process of obtaining an in-depth understanding of rival firms and their offerings

benchmarking
a process of systematic analysis and comparison of one company's performance, measured against another's (the industry leader's), in order to improve business performance

marketing mix
(see 4Ps, 7Ps) the basics of marketing plan implementation, usually product, promotion, place, price, sometimes with the addition of packaging; the services marketing mix also includes people, physical evidence and process

Exhibit 12.10

Key Success Factors	Our company	Competitor company
Strong R&D	1 2 3 X 5 6 7 8 9 10	1 2 3 4 5 X 7 8 9 10
Speed of response	1 2 3 4 5 6 7 X 9 10	1 X 3 4 5 6 7 8 9 10
International marketing experience	1 2 X 4 5 6 7 8 9 10	1 2 3 4 5 6 X 8 9 10
Technological capability	1 2 3 4 5 X 7 8 9 10	1 2 3 4 5 X 7 8 9 10
Financial strength	1 2 3 4 5 6 7 8 X 10	1 2 X 4 5 6 7 8 9 10
Strength of management	1 2 3 4 5 6 7 8 X 10	1 2 3 X 5 6 7 8 9 10

well as your own and it is a lot cheaper! This sort of information can be gathered by talking to customers and other industry or market informants. Sources may include commissioned market research; commercially available market information such as Mintel, Target Group Index and retail audits; the press; suppliers; or other competitors with whom you have contact. Very often, companies will attend high-profile conferences and trade exhibitions with a view to gathering competitive intelligence quite openly, although some may engage in underhand corporate espionage (the latter is obviously not ethical or, indeed, recommended). Clearly, the closer you are to market intelligence, the better you will be able to make decisions – third- or fourth-hand data can be twisted out of all recognition, not unlike a game of Chinese whispers, and result in ineffective decision-making.

competitive intelligence information on rivals, their products and environments compared with one's own

Souhami (2003) has argued that companies must stop 'staring at the same information and get the most out of competitor intelligence' and that 'competitive myopia' sets in when companies do not monitor their competitors systematically, which involves continuously gathering up-to-date information.

Strategic and Competitive Intelligence Professionals (SCIP) is a worldwide professional body whose mission it is to raise the profile and recognition of the importance of competitive intelligence (CI), to get more companies involved in it and maintain and encourage ethical practices in CI. From a marketing point of view, it is not easy to distinguish where, or even if, CI differs from marketing information and intelligence. For our purposes here, it is helpful to consider CI as an important part of the total process of marketing intelligence. An approach to systematic gathering and disseminating competitive intelligence, together with other relevant marketing information, is referred to as a marketing information system (MkIS).

A fundamental function of the MkIS is to provide information when it is needed for decision-making. The information needs to be timely, accurate and trustworthy. The MkIS comprises a number of components:

- data collection and storage
- analysis
- reporting.

Data collection and storage

'Internal continuous data', as the name suggests, is data that is gathered continuously, e.g. financial accounts and salesforce records. The phenomenal growth in cheap computing power has revolutionised the process of information gathering, storage and analysis. Customer transaction data is an important part of any marketing intelligence system and there are many commercially available analytic systems to make greatest use of such data and companies willing to provide consultancy and data services to enhance this. 'Internal ad hoc data' is gathered from activities undertaken for specific events within the business, e.g. to see how well a particular promotion has performed. 'Environmental scanning' monitors the business environment (PRESTCOM factors) and 'marketing research', undertaken either continuously or as needed for particular purposes on an ad hoc basis, determines such things as customer attitudes to and opinions on product offerings.

Analysis

Companies gather huge amounts of data and managers need to make sense of it and turn it into useful information from which decisions may be made. Data needs to be distilled and disseminated to the right people at the right time in order for them to make optimum strategic, tactical or operational decisions.

Reporting

Based on the analysis conducted, reports should be produced from the MkIS on a regular basis, meeting the needs of the different marketing managers. Salesforce requirements differ from those of brand managers which differ from those of the marketing director, etc.

The sheer amount of data now available to managers, however, highlights particular management issues. Data was originally managed manually and sometimes with the assistance of press cuttings agencies, which helped companies to gather data. Now, growth in the range of media, facilitated by the development and growth of technologies, has resulted in the development of specialist computer software, e.g. SAS Textminer (**www.sas.co.uk**). This software helps manage the extraction of key information using techniques that the industry frequently refers to as 'data integration management'. The use of such a wide array of data has given rise to the general term database marketing. Such databases are frequently thought of as holding customer data only, but they often hold much more.

Schultz (1997: 10) comments:

> To integrate marketing you must integrate sales and selling, and to integrate those functions, you must integrate the entire organisation ... The goal is to align the organisation to serve consumers and customers. Databases are rapidly becoming the primary management tool that drives the organisation's business strategy.

e-focus: Customer DNA

Marks & Spencer Financial Services (M&S FS) recognised the need to better understand, track and anticipate the behaviour of M&S customers. The influential authors, Peppers and Rogers (1999) asserted that it is critical to know customers in as much detail as possible: 'Not just names and addresses but habits, preferences, and so forth. And not just a snapshot, but across all contact points, through all media, across every product line, at every location and in every division'. So M&S FS set up their 'Customer Intelligence Framework' to cope with the massive amount of data they already had and all the data they were to collect. The process brought together all the data, technology, marketing and business knowledge,

and statistical skills required. The system has a range of tools for customer profiling; recency, frequency and value segmentation; attitudinal, behavioural, lifestage and lifestyle segmentation; customer profitability and lifetime value analysis; predictive modeling; and event modeling and triggering. MRS FS used specialist outside suppliers to help with campaign management and analysis, data collection, data mining and reporting. The result was a set of customer 'DNA' profiles which identified five macro segments which were further divided into 27 micro segments. The database is in continuous use, updating and modifying as circumstances, competitive activities and the business environment change.

Today's databases are very much more than simple customer listings. Computing power has created the ability to store and cross-analyse vast amounts of data, such as service and sales data, purchasing records, and attitudinal and behavioural data. There are many fields of data, covering millions of transactions and relationships. Without this information, it is unlikely that truly integrated marketing can exist. The database is the heart of a marketing intelligence system.

The aim of an efficient and successful MkIS is to turn data into information that, in turn, can be turned into management knowledge from which decisions can be made and action taken. Exhibit 12.11 illustrates an overview of a marketing intelligence system.

ethical focus: Data theft worries US businesses

Many of us think about the problems of having our own personal data stolen but such worries are not confined to individuals, as businesses are worried too. In a survey released at the end of March 2013, more than a quarter of American businesses reported that their propriety data or trade

secrets were stolen from their China operations. More than 40% of the companies in the survey saw the risk of data breach in their China operations rising. Clearly, security is a major concern.

SOURCE: Tejada, 2013.

Exhibit 12.11   Marketing information/intelligence system

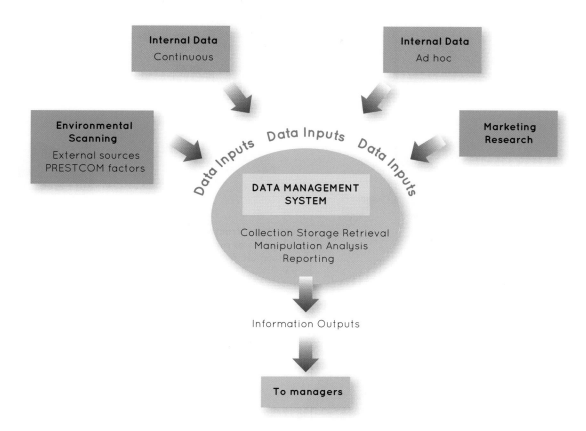

PORTER'S FIVE FORCES MODEL

Porter's five forces model (Porter, 1985) is a useful tool for analysing competitive activity by helping firms determine the strength of competitive threats. This model enables businesses to analyse their competitive environment by focusing particularly on the competition and who has the bargaining power in the supply chain. Assessment can be made of the intensity of competition and the threat of new competitive entrants, the threat of substitute products, and the bargaining power of suppliers and customers (see Exhibit 12.12).

Porter's five forces model
a competitive environment analysis tool

Rolls Royce

Exhibit 12.12   Porter's five forces model

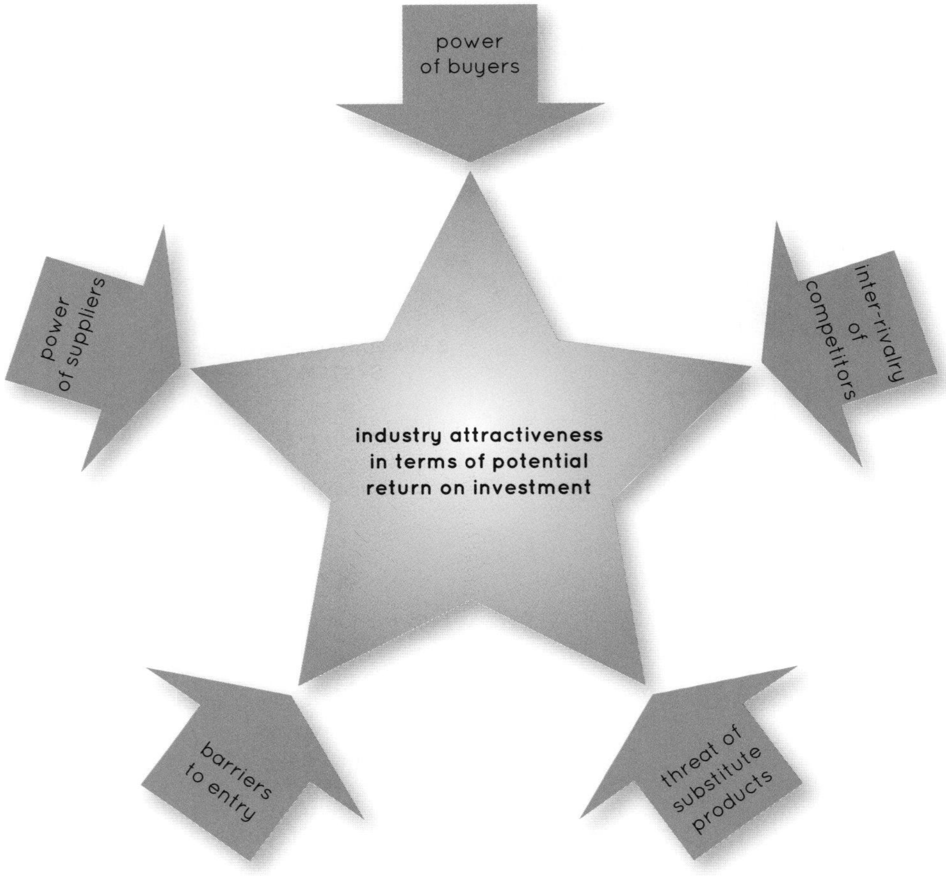

Threat of new entrants

An organisation needs to monitor the activities of potential competitors as well as existing competitors. The lower the market's **barriers to entry**, the more likely it is that these potential rivals will become actual rivals.

Barriers to entry include:

barriers to entry things that make it difficult, or impossible, for new competitors to enter a market, e.g. patents, high set-up costs

- the costs of producing/providing for the marketplace; there may be the requirement for high capital outlay – perhaps to buy expensive production machinery, e.g. the nuclear power industry
- existing powerful brand names within the market, e.g. new entrants into the chocolate market would have to compete with Nestlé, Cadbury's, Mars, Suchard, etc.
- the size of the market – it may be too small to support any more competitors, e.g. a local high street may already have two good bakeries
- legal/regulatory barriers, e.g. a licence may be required to trade (selling alcohol, running a casino); foreign firms are often banned from owning businesses in

key sectors such as defence or the media. Patents are another means by which firms keep out potential rivals

- existing companies that control key resources, e.g. ownership or access to distribution chains or raw materials supplies
- existing companies that are large enough to benefit from economies of scale and therefore have lower cost bases than any new entrant would; this would mean that a new rival would be unable to match their prices without making a loss
- competitor reactions, e.g. fear or concern that competitors may react in ways either singularly or collectively that would make it difficult to enter a market successfully.

Threat of substitutes

The more alternative products and services there are, the harder it will be to maintain a competitive advantage and to make a good profit. For example, when crossing the channel, ferries and planes are substitutes for the Eurostar and Eurotunnel Le Shuttle. The threat of substitutes may be determined by:

- the pricing of substitute products and, therefore, the sensitivity of customers to pricing
- the costs of the customer switching to a competitive product – if these are low, the risk of substitution is higher
- whether customers have a high propensity to substitute or, in other words, customers have low loyalty levels.

Bargaining power of buyers (customers)

Customers will be powerful if, as individuals or buying groups, they are more important to the suppliers than the suppliers are to them. Major grocery retailers such as Tesco and Asda Wal-Mart are able to dictate terms to most of their suppliers because of the bulk of groceries that are sold through their stores. Manufacturers such as Kellogg's and Nestlé have to be seen on these supermarket giants' shelves. Smaller manufacturers actively compete for the supermarkets' shelf space. This has led to pressure on prices and, in some cases, insistence upon manufacturer-funded special offers such as BOGOFs (buy one get one free). Customers (buyers) are powerful when:

- there are few major buyers in the marketplace
- products are commoditised or standardised, i.e. there is little or no differentiation from the customer's perspective
- the company is not a key supplier to the customer and the customer holds the balance of power.

Bargaining power of suppliers

If raw materials or ingredients are scarce, then their suppliers can dictate terms. For example, after a bad coffee bean harvest, the price of coffee rose sharply in the shops (though little of this money went to the smaller coffee growers). Suppliers can redress the balance of power with retailers by developing strong **brands**. It would be a brave supermarket that refused to put Heinz baked beans on its UK shelves. **Market leaders** have a distinct advantage. Suppliers are powerful when:

brand
'the intangible sum of a product's attributes: its name, packaging, and price, its history, its reputation, and the way it's advertised' (David Ogilvy)

market leader
the company with the highest sales within a market (also sometimes used to refer to a groundbreaking firm that others follow)

- there are few other sources of supply for the company
- the suppliers threaten to integrate along the supply chain, in effect becoming a direct competitor to the company
- the costs of switching to other suppliers is great; suppliers have been known to tie in their customers through financial pressure by extending credit terms so that companies they supply become dependent on such extended terms to help manage cash flow
- the company's business is not key to the supplier.

Intensity of rivalry of competitors

Just as some people are more competitive than others, so are some companies. Markets such as grocery retailing and fashion are highly competitive. In the first case, this is shown in price wars and intense **below the line activity**. In the second case, it is apparent in high advertising spend. Just how intensely firms compete with each other depends on a number of factors, one of which is the market growth rate. In a growing market, there is more business available for everyone and so firms do not need to steal each other's market share in order to make more sales. The intensity of rivalry between competitors may depend on:

- the number of competitors in the market – the more there are, the more intense the competitive activity
- the cost structure – high capital investment may actually result in lower unit costs because management will want to ensure that its machinery operates at optimum capacity rather than laying idle, waiting for orders
- the differential advantages between products and brands, i.e. those brands perceived by customers to be differentiated are less likely to attract competitive activity
- the costs involved in customers switching to competing products – if these are high, then customers are less likely to switch, negating the need for such intense rivalry
- the strategic objectives being pursued by the competitors – if a competitor is holding or harvesting its products, then it is not as concerned with highly competitive behaviour
- the exit barriers, i.e. if these are high, then more competition will be encouraged to stay in the market, resulting in highly active competitive behaviour as they try to gain market share.

If a company is to develop a **competitive edge**, then it must understand its competitors' strengths and weaknesses. An in-depth, up-to-date analysis of the competitive environment is the basis of any sound competitive strategy.

below the line
non-commission-paying promotion, typically all forms except advertising

competitive advantage or competitive edge
something about an organisation or its products that is perceived as being better than rival offerings

ACTIVITY

Imagine you are the manager of your favourite football team. Apply Porter's five forces model to identify who has the greatest power in your market. Consider:

- who potential entrants into your market could be
- who the competition is and how competitive the game is
- who could be a substitute for your team
- who your suppliers are, what they supply to you and how important they are
- who your customers are, what they buy from you and how important they are to you and your team.

EXPAND YOUR KNOWLEDGE

Classic article

Porter, M. (1980) 'Industry structure and competitive strategy: keys to profitability', *Financial Analysis*, 36 (4): 30–41.

Michael Porter's name is synonymous with competitive analysis and strategy. Here is an early paper in which he highlights the need to understand the competitive environment and outlines the key forces that drive industry competition.

BUSINESS MISSION AND MARKETING OBJECTIVES

Just as you set out on your studies to obtain a higher qualification, such as a degree or diploma, in order to become, perhaps, a marketing management expert, successful advertising executive or an entrepreneur, so a business will set out to achieve some broad aims. A business mission, or vision as it is sometimes called, is an explicit statement that captures the broad aims of the company. This is used to communicate those broad aims to all its stakeholders, both internal and external. Its purpose, ideally, is to provide an inspirational focus or strategic and operational direction for the whole company. Preferably, it should not be 'a long awkward sentence that demonstrates management's inability to think clearly', a criticism laid by Dilbert, one of the greatest cartoon characters who ever poked fun at business and management.

There are a number of general components to a good business mission statement. It should:

- identify the company's philosophy, i.e. its approach to business
- specify its product–market domain, i.e. where the company will operate in the marketplace
- communicate key values for those involved, i.e. how it will operate
- be closely linked to critical success factors, i.e. the things the company has to be good at to survive.

business mission the broad aims a business hopes to achieve

Kellogg's aims and objectives

ACTIVITY

Your mission

McDonald's mission statement is:

'McDonald's vision is to be the world's best quick service restaurant experience. Being the best means providing outstanding quality, service, cleanliness, and value, so that we make every customer in every restaurant smile.'

How well does this measure up to the criteria for a good mission statement given in this chapter?

- What is McDonald's philosophy, i.e. its approach to business?

- What is McDonald's product–market domain, i.e. where does it operate in the marketplace, what position does it hold?

- What are McDonald's key values, i.e. how it will operate?

- Can you identify **critical success factors** for McDonald's, i.e. the things the company has to be good at to survive – how does this mission statement relate to those? What clues does it give to the critical success factors?

critical success factors
things that the success of an organisation or activity depend upon; they must happen or the objectives will not be met

According to Levitt (1960), who is responsible for having created the concept of the business mission, in order to develop an appropriate mission a company's managers should ask some basic questions: 'What business are we in?', 'What business should we be in?' and 'What business can we be in?' The answers should be given in terms of customer needs, rather than the products the company makes (and are, therefore, another good indicator of market orientation). See the examples in Exhibit 12.13.

Exhibit 12.13   Defining the business from the customer's perspective

Traditional definition of business	Customer need-based definition of business
Electricity	Power/Energy/Heat/Light
Train travel	Transportation
Cinema	Entertainment
Computers	Information processing
Telephones	Communications

This type of approach enables a company to identify much broader-based competition and think about how it could be more competitive and avoid 'marketing myopia' (Levitt, 1960). Marketing myopia is where a company forgets that a customer wants a product to solve a problem. The classic example highlighted by Levitt is a drill – he states that the customer actually wants the holes it makes. This can be taken further, however, because in fact customers do not usually want holes in walls, they want hooks for pictures or brackets for shelves.

Thinking about products, in this way gives the company greater scope in its development of new products as well as highlighting the full range of products that may be competing for its customers. The process of identifying what business it is in, and could be in, will enable a company to develop an appropriate business mission. Having decided on a business mission, a company will use this to inform and develop its business and marketing objectives from which it will decide on specific strategies.

Objectives should conform to three basic conventions (Walker et al., 2003):

- What performance dimensions should the company and employees focus on?
- What is the target level of performance for each of these dimensions?
- What is the time frame in which the targets should be achieved?

Different organisations are trying to achieve different things. However, there are some things that most hope to achieve, for example:

- Survival
- Profits (however, not-for-profit organisations, such as charities or hospitals, might more usually refer to revenue and surpluses)
- A good reputation
- Competitive edge.

Everyone within the organisation is expected to work together to meet these objectives and each business function will set its own objectives which are designed to help meet the overall corporate ones.

Typical marketing objectives include:

- a move into a new market (perhaps another country)
- the launch of a new product
- an increase in sales volume (i.e. quantity of goods sold)
- an increase in market share
- the acquisition of another brand.

Objectives are things that the organisation wants. Businesses then organise their resources (money, people, machinery, etc.) to achieve or acquire those things that they want, i.e. to meet their objectives. Marketing objectives should be SMART:

Specific	clearly worded and directed at specific markets and/or audiences
Measurable	it will be clear that the objective really has been achieved; this normally means that it will be quantifiable, e.g. a percentage or absolute amount to be gained
Achievable	possible to do
Relevant	of value to the organisation and in keeping with other objectives; also objectives should always be challenging enough to act as motivators
Timed	with a deadline.

Objectives are not general across markets or even the whole of one market but directed at specific market segments (see Chapter 4).

So an example of a SMART objective might be to increase sales revenue from the pet food division (specific) by 10% (measurable) by 31 December 2012 (timed). This objective could be relevant if the company was seeking to grow, and achievable if it has the resources (money, people, facilities) to put behind the sales drive. (For more on marketing objectives, see Chapter 11.)

A well-designed marketing mix will:

- achieve marketing objectives
- meet customers' needs
- create competitive advantage
- be well integrated (each element supporting the others)
- fit within the available marketing resources.

The next section will look at setting strategies to achieve the organisation's objectives.

Phillip Kotler talking at the LBS

MARKETING STRATEGY

With a clear picture of the business environment and of the objectives it wishes to achieve, the company can now decide how it is going to take its business forward into the next trading period. It can think about this in terms of shorter or longer time periods. It is often much easier for managers to make decisions for the short term because they will have more detailed and accurate information about the marketplace. There are a number of ways of thinking about possible strategies. **Porter's Generic Strategies**, **Ansoff's Matrix** and Push/Pull Strategies are discussed below. Chapter 11 also highlighted branding strategies and Chapter 6 covered aspects of product portfolio management – the Boston Consulting Group Matrix and the GE-McKinsey Matrix, product development and the product life cycle, all of which should be re-read to more fully appreciate the factors affecting marketing strategy decisions.

Long-term decisions require managers to see into the future. Longer-term success is about being visionary, reading the market, knowing the business well and, sometimes, getting lucky. Even Marks & Spencer's experienced managers have not been able to do this with complete accuracy or total success in the past decade or so and have faced some very difficult times. From a peak in the late 1990s when M&S were reported to be the first British retailer to make pre-tax profits of over £1 billion from their combined international operations, they then immediately went through a period of major crisis which lasted several years. At one point they closed all of their European stores outside the UK and Ireland (although some were re-opened shortly afterwards). However, since that time they have carried out a complete review of their business and hope to make a successful turnaround to become, once again, a leading international clothing and food retailer. The next paragraphs look at how some marketing management tools can be utilised to develop strategic direction for the business (Johnson et al., 2011). It is the choice of strategic direction that provides focus for the company's longer-term continuation.

Porter's generic strategies three main competitive strategies: cost leadership, differentiation or focus

Ansoff's matrix comprises four possible growth strategies: market development, product development, market penetration/expansion and diversification

Exhibit 12.14   Generic competitive strategies

```
                        ╭──────────╮
                        │ generic  │
                        │ strategy │
                        ╰──────────╯
                       ╱            ╲
              ┌───────────────┐   ┌───────────────┐
              │ broad segments│   │     niche     │
              └───────────────┘   └───────────────┘
               ╱           ╲       ╱           ╲
    ┌──────────────┐  ┌──────────────┐  ┌──────────────┐  ┌──────────────┐
    │cost leadership│ │differentiation│ │cost leadership│ │differentiation│
    └──────────────┘  └──────────────┘  └──────────────┘  └──────────────┘
                stuck in                         stuck in
               the middle                       the middle
```

SOURCE: Porter, 1985

PORTER'S GENERIC STRATEGIES

Porter's generic strategies is one model that provides an overview of strategic direction for the company (see Exhibit 12.14).

It highlights that the company can pursue one of three main competitive strategic directions based on its identification of competitive forces and view of the market:

- mass (broad segments) or niche – does the company concentrate on one segment or try to serve many?
- differentiation, where the company chooses to differentiate itself based on some competitive advantage it has identified, e.g. brand or service offering
- cost leadership, where the company is able to offer low prices thanks to its low production costs.

If the company ignores these choices, or attempts to pursue two simultaneously, Porter argues that it could be in danger of being stuck in the middle, i.e. where it has no clear direction and merely reacts to market conditions, therefore making it vulnerable to competitors.

ANSOFF'S MATRIX

Ansoff's matrix (Ansoff, 1957) is another tool managers can use to help determine their strategic direction (see Exhibit 12.15). It is also known as the Ansoff growth matrix because it focuses on the ways companies can grow through increased sales opportunities. It looks at the product in relation to its market and helps managers to identify their potential business opportunities. The matrix is one of

Ansoff's Matrix

Exhibit 12.15   Ansoff's matrix

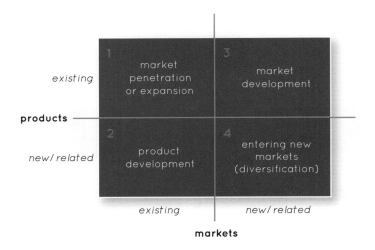

the best-known strategic tools as, despite its simplicity, it is a very powerful way of looking at strategic options. The two-by-two matrix first defined by Ansoff can be made more sophisticated, and other authors have expanded the matrix into a three-by-three matrix that includes categories for modified products and modified markets. The quadrants defined by Ansoff are identified as having different levels of business risk associated with them. In so far as the top-left quadrant is best understood and experienced by the company, it is said to carry the least risk for growth. However, if this proves to be a highly competitive market that is stagnant or declining, and if the company has limited power in the market, this level of risk might become significantly higher and the company might be wise to move into other areas. The top-right and bottom-left quadrants are said to carry greater risk and the bottom-right quadrant carries the greatest risk to the company in that diversification with new products in new markets represents new and uncharted territory in which the company has the least or even no experience.

EXPAND YOUR KNOWLEDGE

Classic article

Ansoff, I. (1957) 'Strategies for diversification', *Harvard Business Review*, 35 (5): 113–24.

Igor Ansoff has had a profound effect on our understanding of business strategies and was one of the early writers on the subject. In this article, he explores the strategies that relate to different diversification approaches.

Quadrant 1: existing products in existing markets – market penetration strategy. This is about focusing effort in existing markets and encouraging existing customers to use the product more (more at each use, or more frequently, or use competing products less). This quadrant emphasises strategies to develop sales from existing customers.

Quadrant 2: new or related products for existing markets – product development strategy. Involves some element of product development or improvement for existing customers. Car manufacturers are continually striving to improve their products, e.g. the Ford Escort has been replaced by the Ford Focus. This quadrant emphasises strategies to gain sales through product development or new products that are marketed to existing target customers (whether they are actual current customers or other potential customers in the target market(s) in which the company currently operates).

Quadrant 3: existing products in new or related markets – market development strategy. This is about finding new uses for products or launching into new markets, e.g. different geographic areas of the world or different market segments. Lucozade was originally a drink for recuperating children, but when the company found that mothers were using it as a 'pick-me-up' during the day, it decided to relaunch the product. It is now firmly established as a 'sports' drink (albeit with a new formulation). This quadrant emphasises strategies related to marketing to newly defined target markets.

Quadrant 4: new or related products in new markets – diversification strategy. Taking new products into new markets is the hardest of the four directions from a company's perspective. This is because it involves moving into an area of business with which it is unfamiliar and, as a result, the risks of potential failure are high. The strategy works best when there is a close match with existing experiences. This quadrant emphasises strategies in which both product development and market development are combined and the consequential diversification can take many forms.

global focus: The Body Shop: a global niche

Some niches are too small to sustain a business in one country alone. Others do not have the desired growth potential, making a focus strategy, i.e. a concentration on a core market segment, difficult. However, they may be viable if multiple countries are taken into account. For example, in order to expand, The Body Shop has spread across the globe.

The means by which a company chooses to adopt any of Ansoff's alternative strategic directions depend on how much the company wishes to control the activities related to the marketing of its products. Such expansion can be achieved through internal development or in unison with other companies through vertical or horizontal integration, which form different types of strategic alliance. Options include the following:

- **A network** – this is a loose association between a company and, for example, a series of distributors, such as pursued by many car manufacturers who sell through a range of different types of outlet. It can also be a network of agents, which is a strategy pursued by some companies when they enter an unfamiliar market or a new country. With a network, the company may have relatively little control over how the third party markets the products to end-users, or how end-users (consumers) are treated.
- **A contract or licence agreement** – here the company imposes conditions on the third party it uses to service its end-user needs. A contract or licence agreement may restrict the marketing operations to specifically those developed by the originating company. This is a strategy pursued by McDonald's. As franchisor, they specify everything from outlet layout to the disposable packaging used by franchisees, and even the training received by counter and waiting staff.
- **A consortium or joint venture** – where two or more companies agree to develop joint operations on a contractual basis. This may be used by companies entering new markets or countries, and enables them to maximise their potential by taking on local working practices. This may also be a situation whereby companies remain focused on their core business but, through utilisation of each partner's specialisms, they develop a new or better product offering for the end-user.
- **An acquisition or merger** – ultimately, complete control of the supply chain is achieved through this route. It does, however, necessitate the company to be cash rich or, at least, able to raise sufficient capital to invest and continue generating a profit. A number of companies have pursued this strategy in order to gain market share only to sell off their purchase at a later date, when they have been unable to realise the expected returns (e.g. EMAP Publications' procurement and then sale of a series of local FM radio stations during the 1980s and 1990s). Of course, the reason for a procurement or merger may be because a firm wants only a part of another company to add to existing operations, such as a brand name, or to achieve economies of scale by focusing on what each are good at, e.g. 3i's Go airline and easyJet merger in August 2002, whereby they have agreed both will use the easyJet flight booking system, among other things.

MOVING INTO OVERSEAS MARKETS

Why do firms trade internationally rather than stick with their familiar home markets? Most commonly, it is as part of a growth strategy. They want to increase sales.

The firm may want to market a wider range of products but has discovered that there is insufficient demand to support this in its home market, or it may be that the converse is true and the firm wishes to specialise in a narrower range of products. Either way, they will need a larger market for those products if they are to maintain sales revenue.

Apart from growth, there are a number of other good reasons for selling products internationally, including:

- as part of a competitive strategy
- risk spreading
- globalisation of markets

- excess capacity
- to extend the product life cycle.

Competitive strategy

Firms may trade abroad because competition has got too hot in their home market and they are looking for an easier market in which to trade. Alternatively, they may be trying to frighten off a new foreign competitor by keeping them busy back home. Internationalisation may be part of either a cost leadership or a focus strategy (see Porter's generic strategies above). Increasing sales is one way to increase profits, but the alternative (or complementary) way is through reducing costs. This can be achieved through the economies of scale that come from dealing in larger volumes of goods – volumes that the international marketplace can deliver. These cost savings can then be passed on to all customers as lower prices.

Risk spreading

Some firms trade in multiple markets in order to reduce risk through geographical diversification. The hope is that although some markets may suffer downturns, the others will make up for it. Unfortunately, as world trade becomes more and more globalised, and trading blocs such as the European Union emerge, the economies of countries are more closely linked and they have a greater tendency to move together. It still remains the case, though, that risk may be spread by marketing a range of products in multiple markets.

Globalisation

One of the upsides of globalisation is that as markets become more similar, and more open to foreign products, it becomes easier to compete globally. It may even be necessary to trade internationally in order to maintain a reputation as a serious competitor.

Excess capacity

If demand is falling, or new technology has made a product easier to produce, or there have been significant productivity gains, then a company may have more products than it can sell. It will either have to downsize (produce less) or find new markets for its products – quite possibly overseas markets.

Extending the product life cycle

Moving to a new, foreign market, is a traditional method of extending a product's life cycle. Car manufacturers used to employ this strategy, selling their old models to third-world countries when their home markets no longer wanted them. With the increase in international communications, this has become harder to do. Consumers the world over see the latest products and styles on television and the Internet. It is harder to fob them off with old products.

Market selection criteria

International marketing managers are constantly screening the international environment looking for threats and opportunities. These often present themselves in the form of new geographic markets for their products. They must select the most promising markets to trade in and reject the rest. They need to consider both the market generally and their own firm's potential within it. Management should set minimum acceptable levels for sales, profit, market share, and then analyse the potential of the new market to assess the likelihood of achieving those levels. This is called market screening. It requires managers to ask the following questions:

- How does the market's potential for profit, sales, market share compare to the company's expectations from an overseas market?
- Does the country have an acceptable legal system (e.g. patent laws)?
- Is the market accessible?
- Is there a suitable marketing infrastructure (e.g. distributors, retailers, agencies)?
- Do existing competitors have too strong a hold on the market?
- Is the level of risk acceptable?

The assessment of political risk is especially important when considering whether to start trading in another country. Some countries have unstable governments that may be able to exercise powers that other governments would not. Economic instability and changing exchange rates are also factors that introduce potential risk.

If the country passes the screening, then the company will then want to assess its own chances of success in that market:

- How much experience does the company have in similar markets and how well has it done there?
- Are there matches in terms of language and other cultural factors?
- Are there opportunities for standardisation?

The answers to these questions, and others like them, will determine whether the new market is likely to be a success.

International strategy: standardisation vs. adaptation

A critical question in international marketing is whether to standardise your offerings worldwide or to adapt them to local needs. Remembering that the marketing philosophy is about satisfying customer needs and wants, it would seem that the best strategy would be to adapt to meet local needs. So if the Spanish want batter mix in smaller pack sizes, with less sugar and all the instructions in Spanish only – so be it. The snag with this approach is that it is expensive.

This is not just about products themselves. It is almost always cheaper to do things the same way everywhere. Promotion is cheaper if you can make one advert for the world; use the same prize draw, the same media. Distribution can be handled more effectively if a company can use the same retailers, the same logistics.

Standardisation is not just about costs. It also fits with a strategy of marketing integration – the philosophy behind which is that if we standardise, then our offering sends the same message the world over, reinforcing the desired positioning and avoiding conflict and confusion. However, most product offerings are difficult to standardise across multiple countries and consequently very few truly global (i.e. standardised) products exist. There are, however, an increasing number of global brands.

Pantene
Pro V
International
Ads

Reasons to standardise internationally

- economies of scale
- the Internet and other technologies have bridged culture and language gaps

- globalised communications media mean that people across the world get the same information and are exposed to the same influences
- some products have no cultural sensitivity – the main barrier to standardisation is national culture but some products really have no cultural values associated with them, e.g. paper clips, raw materials, computer mice
- there are market segments that exist across international boundaries, e.g. the youth market
- members of trading blocs, such as ASEAN, are growing more similar. It would be a big mistake to assume that the citizens of such blocs are all the same though. EU countries, for example, are enormously culturally varied.

Reasons to adapt

- different cultures
- different income levels – this affects product design (number of features, quality of materials) as well as pricing
- different market infrastructure – e.g. different competitors, different types of distribution systems
- different climate – think about clothing, for instance, or duvets
- different legal requirements and regulations
- availability and level of local skills – can a complex product be supported properly?
- differing uses – will a product be used every day or occasionally? By one person or by many? For example, bicycles may be everyday transport (in China) or recreational (USA) or either (UK)
- brand history – sometimes a product is held dear by its customers and is hard to change, e.g. Coca-Cola still markets Thums Up in India though nowhere else. In Europe, Mars sells the Mars bar while in the USA this product is called a Milky Way. Milky Ways can also be bought in Europe, but they, of course, have a different recipe to the US ones.

The above lists are not exhaustive but present the most common arguments on both sides of the standardisation versus adaptation debate. Particular markets or products may have special reasons for choosing one strategy or the other.

EXPAND YOUR KNOWLEDGE

Melewar, T.C., Pickton, D., Gupta, S. and Chigovanyika, T. (2009) 'MNE executive insights into international advertising programme standardisation', *Journal of Marketing Communications,* 15 (5): 345–65.

While the standardisation versus adaptation debate has long raged with expressions of the pros and cons of both approaches, this article sought to identify through in-depth interviews the factors that influence actual executive decisions as determined by experienced and practising international marketing executives themselves and what factors they rated as important in their own businesses. Three areas of standardisation or adaptation were considered: advertising theme, creative expression and media mix.

PUSH AND PULL STRATEGIES

If a company sells its goods or provides its services through third parties (intermediaries), then it needs to consider the roles of push strategies and pull strategies. One of the most significant yet basic strategic marketing decisions centres around the determination of push and pull strategies. These strategies are concerned with the marketing efforts focused towards trade/channel intermediaries (push strategies) and the final customers and consumers, and the decision influencers that affect them (pull strategies). These strategies are also known as 'selling into the pipeline' and 'selling out of the pipeline', referring to push and pull strategies respectively. The 'pipeline' is the channels that facilitate the movement of goods and services through intermediaries (retailers, wholesalers, agents, brokers, etc.). Wherever intermediaries are involved, *both* push and pull strategies should be used in an integrated fashion. To develop one strategy without consideration of the other can result in higher risks of failure.

Push strategies encourage the trade to carry and promote products. They help to achieve distribution coverage, create trade goodwill and partnership. Pull strategies encourage products to be demanded. A combination of push and pull provides a greater synergistic effect than can be achieved in the use of either strategy alone. Often joint promotions between channel members and manufacturers are undertaken to enhance trade partnership and improve pull promotions. Chapter 8 has more details about the promotional aspects of push/pull strategies.

---

 b2b focus: Trade customers for consumer goods

b2c and b2b companies are often treated as though they operate under completely different circumstances. While the balance of their marketing mixes may vary, b2c and b2b companies have a lot in common. FMCG companies are actually amongst the biggest players in b2b marketing. Although their products are targeted towards consumers, their marketing activities have to cover trade customers as well. Push strategies feature strongly in their marketing – although they may seem a lot less exciting than the consumer-focused promotions.

Likewise, b2b companies whose products may never be seen by the majority of consumers, can embark on elaborate pull strategies. In computing, Intel, with its Pentium, Celeron and Core processors, and in textiles, Dupont, with its Lycra fabric, are good examples. Both these companies have heavily branded their products and these are recognised in households throughout the world, yet they have never themselves sold a single product to consumers.

COMPETITIVE STANCE

The company needs to determine the position it wants in the marketplace, based on its assessment of the attractiveness of different market segments relative to business strengths. The company may aim to be:

- a leader
- a challenger
- a follower
- a nicher.

Clearly, these positions will necessitate particular approaches to the market. For example, it would be anticipated that market leader or challenger positions will require aggressive defence or attacking behaviour, actively choosing to engage in pricing or promotional wars. As Ries and Trout (1986) in their marketing warfare book contend, it is far easier to stay on top than to get there. There are clear advantages in being a market leader, however some companies are content not to be in the firing line. A market follower takes a background position, while a market nicher focuses only on a small part of the overall market, thus avoiding direct attention or confrontation with the larger market leaders and challengers. Analogies between war and marketing have been extremely popular and strategic approaches to marketing based on military analogies for attacking and defending against opponents have been developed. See the article below by Kotler and Singh on marketing warfare for further details.

EXPAND YOUR KNOWLEDGE

Classic article

Kotler, P. and Singh, R. (1981) 'Marketing warfare', *Journal of Business Strategy*, 1 (Winter): 30–41.

The analogy of war and military is used here to identify a range of strategic options available to firms from various forms of attack to various forms of defence.

While the application of marketing management tools helps the company to develop its strategic focus, by providing the detail behind the business objectives and strategies, these strategies then need to be operationalised. The next section looks at marketing operations and implementation in more detail.

MARKETING OPERATIONS AND IMPLEMENTATION: TACTICS, RESOURCES AND ACTION

Operational and implementation decisions necessitate the blending of different elements of the company in order to achieve its goals. In other words, they make the goals happen. (This is still part of the 'How are we going to get there?' question.) The broad strategic decisions need to be turned into actual tactics and operational plans. The elements of the marketing mix form the basis of marketing tactics. Decisions have to be made about the specifics of pricing, **marketing communications**, distribution and the product, together with issues of service delivery.

marketing communications another name for promotion; communication designed and implemented to persuade others to do, think or feel something

Resources and timing need to be carefully considered. One way of considering the resource requirements is the 3Ms approach that was first suggested by Smith, Berry and Pulford (1997). The 3Ms stand for:

* money
* men
* minutes.

MONEY

Money refers to budgeting for the plan – the financial requirements needed to put the marketing plan into action. Various methods may be used to set the budget (see Chapter 8) and this may be done as part of the top-down or bottom-up approach referred to at the beginning of this chapter.

The budget is critical in determining what marketing activities can be afforded and also in assessing the overall contribution that marketing has made to the firm. Unless there are some particular and exceptional circumstances, companies expect the returns from marketing to exceed the expenditure so that marketing has made a positive financial contribution to the business. In practice, many related marketing costs may be hidden or placed in other budgets. For example, customer services may be part of a separate department and budgeted separately. Corporate branding, signage, livery and stationery may be a separate budget, PR and publicity may be separated from marketing, and so on. As a consequence, it is not necessarily easy to fully assess marketing contribution.

MEN

This element of the resources relates to the human resources (men and women) required by the plan, not only in terms of numbers of staff, but also their skills and experience and how they are to be organised. The marketing department may need extra staff, more sales staff may be needed, the staffing may need to be restructured, a new call centre may need to be set up, new agencies appointed, and so on. Consideration needs to be given to the extent to which in-house staffing will undertake the marketing activities versus outsourcing.

EXPAND YOUR KNOWLEDGE

Ngo, L.V. and O'Cass, A. (2012) 'Performance implications of market orientation, marketing resources, and marketing capabilities', *Journal of Marketing Management*, 28 (1–2): 173–87.

This paper examines how market orientation, marketing resources and marketing capabilities contribute to a firm's performance. The results show that being market orientated influences the level of marketing resources firms possess and the capability to deploy such resources. The findings show marketing resources and marketing capabilities are significant drivers of a firm's performance, and their impact is greater when they are complementary to each other.

MINUTES

Minutes are to do with the timescale of the plan, the scheduling of activities and the time for tasks to be completed.

CONTINGENCY PLANS

Analysing the market is not just a means to facilitate strategic choice; it also helps to plan for an uncertain future. The theory, of course, is that by analysing the past, one can extrapolate forward. Consider what happens if there is a recession, a war, a new unknown competitor, a new alliance between two firms that wish to steal your market share, a takeover bid for your main customer, further **market fragmentation**, a new form of telepathic media developed, obviating the need for advertising, Internet meltdown, an increase in average life expectancy to 145 years. Clearly, some of these are more likely to happen than others, so events can be ranked by probability of their occurrence and their potential impact on the business. This can be part of the opportunities and threats analysis.

Although marketing research (see Chapter 5) provides good clues as to the nature of the problems that may arise in a market, there is always room for the unexpected. Piercy (2009) coined the term **market sensing**, which is the need for an understanding of the market rather than merely knowledge of it. Understanding is about synthesised knowledge – you may know a lot, but how well do you understand it? Piercy produced a framework to help managers categorise the potential series of events that may impact on their business (see Exhibit 12.16).

market fragmentation
a market characterised by a large number of relatively small players, none of which has significant competitive advantage

market sensing
the need for an understanding of the market, rather than merely a knowledge of it

Exhibit 12.16   Piercy's framework for market sensing

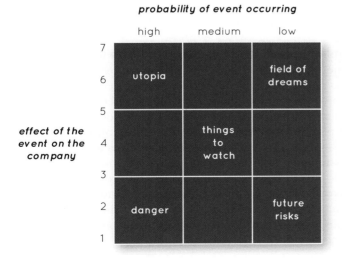

1 = disaster; 2 = very bad; 3 = bad; 4 = neutral; 5 = good; 6 = very good; 7 = ideal

SOURCE: Piercy, 2009: 256.

The purpose, of course, in identifying potential problems is for the company to prepare itself to take some action, referred to as contingency planning (which may be called crisis management in another guise), i.e. plan B through to plan F, etc. should the possible change in outcome apply. In this way, the company is not left wondering what to do and can take the new course of action quickly. It is, however, not possible to develop a great number of options as they will take as much time and effort to develop as 'plan A', but it is prudent to have some rudimentary ideas that can be picked up in a timely manner should things go wrong. The implementation of contingency plans can only be made possible provided there is continuing **environmental scanning**, attention paid to competitor activity and the monitoring of your own plan as it is put into action. This involves tracking of performance and evaluation of the final outcomes at the end of the planned period and this is all part of the next stage of the marketing management and planning process – marketing evaluation and control.

environmental scanning
monitoring the forces that influence the organisation in order to identify changes that may affect performance

EXPAND YOUR KNOWLEDGE

Classic article

Buzzell, R.D., Gale, B.T. and Sultan, R.G.M. (1975) 'Market share: a key to profitability', *Harvard Business Review*, 53 (Jan.–Feb.): 97–106.

This classic article builds on the findings of the extensive PIMS project (Profit Impact of Market Strategies) and highlights the significance and impact of market share on profitability and return on investment. The paper explores the reasons for these links.

MARKETING EVALUATION AND CONTROL

Evaluation and control of marketing activities amount to an understanding of how well the business is performing given the decisions made by its marketing managers. They address two of our strategic questions: 'Are we getting there?' and 'Have we arrived?' This involves ongoing tracking over the period of the implementation of the plan and a final evaluation at the end of the period. Tracking facilitates modifications to the planned activities and, perhaps, the implementation of contingency plans, as described above. If necessary, objectives and strategies can be amended (in more extreme circumstances), as can tactics and operations. The final evaluation is fed back into the next planning cycle. The process requires analysis of the variance between planned (target or budgeted) and actual performance across the range of activities that are affected by the decisions made. It may also, and indeed often does, take into account how well the company has performed in comparison to its competitors, especially the industry leaders. Effective evaluation and control therefore result in successful adjustments to activities in order to

Exhibit 12.17   Marketing evaluation and control process

SOURCE: Chartered Institute of Marketing, 2002.

achieve the intended objectives. Exhibit 12.17 provides a summary of the evaluation and control process.

While it is clearly important to measure the extent to which the desired outcomes are being achieved, or have been achieved, it is also necessary to assess the efficiency and effectiveness of the marketing effort. It should not be the aim to achieve outcomes no matter what the cost. Marketing activities should always be carried out without wasting effort or resources. It is said that efficiency is about doing things right whereas effectiveness is about doing the right things, and both are important. The sort of questions that should be asked include:

- What was expected to happen?
- What did happen?
- What was the effect of each of the marketing elements as well as their collective effect? Can these effects be separated from other factors? That is, are we sure that the results were due to our specific marketing efforts?
- What were the reasons for success or failure?
- What was learned from the plan?
- What does this tell us that we can apply to the next planning period?

The range of evaluation and control mechanisms is vast. The following are just a few examples:

- profitability analysis
- production analysis
- sales analysis
- customer service analysis
- benchmarking and competitor analysis.

All elements of the product offering and the marketing plan can, and should, be examined. Marketing metrics highlight the need to measure and assess all possible aspects of marketing that can be measured. The level and quantity of detail can be extensive. Measurements will include the following and a great deal more.

Exhibit 12.18   Elements of evaluation and control applied to the marketing mix

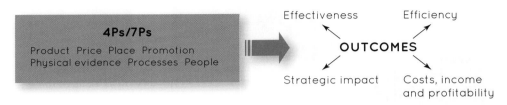

Product

- market share
- sales by segment and customer group
- performance of new products
- level of complaints.

Price

- profit margin
- discounts offered and level
- price analysis by customer segment
- comparisons to competing products
- level of contribution.

Place

- channel costs
- channel volume
- delivery time
- stock levels
- performance of individual channel members.

Promotion

- cost per contact made
- media coverage and levels of exposure to communications
- customer awareness levels; recognition and recall
- attitudes to, and perceptions of, the communication, brand, company
- customer enquiries generated.

Physical evidence

- customer awareness of, and attitudes towards, the physical aspects of service provision
- efficiency of store or outlet layout.

Processes

- length of time from beginning to end
- efficiency and effectiveness of the process
- how well the planning and management were carried out
- the systems and procedures to ensure customer satisfaction.

People

- number of people involved, agencies involved
- performance of the people, agencies involved
- skills and competencies
- training delivery
- qualifications
- rewards and incentives.

Having identified any areas of business that are underperforming, managers must decide how to address the shortfalls – either strategically or tactically – which is where contingency planning comes into force. The decisions, of course, will depend on the nature of the problem identified. For example, if there is a shortfall in sales, the company may decide to:

- target a new segment of the market (strategic)
- temporarily put prices down or up (tactical)
- redirect the sales effort or send salespeople on a training programme (operational).

The speed and efficiency with which shortfalls are addressed is often crucial to the ongoing success of the business.

ACTIVITY

The idea of evaluation and control can also be applied to your own studies. Consider how you measure your performance. You will think about the following:

- the results you have from previous assessments

- your intended results

- the amount of effort you have made to study

- what has given rise to the results achieved and what might have been done to improve them

- whether you monitor your performance regularly and make continual adjustments or just carry on regardless, and whether you have made contingency plans

- whether changes to your inputs should be considered

- the results of your friends' and colleagues' assessments

- how you should plan for improved performance if you did not get the result you expected

- the resource requirements (time, effort and money).

What other aspects of planning should you consider?

SUMMARY

This chapter has reviewed the marketing management and planning process. Consideration has been given to the types of question that managers need to ask. Before addressing the marketing planning process, aspects of organisation and management were highlighted to provide a necessary appreciation that marketing is, above all, a management activity with its corresponding challenges of organising, resourcing and working with people. The McKinsey 7S Framework was used as an overview.

A simple model of the planning process, which can be undertaken through a combination of top-down, bottom-up, outside-in and inside-out approaches, comprising five key stages that should be aligned to corporate mission, objectives and resources, was introduced. This was illustrated in Exhibit 12.7 and was used to provide the outline structure of this chapter. Relevant sections of Chapters 6 and 11 were identified that should be read (or re-read) in conjunction with this chapter.

CHALLENGES REVIEWED

Now that you have finished reading the chapter, look back at the challenges you were set at the beginning. Do you have a clearer idea of what's involved?

HINTS
- Porter's generic strategies, competitive positioning and portfolio analysis
- Marketing planning process model and marketing plan
- Contingency planning and situational analysis and environmental scanning (see also Chapter 2)
- Ansoff's matrix
- Marketing analysis, Porter's 'five forces' model, competitor capability analysis.

READING AROUND

JOURNAL ARTICLES

Ansoff, I. (1957) 'Strategies for diversification', *Harvard Business Review*, 35 (5): 113–24.

Buzzell, R., Gale, B. and Sultan, R. (1975) 'Market share: a key to profitability', *Harvard Business Review*, 53 (Jan–Feb): 97–106.

Ind, N. and Bjerke, R. (2007) 'The concept of participatory market orientation: an organisation-wide approach to enhancing brand equity', *Journal of Brand Management*, 15 (Oct): 135–45.

Kotler, P. and Singh, R. (1981) 'Marketing warfare', *Journal of Business Strategy*, 1 (Winter): 30–41.

Melewar, T.C., Pickton, D., Gupta, S. and Chigovanyika, T. (2009) 'MNE executive insights into international advertising programme standardisation', *Journal of Marketing Communications,* 15 (5): 345–65.

Porter, M. (1980) 'Industry structure and competitive strategy: keys to profitability', *Financial Analysis*, 36 (4): 30–41.

Viet Ngo, L. and O'Cass, A. (2012) 'Performance implications of market orientation, marketing resources, and marketing capabilities', *Journal of Marketing Management*, 28 (1–2): 173–87.

BOOKS AND BOOK CHAPTERS

Ambler, T. (2008) 'Marketing metrics', in M. Baker and S. Hart (eds), *The Marketing Book.* Oxford: Butterworth Heinemann, Chapter 21.

McDonald, M. (2008) *Malcolm McDonald on Marketing Planning.* London: Kogan Page.

McDonald, M. and Mouncy, P. (2011) *Marketing Accountability: A New Metrics Model to Measure Marketing Effectiveness.* London: Kogan Page.

McDonald, M. and Wilson, H. (2011) *Marketing Plans: How to Prepare Them, How to Use Them,* 7th edn. Chichester: John Wiley.

Wilson, R. and Gilligan, C. (2004) *Strategic Marketing Management: Planning, Implementation and Control,* 3rd edn. Oxford: Elsevier Butterworth Heinemann.

JOURNALS

Journal of Strategic Marketing
Marketing Intelligence and Planning
Strategic Change

SELF-REVIEW QUESTIONS

1. What are the main stages of the marketing planning process? (See p. 518)
2. List three marketing planning analysis tools. (See p. 520)
3. How can the product life cycle be used by an organisation? (See pp. 261–8; 479–80)
4. What is portfolio analysis? (See pp. 268–74)
5. What axes are used with the GE matrix? (See pp. 272–3)
6. What are Porter's three generic strategies? (See pp. 535)
7. Define the four generic strategies from Ansoff's matrix. (See pp. 535–8)
8. Name four competitive positioning strategies. (See p. 543)
9. What is 'market sensing'? (See p. 545)
10. Why is marketing control important? (See pp. 546–7)

Mini case study   The lovely, ugly Bug

Read the questions, then the case material, and then answer the questions.

Questions

1 What were VW's objectives in launching the New Beetle? To what extent do you think they succeeded?

2 Applying Porter's generic strategies (see p. 535) how would you classify VW's strategy for the Beetle? Why? Did it change over the years?

3 Using Internet sources and market research reports such as Mintel, Euromonitor and Keynote, as well as the

(Continued)

(Continued)

information below, write a PRESTCOM and a SWOT analysis for the VW Beetle.

4 Discuss the target markets for the Beetle and the Mini. How far do they overlap? Have they changed over the years?

5 Using your answers to questions 3 and 4 above, and drawing on the case material and this chapter, write an outline strategic plan for the VW Beetle for next year. You will have to make some decisions about the direction in which VW should go.

Use the following headings:

- situation analysis (hint: be selective here, only include important factors)

- objectives

- target markets

- marketing strategies

- marketing mix objectives and strategies (hint: an overview of how each of the 4Ps will be used and what you hope to achieve through that)

- evaluation and control.

The VW Beetle has always been loved. Its original design dates back to the 1930s though it was first popularised as the 'People's car' in Germany in the 1940s. Its superior comfort and power made it the small car of choice in both Europe and the USA in the 1950s. Innovative advertising built brand awareness and fed its popular image. In the 1960s, it starred in movies like *The Love Bug* where, as Herbie, it raced to its owner's rescue and saved the day. This personification of the car added fun to its brand values. People just loved their VW Bugs.

© Robert Couse-Baker

In the 1970s, the story took a downturn. Sales declined as more advanced, comfortable and practical cars were launched. In 1974 the Beetle was superseded by the very first model of another VW winner: the Golf. The Beetle was not quite finished however, as production moved to Mexico and the car became a favourite there until its much-lamented withdrawal in the mid-1980s.

In the 1990s, it was back! The New Beetle made its first appearance at the Geneva Motor Show in 1996. It was a sensation: streamlined design, slightly larger and much more comfortable than its predecessor and an updated engine, now more conventionally situated at the front of the car. As a nod to its hippy past, it sported a colourful daisy on the dashboard.

The New Beetle appealed to the young at heart: both those who'd loved it in the 1960s, and those who had never before had the chance. The timing of the launch was just about perfect. Fashion had gone retro as baby boomers got nostalgic about their youth and the youth of the day were intrigued by what seemed to be a golden age. Unfortunately for VW, that sort of opportunity gets noticed by competitors too. In the late 1990s, another German car giant made a surprise investment in an outdated, long dead (but significantly not forgotten) British icon. In 2001, they were ready. The first BMW Mini burst onto a waiting market.

The Mini is quite possibly the most loved little car in the world. It is a piece of British history. A symbol of independence in the 1960s and '70s, it had been the now defunct British Leyland's biggest hit.

The BMW Mini was a massive success story. It played on nostalgia and the driver's sense of fun. For the people who were old enough to have driven one before, it embodied youth and a carefree spirit. For the young, it was an unusual, quirky small car with a BMW engine. Clearly it was major competition for the Beetle.

Both these cars have an enviable heritage. The earlier models were undisputed design classics: the sort of thing that turns up in museums or is used in films to evoke an era. They are both quirky, fun, small and people tend to give them names. They were both film stars back in the day: Herbie was a Beetle and Minis were the cheeky getaway cars in *The Italian Job*. BMW Minis starred in the film's 2003 remake. They've both always been cool, so why did the Mini outsell the Beetle by such a huge margin?

Volkswagen revisited the design. In 2012, a new generation of Beetle with broader appeal hit the road. The 1990s New Beetle, with its Daisy in a vase on the dashboard, had been seen by many as a woman's car. In the twenty-first century this was a drawback. According to Mintel (2012a), most new car buyers are men in the upper income brackets. The 2012 Volkswagen Beetle was intended to appeal to design-conscious, nostalgic, cool men – as well as to women. A 2.0 litre diesel engine made it sportier in terms of performance as well as looks while also seeming greener. The starting price of just over £20,000 kept it relatively affordable – without actually being cheap.

What Car magazine's review of the Volkswagen Beetle concluded:

> It isn't the greatest car to drive and there are other more practical and economical alternatives out there, but there's no doubt that the Beetle will turn heads as it goes past. For some buyers, that could be the clincher. (*What Car,* 2012)

It wasn't the easiest time to introduce a new car. Many of VW's key markets were (and still are) experiencing one of the longest recessions ever. Sales of new cars have fallen as people prefer to buy secondhand or just to make their old car keep going longer.

For many drivers, their car is hugely important to their self-image. Traditionally, cars are thought to confer status and say a lot about who you are and what you value. However, research conducted by Mintel (2012b) found that price is the most important consideration for today's car buyers (for both new and secondhand cars). Other important decision factors are reliability and fuel consumption.

Mintel reported a number of key trends in the car market:

- smaller and medium-sized vehicles are outselling larger ones with cars in the supermini, lower medium and upper medium categories accounting for around three-quarters of UK sales in 2011 (Mintel, 2012a)

(Continued)

(Continued)

- new car buyers in the UK are moving away from mass-market brands towards more individual and especially upmarket brands, leading to a rise in the popularity of German brands such as Audi, Volkswagen, BMW and Mercedes-Benz (Mintel, 2012a)

- value brands, such as Kia, Hyundai, Skoda and Seat, are also selling well (Mintel, 2012a).

BMW have continually innovated over the years and there are now a number of different ranges of Mini, with different price points. The recently introduced Mini Paceman is a cheaper competitor for cars such as the Range Rover Evoque. The Paceman is based on the Mini Countryman but has a re-designed, sloping roof to give it a sportier look. The Volkswagen Beetle will need to be really special, and well supported, if it is to compete.

REFERENCES

Ansoff, I. (1957) 'Strategies for diversification', *Harvard Business Review*, 35 (5): 113–24.

Buzzell, R.D., Gale, B.T. and Sultan, R.G.M. (1975) 'Market share: a key to profitability', *Harvard Business Review*, 53 (Jan–Feb): 97–106.

Chartered Institute of Marketing (n.d.) **www.cim.co.uk (accessed 09/04/13).**

Chartered Institute of Marketing (2002) Marketing evaluation and control process. Available at: **www.cim.co.uk**

Greene, W., Walls, G. and Schrest, L. (1994) 'Internal marketing: the key to external marketing success', *Journal of Services Marketing*, 8 (4): 5–13.

Greenpeace (n.d.) What is Greenpeace's Mission? Available at: **www.greenpeace.org/ international/en/about/faq/** (accessed 04/04/13).

Hooley, G., Piercy, N. and Nicoulaud, B. (2011) *Marketing Strategy and Competitive Positioning*, 5th edn. Harlow: FT/Prentice Hall.

Ind, N. and Bjerke R. (2007) 'The concept of participatory market orientation: an organisation-wide approach to enhancing brand equity', *Journal of Brand Management*, 15 (Oct): 135–45.

Johnson, G., Scholes, K. and Whittington, R. (2011) *Exploring Corporate Strategy: Text and Cases*, 9th edn. Harlow: FT/Prentice Hall.

Kotler, P. and Singh, R. (1981) 'Marketing warfare', *Journal of Business Strategy*, 1 (Winter): 30–41.

Levitt, T. (1960) 'Marketing myopia', *Harvard Business Review*, 38 (Jul/Aug): 45–56.

McDonald, M. (2008) *Malcolm McDonald on Marketing Planning*. London: Kogan Page.

Melewar, T.C., Pickton, D., Gupta, S. and Chigovanyika, T. (2009) 'MNE executive insights into international advertising programme standardisation', *Journal of Marketing Communications*, 15 (5): 345–65.

Mintel (2012a) *Car Retailing – UK – July 2012*. London: Mintel.

Mintel (2012b) *Car Purchasing Process – UK – May 2012*. London: Mintel.

Ngo, L.V. and O'Cass, A. (2012) 'Performance implications of market orientation, marketing resources, and marketing capabilities', *Journal of Marketing Management*, 28 (1–2): 173–87.

Nike (n.d.) *Our Mission*. Available at: **www.nikeinc.com** (accessed 04/04/13).

Peppers, D. and Rogers, M. (1999) *The One to One Field Book*. New York: Doubleday.

Peters, T.J. and Waterman, R.H. (2004) *In Search of Excellence*, 2nd edn. London: Profile Books.

Pickton, D. and Broderick, A. (2004) *Integrated Marketing Communications*. Harlow: FT/Prentice Hall.

Piercy, N. (2009) *Market-led Strategic Change*, 4th edn. Oxford: Butterworth-Heinemann.

Porter, M. (1980) 'Industry structure and competitive strategy: keys to profitability', *Financial Analysis*, 36 (4): 30–41.

Porter, M.E. (1985) *Competitive Advantage: Creating and Sustaining Superior Performance*. Glencoe, IL: Free Press.

Ries, A. and Trout, J. (1986) *Marketing Warfare*. New York: McGraw-Hill.

Schultz, D.E. (1993a) 'Maybe we should start all over with an IMC organisation', *Marketing News*, 27 (22): 8.

Schultz, D.E. (1993b) 'How to overcome the barriers to integration', *Marketing News,* 27 (15): 16.

Schultz, D.E. (1997) 'Integrating information resources to develop strategies', *Marketing News*, 31 (2): 10.

Smith, P., Berry, C. and Pulford, A. (1997) *Strategic Marketing Communications*. London: Kogan Page.

Souhami, S. (2003) 'Competitive myopia', *Marketing Business*, April: 32–4.

Tejada, C. (2013) 'Many US businesses in China cite data theft', *Wall Street Journal*, 29 March. Available at: **http://online.wsj.com/article/SB100014241278873235010 0457838943 3786413300.html** (accessed 08/04/13).

Thomas, D. (2003) 'A good clean fight', *Marketing Week*, 3 July: 20–3.

Walker, O. Jr., Boyd, H. Jr. and Larreche, J.-C. (2003) 'Marketing strategy', in D. Cravens and N. Piercy (eds), *Strategic Marketing*, 7th edn. New York: McGraw-Hill.

What Car (2012) 'New 2012 VW Beetle 2.0 TDI review', 17 September. Available at: **www.whatcar.com/car-news/new-2012-vw-beetle-2-0-tdi-review/263895** (accessed 18/09/12).

Visit the companion website on your computer at **www.sagepub.co.uk/masterson3e** or MobileStudy on your Smart phone or tablet by scanning this QR code and gain access to:

- **Videos** to get a better understanding of key concepts and provoke in-class discussion.
- Links to useful **websites and templates** to help guide your study.
- Access **SAGE Marketing Pins (www.pinterest.com/sagepins/)**. SAGE's regularly updated **Pinterest** page, giving you access to regularly updated resources on everything from Branding to Consumer Behaviour.
- **Daily Grind podcast series** to learn more about the day-to-day life of a marketing **professional**.
- Interactive **Practice questions** to test your understanding.
- A **bonus chapter on Marketing Careers** to not only support your study, but your job search and future career.
- **PowerPoints** prompting key points for revision.

Glossary

4Ps a mnemonic (memory aid) for the marketing mix: product, promotion, place, price

7Ps a mnemonic (memory aid) for the services marketing mix: product, promotion, place, price, process, people, physical evidence

above the line advertising in commission-paying media, e.g. TV, posters, press, radio, cinema

adoption *see* product adoption process

advertising a persuasive communication paid for by an identifiable source and addressed to the whole of a target audience without personal identification

advertising proposition what the overall advert should say to the target audience, the impression that should be left in their minds (this is not the slogan; the whole of the advert should communicate the proposition)

agent represents other businesses and sells products on their behalf; does not usually hold stock or take ownership of the goods, just takes orders and is paid a commission or fee

AIDA a sequential model showing the steps that marketing communications should lead potential buyers through: attention, interest, desire, action

ambient media unusual out-of-home media, e.g. lasers, tickets, promotional clothing, tattoos, pavements

Ansoff's matrix comprises four possible growth strategies: market development, product development, market penetration/expansion and diversification

area or cluster sampling the research population is divided into mutually exclusive groups (e.g. geographical region: perhaps by pastcode) so that a random sample of the groups can be selected

aspirant (aspirational) groups groups to which an individual would like to belong, e.g. a professional football team or a particular club

asset-led *see* asset-led marketing

asset-led marketing basing the marketing strategy on the organisation's strengths rather than on customer needs and wants, e.g. by developing products that can be made with existing equipment or through brand extension

attitude describes a person's consistently favourable or unfavourable evaluation, feelings and tendencies towards an object or idea

audience profile a detailed description of audience characteristics used by marketing communicators to tailor their promotional efforts

awareness set a number of products or brands that may satisfy a customer/consumer need or solve a problem

b2b (business to business) business dealings with another business as opposed to a consumer

b2c (business to consumer) business dealings with consumers

barrier to communication anything that gets in the way of a message and prevents it from being received correctly

barriers to entry things that make it difficult, or impossible, for new competitors to enter a market, e.g. patents, high set-up costs

basic product a bundle of essential characteristics; a product described in terms of the features that deliver its core benefit (e.g. the ingredients of a soft drink – fizzy orange) without reference to service or other more sophisticated elements

behavioural segmentation dividing a market into subgroups (segments) of customers/ users according to how they buy, use and feel about products

belief how or what a person thinks about something, usually based on knowledge, opinion or faith

below the line non-commission-paying promotion, typically all forms except advertising

benchmarking a process of systematic analysis and comparison of one company's performance, measured against another's (the industry leader's), in order to improve business performance

biographical research an individual's story or experiences told to a researcher or found in other materials

blueprint the original, or master, plan for how to make or do something

bogof buy one get one free

boom when an economy experiences a rapid rise in spending, often accompanied by higher prices and raised investment levels

Boston Consulting Group (BCG) portfolio matrix a product portfolio analysis tool involving classifying products or SBUs (strategic business units) according to their relative market share and market growth rate – as stars, cash cows, problem children or dogs

bottom-up approach functions and departments recommend objectives, budgets, strategies and plans to senior management

brand 'the intangible sum of a product's attributes: its name, packaging, and price, its history, its reputation, and the way it's advertised' (David Ogilvy)

brand ambassador someone who is passionate and knowledgeable about a brand and recommends it to others; this may be an employee, a celebrity endorser, or a customer acting independently

brand architecture the structure of an organisation's brand portfolio which shows how their brands relate to one another; it typically includes master and sub-brands

brand communities a group of people, usually consumers, formed on the basis of their shared admiration for a particular branded product or range of products, e.g. the BMW owners' group

brand equity the monetary value of a brand

brand extension offering further products under an existing brand name but in a new category within the same, broadly defined market, e.g. Mars ice cream built on the Mars bar brand

brand identity all the outward trappings of the brand, e.g. logo, name, colours, strap line and packaging

brand image people's perception of the brand

brand leader the brand with the highest sales within its particular market

brand loyalty the attachment that a customer or consumer feels to a favourite product

brand manager responsible for marketing a particular set of branded products

brand map diagram of competing brand positions resulting from the perceptual mapping process; also called perceptual maps, position maps and space maps

brand name the product's, or product line's, given name

brand personality the heart of the brand, the sum of its values, its character traits, e.g. bubbly, elegant, friendly

brand portfolio *see* product portfolio

brand promise the way the brand sets out to fulfil a customer need, e.g. Pepsi Cola might promise to be thirst quenching

brand stretching using an existing brand name on products in a different market

brand values how a brand is perceived by the market

branded entertainment leisure activities, most commonly television or radio programmes, paid for by an advertiser in order to draw attention to its products

branded house a form of brand architecture which uses a single master brand to span a set of products, known as sub-brands

brand-switching buying an alternative brand

break even *see* breakeven point

breakeven point the amount of goods a firm needs to sell in order to cover its costs

breaking down the process of reducing the quantity of product to be moved

bricks and clicks an organisation, usually retail, that operates both online and offline, e.g. John Lewis, Tesco

business mission the broad aims a business hopes to achieve

buying centre comprises all the individuals that participate in the business buying decision process

buying economies i.e. economies of scale; companies may buy goods in large quantities and so obtain favourable terms

c2c (consumer to consumer) business dealings between consumers, e.g. on eBay

capital goods (fixed assets) substantial purchases that are not used up in one go but are expected to be used multiple times

cartel a group of companies that get together and fix prices between them

case study contains in-depth information, built from multiple sources, that forms a detailed picture of a particular situation

cash and carry a wholesaler whose main customers are small retailers who visit the premises, pay for their goods and carry them away; cash and carries do not deliver

cash cows a category within the Boston Consulting Group matrix, products or SBUs (strategic business units) with relatively high market share in low-growth markets

categorical data also known as 'nominal' data, data that has no numerical value and so cannot be statistically analysed although each category may be counted, e.g. gender, star sign, hair colour

cause-related marketing a form of sponsorship whereby funds are raised for a worthy cause, often a charity (e.g. Tesco's Computers for

Schools, Pizza Express's support of the National Trust through sales of its Neptune pizza)

census a survey that includes all members of a population

channel members the businesses that make up a distribution channel; intermediaries

classical conditioning the process of using an established relationship between a stimulus and a response, which can then be used to evoke the same response

classified advertising the small ads, usually placed into specific classifications, e.g. cars for sale, help wanted

closed questions questions that expect a one-word (usually yes or no) answer

co-branding when two companies' brand names appear together, e.g. Intel on IBM computers

cognitive dissonance when a person is troubled by conflicting thoughts; in marketing this is commonly with regard to a purchase decision: a customer may be unsure whether they made the right decision

cognitive learning active learning using complex mental processing of information

cold call when a salesperson calls on a prospect without an appointment

competitive advantage or **competitive edge** something about an organisation or its products that is perceived as being better than rival offerings

competitive advertising highlights and illustrates the uses, features and benefits that the advertised brand has and its rivals do not

competitive edge *see* competitive advantage

competitive intelligence information on rivals, their products and environments compared with one's own

competitive advantage something which gives a brand or organisation an edge over its competitors

competitor analysis the process of obtaining an in-depth understanding of rival firms and their offerings

complementary product one that is required by another product, e.g. a printer needs paper, a DVD player needs DVDs

concentrated marketing where only one market segment is chosen for targeting

consideration set a range of preferred products or brands that may satisfy the need or provide a solution to the problem

conspicuous purchase a product or service that is likely to stand out, perhaps because it has unusual or high status or will be consumed in public

consumer the individual end-user of a product or service

consumer durables products for use by individuals that can be expected to last for some time, e.g. a washing machine

consumer goods goods that are bought/used by individuals rather than by companies

consumer models representations of consumer buying behaviour, usually as diagrams

consumer panels a primary research technique that seeks the views, attitudes, behaviour or buying habits of a group of consumers

consumerism the belief that increasing consumption is economically desirable

consumerist someone who believes in consumerism

contract manufacture when a company employs another company to manufacture its goods, the employing company retains ownership of the goods and rights of sale

contribution the amount of money remaining from the sale, when the variable costs have been paid

contribution pricing a pricing method based on variable costs

controllables events, issues, trends, etc. within the internal environment

convenience goods products that customers buy frequently and think little about

convenience sample a sample picked on the basis of convenience to the researcher, e.g. work colleagues

coopetition when competitors cooperate with each other for mutual benefit, e.g. by sharing research costs

copy text

copywriter someone who writes the words for promotional materials, e.g. adverts

core benefit (core product) the minimum benefits a product should confer, e.g. a pen must write, a car must go

corporate brand a company brand name

corporate image audiences' perception of an organisation

corporate social responsibility (CSR) 'the responsibility of enterprises for their impacts on society' (European Commission, 2011)

costs what an organisation pays for the goods and services it receives; see also direct costs, indirect costs, variable costs and fixed costs

countertrade exchanging goods for other goods rather than for money; there are various forms of countertrade, the best known of which is barter

creative execution the way an advert is designed in order to put a message across

creative team   an art director and a copywriter; they work together to create ads

critical success factors   things that the success of an organisation or activity depend upon; they must happen or the objectives will not be met

CRM   *see* customer relationship management

cross-selling   persuading a customer to buy other products

CSR   *see* corporate social responsibility

culture   the set of basic values, perceptions, wants and behaviour learnt by a member of society from family and other institutions

customer   a buyer of a product or service

customer journey   a customer's experience of the brand, incorporating all the customer's brand-related interactions and emotions; this journey can be mapped as an aid to planning

customer lifetime value   a calculation of the long-term worth of a customer using estimates of expected purchases

customer loyalty   a mutually supportive, long-term relationship between customer and supplier, which results in customers making multiple repeat purchases

customer orientation   the whole organisation is focused on the satisfaction of its customers' needs

customer profile   a description of the firm's customer base, used to target customers more accurately

customer relationship management (CRM)   attracting and keeping the right customers

customer value pricing   pricing a product or service according to the value placed on it by the customer

customised marketing   producing one-off products/services to match a specific customer's requirements, e.g. a made-to-measure suit or the organisation of a product launch party

DAGMAR   an acronym for Defining Advertising Goals for Measured Advertising Results; a hierarchy of effects model describing the stages individuals go through when making a purchase, or consumption, decision

data mining   using specialist software to analyse large amounts of data (held in a database) to identify patterns or relationships in that data

data warehouse   a large database holding copies of customer and environmental data taken from the organisation's other systems and designed specifically to make it easier to raise queries and produce reports

database marketing   the use of computerised information used for targeted marketing activities

decision-making unit (DMU)   all the individuals who participate in and influence the customer's purchase decision

demand   the quantity of goods that customers buy at a certain price

demand-driven   when a surplus, or potential surplus, of goods to be sold gives the buyers more power than the sellers

demographic segmentation   markets segmented by population characteristics such as age, gender, occupation and income

depression   when an economy experiences a severe fall-off in sales, usually accompanied by unemployment, lower prices and low levels of investment; sometimes called a slump

desk research (secondary research)   the search for good-quality data that has been validated and is now published for use by others

destroyer pricing   *see* predatory pricing

differentiated marketing   differences between market segments are recognised and two or more target markets are selected, each receiving a different marketing programme

direct costs   costs that are clearly due to the making of a particular product, e.g. cocoa and sugar are direct costs of chocolate bars

direct export   when a company makes products in its home country for sale abroad and then manages the overseas sales and marketing of them itself

direct mail   promotional material delivered by post

direct marketing   'all activities that make it possible to offer goods or services or to transmit other messages to a segment of the population by post, telephone, email or other direct means' (Chartered Institute of Marketing)

direct marketing communications   promotional materials designed to prompt a direct response from the recipient to the sender

direct sales   when a manufacturer deals directly with customers rather than through intermediaries in the supply chain

direct-response advertising   'advertising, or selling, through any medium inviting the consumer to respond to the advertiser' (*IDM Direct Marketing Guide*)

disassociative groups   groups to which the individual does not want to belong or be seen to belong, e.g. an upmarket shopper may not wish to be seen in a discount store

discount   a deduction from the price

disintermediation the removal of levels of intermediaries in distribution channels, often associated with the trend towards direct sales facilitated by the Internet

display advertising mainstream press advertising, usually with illustrations or other attention-drawing features

distortion a barrier to communication; poor coding skills, e.g. a badly devised ad or a badly worded sales promotion, that prevent the message from being received correctly

distribution the processes involved in moving goods from the supplier to the customer or user

distribution centres large warehouses that repackage goods into smaller units and ship them to trade customers; they may be exclusive to one large retailer

distribution channel a chain of organisations through which products pass on their way to a target market

diversification strategy developing new products to sell to new markets (customers) (part of Ansoff's growth matrix)

dogs a category within the Boston Consulting Group portfolio matrix, products or SBUs (strategic business units) with relatively low market share in low-growth markets

domestic market a company's home market, i.e. markets in the same country as the company itself

dumping an anti-competitive practice whereby a company exports its products at a very low price and so undercuts competitors in the target country

duty an import tax charged by the government

dyadic comparisons a technique used in perceptual mapping in which two products are compared to each other at a time

early majority a substantial group of customers who follow early adopters in buying a new product or service

earned media channels of communication outside marketers' direct control that are used to talk about brands, issues, organisations; traditionally PR media, e.g. newspaper columns/editorials (**not** advert space), an individual's blogs, individual social media pages

economies of scale unit costs fall as larger quantities are produced; a cost advantage associated with large organisations

efficient market a market in which prices adjust quickly, and frequently, in response to new information (economic theory)

elasticity a significant response to changes in a marketing variable, most commonly price; if the demand for a product is price elastic, sales volumes will change by a greater percentage than the percentage change in price, e.g. if the price goes up by 5%, sales fall by 7%; therefore if the price rises the sales revenue actually falls

embargo(es) a ban on the trade of a particular category of goods (e.g. arms) or between certain areas (e.g. the USA and Iraq)

emergency goods goods infrequently purchased but needed at short notice, e.g. rain capes, sun hats, plasters

end-user the person who actually uses the product or service; this is not always the customer, e.g. a computer may be bought by a company's purchasing officer for use by the marketing manager (the end-user)

environmental scanning monitoring the forces that influence the organisation in order to identify changes that may affect performance

environmental variables factors within an organisation's environment that may change, i.e. PRESTCOM elements

EPOS (electronic point of sale) a computerised system that collects sales data at a retail checkout

e-tailers online retailers

ethnocentrism ethnocentric firms have a home country focus; there is an assumption that home country ways are best and that others should adapt to them

ethnography the description, or interpretation, of the patterns of behaviour in a social group or setting; the researcher will immerse himself or herself in a variety of ways into the culture of the group to be studied

evoked set the products or brands from which a person will make their purchase choice

exchange when two parties swap items perceived to be of approximately equal value

exclusive distribution the distribution channel has only one or two specially selected outlets within a specified area

experimentation a primary research technique that seeks to understand the behaviour of specified variables under controlled conditions, i.e. not real-world

exploratory (research) initial research to see whether a more comprehensive study is needed

extension strategies means of prolonging the product life cycle

external environment organisations and influences that are not under the organisation's control, e.g. government, competitors, legislation

extinction pricing *see* predatory pricing

extrapolate use already established data (or experience) to predict the unknown, e.g. using last year's sales figures, adjusted for current conditions, to forecast this year's figures

family brand a brand name that covers a group of related products

family life cycle a form of market segmentation based on the recognition that we pass through a series of quite distinct phases in our lives

feedback a part of the two-way communications process whereby the receiver sends a message back to the original sender

fees payments made for services or for permission to use something, e.g. for a licence or a franchise

field research (primary research) carried out specifically for the research task in question

first mover advantage the first significant company to move into a market often becomes the market leader and can be hard to dislodge from that position

fixed costs costs that do not vary with production levels, e.g. insurance premiums

FLC *see* family life cycle

flyer a short brochure

FMCG (fast-moving consumer goods) low-value items that are bought regularly (the shelves empty quickly), e.g. toothpaste

focus groups a qualitative research technique using a group discussion overseen by a moderator, used to explore views, attitudes and behaviour with regard to a marketing issue; common in advertising research

fragmented industry one in which there are a lot of players, few of whom have any significant power

franchise a form of licence; the franchisee pays for the rights to run a business that has already been successful elsewhere, in a new territory and benefits from the expertise of the original owners (franchisors)

franchisee a person or company who has bought a franchise

franchisor or **franchiser** a person or company who has sold a franchise

free trade trade across international boundaries without government restrictions such as import duties and quotas

frequency the number of times that an average member of the target audience is exposed to an advert during a campaign

full-cost pricing prices are set by adding an amount (usually a percentage) to the full (i.e. total) costs of making and selling the product

functional silo when departments or work groups act as independent entities rather than as components of a much larger system despite having many overlapping activities and information needs

GE-McKinsey a portfolio analysis tool developed by McKinsey & Co and GE involving classifying product lines or SBUs (strategic business units) according to their competitive position and market attractiveness

generic products goods that have no discernible difference from each other; often used to mean unbranded products

geocentrism the middle ground between ethnocentrism and polycentrism; geocentric firms have a worldwide outlook, picking and choosing the best practices from the various countries in which they do business

geo-demographic segmentation markets are segmented by a combination of geographic and demographic approaches using house location and house type

geographic segmentation markets are segmented by countries, regions and areas

globalisation the process of growing to a worldwide scale; it often involves the standardisation of offerings and cultural convergence

goods tangible products, i.e. those with physical substance

grey importing when someone outside the official supply chain buys goods (usually very cheaply) in another country for sale in their home country

grey market *see* grey importing

grounded theory starts from the intention to generate, or to discover, a theory by studying how people interact in response to a particular phenomenon; theoretical propositions are developed from interview data and field research

hard currency freely exchangeable currency, usually from one of the more developed countries, e.g. the euro, pound, US dollar

hedging making a deal to buy or sell foreign currency in advance so that the exchange rate is fixed

hierarchical management structure each manager has a set place within a vertical chain of command

hierarchy of effects models describes the stages individuals go through when making a purchase or consumption decision

high-context culture one where communication must be interpreted according to the situation; much of the message is in the context rather than being explicitly expressed in the words (*see also* low-context culture)

high-involvement purchases purchases that customers expend time and effort on, usually high cost or high risk, e.g. cars, holidays, wedding dresses

high street multiples chains of shops, such as WH Smith and Boots

horizontal communications sideways communications within an organisation, e.g. between work groups or departments

horizontal integration where a company owns a number of different businesses at the same level in the supply chain, e.g. Curry's and Dixons electrical retailers are part of the same company

hospitality hosting clients (e.g. providing refreshments in a private room) at events

house of brands a form of brand architecture which comprises a set of stand-alone brands with their own names and identities, although there may be a reference to the owning brand

hypothesis a proposition put forward for testing

import duties taxes paid when goods are brought into a country from outside

import licence permission, usually granted by a government, to bring specified goods into a country

impulse purchase buying behaviour, made on the spur of the moment

incoterms a set of rules governing the delivery terms for international sales

in-depth interviews one-to-one research interviews; commonly used in qualitative research

indirect costs costs that cannot be attributed to a particular product as they are not directly associated with its production or sale, e.g. the running costs of the chief executive's car

indirect export using a third party (e.g. an export management company), based in the firm's home country, to sell products abroad

inelasticity little response to changes in the marketing variable being measured (commonly price, advertising, competitive products, income); the percentage change in demand is less than the percentage change in price (or other variable), so if price rises, sales rise

infinite elasticity the product can only be sold at one price; there is no demand at any other (this is really just a theoretical term)

inflation when the prices of goods rise without a matching (or greater) increase in their actual value

information framing the ways in which information is presented to people to ensure selective distortion does, or does not, happen

information search identifying the various ways a need or problem can be satisfied

innovative products a really new product, possibly a technological or medical breakthrough

Innovators people who are most receptive to new ideas and are first to try out new products

inside-out approach focuses on the needs of the organisation first, and customers and the marketplace second

instrumental conditioning another term for **operant conditioning;** learning a behaviour that produces a positive outcome (reward) or avoids a negative one

integrated marketing communications the process of ensuring that all elements of the promotional mix are complementary in order to avoid mixed messages and strengthen the brand

intensive distribution products are available at numerous outlets

inter-media decision the choice of media class

intermediaries businesses that form part of the distribution channel, passing goods on towards the end customer

internal environment the organisation itself, its functions, departments and resources

internal marketing also called internal PR, it addresses the needs (particularly information needs) of employees

international organisations there is a head office in the home country which controls overseas sales

Internet worldwide computer network linking smaller networks via satellite and telephone links, and providing access to email services and the World Wide Web

intra-media decision the choice of media vehicle

iTV interactive television

judgemental sample *see* quota sample

junk mail unwanted promotional material sent by post

just in time (JIT) a lean manufacturing technique where little or no stock is held

knowledge-based economy one in which knowledge is the primary wealth creator

lead time the time it takes for an order to reach the customer

learning changes in an individual's behaviour arising from their experiences

legitimate power influence over others conferred by law or regulations

level of confidence   the degree to which the researchers are sure that data are accurate

level of involvement   the extent to which the purchase is important to the purchaser

Likert scale   subjects are asked to indicate their agreement, or disagreement, with a statement by use of a five-point scale

line extension   using the brand name on products within the same category

lobbying   a means of influencing those with power, particularly politicians and legislators

logistics   the flow of goods and services through the supply chain

logo   a graphical device associated with an organisation

loss leader   a product that is sold at a loss, usually to tempt shoppers to make other purchases

low-context culture   the information to be communicated is put into words explicitly; there is little need to take account of the surrounding circumstances (*see also* high-context culture)

low-involvement purchase   products that customers spend little time or effort in choosing, often low cost, low risk or regular purchases, e.g. toothpaste, washing-up liquid, jam

loyalty schemes   ways in which companies try to retain customers and encourage repeat purchases, often accomplished by awarding points (e.g. Tesco Clubcard, Air Miles)

macroenvironment   the broad, external influences that affect all organisations in a market, e.g. the political situation in a country

mailing lists   any list of names and addresses to which mail is sent, often potential customers

marginal cost pricing   similar to contribution pricing, a margin is added to the marginal cost (the cost of making an additional product) to arrive at a price

market   a composite of individuals or organisations that have a willingness and ability to purchase products; a market can consist of single or multiple segments

market attractiveness   an assessment of how desirable a particular market or market segment is to an organisation

market challenger   a company that is trying to take over the market leader position

market development strategy   selling existing products to new markets (customers) (part of Ansoff's growth matrix)

market followers   take their lead from competitors and copy their successful ideas and strategies (*see also* market-led)

market fragmentation   a market characterised by a large number of relatively small players, none of whom has significant competitive advantage

market growth rate   the percentage increase in total sales within a category or market

market leader   the company with the highest sales within a market (also sometimes used to refer to a groundbreaking firm that others follow)

market-led   companies take their lead from competitors and copy their successful ideas and strategies (they are also called market followers), i.e. they are more cautious and wait for more radical ideas to be tested by others first

market orientation   provision of customer value determines an organisation's direction

market penetration pricing   pricing a product lower than competitors in order to gain market share

market penetration strategy   encouraging existing customers to buy more of a product in order to increase sales of existing products in existing markets (part of Ansoff's growth matrix)

market research   the systematic gathering, recording and analysing of customer and other market-related data

market screening   assessing the potential of a new market to achieve desired levels of sales, profit, market share and/or other objectives

market segment   a group of buyers and users/consumers who share similar characteristics and who are distinct from the rest of the market for a product

market segmentation   the process of dividing a total market into subgroups (segments) such that each segment consists of buyers and users who share similar characteristics but are different from those in other segments

market sensing   the need for an understanding of the market, rather than merely a knowledge of it

market share   a firm's sales expressed as a percentage of the total sales of that type of product in the defined market

market skimming   setting a relatively high price to take advantage of limited competition

marketing channel   another term for distribution channel

marketing communications   another name for promotion; communication designed and implemented to persuade others to do, think or feel something

marketing environment   the forces and organisations that impact on an organisation's marketing activities

marketing information system (MkIS) also known as a marketing intelligence system, the systematic gathering and dissemination of competitive and marketing information; this usually involves a computerised system

marketing metrics 'measurements that help with the quantification of marketing performance, such as market share, advertising spend, and response rates elicited by advertising and direct marketing' (Chartered Institute of Marketing)

marketing mix (*see* 4Ps, 7Ps) the basics of marketing plan implementation, usually product, promotion, place, price, sometimes with the addition of packaging; the services marketing mix also includes people, physical evidence and process

marketing opportunity a chance to reach a particular group of customers with a product offer

mark-up pricing the price is set by adding a percentage (a mark-up) to the direct cost

mass customisation tailoring product offerings almost to meet individual needs

mass market a homogeneous market, i.e. there is no distinction between segments

mass marketing delivering the same marketing programme to everybody without making any significant distinction between people

mass media communications channels that reach a large, relatively undifferentiated audience, e.g. posters, the Internet, press; plural of mass medium

McKinsey/General Electric matrix a portfolio analysis tool developed by McKinsey & Co and GE, involving classifying product lines or SBUs according to their competitive position and market attractiveness

media class or **media category** type of media, e.g. television, press, posters, cinema

media vehicle the actual TV programme, newspaper, magazine, film, etc., in which adverts appear

mediagraphic segmentation markets segmented by reading and viewing habits

membership groups groups an individual already belongs to and which therefore have a direct influence on his or her behaviour, e.g. students belong to a class

merchandise *see* merchandising

merchandising (1) selection and display of products within a retail environment; (2) a form of licensing spin-off products often inspired by entertainments (e.g. T-shirts at a concert)

message the impression a promotion leaves on its audience

me-too product a new product that is an imitation of an existing, competitive one

microenvironment comprises an organisation's competitors, distributors, suppliers and its own internal resources

modified rebuy the buyer wants to modify an element of the rebuy, e.g. change colour, size, price or delivery time

monopoly a market in which there is only one supplier

Multi-attribute Attitude Mapping (MAM) a form of perceptual mapping comparing a product's key features (according to their importance to target customers) with features offered by competitive brands

multibranding a strategy employed by companies that have multiple products within the same category

multichannel distribution the use of different types of channel to reach the same target market

Multidimensional Scaling (MDS) a form of perceptual mapping that establishes similarities and differences between competing brands

multinational *see* multinational organisation

multinational organisation has subsidiary companies in other countries which have significant power although they answer to the parent company

multivariate analysis two or more variables are analysed at the same time

new media makes use of modern technologies, e.g. the Internet, iTV, mobile phones, CD/DVD

new task when someone buys a product for the first time

niche market a market segment that can be treated as a target market; a small, well-defined market, often part of a larger market

niche marketing a form of concentrated marketing in which the target market is relatively small, well defined and very focused

noise a barrier to communication, usually from an external source, e.g. technological breakdown

not for profit organisations whose primary goal is something other than profit, e.g. government, charities, clubs, pressure groups

objective a goal or target

observation a primary research technique that involves watching how subjects behave in their normal environment

oligopoly a situation where the market is dominated by a small number of very large companies

omnibus survey a large questionnaire that provides data for multiple clients

one-to-one marketing personalised marketing, typically on the Internet

on-pack promotion a promotional offer printed on the product's packaging

open-ended questions questions that invite the respondent to comment rather than just give a one-word answer

operant conditioning (instrumental conditioning) learning a behaviour that produces a positive outcome (reward) or avoids a negative one

opinion formers individuals with specialist skills or expertise who have influence over others, often through the media

opinion leaders individuals who are often asked by people they know for advice or information

opportunities to see (OTS) a measure of media effectiveness

opportunity cost alternatives that could have been had/done instead, e.g. the opportunity cost of a lunchtime sandwich may be a pre-packed salad, and an evening at the cinema costs a night's study

outside-in approach the organisation looks outwards to focus on the needs of the marketplace to determine appropriate courses of marketing action

outsourcing the subcontracting of a business process, e.g. delivery or maintenance, to another organisation

owned media channels of communication which belong to the client company, e.g. a company website or in-house newsletter

own-label products that bear a retailer's brand name, e.g. Tesco; sometimes called 'private brands'

pack shot a picture of the product, in its packaging, used in an advert to aid recognition

paid media channels of communication in which advertisers buy space, e.g. television, magazines, social media sites

parallel importing when someone outside of the official supply chain sells goods that were bought abroad (usually more cheaply)

participant observation a primary research technique in which the observer becomes involved with their subjects rather than remaining apart

patent a legal protection for inventions that prohibits unauthorised copying

pattern adverts partial standardisation of advertising, useful in international marketing; the adverts have the same look and feel although some images and the slogan may be written for a particular place or purpose

penetration pricing see market penetration pricing

people one of the elements of the marketing mix, concerned with distribution, delivery, supply chain management

perception the process by which people select, organise and interpret sensory stimulation (sounds, visions, smell, touch) into a meaningful picture of the world

perceptual map results from the perceptual mapping process and shows brands' relative positions (also called a brand map, position map or space map)

perceptual mapping the process of visually representing target-market perceptions of competing brands in relation to each other

perfect competition a theoretical market situation in which all product offerings are identical, and there are many small buyers and sellers, none of which is able to influence the market and all of which have perfect market knowledge

peripheral product a secondary product often provided as part of a service, e.g. the complementary mints at the end of a meal, shampoo at the hairdressers

personal selling communication between a salesperson and one or more prospective purchasers

personality a person's distinguishing psychological characteristics that lead them to respond in particular ways

PEST an acronym for the macroenvironment (part of an organisation's external environment): political, economic, social, technological

phenomenological research describes the experiences of individuals concerning some specific phenomena or occurrence

physical distribution the process of moving goods and services between businesses and consumers

physical evidence the tangible aspects of a service, e.g. a bus ticket, shampoo (at the hairdressers); one of the 7Ps of services marketing

piggyback marketing a collective term for a number of joint marketing practices, e.g. co-branding, sharing marketing channels, on-pack promotions, usually for complementary products

piggybacking when one company uses the distribution channels already established by another company, usually, but not always, in an overseas market

pioneer advertising informative advertising, usually for a new product or service

place one of the elements of the marketing mix, concerned with distribution, delivery, supply chain management

PLC most commonly, public limited company but often used in marketing to stand for the product life cycle

point of sale (POS) the place where a product or service is bought

polycentrism polycentric firms have a host country (i.e. the foreign country) focus; they assume that the host country's ways are superior and try to adapt their own business to fit into the other country as perfectly as possible

POP (point of purchase) see point of sale (POS)

population a complete group of people, cases or objects which share similarities that can be studied in a survey

portal a website that acts as a gateway to a number of other sites

Porter's five forces model an industry analysis tool

Porter's generic strategies three main competitive strategies: cost leadership, differentiation and focus

portfolio analysis the process of comparing SBUs (strategic business units) or products/services to see which are deserving of further investment and which should be discontinued

position map graphical representation of brand positions resulting from the perceptual mapping process; also called a brand map, perceptual map or space map

positioning the place a product (brand) is perceived to occupy in the minds of customers/consumers of the relevant target market relative to other competing brands

post-purchase dissonance when a consumer is psychologically uncomfortable about a purchase

post-testing evaluating the effectiveness of an aspect of a marketing campaign with its target audience after release

PR see public relations (PR)

predatory pricing also known as destroyer pricing or extinction pricing, it is when a dominant company sells products at a loss with the intention of driving a rival firm out of the market

pre-emptive pricing setting prices relatively low in order to deter others from entering a market

premium price a relatively high price

press the types of media written by journalists, most commonly newspapers, and magazines and directories

press advertisements adverts placed in printed media such as newspapers and magazines

press conference a meeting at which journalists are briefed

press release publicity material sent to editors and journalists

PRESTCOM an acronym for the marketing environment: political, regulatory, economic, social, technological, competitive, organisational, market

prestige goods high-status goods, e.g. Rolls-Royce, Rolex

prestige pricing pricing a product high in order to enhance its status

pre-testing evaluating the effectiveness of an aspect of a marketing campaign with its target audience before release

price how much each product is sold for

price discrimination charging different prices for the same products/services to different market segments, e.g. off-peak fares

price elastic when the demand for a good changes significantly after a price change e.g. price goes up by 10%, demand falls by 20%

price elasticity of demand a measure of the degree to which demand for a good changes when its price is changed

price followers firms that set their prices in accordance with others in the market, notably a price leader

price inelastic the percentage change in demand is less than the percentage change in price, e.g. price goes up by 10%, but the demand is unaffected or is effected to a lesser extent

price inelastic demand product sales are not very sensitive to price changes (see also inelasticity)

price leaders set prices for a market; other firms follow their lead

price makers another term for price leaders

price premium a high price charged to give the impression of superior quality

price takers another name for price followers

price war two or more firms keep undercutting each other in an attempt to build market share until one or the other backs off or goes out of business

primary data first-hand data gathered to solve a particular problem or to exploit a current opportunity

primary research (field research) research carried out specifically for the research task in question

problem children a category within the Boston Consulting Group portfolio matrix; products or SBUs (strategic business units) with relatively low market share in high-growth markets

process one of the 7Ps of the services marketing mix; the way in which a service is provided

procurement buying of goods and services for use within organisations

product adopters model (product diffusion model) categorises product buyers/users according to their take-up rate of new products

product adoption process the stages a buyer goes through before purchasing a product

product breadth the number of product lines a company supports

product depth the number of items within a product line

product development strategy developing new products to sell in existing markets (part of Ansoff's growth matrix)

product life cycle a product analysis tool based on the idea that a product has life stages: introduction, growth, maturity, decline, deletion

product line a product and all its variants (models, colours, styles, sizes, etc.)

product line pricing coordinated pricing for a group of related products

product manager the person responsible for the marketing of a specific product or product line

product orientation the philosophy of an organisation that focuses on making the best possible product rather than on its customers' needs

product placement arranging for products to be seen, or referred to, in entertainment media, e.g. during TV or radio programmes, films, plays, video games

product portfolio all a company's or strategic business unit's products

product portfolio analysis the process of comparing products/services to see which are deserving of further investment and which should be discontinued

production orientation the philosophy of an organisation that focuses on production rather than marketing

profit the difference between what something costs to make and the price for which it is sold

profit margin the difference between cost and price, expressed as a percentage

promotion another name for marketing communications (one of the 4Ps); communication designed and implemented to persuade others to do, think or feel something

promotion mix traditionally, advertising, PR, sales promotion and personal selling

prospecting looking for prospective customers

prospects prospective (i.e. possible future) customers

psychographic segmentation using lifestyles, values, personalities and/or psychological characteristics to split up markets

psychological price barrier the top price a customer is prepared to pay

public relations (PR) planned activities designed to build good relationships and enhance an organisation's or an individual's reputation

public sector government-owned organisations

publicity the stimulation of demand for goods or services by generating news about them in the mass media

publicity stunt an event designed to capture the attention of the media or other publics

publics PR term for target audiences, the groups of people with whom the organisation communicates

pull common usage descriptor for part of a pull strategy

pull strategy a promotional strategy aimed at end customers or consumers

purchase consideration set the mental shortlist of products or brands from which a person will make their final purchase choice

purchase decision the selection of the preferred product to buy

pure play an organisation that only sells online, e.g. Amazon, eBay

purposive sampling a non-probability sampling method, which means that every member of the research population does **not** have an equal chance of being picked; the researcher uses their judgement to choose the units to be studied

push common usage descriptor for part of a push strategy

push strategy a promotional strategy aimed at distribution channels

qualitative research investigates people's feelings, opinions and attitudes, often using unstructured, in-depth methods

quantitative research seeks numerical answers, e.g. how many people have similar characteristics and views

question marks an alternative name for problem children; also sometimes called wild cats

questionnaire a set of questions for use during a survey

quota a limit on the amount of foreign goods that can be imported into a country

quota sample picks respondents in proportion to the population's profile, e.g. if 25% of the population are under 25 and female, then researchers set a quota of 25% females under 25 for the sample

random sample a probability sample (*see also* simple random sample)

reach the number (or percentage) of the target audience exposed to an advert or other promotion during a campaign; also referred to as coverage or penetration

recall remembering things (e.g. products, brands, adverts); may be prompted (i.e. aided by stimulus material such as part of an advert) or unprompted (i.e. unaided)

recession when an economy experiences reducing sales and investment; if this continues, it may go into a depression

recognition being aware of something, e.g. a product or an advert, when shown

reference groups the groups to which an individual belongs or aspires to belong

referent power influence over others gained through superior knowledge or expertise

relationship marketing a long-term approach that nurtures customers, employees and business partners

repositioning involves moving existing perceptions to new perceptions relative to competing brands

reseller a business that buys products in order to sell them on to another business further down the marketing channel

response a reaction to a stimulus

retail selling goods to customers for their own use, i.e. not for resale

retail audit a research implement that provides information on retail product sales, e.g. value, volume, market/brand share

retailer a sales outlet that deals with end customers, e.g. a shop

retainers regular, contracted payments for services (fees) provided over a specified time span

return on investment (ROI) profit expressed as a percentage of the capital invested

revenue (sales revenue) the income a firm receives from the sale of goods and services

reward cards similar in appearance to credit cards, used to register points given away with purchases (e.g. Nectar card, Tesco Clubcard)

sales orientation strategic view that focuses on short-term sales

sales promotion short-term special offers and other added-value activites, e.g. two for the price of one

sales quota target number (or value) of sales set for a salesperson

sales revenue the income a firm receives from the sale of goods and services

sales value the revenue derived from items sold

sales volume the quantity of goods sold, expressed in units, e.g. 2 million apples

sample a smaller number of people, or cases, drawn from a population that should be representative of it in every significant characteristic

sampling frame a list of the actual members of a population from which a sample is then chosen

SBU see strategic business unit (SBU)

secondary data data previously collected for other purposes that can be used in the current research task

secondary research (desk research) the search for good-quality data that has been validated and is now published for use by others

segmentation *see* market segmentation

segments distinct parts of a larger market; customers and consumers in each segment share similar characteristics

selective attention the process by which stimuli are assessed and non-meaningful stimuli, or those that are inconsistent with our beliefs or experiences, are screened out

selective distortion occurs when consumers distort or change the information they receive to suit their beliefs and attitude

selective distribution the distribution channel is restricted to a few outlets

selective retention the way consumers retain only a small number of messages in their memory

self-liquidating special offer a sales promotion that pays for itself (usually because the company making the offer has bought the promotional items in vast quantities and so obtained a substantial discount)

self-reference criterion (SRC) a person's own cultural values and experience – reliance on one's SRC is a problem when doing business with people from other cultures

semantic differential scale research subjects are asked to indicate the strength of their views by choosing a point between two extremes, e.g. was the Rosannica Restaurant's service: good – poor?

service convenience a measure of how much time and effort consumers need to expend to use the service offered

service encounter the time during which a customer is the recipient of a service, e.g. the duration of a meal in a restaurant

service recovery trying to retrieve a situation caused by a bad product or poor service encounter

services intangible products

servicescape the total environment in which a service is experienced

shopping agents programs which search the Internet and then display a table of comparative prices for a specified item

shopping goods carry a relatively high risk, perhaps because they are a high price or it may be that the cost of product failure is high

SIC (Standard Industrial Classification) a system of classifying products by allocating numbers (codes) to every product category, industry or business sector

simple random sample the Rolls-Royce of sampling methods, every member of the population has an equal chance of being selected; this can be expensive and often difficult

situation analysis an investigation into an organisation or brand's current circumstances to identify significant influencing factors and trends; the most common framework used is SWOT (Strengths, Weaknesses, Opportunities, Threats)

slump when an economy experiences a severe fall-off in sales, usually accompanied by unemployment, lower prices and low levels of investment, sometimes called a depression

SMART a mnemonic for the setting of objectives, which should be: specific, measurable, achievable, relevant and timed

social costs the costs incurred by society generally as a result of business processes or decisions, e.g. the clearing up of pollution, the provision of transport infrastructure

social grading segmentation by occupation of head of household; the typical classifications used are A, B, C1, C2, D and E groups

social responsibility a sense of duty towards all organisational stakeholders

societal marketing meeting customers' needs and wants in a way that enhances the long-term well-being of consumers and the society in which they live

space map *see* position map

spam electronic junk mail

speciality goods unusual, probably quite pricey, products

sponsorship giving financial aid, or other resources, to an individual, organisation or event in return for a positive association with them, e.g. the Coca-Cola Cup

SPSS (Statistical Package for the Social Sciences) a software program for statistical analysis

stakeholders individuals or groups who are involved in, or affected by, the organisation's actions and/or performance

standard error average amount of error introduced through the sampling process

staple goods essential goods, regularly purchased, perhaps always kept in the cupboard, e.g. coffee, milk, shampoo

stars a category within the Boston Consulting Group portfolio matrix; products or SBUs (strategic business units) with high market share in a high-growth market

statement stuffers promotional inserts sent with a statement, e.g. bank statement, credit card statement

stimulus something that provokes a reaction, activity, interest or enthusiasm

stock out when a supplier runs out of a particular product

straight rebuy where the buyer routinely reorders a product or service without any change to the order whatsoever; it may even be an automatic process

strap line a subheading in a press article or advertisement

strategic alliance a form of joint venture in which two organisations work together to achieve their goals

strategic business unit (SBU) a distinct part of an organisation that has an external market for its products and services

stratified random sampling the research population is divided into mutually exclusive groups and random samples are drawn from each group

subscriptions regular purchase payments, usually as part of an ongoing contract to buy something, e.g. a monthly magazine

substitutes other products that might be bought as alternatives; they satisfy the same or similar needs

supply the quantity of goods that sellers are prepared to put on the market at a certain price

supply chain the network of businesses and organisations involved in distributing goods and services to their final destination

supply-led shortages of goods mean that suppliers can dictate terms of business

survey direct questioning of market research subjects

SWOT analysis a situational analysis tool that assesses the organisation's strengths and weaknesses (internal) and opportunities and threats (external)

syndicated data services combine data from responses to questions on various topics, e.g. the British Market Research Bureau's (BMRB) Target Group Index's (TGI) questionnaire

syndicated research data consolidated information from various studies

systematic random sampling uses the whole population as a sampling frame but draws subjects from it at regular intervals, e.g. every 10th name on the list

target audience the people, or organisations, that are selected to receive communications

target market a group of buyers and consumers who share common needs/wants or characteristics, and on whom the organisation focuses

target marketing (targeting) the selection of one or more market segments towards which marketing efforts can be directed; sometimes called market targeting

targeting strategies used to select a single, or group of, target markets

tariffs import taxes charged by governments

telesales making sales calls by telephone

tender (tendering) where firms bid for a contract and, usually, the lowest-priced bid wins

test market a subset of a market in which a product offering can be sold for a short period of time in order to predict demand and to try out and refine the marketing mix

top-down approach senior managers specify objectives, budgets, strategies and plans that are passed down to functions and departments to put into action

total costs the sum of all costs

total product offering the total package that makes up, and surrounds, the product, including all supporting features such as branding, packaging, servicing and warranties

touchpoints all a customer, user or consumer's contacts or interactions with a brand including communications and actual use

tracking marketing effects are monitored over time

trade cycle patterns of economic activity consisting of boom, downturn (recession), slump (depression), upturn (recovery); also known as the 'business cycle'

trade trial promotions sales promotions aimed at members of the supply chain, e.g. a prize for selling 100 cases of wine

trading bloc a group of countries that work together to promote trade with each other and present a common front to outside nations, e.g. the European Union (EU), NAFTA (North American Free Trade Association)

transactional exchange a one-off sale or a sale that is conducted as if it were a one-off

transactional marketing focuses on the immediate sale

triadic comparisons technique used in perceptual mapping in which three products are compared to each other at a time

turf battles when individual managers or departments fight for their own interests at the expense of those of other managers/departments

turnover the monetary value of sales; also called revenue or sales revenue

uncontrollables events, issues, trends, etc., within the external environment

unconvertible currency cannot be exchanged for another currency

undifferentiated marketing where the market is believed to be composed of customers/consumers whose needs and wants from the product are fundamentally the same; in undifferentiated or mass marketing, the same marketing programme is used for all

unique selling proposition (USP) a clear point of differentiation for a product/service

unit costs how much it costs to make a single item (usually worked out on average)

unit elasticity price and quantity demanded change at exactly the same rate; as a result, whatever you do to the price, there is no increase in the company's revenue

up-selling persuading a customer to trade up to a more expensive product

variable costs costs that go up as production increases and down when it decreases, e.g. electricity bills

vendor rating a vetting process to help buyers identify where there may be potential benefits or difficulties associated with a particular supplier

vertical communications happen up and down the hierarchical organisation structure, e.g. sales manager to salesperson, and vice versa

vertical integration where a company owns a number of different businesses above or below it in the supply chain

viral marketing an electronic form of **word of mouth** marketing

white goods large electrical appliances for domestic use, e.g. fridges, washing machines (traditionally coloured white)

wholesaler a reseller, buying products in bulk to sell on to other businesses in smaller quantities

wild cats an alternative name for problem children; also sometimes called question marks

word of mouth individuals passing on information, experiences or promotional messages to each other; *see also* viral marketing

World Wide Web the graphical user interface to the Internet

write-downs goods reduced for sale

zero elasticity completely inelastic; you can do whatever you like to the price (or other marketing variable), as there will be no change in the quantity demanded

Index